BOOK TWO
of Object-Oriented Knowledge:

The Working Object

Object-Oriented Software Engineering:
Methods and Management

S0-FIU-812

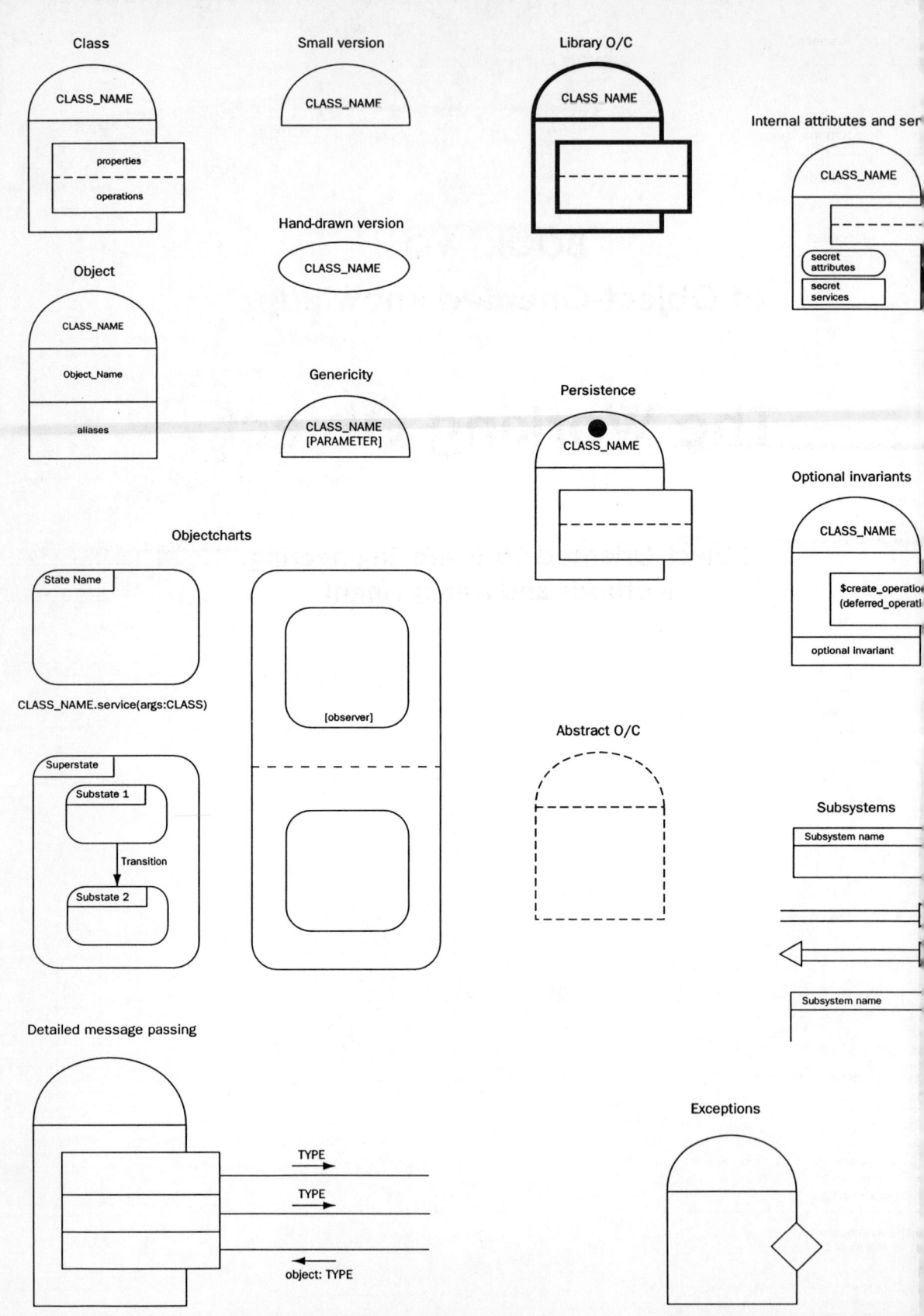

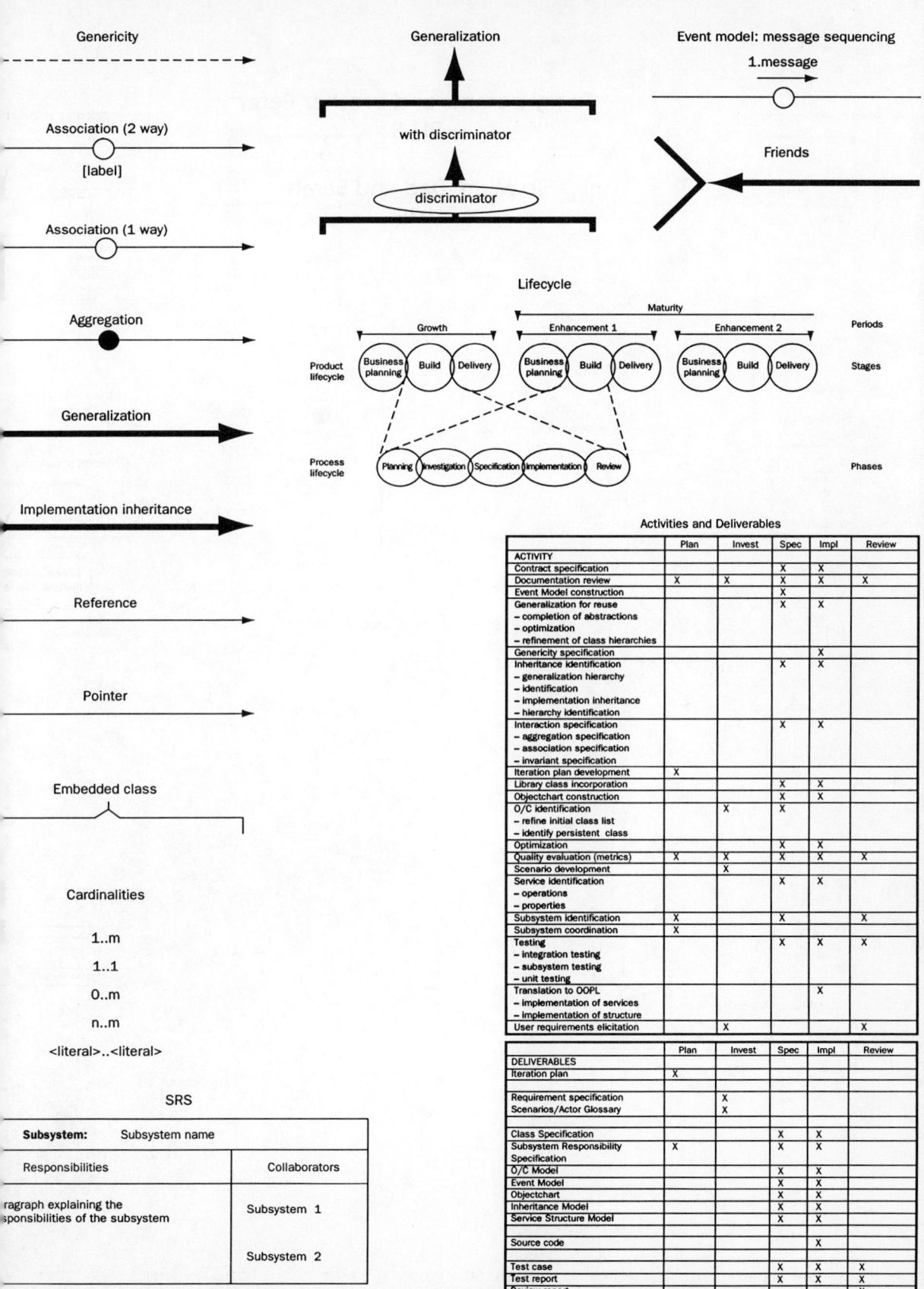

To my parents and brother Peter
BH-S

To Mum, Dad and Sarah
JME

BOOKTWO of
Object-Oriented Knowledge:

The Working Object

Object-Oriented Software Engineering:
Methods and Management

B. Henderson-Sellers and J. M. Edwards

PRENTICE HALL

Sydney New York London Toronto Tokyo Singapore
Mexico City Amsterdam

© 1994 by Prentice Hall of Australia Pty Ltd

All rights reserved. No part of this publication may be reproduced, stored in a retrieval system, or transmitted in any form or by any means, electronic, mechanical, photocopying, recording, or otherwise, without written permission of the publisher.

Acquisitions Editors: Andrew Binnie and Kaylie Smith
Production Editor: Marah Braye
Cover design: The Modern Art Production Group, Prahran, Vic.
Typeset by James Young
Printed in Australia by Ligare Pty Ltd, Riverwood, NSW

1 2 3 4 5 98 97 96 95 94

ISBN 0 13 148404 4.

National Library of Australia
Cataloguing-in-Publication Data

Henderson-Sellers, Brian.
  Booktwo of object-oriented knowledge.

  Bibliography.
  Includes index.
  ISBN 0 13 093980 3.

  1. Software engineering. 2. Object-oriented programming
  (Computer science). I. Edwards, J. M. . II. Title.
  III. Title: Book two of object-oriented knowledge. IV. Title:
  Book 2 of object-oriented knowledge.

005.1

Library of Congress
Cataloging-in-Publication Data

Henderson-Sellers, Brian.
   Book two of object-oriented knowledge: the working object: object-oriented software engineering: methods and management/B. Henderson-Sellers and J. M. Edwards.
       p. cm.
   Includes bibliographical references and index.
   ISBN 0-13-093980-3.
   1. Software engineering. 2. Object-oriented programming
 (Computer science) I. Edwards, J. M. (Julian Marcus). II. Title.
 III. Title: Book 2 of object-oriented knowledge.
 QA76.758.H47   1994
 005.1'1--dc20

Prentice Hall, Inc., *Englewood Cliffs, New Jersey*
Prentice Hall Canada, Inc., *Toronto*
Prentice Hall Hispanoamericana, *SA, Mexico*
Prentice Hall of India Private Ltd, *New Delhi*
Prentice Hall International, Inc., *London*
Prentice Hall of Japan, Inc., *Tokyo*
Prentice Hall of Southeast Asia Pty Ltd, *Singapore*
Editora Prentice Hall do Brasil Ltda, *Rio de Janeiro*

PRENTICE HALL

A division of Simon & Schuster

Foreword

In *A Book of Object-Oriented Knowledge*, Brian Henderson-Sellers presented a concise yet complete overview of object technology. The success of BOOK (the self-referential acronym by which this work has come to be known) showed how well Professor Henderson-Sellers had identified and filled the need for such a practical introduction.

The Working Object is BOOKTWO, this time with two authors rather than one, thanks to the participation of Julian Edwards. Since the appearance of the first book, the object-oriented literature has expanded considerably. The present volume, especially Chapters 2 and 3, is an excellent source of information on the current state of the art and on the available literature. These chapters will be particularly useful for the summaries they give of various authors' answers to such fundamental questions as the proper use of inheritance and the object-oriented software lifecycle. Also notable are the lucid presentations, a few pages each, of the best-known O-O analysis and design methods, as well as the even shorter capsules on major O-O languages.

The next chapters are devoted to a detailed presentation of the authors' own method, MOSES: overview, notation, process, lifecycle, and case study. MOSES is one of the first of what may be called the second-generation O-O methods; describing it in any detail would be stealing the authors' privilege, but it will suffice to say that MOSES remedies many of the limitations of first-generation methods by covering the entire lifecycle, ensures smooth transition between phases ("seamlessness"), integrates the notion of contract to help produce reliable products, has a precise definition of the goals and deliverables of each stage, and emphasizes the use of metrics to assess the results obtained. This book will clearly be the essential reference on MOSES for quite some time.

In the final chapter Henderson-Sellers and Edwards examine a number of managerial aspects of object technology, summarizing a large body of published information about industrial O-O projects. The Postscript, a prudently small venture into forecasting, attempts to sketch what the future of the technology will be.

The book is filled with concrete information—bibliographical references, quotations, figures, glossaries, and addresses. It is particularly notable for its combination of two streams: one which in journalistic terms would be called objective reporting (the description of other people's work), and the other more akin to Op-Ed pieces—the presentation of the authors' views and their own important contributions on such topics as methodology (MOSES), the lifecycle (the fountain model), and others.

Some readers will probably be more attracted to the reporting, others to the innovative thinking; but all will appreciate the breadth and depth of the material and enjoy the view it provides of where object technology stands today.

Bertrand Meyer
Series Editor

Contents

Foreword	vii
Preface	xvii
Glossary of Technical Terms	xxi
Glossary of Abbreviations	xxv

Chapter 1 Introduction — 1
  1.1 Rationale and scope of book — 1
  1.2 Goals of software engineering — 6
  1.3 Managing objects — 22
    1.3.1 Methodologies and notation — 22
    1.3.2 Project management — 23
    1.3.3 The importance of reuse — 23
    1.3.4 Metrics — 24
    1.3.5 Competitive edge technology — 24
  1.4 Recent and emerging issues — 25
    1.4.1 Recent issues — 25
    1.4.2 Current and emerging issues — 27
  1.5 Summary — 38

Chapter 2 The Object-oriented Paradigm — 41
  2.1 Introduction and review — 41
  2.2 Abstraction — 42
  2.3 Nomenclature and definitions — 46
    2.3.1 Objects and classes — 46
    2.3.2 Encapsulation/information hiding — 49
    2.3.3 Responsibilities, services, and behavior — 49
    2.3.4 Properties, operations, and contracts — 51
    2.3.5 Communication — 54

	2.3.6	Relationships	56
	2.3.7	Roles	73
	2.3.8	The object-oriented triangle	75
2.4	Implementation issues	78
	2.4.1	OOPLs—definitions	79
	2.4.2	Comparison of OOPLs	82
		2.4.2.1 Pure OOPLs	90
		2.4.2.2 Hybrid OOPLs	94
	2.4.3	OOP language features	97
		2.4.3.1 Genericity	97
		2.4.3.2 Assertions	97
		2.4.3.3 Exception handling	99
		2.4.3.4 Garbage collection	99
2.5	Summary	99
2.6	Study examples	101

Chapter 3 Object-oriented Development — 103

- 3.1 Software Development Lifecycles (SDLC) — 103
  - 3.1.1 Waterfall model — 107
  - 3.1.2 Fountain model — 111
    - 3.1.2.1 Subsystems fountain lifecycles — 118
  - 3.1.3 Spiral model — 121
  - 3.1.4 Fractal model — 123
  - 3.1.5 McGregor and Sykes — 125
  - 3.1.6 Summary — 126
- 3.2 Hybrid methodologies — 129
- 3.3 Object-oriented methodologies and notations — 133
  - 3.3.1 Rumbaugh *et al.* (OMT) — 137
  - 3.3.2 Booch — 141
  - 3.3.3 Wirfs-Brock *et al.* (RDD) — 146
  - 3.3.4 Coad and Yourdon (OOA, OOD) — 153
  - 3.3.5 Henderson-Sellers and Edwards (O-O-O) — 159
  - 3.3.6 Jacobson *et al.* (Objectory) — 163
  - 3.3.7 Firesmith (ADM3) — 167
  - 3.3.8 Shlaer and Mellor — 175
  - 3.3.9 Berard — 178
  - 3.3.10 Nerson — 182

Contents   xi

        3.3.11 Other methods and notations _____ 184
  3.4 Summary _____ 192

Chapter 4 An Overview of MOSES _____ 193
  4.1 Introduction _____ 193
        4.1.1 Product lifecycle _____ 195
        4.1.2 Process lifecycle _____ 197
  4.2 MOSES: both a product and process lifecycle methodology ____ 199
  4.3 Phases and deliverables of MOSES _____ 200
  4.4 Activities of MOSES _____ 206
  4.5 Lifecycle model of MOSES _____ 206
  4.6 Summary _____ 207

Chapter 5 The MOSES Notation _____ 211
  5.1 Introduction _____ 211
  5.2 O/C Model _____ 212
        5.2.1 Classes _____ 213
        5.2.2 Objects _____ 219
        5.2.3 Relationships _____ 219
                5.2.3.1 Inheritance _____ 220
                5.2.3.2 Association _____ 221
                5.2.3.3 Aggregation _____ 223
                5.2.3.4 Cardinality and existence constraints _____ 225
        5.2.4 OOPL-specific notations _____ 225
                5.2.4.1 Embedded structures (composite classes) ____ 225
                5.2.4.2 Client–server relationships _____ 226
                5.2.4.3 Friends _____ 227
                5.2.4.4 Exception handling _____ 227
        5.2.5 Summary _____ 228
  5.3 Class Specification (CS) _____ 229
        5.3.1 Class Specification diagrams _____ 232
  5.4 Service specifications _____ 234
        5.4.1 Contracts _____ 234
        5.4.2 Service Structure Model (SSM) _____ 236
  5.5 Event Models (EMs) _____ 237
  5.6 Objectcharts _____ 240
  5.7 Inheritance Model _____ 242

5.8	Complexity management techniques	243
	5.8.1 Sheets	244
	5.8.2 Subsystems	247
	5.8.3 Layering	250
	5.8.4 Selective visibility	250
5.9	Practical applications of MOSES notation	253
	5.9.1 CASE tool support	253
	5.9.2 Whiteboarding and brainstorming	254
5.10	Example	254
5.11	Summary and conclusions	261
5.12	Study examples	265

Chapter 6 The MOSES Product and Process Lifecycles — 267

6.1	Growth Period	268
	6.1.1 Business Planning Stage	268
	6.1.2 Build Stage	271
	6.1.3 Delivery Stage	272
6.2	Enhancement Period	273
6.3	Process lifecycle	274
	6.3.1 Planning Phase	275
	6.3.2 Investigation Phase	277
	6.3.3 Specification Phase	279
	6.3.4 Implementation Phase	285
	6.3.5 Review Phase	288
6.4	Summary	291
6.5	Study examples	291

Chapter 7 The MOSES Lifecycle Activities — 295

7.1	Contract Specification	295
	7.1.1 Invariant specification	298
7.2	Documentation Review	299
7.3	Event Model Construction	300
7.4	Generalization for Reuse	302
	7.4.1 Completion of abstractions	305
	7.4.2 Optimization	305
	7.4.3 Refinement of inheritance hierarchies	306
7.5	Genericity Specification	314

Contents

- 7.6 Inheritance Identification — 315
  - 7.6.1 Generalization hierarchies — 316
  - 7.6.2 Implementation inheritance hierarchies — 321
- 7.7 Interaction Specification — 323
  - 7.7.1 Aggregation specification — 323
  - 7.7.2 Association specification — 324
- 7.8 Iteration Plan Development — 326
- 7.9 Library Class Incorporation — 327
- 7.10 Objectchart Construction — 330
- 7.11 O/C Identification — 335
  - 7.11.1 Determine initial class list and refine — 335
  - 7.11.2 Identify persistent classes — 337
- 7.12 Optimization — 338
- 7.13 Quality Evaluation (Metrics) — 338
- 7.14 Scenario Development — 343
- 7.15 Service Identification — 346
  - 7.15.1 Operations — 346
  - 7.15.2 Properties — 348
- 7.16 Subsystem Coordination — 349
- 7.17 Subsystem Identification — 350
- 7.18 Testing — 352
  - 7.18.1 Integration testing — 353
  - 7.18.2 Subsystem testing — 354
  - 7.18.3 Unit testing — 354
- 7.19 Translation to the OOPL — 355
  - 7.19.1 Implementation of services — 355
  - 7.19.2 Implementation of structure — 355
- 7.20 User Requirements Elicitation — 356
- 7.21 Summary — 357
- 7.22 Study examples — 357

Chapter 8 A Case Study Using MOSES — 361
- 8.1 Evaluating MOSES for completeness — 361
- 8.2 Case study: Decision support system for wastewater management — 362
  - 8.2.1 Investigation Phase — 364
    - 8.2.1.1 Initial requirements — 364
    - 8.2.1.2 Identify subsystems and responsibilities — 365

                8.2.1.3 Description of treatment plant subsystem _____ 368
                8.2.1.4 Scenarios _____ 370
        8.2.2 Specification Phase _____ 373
                8.2.2.1 Initial class structure _____ 373
                8.2.2.2 Refined scenarios _____ 381
                8.2.2.3 Identify behavior _____ 382
                8.2.2.4 Dynamic model _____ 386
                8.2.2.5 Refinement _____ 391
                8.2.2.6 Generalization _____ 394
                8.2.2.7 Dividing into sheets _____ 397
                8.2.2.8 Class Specifications _____ 397
                8.2.2.9 Iteration _____ 401
                8.2.2.10 Discussion _____ 401
        8.2.3 Specification of the GUI model _____ 402
                8.2.3.1 Discussion _____ 411
        8.2.4 Implementation Phase _____ 412
        8.2.5 Generalizing the O/C Model _____ 413
  8.3 Summary and conclusions _____ 414
  8.4 Study example _____ 414

Chapter 9 Project Management and Commercial Adoption of OOSE ___ 415
  9.1 Project management _____ 415
        9.1.1 Managing the OO SDLC _____ 415
        9.1.2 Organizational roles _____ 426
        9.1.3 Reuse _____ 427
        9.1.4 Library management _____ 429
        9.1.5 Tool support _____ 438
  9.2 Commercial adoption of OO _____ 447
        9.2.1 Migration paths _____ 447
        9.2.2 Industry case studies _____ 452
        9.2.3 The OMG _____ 459
  9.3 Summary _____ 459

Chapter 10 Object-oriented "Metrics" _____ 461
  10.1 Metrics and measures _____ 462
  10.2 Product and process metrics _____ 464
  10.3 Product metrics (or structural complexity) _____ 471

Contents — xv

        10.3.1 Intermodule metrics (for system design complexity) — 472
        10.3.2 Module metrics (for semantic complexity) — 478
        10.3.3 Module metrics (for procedural complexity) — 479
            10.3.3.1 Size metrics — 480
            10.3.3.2 Logic structure metrics — 492
            10.3.3.3 Other procedural complexity measures — 499
        10.3.4 Composite metrics — 501
   10.4 Cognitive complexity model — 502
   10.5 Process metrics — 511
   10.6 Cost-benefit metrics — 518
        10.6.1 Generalization and reuse — 519
        10.6.2 Simulation of ROI over a number of projects — 521
   10.7 Summary — 526

Postscript   The Future of Object Technology — **529**

Appendix   Suggested Answers to Study Examples — **533**

   Further Reading — 561
   References — 563
   Index — 591

Preface

You may have read BOOK (Henderson-Sellers, 1992a)—we hope you have. This is BOOKTWO.

While BOOK is a basic introduction to the object-oriented approach to software engineering, BOOKTWO is a more advanced text. It is the definitive document for the MOSES methodology (Version 2.1), focusing as it does on a "seamless transition" across the lifecycle stages. The major focus is on analysis and design (which we often refer to collectively as "specification"), emphasizing modeling concepts and project management techniques.

The book contains a detailed description of the role of object technology (OT) in commercial and industrial applications, focusing on analysis, design, *and* implementation, together with many references for more detailed study. It is fashioned on our experience of researching methodologies, notations, object-oriented project management, and metrics. The material it contains has been utilized in student and commercial projects, and in courses aimed at conveying OT concepts and techniques to practitioners—professional MIS executives, managers, and programmers/coders.

It is hard to be definitive about what software skills the reader should possess in order to gain full advantage from this text and from using object-oriented software engineering. Certainly, we will presume that the reader is reasonably familiar with computers, software, and the associated technical terminology. We will also presume that the reader has several years' professional experience in software development (probably largely in a structured development environment) and/or has participated in first-year, university-level courses in at least one programming language and/or information systems course. In addition, the basic concepts of OT will be assumed, although these are summarized and built on in the first two chapters.

The text is useful for a full semester course in OT or for a week-long full-time professional course in which sufficient time is allowed for "hands-on" examples. It is also useful for professionals wishing to update their knowledge *in the context of* the growing OT literature. It is *not* a handbook or "cookbook" for MOSES, although a full description of this methodology is indeed presented.

In preparing and presenting this book, we wish to acknowledge the stimulation and ideas from all seminar participants (now several hundred in number), from students at the University of New South Wales, and from the coauthors of research papers, some of whose material is included herein. In the last category we would like to express our thanks to Larry Constantine for the collaboration on EUON (the precursor of the MOSES notation), and to June Verner, Yagna Pant, Simon Cant, Ross Jeffery, David Monarchi, and David Tegarden for the collaboration on metrics. We are also grateful to, in alphabetical order, Kalpana Bilimoria, Steve Bilow, Tina Case, Jan Drake, Adele Goldberg, Ian Graham, Leith Hayes, Bill Hutchens, David Monarchi, Gail Murphy, Gretchen Puhr, Geoff Rasmussen, Mark Ratjens, Derek Renouf, Madhu Singh, Ray Steele, Rowan Stevens, David Tegarden, Bhuvanesh Unhelkar, and June Verner for commenting constructively on earlier drafts of this book and also to the Series Editor, Bertrand Meyer, for his advice and continuing support. We wish to thank Jim Nelson (of the University of Colorado in Boulder) for providing the code of Figure 2.25 (Smalltalk Bear class) and Tim Menzies (of the University of New South Wales) for providing the Smalltalk example discussed in Figures 7.17 and 7.18. We also wish to thank Trisha Hartley for her help in preparing the final manuscript.

Last, but by no means least, we thank our spouses ("spice"), Ann and Sarah, for being themselves.

In addition, we wish to acknowledge the following copyright holders for permission to reprint copyright material:

ACM for Figure 3.50; Tables 3.2, 3.9, and 9.3
ACM/Addison-Wesley for Figures 3.33–36
Addison-Wesley and AT&T Bell Laboratories for Figure 2.24
Addison-Wesley Publishing Company Inc. for Figures 3.22, 3.31–32, 3.52–53, 3.56, and 9.10; Table 3.7
Barry Boehm/ACM for Figure 3.11
Benjamin Cummings for quotation in Chapter 10, p. 481
Bertrand Meyer for Figures 1.3–5
Computer Language for Figure 5.19
Don Firesmith and ASTS for Figures 3.43–44
ECOOP/Springer for quotation in Chapter 2, p. 58
Grady Booch and The Benjamin/Cummings Publishing Company Inc. for Figure 9.1
Grady Booch/*Computer Language* for Figures 3.23–25
Harvard Business Review for Figure 9.11
Hewlett-Packard for Figure 1.1
IEEE for Figures 3.54, 5.31, 7.20, 10.2, and 10.6; Table 10.3
International Business Machine Corporation for Figure 10.22
John Wiley & Sons, Inc. for Figure 3.1 and Table 7.4
Kent Beck and Ward Cunningham for Figure 9.8
Norman Fenton and Chapman & Hall for Figure 10.1 and Table 10.10

Paul Swatman for the Object-Z Template in the Postscript
Prentice Hall for Figures 2.17, 3.10, 3.20–21, 3.28–29, 3.37–42, 3.45, 3.46–49, 7.10, and 9.7; Tables 3.8 and 9.4
Rob Thomsett and Associates for Figures 9.4 and 10.23
SIGS for Figures 1.2, 1.9, 2.17, 3.46–49, 3.51, 7.10, 7.22, 9.2, and 9.12; Tables 1.6, 9.6, 9.7, and 9.8; Quotations, Chapter 1, pp. 38–39, and Postscript, pp. 529–30
Van Nostrand Reinhold for Figures 3.13–16 and 9.9

Trademarks
The following trademarks are used in the text:

Actor is the trademark of The Whitewater Group
ADM3 is a trademark of ASTS
Apple, Lisa, MacApp, and Macintosh are trademarks of Apple Computer Inc.
C++ and Unix are trademarks of AT&T
Classic Ada is the trademark of Software Productivity Solutions, Inc.
CLU is a trademark of MIT
Domino's Pizza is the trademark of Domino's Home Delivery Pty Ltd
Eiffel is the trademark of the Non-Profit International Consortium for Eiffel
Eiffelbench and EiffelVision are the trademarks of Interactive Software Engineering
HOOD is a trademark of HOOD Working Group
IBM is a trademark of International Business Machines, Inc.
Interleaf is a trademark of Interleaf, Inc.
MetaEdit is the trademark of MetaCase Consulting Inc.
Monopoly is the trademark of Parker Brothers
Objective-C is a trademark of Productivity Products International
ObjectMaker is the trademark of MarkV Systems
Objectcraft is the trademark of Object Craft Inc.
Objectory is the trademark of Objective Systems
OMTool is the trademark of GE
OOATool, OODTool, and OOCodeGen are trademarks of Object International Inc.
PageMaker is a trademark of the Aldus Corporation
Paradigm Plus is the trademark of Protosoft
PTech is a trademark of Associative Design Technology Inc.
ROSE is the trademark of Rational Software Engineering
Scrabble is the trademark of Milton Bradley
Simula is a trademark of Simula AS
Smalltalk80, ObjectWorks, and VisualWorks are trademarks of ParcPlace Systems Inc.
Smalltalk/V is a trademark of Digitalk Inc.
Software-IC is a trademark of PPI
Software Through Pictures is a trademark of Interactive Development

System Architect is the trademark of Popkin Software
Taligent is a trademark of Taligent, Inc.
Teamwork is a trademark of Cadre Technologies Inc.
Turbo Pascal is a trademark of Borland International Inc.
Versant is a trademark of Versant Object Technologies
Ventura is a trademark of Corel
Word is a trademark of the Microsoft Corporation
Word Perfect is a trademark of the Word Perfect Corporation

Glossary of Technical Terms

abstract class A class that cannot be instantiated. It has one or more services left undefined specifically so that subclasses can inherit this/these service(s) and tailor it/them to the specific context.
abstract data type (ADT) A description of a class (q.v.) but without implementation details, thus providing the specification. Perhaps better thought of as a "user-defined" type.
abstraction A cognitive tool for rationalizing the world by only considering *necessary* details for the current purpose of comprehension.
abstraction hierarchy (also often known as inheritance hierarchy) Superclass/subclass relationships. The process of traversing from superclass to subclass is specialization; from subclass to superclass, generalization. The term is also used to refer to a network in which multiple generalization occurs.
activity A technique or an action undertaken during one or more phase(s) of the process lifecycle.
aggregation A relationship in which one O/C has several component parts.
analysis Relates to the "problem space." In MOSES subsumed into the Specification Phase.
association A relationship between two O/Cs describing their interaction.
behavior Sometimes used to describe the dynamic nature of an O/C. In MOSES, synonymous with class services or responsibilities. Implemented by means of a method.
cardinality The number of O/Cs participating in a relationship.
class The term "class" is often used in analysis and design to represent (i.e., specify) a single concept which is an abstraction of commonality between individual items in a collection. It is also used to describe the code (specification plus implementation). Context always eliminates any ambiguity. A "deferred" or "abstract" class (q.v.) is one in which some services are not fully specified, these being deferred to a subclass. Such deferred classes cannot therefore be instantiated (q.v.) themselves, but must be inherited from.
class specification (CS) A formal or informal template that records details of

the class's properties, operations, and relationships. Forms the central source of textual information about a class.

classification Abstract notion of grouping like things into sets or classes.

client–server Broad term used in the Implementation Phase to capture language-dependent relationships between two O/Cs.

cluster A loose affiliation of a number of classes, usually grouped together semantically as well as pragmatically.

complexity The difficulty of comprehension/maintainability.

concept The statement of a shared idea.

conceptual model(ing) A model (or modeling process) that focuses on concepts, i.e., logical descriptors, and not on physical implementation within a computer domain.

contract A binding statement on the pre-/postconditions and invariants that must prevail in an O/C interaction.

deferred class Also known as abstract class (q.v.).

deliverables Documentation (graphical and textual) available for assessment at the end of each phase (q.v.) of each iteration of the process lifecycle.

design Relates to the "solution space." In MOSES subsumed into the Specification Phase.

encapsulation A "chunking" mechanism. An encapsulation may or may not support information hiding (q.v.).

extension The set of individual objects that correspond to the intension (q.v.) of the concept.

framework A group of collaborating classes that provide a high-level abstract view of one specific problem domain. This framework is then available in the library for further tailoring to specific problems within the domain described by the framework. For example, a user interface framework would supply all menu O/Cs, popup dialogue boxes, scroll bars, windows, etc., onto which the developer can then build the application itself.

generalization Creating superclasses within the abstraction hierarchy (q.v.) (upward).

genericity Supporting the use of parameterized types, i.e., a class with an argument that is specified dynamically (even for statically typed languages).

graphical user interface (GUI) Increasingly expected as a "standard" by users.

Implementation Phase Relates to language-dependent "design" and coding.

information hiding Limited scoping in which some information is invisible outside the boundaries of the class.

inheritance Equivalent to a taxonomic relationship between "parents" and "children," possibly over many "generations." Both specification inheritance (subtyping) and specialization inheritance (**is-a** or **is-a-kind-of**) support substitutability. Implementation inheritance does not, but simply permits sharing of code with no semantic implications for the relationship.

instantiation Creation of an individual instance (an "object") from the (coded) class.

Glossary of Technical Terms

intension The intension of a concept is a description of a template/model representing the concept.
Investigation Phase The phase in which the nature of the problem is understood. This involves the customer (end user).
iterative development process (IDP) The sequence of phases within the Build Stage of the product lifecycle. The IDP provides a heuristic framework for the iterative nature of the process lifecycle. Each iteration passes through a maximum of five identifiable phases in MOSES: Planning, Investigation, Specification, Implementation, and Review.
message The request by one object for the services/assistance of a second object roughly equivalent to a subroutine CALL in a procedural language.
metamodel A model that embodies properties abstracted from a family of models (defined at a lower level of abstraction). A metamodel can define the epistemological (knowledge) and design foundations of modeling. Design foundations are the core of more practical methodologies, including MOSES.
method A technique useful for undertaking a particular step within a lifecycle. Also used in OT to mean a procedure or function specified within the class. Also known as a routine.
methodology A set of guidelines for the software development process.
model An abstraction; an artifact used to aid understanding. A model always simplifies the real situation, making assumptions and approximations and confining the domain, often severely.
modeling The process of building a model; it requires cognitive skills and an artistic flair.
object At run-time, a single instantiation; in the real world, a "thing" that is a member of a set that is the extension of the concept.
objectchart Extension of a statechart useful in describing the dynamics of class behavior.
object/class (O/C) The general term for objects and classes across the lifecycle. Context will easily determine whether a single instance or a set of instances is meant. Often, the term used to describe both instances and sets in parallel.
operation The action aspect of an O/C in the sense of being a service that does something.
persistence The ability of an object to continue to exist after the cessation of the running of the program itself.
phase One of the quasi-chronological "steps" of the process lifecycle.
Planning Phase The phase in which work schedules, resource assignments, goals, etc., are set for each iteration of the development process.
polymorphism The ability to refer to an object as an instance either of its class or of any of its superclasses. In many OOPLs, polymorphism is restricted to classes belonging to the same inheritance hierarchy (known as inclusion or limited polymorphism).
property The state aspect of an O/C in the sense of being a service that gives information.

responsibilities   The set of criteria of an O/C that describe the reason for the class's existence. An individual responsibility may result in information being returned (a property) or in an action being performed (operation). Collectively, they describe the "class responsibility." In this text we prefer the term "service" as a synonym.

Review Phase   The phase in which an assessment is made of the quality of the development process.

scenario   A description in natural language of an interaction sequence with a system from which O/Cs, events, and interactions can be identified. Scenarios are also used to formulate testing programs.

service   Sometimes used as a synonym for responsibility (as here) (q.v.).

software development lifecycle (SDLC)   The model underlying the *process* of creating software.

software engineering   The application to software development of engineering principles by which a high-quality product can be achieved.

specialization   Creating superclasses within the abstraction hierarchy (downward) by both restriction and extension.

Specification Phase   The part of the process lifecycle that takes the requirements and turns them into a final design for implementation. This phase is programming-language-independent. Language choice is made at the end of this phase, just before the Implementation Phase. The Specification Phase subsumes "analysis" and "design."

subsystems   Component parts of a system, which is broken down on semantic grounds so that each subsystem is in fact a system itself with very limited coupling to other subsystems but with high coupling and coherence within the subsystem.

system   A set of interacting components that may be closed (no energy crosses the stated boundary) or open (in which external forces have an effect).

taxonomic   A technique in the life sciences for arranging classes of objects in a hierarchy. In biology this is often based on physical structure and other observable characteristics.

use case   Also known as a scenario (q.v.).

Glossary of Abbreviations

3GL third-generation language (a procedural language such as COBOL, FORTRAN, BASIC)
4GL fourth-generation language (many fourth-generation languages are database query languages)
ACM Association for Computing Machinery
ADT abstract data type
AI artificial intelligence
AKO a-kind-of
ANSI American National Standards Institute
API application programming interface
ATM automated teller machine (in banking example)
CAD/CAM computer-assisted design/computer-assisted manufacture
CASE computer-aided software engineering
CBA cost-benefit analysis
COV concept-oriented view
CRC Class, Responsibility, and Collaboration
CS class specification (diagram)
CSF critical success factor
DAG directed acyclic graph
DBMS database management system
DCL data control language
DDL data definition language
DFD data flow diagram
DSS decision support system
EM event model
ER entity relationship (data modeling)
ERA entity relationship attribute diagram
ERD entity relationship diagram
FAQ frequently asked questions
F-O-O functional analysis, object-oriented design, object-oriented programming

GIS geographical information systems
GUI graphical user interface
ID inheritance diagram
IDP iterative development process
IM inheritance model
IS information systems
ISE Interactive Software Engineering
KBIS knowledge-based information systems
LGC library of generalized components
LOC lines of code
MI multiple inheritance
MIS management information systems
MISA mortgage investment savings account
MOSES Methodology for Object-oriented Software Engineering of Systems
MVC model-view-controller
OBMS objectbase management system
ODBMS object-oriented database management system
OLMS Object Library Management System
OMG Object Management Group
OMT Object Modeling Technique
OO object-oriented (adjectival) or object-orientation (noun)
OOA object-oriented analysis
OOD object-oriented design
OOA/D object-oriented analysis and design
OOAD object-oriented application development
OODDes object-oriented domain design
O-O-F object-oriented analysis, object-oriented design, functional programming
O-O-O Object-oriented analysis, object-oriented design, object-oriented programming
OOP object-oriented programming
OOPL object-oriented programming language
OOPSLA Object-Oriented Programming, Systems, Languages, and Applications. This is an annual conference organized by the Association of Computing Machinery (ACM)
OOSD object-oriented structured design
OOSE object-oriented software engineering
OT object technology
PC personal computer
PL programming language
POV program-oriented view
RDD responsibility-driven design
SDLC software development lifecycle
SE software engineering
SLOC source lines of code
SQA software quality assurance

SQL structured query language
SRS subsystem responsibility specification
SSM structured service model
STD state transition diagram
TOOLS Technology of Object-Oriented Languages and Systems. A series of conferences held in Europe, Australia, and the United States
TQM total quality management
UoD universe of discourse
UON Uniform Object Notation
VDU visual display unit

CHAPTER 1

Introduction

1.1 Rationale and scope of book

The last few years have seen an upsurge of interest in object technology (OT). This interest is increasingly of a commercial nature rather than exclusively the domain of academe and research laboratories. Industry in general is beginning to recognize the potential benefits of adopting object technology as it matures into an established subdiscipline of software engineering (SE). The advent of object technology provides a potentially important opportunity for increased productivity and improved quality for software systems—ever more critical factors in today's "fly-by-wire" technological society.

The combination of increasingly more powerful software tools, such as languages and CASE tools, and cheap, powerful workstations (since the mid-1980s) has been enhanced more recently by the growth in maturity of object-oriented analysis and design (OOA/D) methodologies, which are now being complemented by project management and quality guidelines. Without such a methodological framework and management heuristics, large commercial companies have understandably been reticent to adopt object technology. This book provides methodological guidelines for the development process, including a *strong management perspective*, by focusing on *product quality*.

Object technology requires (i) new analysis and design techniques to replace traditional structured techniques; (ii) new object-oriented metrics to complement and, in many cases, supplant the older "metrics"; and (iii) a revaluation of software development project management guidelines that are currently more appropriate to a strict, linear waterfall-type model of software development. At the programmer level, it also requires a new "style" of coding. Although this is an important topic in itself, it will not be discussed in any detail in this book. Indeed, the subject of programming languages will be discussed only briefly (Section 2.4), since this text is aimed at application and management of object technology throughout the lifecycle, not at the technical level of individual languages where specific implementation techniques are paramount.

The essence of object technology is the adoption of a new mindset and for that mindset to be maintained throughout *all* the phases of the lifecycle. Adopting a consistent mindset permits enhancement of a number of quality factors such as reliability and flexibility (Section 1.2) by focusing on (i) a single model throughout (the "seamless transition"); (ii) a highly encapsulated style of analysis and design; (iii) the use of powerful modeling techniques; and (iv) the creation of reusable designs, frameworks, and coded modules, which both demand and enhance quality.

The rapid rate at which computer-based technologies progress leads to pressure on an organization as existing processes change and new technologies, such as CASE and OT, are adopted. Griss (1992) focuses on the factors that need to be acknowledged, and eventually resolved, in an organization attempting to migrate to any new technology. He notes that there are four major factors (Figure 1.1):

1. *High-level endorsement.* The involvement of senior executives underpins the importance of this new technology to the company goals.
2. *Grass roots involvement.* Even with high-level support, success can only be achieved if the technicians are skilled and enthusiastic about the potential success of the new technology. Money and investment cannot buy success without the collaboration of programmers, designers, and analysts.
3. *Visibility.* Here metrics are able to be used to quantify the progress toward a successful adoption.
4. *Success stories.* Even leading edge companies in the vanguard of the object movement would prefer to hear of successful projects elsewhere to encourage them, as well as to learn from the failures of others so that they may avoid such pitfalls as exist. This gives the motivation for both grass roots "do-ers" and high-level "managers."

Grass roots technicians need to acquire new knowledge. As with any other new technique or new technology, there is a "learning curve" along which "novices" must pass to become "initiates" and finally "experts." The path from "novice" to "expert" is typified by the more rapid assimilation of information, the smaller

Introduction

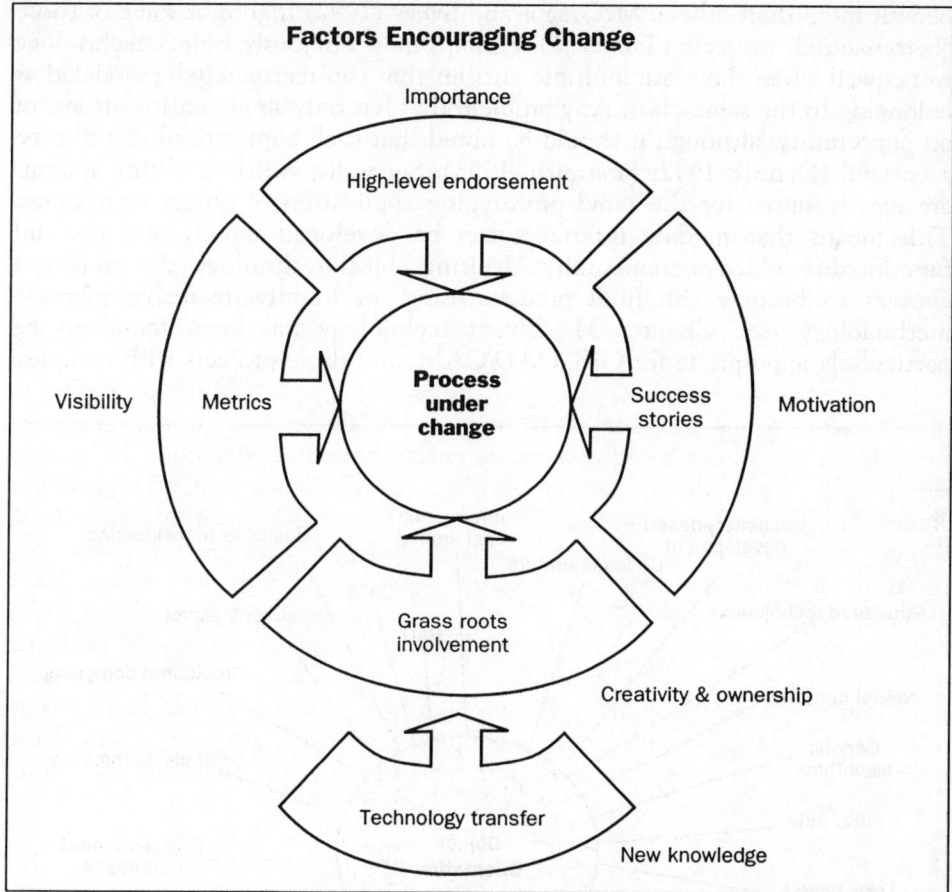

Figure 1.1 *Four major factors involved in migration to any new technology (Griss, 1992)*

numbers of cues utilized, the accuracy of decisions, and the increasing reliability of predictions (van Gigch, 1991, p151). The need for education and training is increasingly stressed (e.g., D'Souza, 1992; Parkhill, 1992; Rossiter, 1992; Bellin, 1992). Concepts need to be emphasized (in education) rather than skills (the realm of training). The effort of learning should not be underestimated—but then neither should the potential benefits!

Object-orientation is often touted as a panacea. Rather than a panacea, it should be regarded as today's best available option for developing high-quality software systems. Odell (1992b) identifies object-orientation more as a facilitating technology, offering interconnectability support for a wide range of systems approaches (Figure 1.2). Some advocates of object technology may try to persuade you that any application can benefit from the adoption of object technology. While this is nearly true, there are some types of projects that can benefit more than others. McGregor and Sykes (1992) highlight some of those "better-suited" projects (Table 1.1). Perhaps most obviously, object technology works well when there are multiple entities that can reasonably be modeled as belonging to the same class. Any problem that has only single entities is less of an opportunity, although it should be noted that such applications can also be successful (Dennis, 1992; Firesmith, 1993). Secondly, swiftly evolving systems are ideally suited for the rapid prototyping application of object technology. This means that module interfaces can be developed rapidly and the full functionality added incrementally. Utilizing object technology, the prototype evolves to become the final product using an iterative/recursive lifecycle methodology (see Chapter 3). Object technology has been found to be particularly appropriate for GIS, CAD/CAM, and those projects with complex

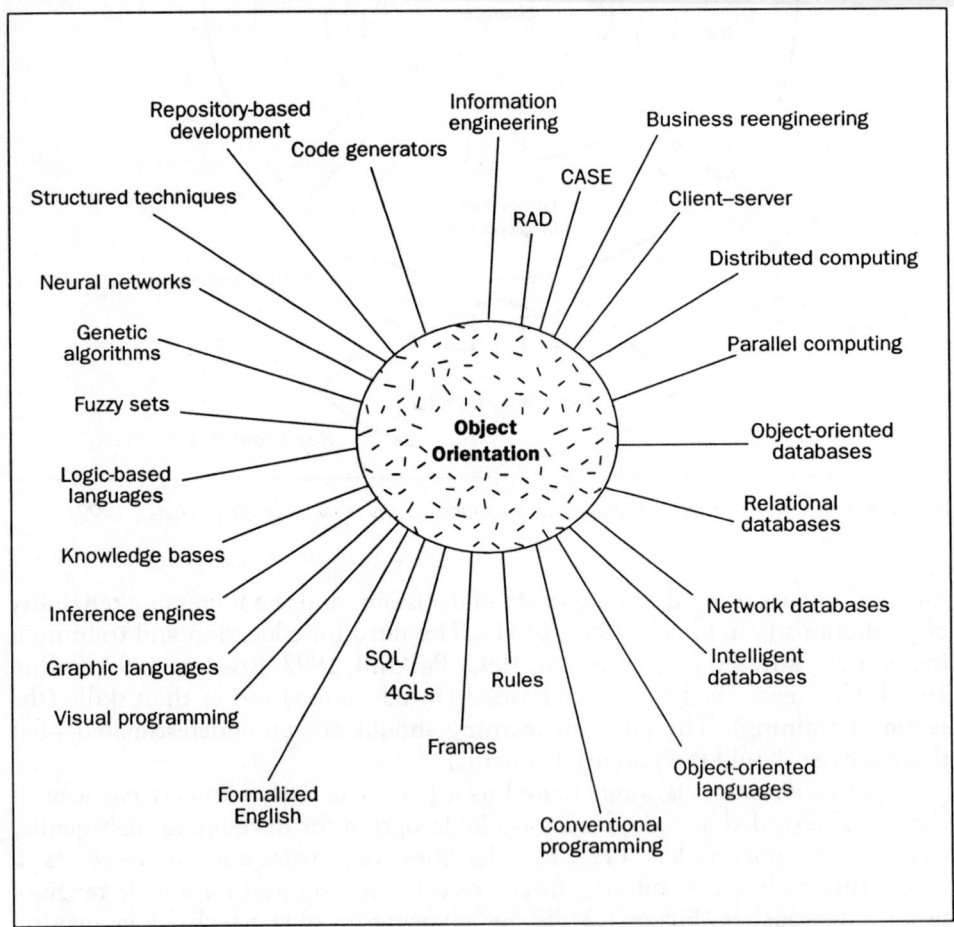

Figure 1.2 *OO can be used as a mechanism that organizes and interconnects many different kinds of system approaches (Odell, © copyright SIGS Publications, 1992)*

data and models to be manipulated (Object Interest Group, 1991), as well as offering potential for enhanced quality to traditional MIS application areas.

Table 1.1 *When to use OO techniques (Adapted from McGregor and Sykes, 1992)*

- When multiple instances of complex entities are part of the solution
- When solutions will evolve over time
- When prototyping leads to quick development of module interfaces
- When a number of related applications will be developed over time
- When large development teams and large applications require partitioning of the system

Organizational contexts must also be considered. For example, an industry that is focused on a single application domain (for example, a large bank's information systems (IS) department) can accrue benefits rapidly through reuse of domain-specific classes, frameworks, and designs. On the other hand, contract software developers who respond to requests for systems over a number of application domains are unlikely to be able to recoup their class library investments rapidly enough to maintain a competitive advantage *in the short term*. In other words, while there are undoubted benefits in the long term, the company must, of course, still be viable in the short term before any long-term benefits can be realized. In such a situation, it is also likely that *not* adopting object technology might lead to short-term advantage but long-term disadvantage—again rendering the long-term viability of the organization suspect. Perhaps the best advice here would be to be more focused in developing both operational and strategic business plans that lead to phased integration of object technology on an economically viable time scale.

Another area likely to yield results rapidly is the solution of large-scale computing problems where there is no option other than to partition the project among several teams. Since object technology offers, particularly in analysis and design, a larger-scale packaging technology (namely, the subsystem or subassembly) than the procedural paradigm, it matches readily the entities present in the problem domain that span a range of resolutions/abstraction levels (see also Section 2.2). In other words, an object-oriented approach provides a sounder and more consistent base for modeling business rules, products, and services than a traditional, functional decomposition strategy. It provides a greater capability for scaling up to larger systems than previously possible (e.g., Booch, 1991) in a way that is understandable to managers and technicians alike.

Graham (1991) sees the key business advantages of adopting object technology as (i) reusability and (ii) extensibility. Reuse decreases costs directly. Coupled with easy extension to existing software modules (decreased "maintenance" costs), object technology permits a company to react quickly to changes in the business environment or to user requests for modifications and enhancements (Humphrys, 1991). This is a key feature of object technology, as business opportunities are changing ever more rapidly.

The rationale for this book (BOOKTWO) then is not solely to gain object-oriented knowledge for its own sake, but to also harness this knowledge to provide "The Working Object." The text goes beyond simply a presentation of a methodology by additionally providing managerial guidelines. Our premise is that strategic investment in object technology requires:

- information on concepts (the "learning curve");
- a workable software development lifecycle (SDLC) methodology;
- a supporting (graphical and/or textual) notation;
- supporting tools;
- management guidelines, deliverables, and case studies;
- a migration path;
- metrics.

In BOOKTWO, we provide just such information. This book is therefore aimed at providing a workable project management methodology, and is *not* an introductory level book (this is available as BOOK: Henderson-Sellers, 1992a). However, in order to make the present volume relatively self-contained, we felt it appropriate to review the basic concepts of the object paradigm (Chapter 2) before describing methodological details (Chapter 3). The central part of the book (Chapters 4–7) is the presentation of the Methodology for Object-oriented Software Engineering of Systems (or MOSES for short) and its associated notation. Indeed, to present MOSES was one of the underlying reasons for writing this work. Chapter 8 presents a case study using MOSES to illustrate some of the fine details of this second-generation methodology and notation.

Of even more recent origin than methodologies are the other tools that industry demands: project management guidelines, consideration of CASE tools and other automated support (Chapter 9), and object-oriented metrics (Chapter 10). Although we cannot promise a complete answer to all (or indeed any) of these major areas of interest to industry, these last two chapters introduce material not found elsewhere.

1.2 Goals of software engineering

In her analysis of object-oriented project management, Adele Goldberg (1991a) asks the question "What do we value in software development project management?" She suggests that satisfaction (to developer and/or end user) derives from (i) delivering the product to the user on time and within budget—

perhaps the key "bone of contention" for IS managers; (ii) ensuring that the products really do meet the user requirements—this requires significant dialogue with the user to be maintained during the development; (iii) responding in a timely fashion to user requests to modify the system and/or fix bugs in the current version of the software—software needs to be extensible to meet changing business needs; (iv) being able to offer increasingly sophisticated applications products to the marketplace and keep a competitive edge; (v) keeping up with changes in standards and delivery technology; and (vi) ensuring the project team feels both well motivated and successful, since enthusiastic team members are generally more productive and more likely to meet quality objectives.

Table 1.2 summarizes the 14 basic advantages of using an OO approach to address the problem areas of software engineering:

1. *Correctness and verifiability.* There is an obvious need for software to be correct and verifiable, although the definition of these terms is not universally agreed upon. Correctness is potentially more attainable using an object-oriented approach (e.g., Henderson-Sellers, 1991c) by the use of assertions (Meyer, 1989b), which tie in tightly with the concepts of contracts and client–server relationships (see discussion in Section 2.3.4). The use of formal methods for verification in OT is also attracting growing interest (Stepney *et al.*, 1992).
2. *Robustness.* This relates to the program's behavior when exposed to abnormal conditions. A robust program will not only be resilient to abnormality but also, when it must fail, do so in a controlled and "graceful" way—"exception handling." Robustness is improved when you can safely

Table 1.2 *Fourteen basic advantages of object-oriented software engineering (Adapted and revised from Henderson-Sellers, 1992a)*

1. Correctness and verifiability
2. Robustness
3. Extensibility
4. Reusability
5. Integrity
6. Quality
7. Increased productivity
8. Data dependency avoidance
9. Better model of real world
10. Seamless transition
11. Maintainability
12. Ease of use
13. Management of complexity
14. Competitive edge

modify a portion of your program without causing repercussions in distant parts of the code.

3. *Extensibility.* Following delivery, the user will often return to the software developer with new ideas about how the original success can be built on and the program developed to undertake new problem solving. That is likely to require the addition of extra program components. Using an object-oriented systems development methodology, this is easier and safer than in a more traditional functional decomposition methodology, most markedly for *large* software developments. Extensibility is achievable, in part, by the availability of inheritance constructs in object-oriented programming languages (OOPLs).

4. *Reusability.* This is seen as so important by Brad Cox (Cox, 1986) that he has trademarked the phrase "software IC" (IC = integrated circuit). His basic idea is to follow the analogy of hardware, which works on the premise that you don't reinvent basic circuits every time; rather you take what already exists, buy chips off the shelf, and plug them together to build your "original" design of a "hardware box." However, Graham (1991) notes that there is in fact one major difference: while hardware goods can be mass-produced by multiple instantiation (manufacturing lines), software products are in essence individualistic. Multiple copies are then created as perfect clones rather than being produced in the manufacturing sense, where perfect reproduction is not assured. Meyer (1989c) characterizes this as a shift from a *project* culture (non-OO) to a *product* culture (OO) (Figure 1.3). Here the short-term goals of projects in which there is little or often no

Shift of Mindset Project culture versus product culture

	PROJECT	PRODUCT
OUTCOME	RESULTS	COMPONENTS, LIBRARIES, TOOLS
Economics	Profit	Investment
Unit	Department	Company, industry
Time frame	Short-term	Long-term
Goal	Programs	Systems
Bricks	Program elements	Software components
Strategy	Top-down	More bottom-up
Method	Functional	Object-oriented
Language	C, Pascal, COBOL, etc.	OOPL–Eiffel, Smalltalk, C++, etc.

Figure 1.3 *Project versus product culture (Meyer, 1989c)*

emphasis on developing reusable code for future projects are replaced by the strategic aims of reusability and software components viable for the whole industry sector, as opposed to the current project team. It is possible to build up libraries of classes and of object-oriented designs that can subsequently be reused. It should be noted that reusability includes not only reusability of code but also reusability of designs. Reusability is one of the major advantages that an OO approach can provide and is consequently discussed further in Section 1.3.2.

5. *Integrity.* Integrity can be discussed in terms of accidental or unauthorized access. Highly encapsulated classes with tightly defined interfaces possess a higher degree of integrity. The resulting coded modules are, as a consequence, difficult to modify accidentally. This is the antithesis of structured languages, which permit (even encourage) globally scoped variables. In such programs, it is very easy to overload a variable name inadvertently, with sometimes disastrous consequences.

6. *Quality.* Product quality is, in general, more important for commercial success than speed or productivity. Quality is difficult to define, but quality products are readily discernible by the user. It requires correctness, robustness, integrity, etc.[1] as prerequisites but enhances these with characteristics less easily quantified. Singh (1990) characterizes quality by (i) how well the model adapts to changes in requirements and (ii) how consistent is the feel of the application—both hard to quantify unequivocally. It is worthwhile emphasizing quality *per se* as a goal of good software engineering practice, but one that has unfortunately been seldom achieved in practice (see, for example, any issue of ACM *Software Engineering Notes*).

Table 1.3 *Attributes of software quality*

(Adapted from Graham, 1991)	
Resilience and Reliability (robustness)	
Correctness	Verifiability
Maintainability	Security
Reusability and generality	Integrity
Interoperability	Friendliness
Efficiency	Describable
Portability	Understandability
(Adapted from Thomsett, 1990)	
Conformity	Portability
Reliability	Usability
Maintainability	Auditability
Reusability	Security
Efficiency	Flexibility

1. Graham (1991, p36) gives a list of 13 quality indicators and Thomsett (1990) 10 (Table 1.3).

Those are the *main* software engineering concerns addressed by object-oriented software engineering. There are other, less obvious, potential advantages, including:

7. *Productivity.* It is becoming increasingly evident that there will necessarily be an increased overhead in the analysis and design stages, with a concomitant decrease in coding/implementation and in maintenance (see detailed discussion in Section 9.1). This contrasts with traditional methods where the maximum effort in design is less but the ensuing phases (implementation, testing, and maintenance) continue to require large amounts of effort (traditional "Rayleigh" curve: Norden, 1958—see Section 10.5). Initial experiments (Lewis *et al.*, 1992) support the contention that use of the object-oriented paradigm "substantially improves" productivity in comparison with a traditional procedural environment. Plews (1993) differentiates between the use of a hybrid OOPL and a pure OOPL (see Section 2.4.2) and concludes that "using hybrid object-oriented languages did not exhibit a statistically significant advantage" over traditional 3GLs, while the use of a pure OOPL gave rise to statistically significant results using standard McCabe and Halstead metrics (see Chapter 10 for details of these metrics). In addition, O'Shea (1992) notes studies in which a 14 to 1 improvement in productivity and a 12 to 1 reduction in code size were achieved. However, it should be noted (Meyer, 1992c) that productivity increases are a *consequence* of gains in quality, not a *raison d'être*.
8. Avoidance of the *data dependency* problem. This problem occurs when data structures are frozen in many parts of the program, e.g., United States zip codes in the address field of several applications. When a change is made (recently United States zip codes were lengthened by a dash and four numerals), *all* occurrences of what is essentially the identical data structure must be changed simultaneously—an error-prone and costly exercise.
9. A *better model* of the real world. This means that the integrated focus on state and behavior is nearer to the way in which humans build abstractions of the world around them. It is more "natural" (e.g., Bennett, 1991) and easily personalized (Ramakrishnan, 1992). This is borne out by the initial emergence of OT within the simulation community (Simula) and as a way of teaching young children the essence of programming (Smalltalk). The ability to incorporate the same modeling techniques *throughout* the lifecycle is seen as a great advantage by many authors (e.g., Rumbaugh *et al.*, 1991; Jacobson *et al.*, 1992), although Odell (1992a) notes that objects model the way in which reality is understood by people rather than modeling reality directly.
10. *"Seamless transition."* This means that the same model applies through the different stages and that there is a more or less one-to-one mapping between the models developed during the requirements and design stages and then between design and coding (Coad, 1991). The models and notations used in design evolve smoothly from those used in analysis. Auditability is also increased. This is illustrated in Figure 1.4, where each ellipse is a

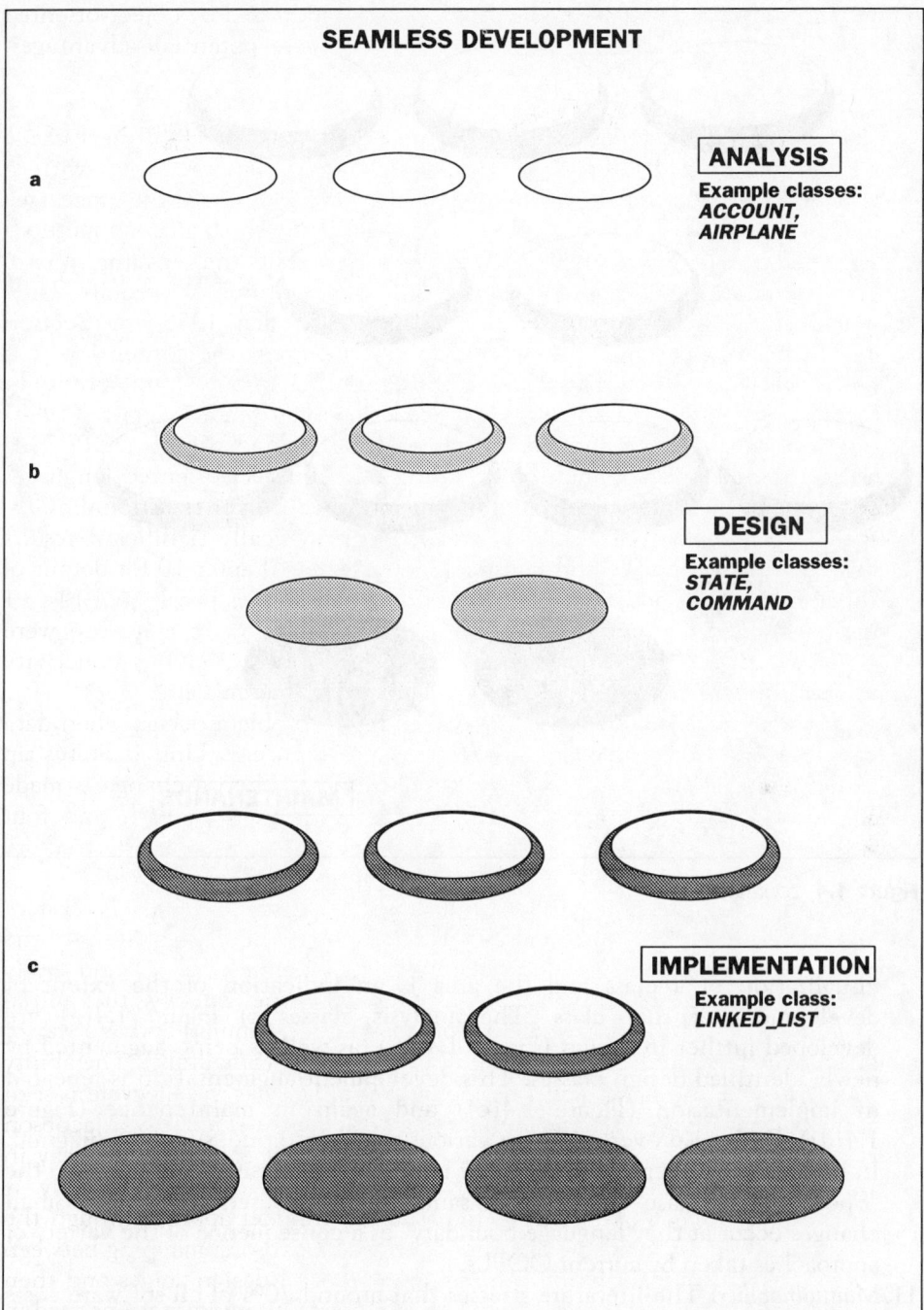

Figure 1.4 *Seamless development visualized in (a) analysis, (b) design, (c) implementation, and (d) maintenance (Meyer, 1992e)*

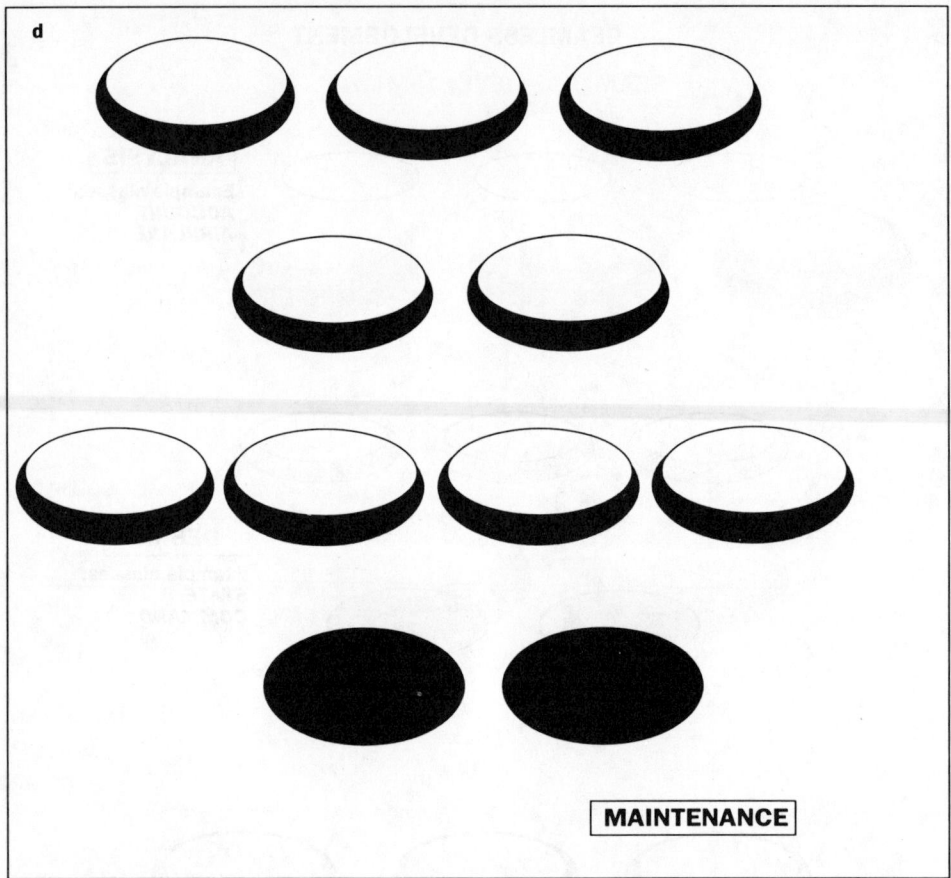

Figure 1.4 *continued*

visualization of a class and the area is an indication of the extent of development of that class. The analysis classes of Figure 1.4(a) are developed further in design (Figure 1.4(b)), as well as being augmented by newly identified design classes. This development/augmentation is repeated in implementation (Figure 1.4(c)) and again in maintenance (Figure 1.4(d)). Figure 1.5 overlays these various stages into one, summary diagram. In MOSES, this is emphasized by the merging of analysis and design into the "Specification Phase" in which the same notation is used throughout. Small changes occur at the "language boundary" as a consequence of the variety of approaches taken by current OOPLs.

11. *Maintainability*. The literature stresses that around 70% of all software costs are maintenance costs (e.g., Boehm, 1975, 1981). With a more reliable, more easily extensible system, maintenance costs should drop substantially

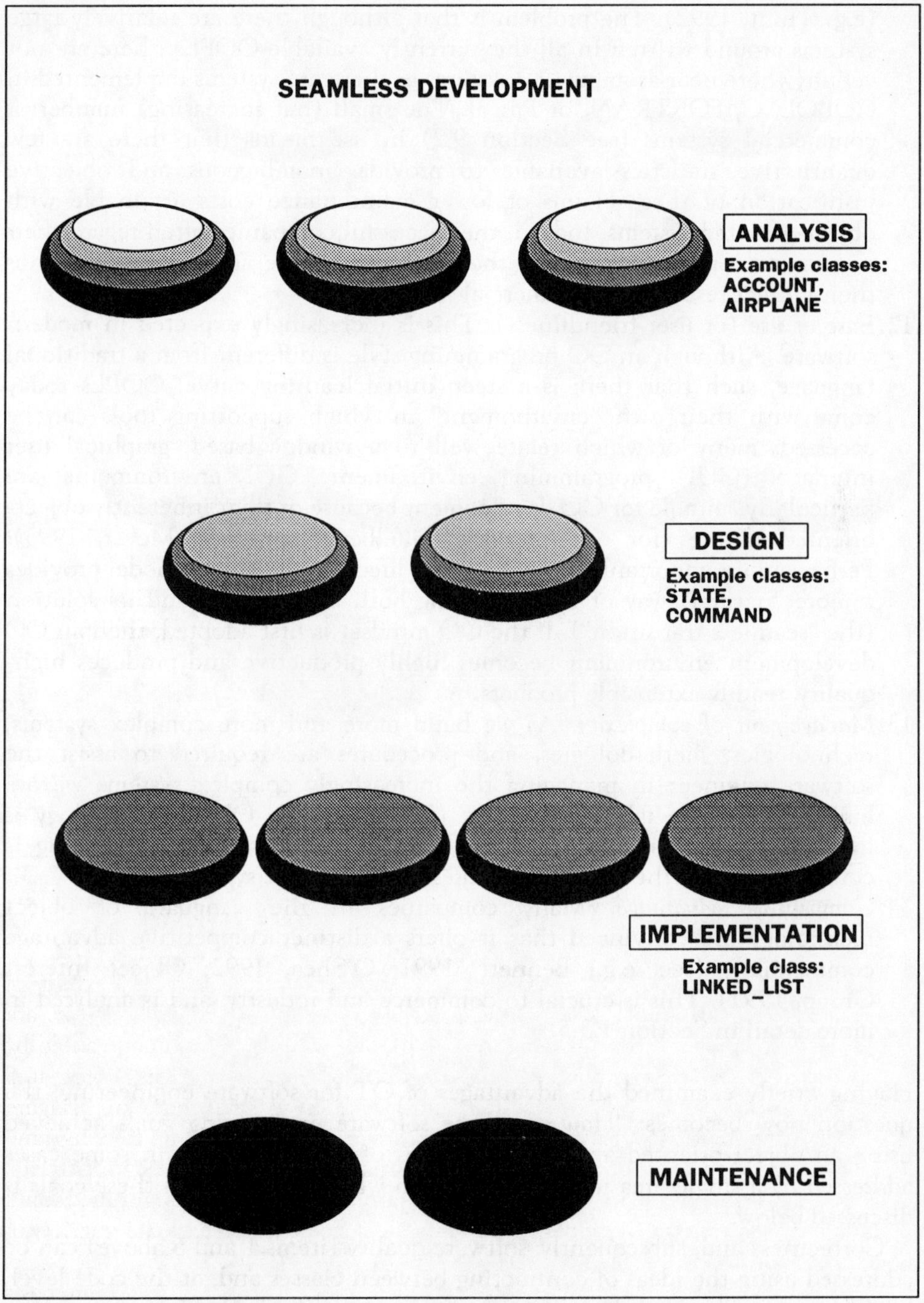

SEAMLESS DEVELOPMENT

ANALYSIS
Example classes:
ACCOUNT,
AIRPLANE

DESIGN
Example classes:
STATE,
COMMAND

IMPLEMENTATION
Example class:
LINKED_LIST

MAINTENANCE

Figure 1.5 *Summary visualization of the "seamless development" of an object-oriented system (Meyer, 1992e)*

(e.g., Hunt, 1992). The problem is that although there are relatively large systems around written in all the currently available OOPLs, there are not yet anywhere near as many OO systems as there are systems implemented in COBOL, C, FORTRAN, or Pascal. The small (but increasing) number of commercial systems (see Section 9.2) in use means that there are few quantitative statistics available to provide unambiguous and objective justification of these claims of lower maintenance costs attainable with object-oriented systems. Indeed, the successful companies often regard their systems as confidential, giving them a "competitive advantage," and thus their project results are "commercial secrets."

12. *Ease of use* (or user friendliness). This is increasingly expected in modern software. Although an OO programming style is different from a traditional language, such that there is a steep initial learning curve, OOPLs today come with their own "environment" in which supporting tools can be accessed, many of which relate well to a window-based, graphical user interface (GUI) programming environment. GUI environments are particularly suitable for OO development because of their inherently object-oriented nature (for example, the Eiffelbench product: Meyer, 1993). Perhaps more important, throughout the lifecycle the object-model provides a more "natural" way of understanding both the problem and its solution (the "seamless transition"). If the OO mindset is first adopted, then an OO development environment becomes highly productive and produces high-quality, readily extensible products.

13. *Management of complexity.* As we build more and more complex systems, technologies, methodologies, and procedures are required to assist the software engineer in managing the increasingly complex systems we are building into the fabric of society (Booch, 1991). Object technology is inherently modular, and in such a way that more semantic meaning is contained within the software modules and hence the system.

14. *Competitive advantage.* Many companies in the vanguard of object technology are convinced that it offers a distinct competitive advantage commercially (see, e.g., Bennett, 1991; O'Shea, 1992; Object Interest Group, 1991). This is crucial to commerce and industry, and is analyzed in more detail in Section 1.3.5.

Having briefly examined the advantages of OT for software engineering, the question now becomes: "*How* are these software engineering goals achieved using an object-oriented approach?" Groups of these goals are in some cases addressed by a single area in OT. The way in which OT supports these goals is discussed below.

Correctness and, subsequently, software quality (items 1 and 6 above) can be addressed using the ideas of contracting between classes and, at the code level, by assertions *within* the class. The increasing use of formal techniques such as assertions enhances quality, although it should be noted that their advent predates OOPLs, in languages such as Alphard and Euclid (see Meyer, 1988a,

Chapter 7). Assertions (a form of *constraint*) include preconditions, postconditions, and invariants. A precondition specifies the conditions under which an operation is initiated and a postcondition specifies what the operation must achieve. Each may be tested in the code to ensure compliance. For example, there may be a business rule stating that a bank balance must exceed some threshold value before a withdrawal is permitted. Class invariants can be used that prevent specified constraints (business rules) from being violated at any time during the use of an object. For example, a bank balance is never allowed to become negative. They should be viewed as part of the class specification, i.e., essentially a part of the semantic specification of the class and *independent* of implementation (see also Section 2.4.3.2 for a language-level view of assertions).

Robustness, extensibility, reusability, and integrity (items 2 to 5 above) are all essentially addressed by the concepts of modularity and encapsulation, as well as by the notion of abstract data types. Encapsulation and modularity have always been considered important in procedural programming. However, identification of modules in a procedural language need not be conceptually or semantically coherent, whereas the module of object technology (the class) is tightly focused upon semantic cohesion.

Encapsulation localizes data and the operations upon those data in one place. Encapsulation combined with information hiding leads to a module with a clearly defined interface typically expressed as an external interface hiding the private parts and hence hiding the implementation. This means that internals of the module are protected against accidental changes in the external environment. Additionally, the module describes a single logical entity: the abstract data type (ADT). This reinforces the focus on quality, reusable code, and the avoidance of redundancy.

Modularity expresses the idea that each chunk of code should be autonomous and self-contained. The rationale in object-oriented systems is not the functional, procedural, or sometimes accidental cohesion that results from such program decomposition but is a focus upon logical or semantic cohesion (see Section 10.3.2). In many OOPLs, classes provide that basic module used as the building blocks of system development containing both data and functionality; in others a class may be split between more than one module (e.g., interface and implementation separately modularized in C++). A class should, however, be more than a module; it should also relate to a meaningful concept or abstraction. In some object-oriented programming languages the software modules are identical to classes. In other OOPLs the primary software module may not be the class, and hence a module may contain more than one class. As can be seen, modules and classes are not identical concepts but in an OO framework they are often regarded as the same, especially during analysis and design and frequently in implementation.

Meyer (1988a) proposes five principles for modularity: decomposability, composability, understandability, continuity, and protection. He suggests that these criteria can be met best by utilizing linguistic modular units, interfaces that are few, small, and explicit, and information hiding (Section 2.3.2).

Reusability, flexibility, productivity, and high quality are key advantages of object-oriented software engineering. They are coupled in one sense: if we reuse existing code and existing designs, then we must become more productive in the sense of achieving the goal with less expenditure of effort. These well-tested library classes are then of higher quality than previously achievable. Reusability, then, aims to provide high-quality software available "off the shelf"; this may be software from the organization's project library or software purchased from a general vendor. The topic of library management is discussed in detail in Section 9.1.4, as it plays a crucial role in the adoption and subsequent management of object technology in organizations.

Data dependency (item 8 above) has long been an area of great concern in software engineering and especially in database management. To illustrate the problem, Figure 1.6 shows some pseudocode in a procedural language, while Figure 1.7 shows the equivalent in an OOPL to illustrate the extent of data dependency in the two paradigms. Here, consider a bank account that is represented as a record with a type of CHECKING or SAVINGS or MISA (Mortgage Investment Savings Account). It has a balance of type MONEY and procedures including *deposit, withdraw, transfer*. In a procedural language, a procedure (module) for *deposit* would be written. With several types of bank account in existence, it is likely that there may be slightly different rules for each type of bank account for each of these procedures. For instance, with the MISA type of account, deposits and transfers may have to be in multiples of, say, $500. In a procedural sense, this would be coded as a procedure *deposit* and a Case statement would be used to select the type of bank account under consideration. Similarly, there would be a Case statement for procedure *withdraw*, etc. In a procedural language, addition of a new bank account with new procedural implementations of *withdraw, deposit*, etc., would require modification to *every* Case structure—easy to miss one in a large program even with automated tools. In this example, each Case structure would have to be changed from a three-way switch to a four-way switch.

In an OOPL (Figure 1.7), on the other hand, there would be a basic BANK_ACCOUNT type with an attribute *balance* and routines *withdraw, deposit, transfer*, etc. Each of the other bank account types would be coded as subclasses—CHECKING, SAVINGS, and MISA—each inheriting (see Section 2.3.6) from class BANK_ACCOUNT and possibly redefining one or more of the procedures. Class CHECKING would inherit everything from BANK_ACCOUNT. Addition of a new account class is then straightforward. The bank decides to start a new STUDENT_SAVINGS account. Rather than having to locate several Case statements scattered around a procedural program, in an object-oriented system a new account is added by declaring a new class STUDENT_SAVINGS that inherits from an existing class, SAVINGS. The declaration simply says, in effect, that this new account class is "just like a savings account" (the inherit clause), "but it has some slight redefinition of some or all the features."

Introduction — 17

Data Dependency

Type
　　BankAccount = Record
　　　　Type:(CheckingAccount, SavingsAccount,
　　　　　　　　MISAAccount);
　　　　Balance: Money;
　　　　. . . .
　　End;

Procedure deposit(account:BankAccount,amount:Money)
Case BankAccount. Type of

　　CheckingAccount:Checkdeposit(account,amount);
　　SavingsAccount:Savingsdeposit(account,amount);
　　MISAAccount:MISAdeposit(account,amount);
End;

Procedure withdraw(account:BankAccount,amount:Money)
Case BankAccount. Type of

　　CheckingAccount:Checkwithdraw(account,amount);
　　SavingsAccount:Savingswithdraw(account,amount);
　　MISAAccount:MISAwithdraw(account,amount);
End;

Procedure transfer (. . . etc.)

New account (e.g., StudentSavingsAccount) must be added separately to Case structure of **all** procedure definitions

Figure 1.6 *The problem of data dependency is seen in the location of similar operations in different subroutines in a procedural language (Henderson-Sellers, 1992a)*

Problem avoided using OO

```
Type
    BANK_ACCOUNT
Attribute
    balance
Routine
    withdraw
    - - algorithm to withdraw
    deposit
    - - algorithm to deposit
    transfer
    - - algorithm to transfer
End

Subtype
    CHECKING
Inherit
    BANK_ACCOUNT
End

Subtype
    SAVINGS
Inherit
    BANK_ACCOUNT
Routine
    - - redefines withdraw
    withdraw
    - - new algorithm to withdraw
End
```

Adding new account, simply add

```
Subtype
    STUDENT_SAVINGS
Inherit
    SAVINGS
Routine
    - - appropriate redefinitions or new features
End
```

Figure 1.7 *The object-oriented approach avoids the data dependency problem seen in Figure 1.6 (Henderson-Sellers, 1992a)*

The proposition that an object-oriented model is a better model of the real world (item 9 above) is supported by the origin of object-orientation in the simulation world, where modeling concerns are paramount. It is also a better model for software development insofar as it provides a relatively "seamless transition" throughout the lifecycle. In other words, the modeling approach used in the Specification Phase (analysis plus design) is essentially the same as that applied in the Implementation Phase (detailed design plus coding) (Figure 1.8). Use of the same underlying modeling paradigm also assists in traceability or auditability because the basic unit ("class") is identifiable in the analysis, the design, and even the code (assuming an object-oriented programming language is used). This is in stark contrast to functional decomposition and structured lifecycle methodologies where different models are used at different lifecycle stages: for instance, an entity relationship diagram and data flow diagram in the analysis phase, a hierarchy chart in the design phase, and a procedural module at the language level. These are all *very* different ways of viewing the world and hence provide a variety of views of each piece of software.

Viewing the world in terms of objects and classes is claimed to be more natural (e.g., Bennett, 1991). It is claimed that when we view the world we tend to see objects, things possessing identifiable and describable characteristics, and have a tendency to classify similar objects into categories (e.g., trees, birds). The most immediate characteristic is what the object looks like (its external interface). Secondarily, we notice how the thing behaves. In other words, we see state and behavior. Objects are thus identifiable in the real world and translated *directly* (i.e., not through some intermediary akin to structure charts or DFDs) into software objects grouped into classes. Objects from these classes then interact with each other.

Although an object-oriented model may simply be described as more data-oriented than a traditional procedural/functional decomposition model, it is much more than a straightforward data-centered approach. Indeed, the distinction is somewhat irrelevant, as an object-oriented approach integrates data and functionality by describing a holistic abstraction in which objects are identified by their behaviors or responsibilities (e.g., Wirfs-Brock *et al.*, 1990; Kilov, 1990; Rubin and Goldberg, 1992). This is succinctly illustrated by Wirfs-Brock *et al.* (1990) in describing a horse using the following approaches:

- The *data-driven* approach describes a horse in terms of its parts: head, tail, body, legs.
- The *procedural* approach describes a horse in terms of operations it can perform: walk, run, trot, bite, eat, neigh.
- The *responsibility-driven* approach describes a horse in terms of its responsibilities: communicate, carry things, maintain its living systems.

There are a number of areas of object technology that have been viewed less positively—for example, compatibility with other languages and software systems. However, although this new technology initially appears to provide incompatible software, there are several, largely unexplored, advantages in

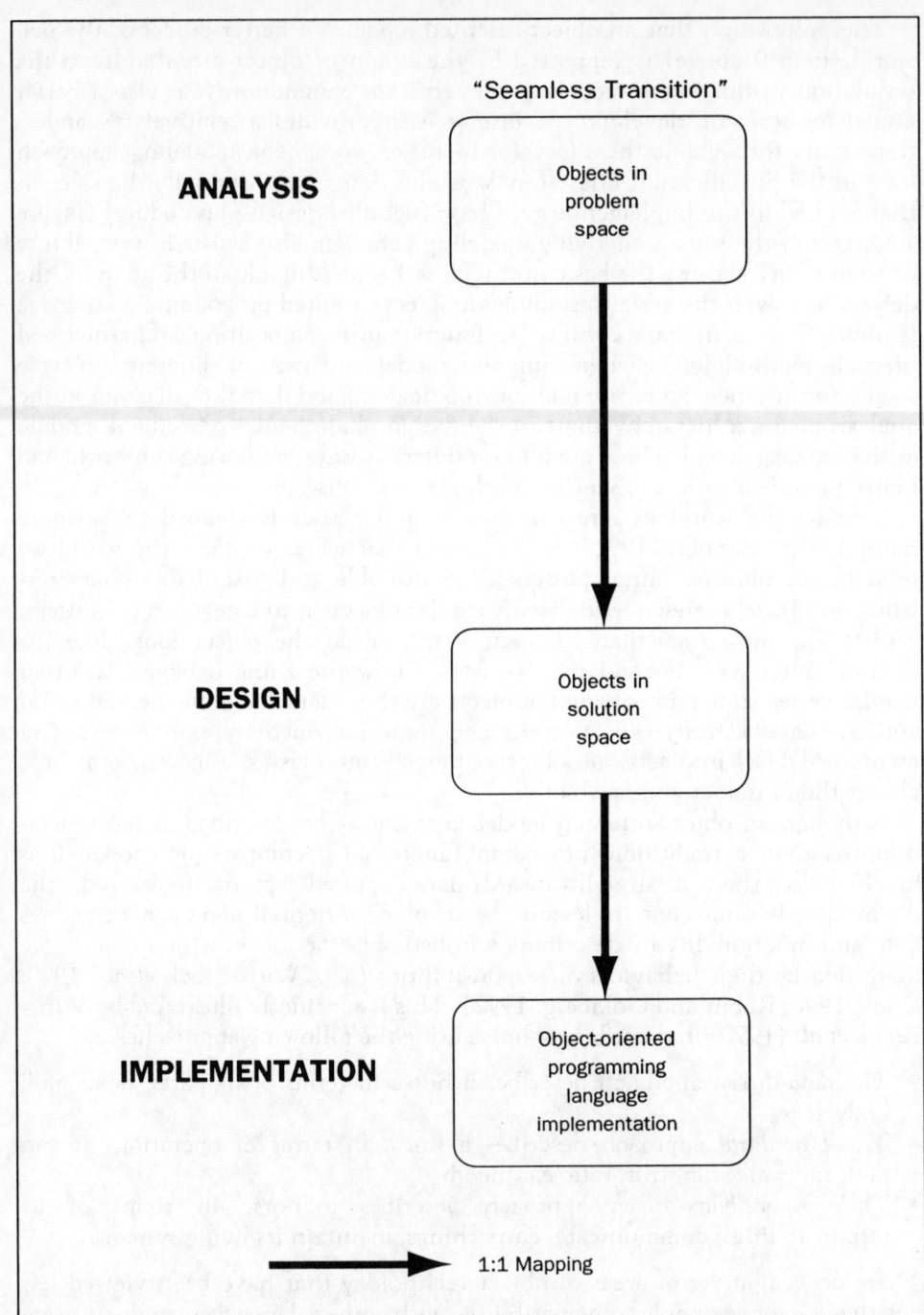

Figure 1.8 *Object technology provides a "seamless transition" across the lifecycle by using objects at each phase*

terms of linkages with other languages. For instance, in Eiffel, Smalltalk, and C++ it is possible to link in subprograms written in C or assembler (and potentially other languages, databases, etc.). This suggests a more open design in software development compatible with and supported by the general trend to open systems computing. Certain packaging approaches can be explored in which procedural modules can be given interfaces compatible with classes in a system. This may provide a migration path from procedures to classes, as such encapsulated procedures gradually require replacement (see Section 9.2.1).

At the language level, efficiency of the early OO compilers was a major concern. This has certainly improved recently, such that although OO languages will probably never be as machine-efficient as low-level languages, their compile-time and run-time characteristics are more than acceptable for most commercial domains of application. Concerns about these characteristics are also fading as higher-powered, low-price PCs and workstations rapidly come onto the market.

Object technology can support open systems computing and portability by encapsulating all platform-specific details into a small number of classes. For example, Smalltalk 80 is portable to any machine without change to the source code, as it uses its own virtual machine (Dellinger, 1992). This encapsulation capability makes object-oriented systems potentially more portable across platforms than traditional systems.

Apart from the concerns discussed above, a number of more obvious constraints and/or caveats that might restrict full exploitation of this new technology include (adapted, in part, from Graham, 1991):

- Reusability (one of the key benefits of object technology) is sacrificed on the altar of expediency when the product delivery dates are near.
- There is a need to change intraorganizational culture to cooperation rather than competitiveness in order to encourage reuse, something that may be difficult for the competitively driven organization.
- Information about available class libraries is not easy to disseminate and there is little incentive for software developers to build them in the first place.
- The relative immaturity of the technology means that we are still at a stage of rapid growth and change which makes industrialists hesitant about investing heavily in the technology.
- The optimum use of inheritance can compromise reusability and industry guidelines are still required.
- Persistence, concurrency, and performance issues have still to be resolved, particularly in the ODBMS arena.
- Stylistic code guidelines are not yet standard for object-oriented programming.
- A significant change in the mindset of the organization is required so that it can benefit effectively from OO solutions.

On the basis of the above discussion, we feel that object technology aims to provide the mechanisms with which to achieve many qualities valued in software. We have briefly discussed these mechanisms and indicated some of the likely impediments to full exploitation of the technology.

1.3 Managing objects

We noted in the opening paragraphs of this chapter the lack of a management slant to many object-oriented texts. In this section we give only a brief introduction to the key management issues, which are then discussed in detail throughout the remainder of this book.

1.3.1 Methodologies and notation

The first key concern is that of appropriate methodologies. We view this as the cornerstone for the adoption of object technologies and devote the major part of this book to that topic: we discuss it first in terms of general concepts, and then in terms of currently available methodologies and notation (Chapter 3), finally presenting the full details of one specific, comprehensive SDLC methodology: MOSES (Chapters 4–8).

A methodology is a set of instructions, guidelines, and heuristics that is *implementable* within a commercial environment addressing technical and managerial issues. An acceptable methodology should span the *whole* lifecycle from initial users' requirements through to delivery and maintenance. It must be well documented (this book provides the prime documentation for the MOSES methodology) and be amenable to creating a flexible development in which recursion, iteration, and rapid prototyping are easily accommodated. This is achieved within MOSES by separating the idea of activities and phases and only integrating them in a final description of the "development process." This approach allows different organizations to adapt the process to different lifecycles (such as prototyping) as necessary.

A number of notations have also been proposed. Some of these are inextricably linked with one methodology; others are effectively stand-alone in that the icons support the object model but are adaptable for various methodological environments. A growing number of these notations are now supported by CASE tools (Chapter 9.1.5), often marketed by the notation developer, but also increasingly by third parties. However, it seems highly unlikely that the global IS community will adopt a single notation worldwide in the foreseeable future. In Chapter 3 we include details of these notations along with our discussions of available methodologies. Chapter 5 presents the notation we have developed for MOSES. This notation builds on the Uniform Object Notation of Page-Jones *et al.* (1990) by incorporation of the systems level ideas of Edwards and Henderson-Sellers (1991, 1993a) and objectcharts developed by Coleman *et al.* (1992).

1.3.2 Project management

In the object-oriented lifecycle, more effort is required in the Specification Phase and considerably less in program building (Implementation) and later Enhancements. Strategic planning is therefore required by organizations, together with concomitant software metrics (see also Caldiera and Basili, 1991) and clearly stated deliverables, so that the actual quality and productivity gains foreseen for large system developments using the object-oriented paradigm can be consistently evaluated.

The learning curve for any object-oriented language therefore relates not just to learning the syntax of the language, which in some cases is relatively easy, but to learning to navigate through the existing libraries of prebuilt classes. Although learning to navigate around a class library of about 200 classes is not trivial, even with the use of available browsing tools, the anticipated advent of corporation libraries of several thousand or hundreds of thousands of classes, and the possibility of third-party class vendors providing off-the-shelf classes for purchase, require techniques for locating the required class. Object-oriented cataloging and retrieval systems (Section 9.1.4) are currently being developed to address this challenge of large-scale reusability (e.g., Meyer, 1990a; Price and Girardi, 1990; Henderson-Sellers and Freeman, 1992; Ma and Edwards, 1991). Finally, the problem of software quality in vendor libraries has yet to be addressed fully (Korson and McGregor, 1992).

1.3.3 The importance of reuse

A significant advantage of object technology is the ease and extent of reuse now possible (e.g., Wegner, 1990, pp15–16; Cox, 1990a,b; Griss, 1991; Graham, 1991, p7; Lewis *et al.*, 1992; Pratap, 1992; Meyer, 1992e). Graham (1991) notes that industrial observers suggest that a reuse strategy could save up to 20% of development costs, and this in an industry where even a 1% saving could give a competitor a major advantage. Many of the benefits of reuse are realized by generalization of coded classes for storage in libraries and subsequent reuse— either directly or via extension using inheritance. Class specialization using inheritance becomes a powerful, robust, and safe way of extending existing modular code without fear of "breaking" existing working modules. In this way, a new class that is semantically just like its parent class, but with slight differences, is created. It should be noted that important levels of reuse also occur through the use of previous classes by instantiation and by new uses in aggregation and association configurations (Section 2.3.6).

However, many see reuse in a more general context, especially in terms of frameworks and designs (Johnson and Foote, 1988; Wirfs-Brock and Johnson, 1990). Reusability in the long term requires the development of a library of classes from both commercially available classes and in-house developments (e.g., Goldberg and Rubin, 1990). Maiden (1991) also urges reuse of specification by analogical reasoning—a potentially useful area in OT still awaiting exploration.

What should be stressed, therefore, is not simply end-lifecycle generalization but a "reuse mindset" *throughout* the lifecycle (McGregor and Sykes, 1992; Menzies et al., 1992). This links closely with a quality mindset. Lack of quality assessment procedures and standards is highlighted by Monarchi and Puhr (1992), who suggest the use of "evaluative" tools that measure not only the technical, software engineering issues but also the less tangible, stylistic evaluation of the semantic modeling embodied in any specific methodology.

1.3.4 Metrics

While there have been several notable treatises on metrics recently (e.g., Conte et al., 1986; Zuse, 1990; Fenton, 1991), almost no work has been published on *object-oriented* metrics (although there are some qualitative summaries in Berard, 1992b). In Chapter 10 we seek to redress that imbalance in an area of critical importance for project management and strategic planning. It is often said that "what cannot be measured cannot be controlled." In the manufacturing environment this involves the use of industrial statistics, such as control charts, and process monitoring and modification. Little attempt has been made to transfer that technology to the software development process, although Card and Glass (1990, Chapter 8) have already initiated such an application in a traditional development environment. Such advances permit the attainment of higher quality.

Without metrics, the software engineer is no engineer. Measurements are needed to control, evaluate, understand, and assess both process and product at different stages of development. Models are needed to build on these measurements in order to be able to forecast costs, defect rates, maintenance costs, etc., with increasing confidence.

Card and Glass (1990, p104) conclude that "measurement makes productivity and quality improvement meaningful." These increasing emphases on software quality and links between OT and the quality (especially TQM) movement (Henderson-Sellers, 1991c; Howard, 1992a) are very welcome. The vehicle of object technology to achieve these quality goals appears to many (e.g., McGregor and Sykes, 1992; Bellin, 1992) to be the best currently available.

1.3.5 Competitive edge technology

Object technology is undoubtedly seen by many as today's leading edge technology and one that will grow over the next decade to become "The Computing of the 90s" (Atwood, 1990; Object Interest Group, 1991; Plant, 1992a). There are a growing number of commercial ventures, of increasingly large scale. It is estimated that about one-third of the major corporations in the United States are investigating the technology (Connell, 1991), and Adams (1992a) reports that 75% of the Fortune 100 companies have one or more OT projects under way. Many of these projects are covered by commercial confidentiality agreements so that the organization can maintain its competitive advantage. Naturally, this makes it difficult for another, competing organization to learn from others' mistakes, but of course gives the initiating company a lead-time over its competitors. Although many companies still ask their employees, consultants, and contractors to sign nondisclosure agreements, an increasing number of companies are now so happy with their use of object technology that they are prepared to advertise their success in forums such as the TOOLS and ObjectWorld conferences and OOPSLA workshops, or locally in national computer societies' object-oriented special interest groups.

In addition, 1989 saw the formation of the Object Management Group (OMG), which is an industry organization whose aim is to provide collaboration in the definition of object nomenclature and models (see Section 9.2.3). In 1992, the ANSI X3H7 committee was formed for object standardization.

1.4 Recent and emerging issues

1.4.1 Recent issues

Some areas of recent interest and concern are shown in Table 1.4. Although some of these are now fading as we learn more about object technology in the commercial (as opposed to the research) world, it is still worth bringing them to the reader's attention as an indication of both the state of the art and the great speed at which the technology is currently moving.

Table 1.4 *Issues of recent concern*

Top-down versus bottom-up
Object and class relationships—client–server or inheritance?
Multiple inheritance
Object and class relationships
Learning curve
How to find objects and classes

Top-down versus bottom-up
The top-down versus bottom-up debate stemmed partly from the ideas over the last few decades that we should all be doing top-down decomposition. In OT it is necessary to utilize both top-down *and* bottom-up development in order to optimize on design and reuse. Indeed, many of the OO lifecycle methodologies discussed in Chapter 3 start off being top-down and then migrate to being bottom-up. The merging of these two approaches is useful and essential in OT.

Object and class relationships—client–server or inheritance?

Meyer (1988a, p332) asked the question "Would you rather buy or inherit?" This question relates to the ongoing discussions about the apparent trade-offs between using client–server and using inheritance. In general, most cases are relatively clear-cut. They are either **uses-a** or **is-composed-of**, both of which use client–server, or they are **is-a**, which is inheritance. Meyer (1988a) certainly notes that inheritance is a "more committing decision than 'buying' "— another variable in the equation. Further discussion on this topic is also to be found in Rumbaugh et al. (1991, Chapter 10) and later in this book (see Section 2.3.6).

Multiple inheritance

In a somewhat similar vein are discussions on the need for multiple inheritance in a language. While most languages have aimed to add multiple inheritance as an extra, much-needed language feature, there are still debates regarding appropriate cases of multiple inheritance (MI), especially since the overuse of MI does lead to complex networks of classes that are likely to thwart class reusability. Meyer (1988a, 1990a) gives many examples of the use of MI in the Eiffel library classes. On the other hand, it has been argued that an apparent need for MI can equally well be coded using single inheritance (see also Snyder, 1986). There is, however, a growing consensus that MI is a valuable and powerful tool, yet like all powerful tools it can be misused and should perhaps be used sparingly.

Object and class relationships

Relationships between classes have been much discussed recently. The client–server metaphor, together with an inheritance hierarchy, is now well established for OOP. In analysis and design, the influence of data modeling through seminal works such as that of Rumbaugh et al. (1991) has led to the recognition of different relationships. Rumbaugh et al. (1991) and Edwards and Henderson-Sellers (1991) identify three: association, aggregation, and generalization/specialization, although the semantics of these relationships may be different between authors. Indeed, it is increasingly clear that a definitive definition of aggregation is hard and perhaps not even a fruitful topic of discussion. Rather, it should be viewed as a potentially useful modeling tool and seen as a "special sort" of association rather than as a distinct relationship.

Learning curve

The time taken to learn the syntax of a language differs between languages and varies according to prior experience. It is said that learning an OOPL that is an extension of a language you already know is tantamount to admitting defeat, since you will tend to continue to code in the paradigm with which you are already familiar (e.g., Antebi, 1990), rather than adopting the powerful new concepts embodied in the OOPL itself. Burton Leathers (pers. com., 1990) wisely suggests that if you want to learn C++, learn Smalltalk or Eiffel first, a sentiment echoed by Thomas (1989b), LaLonde and Pugh (1990), Gibson (1991), Graham (1991), Jacobson *et al.* (1992), and Page-Jones (1992a). C programmers might automatically drift toward C++, and indeed managers find it easier to support such a transition. However, experience is building (e.g., Waldo, 1990) to suggest that this can be a painful transition for the reasons outlined above. The need for *good* training has been noted by Leathers (1990b), Wybolt (1990), Stewart (1991), and by many others at international conferences, such as OOPSLA, TOOLS and ObjectWorld.

Rather, as we advocate throughout this book, learning an OOPL should take second place to learning object-oriented concepts in a programming-language-independent manner—the change of mindset that is necessary (e.g., Cox, 1990a). This is supported by recent documentation from Taligent (1993a, b), the company set up specifically by IBM and Apple to exploit object technology, in which three learning curves are identified: a steep curve for concepts, a second, less steep curve for environments (libraries and frameworks), and a relatively shallow and final learning curve for any chosen OOPL.

How to find objects and classes
An area of intense discussion in all areas of modeling is how to find the "x," in this case objects and classes. Although we will clarify later the distinction between objects (individuals) and classes (sets), we also find the need for the general "all-inclusive" term object/class, or O/C. Finding O/Cs is really no more of an issue than finding entities in ERDs or finding processes in DFDs. The same issues and problems arise, and guidelines are becoming increasingly formalized as experience with "real" systems is gathered. Finding the O/Cs is often loosely based upon identifying the nouns (Abbott, 1983; Booch, 1983) in the requirements specification, i.e., the user's description of the system. This usually contributes a "first pass" for the top-level O/Cs in the system. These tend to be O/Cs identifiable by substantive nouns. However, abstract nouns are just as likely to be candidates for becoming O/Cs (e.g., Harmon, 1990). Indeed, as systems are analyzed and designed, it is often those more abstract concepts that emerge during system refinement. During system development those "first pass" O/Cs (substantive and abstract) will be significantly augmented by O/Cs created as artifacts of the conceptual model.

An increasing number of formalized guidelines and techniques are being developed for "finding the classes" in the problem space and the solution space. A number of these guidelines are discussed in Chapter 7.

1.4.2 Current and emerging issues

Many of the issues raised in this section (Table 1.5) are discussed in full detail elsewhere in this book; others are still emergent and therefore little is known about them. The issues identified in Table 1.5 are, in part, influenced by discussions at the February 1992 Workshop on Object-Oriented Software Engineering Practice held in Denver, Colorado. Many of the items were

Table 1.5 *Issues of current and emerging concern*

Object model
Lifecycle methodologies and clarification of OOA/OOD border
Notations
Commercial programming in the large (complexity management)
Project management
Metrics
Reuse
Library management
Objectbases
Migration paths
Style
Testing
Maintenance
Formal aspects
Emerging methodologies and metamodels
Standards

---

identified in a brainstorming session as being those current/emerging issues most likely to be retarding the adoption of object technology by industry. This list is therefore very germane to the tenets of our text.

Object model
There is currently no standard object model, i.e., a set of definitions of objects and classes, and of rules for behavior, inheritance, etc. All languages, methodologies, and notations therefore are based on one of a small number of slightly different conceptual models for O/Cs. There is extensive work on rationalizing these different views, some of which is discussed in Section 2.3.1.

Lifecycle methodologies
Another area of recent and current concern is that of devising and testing design and analysis methodologies. Since the object-oriented "(r)evolution" was led initially by the computer scientists, the areas of analysis and design methodologies were somewhat neglected until about 1990. Special issues of *Communications of the ACM* (September 1990; September 1992) and of the *Journal of Object-Oriented Programming* (e.g., January 1991 and February 1993), as well as a growing number of good texts, are beginning to address the dearth of information in these important information systems areas. Methodologies are most important for large, team projects, especially those focused on developing software critical to the organization's success (Berard, 1992b, Chapter 4). Some of these methodologies and guidelines are discussed in Chapter 3.

One of the debated issues in methodologies is the transitions along the lifecycle phases—is there OOA and then OOD, or do we now have a single lifecycle phase (OO_D^A perhaps!)? As you will see in Chapter 4, we believe that while in many ways analysis and design remain two distinct mindsets as a consequence of their different focus—the one "backward" to the user and the problem and the other "forward" to the software implementation of the solution (see also Jacobson *et al.*, 1992)—there is no longer a need to translate the model into a different formalism between the two phases. In "analyzing" a problem and creating a requirements specification, the very act of documentation imposes a "design." Thus the two mental activities of analysis and design become intertwined in this new "specification" phase. The analyst/designer undertakes both activities, often switching between them rapidly. However, at the subsystem level there may be more of a distinction between these mental activities (Chapter 3).

Notations

Notations are often closely linked with methodologies; indeed, it is often stated that every methodology should contain a notation so that the results of the methodological steps can be adequately expressed. The debate here is whether any one of the existing notations is adequate to adopt as a "standard," how many notations we expect to be supported and used in the OOSE industry worldwide now or in ten years' time, and whether the industry should attempt to standardize. As you will see in Chapter 3 from the plethora[2] of notations currently available, we are still far from global rationalization. We envisage that testing of the notations in large commercial ventures will lead to the identification of a small number (probably around three or four) worthy of a long life. It is not, at this stage, possible to be prescriptive.

Programming in the large

Object technology offers the opportunity for methodological, notational, conceptual, and managerial support on significantly larger projects than currently attempted. The issue here is both of project management and complexity management. They are subthemes of this book. For other views on large-scale commercial systems, the experiences of the Ada, object-based, community can provide useful guidelines on what is currently possible (see, e.g., examples in Booch (1991) and Firesmith (1993), both of whom have experience in both the Ada community and the object-oriented community). Many other large-scale OO projects are currently under way or have been recently initiated, the best information source for these being brief statements in journals such as *Journal of Object-Oriented Programming*, *Hotline on Object-Oriented Technology* (until its demise in early 1993) and *Object Magazine*.

Project management

Moving from technical issues to managerial issues is of crucial relevance to commercial adoption of object technology. Little work has yet been published on this important area, and in this book we devote Chapter 9 to these issues.

---

2. Plethora = "any unhealthy repletion or excess" (Shorter Oxford English Dictionary).

Metrics
Little is known about what object-oriented metrics are most relevant to gaining an understanding of good classes or to providing cost estimates to project managers. An introduction has already been given in Section 1.3.4 and a full assessment of the state of the art is given in Chapter 10.

Reuse
Reuse is seen as one of the prime benefits of object technology (e.g., Graham, 1991; McGregor and Sykes, 1992). The importance of reuse has been outlined in Section 1.3.3 and is discussed more fully in Section 9.1.3. It links closely with the next topic.

Library management
Reuse is effective only if libraries of classes are managed well (e.g., Adams, 1992a). Libraries will be built up not only from in-house developments but also from library classes bought from third-party vendors. Vasan (1992) asks the question "to build or buy?" He argues that the growing number of quality libraries militate in favor of purchase rather than in-house development, although he highlights a number of potential problems in adopting such a strategy. These include the cost of maintenance (especially for "free" software), a large potential for name space clashes, the financial stability of the vendor company, and potential licensing/royalty pitfalls. Further issues concerning library class quality are addressed by Korson and McGregor (1992), discussed here in Section 9.1.4.

Objectbases
These were originally called object-oriented databases. It has been pointed out, however, that the juxtaposition of "object" and "data" is essentially oxymoronic and therefore that the new appellation of "objectbase" (e.g., Rossiter, 1992; Plant, 1992b) is clearer and more apt.

As the object-oriented philosophy is increasingly adopted across all facets of an organization's software operations, the requirement for an objectbase management system (OBMS) will be paramount in a significant number of commercial, MIS groups. The arrival of commercially available OBMSs in recent years, although they are generally acknowledged as being in their infancy, provides this opportunity. In an OBMS, the characteristics of object technology (as discussed here) need to be combined with database management requirements of persistence, secondary storage management, concurrency, recovery, and an *ad hoc* query facility (Loomis, 1990a), coupled with reasonable performance (at least as good as currently available relational database management systems), schema modification (e.g., Dobbie, 1991), and security (Loomis, 1991). Ullman (1988) identifies six key features of database systems. They need to support (i) an abstract data model, (ii) high-level access/query language(s); (iii) transaction management in a multiuser environment; (iv) access control and data ownership; (v) data validation and consistency checking; and (vi) recovery following system failure that minimizes data loss.

Three approaches are possible (e.g., Hurson *et al.*, 1993; Manola, 1993): (i) to extend an OOPL by adding persistence,[3] data sharing control (concurrency), and a query facility, etc. (e.g., Lahire and Brissi, 1991); (ii) to rework existing relational DBMSs to support object-oriented structures (e.g., Premerlani *et al.*, 1990); and (iii) to design an OBMS totally on object-oriented principles.

In this context, McGregor and Sykes (1992, pp318–319) list five areas of especial interest:

- unique object identifiers;
- support for the object model;
- compatible database and programming language representations;
- efficient system performance; and, finally,
- representation for ordered aggregates.

An OBMS requires the interaction of an object manager (to ensure integrity and to process messages), an object server (to interface with the outside world), and an object store. Three languages are conventionally required (McGregor and Sykes, 1992, p323): a data definition language (DDL) that describes the classes; a data manipulation language (DML) for creation, destruction, etc., of instances; and a data control language (DCL) to support the integrity constraints. However, in most cases in an OBMS these language roles are supported by one OOPL, possibly acting in the role of an Application Programming Interface or API (Thurston, 1993).

Detailed examples of objectbase products can be found in, e.g., Heintz (1991) and Bancilhon and Delobel (1991), and general discussions in, e.g., Stein (1988), Dittrich (1988), Kim and Lochovsky (1989), Winblad *et al.* (1990), Loomis (1990b), Khoshafian (1990, 1993), Hughes (1991) and Cattell (1992). A recent comparison (Ahmed *et al.*, 1992) of five commercial products is given in Figure 1.9, in which the various features of the systems are rated on a scale of 0 (poor) to 10 (excellent).

An understanding of what objectbases actually are is still evolving. A formal proposal for what constitutes an objectbase was developed in 1989 at the First International Conference on Deductive and Object-oriented Databases. At this conference the Object-oriented Database Manifesto was developed (Atkinson *et al.*, 1989). This outlined the key features that an object-oriented database must support in order to be called object-oriented. This manifesto was followed by the Third Generation Database Manifesto, which outlined the key features that a database must support. The difference between the two manifestos is that one concentrates on the "object orientedness" of the database, while the other concentrates on the database features required, such as concurrent access, locking mechanism, and so forth. Together, the manifestos detail the features that an objectbase should support (Table 1.6). Work is continuing on standards

---

3. For instance, there is a class ENVIRONMENT in the language Eiffel that can be used to save objects "as is" rather than to translate them into flat files, although fully persistent object support is not yet available commercially in general-purpose OOPLs.

FEATURE	ORION (ITASCA)	GEMSTONE	ONTOS	ObjectStore	VERSANT
Operating platforms	9	9	9	9	9
Availability/customer support	?	8	8	8	8
Performance/price	?	6	6	7	7
External language interface	10 (LISP) 6 (C)	10 (Smltk) 6 (C) 5 (C++)	9 (C++)	9 (C++) 5 (C)	9 (C++) 7 (C)
Multiple inheritance	10	0	8	10	10
Composite object facilities	10	1	2	4	2
Dynamic schema evolution	10	5	4	2	3
Storage management	10	9	10	9	9 (?)
Lock management	9	6	6	6	8
Change notification and communication	8	1	2	2	3
Version management	10	0	0	9	9
Flexibility of concurrency management	6	4	4	5	6
Facilities for cooperative engineering	6	4	3	5	6
Query management	9	9	9	8	7
Security and authorization	9	8	1	2	3
Multimedia support	10	1	2	2	2
User interface	8	10 (Smltk) 2 (OPAL)	8 (Studio)	6	5

Figure 1.9 *Comparative ratings of features of current (as of late 1991) OBMSs (Ahmed et al., © copyright SIGS Publications, 1992)*

Table 1.6 *Synthesis of features possible in an OBMS (Barry, 1993)*

Transaction Properties
    Atomicity—everything is done or nothing is done
    Consistency—a transaction changes a database from one consistent state to another consistent state
    Isolation—the internal state of a transaction is not visible to other transactions
    Durability—the results of a transaction are lasting
    Long Transactions
    Nested Transactions
    Shared Transactions
    Nonblocking read consistency

Locking and Concurrency Control
    Concurrency control
    Lock escalation
    Promotable locks
    Locks set and release
    Granularity of locks
    Deadlocks

Security Authorization
    Role authorization
    Implicit authorization
    Positive authorization
    Negative authorization
    Strong authorization
    Weak authorization
    Authorization objects
    Private database
    Time and day

Query capability
    Query language
    Query optimization
    Indexing
    Queries in programs
    Queries preferred
    Query language completeness
    Specification of collections
    SQL

Table 1.6 *continued*

Data Independence/Schema Modification
    Runtime types
    Tools for schema transformations
    Update time
    Changes to attributes or data members
    Changes to database methods
    Changes to superclass/subclass relationships
    Versions of schema

Distributed Database Systems
    Location independence
    Local autonomy at each site
    No reliance on a central site that can result in a single point of reference
    Fragmentation independence
    Replication independence
    Distributed query processing
    Distributed transaction management
    Hardware independence
    Operating system independence
    Network independence
    Wide-area network support
    DBMS independence
    Continuous operation

Object Model
    Objects
    Binding and polymorphism
    Encapsulation
    Identity
    Types and classes
    Inheritance and delegation
    Relationships and attributes
    Literals
    Nontraditional objects
    Aggregates
    Composite or complex objects
    Integrity
    Schema extensibility
    Database operation extensibility
    Object languages

Architecture
    Architecture type
    Methods execution location
    Query processing location

Table 1.6 *continued*

> Shared access coordination location
> Multiple interfaces
> Memory utilization
> Safety
> Disk media protection
> Backup/recovery facilities
> Change notification
> Version
> Configuration management

and implementations both in relational extensions to support the object model and in pure objectbases. For example, standards to develop an Object SQL are already being prepared and the ANSI committee for SQL is currently working on the next version of SQL, which may well incorporate object-oriented features (known as SQL 3; Loomis, 1993). To try to influence those standards and to hasten their completion, efforts have been made by a number of vendor groups, such as the Object Database Management Group, which is working on an Object Query language. The group was expected to begin work on the objectbase area in 1993 (Loomis, 1993).

Migration paths
Once you have decided that the future for your company lies with object technology, there arises the question of the best migration path from current to future technology. This is an important commercial question with a growing number of real answers. We deem it sufficiently important to devote Section 9.2.1 to a full discussion of it.

Style
Style can relate to, for example, coding style and naming conventions. Lorenz (1993) stresses the need to spend time deciding on useful and meaningful names that are appropriate beyond the domain of the current systems development. Normally, use singular names for classes (although Lorenz suggests plural names for container classes, which seems to us to be unnecessarily constrictive and committing one to implementation too early). Good names are certainly very important, as is a well-laid out code with consistent rules for indentation and upper/lower case combinations for class names, instance variables, and formal parameters. Code should, of course, be well commented—at the very least so that it can be easily understood by someone other than its developer.

Rumbaugh *et al.* (1991, Chapter 14) identify four major categories of concern: (i) reusability (Table 1.7), (ii) extensibility (Table 1.8), (iii) robustness (Table 1.9), and (iv) programming-in-the-large (Table 1.10). Other stylistic guidelines are provided by the "Law of Demeter" (Lieberherr *et al.*, 1988; Lieberherr and

Table 1.7 *Style rules for reusability (Adapted from Rumbaugh et al., 1991)*

- Keep methods coherent
- Keep methods small
- Keep methods consistent
- Separate policy and implementation
- Provide uniform coverage (supplying methods for all reasonable scenarios, not just those required in the present application)
- Broaden the method as much as possible (aim to generalize and use domain analysis/design methods)
- Avoid global information
- Avoid modes (i.e., those whose behavior depends critically upon the current context).
- Factor out common code into single method
- Factor out common code into "parent"
- Use delegation (avoid implementation inheritance as poor substitute)
- Encapsulate external code

Table 1.8 *Style guidelines for extensibility (Adapted from Rumbaugh et al., 1991)*

- Encapsulate classes
- Hide data structures
- Avoid traversing multiple links or methods
- Avoid case statements on object type
- Distinguish between public and private operations

Table 1.9 *Style guidelines for robustness against improper handling (Adapted from Rumbaugh et al., 1991)*

- Protect against errors, especially incorrect user input
- Optimize after the program runs
- Validate arguments
- Avoid predefined limits
- Instrument the program for debugging and performance monitoring

Holland, 1989), which suggests *inter alia* that the number of classes accessed by a method should be greatly limited. For example, chained messages, such as *library.book.page.display*, which are perfectly legal syntactically in many OOPLs, are poor stylistically since the first client utilizes internal information from the first supplier object in order to send this message.

Table 1.10 *Style guidelines for programming-in-the-large (Adapted from Rumbaugh et al., 1991)*

- Do not begin programming prematurely
- Keep methods understandable
- Make methods readable
- Use exactly the same names as in the object model
- Choose names carefully
- Document classes and methods
- Publish the specification

Testing
As part of quality control, a significant activity after coding must be testing, including verification and validation procedures. Any methodology needs to support both notions strongly. In current methodological instantiations, neither verification nor validation is well described; in fact, both are generally omitted totally! However, testing procedures for class hierarchies are currently under development (Harrold and McGregor, 1992), and verification and validation (V&V) techniques are increasingly stressed (Drake *et al.*, 1992a; Arnold *et al.*, 1992). V&V techniques must address both technical (software) competency and user satisfaction, the latter in particular being relevant throughout the lifecycle. Methodologies should therefore support peer, expert, and customer review, as well as consistency and completeness checking (Drake *et al.*, 1992a) plus a mechanism to support auditability.

Maintenance
Maintenance costs in software are high. Object technology offers a route to potential savings. An essential component of maintenance is fault discovery, which requires comprehension of the program—which is likely to have been written by someone else. Although significant work has been undertaken on the cognitive psychology of programming, it has often not been transferred from the psychological domain to the software engineering (maintenance and metrics) domain (but cf. Section 10.4). Program plans are delocalized (Letovsky and Soloway, 1986), thus often making comprehension more difficult. Stylistic guidelines are still being developed. In the meantime, maintenance strategies and maintenance metrics are required for *current* systems, not idealistic ones (Wilde and Huitt, 1992).

Formal aspects
The use of formal methods in information systems development is scant, although there seems to be more openness to them in Europe and the Pacific Region than in North America. Formal languages such as Z have been extended to the object paradigm. Carrington *et al.* (1990) and Duke *et al.* (1991) describe Object–Z, which has a potentially significant contribution to make to the

rationalization of the underlying object model. OOPLs may also include the notion of assertions as a means of formally specifying a contract. A review of formalism within the OO approach can be found in Stepney *et al*. (1992).

Emerging methodologies and metamodels
As an additional contribution to formalizing object technology (as has been done, for example, in the normalization theories in database), new full lifecycle methodologies are emerging that can be examined, and ultimately described, by a metamodel for object-oriented methodologies. The concept of a methodology metamodel or generic methodology is not yet fully developed. It is discussed very briefly in Section 3.1 and in the Postscript.

Standards
International standards are useful and emerging although some consider this to be too premature (Mellor *et al*., 1993). The Object Management Group (OMG) (see Section 9.2.3) is currently working to create an environment in which standards can be set, while maintaining sufficient flexibility for vendors to adopt the standard and yet provide their own line of products. In this sense, the OMG is driven by opportunity rather than prescription. Currently, they have developed the Common Object Request Broker Architecture (CORBA) (Stone, 1992) for distributed object systems and are soon to release a standard object reference model.

Perhaps of more importance to early adoption of object technology is the establishment of (and adherence to) *organizational* standards. It is crucial for an individual organization to maintain consistency across development teams and across projects, and to set stylistic guidelines for methodologies, documentation, and quality evaluation that are independent of the actual personnel performing the tasks and their departmental/divisional allegiance. Standards are likely to be derived from published methodologies and development "hints" and heuristics, adapted specifically for the development tasks of the business.

Those with access to internet bulletin boards can find generally agreed definitions of and discussions on all aspects of object technology. The "frequently asked questions" (FAQ) from the comp.object news group is available on the anonymous ftp site zaphod.uchicago.edu.

1.5 Summary

Software engineering concerns that need to be addressed by object technology are summarized by Grochow (1992) as:

1. a defined lifecycle (phases and tasks)
2. methods and techniques for performing those tasks
3. tools and languages
4. a "design repository"

5. estimating methods for development effort and cost
6. estimating methods for operating costs of systems
7. training and educational curricula.

We believe that the objectives of software and software engineering can best be met through the use of object technology, which provides the mechanism to achieve them.

Although we are not yet able to satisfy in detail all these criteria (especially 5 and 6), we believe that object technology, as outlined in this book, is well on the way to providing secure lifecycle methodologies, techniques, and tools; supporting reuse of code and design; offering project management and metrics; and forming a sound educational curriculum for training. MOSES, as presented in Chapters 4–8, is the embodiment of these factors in an integrated OO software development methodology.

• CHAPTER 2 •

The Object-oriented Paradigm

2.1 Introduction and review

In this chapter we address the issues of the object model from a conceptual viewpoint in order to provide a reasoned background to the methodological and management issues discussed later. The object-oriented paradigm requires a new mindset for all those participating—either managerially or technically. Although this book is not aimed at an introductory level, this chapter presents a "potted description" of the basic ideas of OT (e.g., Winblad et al., 1990; Henderson-Sellers, 1992a; McGregor and Sykes, 1992), extending them in part to more detailed discussion than normally found at an introductory level.

The key underlying ideas are those of abstraction (Section 2.2) and focusing our understanding on objects/classes or O/Cs (Section 2.3). Together, these ideas bring about a novel perspective on software engineering. As part of our review, we feel it appropriate to include a section (Section 2.4) on implementation (programming language) issues. However, since we firmly believe that using a programming language without understanding the concepts is worse than useless—after all, natural language was developed solely *to express concepts*—and that implementing in an OOPL is almost an automatic, mechanistic procedure from a good OO design, programming language issues will be generally confined to that section. In the rest of the book we concentrate on concepts, their employment in software development and their management implications.

2.2 Abstraction

Abstraction is "The principle of ignoring those aspects of a subject that are not relevant to the current purpose in order to concentrate more fully on those that are" (*Dictionary of Computing*, Oxford University Press, 1986). Thus "a particular characteristic, property, or element is given special attention compared with (isolated conceptually or separated from) all others" (van Gigch, 1991, p234).

Abstraction is thus a mental process to manage complexity, although the same word can also be used to represent the artifact that is abstracted (an abstraction). *Concepts* result from this abstraction process (Martin and Odell, 1992, pp247–257). Concepts become useful once they are shared among many human beings, that is, they have a shared *intension*. In OO terms, that shared concept is formalized as a class or "object type." The set of objects (instances) satisfying this shared notion is the *extension* to which the concept applies.

Abstraction as a process is thus closely linked both to human perception of the world and to traditional modeling techniques. In both, we extract the essential properties while omitting inessential details (Ross et al., 1975; Ghezzi et al., 1991; Booch, 1991; Rumbaugh et al., 1991, p16; Henderson-Sellers, 1992b; Firesmith, 1993). The model we build using this process of abstraction is itself an abstraction of reality at a selected degree of granularity (level of abstraction). For example, we can consider our home surroundings at differing granularities/abstraction levels as (i) a point on a map; (ii) an entity (item) in a housing development; (iii) a house that contains our belongings; (iv) a set of rooms containing a set of furniture; (v) a collection of bricks and mortar. However, the chemist or physicist in the family might prefer to "see" the bricks as composed of various materials, each of which is composed of molecules that are primarily empty space. Do we consider all these abstraction levels all at once? We suggest to you that that is the road to insanity! Humans choose the relevant abstraction level for a given time and a given purpose. If we are indicating our location, we consider the house as a point on a map. If we are building a house, we do *not* consider the chemists' view that the atoms and molecules of the bricks are mostly space!

Firesmith (1993) notes the need to evaluate the number of abstractions or distinct ideas that the typical person can comprehend simultaneously. Here the application of the limit of 7±2 in Miller (1956) suggests an approximate upper limit of nine different abstractions that can be thought about at any given time.

Abstraction thus operates over a range of levels. Indeed, the whole development process and the techniques used in object technology can be described in this way. Figure 2.1 starts with top-level abstractions that model

The Object-oriented Paradigm 43

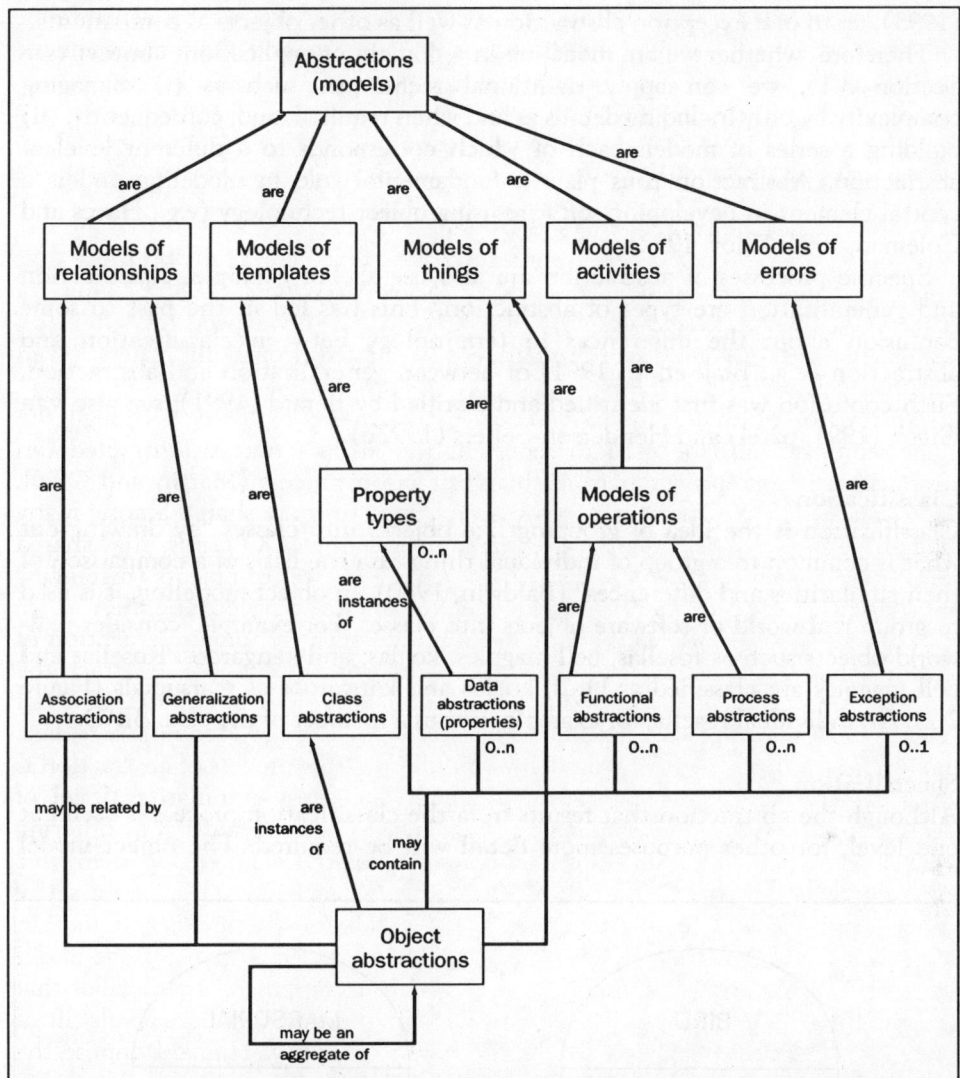

Figure 2.1 *Various types of abstractions needed in a discussion of object technology (Adapted from Firesmith, 1993)*

the overall system. At the next lower abstraction level are models of (i) templates, (ii) things, (iii) activities, (iv) errors (Firesmith, 1993), and (v) relationships. These are all, in fact, types of models.

At the next level of abstraction, more specificity is seen. Property types are types of models of templates; functional abstractions are types of models of operations, etc. Also shown are object abstractions that may contain (aggregation relationship—see Section 2.3.5) property types, data abstractions, functional abstractions, process abstractions, and, according to Firesmith

(1993), up to one exception abstraction as well as other objects as components.

Therefore, whether we are modeling in a domain or applications context (see Section 3.1), we can apply traditional techniques such as (i) managing complexity by only including details as and when required, and, consequently, (ii) building a series of models each of which corresponds to a different level of abstraction. Abstraction thus plays a fundamental role in modeling and is a central element in developing software using object technology (e.g., Hayes and Coleman, 1991; Kilov, 1992).

Specific processes of abstraction are also useful. For example, classification and generalization are types of abstraction. This has led in the past to some confusion about the differences in terminology between classification and abstraction (e.g., Blair *et al.*, 1991) or between generalization and abstraction. Such confusion was first identified and clarified by Berard (1991); see also van Gigch (1991, p234) and Henderson-Sellers (1992b).

Classification
Classification is the idea of grouping like objects into classes "by drawing out what is common to a group of individual things, on the basis of a comparison of their similarities and differences" (Baldwin, 1940). In object modeling, it is used to group real-world or software objects into classes. For example, consider real-world objects such as rosellas, bell magpies, koalas, and kangaroos. Rosellas and bell magpies are classified as birds, koalas and kangaroos as marsupials (Figure 2.2). An individual rosella, for example, is thus a member of the class BIRD.

Specialization
Although the abstraction that results from the classification process is useful at one level, for other purposes more detail will be required. The object model

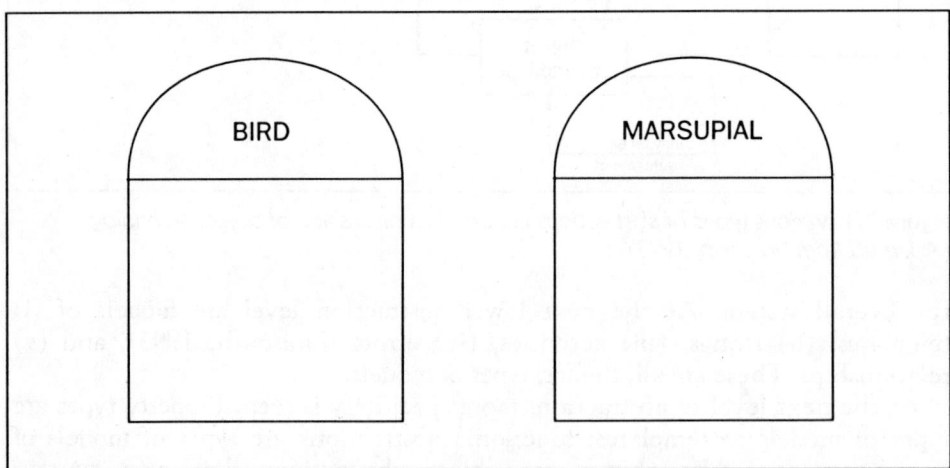

Figure 2.2 *Two classes: birds and marsupials represented by class icons (here MOSES "tablets")*

The Object-oriented Paradigm

permits further refinement of abstractions (classes) by the use of specialization. For example, we might classify rosellas (at a more detailed level than simply BIRD) as being of the class PARROT. PARROT is a more specialized (and hence more restricted) class than BIRD, but the class PARROT inherits directly from (is a subclass[4] of) the class BIRD (Figure 2.3). Any individual rosella is then an example of the PARROT class. Specialization is the process of creating new, more specialized subclasses from an existing class. Finally, one might wish to differentiate in the model between rosellas and other parrots (e.g., cockatoos) rather than make them all examples of a class PARROT. Two new subclasses for PARROT could then be introduced: ROSELLA and

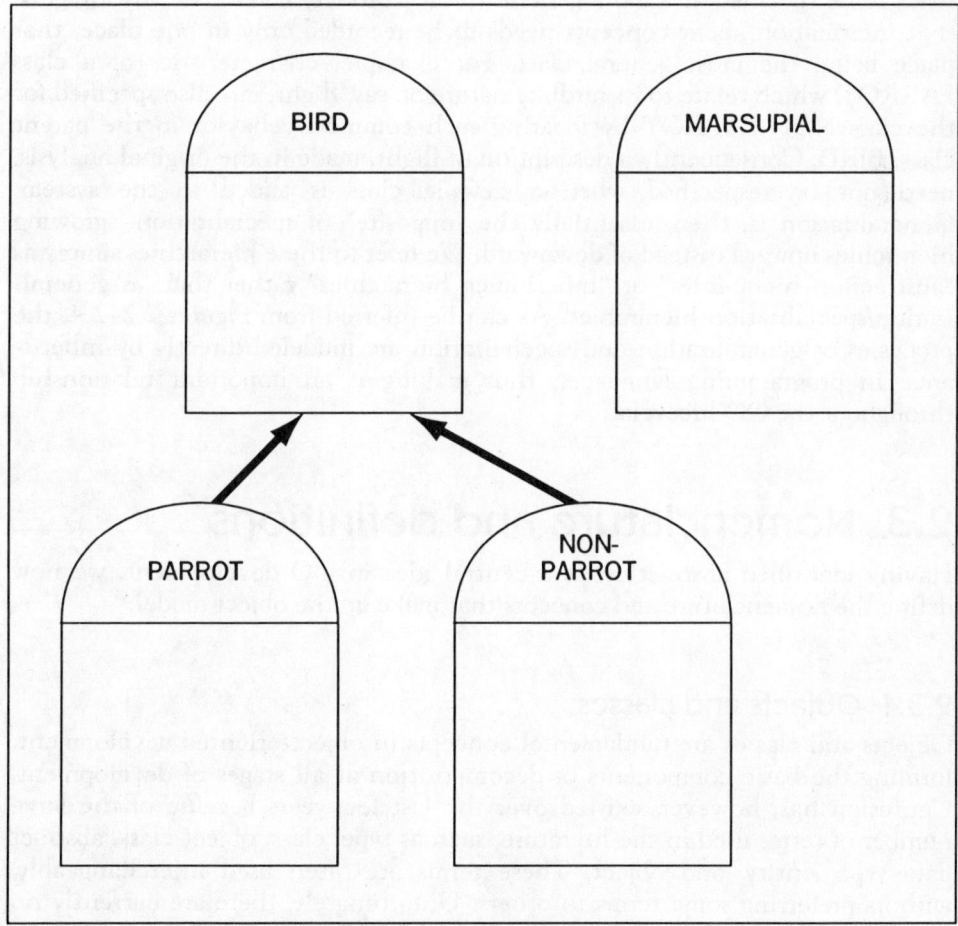

Figure 2.3 *Parrots and non-parrots are specialized sorts of birds*

---

4. For the present, we do not distinguish between classes and types. This distinction will, however, be discussed in Sections 2.3.1 and 2.4.2.

COCKATOO. Any individual rosella is then a typical example of (is an instance of) the ROSELLA class, which itself is a subclass (specialization) of PARROT, a subclass (specialization) of BIRD.

Generalization

Generalization can be regarded as another type of abstraction process. Generalization is the identification of commonalities between classes leading to the creation of a more general, "parent" class or superclass. Such relationships are applied extensively in (biological) taxonomies.

The class BIRD and the class MARSUPIAL in Figure 2.3 have a common superclass of ANIMAL (Figure 2.4). This type of abstraction allows characteristics to be specified at a more general (more abstract) level. The advantage is that information about concepts needs to be recorded only in one place, that place being the most general class. For example, characteristics of a class PARROT, which relate to its birdlike nature of, say, flight,[5] are also specified for the class NON-PARROT by locating such common behavior in the parent class, BIRD. Consequently a description of flight, made in the original analysis, need not be respecified when a new subclass is added to the system. Generalization is, then, essentially the "opposite" of specialization—growing hierarchies upward instead of downward. We refer to these hierarchies simply as "abstraction hierarchies" or "inheritance hierarchies" rather than as generalization/specialization hierarchies. As can be inferred from Figures 2.2–2.4, the processes of generalization and specialization are modeled directly by inheritance in programming languages, thus making it an important relationship throughout the OO lifecycle.

2.3 Nomenclature and definitions

Having identified abstraction as a central idea in OO development, we now define the nomenclature and concepts that make up the object model.

2.3.1 Objects and classes

Objects and classes are fundamental concepts in object-oriented development, forming the basic components of decomposition at all stages of development. Confusion has, however, existed over the last few years because of the large number of terms used in the literature, such as type, class, object-class, abstract data type, entity, and object. These terms are often used interchangeably, authors preferring some terms to others. Unfortunately, there are currently no standards for terminology and definitions that are accepted and used by the industry as a whole.

---

5. In this very simple example, we have taken the extreme liberty of excluding the existence of flightless birds from our Universe of Discourse (UoD).

The Object-oriented Paradigm

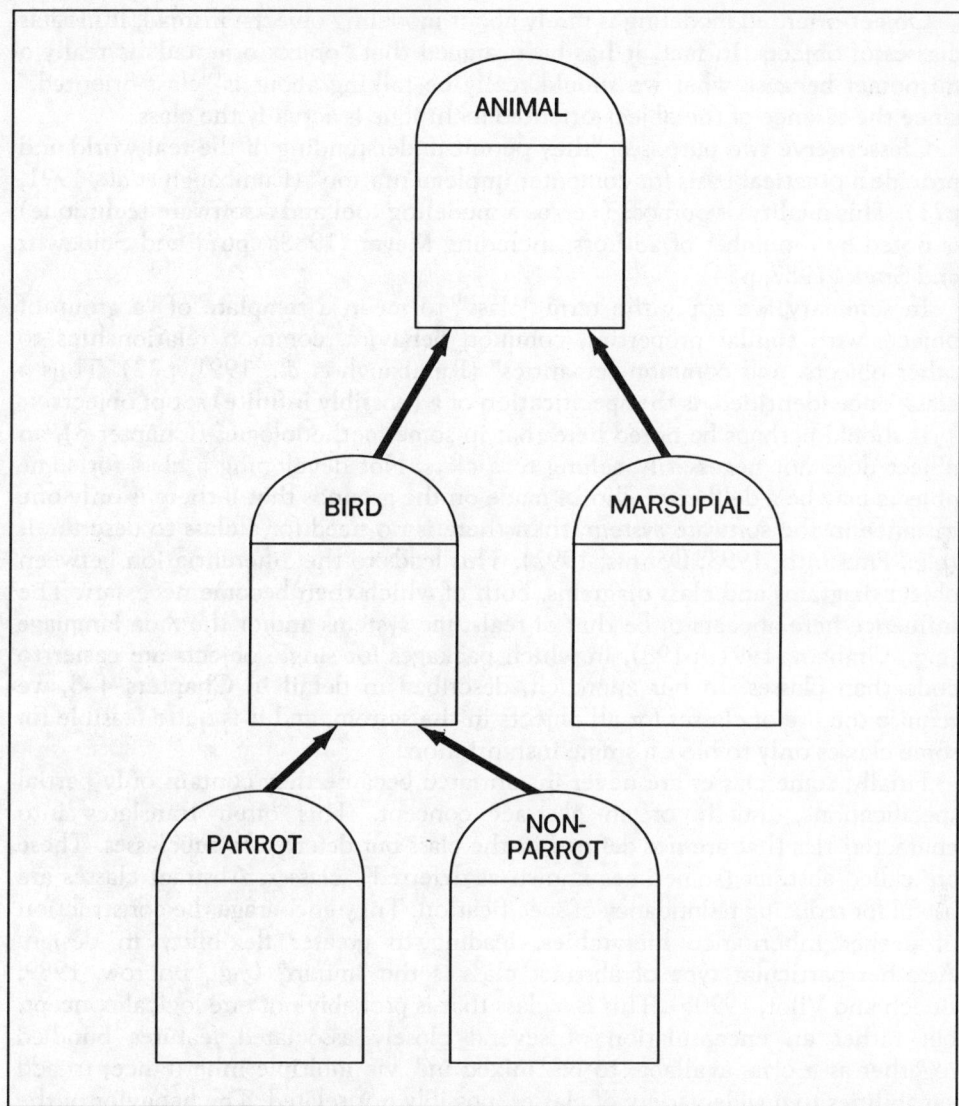

Figure 2.4 *Both birds and marsupials can be generalized into animals*

Essentially, we view a class as modeling the common characteristics of a set of objects that may be concrete or abstract concepts in the Universe of Discourse (UoD). Hence a class is an abstraction. It is an encapsulation of those common characteristics into a conceptual unit. A class provides a "template from which objects can be created" (Wegner, 1989, p10). An object is a particular instance of a class; and, as such, objects have *identity*, which classes do not.

Object-oriented modeling is rarely about modeling objects; instead, it models classes of objects. In fact, it has been argued that "object-oriented" is really a misnomer because what we should really be talking about is "class-oriented," since the essence of the object-oriented technique is actually the class.

Classes serve two purposes: "they permit understanding of the real world and provide a practical basis for computer implementation" (Rumbaugh et al., 1991, p21). This duality of purpose (i.e., as a modeling tool and a software technique) is noted by a number of authors, including Meyer (1988a, p67) and Seidewitz and Stark (1987, p54).

In summary, we apply the term "class" to mean a template of "a group of objects with similar properties, common behavior, common relationships to other objects, and common semantics" (Rumbaugh et al., 1991, p22). Thus a class, once identified, is the specification of a (possibly infinite) set of objects.

It should perhaps be noted here that in some methodologies (Chapter 3), an object does not necessarily belong to a class. Not developing a class for some objects may be a deliberate choice made on the grounds that if there is only one instance in the software system, then there is no need for a class to describe it (e.g., Firesmith, 1993; Dennis, 1992). This leads to the differentiation between object diagrams and class diagrams, both of which then become necessary. The influence here appears to be that of real-time systems and/or the Ada language (e.g., Graham, 1991, p198), in which packages for single objects are easier to code than classes. In our approach, described in detail in Chapters 4–8, we require the use of classes for all objects in the system, and it is quite feasible for some classes only to have a single instantiation.

Finally, some classes are never instantiated because they contain only partial specifications, usually of an abstract concept. This often translates into characteristics that are not defined in the class but deferred to subclasses. These are called abstract (sometimes known as deferred[6]) classes. Abstract classes are useful for reducing redundancy of specification. They encourage the construction of deeper inheritance hierarchies, leading to greater flexibility in design. Another particular type of abstract class is the "mixin" (e.g., Bobrow, 1989; Booch and Vilot, 1990b). This is a class that is probably not one logical concept, but rather an encapsulation of several closely associated features bundled together as a class available to be "mixed in," via multiple inheritance, to add capabilities to a wide variety of classes, possibly not related. The behavior of the mixin is seen as orthogonal to the behavior of the classes with which it is to be combined, insofar as they add extra characteristics in "sideways," thus not requiring *all* classes in the inheritance hierarchy to support the mixin behavior. Bracha and Cook (1990) view a mixin as an "abstract subclass"—for example, a subclass that might add a border to a wide variety of window classes.

---

6. Firesmith (1992b) differentiates between these two terms: abstract classes are superclasses with missing necessary declarations, and deferred classes are abstract classes that include stubs for the missing declarations that must be supplied by a subclass. Here, however, we will use the terms as synonyms.

The basic dichotomy, then, is between individuals, which we term objects, and templates or sets of objects, which we term classes. OOPLs support this dichotomy directly; and this means that OO designs are easily expressed in those languages. A coded module that represents a class is, however, slightly different from the class as a concept because it also contains an implementation. In a sense, the OOA/D class is strictly an abstract data type (ADT) and the coded module simply one possible implementation. Since the meaning of the words "class" and "object" are (i) always clear in a particular context and (ii) may need to be merged when discussing high-level, system overviews, we often prefer the "umbrella" term "object/class," or O/C for short. If we specifically wish to identify individual objects, ADTs, and so forth, we will select the specific terminology.

2.3.2 Encapsulation/information hiding

Encapsulation and information hiding are not especially new, but the degree to which they are used by object technology is new. Some authors equate them (e.g., Booch, 1991; Smith, 1991; and Thomas, 1989b, who says that "encapsulation is the technical name for information hiding"); others try to differentiate them conceptually—one an idea and the other an implementation of the idea. More correctly, at the implementation level, code and data can be *encapsulated* together into a class (i.e., gathered together in a code module), yet remain visible to other classes (Figure 2.5) (e.g., Wirfs-Brock *et al.*, 1990, p18). Within a procedural language, encapsulation can be accomplished simply by using subprogram modules. However, in a language such as C or FORTRAN with global COMMON blocks (or the equivalent), the data are widely available to other parts of the program external to the encapsulated subroutine. On the other hand, *information hiding* requires the visibility of data to be restricted to within the (encapsulated) module. In other words, encapsulation does not guarantee information hiding. Similarly, information hiding does not necessitate encapsulation of the concept in a module. In OT the aim is to use both mechanisms to encapsulate a concept within one module and to hide the details of that concept's implementation via information hiding.

2.3.3 Responsibilities, services, and behavior

A class is defined by, and encapsulates, a set of responsibilities or services.[7] Responsibilities are characteristics of a class; that is to say, it is the responsibility of the class to know the characteristics that define it. Wirfs-Brock and Wilkerson (1989b) stress the need to adopt a responsibility-driven approach to OO development, an approach supported by Rubin and Goldberg's (1992) behavioral analysis model and compatible with Meyer's (1989b) contracting metaphor.

---

7. Here "services" and "responsibilities" are used as synonyms.

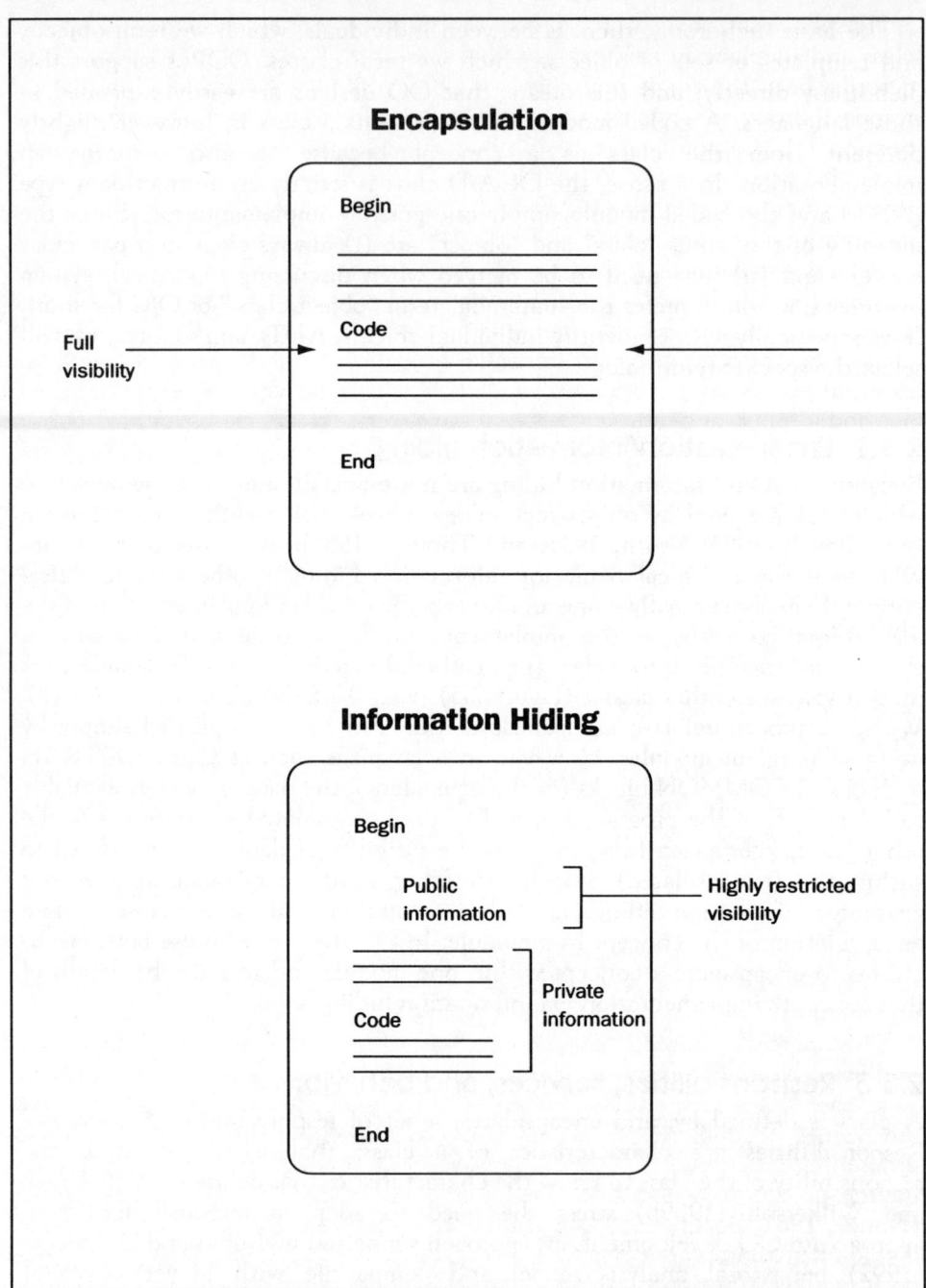

Figure 2.5 Encapsulation places a boundary around a chunk of code; information hiding makes that boundary opaque, except for those small pieces deemed to be transparent (public information) (Henderson-Sellers, 1992a)

The Object-oriented Paradigm

"Responsibilities" is a broad term that conveys the sense of purpose of the class and its place in the system (Wirfs-Brock *et al.*, 1990, p62). It is used to describe both the single high-level "responsibility of the class" and individual responsibilities or services, each of these being described using a contract (see Section 2.4.2). Individual responsibilities describe the knowledge an O/C keeps about itself (properties), as well as the actions it can perform (operations). Responsibilities/services define how an object of a class responds to changes in its environment and together are often termed a class's behavior.

Behavior is defined by Snyder (1989, p2) as "the set of services provided by an object to its clients" where "services are carried out by executing code that accesses or manipulates the actual data." Loomis *et al.* (1987, p195) define a class as having a set of operations (also known as methods) where "a method's external effects are its behavior" and the "behavioral description specifies the method's input and output parameters, effects on attributes of the classes involved, the names of other methods invoked by this method, and the sequence of their invocation." Similarly, Wegner (1990, p8) suggests that class behavior is a collection of operations or methods that define the interface of the class, and that "the operations determine the messages (calls) to which the object can respond." Behavior, responsibilities, and services are therefore viewed as synonymous terms. In MOSES, we use the term "services" to describe the O/C's total behavior.

2.3.4 Properties, operations, and contracts
Properties
Properties are services (responsibilities) of a class that involve information being disclosed about the state of an object. Properties may be viewed as queries about the state of an object and hence should not have side effects on state (Meyer, 1988a). Properties that return objects are viewed no differently from properties that return "values." In fact, following the Smalltalk model, there is no conceptual distinction between "values" and "objects" (Beeri, 1990). Properties that return "values" are often termed "attributes," although this does not necessarily imply a physical piece of stored data. Properties may also take any number of arguments.

This approach simplifies some confusion in the literature regarding attributes and basic types. For example, it has been argued that an attribute may only be of a "basic" type (e.g., REAL, CHARACTER) and thus instances of attributes are values (Rumbaugh *et al.*, 1991). On the other hand, many authors differentiate between complex attributes and "basic" attributes, the former having objects as values and the latter having "simple quantities" as values (Nance, 1981; Booch, 1991). A third approach taken in some of the literature is that *all* attributes are complex classes (Beeri, 1990). The first two approaches both employ a notion of attribute that is similar to the traditional notion of attribute from data modeling. In this case an attribute is in some sense an atomic construct. The values of these attributes are "simple quantities." Examples are attributes such as INTEGER, REAL, and STRING with values such as 1, 2.7, and "John." The third approach, and the one adopted here, provides for a conceptually simpler model.

This issue of attributes in the object model is made even more complex by the overloading of the term "attribute" to mean both "logical attributes" and "physical attributes," i.e., stored data. Physical attributes and functions (without side effects upon the abstract state) of the implementation can together model the logical attributes of the conceptual model. An added complication is that further physical attributes may be introduced by a designer for implementation reasons, implementation attributes being simply a subset of the physical attributes.

In MOSES (Chapters 4–8) we use the word *properties* to denote a "logical," rather than an implementation, characteristic. The word *attribute* is reserved for those data stored privately (private services)—the decision to define the internal data structure may be taken at almost any stage of the lifecycle, although it is preferably left until late in the design process.

A class should not make attributes visible in its interface (e.g., Snyder, 1986; Wirfs-Brock and Wilkerson, 1989a), although information can be accessed by means of services (properties). This does not imply that these properties are actually physical attributes (data); rather, they represent state knowledge held by the class.

In the Implementation Phase of the lifecycle (Chapter 4) when these properties are coded, they may become data or functions and are known by whatever OOPL-specific term is used to describe the mechanism by which attributes (private data) are accessed.

Operations
Operations are services of a class that lead to changes in the state of an object of that class. Operations may be viewed as commands on the object, that is, requests for the object to do something. They should not return information about the outcome of the operation; this should be visible only via the services termed properties. The behavioral specification is written using structured English (Hawryszkiewycz, 1988), formal specification languages (Duke *et al.*, 1991), or simple text. It specifies what effect the operation has on the state of the O/C.

O/C behavior, in the Implementation Phase, is modeled by a set of operations defined on a class. At this phase, the terminology of the OOPL is applied.

Contracts
Each responsibility or service, whether a property or an operation, has an associated contract. Contracting is based on a metaphor of business world contracting (Meyer, 1992e). An agreement for two parties to interact is underlain by an understanding of how both parties will benefit and their ensuing obligations. In general, an obligation for one party is a benefit to the other. The terms of these contractual obligations/benefits may be visualized in a 2×2 matrix (Figure 2.6), which we will refer to as a contract matrix. In this example,

The Object-oriented Paradigm 53

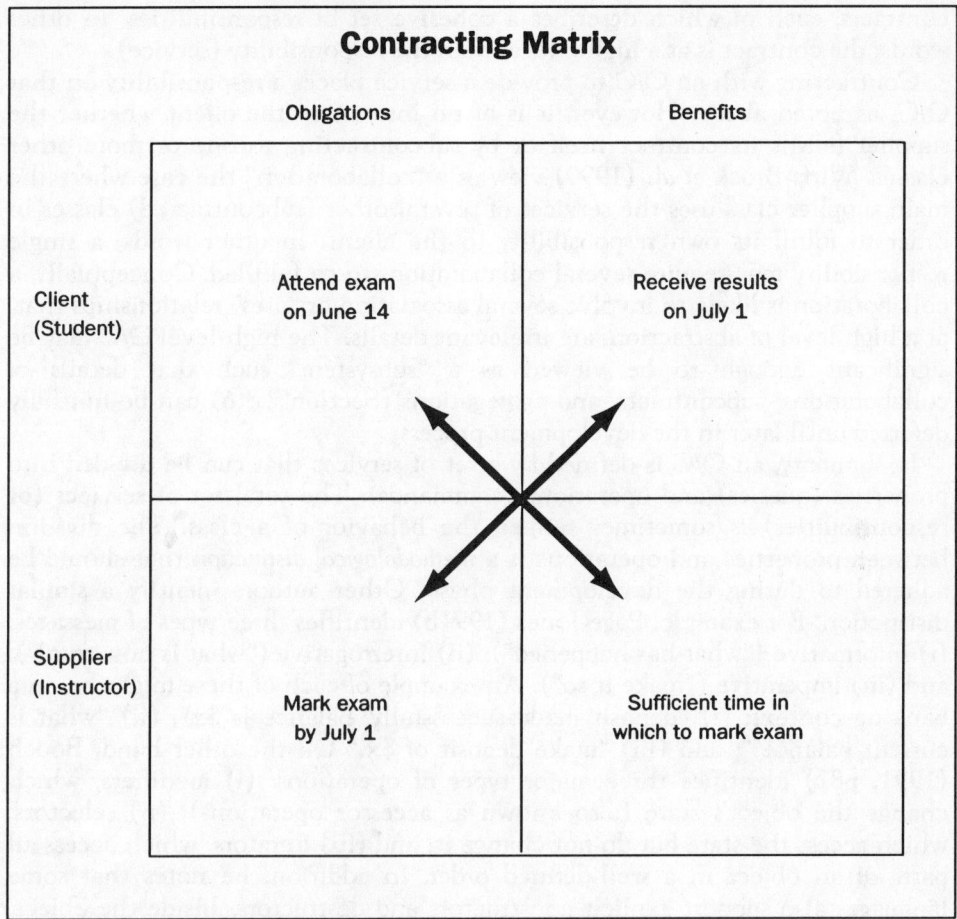

Figure 2.6 *Contract matrix spelling out contractual obligations and benefits to client and server (Henderson-Sellers, 1992a)*

the matrix describes the relationship between a STUDENT O/C and an INSTRUCTOR O/C. The obligation of the student to attend the examination on a given date is mirrored by the benefit to the instructor of having sufficient time to mark the exam (indicated by the diagonal arrow). Hence the supplier (instructor) can fulfill his or her own obligation. If the client (student) breaks the contract (by not attending the exam), then the instructor need take no action. The benefit to the student of meeting the obligation is that he or she receives the results by the stated date. Contracts therefore specify the terms of these obligations and thus add meaning to the O/C.

It should be noted that in this description (used in MOSES), a contract is associated with each service. This is different from the use of the word "contract" in Wirfs-Brock's work in which classes support a number of contracts, each of which describes a cohesive set of responsibilities. In other words, the contract is at a higher level than the responsibility (service).

Contracting with an O/C to provide a service places a responsibility on that O/C, as noted above. However, it is of no interest to the client whether the supplier fulfills its contract itself or by subcontracting to one or more other classes. Wirfs-Brock *et al.* (1990) view as a "collaboration" the case where the main supplier class uses the services of several other (subcontracted) classes in order to fulfill its own responsibility to the client. In other words, a single responsibility may require several collaborations to be fulfilled. Conceptually, a collaboration is likely to involve several association or "uses" relationships that, at a high level of abstraction, are irrelevant details. The high-level O/C may be significant enough to be viewed as a "subsystem" such that details of collaborations, subcontracts, and aggregations (Section 2.3.6) can be fruitfully deferred until later in the development process.

In summary, an O/C is defined by a set of services that can be divided into properties (queries) and operations (commands). The total set of services (or responsibilities) is sometimes termed the behavior of a class. The division between properties and operations is a *methodological distinction* that should be adhered to during the development phase. Other authors identify a similar distinction. For example, Page-Jones (1991b) identifies three types of messages: (i) informative ("what has happened"); (ii) interrogative ("what is now true?"); and (iii) imperative ("make it so"). An example of each of these might be, in a banking context: (i) "deposit made successfully, balance is $x"; (ii) "what is current balance?"; and (iii) "make deposit of $x." On the other hand, Booch (1991, p82) identifies three major types of operations: (i) modifiers, which change the object's state (also known as accessor operations); (ii) selectors, which access the state but do not change it; and (iii) iterators, which access all parts of an object in a well-defined order. In addition, he notes that some languages also support explicit constructors and destructors. Inside the object, Meyer (1988a) identifies three types of functional behavior: (i) a constructor function, (ii) an accessor function, and (iii) a transformer function, which are available to fulfill the message requests identified above for the client class. Such a distinction may blur during the Implementation Phase when a specific OOPL is chosen. This choice influences the fine detail of the design and the coding style.

2.3.5 Communication

In the literature there is a wide range of terminology and meanings assigned by different fields to describe communication between objects. Events, messages, state changes, triggers, and transactions are all terms used in the discussion of O/C behavior. These terms will be discussed below.

Message passing is a widely used term in the software engineering literature and relates to the dynamic nature of objects (as opposed to static classes), the relationships established in analysis and design being essentially the routes by which messages will finally be passed. Such interobject communication is roughly equivalent to subprogram CALLs in a procedure language: in other words, message passing determines the flow of control, although of course in object-oriented systems such threads of control need not be sequential but can also be concurrent. Messages consist of the name of the target object (supplier object), the name of the service required of it, and any optional arguments. For example, in some languages the message to open a bank account with an initial deposit of $500 would be written as *myaccount.open(500)*.

In the conceptual modeling community, the view of communication is somewhat different. Instead of a class having a set of services, a set of events is specified for the system. Wand and Weber (1989, p87) term these external and internal events. An external event "can be viewed as an 'input' to the system" and "occurs because of an interaction with other things." An event is defined as a pair of states. "An event will be designated by e = <s1, s2>, where s1 and s2 are the states before and after the event, r, respectively" (Wand and Weber, 1989, p85). An event therefore specifies the transitions that are to occur on the state of an object. Both the before and after states must be stable states for the system; that is, they must not violate any laws or constraints of the system. Similarly, Wieringa (1991, p14) discusses the changes in a system as being a result of events. "In general there are two kind of events, change of role ... and change of attribute value." Fowler (1991, p208) also sees behavior in terms of events, saying that "the focus of the behavioral view is the event. An event is a change of state of an object."

The common theme is that an event is instantaneous in time or, as Rumbaugh *et al.* (1991, p85) rightly argue, "[since] nothing is instantaneous; an event is simply an occurrence that is fast compared to the granularity of the time scale of a given abstraction." Also, an event contains information or has a specification. This specification details the effect upon an object's state once the event has occurred. Thus an event can in fact be considered as a pair of states, i.e., a pre- and poststate expression for the object. External events are those events that occur externally to the object, that is, the object has no control over the event; while internal events are those that the object initiates upon receiving an external event and over which it does have control. Quite often internal events are triggered by an object in response to an external event in order to fulfill the external event specification.

However, not all objects in a system can respond to all events. A certain object can only respond to a certain set of events. If an event occurs that does not have a defined response by an object in the system, an error in the system specification has occurred. Events and states have been examined in detail by a number of authors (e.g., Wieringa, 1991), and Harel's statecharts have recently received a great deal of attention in the literature (e.g., Coleman *et al.*, 1992) as a way of specifying the events that an object can respond to and the way in which it is affected by them.

In MOSES (Chapters 4-8), the basic model of communication between objects is taken from Coleman *et al.* (1992). In this model, services are requested from a client object such that the provider of the service is directly named by the client. Information flow can also be bidirectional such that the result of a request is returned to the client. The communication mechanism is synchronous such that a "single service request and complete service execution are treated as a single atomic event" (Coleman et al., 1992). This model seems appropriate for most developments, although more complex communication protocols such as balking, time-out, and asynchronous communication may be added to the model by the developer (Booch, 1991).

Services either specify the change in state of an object resulting from a request (operation) or return information (properties). Messages are the triggers for activating services. Messages are instantaneous in time. They may be generated by objects internal to the system or by external objects, e.g., users and devices. An external object may generate a message that requests a service. This service may, in turn, generate a number of internal messages that are sent to other objects. To the sending object these are internal messages, whereas to the receiving objects they are external messages. Once a message has been received, the appropriate service is activated. If the temporal resolution of the service is small compared with the system being modeled, it can be assumed to be instantaneous. A service that is instantaneous implies that control reverts to the caller immediately upon receipt of the message. As no other messages can occur in the intervening period, it can be viewed as instantaneous.

In summary, then, the communication model (sometimes called the dynamic model) of objects is currently somewhat different in the different fields of literature. These approaches to modeling communication and system behavior once again reflect the focus of the research community in each field. Understanding of the dynamic nature of object-oriented systems still lags considerably behind our understanding of the static relationships of the system. The model employed in MOSES is a simple yet effective one to which more sophisticated communication protocols may be added.

2.3.6 Relationships

Relationships between classes during the Specification Phase (effectively analysis and design) are association, aggregation, and generalization. Generalization is directly supported in OOPLs by the inheritance mechanism, while in OOPLs the relationships of association and aggregation are modeled indirectly by a client–server relationship.

Association is a meaningful relationship between two O/Cs such that one O/C may request a service from another. This represents the direct use of the services of one O/C by another (e.g., a CUSTOMER O/C uses the services of a BANK O/C). Aggregation represents the **has_a** or **consists_of** relationship (e.g., a room consists of four walls, a floor, and a ceiling), and generalization represents a taxonomic hierarchy or **is_a** relationship.

Association

An association is a relationship between two O/Cs showing the static structure. They are usually named to provide meaning to the relationship. Association may be a unidirectional or a bidirectional relationship. Bidirectionality is modeled by the use of property symmetry (Velho and Carapuca, 1992). For example, in an association between the O/Cs WINDOW and TEXT_BOX, the WINDOW may know of the TEXT_BOX but not vice versa. On the other hand, in an association between an EMPLOYEE O/C and a COMPANY O/C, a unidirectional relationship such that an EMPLOYEE *Works-for* a COMPANY means that a COMPANY would not know its EMPLOYEEs (not a suitable situation in this case). Therefore, it would be necessary to model the *Works-for* association as bidirectional. This is done by making the property *Employs* in COMPANY the symmetric function of the *Works-for* property in EMPLOYEE. This approach is called the inverse function approach in Martin and Odell (1992). Thus the association may be read as an EMPLOYEE *Works-for* a COMPANY or the inverse, a COMPANY *Employs* an EMPLOYEE. Relationships may in fact be ternary or more (n-ary); that is, the relationship between three or more O/Cs cannot be broken down into binary relationships without losing information.

Many authors have suggested that n-ary relationships rarely occur in practice (Rumbaugh *et al.*, 1991, p28). The ternary relationship may be modeled as a new concept, a class, with each related class having a symmetric property with the new "relationship" class. Martin and Odell (1992) suggest the use of a relationship when the analyst wishes to view objects as tuples. Alternatively a relationship may be viewed as a function, interpreted as a mathematical mapping, when one object is known and it is desired to determine other objects with which it is associated. Both tools model an association. However, Martin and Odell consider that they differ only insofar as a functional association could be implemented as a query or pointer and a relation as a record or group item.

An association between O/Cs implies that each O/C plays a role in that association. For example, a person may play the role of a student in a *Study* association but the role of employee in a *Works-for* association. Roles (Section 2.3.7) are useful in understanding the nature of the relationship being modeled and add extra information to the association name (Rumbaugh *et al.*, 1991, p34). Roles are a useful concept that can be applied at the conceptual modeling phase (the Specification Phase of MOSES). They can be modeled as names of the association property or as subclasses using dynamic classification (Fowler, 1991).

Aggregation

Aggregation can be seen as a special type of association (Rumbaugh *et al.*, 1991; Henderson-Sellers *et al.*, 1992) to represent a "composed-of," "part-of," or "has-a" relationship (see also Pun and Winder, 1990).

The relationship is especially useful in parts hierarchies—for example, an engine is-part-of a car, or a car has-an engine—although, if knowledge of the parts themselves is critical (e.g., mechanics pulling cars apart), aggregation may be inappropriate (Ratjens, pers. com., 1993). The specification of the aggregation construct is based on the observation that parts hierarchies and the **has-a** relationship generally are much used relationships in modeling. Although ill defined, the aggregation relationship is best characterized as one in which antisymmetry and transitivity constraints apply. So, for example, a room usually consists of four walls, a floor, and a ceiling. Since a wall is part of a room, a room cannot be part of a wall (antisymmetry constraint) and, if a brick is part of a wall (which is itself part of a room), then the brick is part of the room (transitivity constraint) (Rumbaugh *et al.*, 1991). If these constraints are not true for the particular case, then it is unlikely that the relationship is aggregation.

Care needs to be applied when using aggregation, to be sure that it is the correct means of expressing the relationships within the UoD. De Champeaux (1991, p11) presents an example of a misuse of aggregation, and the ambiguities that result. He says:

> Can we have the inference:
>
> John Young's hand is part-of John Young;
>
> and
>
> John Young is part-of HP (in fact he is CEO of HP);[8]
>
> therefore we have:
>
> John Young's hand is part-of HP?
>
> Obviously, we have applied transitivity erroneously due to using the part-of in two incompatible senses. Detecting these anomalies is more difficult in large systems with multiple analysts.

The question that is posed is that of transitivity—namely, is it true that John Young's hand is part-of HP? The answer given by de Champeaux and Faure (1992) is that this is misuse of transitivity, since there are two different usages of the phrase "is part-of." We would go further and suggest that the error is not in the use of the transitivity functionality; rather, it is the misidentification of "John Young is part-of HP" as an aggregation relationship. In fact, it is an association relationship disguised as an aggregation, since the real relationship is "is-employed-by." As we have noted, aggregation is a type of association that enforces not only a transitivity rule but also an antisymmetry rule. If a SENTENCE is made up of WORDs, then the reverse is obviously false—antisymmetry.

---

8. Since the publication of de Champeaux and Faure's paper in early 1992, John Young has in fact terminated his role as Chief Executive Officer of Hewlett Packard.

Since aggregations are a type of association, all aggregations could be replaced by associations. Indeed, some developers may find it easier to do just that. However, in our experience many analysts and designers find it extremely valuable to have the option of using aggregations, simply as a modeling tool. It is a fairly natural logic to describe things made up of component parts. If it is a natural description, then aggregation should be utilized. Once the developers begin to agonize over whether a specific relationship is aggregation or association, this indicates that the "added value" of aggregation has become minimal and associations should be used.

In most OOPLs, however, aggregations and associations cannot be represented distinctly. Both may be modeled using a relationship available in most languages that is termed either client–server (Wirfs-Brock *et al.*, 1990) or client–supplier (Meyer, 1988a).

Inheritance

Inheritance is a unique and powerful feature of the object model and also one of the most hotly discussed. Debates rage over the use of inheritance, of multiple inheritance (MI), and of their semantics; furthermore, the AI community has been debating the meaning of inheritance for over a decade.

Inheritance is a technique that can be used to inherit the interface (specification inheritance) and also to inherit code (implementation inheritance). Winkler (1992) calls these the "concept-oriented view" (COV) as opposed to the "program-oriented view" (POV). The differentiation between these two basic "flavors" of inheritance is discussed by, e.g., LaLonde and Pugh (1991). Specification inheritance is often taken (e.g., Rumbaugh *et al.*, 1991) to be the equivalent of the generalization/specialization relationship in which specialized classes are behavior-compatible with their parents—often known as subtyping. In other words, these classes offer a similar set of services such that the specialization can always be substituted for the parent. Dynamic substitution can also be supported such that polymorphic structures (see later in this section) can be successfully employed. The specialized class is often regarded as **a-kind-of** (AKO) its parent. We term this relationship "generalization." Alternatively, it is frequently termed an **is-a** relationship (e.g., Lalonde and Pugh, 1991). More strictly (e.g., Graham, 1991, pp23–25), the **is-a** relationship is an instance–class relationship, whereas the correct term for the class–class relationship is "isakindof" or simply AKO. Here we will use the terms **is-a** and AKO synonymously, since both reflect a traversal up one abstraction level: context will determine the strict interpretation as **is-a** or AKO.

Probably the most common view of inheritance within the OOP field is that the subclass inherits *all* the properties and operations defined for the superclass, and will probably add more (Coad and Yourdon, 1991b). This view is extended to allow for modification of properties and operations in the subclass. How this modification occurs varies with the approach taken. A class inherits all the services and contracts of another class, which should not be arbitrarily canceled (see discussion later in this chapter).[9] Thus any services that are applicable to a class A are applicable to a class B, where A is a generalization of B. This implies that wherever an object of class A appears, an object of class B can substitute for it, as class B **is-a** class A. Class B may also add operations, properties, and constraints.

Therefore, we can see that the descendant class is both an extension and a restriction of the ancestor: an extension in the sense that it has at least those services of the ancestor, and probably more, and a restriction in that it applies to a smaller set of likely instances. This apparent duality of generalization has been noted by Meyer (1988a, p233), Rumbaugh et al. (1991, p63), and Jacobson et al. (1992) among others.

In contrast to generalization, a class may inherit data representation and operations from another class, but these may be changed in the subclass (e.g., Leavens, 1991). Indeed, the resulting subclass may no longer support the interface of the superclass. This approach to inheritance, because it focuses on code inheritance rather than on behavior and substitutability, is called "implementation inheritance" (see also Atkinson in McCullough et al., 1992), a term we also adopt.

Consequently, it is technically possible in OOPLs to use implementation inheritance to inherit from a class with no semantic connections. For example, suppose that there is already a BIRD class. The design calls for the addition of a BAT class. One might be tempted to use implementation inheritance in order to inherit the code for the operation "fly," since both bats and birds (with exceptions) possess the capability of true flight (unlike other flying mammals, which really glide rather than fly). But is a BAT **a-kind-of** BIRD? No; rather, it is classed in a different taxonomy: of mammals, which are distinct from birds. Such implementation inheritance destroys the semantics of the abstraction hierarchy, endangering reusability based on specification (as it should be). For example, the BAT class described above presumably inherits "feathers" from class BIRD. Taken to this extreme, the use of implementation inheritance has given me a bat with feathers!

It is possible that generalization/specialization relationships depicted in the modeled abstraction hierarchy may diverge from the finally implemented class hierarchies. The reasons for this divergence lie in the objectives of the designers and implementors of class hierarchies and other ways in which they use inheritance. As noted by Rumbaugh et al. (1991, p326) and Reed (1992), the aims of one C++ library can differ significantly from another (it is justifiable to extrapolate this to libraries implemented in all other OOPLs). Consequently, Reed contends that "no single construction technique satisfies the needs of all libraries" (1992, p24), this resulting in design differences across class hierarchies.

LaLonde and Pugh (1991) extend these ideas and identify three (rather than

---

9. This is unlike semantic nets in some branches of AI where the descendant (the subclass and all its subclasses) can cancel out a property of the ancestor (the superclass and all its superclasses) (Wegner, 1990, p39).

two) distinct inheritance relationships useful for OT: implementation inheritance (subclassing), specification inheritance (subtyping), and **is-a** (called here specialization inheritance) (Yap and Henderson-Sellers, 1993b). While the first of these is programming-specific, the second two are typically used in the Specification Phase. Specification inheritance describes inheritance use of the interface, which leads to dynamic substitutability, where a class represents a type and correspondingly a subclass is a subtype of its superclass (supertype). In this case, the subclass must be an extension of its superclass so that in every case where the superclass can be used, its subclasses can take its place. For substitutability, a subclass must be able to respond to any messages that its superclass can. Consequently, its superclass's interface is a subset of its own, and each service's arguments in the subclass must not be more specific than the corresponding service in the superclass; and the result type returned by the subclass must not be more general than that returned by the superclass. This corresponds to covariance (Harris, 1991). A subclass must also be able to fulfill any contracts that its superclass can, which means that it cannot fail to perform a requested method that its supertype is capable of fulfilling (Meyer, 1988a). It is important to note that a subtype does not have to be related to its supertype in any other sense than that the subtype has the behavior of its supertype. In other words, an inheritance structure is not absolutely necessary. To illustrate this, consider the following simplistic model (assuming, for simplicity, no assertions for any of the following behavior):

The specification of the type VEHICLE is limited to move and stop.
The specification of the type PERSON is move, stop, and eat.
The specification of the type DOG is move, stop, and bark.

In this case, both PERSON and DOG can be regarded as subtypes of VEHICLE since both exhibit move and stop behaviors—they both have a superset of VEHICLE's specifications. However, as PERSON and DOG have additional different behaviors, eat and bark respectively, they cannot be substituted for each other. Note that the PERSON and DOG do not have to inherit from VEHICLE to be its subtypes. If they do inherit from VEHICLE, they are inheriting the specification of VEHICLE, hence the term "specification inheritance."

Often equated with specification inheritance is specialization inheritance, which is the **is-a** relationship of LaLonde and Pugh (1991) and one they support for design use. Again substitutability at the semantic level is supported. Specialization inheritance is the mechanism underlying an abstraction hierarchy derived by conceptual modeling of generalization and specialization relationships in the UoD.

Using specialization inheritance should result in no difference between classification structures and their resultant class hierarchies. As proposed by LaLonde and Pugh (1991), the specialization relationship is important for understanding logical relationships and is more intuitive. Therefore, this form of class hierarchy should be the easiest to extend at the class level: for someone to know how to introduce a new class into the existing structure, all that he or she would be required to do is to think of how the class fits in conceptually (that is, consider the taxonomy or abstraction hierarchy). If abstraction hierarchies are created through specializations only, that is, every time inheritance is used between two classes, an **is-a** relationship exists between the two classes, then a form of organization exists that satisfies to some extent Wirfs-Brock's (1992) request that "components be organized and described in ways that are understandable without resorting to reading code."

The realization of specialization hierarchies may not be as straightforward as presented, however, since Gibbs *et al.* (1990) believe that "classes are difficult to arrange in predefined taxonomies." Concurrence with this view comes from Booch (1991), whose discussion of classification concludes that it is a highly subjective exercise. Booch suggests as a caveat that perhaps, up to a point, greater knowledge of the problem domain leads to a more intelligent classification.

These ideas are summarized in Figure 2.7. Inheritance is the overall term for the relationship. During the Specification Phase (roughly analysis and design), the relationship is termed generalization. This becomes equivalent to specification inheritance in the Implementation Phase, in which substitutability, polymorphism, and user reuse are the key aspects. In addition, in Implementation, use may be made of implementation inheritance, which is not generally used in the Specification Phase and which focuses on reuse for the code developer.

In general, however, it is probably adequate to differentiate between a substitutability relationship (specification or specialization inheritance) and a code reuse relationship (implementation inheritance).

Multiple inheritance
Some methodologies and OOPLs include the concept of multiple inheritance (Meyer, 1988a; Booch, 1991; Rumbaugh *et al.*, 1991). This is where a class inherits from two or more parent classes forming a class lattice. Therefore, the subclass inherits all the services of the parent classes. For example, if class C inherits from A and B, then class C has all the services of class A and B. Thus an object of class C can substitute for an object of class A or an object of class B. Multiple inheritance (MI), used correctly, is a powerful mechanism. Various OOPLs handle the resulting issues of multiple inheritance in different ways.

Although in the majority of cases a well-planned single inheritance hierarchy will suffice, the availability of multiple inheritance provides extra leverage (Meyer, 1988b). One good example can be found in the technical environment of wastewater treatment (Edwards and Henderson-Sellers, 1993b), where a wastewater plant is viewed both by an engineer (as a piece of plant) and by an economist/accountant as an asset, thus illustrating the simplicity of design based on this "dual parentage" (Figure 2.8) that could not be accomplished succinctly without the use of multiple inheritance (see Chapter 8 for a case study of this wastewater costing problem).

The Object-oriented Paradigm

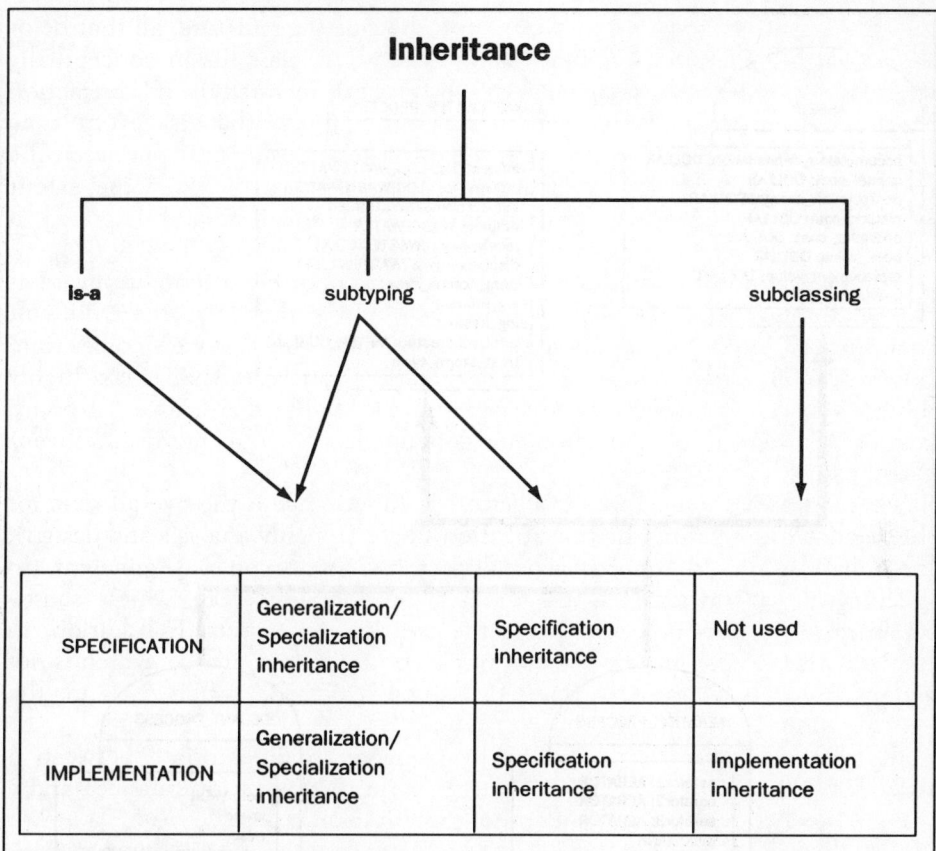

Figure 2.7 *The various faces of inheritance*

In the use of MI, the issue of name clashes arises (Knudsen, 1988). When two parent classes have services with the same name, how should the subclass interpret this clash? Should the subclass inherit both services, or combine them? Resolution of the conflict depends upon the domain being modeled by the classes. In some cases the service will model one thing only in the UoD and there should be no duplication in the subclass; alternatively, it may be that there is simply a name clash and that in fact both services are required. Knudsen (1988, p11) terms these two situations unification and intersection.

In unification, where the same name is used by two parent classes to model two different services and these are inherited by a subclass, the name clash is casual and thus some qualification or renaming is required (Meyer, 1988a). Intersection occurs when two services with the same name do in fact model the same phenomenon and are inherited by a subclass. In this situation the name clash is intended and the services must be combined. These two situations require the renaming of services to avoid a name clash. Although this is not a

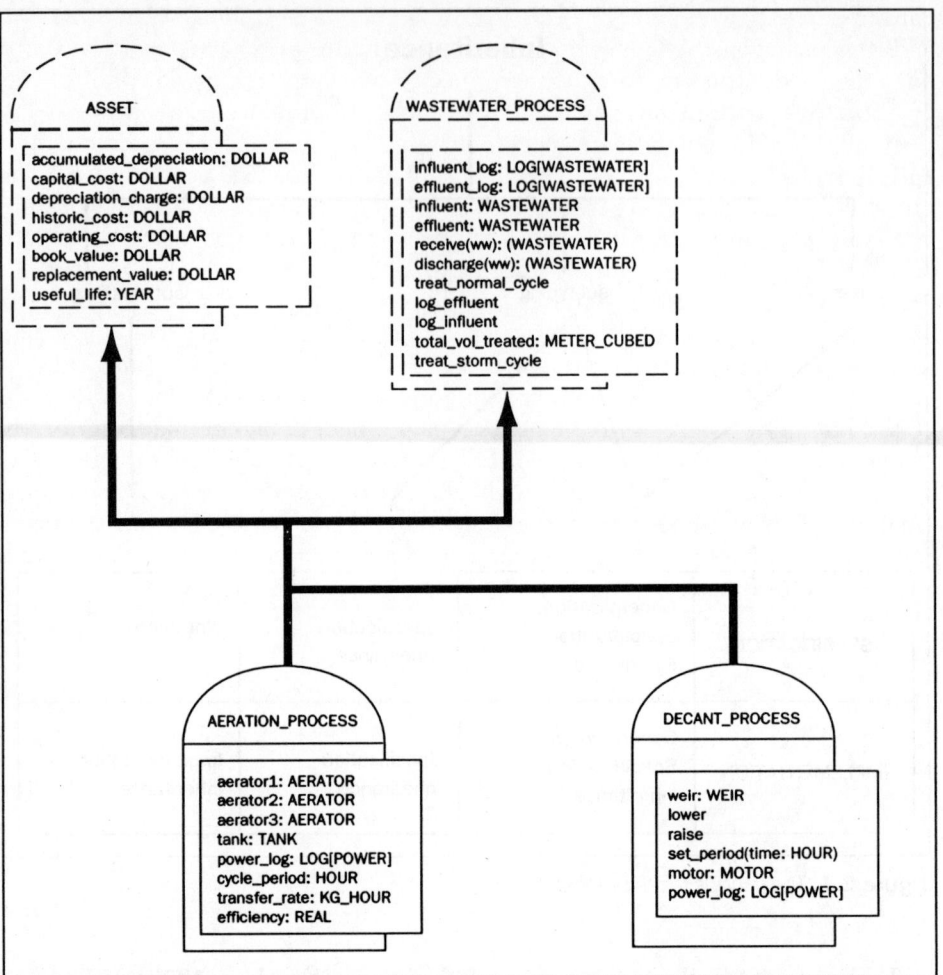

Figure 2.8 *Inheritance Model showing the multiple inheritance relationships for the AERATION_PROCESS, which is both an ASSET and a WASTEWATER_PROCESS*

problem during development of new classes, it may present a problem if two sets of libraries are to be integrated.

A possible consequence of the use of multiple inheritance is that one subclass may inherit from an ancestor class by two or more routes (Figure 2.9)—"repeated inheritance." Although this presents no problem if all the inheritances are unmodified, it is likely that, say, class B has modified a service, say print, inherited from class A and class C has not (or has modified the same service differently). In either case, class D, inheriting both from class B and class C, will inherit the service *print* (from its grandparent A) by two routes (via B and via C). Class B modified this service, while class C did not. Thus there

The Object-oriented Paradigm

are apparently available to class D two copies of the *print* service *but with different definitions!* A language that permits MI must also have a rational way of dealing with this repeated inheritance. Following the style rule of not permitting negations can help here, but it does not provide all the answers.

Guidelines for the correct support of services in abstraction hierarchies are given by Wirfs-Brock *et al.* (1990, pp112–113). The services of a subclass inheriting from multiple parents should be equal to or greater than the sum of the superclass's services. If there are services of the superclass *not* applicable to the subclass, then the hierarchy must be revised.

Multiple inheritance therefore raises a number of important issues for modeling the semantics of a situation. Many OOPLs do not provide adequate support for implementing these semantics. It is therefore very important to understand the domain when employing multiple inheritance, especially if the class hierarchy is to be implemented in an OOPL lacking support for the intended semantics. Within MOSES a renaming facility is provided that enables the developer to deal with these name clashes in an appropriate manner. This is important if the *designs* are to be reused between projects. Merging of services also requires the merging of their contracts and not simply their names (Section 2.4.3.2).

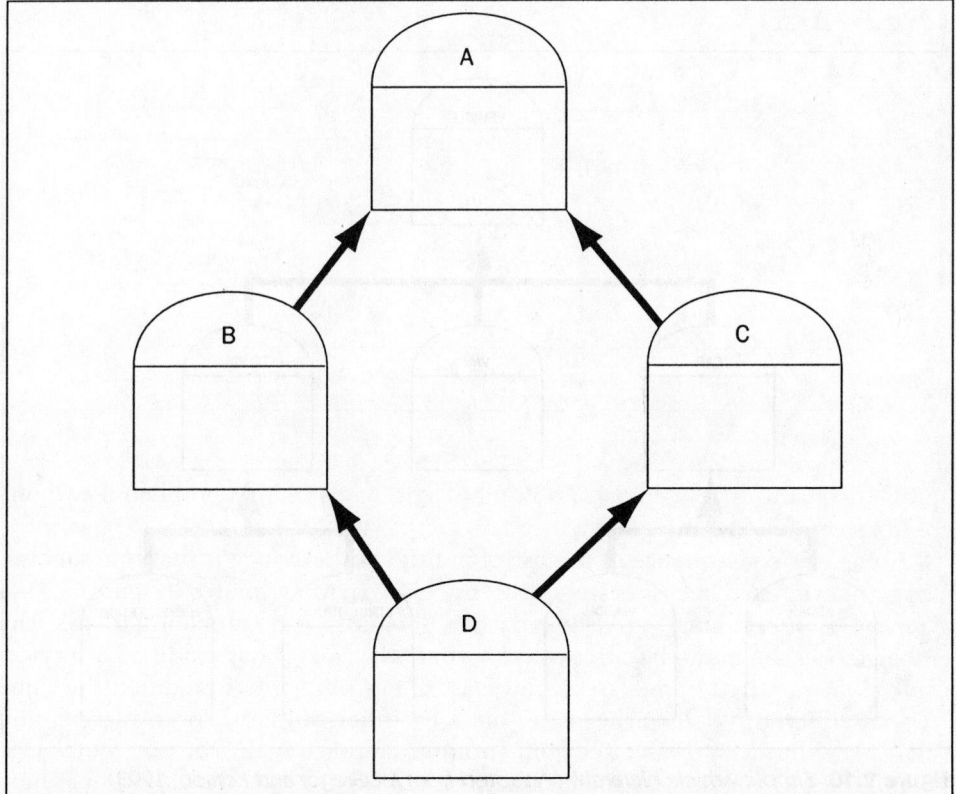

Figure 2.9 *An inheritance hierarchy in which repeated inheritance occurs*

Dimensions of inheritance

One serious concern raised by both Rumbaugh *et al.* (1991) and McGregor and Korson (1993) is that of multiple dimensions used for classification and hence for construction of inheritance (abstraction) hierarchies. For example, Figure 2.10 shows an inheritance hierarchy that would seem intuitively acceptable. Vehicles are cars, vans, or trucks. Furthermore, cars may be either sedans or wagons (estates) and trucks may be petrol-engined trucks or diesel-engined trucks. This manufacturer/rental company now introduces diesel cars into the fleet, initially for wagons only. The software designer may now begin to have concerns, since the hierarchy of Figure 2.11 contains repetition. If we skip a few stages to the more elaborate example of Figures 2.12–2.14, we see that Figure 2.12 shows an apparently (at first glance) sound inheritance hierarchy, since *all* the relationships shown are indeed **is-a-kind-of**. However, further consideration reveals that among the seven second-tier classes, there are strong overlaps. In other words, any instance will (within the stated Universe of Discourse) be a member of three of these classes simultaneously (e.g., a Ford petrol-driven sedan). This (standard) notation obfuscates the fact that classification has actually been performed three times, using three different specialization criteria. CAR has been specialized first by manufacturer, secondly by engine/fuel type, and then by body style. McGregor and Korson (1993) stress the need to make

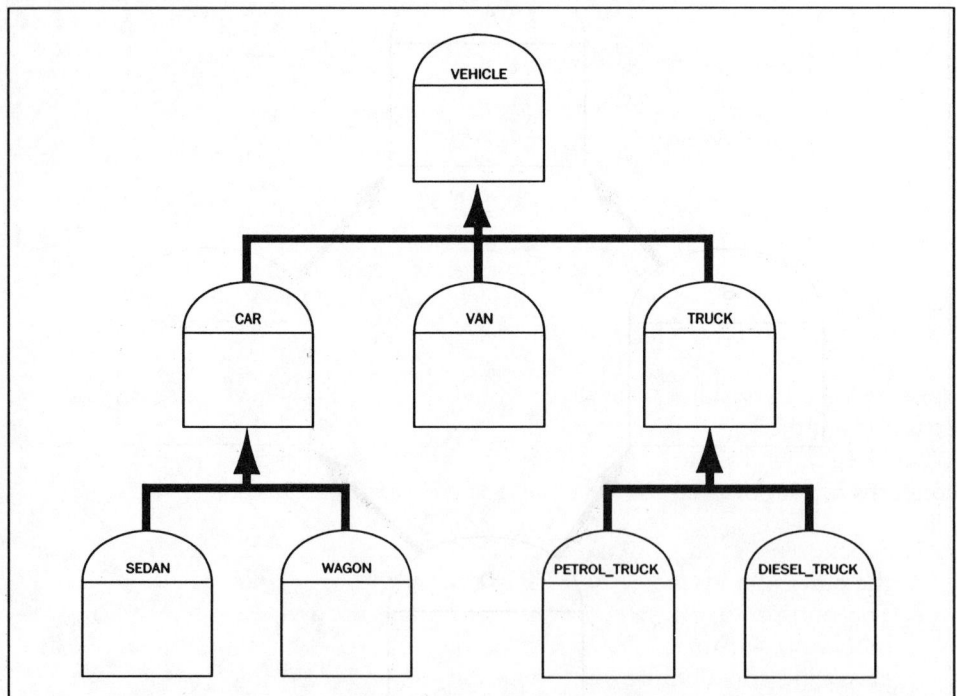

Figure 2.10 *Simple vehicle hierarchy (Adapted from McGregor and Korson, 1993)*

The Object-oriented Paradigm

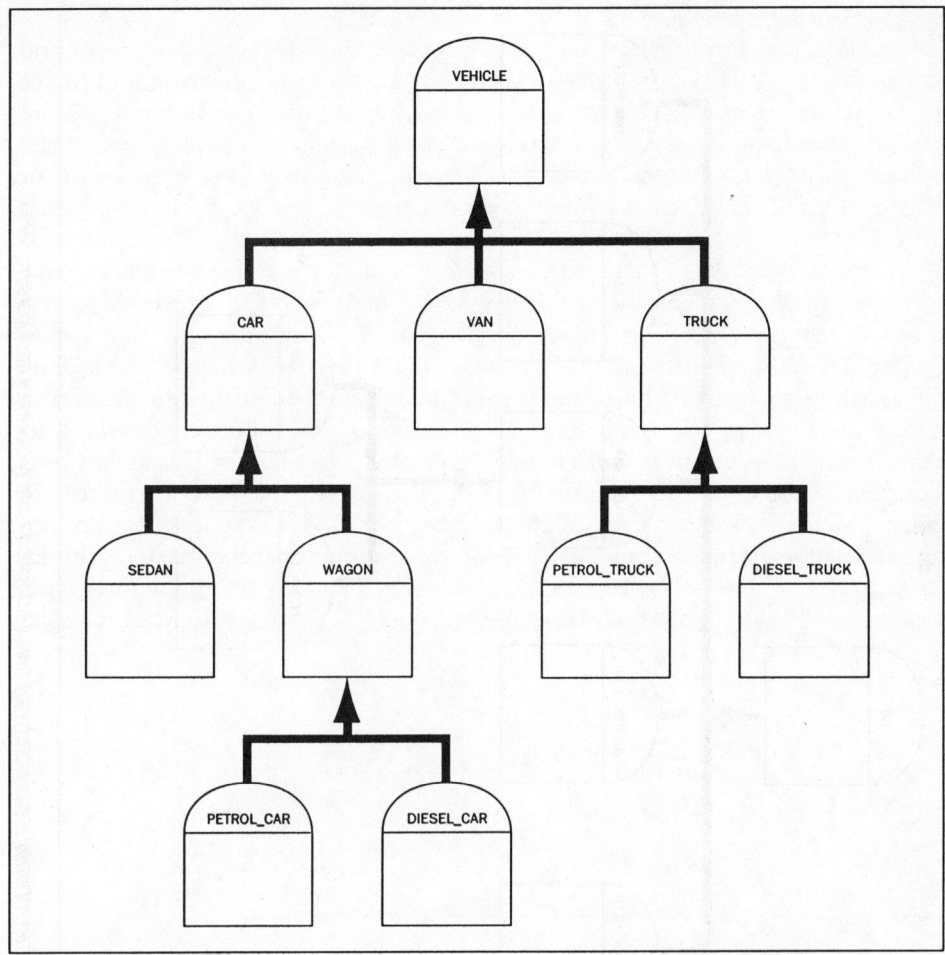

Figure 2.11 *The vehicle hierarchy of Figure 2.10, now allowing for two types of internal combustion engine (ICE) for power. (Adapted from McGregor and Korson, 1993)*

these three "dimensions" (specialization criteria) of classification/specialization *explicit* (Figure 2.13).

McGregor and Korson (1993) summarize these advanced inheritance concerns by four design guidelines, which are worth summarizing here:

1. Subclasses within a dimension should be defined so that any instance of the particular class clearly belongs to exactly one subclass.
2. The portion of the specification of a class that is specialized to form the subclasses within a dimension should be disjoint from the parts of the class's specification used to form other dimensions.
3. A subdimension should be a specialization of the dimension which it partitions.

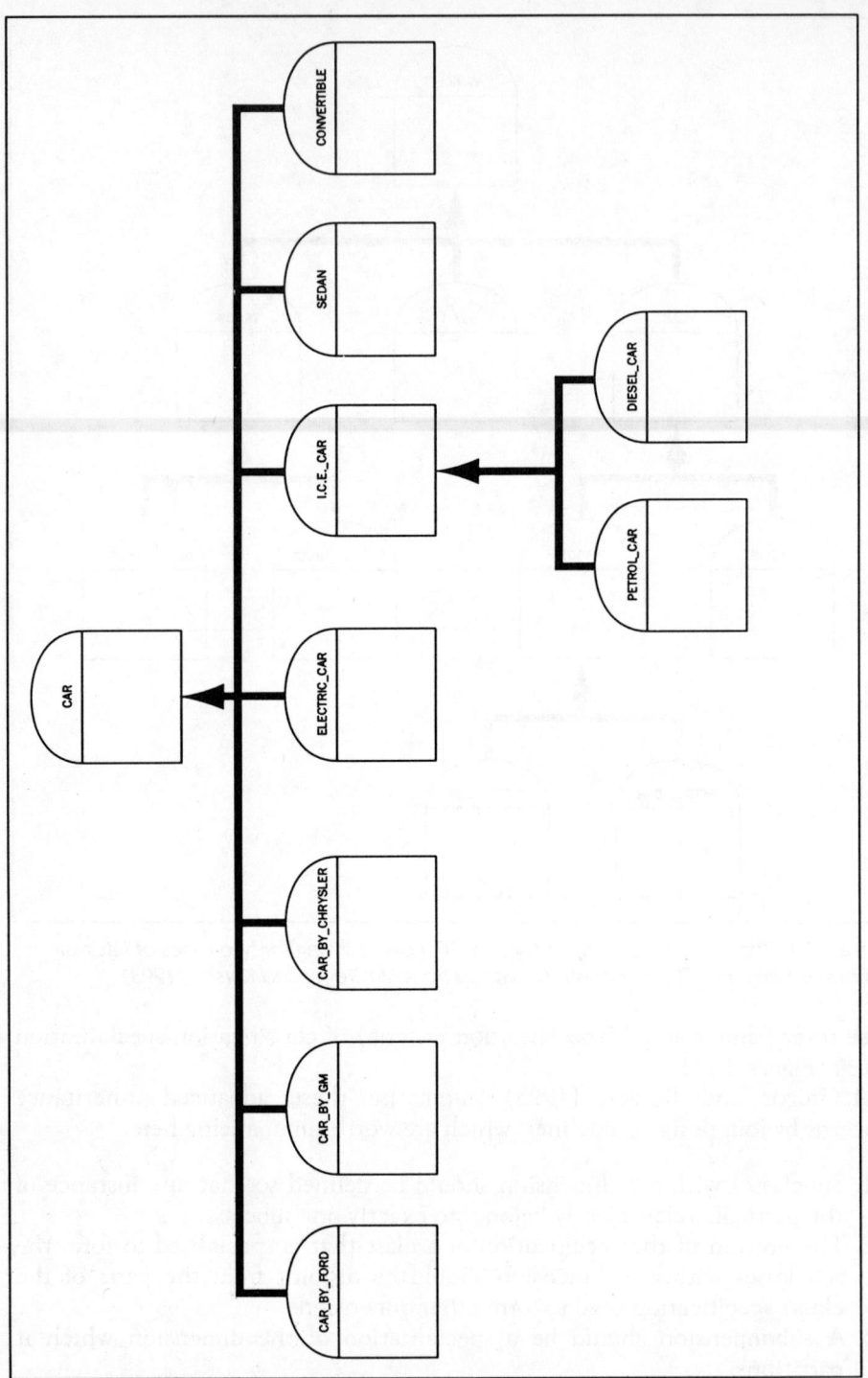

Figure 2.12 Standard notational description of an inheritance hierarchy of cars (Adapted from McGregor and Korson, 1993)

The Object-oriented Paradigm

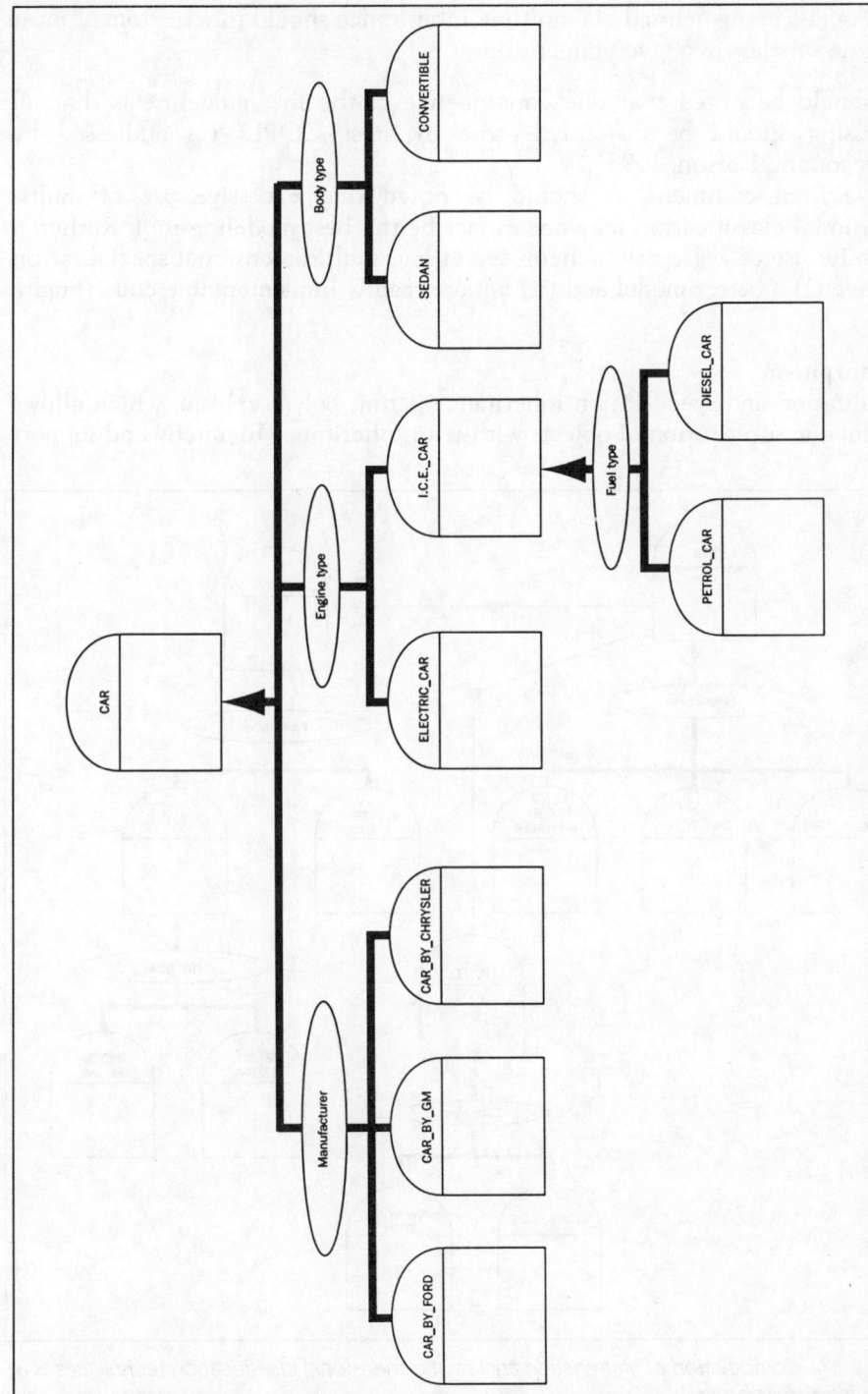

Figure 2.13 Explicit depiction of multidimensional classification/specialization criteria being used to clarify the hierarchical model (Adapted from McGregor and Korson, 1993)

4. A class being defined via multiple inheritance should inherit from at most one subclass in a given dimension.

It should be noted that one consequence of the first guideline is that all subclassing should be disjointed—true in most OOPLs (as addressed by McGregor and Korson, 1993).

As a final comment, it should be noted that excessive use of multi-dimensional classification may not in fact be the best modeling tool. Rather, a composite use of aggregation/client–server and multidimensional specialization may give (i) a better model and (ii) a more readily implementable code (Figure 2.14).

Polymorphism

Specialization and specification inheritance permit polymorphism, which allows the dynamic substitution of objects within an inheritance hierarchy and support

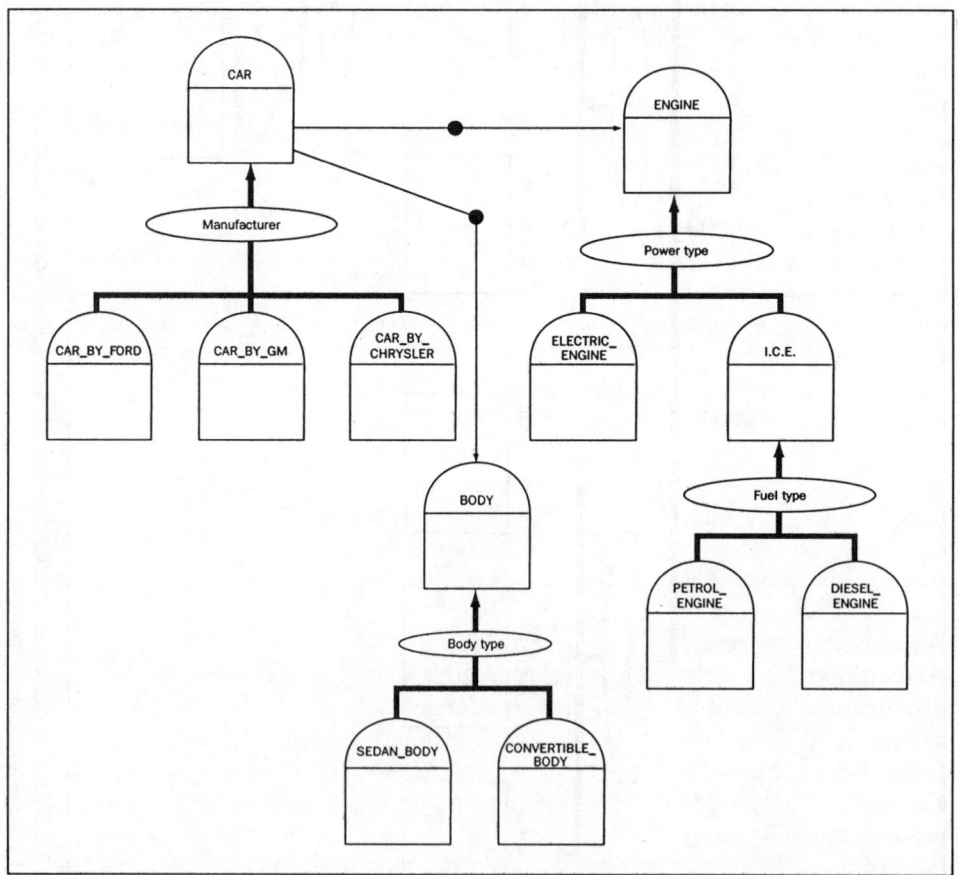

Figure 2.14 *Combination of aggregation and multidimensional classification techniques is a recommended approach*

reusability by the application developer and user. Polymorphism is the ability of abstractions to share services. It can be defined as "a concept in type theory in which a name may denote objects of many different classes related by some common base class. Thus, any object denoted by this name is able to respond to some common set of operations in different ways" (Booch and Vilot, 1990b). In other words, the assignment $a:=b$ is valid not only when a and b are of the same class but also if the class of b is a descendant of the class of a (but *not* vice versa). For example, using the library class COMMAND and a hierarchy of subcommand classes (Figure 2.15(a)), if a class wishes to use objects of this COMMAND hierarchy dynamically, say in a graphic user interface (GUI) development, then the code fragment of Figure 2.15(b) illustrates, firstly, the static definition of *answer* as of type COMMAND and then, following the call to the operation *getRequest*, the actual command executed could be any one of the subclasses shown in the figure. It is possible, for instance, to have an operation called *print*; if a message is sent to an object that happens to be a circle, or to an object that happens to be a square, then those objects will respond correctly (but differently) to the same message, *print*. In other words, the operation *print* can be overloaded, giving it different realizations in different classes.[10]

Furthermore, if more classes, such as LINE, SQUARE, POLYGON, etc., are required, in a language with no polymorphism, each new class requires an extra Case statement—here an additional three lines of code per new class. No additional lines of code are required in a language with polymorphism.

In most object-oriented languages, polymorphism is frequently (but not exclusively) linked with dynamic or late binding. The use of dynamic binding allows binding to be deferred until run-time. Binding is the specification of the exact nature of the service—its name, type, and storage location—and can occur at various stages. It may occur at language definition time; for example, INTEGER in FORTRAN is part of the language. It can occur at compile time (early or static binding) and consequently doesn't permit the use of polymorphic calls. Sometimes the use of dynamic binding is mandatory; in other languages it is optional (e.g., throughout the use of the keyword "virtual" in C++). Operator overloading is an associated concept that is a syntactic mechanism allowing use of the same name for two services in a class.

Association, aggregation, and inheritance
Association and inheritance relationships have often been confused (see discussion in Thomas (1989a) and Henderson-Sellers (1992a, p247)). In a large system, a combination of the two types of relationships into the same diagram (such as the Structure Layer of Coad and Yourdon (1990) or the diamonds of Korson and McGregor's (1990) Figure 7, which are used in an ER diagram to represent both generalization and association) could be unnecessary and confusing.

---

10. Note that overloading is more than simple name overloading.

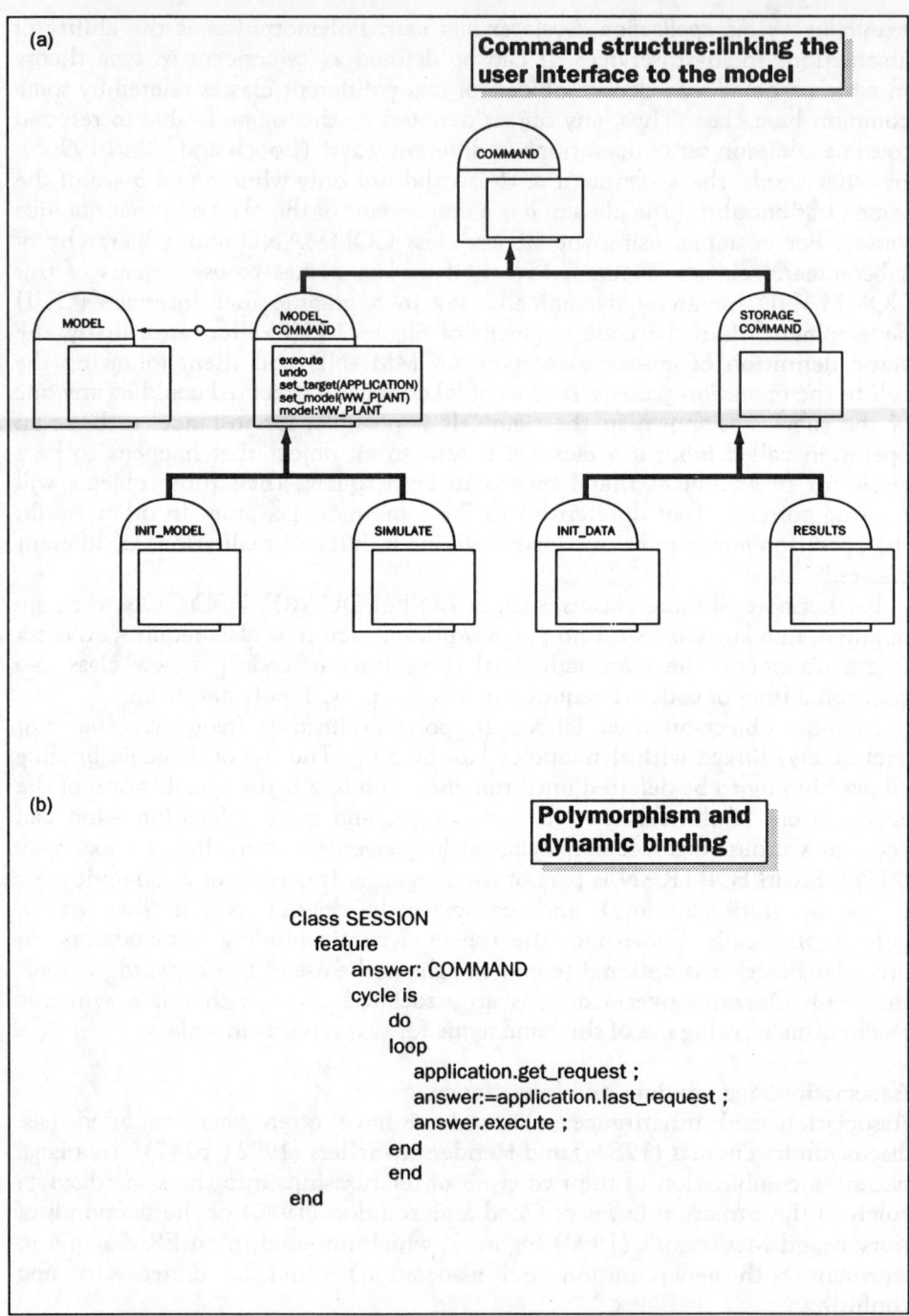

Figure 2.15 Hierarchy of commands: (a) shown graphically and (b) the polymorphic use of those commands

The Object-oriented Paradigm

A clear conceptual distinction can perhaps best be drawn by visualizing association essentially as a "horizontal" relationship and the generalization mechanism as orthogonal to this. In some cases, access may be made to a parent class, in others (especially when the upper-layer classes are abstract classes) to one of the descendants. In yet other cases, different members of the inheritance hierarchy may be required at different portions of the design. Nevertheless, the actual class required should be within the plane of the full system. "Vertical" description of the hierarchy may well be described separately rather than as a third dimension (cf. Figure 2.16, which uses basic MOSES notation); again, choice will be influenced strongly by the need for clarity. In this visualization of the mutual orthogonality (a summary diagram rather than one likely to occur in a real software development process and used here merely to reinforce the necessary conceptual views), aggregation is shown on the left as an "expansion" to a lower-layer design diagram; association connections are essentially horizontal and generalization vertical but rotated through 90 degrees. In this case, two members of the same hierarchy are accessed at the topmost layer.

2.3.7 Roles

We discussed a number of methodological guidelines in the previous sections, including the distinction between operations and properties. In this section, we discuss guidelines for describing *roles* with the object model.

Roles may be modeled in a number of ways. Firstly, an O/C may have all the services for all the roles that its instances play. Then when it is playing a specific role, only those services relevant to the role are visible or operational. This may be implemented by making a role part of the state of the O/C and a status flag to indicate whether that role is currently operative. The problem with this approach is that the O/C can become very large very quickly and tends to hide the different aspects of the O/C in one concept. An alternative approach is to model a role as a subclass. Thus only those extra services required for the role are added to the subclass, the other services being inherited. This is the solution that many OO methodologies propose. The problem with this approach is that in many OOPLs an object may be of only one class during its life. The programming language solution might be the creation of an object of the new class and the corresponding copying from and deletion of the old class whenever an object is reclassified. As a role is of a transitory nature and is frequently found in external-world models, there is a need in future languages to support some sort of dynamic classification.

Another approach is delegating the services to a separate O/C (Rumbaugh *et al.*, 1991). An O/C is then a composition of O/Cs that describes its different roles. This approach may be used in prototype or delegation-based systems but is not yet widely discussed in the mainstream object-oriented literature. It also suffers from the need to break an O/C into many separate O/Cs, thus destroying the single conceptual integrity of an O/C that the class concept brings.

Kilian (1991) suggests the notion of a role type. A role type models the set of services needed for a role but is not part of the normal class hierarchy. Instead,

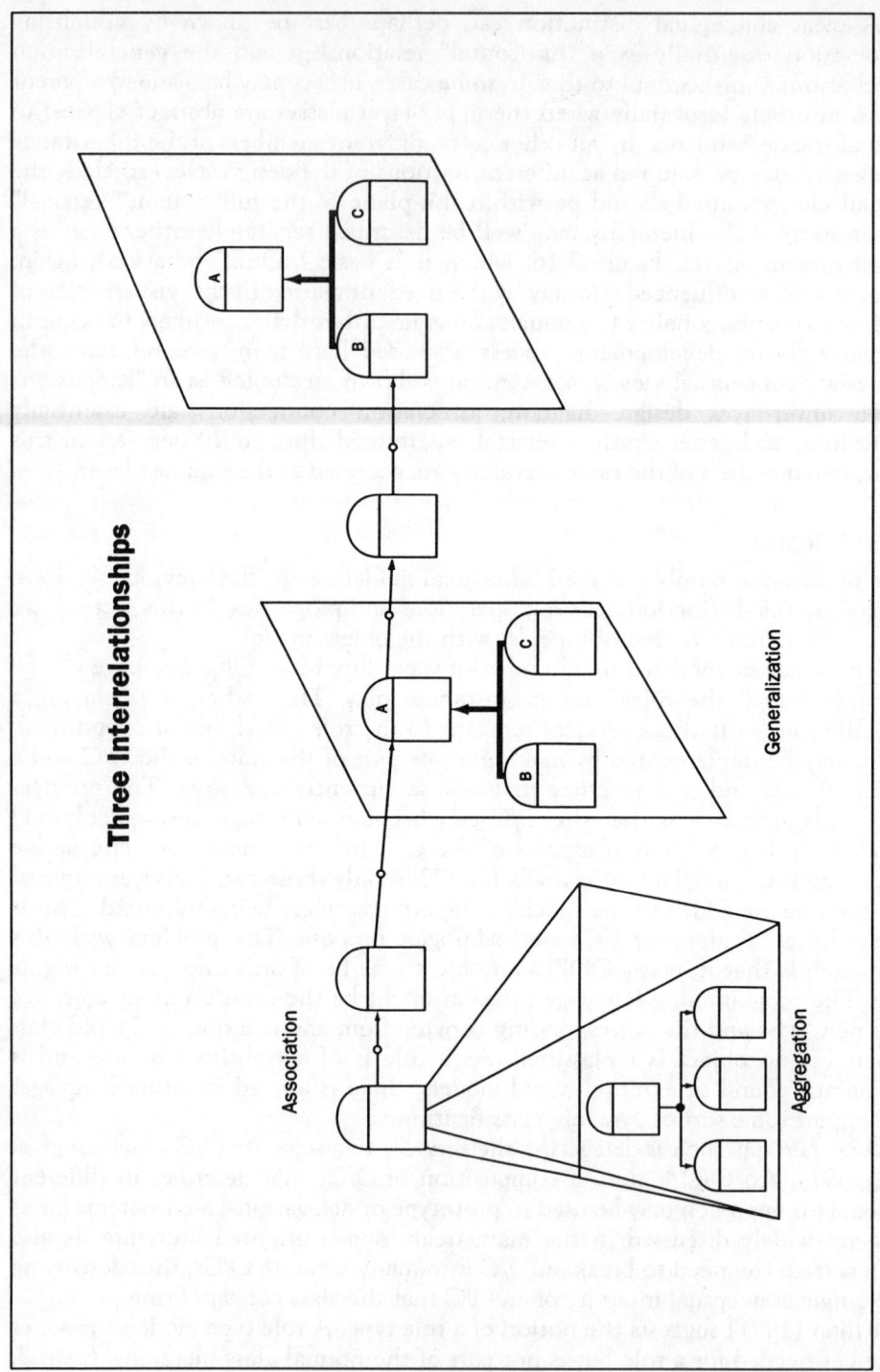

Figure 2.16 *The three relationships of association, aggregation, and inheritance, showing their mutual orthogonality*

it specifies what services an O/C must support in order to be considered in this role. The services are specified in the role type but implemented in the O/C.

In general, roles are shorter lived and more transient than objects, yet longer lived than individual states (Ratjens, 1994). A role may imply a large number of extra services or none at all. A role that implies no extra services can be modeled simply as a property of the basic O/C. For example, the role of employee may not imply any further services and thus can be easily modeled as a role name only on the association. However, the role "student" may imply a number of services such as "subjects taken," "enrolment type," etc. These extra services imply that the situation can be modeled better using a subclass of PERSON named STUDENT. The relationship *Studies-At* is then an association between classes STUDENT and UNIVERSITY. On the other hand, the extra services could have been modeled as services of the class PERSON and the responsibilities would have been only relevant to a state of *Studying* in class PERSON. However, this would not take advantage of the benefits of the inheritance hierarchy and classification discussed earlier. Therefore the former approach, although no more correct than the latter, is a better model in terms of reducing complexity and its use of abstraction. That no current popular OOPLs support the transition of an object between classes should not constrain our use of roles as a modeling tool (D'Souza, 1992).

A further complication (Odell, 1992a) is that of multiple classification where two or more roles are played concurrently. Although foreign to most data processing environments, it is common in models of business and personal situations. For example, a PERSON may be both a WIFE and a SCIENTIST. While not part of the inheritance structure of current OOPLs, multiple classification can be simulated via multiple inheritance, although the combinations needed can be high (Odell, 1992a). Metaphorically, Odell recommends class slicing as a conceptual representation of multiple classification, the slice being represented by surrogate classes (Figure 2.17). Here the unsliced object Alice is represented as an instance of CONCEPTUAL_OBJECT class. Pointers link this with the surrogate objects, which are instances of the IMPLEMENTATION_OBJECT class. The instances in PET_OWNER and EMPLOYEE classes are then slices of the Alice object. Each object slice is thus also an Alice object. Finally, slices comply with conventional OOPL requirements that each instance be a member of only one class: IMPLEMENTATION_OBJECT.

2.3.8 The object-oriented triangle

A literature survey (Figure 2.18) suggests that on the surface there is no precise agreement about what features are vital for "object-orientation." However, when one groups the terms frequently used, some consensus begins to emerge. In the first group are the terms "information hiding," "encapsulation," and "objects." These all describe the modularization process. They relate to the informal notion of expressing everything about an identifiable "thing" in one place and one place only. This translates to having a piece of code relate to that

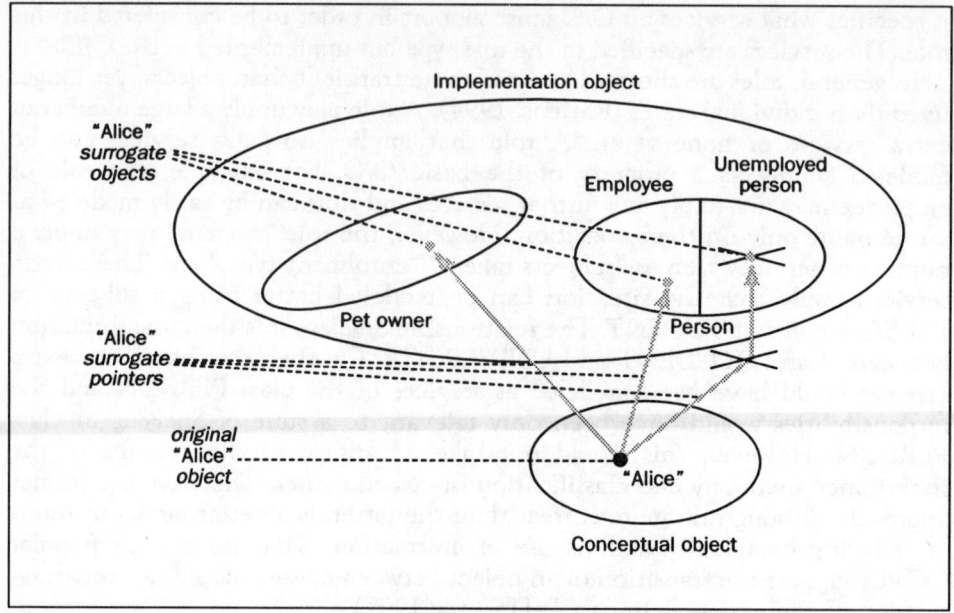

Figure 2.17 *Object slicing supports dynamic and multiple classification (Odell, 1992a)*

identifiable "thing." Figure 2.18 shows that all sources identify one of these three "modularization" terms as a key concept for OT.

In the second group (Figure 2.18) are "classification," "classes," and "abstraction," which all relate to the rationalization of the world by *grouping into collections* of like "things"—although "class" also has some modularization aspects, of course. Almost all authors include this "classification" notion as of importance for OT.

The third major grouping, agreed by all, is the inheritance/polymorphism/dynamic binding trio. While both Winblad *et al.* (1990) and Blair *et al.* (1990) identify inheritance as a basic *mechanism*, they identify polymorphism as the basic *concept*. Blair *et al.* (1990) suggest that polymorphism is nearer the conceptual level, and this is the approach adopted here. Dynamic binding is a technical mechanism by which polymorphism becomes possible in today's OOPLs.

It thus seems reasonable to summarize this broad consensus diagrammatically using the "Object-Oriented Triangle" (Henderson-Sellers, 1992a) (Figure 2.19).

In final summary, a class is the template for a set of objects. A class has services that may be divided into properties and operations. Each service is described by a contract. Classes may be interrelated by the relationships of inheritance, which is divided into specification inheritance, specialization inheritance, and implementation inheritance, or by the relationships of aggregation and association. Communication between objects is via message passing, which is viewed as a single atomic event.

The Object-oriented Paradigm

Main Characteristics of Object-Orientation

	INFORMATION HIDING	ENCAPSULATION	OBJECTS	CLASSIFICATION	CLASSES	ABSTRACTION	INHERITANCE	POLYMORPHISM	DYNAMIC BINDING
Pascoe, 1986	Y					Y	Y		Y
Meyer, 1988a			Y		Y	Y	Y	Y	Y
Stroustrup, 1988	Y	Y				Y	Y		
Wegner, 1989			Y		Y	Y			
Collins, 1990		Y			Y	Y			
Winblad et al., 1990		Y				Y		Y	
Duff & Howard, 1990		Y					Y	Y	
Korson & McGregor, 1990			Y		Y		Y	Y	Y
Potter, 1990			Y		Y		Y		
Borland, 1990		Y					Y	Y	
Loy, 1990		Y		Y			Y		
Blair et al., 1990		Y				Y		Y	
Booch, 1991		Y + modularity					Y	Hierarchy	
Sutcliffe, 1991		Y				Y	Y		
Rumbaugh et al., 1991			Y	Y			Y	Y	
Graham, 1991						Y	Y		
Henderson-Sellers, 1992a		Y				Y		Y	
Hunt, 1992		Y					Y	Y	Y
Martin & Odell, 1992		Y	Y		Y		Y		
Wang, 1992		Y					Y	Y	

Figure 2.18 *The main characteristics of object-orientation can be gleaned from a study of the literature*

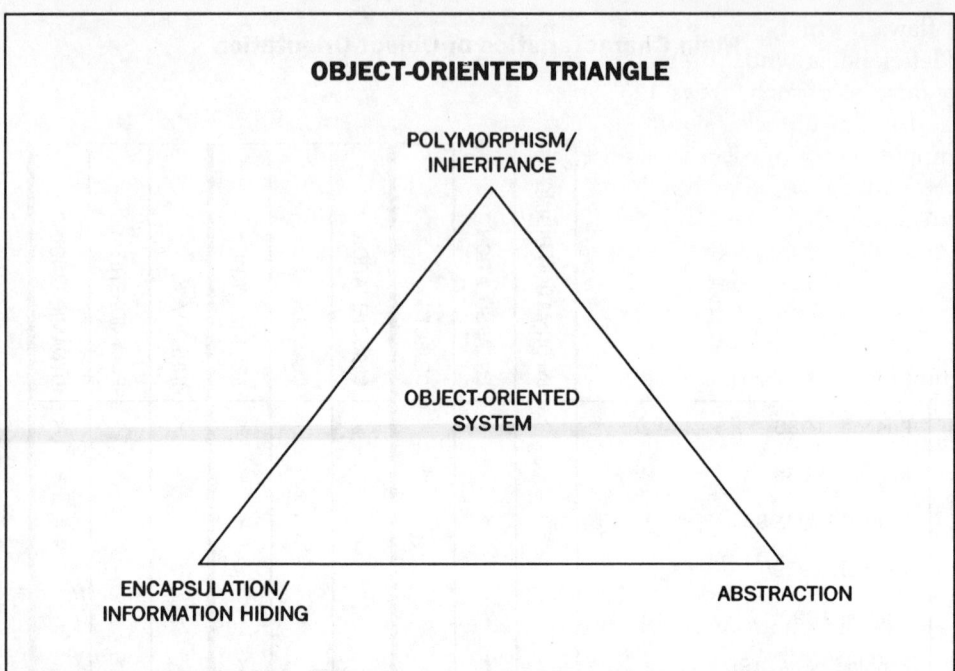

Figure 2.19 *The object-oriented triangle (Adapted from Henderson-Sellers, 1992a)*

2.4 Implementation issues

Implementation or construction is the phase of the systems development lifecycle when the proposed solution, derived from a systems design, is implemented in a programming language; that is, the constructs of the Specification Phase (analysis and design) are translated into the constructs of the programming language chosen for the implementation. The boundary between Specification and Implementation in object-oriented systems is a blurred one, although perhaps more identifiable than any OOA/D boundary in that the nature of design documentation is very different from that of implementation documentation (namely, code). In addition, especially in MOSES, the former is OOPL-independent; the latter fully encompasses the constructs of the chosen OOPL. However, it may be that in some projects or organizations the development is actually undertaken using the final implementation language and that it is consequently somewhat harder to distinguish between the two phases of Specification and Implementation. This may be especially true when the language provides a very close mapping to the model used in development. For example, the language Eiffel, or at least subsets of it, could be used as a Specification Phase language for OO systems (Nerson, 1991). This compatibility between programming language and analysis/design mindset is also stressed by Berard (1992b, p283), who notes that language "flaws", which are of no importance in small systems, may become glaring deficiencies while programming in the large (although he gives no specific examples of such "flaws").

In addition, decisions on algorithms and data structures, which are strictly implementation decisions regarding the way in which a particular service is to be coded, may first require documenting using structured techniques. So, for instance, the details of a particularly complicated algorithmic procedure in one class may require thought and documentation akin to design using structure charts. Consequently, an appropriate appellation for this activity might alternatively be "implementation design" (Firesmith, 1993).

The implementation stage is generally language-specific and therefore will employ terminology specific to the particular language. However, there are obviously a number of common concepts between languages and hence we can apply a common terminology when discussing implementation.

2.4.1 OOPLs—definitions

Wegner's (1989) classification of OOPLs is well accepted (Table 2.1). A language, such as Ada, is said to be *object-based* when it supports objects but not classes or inheritance. In other words, encapsulations representing individual objects are possible (akin to multiple-entry subroutines). *Class-based* languages, such as CLU, support not only objects but also classes, thus giving a degree of object management. An *object-oriented* language then adds inheritance. This, then, gives us a basic working definition of an OOPL. Wegner then goes further and adds other refinements. Object-oriented languages that support data abstraction and strong typing are a narrower set of OOPLs, which incidentally exclude two of the most well regarded (Smalltalk and CLOS). A further subset of those strongly typed languages are those with types determinable at compile-time. An example here would be Eiffel. Then we could also consider concurrency and persistence—not characteristics generally found in OOPLs,

Table 2.1 *Definition of an OOPL following Wegner (1989)*

1. Object-based: objects are supported, e.g., Ada
2. Class-based: objects belong to classes, e.g., CLU
3. Object-oriented: classes support inheritance, e.g., C++, Eiffel, Smalltalk

Further refinements

4a. OO data-abstraction: classes support information hiding, e.g., Smalltalk
4b. Strongly typed OO: types determinable at compilation, e.g., Simula 67
4c. OO + data-abstraction + strong typing, e.g., Eiffel
5a. + Concurrency
5b. + Persistence

but nevertheless topics of much current research and development (Wyatt et al., 1992). Persistence (the storage of an object instance beyond the lifetime of the program), especially for the database community, is also likely to be important in the next few years.

As a contrast to Wegner's language classification, consider Meyer's (1988a) "seven steps to OO happiness" (Table 2.2). These steps describe seven levels attained along the way to becoming fully object-oriented, although, unlike Wegner, Meyer does not give names to these stages. At level 1 there is an "object-based modular structure." At this stage, many 3GLs, such as FORTRAN77 using tightly encapsulated subroutines, pass this test. As we encounter successive levels in Table 2.2, more of these languages fall by the wayside. At level 2, data abstraction is introduced. Again many 3GLs are still in this category. At level 3, automatic memory management is introduced. This entails automatic allocation and deallocation of memory space when objects are no longer referenced, rather than leaving the onus on the programmer of avoiding dangling pointers. Although there is some overhead (1–3%) with automatic garbage collection, it is easier to use than *malloc* in C or *NEW* in C++ and can prevent the program running out of memory at a crucial time. In some language environments (such as ISE's Eiffel, ISE, 1988) there is an On/Off switch in the configuration file; in others, such as Smalltalk, the garbage collector is always available. When operational, the garbage collector runs in the background, reclaiming memory incrementally when the CPU has less work.

The idea of ADTs (which can be seen in procedural languages such as C and FORTRAN) leads to classes and hence to Meyer's level 4. Classes are sets of objects from which can be generated many instantiations by using the class as a "template." Few procedural languages meet this level. For example, while the

Table 2.2 *Definition of an OOPL following Meyer (1988a)*

Level 1 (*Object-based modular structure*): Systems are modularized on the basis of their data structures.
Level 2 (*Data abstraction*): Objects should be described as implementations of abstract data types.
Level 3 (*Automatic memory management*): Unused objects should be deallocated by the underlying language system, without a programmer intervention.
Level 4 (*Classes*): Every nonsimple type is a module and every high-level module is a type.
Level 5 (*Inheritance*): A class may be defined as an extension or restriction of another.
Level 6 (*Polymorphism and dynamic binding*): Program entities should be permitted to refer to objects of more than one class, and operations should be permitted to have different realizations in different classes.
Level 7 (*Multiple and repeated inheritance*): It should be possible to declare a class as heir to more than one class and more than once to the same class.

attribute values of a number of individual instantiated objects can be mimicked in FORTRAN77 by using an array for each attribute with the array dimension equal to the number of extant objects (Wampler, 1990), such arrays are not readily extensible when a new instance needs to be created; neither is there any identifiable entity representing the class template itself.

Meyer also states that every nonsimple type (i.e., excluding simple types such as CHARACTER, REAL, and INTEGER) is a module and every module is a type. An example might be ACCOUNT or CUSTOMER. Each of those nonsimple types is a module. This means that the collection notion of classes and the semantic view of classes as abstract data types are fused together. Level 4 says that modules that are not types are not permitted—this is in contrast to procedural languages such as FORTRAN77 and COBOL85. Although these languages have modules with (potentially) high information hiding, these modules may be conceptually and semantically unrelated and therefore have no relevance whatever to the concept of type. They are just conglomerates of code fragments that were aggregated for some, often arcane, reason. Once we have reached level 4, we have a class-centered language that is the very basis of object-oriented programming.

Inheritance (level 5) is the key new idea that most consider must be present in an OOPL, while polymorphism and dynamic binding belong to level 6. Polymorphism is essentially the ability to refer to an object at run-time that may be from more than one class, and for operations to have realizations from different classes.

Multiple and repeated inheritance is level 7. The extent to which these ideas should be utilized in practice is arguable, but it is undeniable that the trend in languages is toward inclusion of multiple inheritance (MI). It is probably good to have as a feature of any language, but a feature that should not be overused. Meyer's typical example is that of a windowing environment where a window has "graphical" features and thus inherits from some graphical or geometric type of hierarchy (for instance, including class RECTANGLE), yet also has the capability of nesting windows on the screen and therefore must also belong to a tree/node-type hierarchy (for example, inheriting from a TREE superclass). However, others argue that such implementation inheritance, especially in this MI lattice, is dangerous and prevents reusability by destroying the semantic integrity.

Although Meyer considers that these features are in increasing order of sophistication, there are obvious incompatibilities with Wegner's classification, which would give a different classification under the two schemes. Perhaps the most notable of these is the position of automatic memory management available in Smalltalk and Eiffel but not in C++—three languages commonly regarded as OOPLs. Whether Meyer's levels 5–7 simply enhance a level-4 OOPL, or whether only languages at level 7 can justly be called OOPLs, is a matter of debate. For our purposes (Table 2.3), a combination of Meyer (1988a) and Wegner (1989) does, we feel, give the proper perspective of increasingly sophisticated OOPLs.

2.4.2 Comparison of OOPLs

The *definition* of a run-time object is an instantiation of a class (in the sense of a coded module), created as and when required (Figure 2.20). On the other hand, in programming terminology the class is an implementation of an abstract data type (ADT). The ADT describes the external view. It is a generic template (for the instantiation of objects) with which to describe shared characteristics. Object-oriented systems comprise coded classes. With this highly specific terminology, classes exist at *compile-time*. A class could represent all bank accounts, whereas what exist at *run-time* are individual bank accounts. Since the ADT is the *specification* and the class the *implementation* of the ADT, it is in fact possible to construct more than one version of a class that implements the same ADT (in the same way as at a lower level one of several algorithms would be used to implement say a "sort" functionality).

Considered from a programming language point of view, an ADT extends the basic language types, such as INTEGER, CHARACTER, REAL, etc., by allowing the user to define his or her own (user-defined) types. User-defined types can be anything, e.g., TABLE, CHAIR, or BANK_ACCOUNT. This focus on classes therefore permits the extension, by the user, of the programming language, allowing use of the same concept during the earlier Specification Phase as well as maintaining a close relationship with the user's original problem.

The set of messages to which the class responds is called the protocol. It essentially represents those services defined in the class interface, together with some notion of contract or class responsibility (see also earlier discussion in Section 2.3.3).

Sending a message to an account object from a customer object requesting withdrawal of an amount would be written in many languages as *my_account.withdraw(5000)*, etc. This format is common to Eiffel and C++, for example, which use the same sort of dot notation. The messaging notation in Smalltalk and Objective-C is *my_account withdraw(5000)*, whereas in CLOS the object to which the message is directed becomes the argument to the method:

Table 2.3 *Composite of Wegner and Meyer definitions of an OOPL*

Object-based Systems modularized on the basis of their data structures. Objects are supported. Example PL: Ada.

Class-based Classes, as well as objects, are supported. Example PL: CLU.

Object-oriented Classes and objects can be related through inheritance structures. Information hiding is enforced. Dynamic substitutability (polymorphism) should be readily available and easily used. Example PL: C++ (but note default static binding), Smalltalk.

Preferable characteristics: multiple inheritance, genericity, automatic garbage collection. Example PL: Eiffel.

Future characteristics: support for concurrency and persistence.

The Object-oriented Paradigm

What is an Object?

Object = Data + Functionality + Encapsulation

LIFECYCLE STAGE	NOMENCLATURE	EXAMPLE
Analysis and design	Objects or classes or entities or object classes (O/Cs)	Bank accounts
Design → Code/PL	Classes or objects A class is an implementation of an Abstract Data Type (ADT)	Code describing *all* personal bank accounts ADT describes "Account" type: interface and features, but not implementation
Run-time	Object A run-time object is an instantiation of a class	One specific bank account, belonging to one specific person

Figure 2.20 *Object and class terminology as a function of lifecycle phase (Henderson-Sellers, 1992a)*

withdraw (my_account,5000). Arguments are in parentheses when required. In C++ it is possible to have default arguments, especially useful for constructors.[11] In Eiffel the principle of uniform reference holds for both properties and operations and allows the implementor to change from an implementation as an operation to an implementation as a property. The message invokes the services (operations + properties), but only those services declared in the server class's interface. Invocation may of course result in the use of other services, hidden within the class (such as *minimum_balance*). The message name is also sometimes referred to as the "selector."

Furthermore, messages can be nested. For example, we might wish to ask a book to print its authorship details where books are stored in a list contained in a library (Figure 2.21). The classes here are AUTHOR, BOOK, SHELF, and

---

11. There are strict rules concerning whether a default argument can be placed in a C++ member function signature.

LIBRARY, and a generic container class to store the variables of type SHELF. In other words, shelf would be a "variable" in class LIBRARY, which is of type LINKED_LIST that contains lists of books of type BOOK, each of which has an attribute AUTHOR. Thus a message (using Eiffel syntax) would be:

library.shelf.item.author.display

although, as noted previously, this is not regarded as good style (Law of Demeter).

Taking now an *internal* perspective to the class, the component parts are features—some typical terminology is shown in Figure 2.22, although this terminology is language-dependent to a degree. Features may be attributes (the code version of a property describing a "logical attribute") or methods (also known as routines or member functions). (Method is essentially the Smalltalk word, routine Eiffel, and member function C++.) Methods include both functions, which return an object, and procedures, which don't return anything but just do something. In other words, functions provide a query facility on the state of the object, whereas procedures implement commands, thus changing the state of the object. In Smalltalk, a method is always a function; you just may choose to ignore its returned object.

Methods are implemented essentially using procedural code and can be designed (if necessary) using functional decomposition techniques. However, the style of programming, even within a class, should be in sympathy with the overall aim of object-orientation. This does lead to the development of a new programming style, even in designing and coding internal procedural elements. The use of inheritance, at the code level, requires acquisition of new skills, as does the use of complex types and of instance variables, and of message sending.

Figure 2.23 shows Eiffel code (Version 2.3) for a class ZOO_ANIMAL. It has an export clause delimiting the interface, exporting the methods *draw*, *locate*, *inform*. Each of these is then defined in the body of the code, although since this is in fact an abstract class, some definitions will be deferred to subclasses. Following the export clause is the inherit clause (seen in the subclass BEAR). Class BEAR inherits from one other class: ZOO_ANIMAL. Features are listed next and basically occupy the remainder of the class code. The first four features are physical attributes in this particular class: variables that have a value stored here (i.e., not a reference/pointer to another class/object). The remaining features are all routines. The Eiffel syntax for routines is **is do end**. Routines defined in subclasses are indicated by the keyword **deferred**. There are a few other keywords in the language, but they are beyond the scope of our present discussion (for further details see, e.g., Meyer, 1988a, 1992a).

Figure 2.24 shows a brief example of the code for the same class written in C++ (adapted from Lippman, 1989, pp308–309). This is an early prototype for the class ZooAnimal and its derived class Bear. The C++ class is split into public, protected, and (here not shown explicitly) private—the default. Member functions are contained in the class body and may be defined in-line, after the main class definition in a separate section or even in a separate file. In this example,

The Object-oriented Paradigm

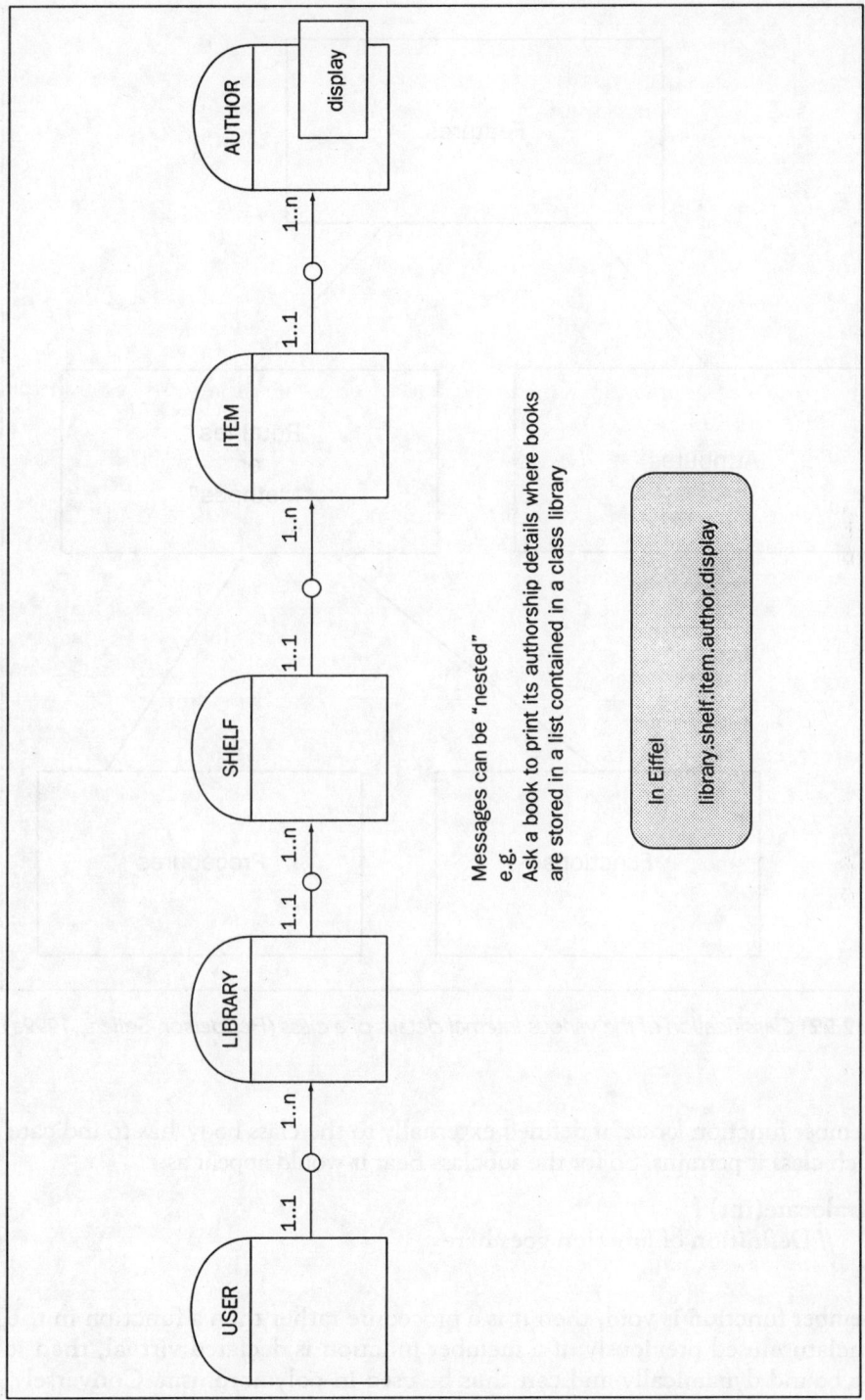

Figure 2.21 Nesting of messages is reflected in a chain of links between a number of O/Cs. The use of such a message chain (not generally recommended) is indicated using Eiffel syntax.

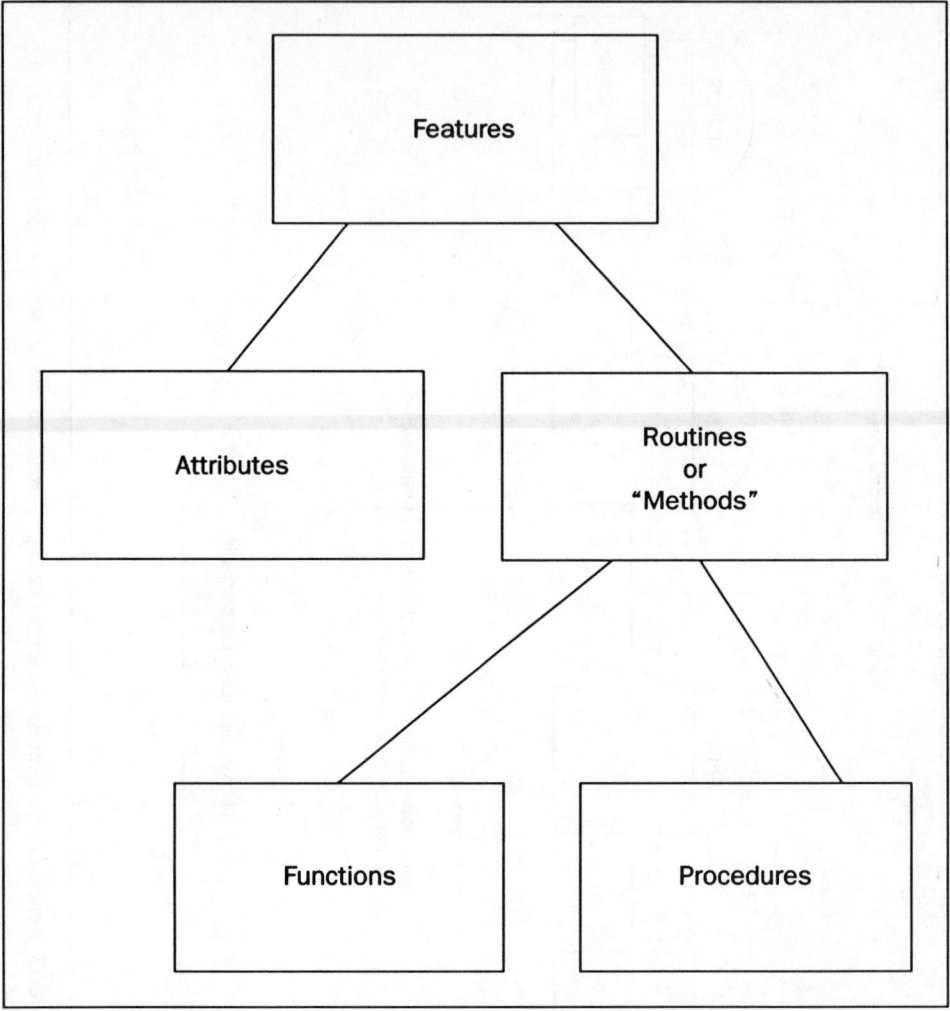

Figure 2.22 *Classification of the various internal details of a class (Henderson-Sellers, 1992a)*

the member function *locate*, if defined externally to the class body, has to indicate to which class it pertains. So for the subclass Bear it would appear as:

```
Bear::locate(int) {
     // Definition of function goes here
}
```

If a member function is void, then it is a procedure rather than a function in the nomenclature used previously; if a member function is declared virtual, then it will be bound dynamically and can thus be used in polymorphism. Conversely,

The Object-oriented Paradigm

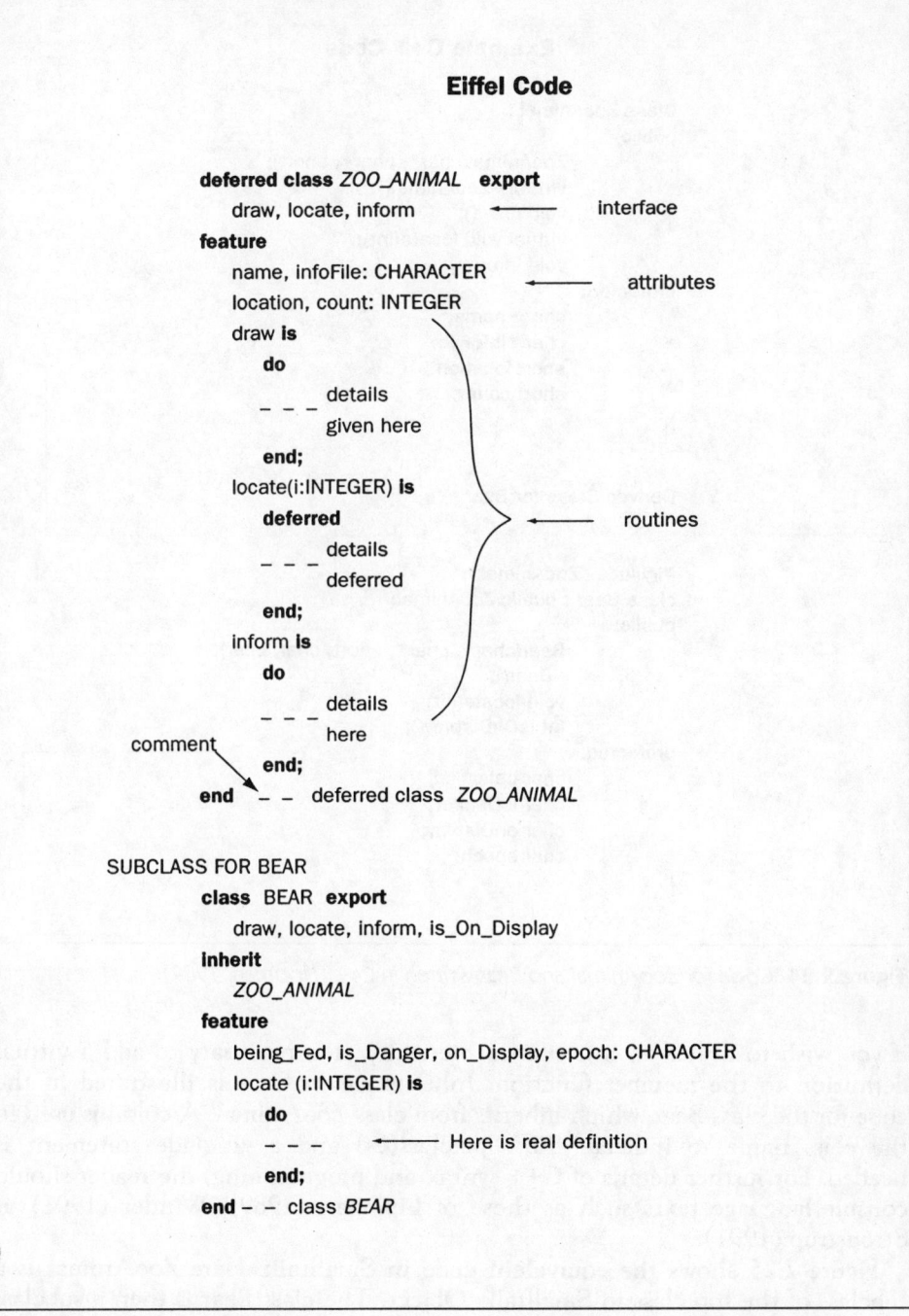

Figure 2.23 *Eiffel code representing a class for ZOO_ANIMAL and a subclass BEAR (Henderson-Sellers, 1992a)*

Example C++ Code

```
Class ZooAnimal {
public:
          ZooAnimal(char*, char*, short);
          virtual ~ZooAnimal();
          void draw();
          virtual void locate(int);
          void inform();
protected:
          char *name;
          char *infoFile;
          short location;
          short count;
};


Derived Class for Bear


#include "ZooAnimal.h"
class Bear : public ZooAnimal{
public:
          Bear(char*, char*, short, char, char);
          ~Bear();
          void locate(int);
          int isOnDisplay();
protected:
          char beingFed;
          char isDanger;
          char onDisplay;
          char epoch;
};
```

Figure 2.24 *Code for ZooAnimal and Bear written in C++ (Lippman, 1989)*

if you wish to utilize an inheritance hierarchy, it is necessary to add a virtual definition to the member function. Inheritance in C++ is illustrated in the code for the class Bear, which inherits from class ZooAnimal. A colon is used in the class name to indicate the superclass(es) and a #include statement is needed. For further details of C++ syntax and programming, the reader should consult language texts such as those of Lippman (1989), Winder (1991) or Stroustrup (1991).

Figure 2.25 shows the equivalent code in Smalltalk. Here ZooAnimal is a subclass of the top class in Smalltalk: Object. The class Bear is then a subclass of ZooAnimal. Texts on Smalltalk include those of Goldberg and Robson (1983) and Pinson and Wiener (1988).

The Object-oriented Paradigm

At the language level, attributes (Figure 2.22) are essentially the variables of the class that represent the characteristics of the class (i.e., its state) rather than its behavior. Often the data values are of a basic type, such as INTEGER, CHARACTER, STRING, etc., which in most OOPLs are themselves regarded as classes. This conforms with the underlying notion of a "pure" OOPL such as Smalltalk, in which *everything* is an object. Attributes are also referred to as slots (e.g., Bobrow, 1989; Harmon, 1990), especially in languages, such as CLOS, with an artificial intelligence (AI) basis, and the idea of an instance variable is sometimes referred to as an entity (Meyer, 1988a).

Within the OOPL arena, concerns such as persistence and concurrency are

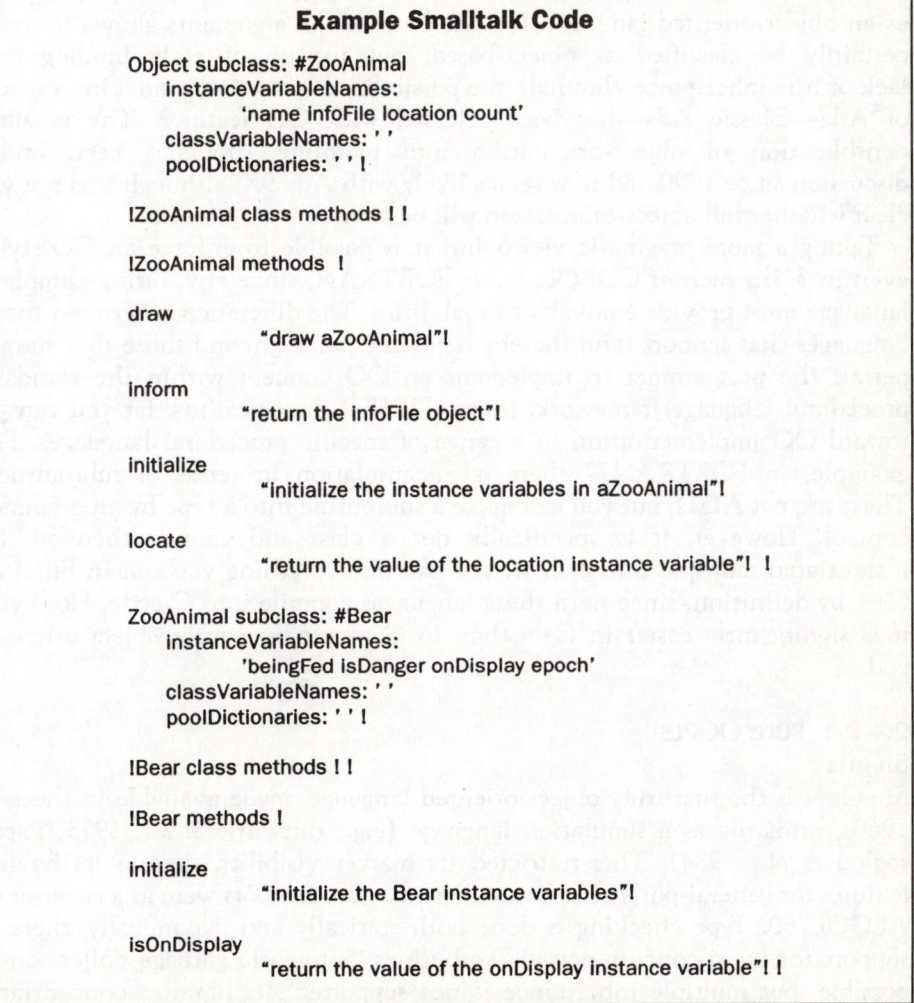

Example Smalltalk Code

```
Object subclass: #ZooAnimal
    instanceVariableNames:
        'name infoFile location count'
    classVariableNames: ' '
    poolDictionaries: ' ' !

!ZooAnimal class methods ! !

!ZooAnimal methods !

draw
    "draw aZooAnimal"!

inform
    "return the infoFile object"!

initialize
    "initialize the instance variables in aZooAnimal"!

locate
    "return the value of the location instance variable"! !

ZooAnimal subclass: #Bear
    instanceVariableNames:
        'beingFed isDanger onDisplay epoch'
    classVariableNames: ' '
    poolDictionaries: ' ' !

!Bear class methods ! !

!Bear methods !

initialize
    "initialize the Bear instance variables"!

isOnDisplay
    "return the value of the onDisplay instance variable"! !
```

Figure 2.25 *Code for ZooAnimal and Bear written in Smalltalk*

not yet addressed in commercial releases of language compilers. While Eiffel has some ability to store objects *as* objects, true persistence (in the database sense) is yet to be incorporated. These and other features are summarized in Table 2.4 for some of nine OOPLs in the full range from object-based to pure OOPL. Some of these are described in more detail in Sections 2.4.2.1 and 2.4.2.2. Table 2.5 compares the terminology for a subset of these OOPLs.

There are many other object-oriented languages. In early 1989, a survey by Saunders (1989) revealed the existence of 69 general-purpose OO languages. These include languages associated with database management systems still under development, AI-based languages, and LISP-based languages. In this last category are LOOPS and CLOS. Several hypermedia products and the Apple Mac interface have object-oriented roots. Finally, Ada is often put forward as an object-oriented language. On the basis of the arguments above, it could certainly be classified as object-based, but its use of early binding and lack of true inheritance eliminate the possibility of polymorphism. One version of Ada—Classic Ada—has been released with OO features. The possible consolidation of object-orientation into mainline Ada has been under discussion since 1990 and now seems likely with Ada 9X, although it is not yet clear whether full object-orientation will be offered.

Taking a more pragmatic viewpoint, it is possible to enforce an OO style, even in 3GLs such as COBOL, C, or FORTRAN, since any Turing-complete language must provide equivalent capabilities. The difference is between those languages that support (and thereby help) the paradigm and those that simply permit the programmer to implement an OO concept within the standard procedural language framework. Meyer (1988a) discusses how far you can go toward OO implementation in a range of specific procedural languages. For example, in FORTRAN77 there is encapsulation in terms of subroutines. These are *not* ADTs, but you can make a subroutine into a type by programmer control. However, it is specifically not a class and cannot therefore be instantiated multiple times. In C, you can do everything you can in Eiffel or C++ by definition, since both these languages compile into C code. However, it is significantly easier in C++ than in C to produce truly object-oriented code.

2.4.2.1 Pure OOPLs
Simula
Simula was the first truly object-oriented language, made available in the late 1960s, primarily as a simulation language (e.g., Birtwistle *et al.*, 1973; Papazoglou *et al.*, 1984). This restricted its market visibility, despite its having features for general-purpose software construction. Its roots were as a superset of ALGOL–60. Type checking is done both statically and dynamically, there is support for quasi-concurrency via coroutines, automatic garbage collection is possible, but multiple inheritance is not supported. Its libraries concentrate, naturally, on simulation primitives.

The Object-oriented Paradigm

Table 2.4 Comparison of OO language features

Feature	Smalltalk	C++	Eiffel	Turbo Pascal	CLOS	Simula	Objective-C	Ada	Object Pascal
Persistence	Some (whole system)	No	Yes	No	No	No	No	As any 3GL	No
Multiple inheritance	No	Ver 2.0	Yes	No	Yes	No	Yes	No SI only	Class-based SI only
Typing	Dynamic	Static	Static	Static	Weak	Either	Late or early	Early	Late
Binding	Dynamic	Default static Optional dynamic	Dynamic	Default static Optional dynamic	Dynamic	Either	Late or early	Early	Late
Autogarbage collection	Yes	No	Yes	No	Yes	Yes	Yes	No	Yes
Exception handling	No	Promised	Yes	No	No	No	Yes	Yes	No
Assertions	No	Limited	Yes	No	No	No	No	No	No
Libraries	Yes	Yes	Yes	Yes	Yes	Simulation only	Few	Few	Few
Polymorphism	Yes	Yes	Yes	Yes	Yes	Yes	Yes	Yes	Yes
Information hiding	Yes	Yes	Yes	Yes	Yes	Yes	Yes	Yes	Yes
Concurrency	Not at present	Not at present Ver 3.0	Not at present	No	No?	Yes	Poor	Yes	No
Genericity	No	Yes	Yes	No	Yes	No	No	Yes	No

Table 2.5 *Language comparison of OO terminology (Adapted from Henderson-Sellers, 1992a)*

Smalltalk	C++	Objective-C	Object Pascal	Eiffel	CLOS
Object	Object	Object	Object	Object	Instance
Class	Class	Factory	Object type	Class	Class
Method	Member function	Method	Method	Routine	Method Generic function
Instance variable	Member	Instance variable	Object variable	Attribute	Slot
Message	Function call	Message expression	Message	Applying a routine	Generic function
Subclass	Derived class	Subclass	Descendant type	Descendant	Subclass
Inheritance	Derivation Templates	Inheritance	Inheritance	Inheritance Generic class	Inheritance

Smalltalk

Smalltalk is the archetypal OO language (Goldberg and Robson, 1983; Goldberg, 1985), although the first OOPL, as noted above, was Simula. In Smalltalk, everything is an object. Even classes are objects, being members of a metaclass. Smalltalk is more than a language, it is a complete environment. It is well supported by the availability of extensive class libraries, debuggers, inspectors, and interactive browsers. It is type-checked at run-time (dynamic typing), which means that it is possible to be running the system and get a type violation while running. If type checking is done at compilation, as in Eiffel or C++, these errors will be trapped then. Meyer (1989d) notes that "wherever $x.f$ appears in a class text and the compiler accepts it, it is guaranteed that any object associated with x at run-time will have at least one feature corresponding to f." Smalltalk is particularly regarded as useful for introducing OO ideas (e.g., LaLonde and Pugh, 1990), for a prototyping environment, and for GUI-based work. The underlying model for much of the Smalltalk environment is that of the Model-View-Controller (MVC) triad, which is an example of a framework (Wirfs-Brock and Johnson, 1990). For example, any Smalltalk window contains a *model*, which is the data to be displayed; a *view*, which determines how the data are to be displayed; and a *controller*, which provides the protocol for the user interaction with both the view and its model (for further details see, e.g., Pinson and Wiener, 1988, p336 *et seq.*).

A number of dialects of Smalltalk exist. The originators at ParcPlace sell Smalltalk-80, while the lower (PC) end of the market is targeted by Digitalk with their Smalltalk-V. A GNU Smalltalk, an implementation of Smalltalk-80, is also available from the Free Software Foundation (Byrne, 1992), and Enfin is a new version of Smalltalk that extends its capabilities to 4GL tools.

Eiffel

Eiffel is a pure object-oriented language (Meyer, 1988a, 1989a, 1992a) with syntax derived (ancestrally) from Simula67, Algol, CLU, Ada, and Z. It uses C code as an intermediate stage for enhanced portability. The language was released to the Non-profit International Consortium for Eiffel (NICE) in 1992. Several Version 3 compilers are available on a variety of platforms. ISE's Version 3 employs new "melting-ice technology," which offers incremental compilation using an interpreter as well as fully compiled options, thus offering facilities for rapid prototyping and the advantages of a fully compiled production system. Version 3 also offers bridges to both relational databases and objectbases (e.g., Bielak, 1992) and external calls at the language level to and from 3GLs such as FORTRAN and C. The supporting environment from ISE is elaborate and extensive. Eiffelbench provides sophisticated browsing, debugging, and management facilities with connections to EiffelBuild—a visual application generator—as well as to an extensive range of tools, both textual and graphical, such as EiffelVision.

The language itself has many advanced features rarely found elsewhere—notably, constrained genericity, an assertion language (for correctness), renaming and redefining for multiple and repeated inheritance, static (and strong) type checking and dynamic binding (with static binding for nonpolymorphic use), automatic garbage collection, and extensive supporting library classes.

Eiffel's syntax (Meyer, 1992a; Jones, 1992) and structure are seen by many as being "clearer" and easier to learn than, say, C++. However, that same characteristic (of a readily learnable yet brand new syntax) makes many managers cautious of endorsing what they see more as an abrupt change in programming environment than as a perceived smooth evolutionary transition to a hybrid language such as C++ or Objective-C. In the long run, however, it is likely that many programmers, encouraged by their managers to follow this evolutionary course, will never come to appreciate and utilize the full power of the OO paradigm, compared with their compatriots/competition that adopt one of the "pure" OOPLs such as Eiffel or Smalltalk.

Sather

Eiffel is seen by many software engineers as providing a good model for an OOPL. For example, Steve Omohundro has taken the Eiffel framework and, by slimming it down to its bare bones, has created the language Sather.[12] Sather is a simpler language than Eiffel (41 keywords being removed: Omohundro, 1991). Inheritance is simply "textual replacement," with no rename facility and a contravariant rule (Eiffel uses covariance). Unlike in Eiffel, more than one class can be stored in a single file. This simplicity and speed, of course, come at a price: invariants have been removed and assertions simplified. Expanded classes are missing and exception handling is done using library classes rather

---

12. Named after a tower on the Berkeley campus, unlike Eiffel, which is named after the French engineer Gustave Eiffel.

than being built into the language (Omohundro, 1991). Arrays use a traditional indexed notation rather than using object references. The libraries are useful, both they and the language still being further developed. Sather is freely available and is not a commercially supported product. The current implementation is evaluated by Thorup (1992).

Actor
Actor is a windows-based object-oriented language that runs on the PC platform. It is currently available from a single vendor[13] (Whitewater Group, 1989) and contains an extensive class library, debugger, and browser. The language supports encapsulation, single inheritance, late binding, incremental compilation, and garbage collection. Dynamic linking to programs in C and other procedural languages is supported using a **CStruct** class. The environment is focused on a graphical user interface with three types of graphical classes: rendering tools, platform encapsulators, and drawables (Urlocker, 1990). The syntax is modeled on C and Pascal (Urlocker, 1989).

2.4.2.2 Hybrid OOPLs
Extensions of non-object-oriented designs, typically C++ and Objective-C, are well-accepted OO languages in which OO ideas are grafted onto existing procedural languages. In addition to C, base languages used in this way include Pascal (OO version in Turbo Pascal) and, forthcoming, COBOL (see Adams and Lenkov, 1990). The new language definition for FORTRAN90 (Fortran Forum, 1989) also has some object-oriented features. The rationale is that of upward compatibility and of learning the OO version as an "add-on" to the basic procedural language, and is "very appealing to those who do not want to fully commit to using object-oriented techniques" (Hunt, 1992). The availability of two language paradigms may be beneficial to excellent programmers, but a notable hazard for beginners who find it difficult to avoid "dropping back" to the traditional, procedural mindset.

C++
The C++ language (Stroustrup, 1986) is the most popular of these so-called hybrid languages at present, with a strong worldwide user-base. It is a language that has been widely adopted, especially in areas where organizations are already using C, where it is seen by many as a natural successor; although it is more often seen as a systems programming language rather than an applications development language (e.g., Love, 1993). Indeed, many programmers have adopted C++ simply as a newer, better version of C—with no intention of adopting the OO paradigm (e.g., Shaw, 1991; Love, 1993). It has been estimated that only one in ten of the C++ compilers sold are actually used for OOP (Graham, 1991). C++ adds the **class** construction as an extension to **struct**.

---

13. At the time of writing, this vendor has been taken over by Symantec and the future of the Actor product is uncertain.

The features of the class are known as data members (instance variables) and member functions (methods) (e.g., Dewhurst and Stark, 1987). Member functions are private by default, when they are available only to the class itself and to friends, and may be declared as public (total visibility) or as protected (available only to the class and to derived classes). Although there is no strict compiler-enforced ordering of these various elements, it is recommended that interface information is declared first and then protected and private parts (hidden information), followed by implementation details of data members.

Furthermore, member functions are statically bound by default but may be declared as *virtual*, which indicates that they will be bound dynamically to permit polymorphic usage. Meyer (1990b) notes that this need for the programmer to choose to define member functions as virtual in order to be useful in an inheritance context is likely to lead to violations of the "Open–Closed Principle of OOP" (Meyer, 1988a, p23)—see also Section 9.1.3. In C++, deciding to extend a previously isolated class is likely to require opening and modifying the base class. In addition, Antebi (1990) suggests that the use of "friends" in C++ "is a violation of the discipline of information hiding, but it is a disciplined violation."

Genericity and exception handling are not supported in Version 2.0 but have been made available in Version 3.0, generic classes being known as "templates."

Being a language nearer to the machine, explicitly using pointer arithmetic (as does C), C++ has been criticized by Meyer (1990b) as potentially unsafe and compared by Potter (1990) to a dragster alongside Eiffel's Porsche (the dragster may be faster, but when it comes to cornering ... !). Joyner (1992) also questions the efficacy of C++ as a language to support quality of software production using OO techniques.

Objective-C

Objective-C was developed by Brad Cox as an upwardly compatible extension of C, but with a significant flavor of Smalltalk. The compiler acts as a preprocessor for C. Terminology is nonstandard: classes are called "factories"— to retain Cox's metaphor with factory mass production. MI is not supported. Objective-C is bundled with the NeXT machine and has a user base smaller than that of C++.

Fortran90

Two other OO extensions to existing procedural languages deserve additional discussion: FORTRAN and COBOL. The new Fortran90 standard has been published (Fortran Forum, 1989) and supporting compilers are available. As well as syntactic modifications to the language, the addition of array processing constructs, and the availability of free-format source code, Fortran90 introduces object-oriented features such as user-defined types, pointers, dynamic structures, a de-emphasis of global COMMON block structures, and new modularization/packaging constructs, including a USE statement.

OO COBOL

The CODASYL standards committee began work on determining a standard for object-oriented COBOL in November 1989. Already there have been articles describing how this "stalwart" of a language is to be brought up to date. Adams and Lenkov (1992) note that any new standard must permit current COBOL to remain legal in object-oriented COBOL. The new syntax will introduce a class construct, inheritance, and interfaces (to support modularity and genericity). Data will always be private, accessible only through procedures, thus enforcing the good stylistic guidelines of Wirfs-Brock and Wilkerson (1989a). Polymorphism will be supported and the language seems likely to be statically typed.

Adams and Lenkov (1992) also note that "We have chosen to separate subtyping from inheritance and base subtype on interface containment," thus removing the restriction of inheritance to a strict type/subtype relationship. Methods have one of three attributes: PRIVATE, RESTRICTED, or PUBLIC and there are four predefined methods: CREATE, INITIALIZE, FINALIZE, and DESTROY (Belcher, 1991). Graham (1991, p83) predicts that the emergence of object-oriented COBOL will be "welcomed and embraced" and is seen to be "of critical importance for the future of object-oriented programming in the world of mainframes and commercial systems." At the time of writing, OO options for well-known PC COBOL environments had already been announced.

AI languages

We have specifically not mentioned languages for the artificial intelligence (AI), knowledge-based information systems (KBIS), or object-oriented database (OODB) environments; rather, the languages described are all "procedurally" based. These are the languages that currently dominate commercial applications.

Language choice

In choosing a particular OO language, the characteristics mentioned below should be borne in mind and ranked according to your particular industry demands. If real-time or transaction-based processing is required, a type-safe (statically typed) language might lead you to C++ or Eiffel. If performance and ability to access low-level instructions are the highest priority, probably C++ should be considered (e.g., Gabriel, 1992). If safe software engineering and pure object-oriented development are the main criteria with language support to prevent the coders from slipping into a procedural paradigm, Eiffel or Smalltalk should be suggested. If GUIs and a visual programming environment are of concern, Smalltalk/VisualWorks or VisualC++ may be the appropriate choice. Compatibility with your current organizational culture should be evaluated. In the past, this has led many C shops to move, without due consideration of the

The Object-oriented Paradigm ─────────────────────────────────────── 97

consequences, to C++ (less than one in ten of C++ programs in AT&T were found to contain even a single class—Graham, 1991, p61). What is missing here is the "object-oriented mindset." Acquire this first, and then choosing the language is essentially irrelevant; you will write good object-oriented code in any language!

In general, OOPLs run on PC and Unix workstation platforms. Little support for OOPLs is found in the mainframe environment. C++, Smalltalk, Eiffel, and Actor are all available on a DOS platform; there is widespread Unix support; and Macintosh and Windows versions of Eiffel have been announced as imminent at the time of writing.

2.4.3 OOP language features
2.4.3.1 Genericity
A generic class (e.g., Meyer, 1988a) or parameterized type (e.g., Stroustrup, 1988) is a special type of class that has one or more arguments of unspecified type. Using this feature of an OOPL allows, for instance, a generic array to store sometimes integers, sometimes reals, and sometimes bank accounts. It is also possible to have a mixed set of types, so long as they are all part of the same inheritance hierarchy. Genericity is available in CLU, Eiffel, and Ada and in Ver. 3.0 of C++ (keyword **template**), but not in Ver. 2.0 of C++, where it must be simulated using type conversions, or casts, a technique viewed by Meyer (1990b) as defeating any attempt to maintain a secure static typing system. In addition, some languages support constrained genericity, which permits collection classes to restrict the parameter classes to those of a particular class or its descendants.

2.4.3.2 Assertions
Quality software can be created more easily using the concepts of assertions (Meyer, 1988a; Masotti, 1991). Currently, this is only really feasible in the language Eiffel by the use of pre- and postconditions and class invariants (Figure 2.26). Assertions are not yet available in C++ (but cf. ANSI C library header file **assert.h**; e.g., Eckel, 1989, p128), Objective-C, or Smalltalk. In Figure 2.26, the class description contains a constraint to reflect the business rule that a deposit is valid only when the amount being deposited is positive. Before a client object can use the deposit routine, it must ensure that the amount is positive. This precondition (here expressed by **require**) places the responsibility for checking this rule on the calling object. The point is that such a contract makes explicit whose responsibility it is to make such checks.

In addition to a precondition tested upon routine entry, there may also be a postcondition at the end of the routine (in Eiffel, this uses the keyword **ensure**). Although trivial in this example, in a lengthy procedure it is useful to ensure at the end of the routine that (here) balance equals old balance + amount. Again, postconditions are aimed at correctness and thus quality software engineering (Meyer, 1988a). The set of assertions can be related to the software contract in the design, the contract specifying the class obligations in

Brief Code for Class Account

Use of Assertions:
    Preconditions
    Postconditions
    Invariants
within class definition

```
class ACCOUNT export
    open, deposit, withdraw, balance, owner
feature
    balance: INTEGER;
    owner: STRING;
    min_balance: INTEGER is 1000;
    open (who:STRING) is
        do
            owner:=who
        end;
    deposit (amount:INTEGER) is
        require
            amount>0
        do
            balance:=balance+amount
        ensure
            balance=old balance+amount
        end;
    withdraw (amount:INTEGER) is
        do
            balance:=balance-amount
        end;
    invariant
        balance>=min_balance
end   - -  class ACCOUNT
```

Figure 2.26 *The use of assertions in Eiffel*

terms of each of its features (known as services in the Specification Phase). Violation of the contract, in terms of its pre- and postconditions, must be dealt with "gracefully" (see next section). Postconditions and preconditions could be violated in the middle of a routine, as can the class invariant, but on exit from a routine the postcondition and class invariant must be satisfied.

When MI is used, contracts must be merged. In doing so, a contract may only weaken a precondition and strengthen a postcondition so that the service in the subclass can achieve at least the superclass service under the same or weaker circumstances.

2.4.3.3 Exception handling

Exception handling is important in providing graceful failure whenever anything goes wrong. It is done in Ada, CLU, Eiffel, Smalltalk, and CLOS, but not in Objective-C and not in C++ (but see Koenig and Stroustrup, 1990). The use of assertions, preconditions, postconditions, and class invariants, as already mentioned, is vital in ensuring safety. Violation of one of these assertions will result in a run-time error, and the program will terminate with a clear message using the exception handling capabilities of a language (when available). Violation of the precondition implies a bug in the client class; violation of the postcondition implies a bug in the class's own service (Meyer, 1989b).

In addition, in Eiffel the exception handling mechanism includes both an optional retry and/or rescue clause (Meyer, 1988a). If an exception/error occurs, you may wish to try again before terminating the program, for example. If you were ringing a number via a modem and the number was busy, you might well wish to try again after a short interval rather than abort your attempt to connect to the remote computer. The rule might be "if tried to connect < 3, wait 10 seconds and retry." Only on the fourth attempt might you decide that today was a bad day (perhaps there was system maintenance time scheduled on the mainframe) and abort the service, reporting the failure to the calling service.

2.4.3.4 Garbage collection

Meyer placed automatic garbage collection high on his list of important characteristics of an OOPL (Table 2.2) in which the release and reuse of memory locations that are no longer required are undertaken automatically, rather than by means of a manual system such as *free* (after a *malloc*) in C or *delete* in C++. Unused objects have space reallocated at run-time, as soon as there are no references (not just deletion of the present reference) to that object (Figure 2.27). This also prevents clogging up of memory with unused (and no longer usable) objects. Hence, if all the references to an object are cut, then the object is no longer needed as a run-time object. Garbage collection does have some run-time penalty, so it may be preferable to use it as an option, especially for system development and debugging. Automatic memory management exists in Smalltalk and CLOS (Thomas, 1989b) and in Eiffel (Meyer, 1988a), but not in C++ (Stroustrup, 1988) or Objective-C.

2.5 Summary

This chapter has aimed to provide not simply an overview but also a more detailed discussion of certain concepts than is found in many textbooks. The concepts of OT have been introduced and discussed in detail through the three

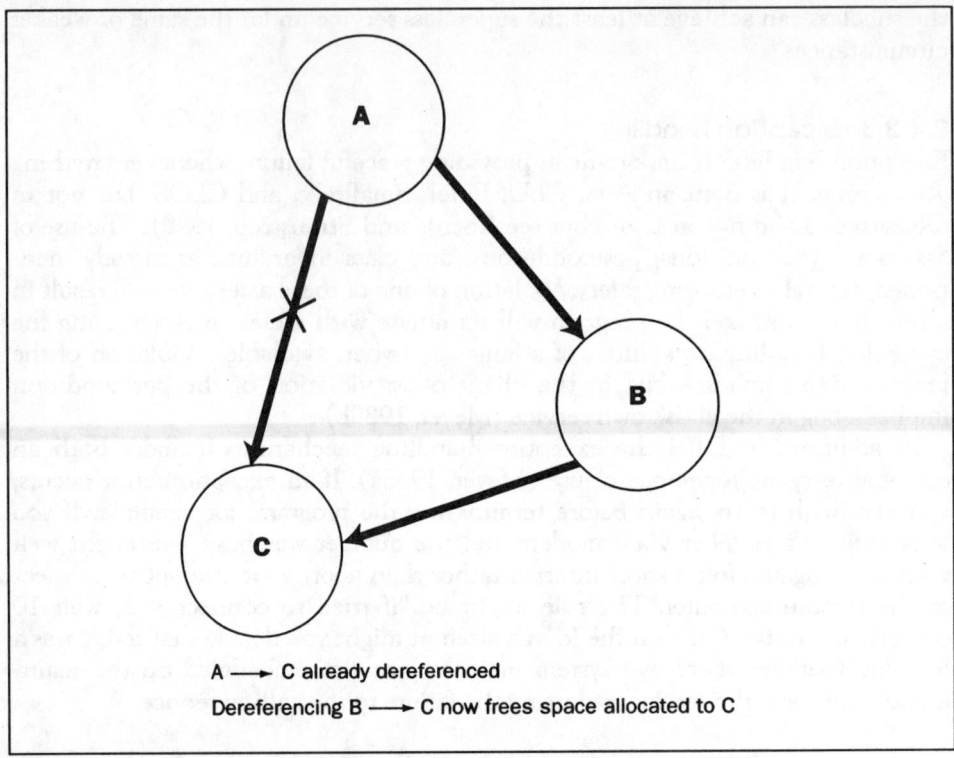

Figure 2.27 *Garbage collection (Henderson-Sellers, 1992a)*

cornerstones of OT: abstraction, encapsulation/information hiding, and polymorphism/inheritance. Abstraction permits the processes of classification, generalization, and specialization; encapsulation and information hiding support tight modularization leading to clear interfaces and "responsible" code modules; and inheritance allows classes to be linked through their commonly identified services or (at the code level) implementation details. However, it should be remembered that the degree to which each of these techniques (and their variants) is used varies. Powerful tools sometimes need treating carefully and indiscriminate use is more likely to be damaging rather than constructive. (A hammer is a useful tool in construction, but wielded in anger can be extremely dangerous!)

The object model, as will be utilized in MOSES (Chapters 4-8), itself builds on these concepts and specifies the semantics of classes, their responsibilities, and their inter-relationships, and how roles will be described. Part of that model is the critical idea of services or responsibilities and software contracting (Dué, 1993).

Our intention is to provide the reader with a clear understanding of all OO concepts and where they are applicable in the lifecycle. This has been achieved by explicitly separating programming language-independent concepts (Specification Phase) from specific OOPL models (Implementation Phase).

This chapter has also examined in brief some implementation (language-level) issues, discriminating between hybrid and pure object-oriented programming languages and comparing their syntax and terminology.

2.6 Study examples

The study examples found after the summary in a number of chapters follow a single example. This is in the musical domain and is built up recursively and iteratively.

In this first exercise (some suggested answers to which are to be found at the end of the book), we offer the following short requirements specification:

> A piece of music consists of several movements, each movement consisting of many notes. Each composition may be assumed to be either a solo piece or an orchestral piece and is therefore performed by a soloist or by a full orchestra.

Exercise 1   What are the O/Cs and their relationships here?

• CHAPTER 3 •

Object-oriented Development

3.1 Software Development Lifecycles (SDLC)

In the development of software engineering principles and practices, the goal has been to determine descriptions of the software process. Initially, specific process models were outlined to give software engineers heuristics and/or manual-type instruction lists that they could follow in either unstructured or structured formats. The imposition of strong guidelines, such as those of the linear, sequential waterfall model (Royce, 1970), *did* provide a strong direction to the software development process, especially to inexperienced software engineers. However, for more experienced developers, who perceived quite rightly that software development was part science/technology (which could be documented as a list of steps) and part art (which is more creative and less readily specifiable), the constraints of the rigidity of such a model were rapidly seen as more detrimental than beneficial. Consequently, more flexible models of the development process have been sought (e.g., Davis *et al.*, 1988; Sutton, 1989). This has led to proposals for prototyping, which allows explicit feedback loops; transformational approaches (e.g., Balzer, 1981; Balzer *et al.*, 1983; Lehman *et al.*, 1984); and evolutionary approaches (e.g., Basili and Turner, 1975; Boehm, 1986; 1988).

The lifecycle approaches outlined above are all prescriptive in the sense that they provide a fixed set of guidelines, stages, and phases for the software developer to follow. All these models share characteristics that can be abstracted out at a higher level, sometimes referred to as a metamethodology. This idea that there might be an underlying metamethodology for the software process was discussed recently by Madhavji (1991). The metamethodology gleans knowledge from this commonly shared knowledge and represents it essentially as a generic model that can be instantiated to give any specific software process. Such ideas of metamodeling are attracting increasing interest (see Postscript for further discussion) and have been applied to the object model as well as to the methodological process. Madhavji (1991) has introduced the term "software process engineering" to describe a range of activities, listed here in Table 3.1.

Table 3.1 *Range of activities identified within software process engineering (Derived from Madhavji, 1991)*

- Determination and specification of system and software requirements
- Analysis and management of risk
- Software prototyping
- Design
- Implementation
- Verification and validation
- Software quality control and assurance
- Integration of components
- Documentation
- Management of software configurations and versions
- Management of data
- Evolution of software
- Project management
- Software evaluation
- Software contracting
- Software acquisition
- Commissioning and decommissioning of software

Identification of the correct terminology also provides some problems. A description of the full lifecycle framework is often referred to as a "methodology" and in this context is defined as an ordered collection of methods as suggested by a framework, for example, a set defining a lifecycle model (Smolander *et al.*, 1991a, b), unified by the same general philosophical approach (Booch, 1991, p18). Methods are then "explicit prescriptions for achieving an activity." Although this terminology is in widespread use in information systems, it is not in accord with the etymology of the word "methodology," which strictly means

Object-oriented Development

"the study of methods." Although we know we will offend some sensibilities, we will use the term "methodology" as a description of the lifecycle framework. This choice also avoids the complication of the use of the word "method" in some OOPLs in a totally disjoint context as a synonym for "service."

Table 3.2 summarizes the current weaknesses in state-of-the-art methodologies. Although these comments were gleaned by Monarchi and Puhr (1992) from a study of extant methodologies, we feel that they reflect an underlying lack of comprehension at the metamethodology level (see above). It is interesting to contrast them with the analysis of weaknesses in non-object-oriented methodologies given by Madhavji (1991) (see Table 3.3).

Table 3.2 *Strengths and weaknesses of current object-oriented methodologies (Monarchi and Puhr, 1992)*

Strengths	Weaknesses
Identifying semantic classes	Identifying interface, application, and system classes
Identifying attributes and behavior	Determining when an attribute, relationship, or behavior should be a class
Placing methods (Law of Demeter: Lieberherr et al., 1988)	Placing classes
Identifying and representing generalization and aggregation structures	Identifying and representing other kinds of relationships
	Maintaining consistent and correct semantics for relationships
Representing static views (structure)	Representing dynamic views (message passing, control, etc.)
	Integrating static and dynamic models
	Maintaining consistent levels of abstraction/granularity

The object-oriented paradigm emphasizes *modeling* of the real world in terms of concepts that may be implemented as software classes. More specifically, we are concerned not with the whole of the real world but with that part of it that pertains to our problem. We can define a Universe of Discourse (UoD) that partitions the real world in such a way that our UoD represents that clearly delineated fragment with which we are currently concerned. For example, if we are trying to solve an accounting problem for a firm, our UoD would contain not only general ledgers and journals but also customers, products, shipment timetables, etc., but would obviously not include rosellas, koalas, or kangaroos.

Furthermore, it is becoming increasingly obvious that we can superimpose two views (subsets) of the UoD and discuss "domain" analysis, design, etc., and "application" analysis, design, etc. (e.g., McGregor and Sykes, 1992; Firesmith, 1993). The "domain" analysis relates to the UoD as defined above in that it will contain more generally applicable concepts; in other words, objects that may not be relevant to this particular software product but are so closely linked that if we are aware of their existence we can more easily build up reusable components. An example here, adapted from McGregor and Sykes (1992), will assist.

Table 3.3 *Weaknesses of current, structured methodologies (Adapted from Madhavji, 1991)*

Current non-OO methodological models are too abstract to convey:

- The process steps required to resolve customer-reported software problems
- Triggering and terminating conditions of an activity
- The state of a product component before, during, and after a process step
- The notational, methodological, operational, and other tools to be used in different process steps
- The inputs and outputs of an activity and the sources and destination of the data
- The manner in which data flow from one activity to another
- The roles played by humans in the process
- The constraints on the process steps
- How communication among humans is supported
- Where parallel and sequential process steps exist

Consider the problem of building software for a game of noughts and crosses (or tic-tac-toe). Such a project is a piece of applications software, since it is highly focused on one very specific problem. This pencil-and-paper game has a set of rules, including a decision rule for winning the game, and involves two players. A software version of the game could be developed based simply on this information. However, the likely success of the software will lead to requests for other "games," such as draughts (checkers), chess, go, and hangman, or to requests for board-based games such as Scrabble™ or Monopoly™.

A more useful approach (and one more likely to lead to significant reusability) would be to widen one's perception of the "problem space" by analyzing other similar problems. When building noughts and crosses software, consider similar software design considerations for other board/pencil-and-paper games. A wider approach such as this would be termed domain analysis (e.g., Neighbors, 1984; Adelson and Soloway, 1985; de Champeaux *et al.*, 1991; Gomaa, 1992). Domain analysis thus extends the boundaries beyond the current problem and is therefore best exploited when future reuse and new initiatives *within the same domain* are foreseen (Iscoe, 1988; McGregor and Sykes, 1992, p60; Berard, 1992b, Chapter 10). It thus takes a broader approach to the current problem as opposed to the more limited view of applications analysis and can be used to elucidate and/or uncover the "business rules" of the organization (Berard, 1992b, p213). In some senses, domain analysis provides a "more idealized" approach, since it aims to provide a broader and therefore stronger base to the software to be developed. It reflects an industrial software engineering approach as opposed to an individually crafted project-specific approach. Domain analysis thus suggests the need for the tighter inclusion of both users and knowledge engineers in the systems development team. People with specific knowledge of the domain rather than just the current problem thus become highly respected team members (Wirfs-Brock et al., 1990).

A domain approach more easily accommodates changes in user requirements, since it is more flexible and the development process will have already considered many of the possible avenues of extension even before the change request is registered. Domain analysis is thus a long-term investment (McGregor and Sykes, 1992, p50) and gels well with an object-oriented software engineering lifecycle approach.

Returning to McGregor and Sykes's (1992) "games" example, we can see that our domain of interest could encompass all "board games" (including pencil-and-paper games). What common features might delineate this domain, presumably excluding other games such as basketball or poker? "Board games" could include characteristics such as (i) board, (ii) cards, (iii) dice, (iv) tokens, (v) players, and (vi) rules, although any single game (an application) would have only a subset of these.

Figure 3.1 discriminates visually between these two (high abstraction level) views of software development: domain development and applications development. Firesmith (1993) here illustrates that it is possible to undertake a full lifecycle development (analysis, design, and programming) at the domain level of abstraction as well as in applications development, although he includes more "stages" in his applications development lifecycle than in the domain development lifecycle. In domain analysis, the design phase (OODDes) covers the design of common reusable classes within the full domain, whereas in OOAD (Figure 3.1), the design details focus on classes within the application-specific domain. In the following sections, we discuss a number of SDLC models that have been discussed as being appropriate for OO development.

3.1.1 Waterfall model

Figure 3.2 shows a simplistic view of the familiar "waterfall" (Royce, 1970). Shown here is a broad division of the lifecycle into very roughly three stages: an analysis, a design, and an implementation phase (left-hand side). Despite the recognition of the need for some iteration between *consecutive* phases of the

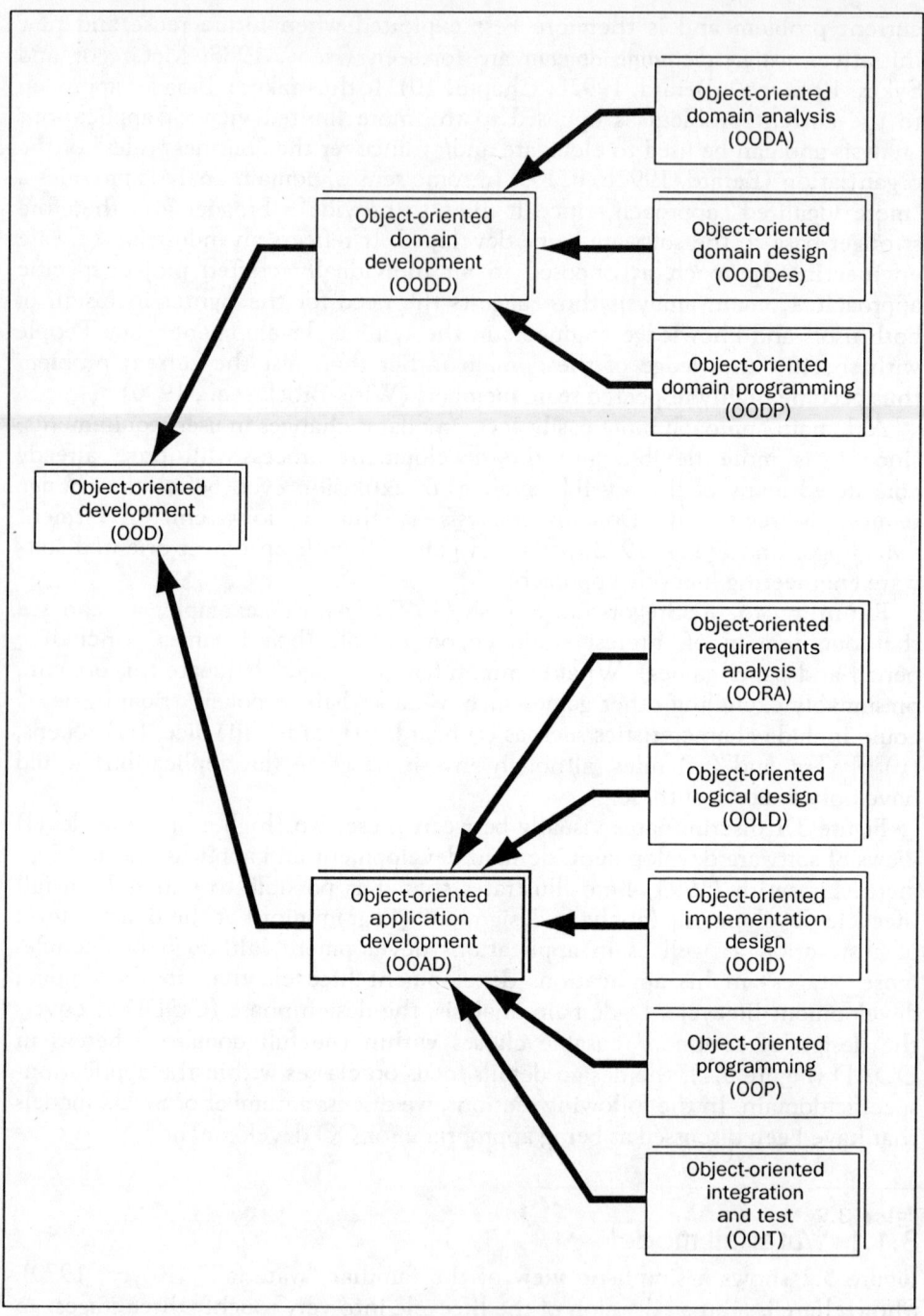

Figure 3.1 *Classes of object-oriented methods (Adapted from Firesmith, 1993)* © John Wiley & Sons, Inc.

Object-oriented Development

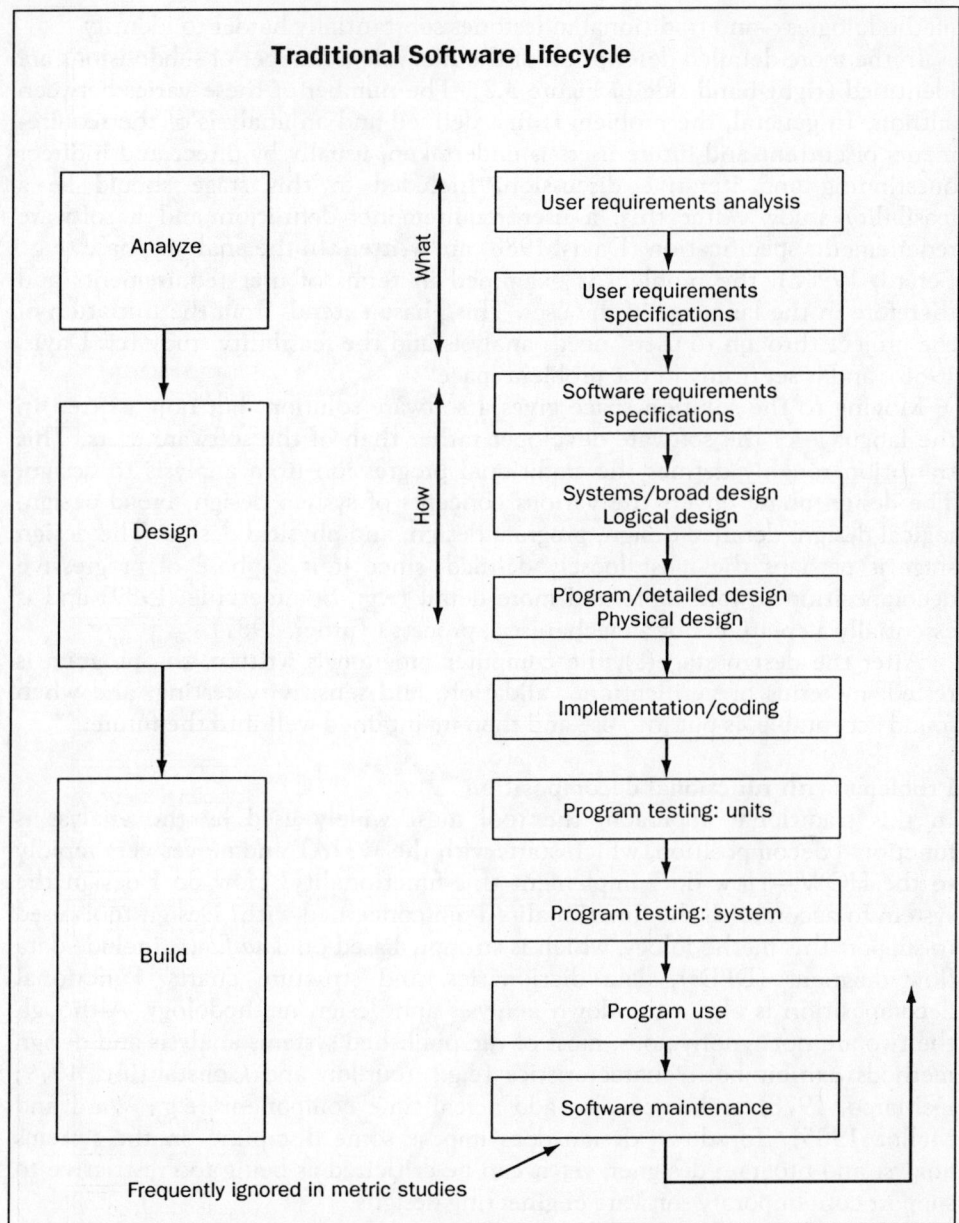

Figure 3.2 *The waterfall model of the systems lifecycle (Henderson-Sellers, 1992a)*

waterfall SDLC, many company methodologies still have rigid milestones: stages that must be reached successfully before the "next" phase can be started. In OT, as we have seen, overlaps become even more evident than in traditional methodologies—and traditional milestones substantially harder to identify.

In the more detailed description of the lifecycle a number of subdivisions are identified (right-hand side of Figure 3.2). The number of these varies between authors. In general, the problem is first defined and an analysis of the requirements of current and future users is undertaken, usually by direct and indirect questioning and iterative discussion. Included in this stage should be a feasibility study. After this, a user requirements definition and a software requirements specification (Davis, 1988) are written. In the analysis phase (e.g., Berard, 1990c), the problem is examined in terms of user requirements and therefore in the language of the user. This phase extends from the initiation of the project through to users' needs analysis and the feasibility study (cf. Davis, 1988), and is set firmly in the problem space.

Moving to the solution space gives a software solution, but now written in the language of the software developer rather than of the software users. This transition roughly defines the traditional progression from analysis to design. The design phase covers the various concepts of system design, broad design, logical design, detailed design, program design, and physical design. The design stage is perhaps the most loosely defined, since it is a phase of progressive decomposition toward more and more detail (e.g., Sommerville, 1989) and is essentially a creative, not a mechanistic, process (Turner, 1987).

After the design stage(s), the computer program is written, the program is tested, in terms of verification, validation, and sensitivity testing, and when found acceptable, is put into use and then maintained well into the future.

Problems with functional decomposition
In this traditional approach, the tool most widely used by the analyst is functional decomposition, which starts with the WHAT and moves very rapidly to the HOW—How do I implement this functionality? How do I design the system to accomplish the functionality I am concerned with? Design tools used to support this methodology, which is strongly based on *data flows*, include data flow diagrams (DFDs), data dictionaries, and structure charts. Functional decomposition is also a top-down analysis and design methodology. Although the two are not synonymous, most of the published systems analysis and design methods exhibit both characteristics (e.g., Yourdon and Constantine, 1979; DeMarco, 1978) and some also add a real-time component (e.g., Ward and Mellor, 1985). Top-down design does impose some discipline on the systems analyst and program designer, yet it can be criticized as being too restrictive to support contemporary software engineering designs.

Meyer (1988a) identifies four basic flaws in a top-down functional decomposition. First, it tends to freeze in the requirements very early. Very little account is taken of evolutionary change and it is commonly accepted that systems evolve. In traditional methodologies this evolution is very difficult to accomplish. Second, it is difficult to identify a single functionality of a system. When a system has been designed, usually *the* functionality becomes modified to several functionalities. Third, on the basis of a functional mindset, top-down functional decomposition identifies functionality and algorithms very early in the lifecycle, indeed basing the whole design methodology on that construct. Meyer suggests that top-down functional decomposition often neglects the data structure, although it is perhaps more realistic to say that data structures are deferred until *very* late in the decomposition and design. Finally, there is little encouragement to develop reusable modules.

Functional decomposition is well supported by the older procedural languages and is therefore a natural mode of design expression in that context. The incorporation of subroutines into these languages led to the ability to create some degree of autonomy and information hiding, while at the same time shared data tended to be placed in globally accessible data storage areas (e.g., COMMON blocks in FORTRAN, externals/fileblock declarations in C). This leads to the "stack of dominoes" effect familiar to anyone working in program maintenance, whereby changes to one part of a software system often cause a problem in an apparently dissociated program area. Furthermore, a system envisaged as providing a single service (single function) is unable to evolve to take into account new data structures or new functions with any degree of robustness.

Other problems with the waterfall lifecycle model are manifested in the disjoint mappings between lifecycle phases. This results from the use of very different underlying models for analysis (e.g., DFDs), design (e.g., hierarchy charts), and coding (e.g., flow charts). On the left-hand side of Figure 3.3 is shown schematically the disjoint mapping, evident in traditional functional decomposition, between analysis and design and possibly between design and implementation. (The "seamless transition" of a lifecycle based on a single (object) model is contrasted with this on the right-hand side of the figure.)

3.1.2 Fountain model

In an OO lifecycle, there is significant merging between various stages of the lifecycle and thus a high degree of iteration. Therefore, rather than the waterfall model, the fountain model has been proposed (Henderson-Sellers and Edwards, 1990)—a graphic image (Figure 3.4) to remind us that although some activities cannot start before others (for example, coding must follow design; and design should not begin before the elicitation of requirements from the user), there is a considerable overlap and merging of activities. In a fountain, water rises up the middle and either falls back to the ground or is reincorporated at an intermediate level. Similarly, in an object-oriented software development the general flow from analysis through design to implementation is overlain with iterative cycles across two (or all three) of these "phases."

Figure 3.4 outlines the general characteristics of the *systems* level perception of an object-oriented development. However, as we have noted elsewhere (Henderson-Sellers and Edwards, 1990), development of an object-oriented system is much more likely to lead us to focus on sections of the whole, such as subsystems (Wirfs-Brock *et al.*, 1990) (see later discussion). These subsystems are small collections of classes that work closely together. Some of them can usually

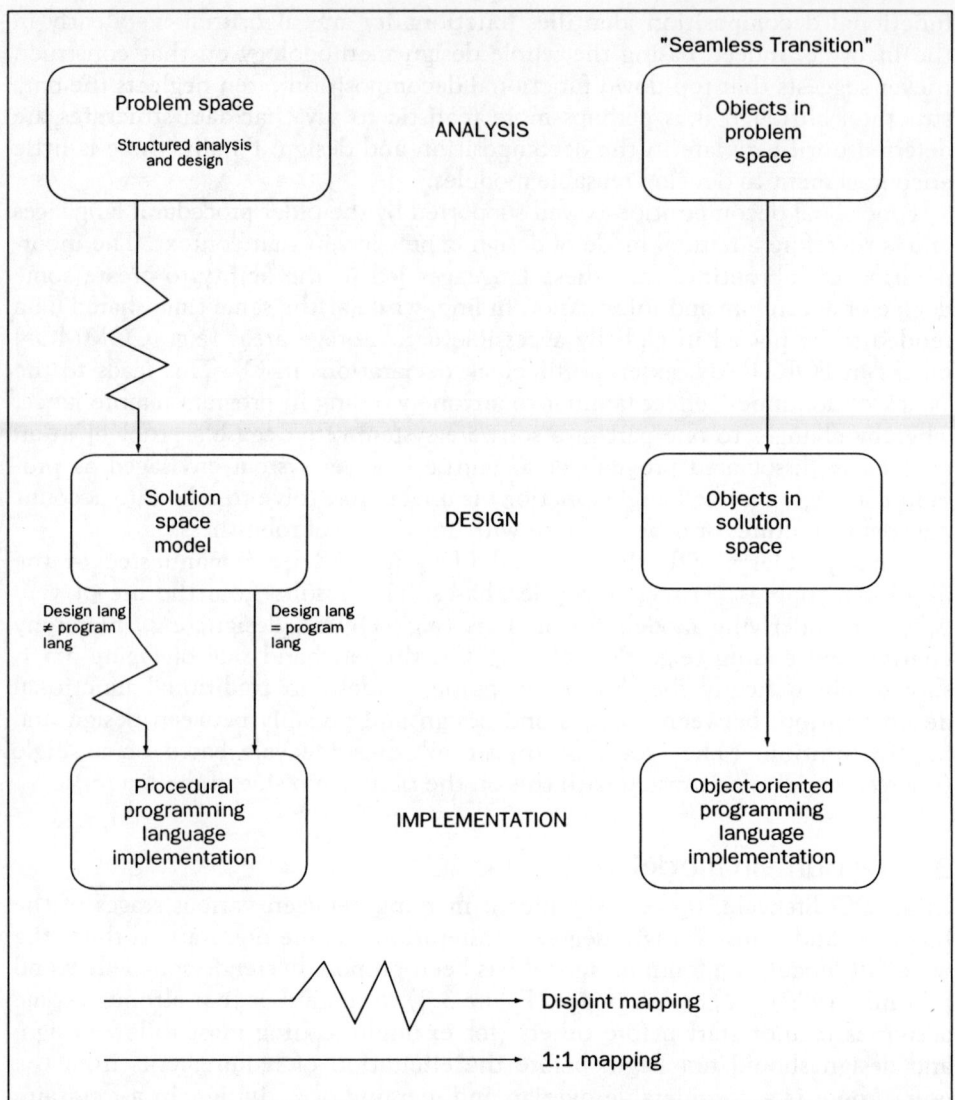

Figure 3.3 *Contrast between the disjoint SDLC mappings of the traditional development environment and the seamless transition of the object-oriented environment (Henderson-Sellers, 1990)*

be identified fairly early in the analysis and design; others appear much later in the design. The stage of development of each of the classes in one subsystem proceeds at the same rate, yet the lifecycle stage of different subsystems within the software system being developed or modified could be very different. Each subsystem represents a coherent or related set of identified classes. Thus there is

Object-oriented Development 113

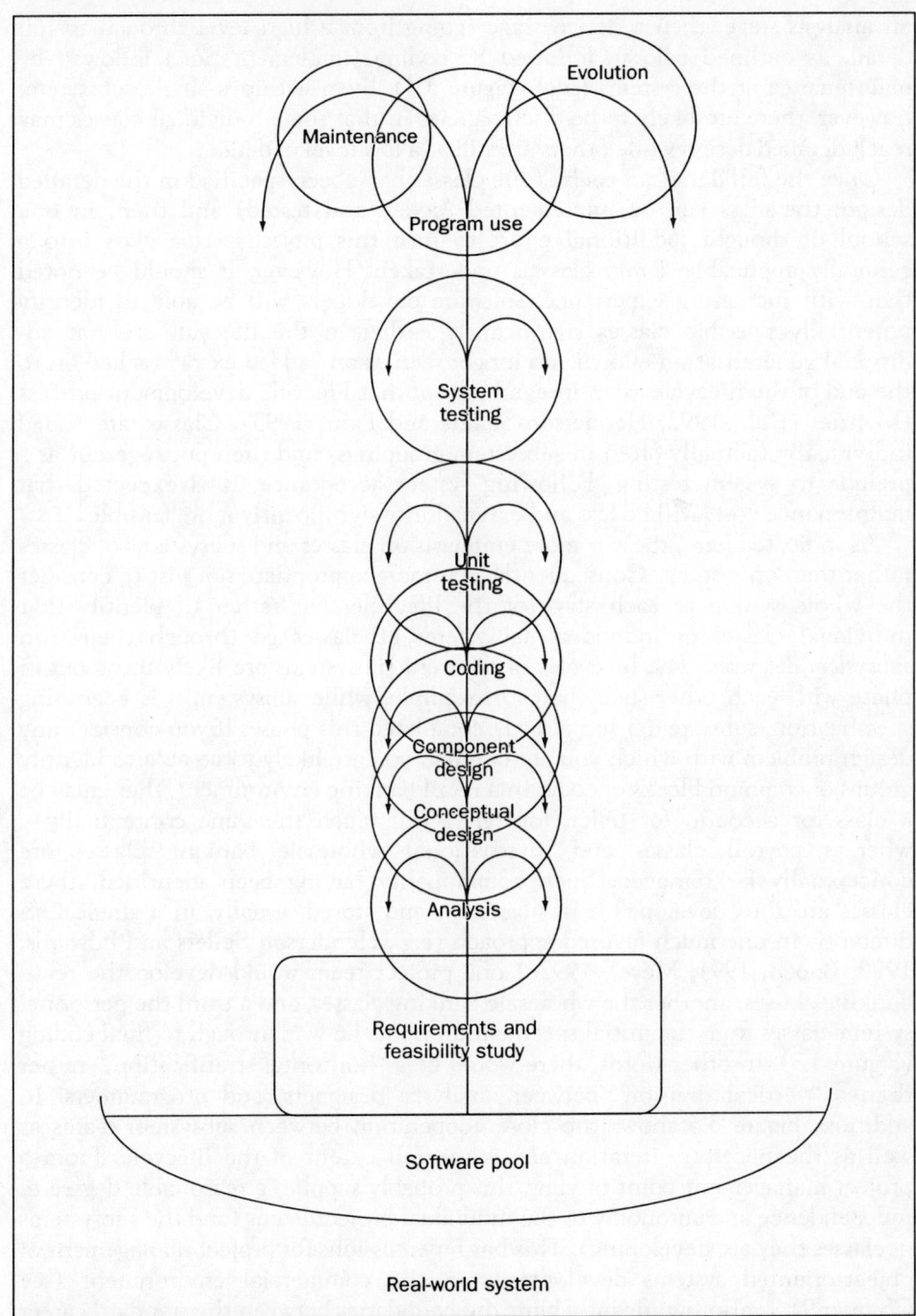

Figure 3.4 *The fountain model for system development (Henderson-Sellers and Edwards, 1993a)*

an analysis stage, then a design stage (going from a high level through to full detail, as outlined below), followed by coding (implementation) followed by maintenance at the systems level (Figure 3.4). Even within a single subsystem, however, there are likely to be discrepancies in that some individual classes may reach detailed design while others are still at a low level of detail.

Once the full details of each of the classes have been specified in the detailed design, the class can be implemented (coded and tested) and then, in one school of thought, additional effort to turn this *project-specific* class into a generally applicable *library* class is undertaken. However, it should be noted that with increasing experience, software developers will be able to identify potentially reusable classes significantly earlier in the lifecycle so that additional generalization effort is no longer seen as an "added extra" tacked on to the end of the lifecycle as an integral part of that lifecycle development process (Menzies et al., 1992; Henderson-Sellers and Pant, 1993). Classes are coded individually (actually often in subsystem groupings) and then put together as a prelude to system testing. Following system acceptance, it is expected that maintenance costs will be less and extensibility significantly more feasible.

As indicated here, there is more emphasis on classes and subsystems of classes rather than on systems. Consequently, it is more appropriate not just to consider the whole system at each stage of the lifecycle, but rather to identify that individual classes or individual subsystems of classes go through their own *subsystem lifecycles*. The lifecycles of different subsystems are likely to be out of phase with each other such that, for example, while subsystem n is beginning specification, subsystem 3 has already completed this phase. If you consider any design problem with which you are familiar, you are likely to be able to identify groups of common blocks of code. In a retail banking environment, there may be a class for account, for teller, for ATM—all much the same contextually—whereas payroll classes and international wholesale banking classes are conceptually far removed. Such commonality having been identified, these classes are thus developed as a subsystem and stored, usually, in a single O/S directory. In one much-favored approach (e.g., Henderson-Sellers and Edwards, 1990; Booch, 1991; Meyer, 1992c) one project team would develop the retail banking classes, another the wholesale banking classes, and a third the personnel system classes from the initial specification right the way through to final coding (Figure 3.5). In other words, there would be a "horizontal stratification," rather than a "vertical division" between analysts, designers, and programmers. In addition, Figure 3.5 shows the close cooperation between subsystem teams as well as the necessary iteration across the full extent of the lifecycle. From a project management point of view, this probably supplies a reasonable degree of independence and autonomy to the individual project teams (and the subsystems of classes they are developing). This has repercussions for project management of object-oriented systems development in the commercial environment (see Chapter 9). It also significantly blurs the boundaries between the standard career grades of programmer, designer, and analyst, although in some organizations these distinctions will likely be retained.

Object-oriented Development

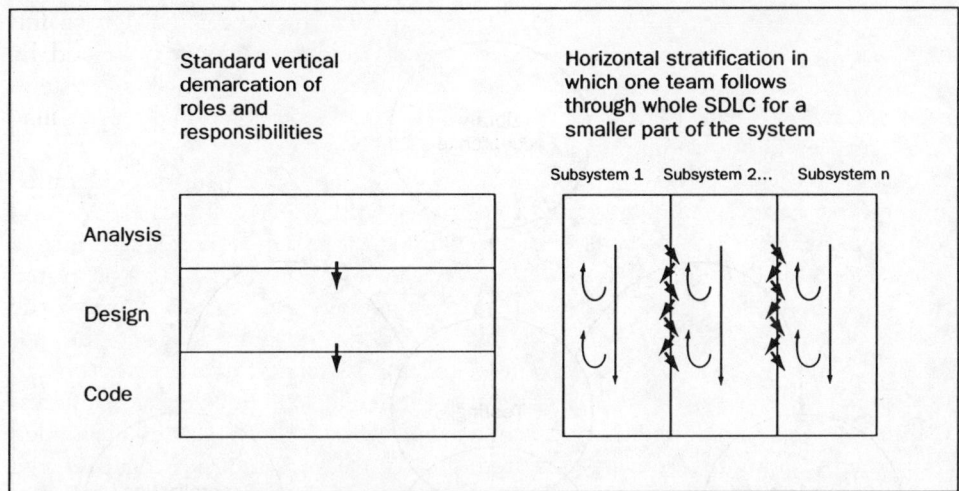

Figure 3.5 *Two approaches to project management and team composition in an object-oriented development environment: (left-hand side) standard demarcations based on lifecycle phase and (right-hand side) division along subsystem lines rather than lifecycle phases*

Figure 3.6 shows how the fountain model can be adapted for this subsystem development approach. This reflects ideas similar to those in the systems fountain model of Figure 3.4, but here the cases of generalization and clustering/reevaluation are now included as a model for the fine-tuning of those classes for future use. Again that part is difficult. Meyer (1990b) describes his experiences in generalizing classes for the Eiffel library, which give genuine insight into the degree of difficulty in obtaining really generic and useful library classes. Finally, superimposed on these steps is the concept of iteration: a return from a "higher" to a "lower" phase, sometimes contiguous, sometimes further removed.

Putting all this together gives a relatively complicated, yet useful, diagram (Figure 3.7). Time is shown on the ordinate depicting evolution, with time, of both requirements and global design. Typically, requirements tend to evolve. As the design process progresses, feedback is often given that could offer the opportunity for the requirements analyst to identify some potential improvement. The worst consequence of permitting iterative modifications to user requirements is that some classes, identified from the original requirements specification, may become redundant, although the extent of this will vary depending on the nature of the revision. It is most unlikely that the whole system design will be scrapped. In any case, the classes already implemented may be of use in future projects. Further capabilities include (i) not having to freeze the requirements too soon; (ii) having many more interactions between the design and the requirements than in a traditional lifecycle; and (iii) being able to start the coding at an early design stage. It should also be noted that the

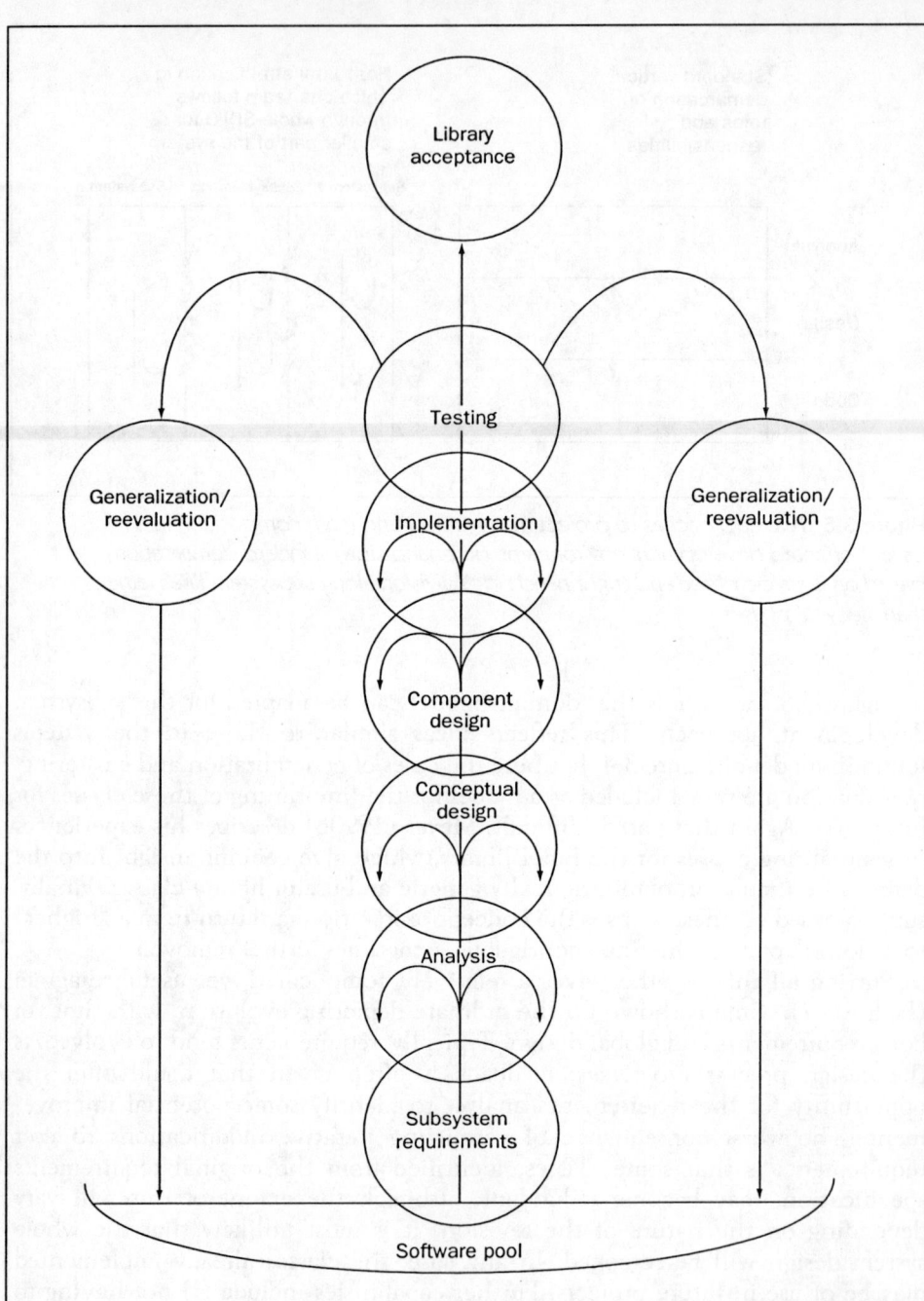

Figure 3.6 *The fountain model for the object-oriented lifecycle of an individual class or cluster of classes. This basic model is appropriate when a class needs to be specified from scratch. (Adapted from Edwards, 1992)*

Object-oriented Development 117

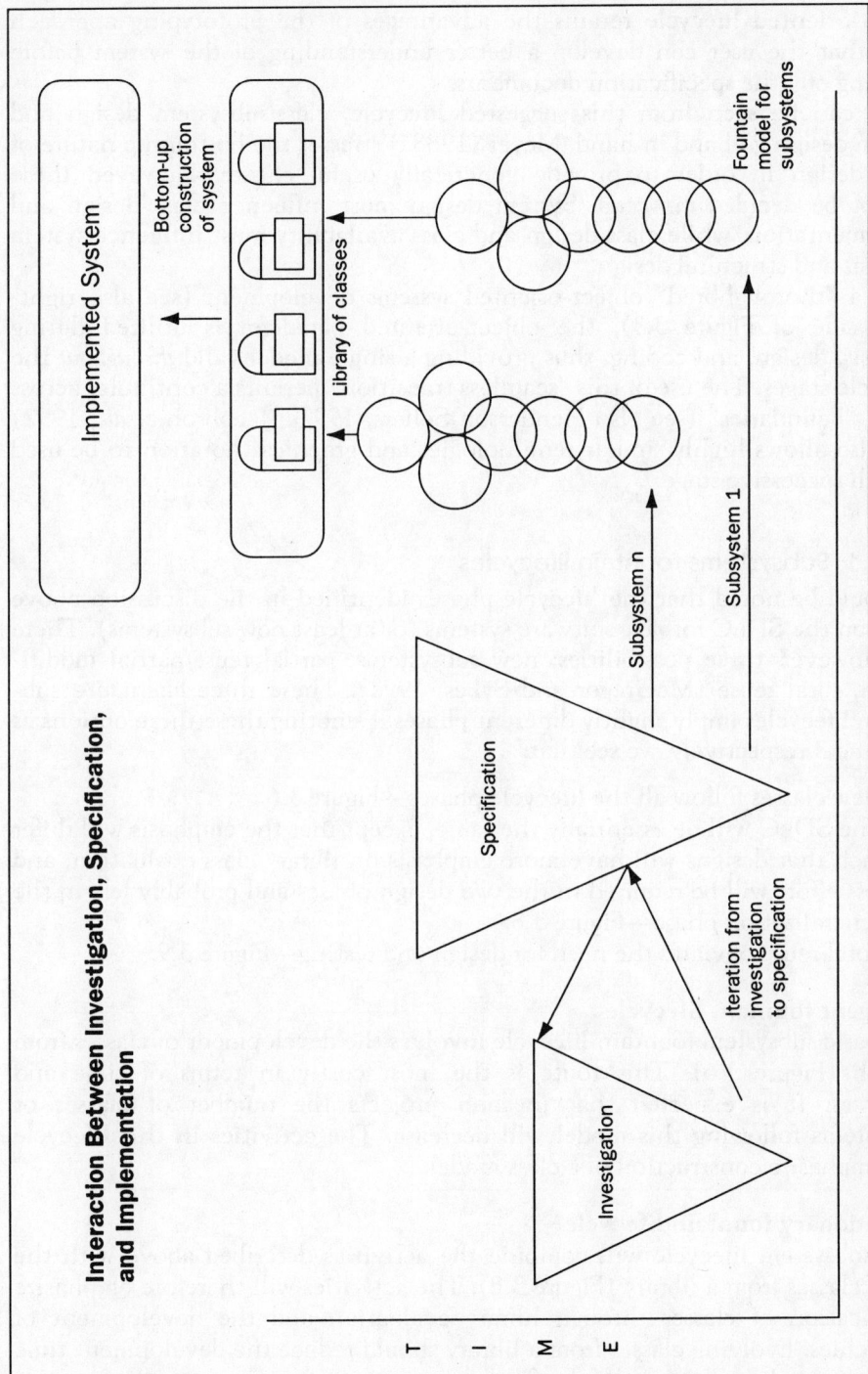

Figure 3.7 *Interaction between requirements analysis, design, and implementation in an object-oriented systems development (Adapted from Henderson-Sellers and Edwards, 1990)*

object-oriented lifecycle retains the advantages of the prototyping approach such that the user can develop a better understanding of the system before "signing off" the specification documents.

As can be seen from this suggested lifecycle, class/subsystem design and system design go hand in hand. Meyer (1988a) stresses the bottom-up nature of class design in order to provide generically useful classes. However, these cannot be decided *in vacuo*. System design must influence class design and implementation, while class design and class availability must influence system analysis and structural design.

In a "thoroughbred" object-oriented systems development (see also right-hand side of Figure 3.3), the object-oriented paradigm is utilized during analysis, design, and coding, thus providing a single model valid *throughout* the lifecycle stages. The use of this "seamless transition" permits a continuity across phase "boundaries" (see also Henderson-Sellers, 1992a; Jacobson et al., 1992) and also allows highly similar terminologies and graphical notation to be used at each successive stage.

3.1.2.1 Subsystems fountain lifecycles

It should be noted that the lifecycle phases identified in the discussion above focus on the SDLC for *new* software systems (or at least new subsystems). There are, however, three possibilities: new subsystems, partial reuse/partial modification, total reuse (McGregor and Sykes, 1992). These three *alternative* subsystem lifecycles imply slightly different phases. Denoting these three options as 1, 2, and 3 respectively, we see that:

1. New classes follow all the lifecycle phases—Figure 3.6.
2. The SDLC will be essentially the same, except that the emphasis will differ such that designs will have more emphasis on library class evaluation; and less effort will be required in the two design phases and probably less in the generalization phase—Figure 3.8.
3. Total reuse obviates the need for design and testing—Figure 3.9.

Emergent fountain lifecycle

The basic subsystem fountain lifecycle involves the development of classes from scratch (Figure 3.6). This route is the most costly in terms of time and resources. It is expected that in later projects the number of classes or subsystems following this model will decrease. The activities in this lifecycle will emphasize construction of a class model.

Evolutionary fountain lifecycle

This subsystem lifecycle will combine the activities described above with the use of classes from a library (Figure 3.8). The activities will therefore emphasize modification of classes through library evaluation and the development of hierarchies. Evolving classes from a library should reduce the development time and increase the robustness of the final system.

Object-oriented Development — 119

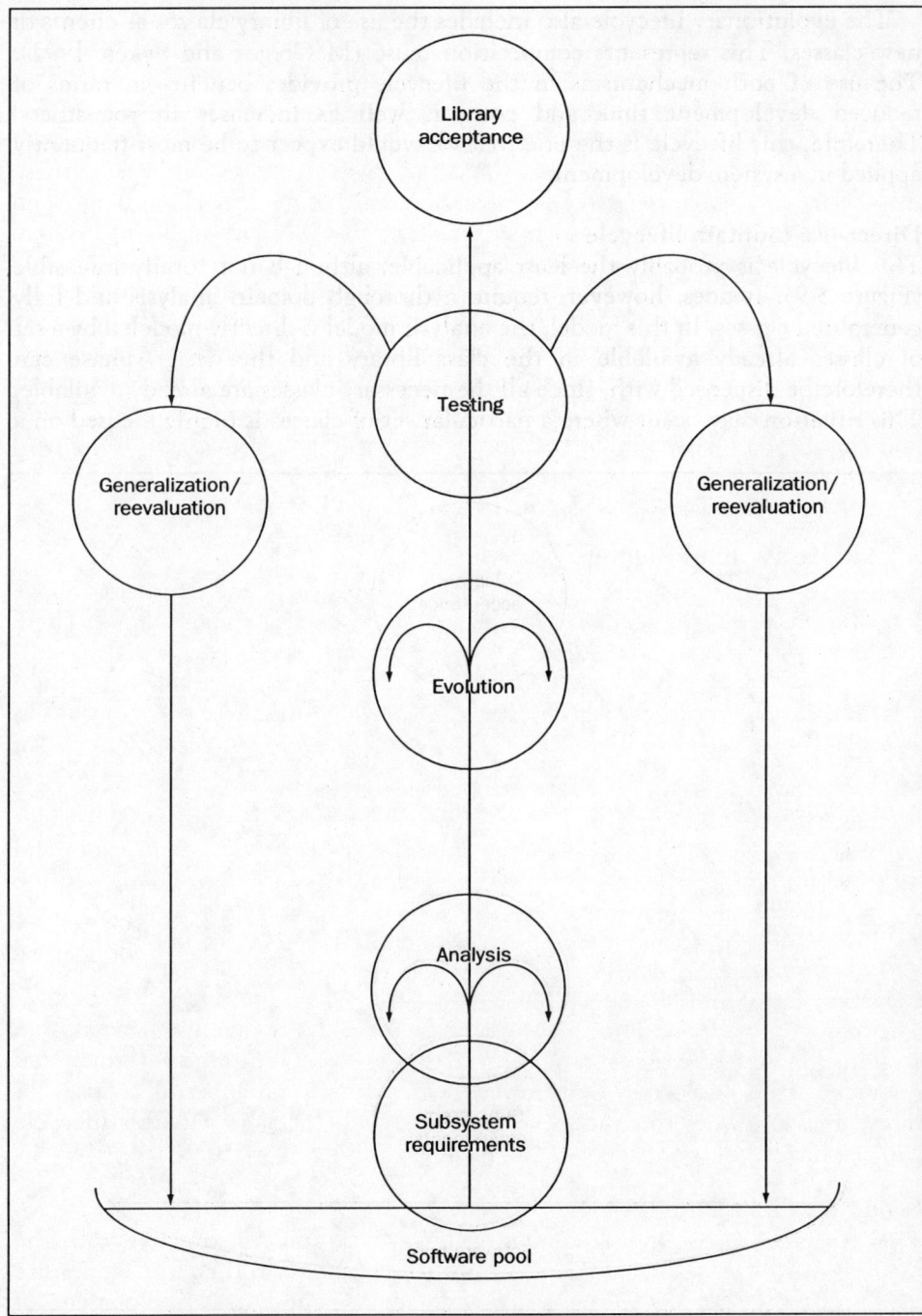

Figure 3.8 *Module fountain model where a class needs evolving from the software pool (Adapted from Edwards, 1992)*

The evolutionary lifecycle also includes the use of library classes as clients of new classes. This represents composition reuse (McGregor and Sykes, 1992). The use of both mechanisms in the lifecycle provides benefits in terms of reduced development time and cost, as well as increases in robustness. Therefore, this lifecycle is the one that we would expect to be most frequently applied in a system development.

Direct-use fountain lifecycle
This lifecycle is probably the least applicable, although not totally infeasible (Figure 3.9). It does, however, require a thorough domain analysis and fully generalized classes. In this model, the analysis model is directly modeled by a set of classes already available in the class library and the design phase can therefore be dispensed with, since all the necessary classes are already available. This situation may occur where a particular set of classes is highly focused on a

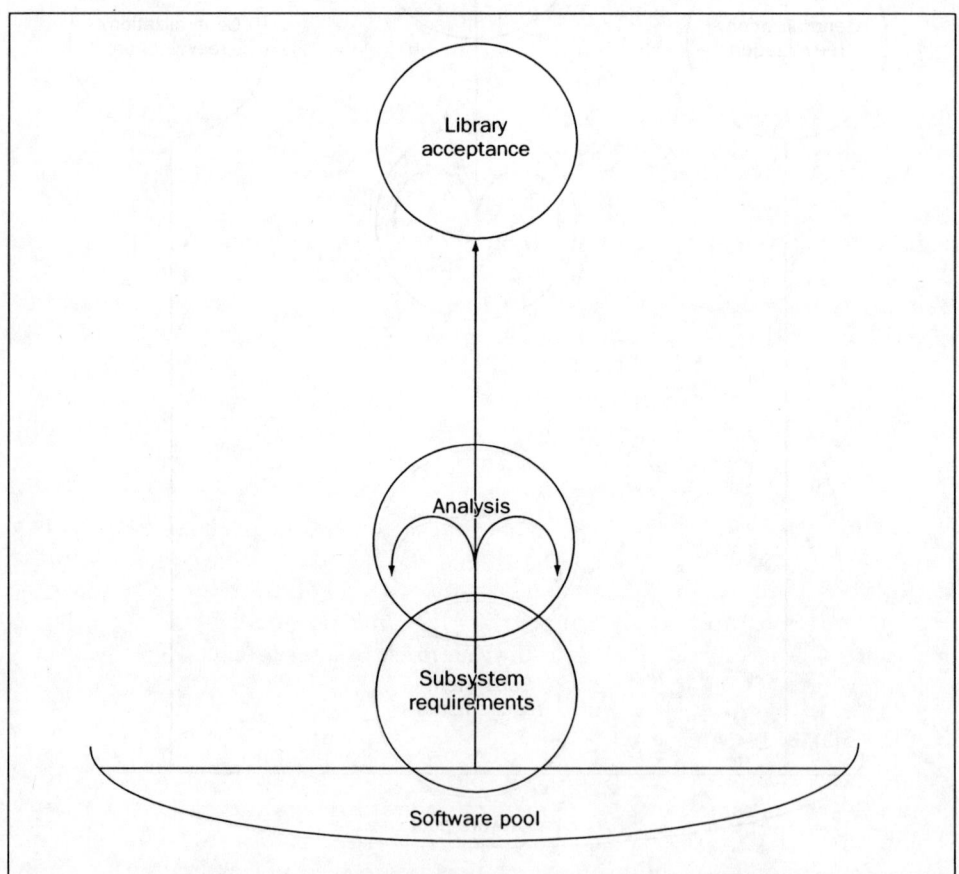

Figure 3.9 *Module fountain model when a class/cluster can be used directly from the software pool (Adapted from Edwards, 1992)*

domain that recurs repeatedly for an organization. Such a situation is possible, although unlikely, and is included largely for completeness. In this model the only activity is really that of validation, ensuring that the class meets the necessary requirements of the model. Validation is therefore the major emphasis throughout this lifecycle.

The fountain lifecycles provide a view of systems development that incorporates iteration and recursion in a controlled manner. In particular, the identification of a lifecycle applicable at two levels of abstraction—the system and the subsystem—leads to a flexible approach to project management.

Cluster model
One of the earliest models to be proposed for an object-oriented lifecycle was the cluster model of Meyer (1988a). Meyer noted that object-oriented systems were composed of "equal" classes that communicated for performing a task rather than being composed of hierarchically decomposed functions. This "flat" architecture allowed parallel development of groups of classes, called *clusters*. Meyer also noted the considerable overlap between the phases of development that occurs when the object model is applied. This results from the fact that the object model can be used at all phases of the development process and does not require the developer to change formalisms from one phase to the next.

These factors of parallel development and blurred lifecycle phases led Meyer to propose the *cluster model* as a lifecycle for a tightly related group of classes in which three phases are identified. It should be noted that this model applies to software *classes* and not software *systems*. First, a specification is written by the system designer (SPEC); it is then designed and implemented (DESIMPL) (Meyer views this as one process in a language such as Eiffel), and finally it is validated and generalized (VALGEN). This latter phase has been divided into two separate phases in later versions (Meyer, 1992g) (Figure 3.10).

This lifecycle occurs for different clusters at different times. The specification of a class is refined from a specification of the system and describes, in as much detail as possible, the services and semantics of the class. This would be best expressed theoretically by the formal specification of an Abstract Data Type (ADT), with the final algorithmic detail being deferred until implementation of the class. This model is one that evolved from experience at Interactive Software Engineering Inc. (ISE) in the development of large, industrial-strength class libraries and was refined in later projects.

3.1.3 Spiral model
Figure 3.11 illustrates the risk-driven "spiral" model (Boehm, 1986) in which iterative and incremental development revolves through four basic "activities." These are (i) assessment of objectives, (ii) risk assessment, (iii) product development, and (iv) planning. The first phase in each circuit of the spiral, progressing from a system level viewpoint on through to coding, is an assessment of objectives, constraints, etc., for this next "circuit." A cost-effective

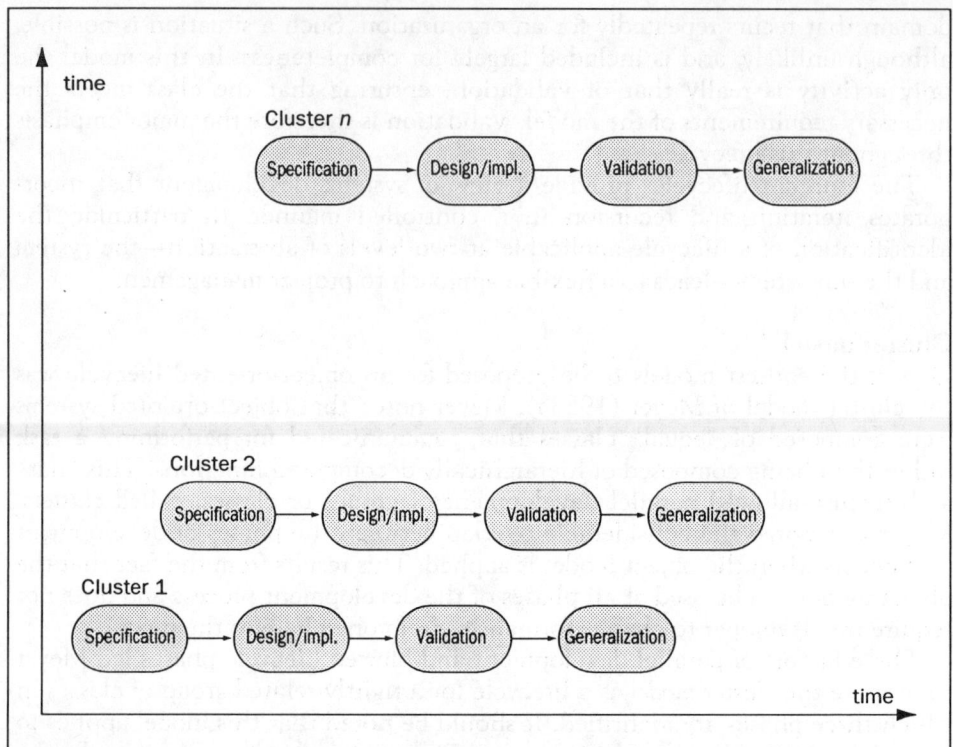

Figure 3.10 *The cluster model for the SDLC (Meyer, 1992g)*

strategy is identified, which may involve prototyping, simulation, and user questionnaires. Next, risks are identified explicitly. Depending on this risk evaluation, the next stage may be evolutionary development, a more detailed prototype, or a traditional waterfall progression. Planning may include partitioning of the system as well as system reviews, including walkthroughs. Roughly each circuit corresponds to a phase of the waterfall model, e.g., feasibility, requirements analysis.

Williams (1988) notes that this model also subsumes other process-driven development approaches, including prototyping and specification-driven, while Boehm (1986) notes its shortcomings with respect to its applicability for software developments undertaken under external contract.

The applicability of the spiral model to object-oriented developments is being increasingly explored (Wirfs-Brock *et al.*, 1990), although a number of concerns (e.g., Berard, 1992b, Chapter 4) have been raised regarding its truly iterative and recursive nature. For example, although depicted as a spiral, it is in fact a linear description (Figure 3.12) in which some activities are returned to. However, these are *prescribed*, whereas in a truly iterative/recursive OO development one could expect the need for more flexibility in decisions taken on

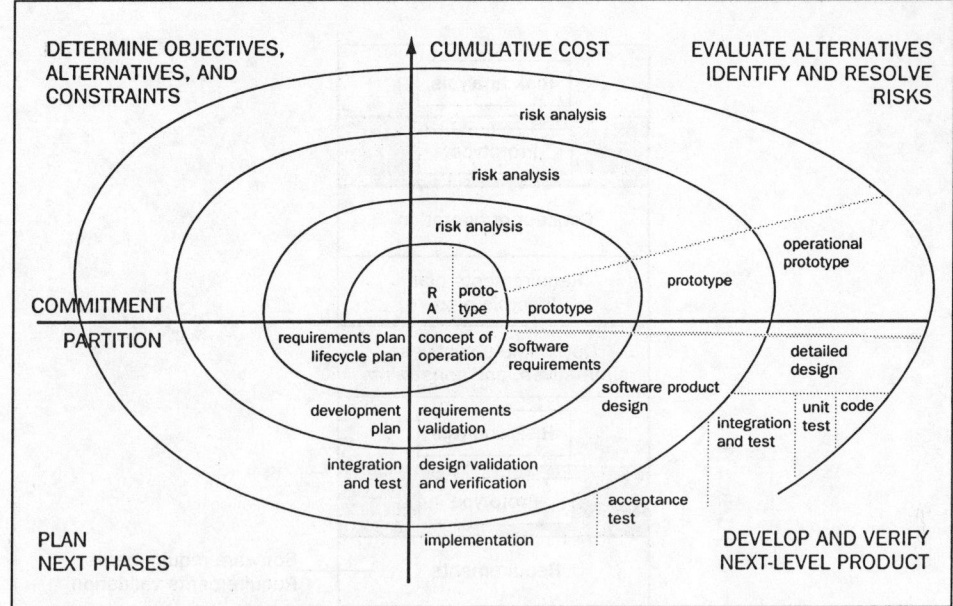

Figure 3.11 *The spiral model for the SDLC (Boehm, 1986)*

when to iterate back to an early stage. Nevertheless, the spiral model provides a significant improvement on a linear waterfall model and has also been embodied in the proposals of Iivari (1990) for an "hierarchical spiral model" and Rumbaugh (1992b) for a whirlpool-like development.

3.1.4 Fractal model

Another alternative that has an immediate, superficial appeal is the "fractal model." Unfortunately, it does not stand up to detailed scrutiny as a useful candidate for describing the OO SDLC. Originally proposed by Foote (1991) and refined by McGregor and Sykes (1992, p41), it is designed to describe the recursive self-similarity of the software development process, in which three phases of Prototype/Initial Design, Expansionary/Exploratory Design, and Consolidation/Design Generalization are applied. However, fractals are deterministic and infinitely recursive, and in them detail at *every* "abstraction level" is *identical*. This is clearly not true for the development process. It has some appeal for the recursive layers of aggregated objects; but again detail at lower levels is *not* reminiscent of that at higher levels, as would be the case in a fractal surface. An analogy is useful only if it both describes *and elucidates* the real world that we are modeling, as well as providing a supportive analog to a reasonable depth. Unfortunately, a fractal model provides neither, whereas both the fountain model and the spiral model do pass these "tests."

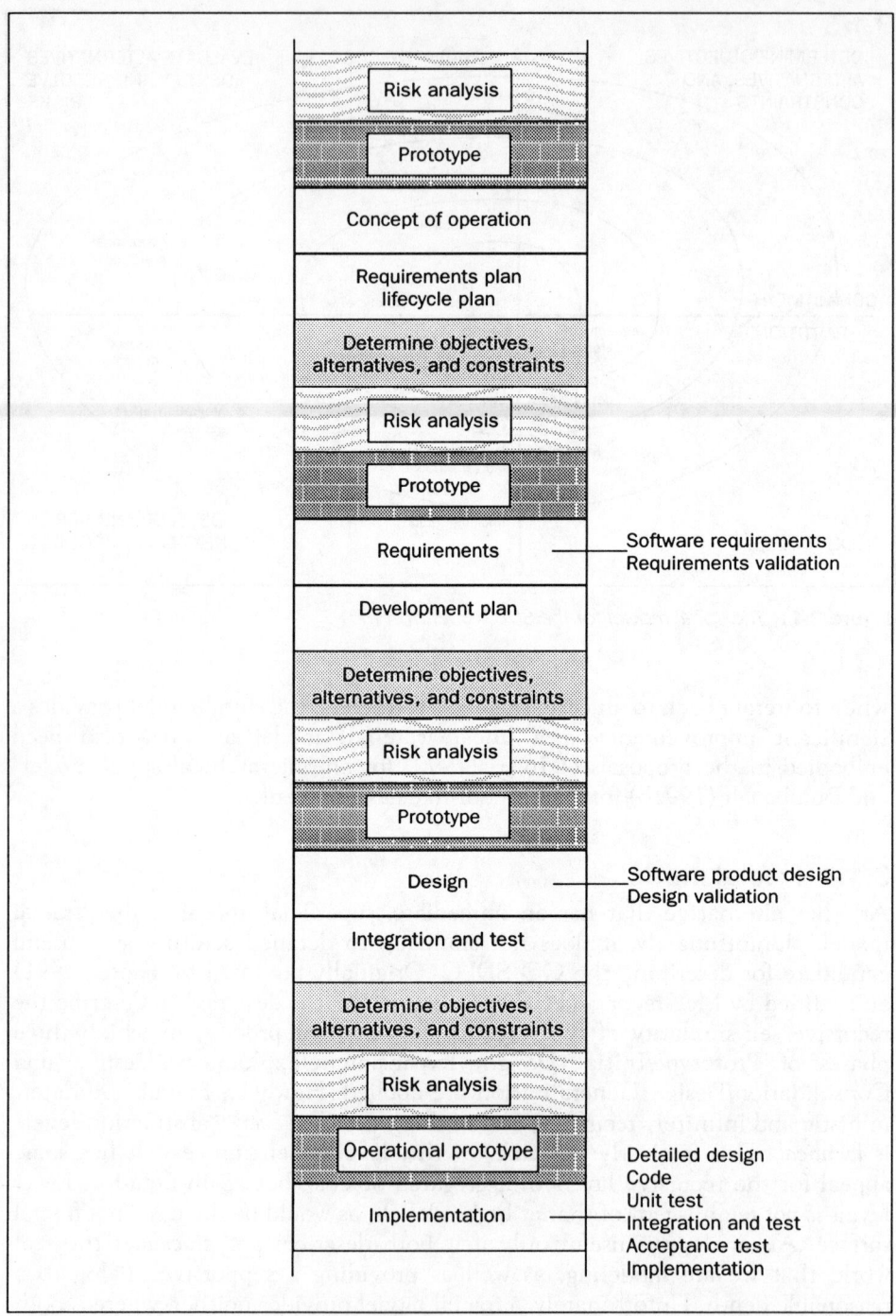

Figure 3.12 *"Unwrapping" the risk-driven spiral model*

Object-oriented Development — **125**

3.1.5 McGregor and Sykes

McGregor and Sykes (1992) develop a lifecycle variant based on the application lifecycle progression shown in Figure 3.13. Embedded in this is the smaller scale "Class Development" lifecycle—based on the subsystem lifecycle models described earlier by Henderson-Sellers and Edwards (1990). They note (Figure 3.14) the smooth transition of classes between analysis, design, and implementation, while drawing the reader's attention to classes that originate

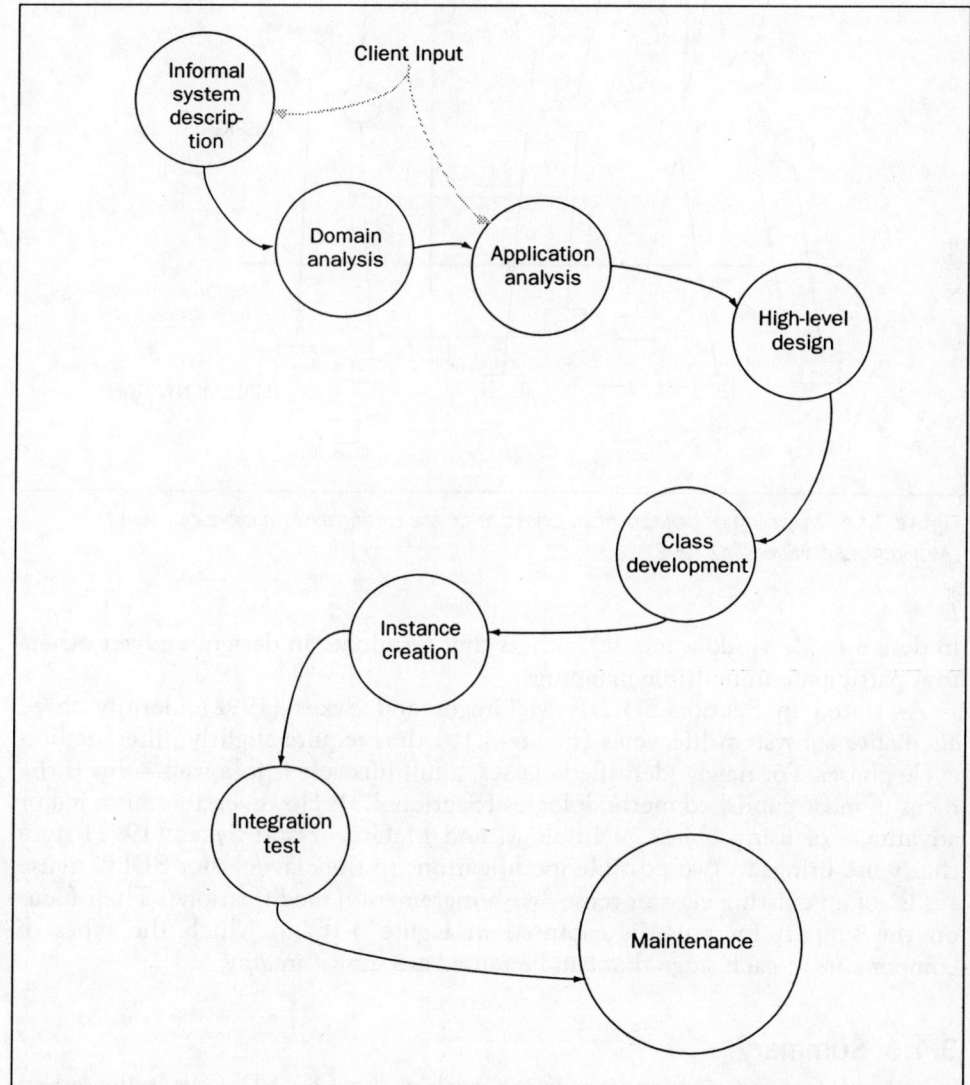

Figure 3.13 *An application lifecycle model proposed by McGregor and Sykes (© 1992)*

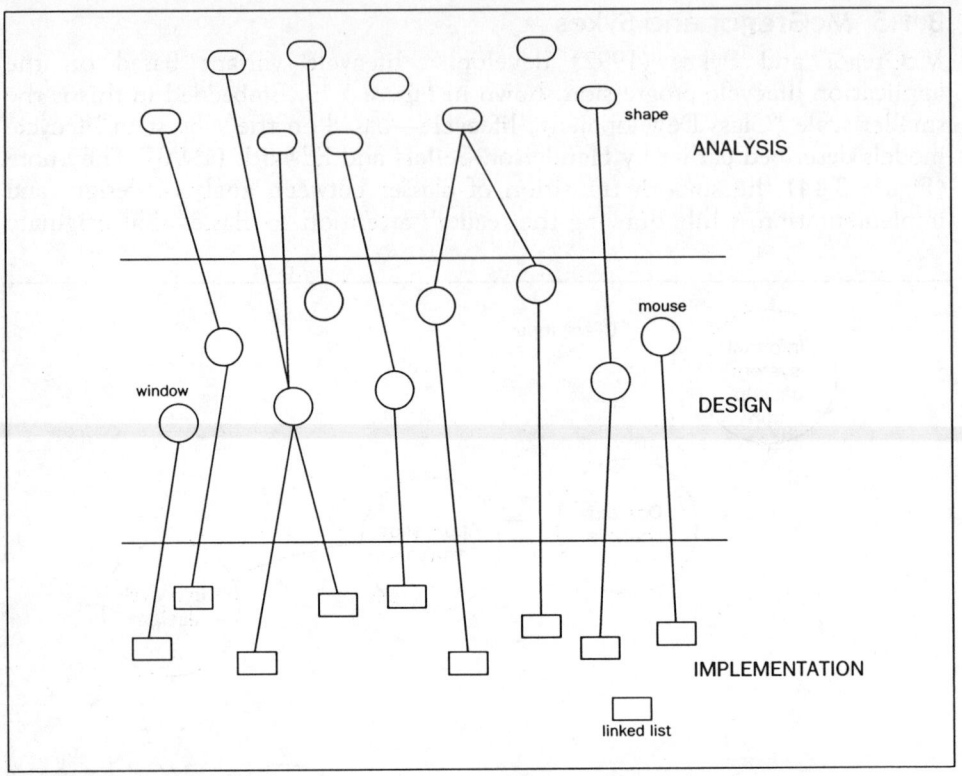

Figure 3.14 *Mapping of objects from phase to phase during system development (McGregor and Sykes, © 1992)*

in design (e.g., window, mouse), others that terminate in design, and yet others that participate in multiple mappings.

As noted in Section 3.1.2.1, McGregor and Sykes (1992) identify three *alternative* subsystem lifecycles (Figure 3.15) that require slightly different lifecycle phases. For newly identified classes, a full lifecycle is followed—this is the focus of most published methodologies (Section 3.3). However, reuse is a major advantage of using object technology, and McGregor and Sykes (1992) note that reuse brings in two possible modifications to the class/cluster SDLC: reuse "as is" of an existing class or reuse "with incremental modification." Their focus on the support for reuse is captured in Figure 3.16, in which the types of components at each stage that can be reused are shown in gray.

3.1.6 Summary

The need for iteration and recursion within the OO SDLC is reflected in current instantiations, especially the spiral (Boehm, 1986, 1988) and the fountain (Henderson-Sellers and Edwards, 1990, 1993a) lifecycles. Progression

Object-oriented Development

from analysis to design is initially sequential, i.e., the basic, underlying model of analysis, then of design and implementation, is still linear—one cannot implement before analyzing (Figure 3.6). Overlain on this basic structure, a methodology must be able to describe and incorporate "reverse flows," say from design to analysis. In object systems, this tends to occur at a finer granularity than the whole system. There are several terms to describe such finer granularity, including Meyer's (1988a) cluster model, subsystems (Wirfs-Brock *et al.*, 1990), ensembles (de Champeaux, 1991), and subassemblies (Firesmith, 1993).

The fountain lifecycle (Henderson-Sellers and Edwards, 1990, 1993a) may also

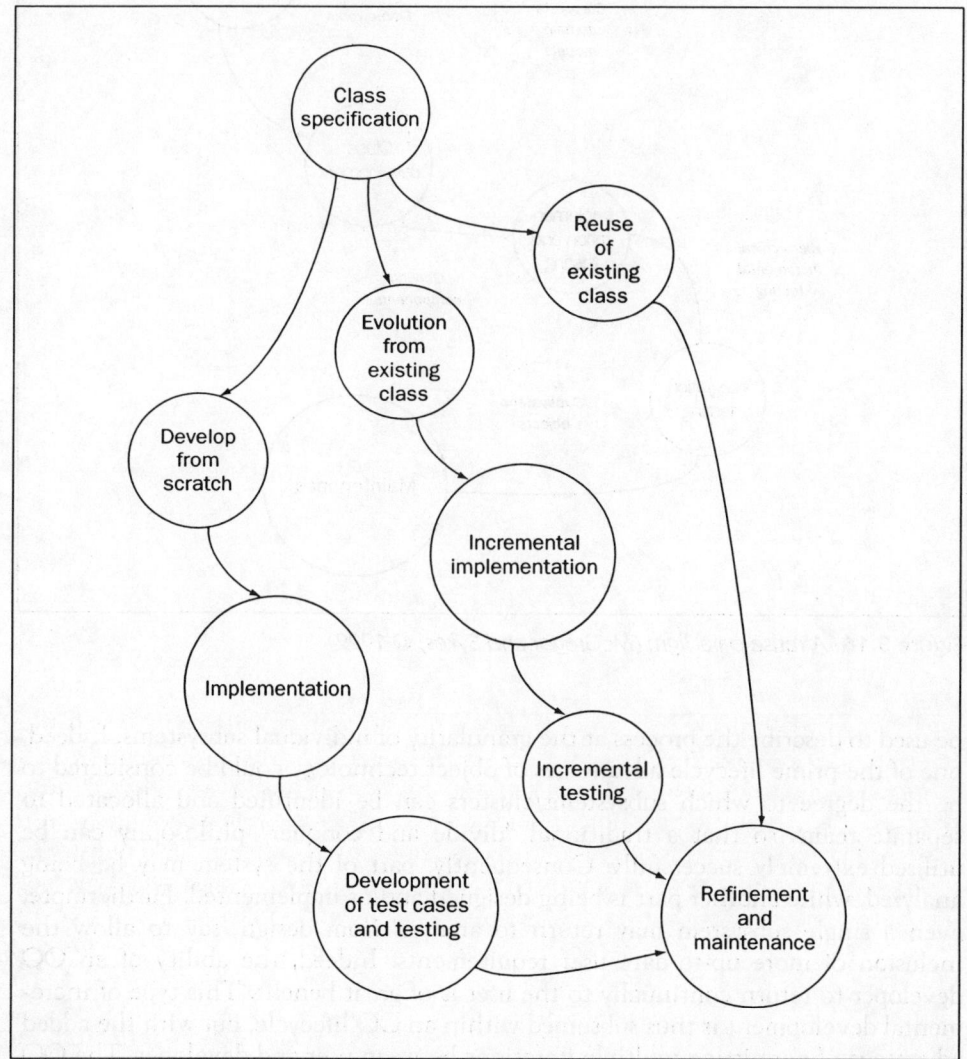

Figure 3.15 *Three optional class lifecycles (McGregor and Sykes, © 1992)*

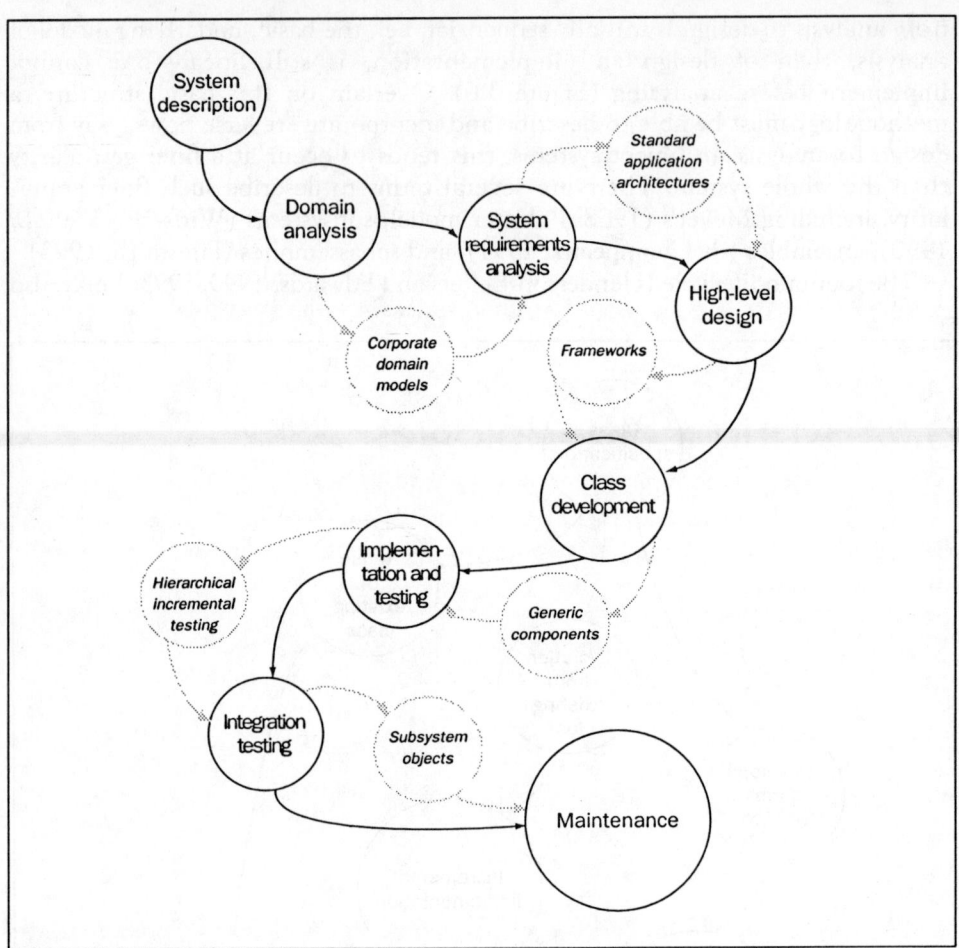

Figure 3.16 *A reuse paradigm (McGregor and Sykes, © 1992)*

be used to describe the process at the granularity of individual subsystems. Indeed, one of the prime lifecycle advantages of object technology could be considered to be the degree to which subsystems/clusters can be identified and allocated to separate teams so that a traditional "divide and conquer" philosophy can be utilized extremely successfully. Consequently, part of the system may be being analyzed, while another part is being designed and/or implemented. Furthermore, even a single subsystem may return to analysis from design, say to allow the inclusion of more up-to-date user requirements. Indeed, the ability of an OO developer to return continually to the user is of great benefit. This type of incremental development is thus subsumed within an OO lifecycle, but with the added advantage of permitting multiple iterations between user and developer. The OO SDLC is therefore an incremental development methodology rather than a traditional "throw away" prototyping approach, although the latter may be applicable in some situations. This incremental delivery approach removes the "big bang" approach to applications development.

In Chapter 4, we discuss the approach adopted by MOSES to OO development lifecycles in which systems development is divided into a product and a process lifecycle. The former represents the whole history of the product from initiation to decommissioning, while the latter is the actual phases and process of constructing and enhancing a product's functionality. The lifecycles discussed in this chapter are, to a large extent, applicable to the process lifecycle and can be interchanged as project schedules and organization requirements demand.

3.2 Hybrid methodologies

Although the ideal process for adopting object technology into *commercial* information systems development environments is to replace existing functional decomposition and procedural implementation tools and methodologies with their object-oriented equivalents (an O-O-O[14] approach), thus providing a "seamless" transition throughout the lifecycle (Henderson-Sellers and Edwards, 1990), it is recognized that many software developers will take a more pragmatic approach. In this they will *incrementally* adopt the emerging technology by deciding to "mix and match" object-oriented techniques with functional decomposition techniques to create a hybrid object-oriented/functional decomposition software systems development methodology (Henderson-Sellers, 1991b). This pragmatism may be a result of the large current investment in top-down functional decomposition, in terms of both expertise and front-end CASE tools (e.g., Ward, 1989). Secondly, even if the OO design methods are viewed as "more natural," the investment in code in, say, COBOL leads to the question, Can an object-oriented design (viewed as a better design) be implemented in a non-OO language? The two most likely paths (Figure 3.17) are to adopt object-oriented design and implementation while retaining functional specification and analysis (Booch, 1987; Alabiso, 1988) (the F-O-O[14] methodology—Henderson-Sellers, 1991b), or to retain implementation in a procedural language (for code compatibility) and precede this with object-oriented analysis and design (the O-O-F methodology) (Figure 3.18).

The F-O-O methodology

The rationale for the F-O-O methodology is that since much of the enthusiasm in object techniques was generated in the latter stages of the lifecycle with the advent of new object-oriented programming languages (OOPLs), software developers may have adopted the new paradigm at implementation and probably design stages. As these ideas start to percolate "upward" to the earlier

---

14. In each case, F = functional/procedural, O = object-oriented. The first letter refers to the analysis phase, the second to design and the last to implementation.

lifecycle phases (Loy, 1990), the question remains whether functional decomposition techniques will be retained or whether a fully object-oriented (O-O-O) methodology, using object-oriented analysis methods, such as that of Bailin (1989) or Coad and Yourdon (1990), will be developed. In the *transition period*, therefore, it is likely that structured techniques will continue to be used at the requirements specification and analysis stage and that techniques for "translating" these analyses into object designs will be sought.

Nevertheless, proceeding from a structured analysis to an object-oriented

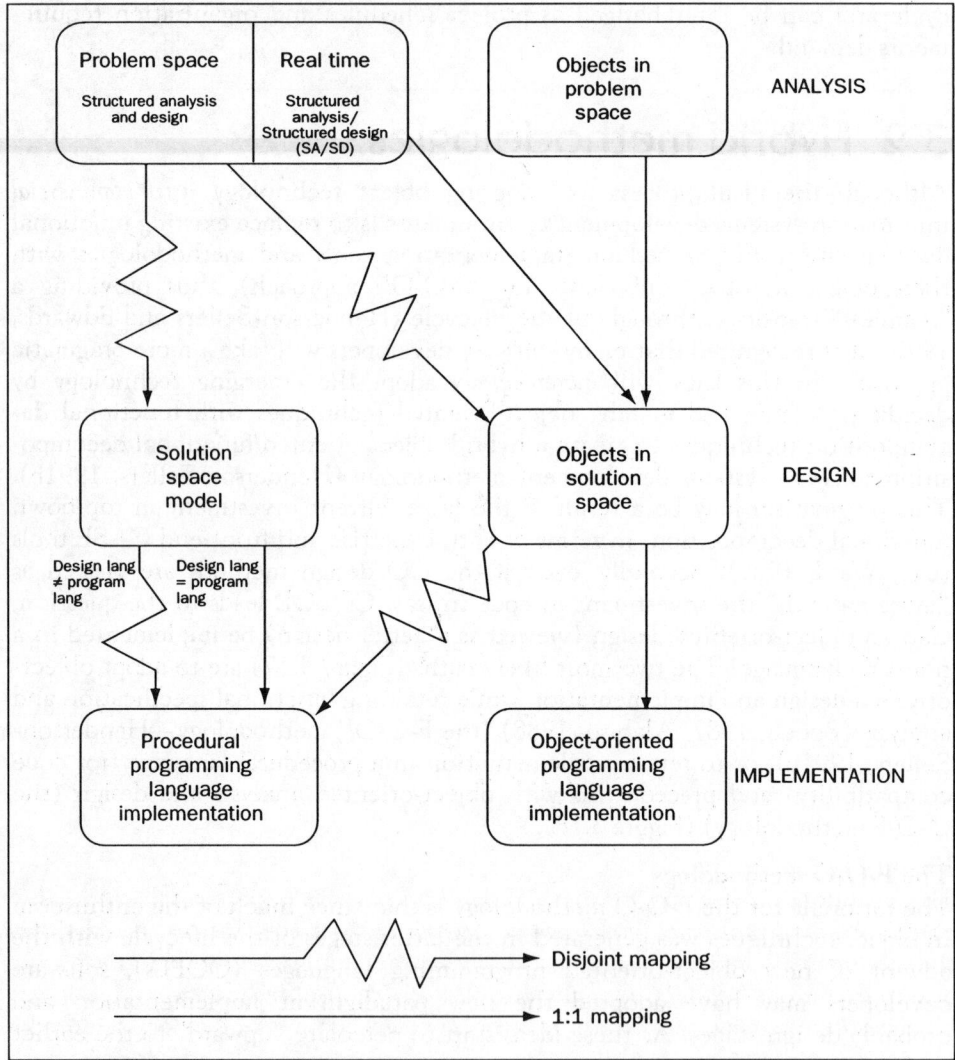

Figure 3.17 *The possible paths between the traditional and the OO SDLCs (Henderson-Sellers and Edwards, 1990)*

Object-oriented Development

Hybrid Approaches		
O-O-F	O-O-O	F-O-O
1. Object-oriented systems requirement specification		Functional systems requirement specification
2.	Identify objects	Draw DFDs
3.	Establish interactions	Semantic data modeling
4.	Lower-level, detailed design	Transform to lower-level detailed design
5. Use of libraries and simulation of inheritance	Bottom-up use of library classes	
6. Revision to transform into a design compatible with procedural code	Add inheritance hierarchies	
7. Code using procedural models	Aggregation/generalization	

Figure 3.18 *Summary table of seven-step methodological frameworks for O-O-F, O-O-O, and F-O-O approaches (Henderson-Sellers, 1990)*

design can be awkward (Bailin, 1989; Coad and Yourdon, 1990) since different aggregation principles are involved in a functional-oriented, as compared with an object-oriented, analysis. This is illustrated in Figure 3.18 by the wavy arrow from functional analysis to object-oriented design. In this diagram one-to-one ("seamless") mappings are indicated by straight arrows and disjoint mappings by wavy arrows. Each transition indicated by a wavy arrow in Figure 3.17 thus requires the development of a technique to "translate" between the functional and object worldviews. Techniques for this translation are discussed by, e.g., Seidewitz and Stark (1987) and Alabiso (1988).

The O-O-F methodology

The rationale for the O-O-F methodology is that the novel ideas behind the object-oriented philosophy that permit the use of the same "model" throughout the systems development lifecycle will be implemented to provide an object-oriented analysis (OOA), merging into an object-oriented design (OOD). As has been stressed by many authors (Mullin, 1989), the term "object-oriented" relates to this modeling philosophy; and it is essentially coincidental that, today, new languages structured on the same paradigm are available to complete the software development lifecycle *entirely* within the object-oriented paradigm.

Nonetheless, with current large investments in procedural code and coding tools, especially the investment in COBOL in the commercial environment and Ada in the Defense environment, organizations may well be reticent about replacing their language environment with one of the new OOPLs. A further concern is the nonstandard and evolving nature of these new programming environments.

Pragmatically, however, it should be recognized that the organization policy may be to implement in a 3GL, such as COBOL, or in a 4GL. Millikin (1989) recommends that even in this cultural environment, object-oriented analysis and design techniques still provide a valuable precursor to implementation in a traditional language environment. The ease or difficulty of doing this implementation will, of course, be determined not only by the success of the OOA and OOD steps in producing a good detailed design but also by the extent to which such design features are supported by the chosen language. Procedural languages traditionally support only procedural abstraction directly, so that data abstraction and encapsulation, while feasible, are the full responsibility of the programmer (an approach that has often been realized successfully within a non-object-oriented development environment). Conversion to procedural code may require a reevaluation of the total set of objects identified in the design phase, and perhaps a regrouping of the objects and the addition of more procedural detail so that object-oriented concepts can be simulated within the target procedural language. However, Henderson-Sellers and Constantine (1991) suggest that robust object-oriented designs can survive virtually intact when mapped into languages as diverse as Smalltalk and COBOL. The O-O-F methodology is certainly one that has been adopted by some organizations (Coad and Yourdon, 1990, p173).

Summary
The two hybrid approaches that have been described have been labeled the F-O-O and the O-O-F approach: the three letters emphasizing the lifecycle stages at which either object-oriented (O) or functional (F) approaches are being utilized. MIS departments are certainly utilizing such hybrid approaches, sometimes seen as one step toward a full adoption of object technology, and sometimes as a pragmatic approach in which it is realized that full adoption is unlikely in the near future because of current investments in structured CASE tools (either analysis/design or for code generation). Since it is evident (from discussions with practitioners) that the hybrid methodologies being used are essentially *ad hoc*, the summary in this section provides a methodological framework for each of the O-O-F and F-O-O lifecycles that can be used by software developers and with which the best gains can be made from these types of approach. In addition, convergent methodologies, using parts of object-oriented techniques and parts of structured techniques within the same lifecycle stage, may be useful, if care is exercised, in some circumstances (Henderson-Sellers and Constantine, 1991).

Finally, we should stress that the discussion in this section is included from a pragmatic point of view only. *We do not recommend* either O-O-F or F-O-O in preference to O-O-O. Rather, we acknowledge the practical and political difficulties present in some commercial MIS departments that might otherwise prevent *any* serious consideration from being given to the adoption of object technology (see also discussion on migration paths in Section 9.2.1).

3.3 Object-oriented methodologies and notations

Methodologies are a combination of concepts, guidelines, steps, and formalisms in the context of an underlying process description. They may also include graphical and textual notations, documentation standards, and deliverables. They should certainly be able to be closely linked to project management concerns, including metrics. This is an extension of the definition of Monarchi and Puhr (1992), who described methodologies essentially as an integrative combination of tools and techniques. Here we complement this by superimposing the ideas of software process engineering (Madhavji, 1991) and project management. In other words, methodologies should be seen essentially as dynamic descriptors of software development. In addition they need to support specific techniques (which might also include notations).

Although size is an important driving force in the application of methodologies (e.g., Berard, 1992b, Chapter 4), it is not the only one. Complexity of applications is increasing, requiring a rigorous approach to problem solving. Complexity may be correlated with size, but there is not necessarily a causal relationship. Thus what may be considered small, but complex, systems can gain from the application of a rigorous methodology. These types of systems are found particularly in research environments or more unstructured decision environments.

Methodologies are aimed at providing the user with a means of developing "better" systems than if they were not used, although management support is also needed. "Better" here usually means one or more of the following attributes: more complete, correct, robust, economical, maintainable, and understandable (Meyer, 1988a). If this were not the case, there would be no need for methodologies; it would simply be sufficient to learn a programming language and code the required system. Large systems require a team of people to decompose, design, and implement the system. Thus effective communication between different groups, possibly separated in time and space, concerning the details of a problem and the system solution is essential. By following a standard approach to design, documentation, and communication, risks of a possible mismatch between different groups in system development are reduced.

A methodology, therefore, as well as producing "better" software engineered systems, should enable people to communicate more effectively about a problem and its solution. It should support people in thinking more incisively about the nature of the problem and solution, hopefully leading to "better" solutions, and it should aid in the documentation of a solution. Methodologies are not a recipe to be followed blindly, but need to be understood and combined with a good deal of experience on behalf of the user before they will yield their promised benefits. Indeed, poor or nonexistent training in the methodology or the use of the wrong methodology or a poorly defined one may make any use of the chosen methodology ill advised (Berard, 1992b, Chapter 4).

Commercial adoption of the object-oriented paradigm for software development has been hindered by the lack of validated development methodologies (Dock, 1992b). Although a number of analysis and design approaches appropriate for specific aspects of object-oriented software engineering have been developed over the last few years, few have been widely tested outside a research environment (although this is rapidly occurring) and little evaluation has been made of their strengths and weaknesses. What little has been presented has been focused on direct comparison, at the technique level rather than the methodology level, of specific OOA/D methods (Edwards, 1992; Berard, 1992a; Walker, 1992). For example, de Champeaux and Faure (1992) tabulated 13 OOA methodologies/methods under 14 characteristics. They noted firstly that, of the 13, three did not support inheritance and could therefore not be described as object-oriented, but rather as object-based. Of the remaining ten OOA methods, for example, three did not support aggregation, four did not address parallelism, and only one offered the support of an integrated tool set (for more details see de Champeaux and Faure, 1992).

Similarly, Arnold *et al.* (1991) list a number of design methods and their characteristics in their tabulated comparison of five methodologies: Booch, Rumbaugh *et al.*, and Wirfs-Brock *et al.*, supplemented by HOOD and Buhr. Their conclusions were similar in that the last two do not support inheritance, thus disqualifying them from being considered fully object-oriented. Of the remaining three, Booch and Rumbaugh *et al.* supported metaclasses, while Booch supported generic classes and packages (the Ada influence). With respect to communication, several differences were listed. Booch and Wirfs-Brock *et al.* support synchronous communication, while Booch and Rumbaugh *et al.* support asynchronous communication. Notations used to describe the logical and physical model are also very different. These differences are summarized by Arnold *et al.* and reproduced here for the three OO methodologies as Table 3.4. With respect to accompanying notation, Arnold *et al.* (1991) comment that all notations are informal, expressive, and tend to be verbose (especially that of Booch). All three OO notations were found to be well documented, but tend to rely on informal examples to explain their semantics. Lifecycle coverage varies: Booch was considered not to address analysis and responsibility-driven design (RDD) (Wirfs-Brock *et al.*, 1990) not to address implementation issues. Arnold *et al.* (1991) concluded that all three methods were workable but not without flaws and deficiencies, highlighting particularly lack of support for the dynamic modeling aspects.

Table 3.4 *Comparison of three object-oriented methodologies (Compiled after Arnold et al., 1991)*

	Booch	Rumbaugh et al.	Wirfs-Brock et al.
Objects and classes			
Package	Y		
Class	Y	Y	Y
Generic	Y		
Metaclass	Y	Y	
Visibility			
Aggregation	Y	Y	
Global scope	Y	Y	Y
Restricted scope:			
Static	Y		
Dynamic	Y		
Inheritance			
Single inheritance	Y	Y	Y
Multiple inheritance	Y	Y	Y
Subtype	Y	Y	Y
Unrestricted inheritance	Y		
Abstract class	Y	Y	Y
Lifetimes			
Creation	Y	Y	
Destruction	Y	Y	
Persistence	Y		
Concurrency			
Passive	Y	Y	Y
Active	Y	Y	
Internally concurrent		Y	
Mutual exclusion		Y	
Communication			
Synchronous	Y		Y
Asynchronous	Y	Y	
Event	Y	Y	
Procedure	Y	Y	
Rendezvous		Y	
Mutual messaging		Y	
Notation			
Expressivity	Y	Y	Y
Syntax	Y	Y	Y
Semantics	Y	Y	Y
Reasoning and transformation		Y	
Partitioning	Y	Y	Y
Scoping	Y		

Another discriminator often used to characterize methodologies is whether their prime focus is (i) data-driven, (ii) responsibility-driven, (iii) event-driven, or (iv) process-driven (e.g., Sharble and Cohen, 1993). Data-driven approaches are extensions of data modeling and/or information modeling; a responsibility-driven approach is a "pure" OO approach focusing on contracts, services, collaborations, and responsibilities that synergistically help to carry out the overall purpose of the system. Event-driven methodologies are based on states of objects and the events that trigger changes in these states; process-driven methodologies begin by focusing on the functional aspects of objects.

In a comparison of notations, Barrett and Simsion (1992) highlight issues of particular relevance to practitioners. They present comparison tables for a number of concerns raised regarding the practical application of notations, including expressive power and communication, degree of detail and number of symbols to be learned, management of complexity, and ease of use. They conclude that "no one method is clearly 'better' than the others" at present.

De Champeaux and Faure (1992) note that the greatest diversity among existing specific methodologies is seen in their description of the dynamic dimension. Notions such as "transition," "event," "triggers," and "timing" can all be used to discriminate between specific methodological instantiations. Of complementary, and also crucial, importance is how the static nature and dynamic nature of classes are integrated, and rules are needed for checking consistency between these different views (Arnold *et al.*, 1992). This is of especial importance in light of the observations that several current, established methodologies (e.g., Rumbaugh *et al.*'s (1991) OMT) fail to do a convincing job on this integration (Monarchi and Puhr, 1992).

As noted above, the real world is inherently parallel or concurrent and thus analytical techniques must support concurrency (de Champeaux and Faure, 1992; Arnold *et al.*, 1992). Support for concurrency, especially in analysis, is thus seen by many as a necessary part of a methodology. In addition, techniques to transform this to a sequential design (for single CPU hardware) must also be incorporated. As well as concurrency, some methodologies are oriented toward real-time software.

The first attempt to generalize beyond such method-by-method comparison (an observational or descriptive approach) and to conceptualize about the *necessary requirements* for a methodology (prescriptive or normative approach) was undertaken by Monarchi and Puhr (1992), in which they derived some general principles by analysis of existing techniques, representations, and methodologies. They identified critical components of an OO development methodology against which 23 methodologies, notations, and techniques were evaluated. From this they summarized current strengths and weaknesses in OOA/D methodologies. In their comparison of six analysis and design methodologies, Hong *et al.* (1992) develop a "meta-model" that is really the conceptual model of the methodology expressed as a "smallest common denominator" or "supermethodology" of the six methodologies evaluated.

In the next sections, we describe some of the most frequently cited and frequently used methodologies and notations for which adequate documentation exists. Unfortunately, it is not possible to be complete and we apologize if we have inadvertently omitted any particular methodologies or notations. We have focused on those that we feel have either influenced (for better or worse) commercial information systems developments or are likely to do so in the near future. Their associated CASE tools (when applicable) are also discussed briefly.

3.3.1 Rumbaugh et al. (OMT)

The Object Modeling Technique (OMT) of Rumbaugh et al. (1991) consists of a full lifecycle methodology woven around three complementary models that act as three relatively independent views on an object-oriented system. These three parts are:

1. object model
2. dynamic model
3. functional model

The methodology is well thought out and consistent. It is based on an extended entity relationship model with dynamic modeling capability. However, it has an acknowledged weakness in terms of its poor consistency checking mechanisms and integration between these three models (Shelton, 1991). Rumbaugh et al.'s original text was unclear about the relative weights of these models and how they related to each other. In fact, the object model is the most important, with the dynamic and functional models being less significant until much later in the lifecycle (Eddy, pers. com., 1991; Rumbaugh and Blaha, 1991). Indeed, the use of DFDs has been criticized by Hayes and Coleman (1991) as being inappropriate, causing a poor integration of the dynamic and static aspects of the object model (Huneke, 1991). Hayes and Coleman (1991) eliminate DFDs, replacing them by specifications of pre- and postconditions over the class structure model. They also replace Rumbaugh et al.'s dynamic model by objectcharts (Section 7.10).

The object model is fully supported in this approach (de Champeaux, 1991) and a number of more advanced features are included from the world of semantic data modeling. The model also supports concurrency in the definition of class behavior. The notation supporting the models is concise and clear and reflects traditional information modeling notations (see below). The methodology provides limited support for large-scale concepts and models, such as subsystems and the categories of Booch, although modules and sheets are discussed. This may be an important weakness for large or complex models. Also, documentation of the model seems to rely entirely on the diagrams.

The underlying process is probably the best defined for all the published methodologies. It provides step-by-step activities and guidelines in the development and implementation of an object-oriented model. In this process, the authors explicitly separate analysis and design as distinct phases of development. The methodology concentrates on the analysis model (see also Rumbaugh, 1992b) but does provide a discussion for a number of design mappings to different implementations. The method is fairly rigorous and may not be appropriate for smaller-scale exploratory developments if followed exactly, as the analysis and design phases seem to imply a sequential development of the model. Also, the work does not really consider reuse to any great degree (Huneke, 1991) either in the development of reusable components or in the use of components.

Overall, the approach is fairly complete with an emphasis on the OOA model and high-level OOD architecture of systems. It supports a concise model and notation and a well-defined process. Weaknesses are identifiable particularly in reuse, in concepts for managing large-scale complex models, and in the flexibility of the process.

The steps of Rumbaugh *et al.*'s (1991) methodology are as follows:

Analysis Phase
1. Develop a natural language description of the problem.
2. Build an object model together with a data dictionary of classes, relationships, and attributes.
3. Build a dynamic model together with diagrams showing examples of how events flow through the system in response to system operations.
4. Build a functional model together with any constraints that may apply between objects.
5. Iterate through the steps, looking for missing classes, relationships, attributes, events, etc.

Each of these five stages is then further elaborated. In building the object-oriented model it is necessary to identify classes, add associations and attributes, use inheritance to simplify classes, and use scenarios to test access paths. The result is an object-oriented model documented by a class model diagram and a data dictionary.

In developing the dynamic model (stage 3), events and event traces are identified and an event flow diagram is drawn. Each class that has a dynamic component requires a state diagram and, finally, consistency checks are undertaken. The documentation is a set of state diagrams and a global event flow diagram.

In the functional model, standard data flow diagraming techniques are advocated. Inputs and outputs are identified. Constraints and processes are described and added to the diagram, creating a set of DFDs showing any constraints.

In the final analysis stage, key operations discovered during preparation of the functional model may need to be added to the object model. Consistency checking is undertaken between the three models in an iterative fashion.

System Design Phase
1. Identify subsystems.
2. Identify concurrency.
3. Allocate subsystems to processors and tasks.
4. Choose strategy for implementing data stores (e.g., files, databases).
5. Identify global resources and access controls.
6. Choose implementation strategy (e.g., concurrency, state machines).
7. Consider boundary conditions.
8. Establish trade-offs necessary.

The resulting documentation (the "system design document") describes the overall architecture of the system before the next stage, that of object design.

Object Design Phase
This is the detailed design phase, which retains language independence while providing a design that is readily implementable. The eight stages are:

1. Extract operations for object model from other models, using processes in functional model and events in dynamic model.
2. Design algorithmic detail of operations, selecting data structure, defining private services needed, and assigning responsibilities not previously delineated.
3. Optimize access paths to data, if necessary adding redundant associations to maximum access efficiency (convenience and costs).
4. Implement software control by adding detail to system design.
5. Optimize use of inheritance, which often requires rearrangement of classes in various hierarchies, creating new classes by generalization. In other cases, delegation may be used to replace semantically invalid inheritance relationships.
6. Design implementation details for associations, implementing each as a distinct object or as class attributes.
7. Determine exact representation of attributes.
8. Package classes and associations into modules.

The products of this phase are a detailed and integrated class model specifying the behavior and structure of the classes of the application in a form appropriate for final implementation/coding.

The OMT notation for the object model is based on earlier work by Loomis et al. (1987) and Rumbaugh (1987) and is a considered extension of entity relationship modeling. The basic icon is a rectangle divided into three areas: name, attributes, and operations. It remains the same for analysis and design. Relationships, which are considered a separate concept in OMT, are lines with graphical cardinalities and labels to indicate the name of the relationship. In addition, associations may be "qualified" and/or have role labels. Links between objects (a link being an instance of an association) and link attributes are also used, as are discriminators on superclass/subclass relationships. Inheritance is indicated by a triangle at the junction of the two lines (Figure 3.19).

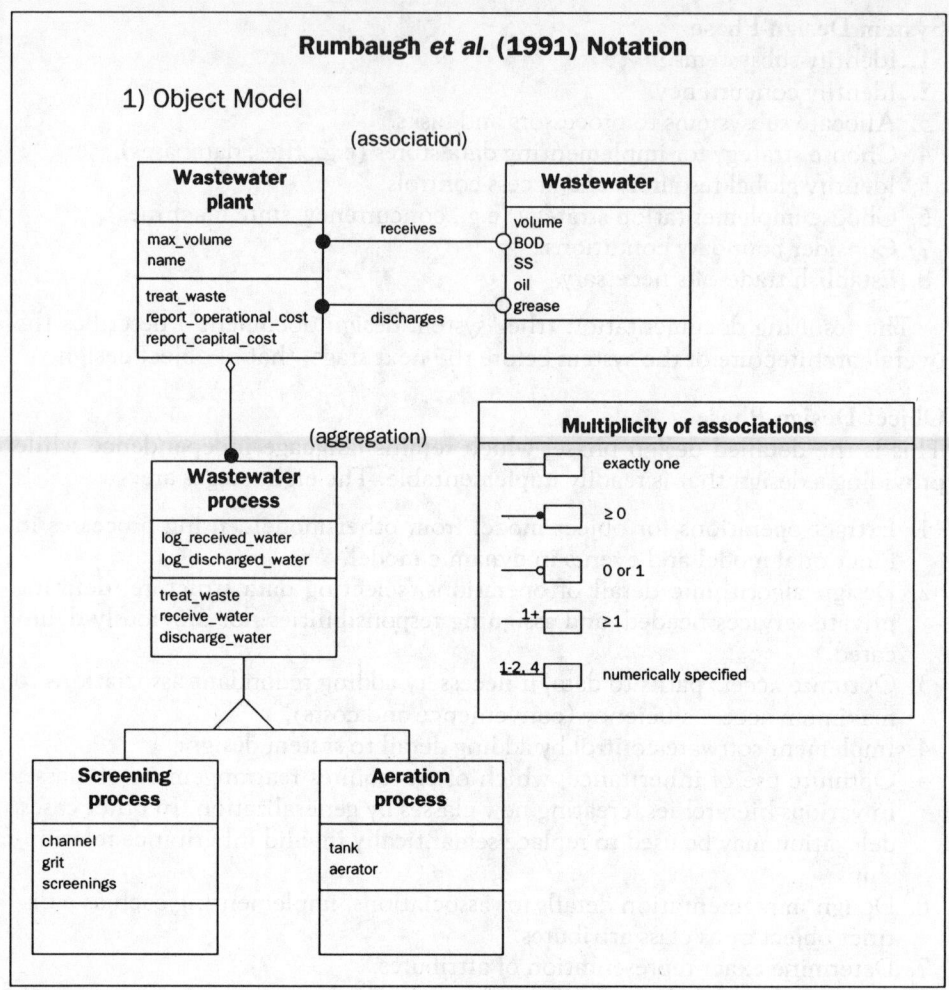

Figure 3.19 *Example of OMT notation*

OMT notation for the dynamic model depicts states as ellipses with arrowed and labeled lines indicating the direction of the transition between the states. Initial states are shown as small black dots and final states by small black dots encased in larger white dots (Figure 3.20).

OMT notation for the functional model is reasonably standard except that splitting of data flows is permitted—something not allowed in structured DFDs. Processes are indicated by bubbles and data flow by solid lines (Figure 3.21). Control flows are also allowed, being represented as dotted lines. Data stores are two parallel lines.

An application of the analysis notation is given in Rumbaugh (1992b), in which the "OOPSLA Conference Registration Problem" is discussed in detail,

Object-oriented Development

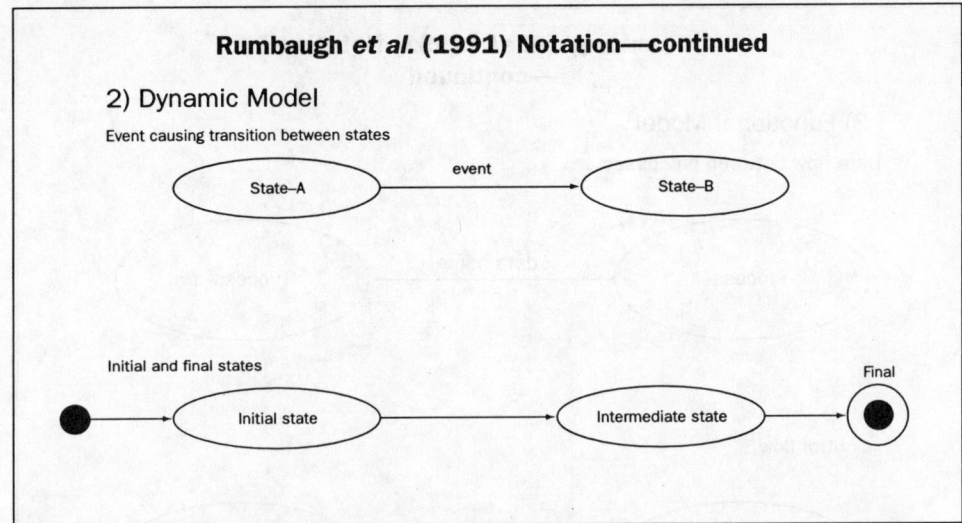

Figure 3.20 *Rumbaugh* et al.*'s notation for their dynamic model (Rumbaugh et al., 1991)*

with results from various iterations being illustrated. It provides illuminating insights into the analysis and notational aspects of OMT.

The methodology and notation are supported by the CASE tools, OMTool, ObjectMaker, Paradigm Plus and Software through Pictures (see Section 9.1.5). These tools provide good browsers, a significant amount of consistency checking and configuration options; for example, duplicate names are trapped (unlike with many other CASE tools). Dragging connections around an outline does drag anchor points, although it is still possible to convolute the path itself. Code generation to C++ and DSM (Shah *et al.*, 1989) is possible in some tools, and diagram output is available for Postscript, Interleaf, and Framemaker. OMTool can also be used to generate relational database schemata.

3.3.2 Booch

One of the earliest writers in the field of OO methodologies was Booch (1987), originally focusing on the Ada environment. Booch's (1987) OO methodology can be described as follows:

1. Identify objects and attributes.
2. Identify operations/functionality *after* the data/objects.
3. Establish the visibility/interfaces.
4. Establish that interface more closely.
5. Implement.

In the first edition of *Software Engineering with Ada*, he suggests that object identification can be done by underlining the nouns, an idea first proposed by

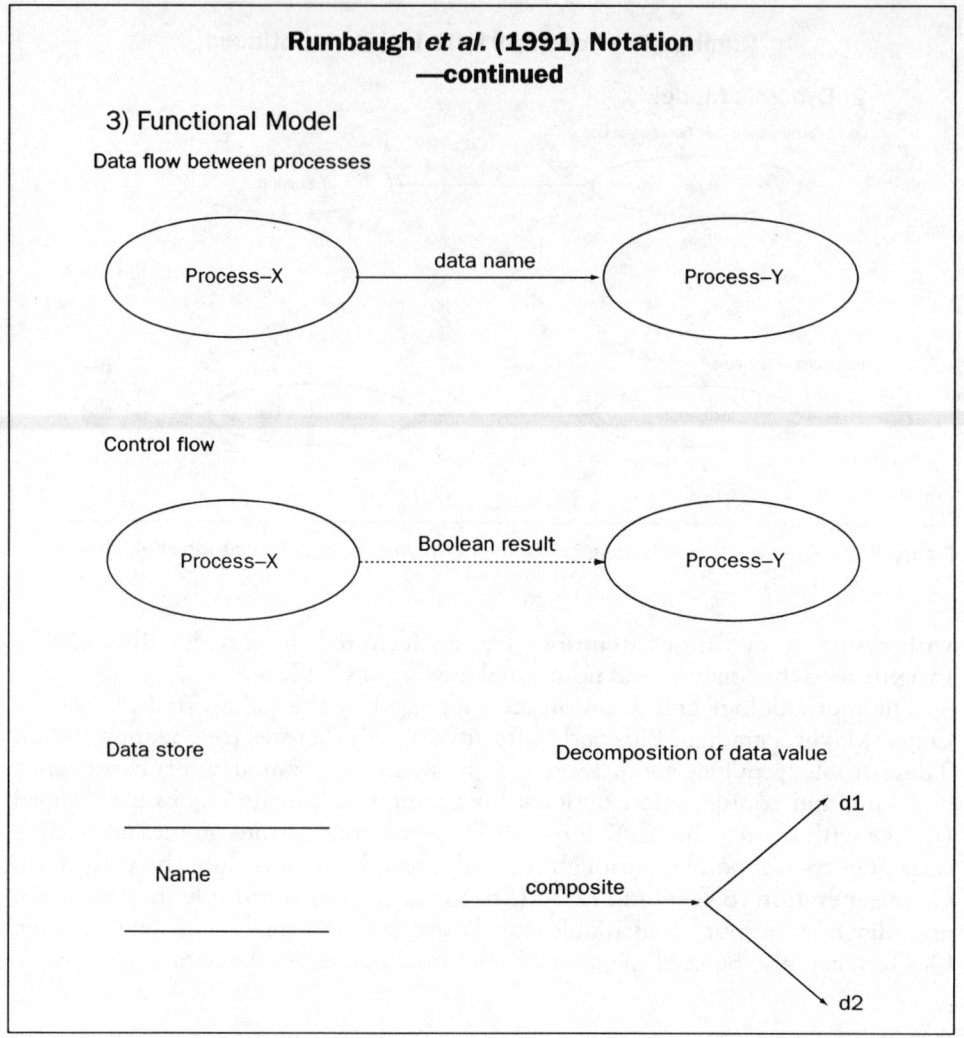

Figure 3.21 *Rumbaugh* et al.*'s notation for their functional model (Rumbaugh et al., 1991)*

Abbott (1983). This is now seen as oversimplistic, being unlikely to scale well beyond the trivial, although still providing a useful "first cut." There are also problems implicit in the modern (bad) habit of turning nouns into verbs and verbs into nouns indiscriminately and to excess (cf. Booch, 1991, p143 *et seq.*). There are unlikely ever to be clear methodologies on object identification, but many guidelines and techniques do currently exist.

Booch divides the interface into three parts: public, protected, and private. Only the public interface is visible, generally, while the protected interface is visible only to subclasses.

Booch's earlier work tended to concentrate more on design rather than the full lifecycle. Even in his 1991 book, the title suggests that analysis is disregarded, although many point out the applicability of Booch's method to analysis as well as design. Indeed, in the recent (mid-1992) release of the supporting CASE tool, ROSE, both analysis and design are indeed supported, although not differentiated. Analysis and design are seen as nothing more than two views ("what" versus "how" or "discovery" versus "invention").

Booch's (1992) current methodology, modified a little since the publication of his book (Booch, 1991), is known as a "round-trip gestalt design," which is essentially another version of a spiral development model (perhaps reminiscent a little of Berard's "analyze a little, design a little, implement a little, and test a little"; see below).

Booch's four recommended steps are:

1. Identify the classes and objects at a given level of abstraction.
2. Identify the semantics of these classes and objects.
3. Identify the relationships among these classes and objects (perhaps using CRC cards).
4. Implement these classes and objects.

The process of the methodology, however, is not well defined, and there is little breakdown of phases or activities. The process is aimed at an iterative and exploratory type of development and lifecycle models, activities, and project plans are not really discussed, although a large number of useful heuristics and guidelines are provided.

The object model supported by Booch is comprehensive and fully object-oriented, and includes advanced communication protocols for modeling concurrency. The methodology also supports a large number of other concepts and models for physical design, such as packages, and for large-scale systems development, such as categories and subsystems.

The notational description applied in the method is rich, especially in relation to real time and concurrency (perhaps influenced by Booch's early work on Ada), where it is matched only by Firesmith (1993), who himself has taken Booch's ideas as a starting point.

Figure 3.22 shows the basic iconic notation and Figure 3.23 some of the relationships and cardinality labels. These icons are used in three basic notational constructs—class diagrams, object diagrams, and state transition diagrams—with other icons being used in the module diagrams and process diagrams, the first three diagram types representing the logical structure and the last two the physical structure. Each diagram is supplemented by a specification (Booch, 1992) that gives greater detail. The icon for a class is a "blob" (also called a "cloud"), which can be substituted by an ellipse (Booch, 1992). Class utilities represent freely standing function subprograms.

Class relationships are association, has, using, inheritance, instantiation, and metaclass (Figure 3.23); cardinalities are indicated numerically; and the

Booch (1991) Class Notation
Class
Name

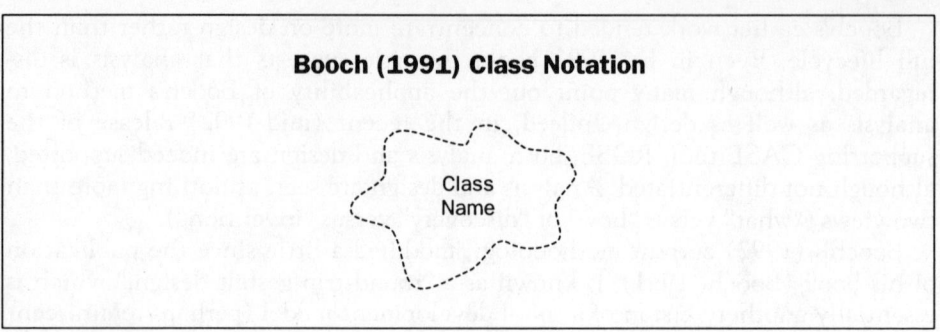

Figure 3.22 *Booch's notation for classes (Booch, 1991)*

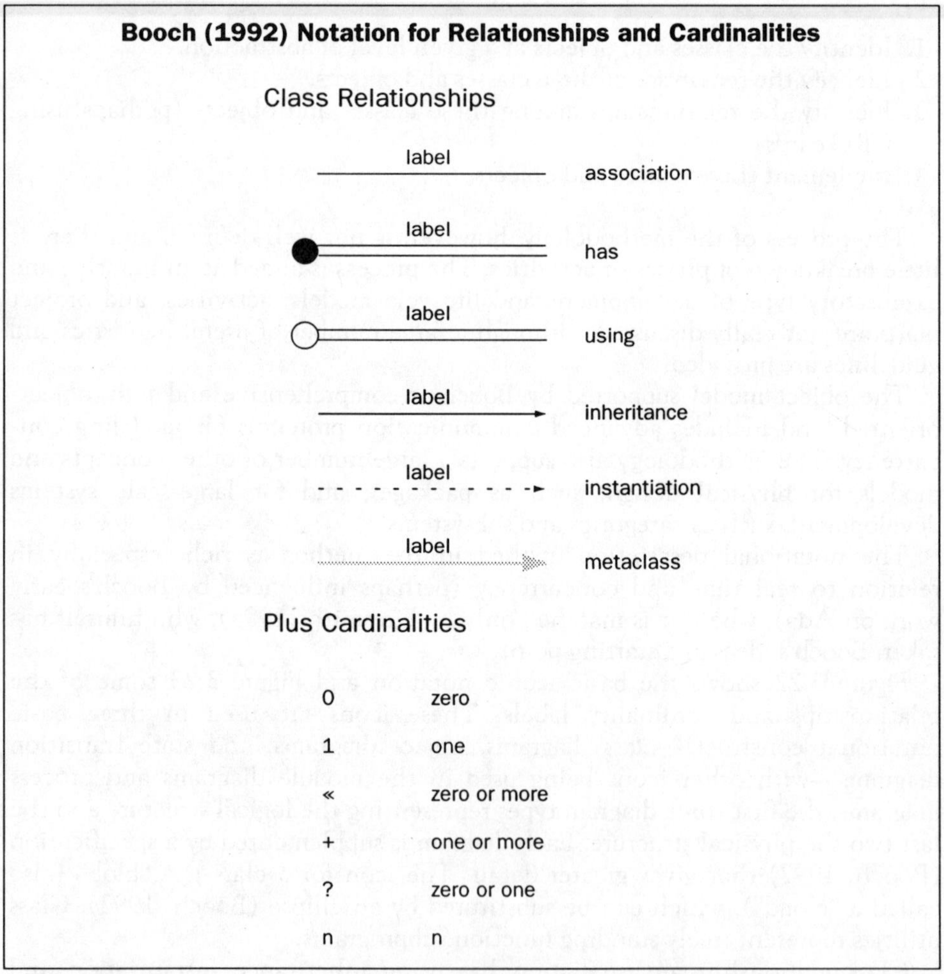

Booch (1992) Notation for Relationships and Cardinalities
Class Relationships
label
association
label
has
label
using
label
inheritance
label
instantiation
label
metaclass
Plus Cardinalities
0
zero
1
one
«
zero or more
+
one or more
?
zero or one
n
n

Figure 3.23 *Booch's notation for class relationships (Booch, 1992)*

relationships may be labeled with text. Various types of inheritance (relevant mostly to the C++ language implementations) are given in Figure 3.24. Other adornments indicate friend, virtual, and static functions.

For large systems, class categories offer a higher abstraction level of grouping. The icon for a class category is a plain rectangle.

Object diagrams document instances of classes and must be semantically consistent with the class diagram. Class diagrams and state diagrams capture the logical semantics, while object diagrams illustrate the runtime structure and behavior of the model (Booch, 1992). Object diagrams are used to capture particular method calls and their ordering is known as a scenario diagram. The icon for an object is similar to that for a class except that it has a solid outline to indicate a concrete instance. Class–class relationships are indicated by solid lines for message interactions and by labeled dotted (gray) lines for communication to and from entities outside the software system. Connecting lines can also be arrowed to indicate the direction of the message pass. A variety of arrow types can be used to indicate concurrency concerns such as balking, time-out, synchroneity, and asynchroneity. Extensive options are available as adornments to indicate object visibility.

State transition diagrams, adapted from Harel (1987), and timing diagrams are used to describe the system dynamics.

Module diagrams are used to allocate classes and objects to modules in the physical model of a system. These are most useful in languages that do not support the concept of a class directly but may support a module (e.g., Ada packages, Modula2), and the notation used (Figure 3.25) is that originally devised for object-based design in Ada (Booch, 1986). Clusters of logically related modules are grouped into subsystems (the icon is a rounded and shadowed rectangle).

Overall, the Booch method is generally recognized as one of the more complete OO design methods available, being thorough and well integrated for

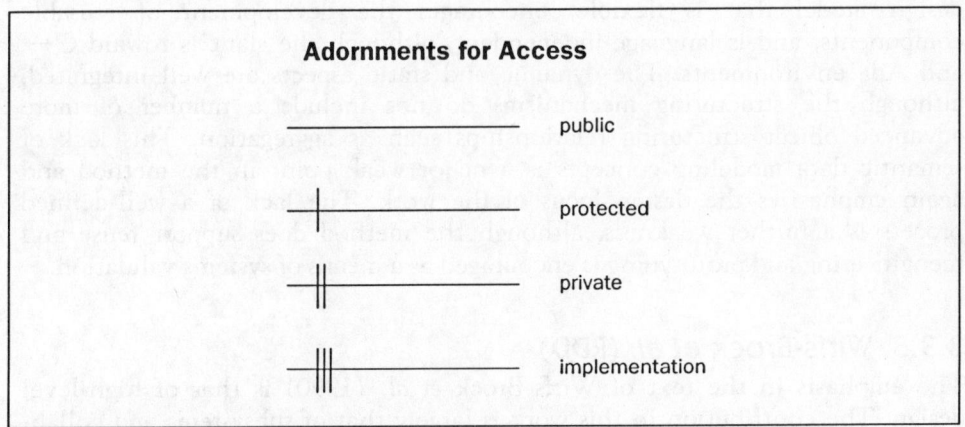

Figure 3.24 *Booch's notation for access (Booch, 1992)*

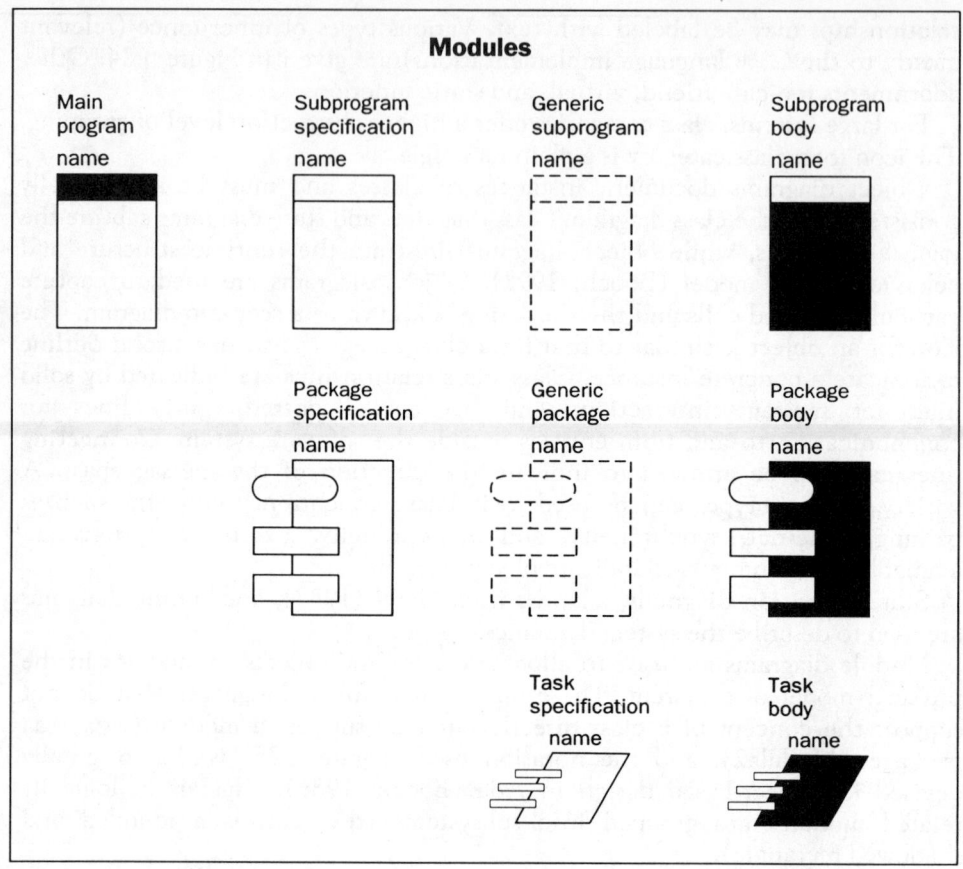

Figure 3.25 Booch's notation for modules (Booch, 1992)

development of large complex systems. The methodology supports a strong design model that is flexible, encourages the development of reusable components, and is language-independent, although the slant is toward C++ and Ada environments. The dynamic and static aspects are well integrated, although the structuring mechanisms do not include a number of more advanced object structuring relationships such as aggregation. This lack of semantic data modeling concepts is a major weak point in the method and again emphasizes the design focus of the work. The lack of a well-defined process is a further weakness, although the method does support reuse and reengineering and prototyping is encouraged as a means of systems validation.

3.3.3 Wirfs-Brock et al. (RDD)

The emphasis in the text of Wirfs-Brock et al. (1990) is that of high-level design. The contribution in this work is largely that of subsystems and collaborations, and the authors use three techniques of modeling: responsibility-

Object-oriented Development

driven design (RDD), client–server, and contracting. In support, they recommend the use (in the appropriate context) of CRC cards, Venn diagrams, subsystem notation, graphs, and contract specifications. Their major steps are:

1. Identify classes.
2. Identify responsibilities.
3. Identify collaborations.
4. Refine design in terms of hierarchies and subsystems.
5. Construct protocols.

In "responsibility-driven" design (Wirfs-Brock and Wilkerson, 1989b; Wirfs-Brock et al., 1990) the behavior, as opposed to the structure, of objects is emphasized. Object structure is a relatively minor part of the approach. The object model is fully object-oriented (de Champeaux, 1991), supporting multiple inheritance and subtyping. The approach does not mention concurrency issues or more detailed semantic modeling issues.

Their methodological process has two identifiable phases (Wirfs-Brock et al., 1990, pp235–238): the exploratory phase and the analysis phase. The steps of the exploratory phase are summarized as:

1. Read and understand specification.
2. Explore several scenarios using the following steps, recording results on design cards.

Classes
3. Construct list of noun phrases from specification.
4. Look for "hidden" nouns.
5. Identify candidate classes from these noun phrases.
6. Identify candidate abstract superclasses.
7. Use categories to identify missing classes.
8. Write short description of purpose of each class.

Responsibilities
9. Identify responsibilities.
10. Assign responsibilities to appropriate classes.
11. Find additional responsibilities arising from relationships.

Collaborations
12. Identify collaborations based on responsibilities.
13. Identify additional collaborations arising from relationships.
14. Discard classes if they do not participate in any collaborations.

The second of the two phases, the analysis phase, is described by the following 12 steps:

Hierarchies
15. Build hierarchy graphs of inheritance relationships.
16. Identify abstract versus concrete classes.
17. Draw Venn diagrams for shared responsibilities.
18. Construct class hierarchies.
19. Construct contracts.

Subsystems
20. Draw a complete collaborations graph for system.
21. Identify possible subsystems.
22. Simplify collaborations between and within subsystems.

Protocols
23. Construct protocols for each class and refine responsibilities into sets of signatures.
24. Write design specification for each class.
25. Write design specification for each subsystem.
26. Write design specification for each contract.

The process tends to be very flexible and particularly appropriate for exploratory developments, prototyping, or small team projects, providing a large number of guidelines and heuristics for systems development. However, it does not tackle the broader project management aspects of software development.

Advantages of the approach are its holistic and flexible approach to development that also encourages reuse with an emphasis on prototyping and responsibilities. Disadvantages include the lack of object structuring and semantic data modeling ideas, which limits the approach in the model construction phase, and the poor notational expressiveness. The methodology is most appropriate for design but does provide a useful mindset for analysis based on the ideas of object responsibility.

The notation is spartan (Figure 3.26), consisting of simple rectangular boxes containing the class name. Inheritance is achieved by nonarrowed lines, the subclass/superclass relationship being indicated by placing superclasses higher (on the paper/VDU screen) than subclasses. Abstract classes are indicated by filling in the upper left corner of the class icon. The authors' emphasis on collaborations introduces a notation not found elsewhere: numbered semicircles for each contract. Their use of Venn diagrams is not inappropriate. However, care must be taken with this type of visualization (Figure 3.27), since the same visual has been used for both inheritance and aggregation in the literature. It seems unlikely that the notation would scale up to large systems. Other tools they recommend are CRC cards (Section 9.1.5), collaboration graphs (showing classes, contracts, collaborations, and superclass–subclass relationships), and walkthroughs.

The deliverable of this responsibility-driven design (RDD) is a design document comprising (i) a graph of each class hierarchy; (ii) a graph of the

Object-oriented Development

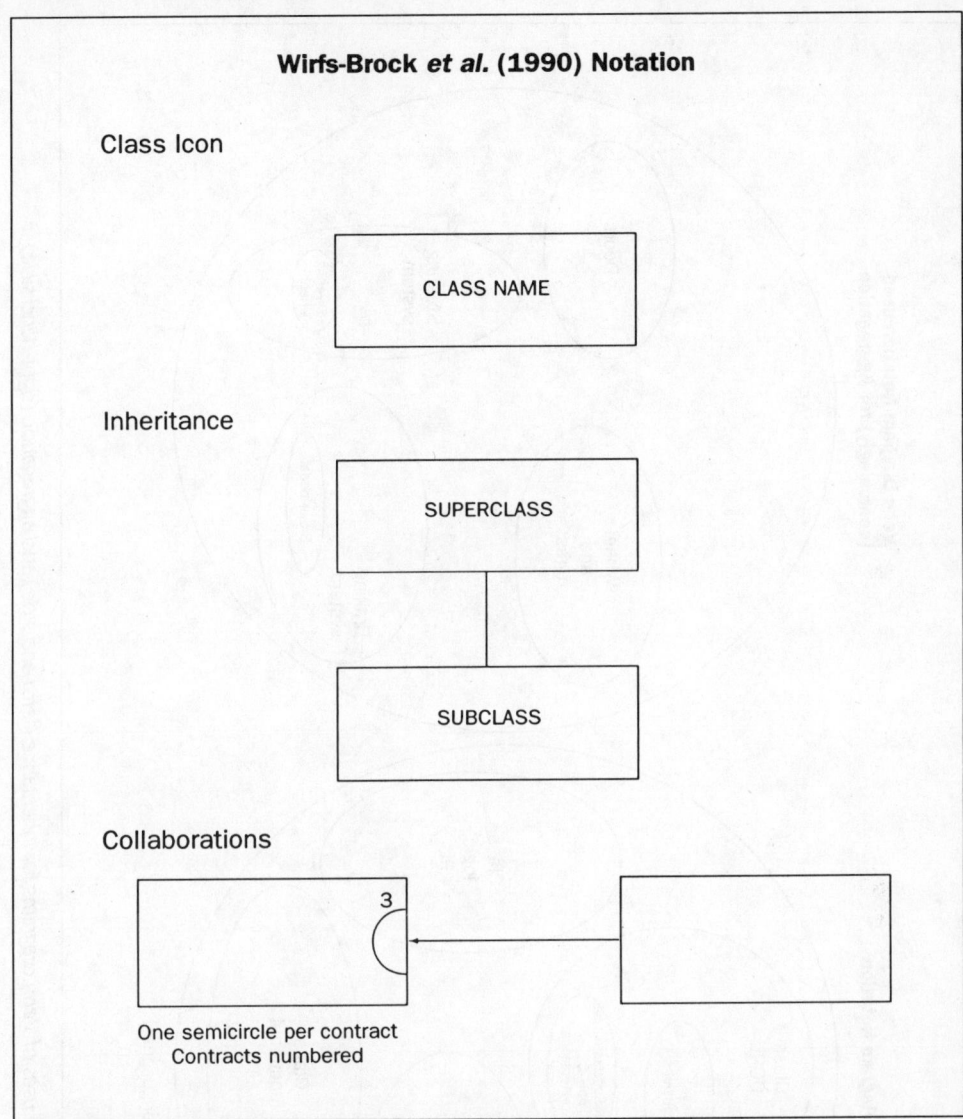

Figure 3.26 Wirfs-Brock et al.'s notation for classes, inheritance, and collaborations

collaboration paths for each subsystem; (iii) a specification for each class; (iv) a specification for each subsystem; and (v) a specification of the contracts for all classes and subsystems.

Lorenz
The work of Lorenz (1993) builds upon that of Wirfs-Brock *et al.* (1990). Lorenz discusses a number of broader lifecycle issues such as Business Planning,

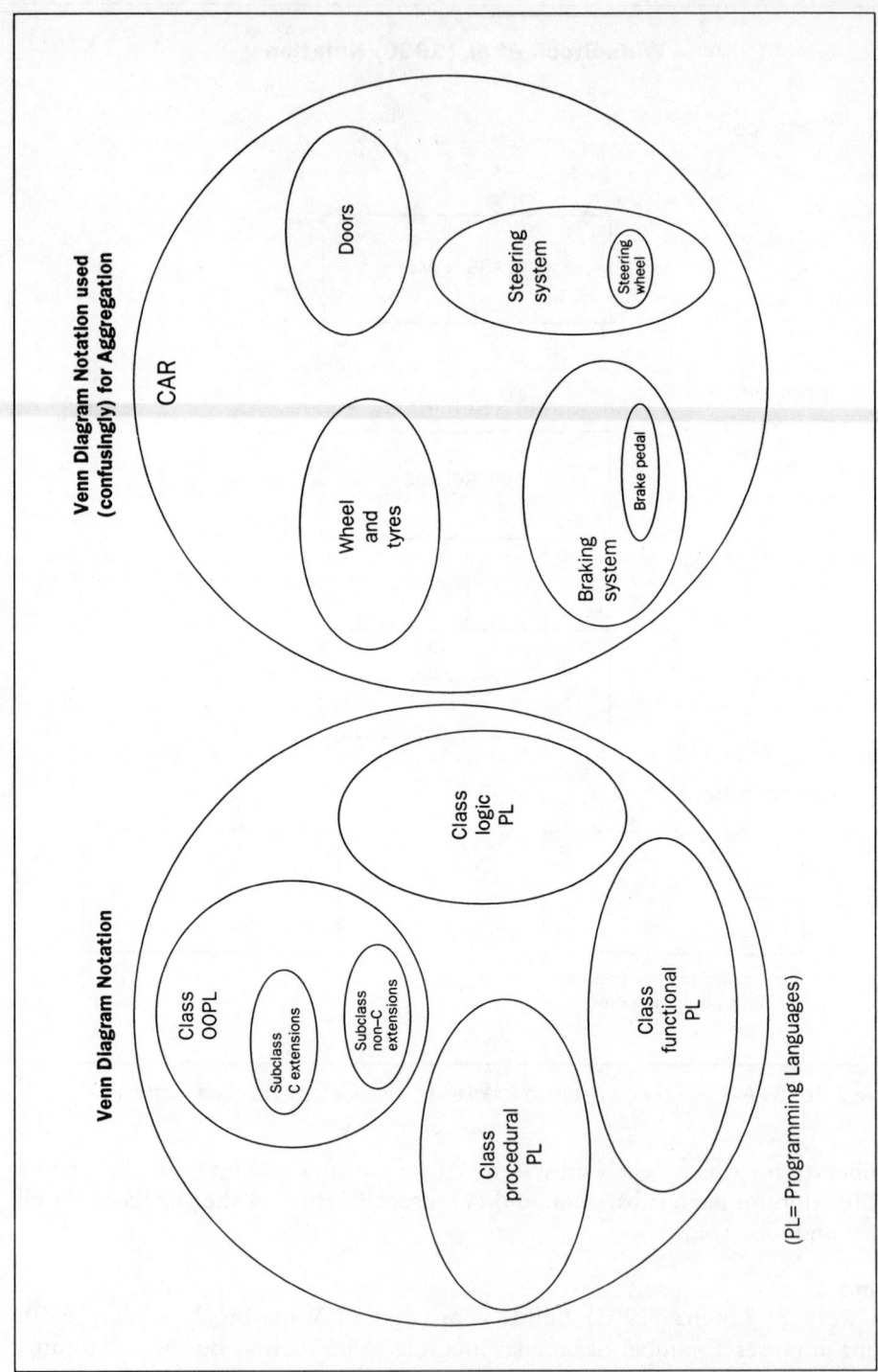

Figure 3.27 *Comparison of two uses of Venn diagrams for inheritance (left-hand side) and aggregation (right-hand side).*

Object-oriented Development

Testing, and Delivery. He views his OO methodology, which is essentially a derivative of RDD, as being applied within the production phase of an iterative development process that itself is part of a software development phase.

Figure 3.28 illustrates the way Lorenz views the interaction between phases, the development process, and the methodology. Essentially, the complete lifecycle is composed of four software development phases: Business, Analysis, Design & Test, and Packaging. The Analysis and Design & Test phases are completed through an iterative development process (IDP). The IDP is made up of three periods: Planning, Production, and Assessment. The production phase is where the methodology of Wirfs-Brock *et al.* is applied. The actual

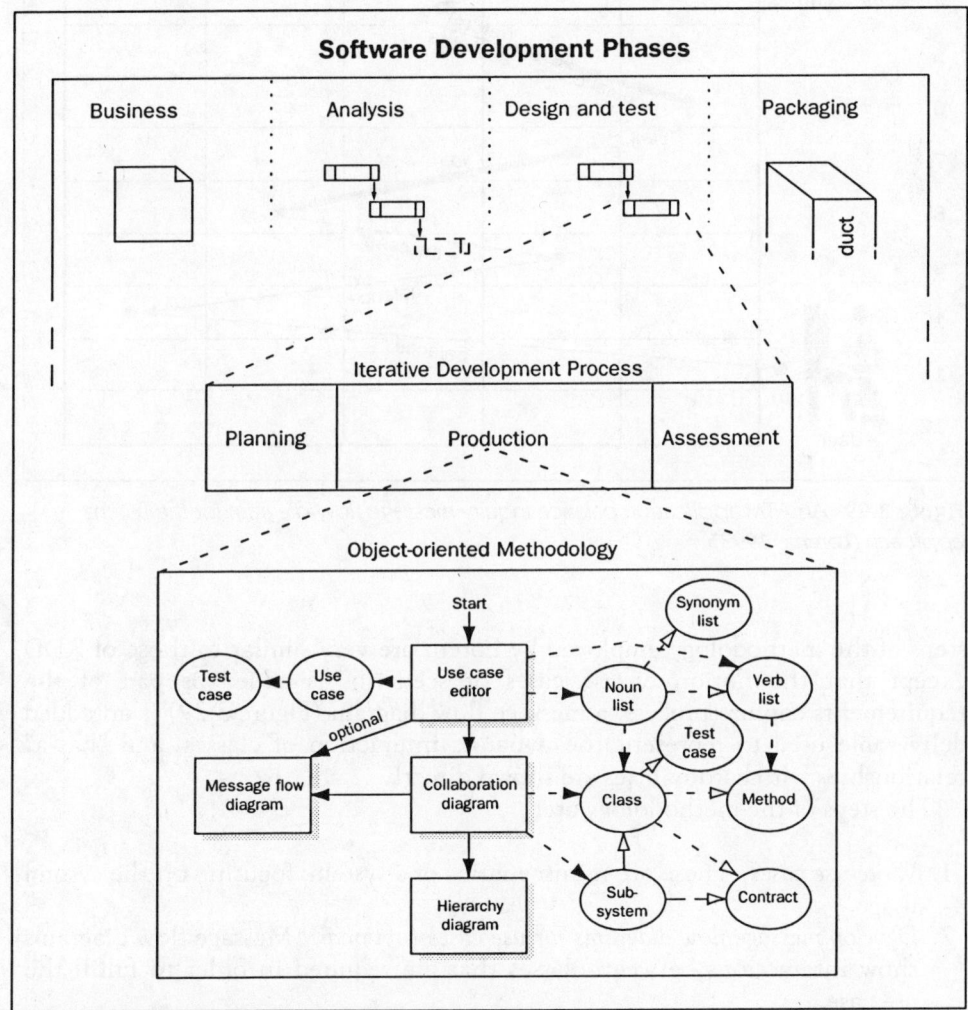

Figure 3.28 *The Iterative Development Process (IDP) of Lorenz (1993)*

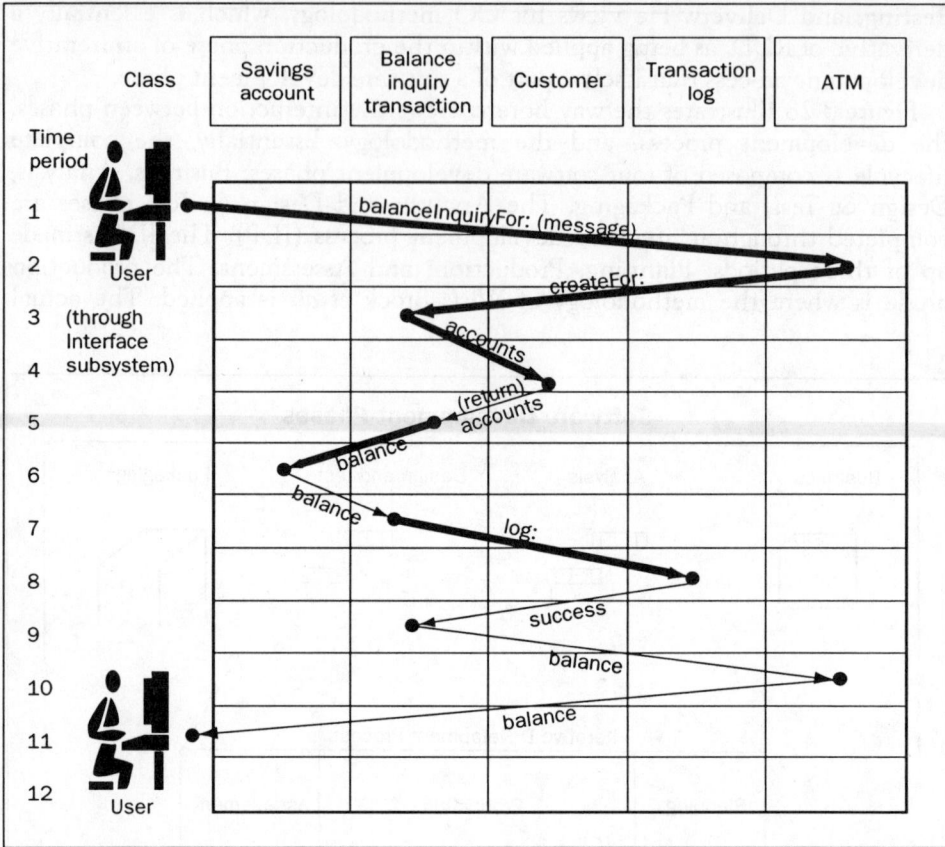

Figure 3.29 *An ATM application balance inquiry message flow diagram for the Lorenz approach (Lorenz, 1993)*

steps of the methodology employed by Lorenz are very similar to those of RDD except that the notion of use cases or scenarios is added as part of the requirements capture process, a message flow diagram (Figure 3.29) is an added deliverable used to represent the dynamic interaction of classes, and "has-a" relationships with cardinalities are shown directly.

The steps of the methodology are:

1. *Write use cases*. These are miniscenarios of a system, focusing on the system usage.
2. *Develop message flow diagrams for use cases (optional)*. Message flow diagrams show interactions between classes that are required in order to fulfill the use case.
3. *Develop collaboration diagram*. During this step classes, attributes,

responsibilities, systems, and contracts are all defined in collaboration diagrams derived from the message flow diagrams and use cases.
4. *Place classes in the inheritance hierarchy*. This step reorganizes classes into a hierarchy to reduce redundancy and optimize reuse.
5. *Develop message flow diagrams for methods*. Methods can be represented as a message flow diagram or simply as pseudocode.
6. *Implement methods*. The public methods are implemented on the basis of the message flow diagram. Private methods are implemented later.
7. *Test methods*. Methods are tested by the developer to ensure that they meet the requirements.
8. *Develop function test*. Function tests are achieved by applying the use cases to the collaboration diagram.

The steps and particularly the extensions to the methodology address a number of weaknesses in RDD, such as the lack of a requirements-capturing mechanism and a general weakness in expressing dynamic interactions of O/Cs. The work of Lorenz is significant, as it is one of the few methods to address the broader issues of the lifecycle in a comprehensive manner. For example, a number of project management hints are provided to manage iterations and incremental development of systems, and the issues of testing, metrics, and standards are addressed to varying degrees.

One criticism of Lorenz's approach is that it appears to advocate a waterfall approach throughout the *software development phases*; that is to say, iteration occurs within a phase, e.g., Analysis, but not between Analysis and Design & Test. This is a somewhat restrictive view of the IDP as discussed by Booch, Berard, and many other authors in the OO field. The MOSES lifecycle is therefore somewhat different in its approach, advocating an IDP across both Analysis and Design. In fact, as discussed in Chapter 4, it identifies a Specification Phase rather than an Analysis and Design phase.

3.3.4 Coad and Yourdon (OOA, OOD)

In the first edition of Coad and Yourdon's OO analysis book (Coad and Yourdon, 1990), the emphasis was heavily on extensions from data modeling, especially ER modeling (Frank, 1991; Beynon-Davies, 1992). Their model consists of a single depiction in which are described five layers: the Subject Layer, the Object Layer, the Structure Layer, the Attribute Layer, and the Service Layer. They choose to show these layers using "overlays" so that all relationships are shown in the plane, but the method and the supporting CASE tool (see below) permit the temporary removal of one or more of these five layers to assist in clarity.

From the five model layers are derived five steps in the OOA methodology. Assembly Structures are proposed in order to represent aggregation of classes. Coad and Yourdon (1990) differentiate between class–class interactions of such aggregates, or component parts of a larger class, and a Service Layer of interaction where, for example, a CUSTOMER class uses the services provided by a (conceptually discrete) BANK class. At the OOA stage this differentiation may be reasonable, since the implementation details, especially in a procedural language, may be different. However, for a fully object-oriented lifecycle, coding in an OOPL, such as Eiffel, of Coad and Yourdon's (1990) Assembly Structure and the message-passing Service Layer falls within a single implementation technique.

In addition to the basic structure shown here, explicit addition of attributes and services permits the adoption of an entity relationship (ER) notation (Coad and Yourdon, 1990) to illustrate n-ary relationship constraints and mandatory/optional links. Exploring in full detail such synergism between object-oriented notation and data modeling notation is of current concern (Bailin, 1989; Brown, 1992; Beynon-Davies, 1992; Edwards and Henderson-Sellers, 1993a).

In the second edition of their OOA book, Coad and Yourdon (1991a) revised their notation and concepts so that their five layers became:

- Subject Layer
- Class-&-Object Layer
- Structure Layer
- Attribute Layer
- Service Layer

This reorganization recognizes the similarity (at analysis and design) of objects and classes (but cf. the discussion of Firesmith (1993) in Section 3.3.7). Interpreting these five layers as five methodological phases/activities (Graham, 1991, p226), we can describe their methodology as follows:

1. The system is decomposed into a small number of "subjects" (subsystems). Each subject should contain about 5–9 objects (Graham, 1991).
2. Objects and classes are identified from the business specification.
3. Two orthogonal structures need to be identified: classification (specialization/generalization) and assembly or composition structures.
4. Attributes and their multiplicity relationships are detailed using a version of extended relational analysis (ERA).
5. Each object type requires specification of its services.

A slightly different interpretation is offered by Coad and Yourdon (1991a), and echoed by Jacobson et al. (1992), who suggest five activities (and not sequential steps) to be followed:

1. Find classes-&-objects.
2. Identify structures.
3. Define subjects.
4. Define attributes.
5. Define services.

Object-oriented Development

This has more bottom-up flavor to it than Graham's (1991) interpretation. Here subjects are not defined by partitioning the problem space, but rather by aggregating the Class-&-Object model. Each of these steps/layers tends to be a deliverable associated directly with that layer. The notation (see below) and object model are less expressive in both the static domain and dynamic domain than either those of Booch or OMT, although an interesting addition is the use of "subjects" that provide a way of organizing large models into small, more manageable systems.

The icon (Figure 3.30), originally much like that of Rumbaugh *et al.*, but now a double-boxed enclosure, was revised to permit relationship arrows to join either to the outer icon (object) or to the inner box (class). Inheritance and aggregations are shown in Figure 3.31. Graham (1991) notes the confusion between composition and association and between classes and objects, but comments that the second edition (Coad and Yourdon, 1991a) did contain clarifications.

Another difference between the first edition and the second edition of their OOA method lies in the replacement of the graphical notation for cardinalities by a numerical notation for cardinalities. The design icon is identical. Indeed, reading their OOD book (Coad and Yourdon, 1991b) we find little differentiation between analysis and design, the most important being the introduction in design of four components:

1. Problem Domain.
2. Human Interaction.
3. Task Management.
4. Data Management.

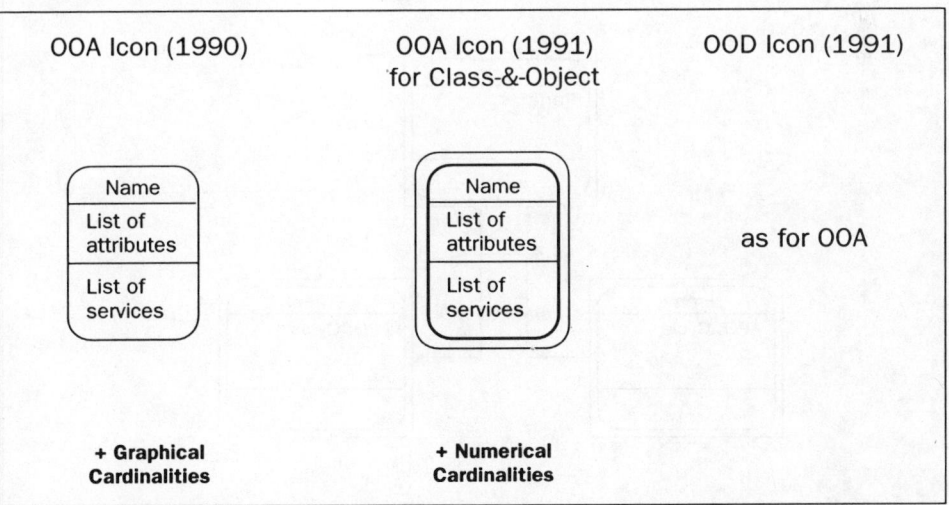

Figure 3.30 *OOA and OOD class and object icons for the Coad and Yourdon methodology*

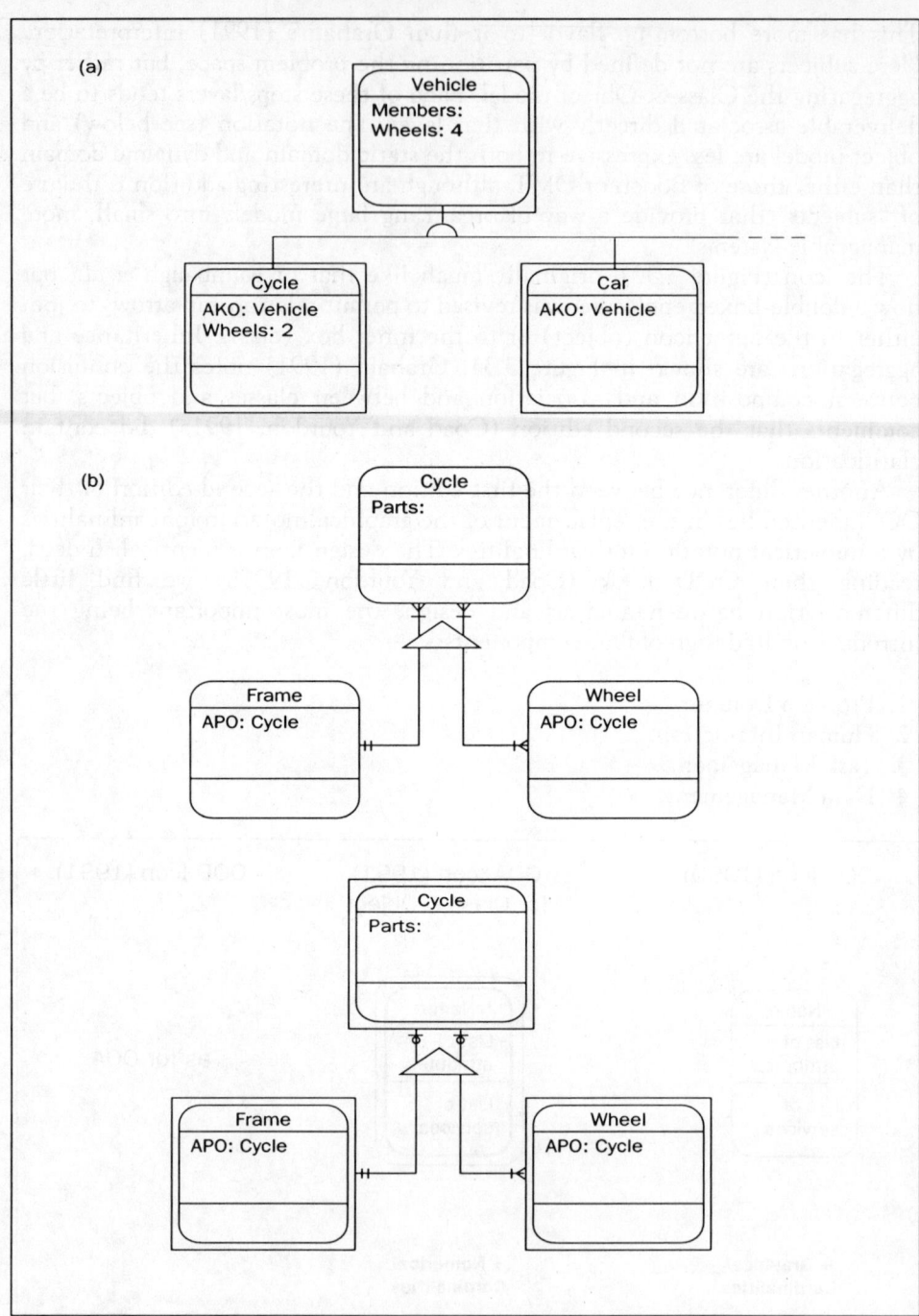

Figure 3.31 *(a) Inheritance hierarchy in Coad and Yourdon notation; (b) aggregation hierarchy for class level and instance level (Graham, 1991)*

Object-oriented Development 157

Although it is recognized that these subcomponents are likely to exist in almost all systems, it is hard to see that their weights are likely to be equal. Rather, in most IS applications the first component would dominate. The Human Interaction component relates to the GUI, and the task management relates to the classes unearthed in design for the sole purpose of computer-level management (e.g., file managers). The Data Management component includes options to convert storage in a relational database or use of a fully object-oriented (data)base (OB).

The OOD work is closely related to the OOA work and is essentially a difference of emphasis and guidelines rather than model, process, and notation. Indeed, Coad and Yourdon (1991a, p178) argue that "moving from OOA to OOD is a progressive expansion of the model." Thus they see OOD as involving essentially the same constructs, notation, and process but also involving the discovery of new and different objects to manage the computer domain. The OOD work is probably slightly weaker than the OOA material, since it relies heavily upon the static architecture as opposed to understanding object dynamics. Reuse, reengineering, interface design, and concurrency are not discussed. The work is aimed more at overall system specification and architecture in design than at detailed class design. This is discussed in the later sections of their work and seen more as implementation than design.

There is also the question as to how closely these components resemble Wirfs-Brock's subsystems or Firesmith's subassociations. It is our conjecture that within most sizable systems the problem domain cannot be covered in a single component and that this would require further division (not discussed by Coad and Yourdon, 1991b) into a number of (probably recursive) subsystems.

Modifications

Murphy's (1991) commercial case study of the use of OOA is revealing. In the domain of network management, she found two areas of deficiency in OOA: (i) the method was noted as being incomplete and (ii) the data-driven approach of OOA is contradictory to the more normal behavioral or responsibility-driven approach of the object paradigm. Consequently, Murphy (1991) supplemented OOA by Berard's OCS entity template and restructured OOA using the behavioral approach as described in ParcPlace documentation. This led to the semantically important replacement of OOA's instance connections by relationships. This was necessary, since a split between two of the OOA layers of relationship-associated information was identified by Murphy. Such a split, it was proposed, forces a design decision to be made during analysis.

In a similar vein, Graham (1991) found Coad and Yourdon's methodology inadequate for his purposes, criticizing the "muddled" uses structure (p228). Consequently, he extended it by (i) differentiating between object and class composition (Figure 3.32; cf. Figure 3.31(b)); (ii) differentiating between instance methods and class methods; (iii) permitting relationships as objects; (iv) using an ER notation for both classification and composition structures; and (v) adding a fourth partition to the object class to display business

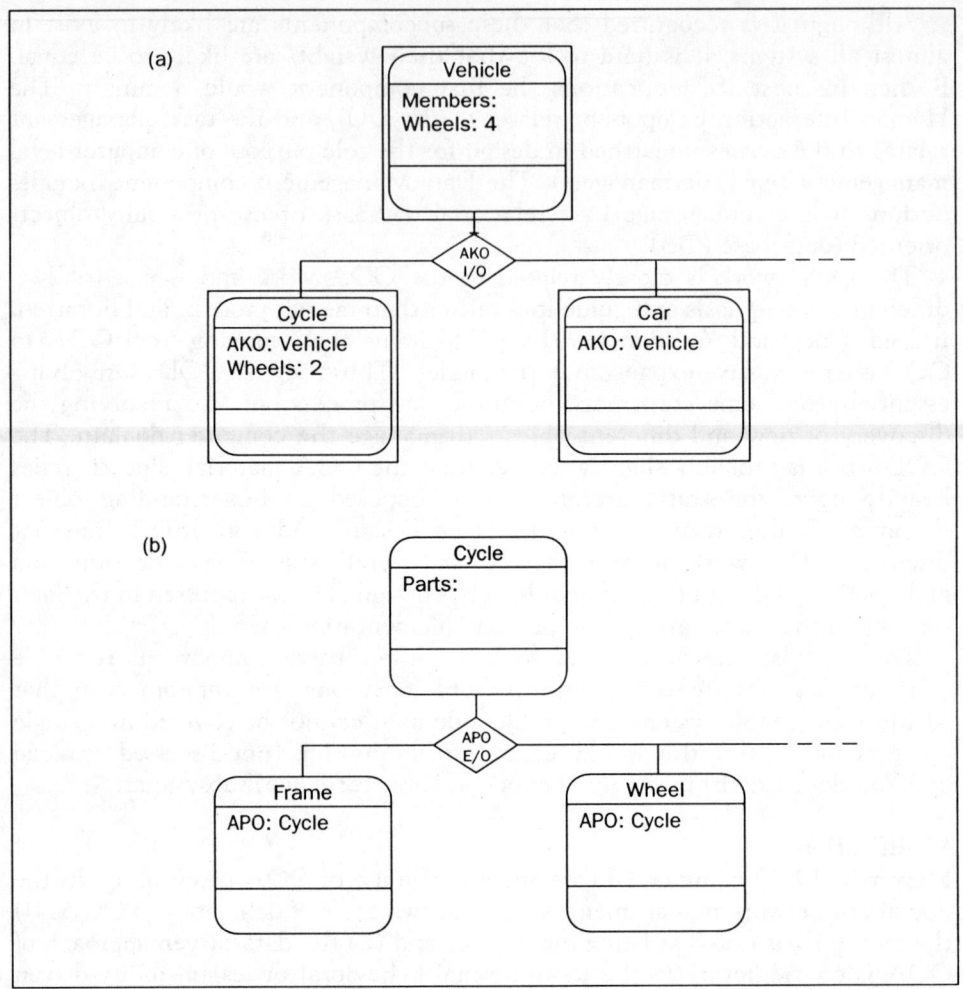

Figure 3.32 *SOMA notation for (a) classification/inheritance and (b) composition (Graham, 1991)*

rules/constraints. The revised methodology, known as SOMA (Semantic Object Modelling Approach) (Graham, 1994), extends Coad and Yourdon's SOSAS mnemonic to LOSAMDR (Table 3.5), the stages being roughly sequential, overlain with appropriate amounts of recursion, and described loosely in terms of a spiral model.

Supporting CASE tools for Coad and Yourdon's notation—OOATool, OODTool, and OOCodeGen—are available from Object International Inc. either as a cut-down version for evaluation and use on small projects or as a (much more expensive) unrestricted version. Early versions of this tool were very unstable (Firesmith, 1991) and used line drawing algorithms that led to

Object-oriented Development

some peculiar results. As with so many of these CASE tools, there is little optimizing for layout. This must still be done manually.

Since OOA is a "flat" notation, layering considerations are not supported. Selective visibility is, however, usefully available so that one can view all the attributes only, or all the gen/spec relationships only, etc. OOA notation is also supported by ObjectMaker (Section 9.1.5).

Table 3.5 *Comparison of Coad and Yourdon's SOSAS with Graham's LOSAMDR*

Coad and Yourdon SOSAS	Graham LOSAMDR
Subjects	Layers
Objects	Objects
Structures	Structures
—classification	—classification
—composition	—composition
	—use
Attributes	Attributes (+ validation, security, defaults)
Services	Methods (+ exceptions, assertions, parameter passing)
	Data semantics
	Rules
	—control
	—business
	—exception handling
	—contention
	—triggers

3.3.5 Henderson-Sellers and Edwards (O-O-O)

The seven activities of the O-O-O methodology (Table 3.6) (Henderson-Sellers and Edwards, 1990, 1993b; Henderson-Sellers, 1992a; Henderson-Sellers et al., 1992) essentially cover the lifecycle as far as the final production of the software product and release to the customer/user. After that, the program is used and maintained for its useful lifetime. Maintenance and extension will often require the development of new classes, each of which will then go through its own O-O-O lifecycle. Generalization and reuse are addressed specifically in Activity 7 but should also pervade the OO development as a "reuse mindset." The O-O-O methodology provides an instantiation of the fountain model.

1. The *systems requirement documents* are prepared in the language of the user, as normal, but discussed and analyzed in terms of classes, properties, and

operations (services) rather than functionality. These documents could include timing details, hardware usage, cost constraints as well as problem specification and strict user requirements. Consequently, interviewers who elicit the requirements from the user/customer need to phrase their questions using object-oriented concepts, though not specific object-oriented terminology (so as not to confuse the users themselves). In other words, the user should be strongly encouraged to outline the problem in terms of the behavior of participating external world objects rather than overall system functionality.

2. *Identify the candidate classes*. Analysis (first domain analysis and then applications analysis) begins with identification of real-world classes (Activity 2.1), concentrating on identifying those that are likely to provide good user-defined types (abstract data types, or ADTs) at the later design and implementation stages.

As classes become evident the analyst will also label them with obvious properties (state) (Activity 2.2) and operations (functionality) (Activity 2.3), as well as a class name. Although they are labeled 2.2 and 2.3 for convenience, it is noted that these two activities can occur in either order—or more likely concurrently across the cluster. As properties and operations are identified they are noted on the class that is to provide the service.

These techniques provide the beginning of a merging toward Activity 3; and indeed Activities 2 and 3 are frequently found to occur in parallel.

Table 3.6 *The seven activities of the O-O-O methodology*

Activity
1. Prepare systems requirement document
2. Identify candidate object classes
2.1 Identify classes
2.2 Identify attributes
2.3 Identify operations
3. Identify interactions between classes
3.1 Identify association relationships
3.2 Identify aggregation relationships
3.3 Possibly identify generalization relationships
4. Prepare design diagrams for the top few layers
5. Add more details, especially in terms of library classes (bottom-up). Prepare class interface diagrams and contract diagrams. Begin to code.
6. Reevaluate design and identify and freeze inheritance hierarchies. Finalize coding and testing
7. Generalize for future projects by producing *good* library classes in order to capitalize on reuse

3. *Establish interactions between classes* in terms of services required and services rendered. The initial relationships identified are depicted in a (top layer) class diagram (Edwards and Henderson-Sellers, 1991). The interactions identified at the analysis stage, as opposed to the later design stage, are association (Activity 3.1), aggregation (Activity 3.2), and generalization (Activity 3.3). The authors note that most of the relationships identified at this stage should in fact be associations, although some aggregations and generalizations will be identified fairly early.

   Modeling is first undertaken at a high level of abstraction (little detail, few classes) and iteratively refined to finer and finer detail. The upper layer relates to the subsystem associative interactions and the lower layers to aggregation details. In this, a high-layer class is "decomposed" into its components using a layering approach, often several such nested decompositions being necessary.

   When the services of a class are used, software quality is enhanced if there is a protocol for the interaction: a "software contract" between client (customer) and server (supplier) classes. Contracts are documented using tables that should be filled in using a more formal version of a natural language (e.g., a subset of English).

   The main results of the analysis phase are a set of relatively high level classes with clearly defined properties and operations and their associated contracts, interlinked with (primarily) associations. The analysis is likely to be encapsulated and documented in a set of analysis diagrams using a suitable notation, ready for further elaboration and refinement during design.

4. As the analysis stage merges into the design stage, high-level design diagrams (DDs) and increasingly lower level DDs can be drawn to illustrate more details of the classes. The design activity deals with class "services" rather than the state/behavior dichotomy useful in the analysis modeling activity.

   Low-resolution (upper-layer) design diagrams (DDs) can be drawn directly from the analysis diagrams. Associations and aggregations are both transmuted into client–server relationships while the class icons at design are still closely related to the classes of the analysis phase, which are close replicas of the real-life objects. Auditability is obvious. However, as the design stage is entered, especially detailed design and refinement of the inheritance hierarchy, further design-specific classes will be created that have no immediate traceback to external world objects. These relate to resource and efficiency constraints and introduce "software and hardware world" classes.

   Client–server relationships (possibly related to the aggregation structures identified in analysis) will be added recursively and lower-layer (higher-resolution) descriptions of classes will be introduced. At this stage a fully object-oriented, relatively detailed design has been created.

5. At this detailed design stage, where Activity 5 overlaps strongly temporally with the later, detailed design subactivities within Activity 4, it is also

necessary to identify library classes. Classes are themselves often constructed from libraries (the successful outcome of this proposed development methodology) of more primitive classes using concepts of inheritance as well as of client–server. This leads to coding directly from the class specification diagrams. Implementation (coding plus testing) of low-level modules may begin at this or the next stage.

When the subsystem DDs have been refined down to their most detailed resolution, we are left with classes that are awaiting final specification and implementation.

The class specification (CS) is the lowest (i.e., most detailed) design layer notation (before source code). This shows the class interface in full detail, specifying method names, arguments, and results, as well as a synopsis of the contract, either in the form of comments or, in a language such as Eiffel, using assertions.

These class internals will tend to be methods that are relatively short, requiring little logical description. However, for larger methods they are documented by structured design techniques, including structure charts, etc., and can thus be viewed as structured programs in miniature. This dynamic view of classes is a vital complement to the static view described above. The communication model assumed here is message passing along relationship paths supplemented by structural techniques together with appropriate object-oriented versions of statecharts. In addition, more work on inheritance at the larger system and subsystem level is needed in Activities 6 and 7, which will *also* lead to coding demands.

6. As more classes are identified within the detailed design, reevaluation of the total set of classes will require an iterative analysis of whether new superclasses (parents) or new subclasses (children) will be useful. Consequently, inheritance diagrams will be further developed and refined. The authors stress that inheritance hierarchies should not be sought too early, since this could eliminate the flexibility that one would look for in an SDLC.

    Detailed design documents are prepared, usually at the granularity of the subsystem, for peer and customer review. These together with the documented (and well-commented) final code form the basic maintenance support documentation, as well as being available for quantitative evaluation using metrics.

7. At the end of the basic system development, then, further work is necessary to guarantee reusability for future projects—although if the goal of reusability is borne in mind *throughout* the preceding six activities (as it should be), the work of Activity 7 will be much less. This refinement work is needed to ensure that classes are really reusable, and augments the project-specific refinement of the inheritance hierarchy of Activity 6. Such refinements may, of course, lead to iteration back and a reconsideration of the system design (and associated design diagrams). Subsystems may be identified and/or consolidated and documentation prepared.

At this stage, the product is generally delivered and put into operation. Subsequent maintenance, involving not only error correction but also extensions, modifications, or enhancements, and supported by metrics collection, is now undertaken at the systems level (Figure 3.6) rather than at the subsystem or class level. Changes undertaken to small portions of the system will effectively return the class to an earlier lifecycle activity in the recursive manner supported by the O-O-O methodology.

In the analysis diagrams, association, aggregation, and some generalization relationships are used between classes that themselves exhibit an external interface in terms of properties and operations. These are then easily translated into a design using services and client–server relationships as well as inheritance hierarchies. To complement these, more detailed information needs to be expressed in terms of class contract diagrams (CDs) and finally each class needs to be fully specified by a class interface that provides the basis for coding. The O-O-O methodology allows for these differing features but maintains a smooth transition between analysis and design, in accordance with the underlying object model.

The methodology also provided a detailed notation, which is summarized in Edwards and Henderson-Sellers (1993a). This notation has since been further refined and is discussed in some detail in Chapter 5.

Weaknesses of the approach include the concentration on the static aspect in the model and notation, the lack of guidelines and heuristics to guide the designer, and the paucity of documentation mechanisms. Since this early work, and as a result of further research and industry feedback, a more comprehensive, second-generation methodology has been developed. This methodology, called MOSES, is described in Chapters 4–8 and involves a theory of the object-oriented lifecycle developed by Henderson-Sellers and Edwards (1990, 1993a). This approach to OO development encourages an iterative approach to class development, something that many authors note but few really discuss.

3.3.6 Jacobson *et al.* (Objectory)

Objectory (the *Object* Factory for Software Development) has been pioneered by Ivar Jacobson and colleagues in Sweden (Jacobson *et al.*, 1992). A methodology for object-oriented analysis and design, Objectory has been continuously refined over many years. It has had industrial exposure with 15 successful projects around the world. Its novelties lie in its focus on the "use case": a sequence of transactions that are performed by a user of the system. A use case is an exemplar or pattern. Each use case thus outlines a likely thread of control through the many objects in the system, providing a potential unification between the static and dynamic views of the system—an integration lacking in some other methodologies, as noted elsewhere in this chapter. It is argued that by structuring methodologies to build systems around action patterns of likely users, a greater degree of reusability and flexibility will be built into the system.

Three totally different techniques are synthesized by Jacobson *et al.*: object-oriented programming, conceptual modeling, and block design. The last of these has widespread use in the telecommunications area, based on original hardware applications. Blocks collect together programs and data into modules and describe their mutual communication with signals.

Objectory focuses on the full lifecycle, emphasizing the user, the engineering process, and the seamless transition between lifecycle phases. Five models are identified—requirements, analysis, design, implementation, and test (Figures 3.33–3.35)—developed during the analysis, construction, and testing processes. The requirements model specifies the required functionality, which focuses on the use of "use cases." This provides a basis for the analysis process in which the system's structure is described in the analysis model. This description is a logical description of the classes in the system. Full specification is then undertaken in the design model, the implementation model consisting of the source code. Testing results of the code are described in the testing model.

Actors are concepts to represent the various roles a user can play, and they figure prominently in the use case description. The concept of use case, similar to that of scenario (Rumbaugh *et al.*, 1991), focuses on how an individual user might use the system and is a set of possible traces through the system. The use case model is the underlying thread for Objectory (Figure 3.36).

In the analysis model, the information space has three axes of information, behavior, and presentation (Jacobson *et al.*, 1992, p133). The single axis of information, perhaps equivalent to function/data methods, offers a restricted view. This three-dimensional view emphasizes the synergy of function

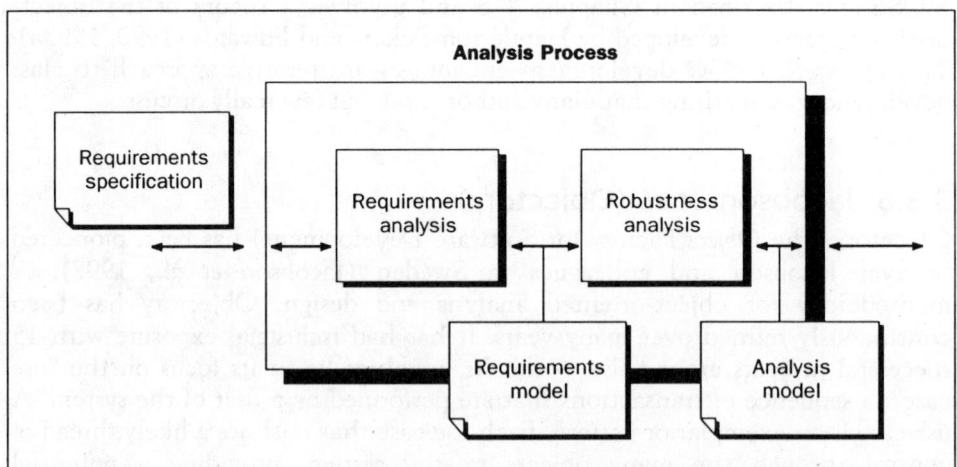

Figure 3.33 *The analysis process and subprocesses and the models they produce. Note that the arrows between processes are bidirectional to illustrate that information may flow in both directions. (Jacobson et al., 1992)*

Object-oriented Development

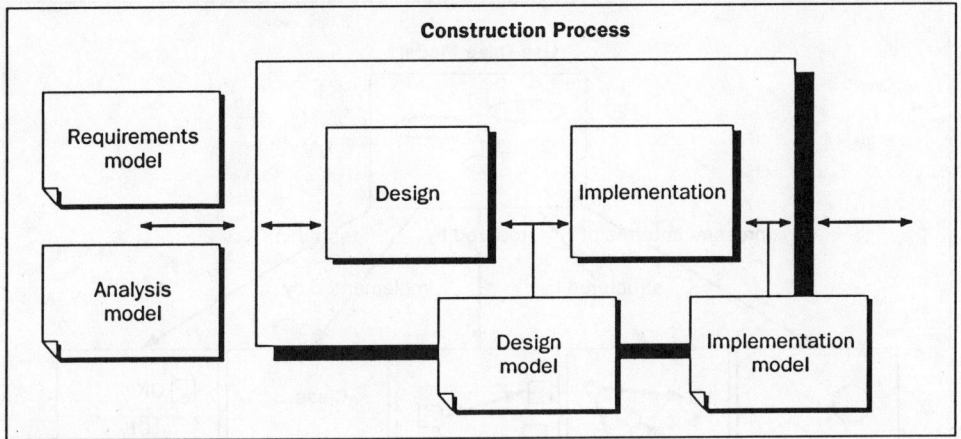

Figure 3.34 *The construction process of Objectory with its major subclasses and models (Jacobson et al., 1992)*

(behavior axis) and data (information axis) overlain with the very important presentation axis, although Jacobson notes the propensity for classes to be largely two-dimensional.

The design model is regarded as a formalization of the analysis space (Jacobson et al., 1992, p139). This is seen to have four dimensions, the fourth being the implementation environment. Thus the completed design should be readily identifiable.

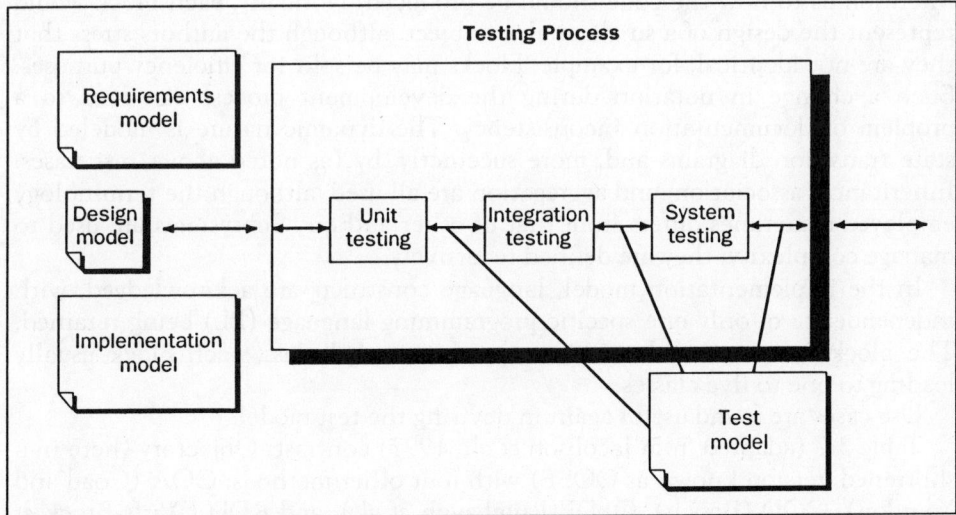

Figure 3.35 *The testing process of Objectory with its major subprocesses (Jacobson et al., 1992)*

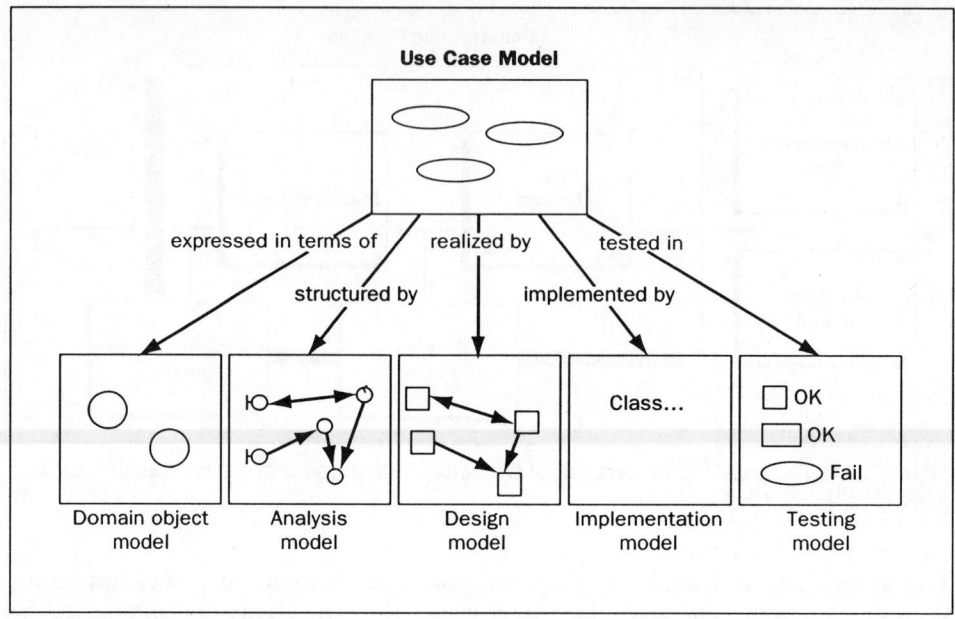

Figure 3.36 *The use case model of Objectory (Jacobson et al., 1992)*

There is a distinct shift of viewpoint in moving from analysis to design, reflected in both the mindset and the static notation (circles for analysis, rectangles for design). Each block in design (rectangular symbol) describes the intention as to how the code should be produced. Normally, each block would represent the design of a single analysis object, although the authors stress that they are not identical; for example, blocks may be split for efficiency purposes. Such a change in notation during the development process can lead to a problem of documentation inconsistency. The dynamic nature is modeled by state transition diagrams and, more succinctly, by (as noted above) use cases. Inheritance, association, and aggregation are all used, although the terminology employed sometimes differs from that of other authors. Subsystems are used to manage complexity; they are defined recursively.

In the implementation model, language constructs are acknowledged, with independence of only one specific programming language (PL) being retained. The block structure of design is mapped to coded class, each block usually leading to one to five classes.

Use cases are found useful again in devising the test model.

Table 3.7 (adapted from Jacobson *et al.*, 1992) contrasts Objectory (here in a shortened version known as OOSE) with four other methods: OOA (Coad and Yourdon), OOD (Booch), OMT (Rumbaugh *et al.*), and RDD (Wirfs-Brock *et al.*). It excludes HOOD from the original table, since it is object-based and not object-oriented.

Object-oriented Development

Table 3.7 Comparison of five OO SDLC methodologies (Jacobson et al., 1992)

OOSE	Coad & Yourdon	Booch	OMT	RDD
Class	Class	Class	Class	Class
Object	Object	Object	Object	Object
Inherits	Gen-spec structure	Inherits	Generalization	Inheritance/ hierarchy
Acquaintance	Instance connection/ whole-part	(Uses relationships)	Link	(Collaboration)
Communication	Message connection	(Uses/instantiates rel.)	(Data flow)	
Stimuli	Message	Message	Event	
Operation	Service	Operation	Operation	Method
Attribute	Attribute	Field	Attribute	Attribute
Actor	(User)	—	—	—
Use case	(Threads of execution)	(≈Mechanisms)	Scenario	(Scenario)
Subsystem	(Subjects)	Class categories/ subsystems	Subsystem	Subsystem
Service package	—	—	—	—
Block	—	Module/class category	Module	—
Object module	—	Class	Classes	Classes
Public object module	—	(visibility of class categories)	(Service)	Responsibility/ contract

3.3.7 Firesmith (ADM3)

Firesmith (1992a) describes the ASTS Development Method 3 (ADM3)[15] as a full object-oriented methodology developed from earlier versions focused solely on an Ada programming environment. Its individualistic features are as follows:

1. It focuses on domain analysis, concurrency, and subassemblies.
2. It contains a state model, a control model, and a timing model.
3. It differentiates between objects and classes in both analysis and design as well as in implementation/running.

---

15. ASTS stands for Advanced Software Technology Specialists. The current version of the methodology, ADM3, is soon to be updated to ADM4.

Figure 3.37 depicts an overview of the ADM4 development process (Firesmith, 1994). The first two steps are performed once at the beginning of the project, the remaining three steps once for each build of the system (recursion). Thus the iteration appears to be across several versions and the recursion inside lifecycle phases. These basic steps can be described as follows:

1. *Initial planning* (Figure 3.38). This is part of the proposed process in which project management details, risk management, and training plans are incorporated into the project software development plan. User agreement on these plans is required.
2. *Systems requirements analysis and design* (Figure 3.39). In this phase the software requirements specification is analyzed to find the assemblies. It has seven substeps, which are linear, as detailed in Figure 3.39.
3. *Preparation for globally-recursive development* (Figure 3.40). This involves the project manager and team members in developing assembly and context diagrams, and event lists, discovering the initial subassemblies in each assembly, and carrying out an initial progress review.
4. *Globally-recursive development* (Figure 3.41). This is the core of the method, in which each subassembly undergoes a "mini-waterfall" development cycle of (i) OO requirements analysis and logical design; (ii) implementation design; (iii) coding and unit testing; (iv) subassembly integration and testing; and (v) assembly integration and testing. These are discussed in detail below.
5. *Completion of the build*. Firesmith (1992a) describes this stage only pictorially, with no associated textual description, as follows: (i) baseline each assembly; (ii) perform formal assembly testing; and (iii) perform system integration and system testing. No other details of this phase are given.

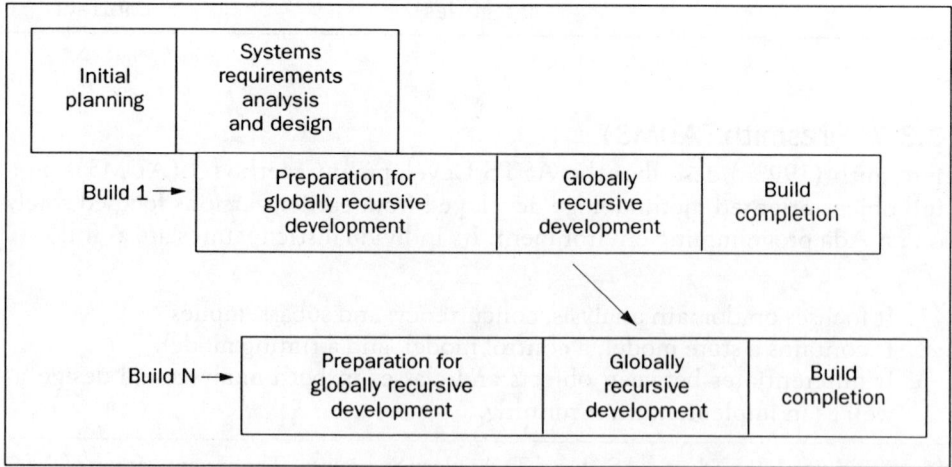

Figure 3.37 *ADM4 development cycle and activities (Firesmith 1994)*

Object-oriented Development 169

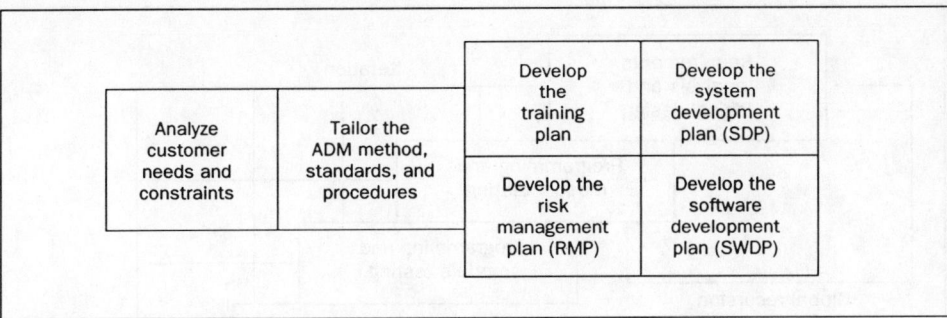

Figure 3.38 *ADM4 Activity 1: Initial planning (Firesmith, 1994)*

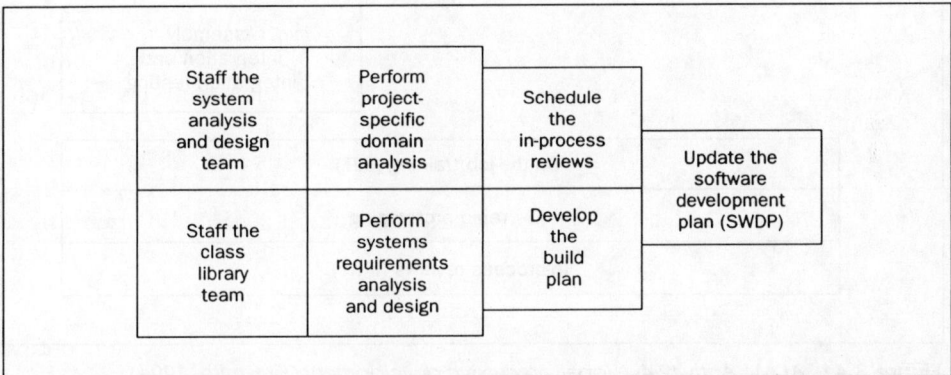

Figure 3.39 *ADM4 Activity 2: Systems requirements analysis and design (Firesmith, 1994)*

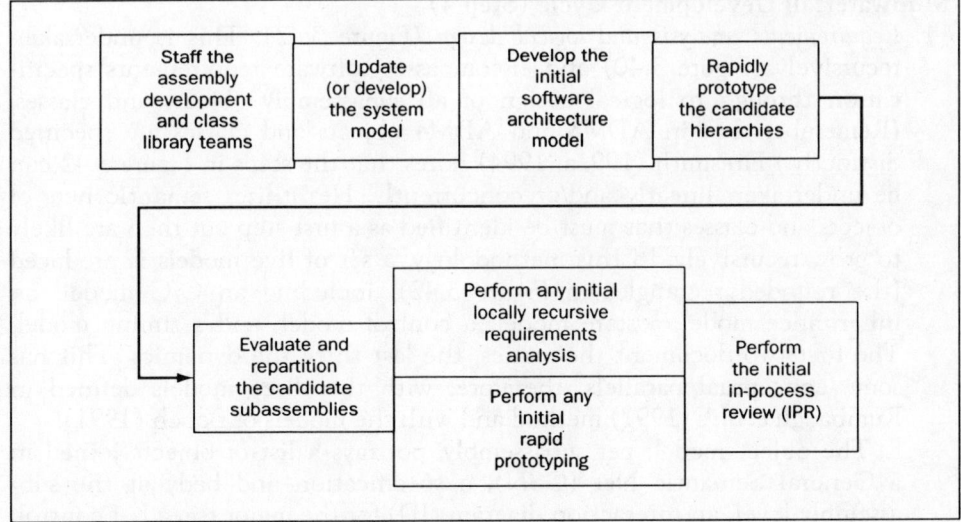

Figure 3.40 *ADM4 Activity 3: Preparation for globally-recursive design (Firesmith, 1994)*

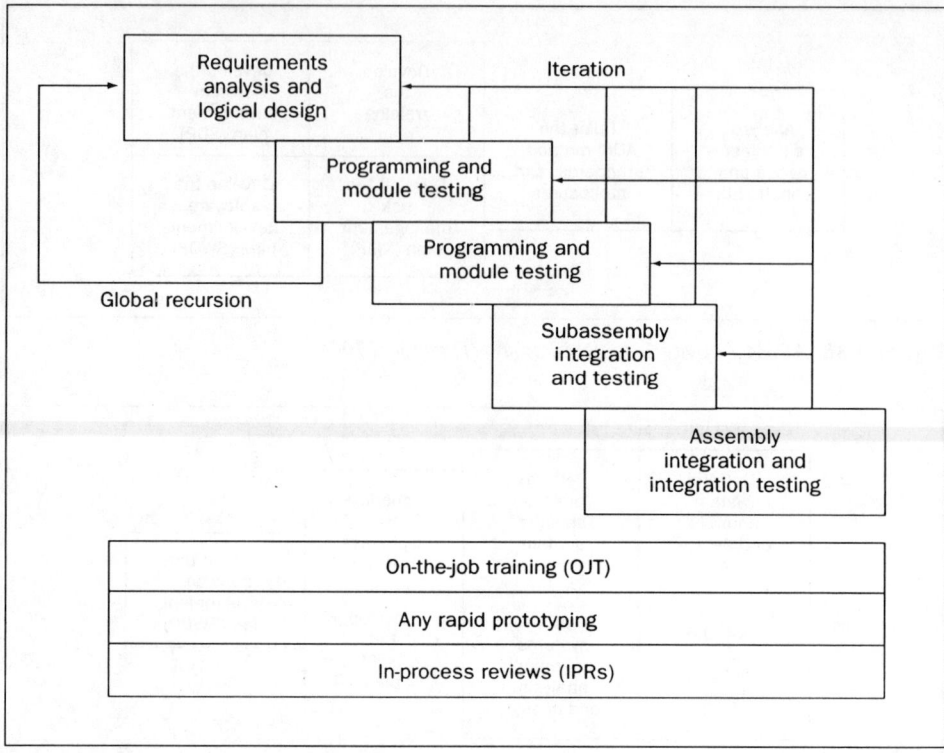

Figure 3.41 *ADM4 Activity 4: Globally recursive development (Firesmith, 1994)*

Miniwaterfall Development Cycle (Step 4)
1. *Requirements analysis and logical design* (Figure 3.42). This is undertaken recursively (Figure 3.40) and encompasses software requirements specification through to logical design of all subassembly objects and classes. (Remember that in ADM3 and ADM4 objects and classes are specified distinctly.) Firesmith (1992a, 1994) notes that the steps in Figure 3.42 can be undertaken linearly and/or concurrently. He utilizes semantic nets of objects and classes that must be identified as a first step but then are likely to grow recursively. In this methodology, a set of five models is produced (the rounded rectangles in Figure 3.42), including an O/C model, an inheritance model, a state model, a control model, and a timing model. The first two document the statics, the last three the dynamics. This has some conceptual parallels, therefore, with the three models defined in Rumbaugh et al.'s (1991) method and with the models of Booch (1991).

The object model, per subassembly, portrays a list of objects joined in a General Semantic Net (GSN), a specification and body at the subassembly level, an interaction diagram (ID) for the major thread of control, a description of all messages, a composition diagram (CD) for each

Object-oriented Development

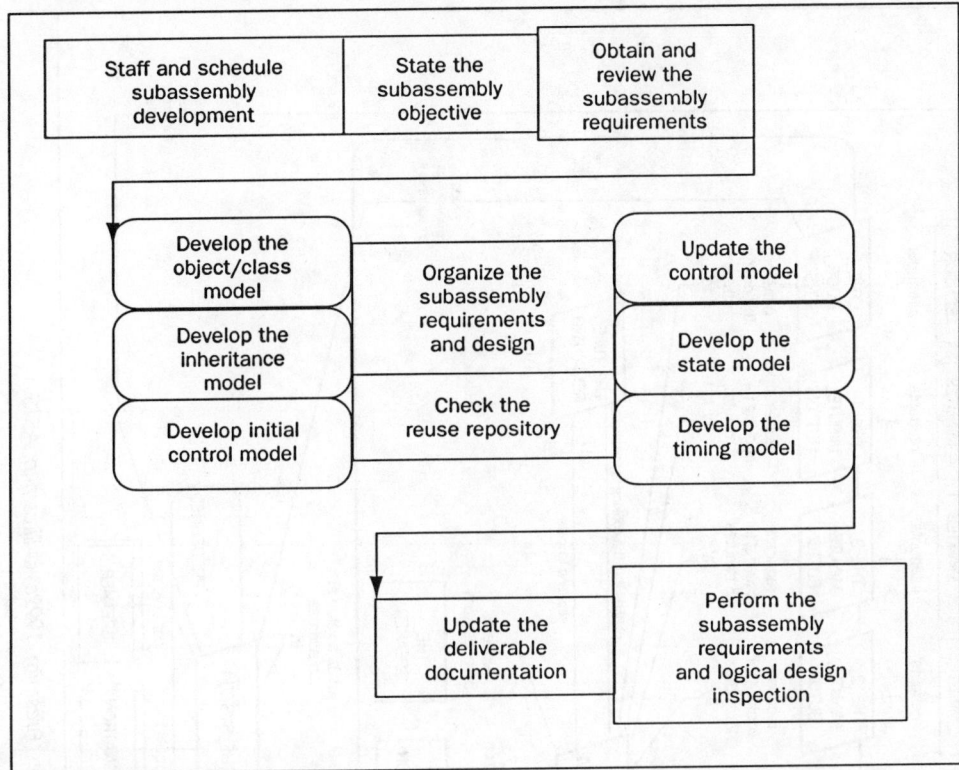

Figure 3.42 *Overview of requirements analysis and logical design of ADM4 (Firesmith, 1994)*

"subassembly aggregation hierarchy," a textual description of the logical cohesion of each object as well as a description of its specification and body, and a description of each attribute type and of all messages, operations, and exceptions. (Further details of these iterative and recursive steps are given in Firesmith, 1992a, 1993.)

The notation used is illustrated in Figure 3.43. The emphasis on real time requires icons for concurrent objects, and objects and classes are depicted differently, the notation being known as OOSDL. Since this is an object model, only single instantiations exist and Firesmith (1993) therefore suggests a naming convention with a prefix THE_; he similarly inverts the normal order for representing message passing to SERVICE.TARGETOBJECT in order to make English sentences. Consequently, a standard message of *light.off* to turn off a light becomes TURN_OFF.THE_LIGHT in ADM3/4.

The second model is the class model, which consists of a list of all classes in the subassembly, a classification diagram (CLD) for each associated inheritance hierarchy, a textual description at the ADT level, and a

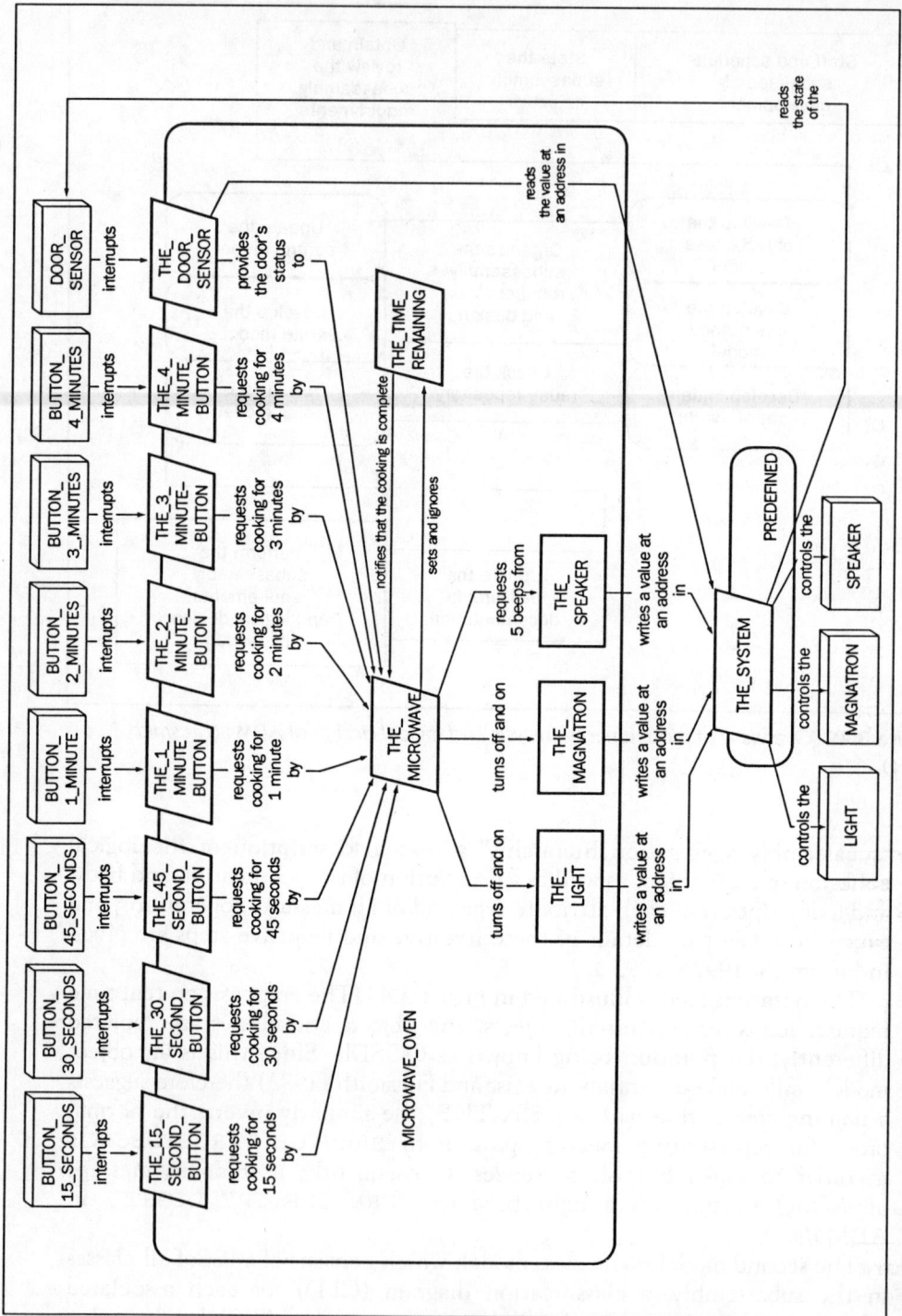

Figure 3.43 Software semantic net illustrating the ADM3/4 notation (Firesmith, 1992a) © Firesmith, ASTS

Object-oriented Development

specification and body of each class. This model introduces the notion of inheritance, which is absent from the object diagram. An example is given in Figure 3.44.

At the same time, subassembly requirements are allocated to objects and classes to assist in their final design, potential for reuse from existing library classes is examined, and the dynamic models are developed.

The state model used in ADM3/4 is a state transition diagram for each object and class that requires one. The control model details important threads of control in each subassembly and requires predevelopment of expected error-handlers and their threads of control. Real-time considerations lead to the use of messages that may be sequential, synchronous (Ada rendezvous), or asynchronous. Concurrency problems such as starvation and deadlock are also considered. The third of the dynamic models is a standard timing model, similar to that of Booch (1991) but rotated through 90 degrees. There seems (from the documentation) to be no explicit connections between these three dynamic models, or between the dynamic and the two static models.

2. *Implementation design.* In this step, the logical design is translated into a design suitable for coding (implementation). This would be regarded in other circles as the "physical design." The steps in implementation design are also extensive (Figure 3.45). In Firesmith (1992a) the target language is Ada. Although this is still the dominant language environment for application of ADM3/4, it has been applied to projects written in C++ and Smalltalk. Since much of the documentation is Ada-specific, which is deemed to be outside the scope of this book, no synopsis will be given here.

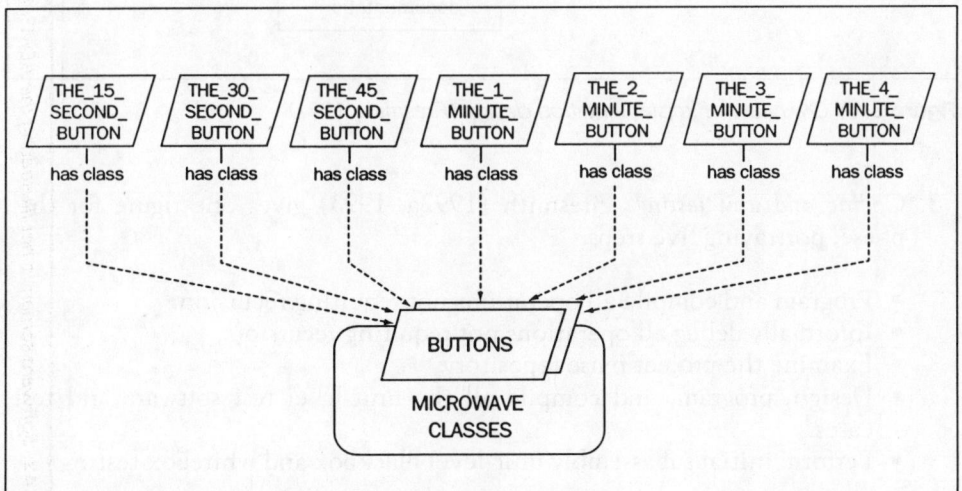

Figure 3.44 *Detailed classification diagram of the ADM3/4 notation (Firesmith, 1994)*
© *Firesmith, ASTS*

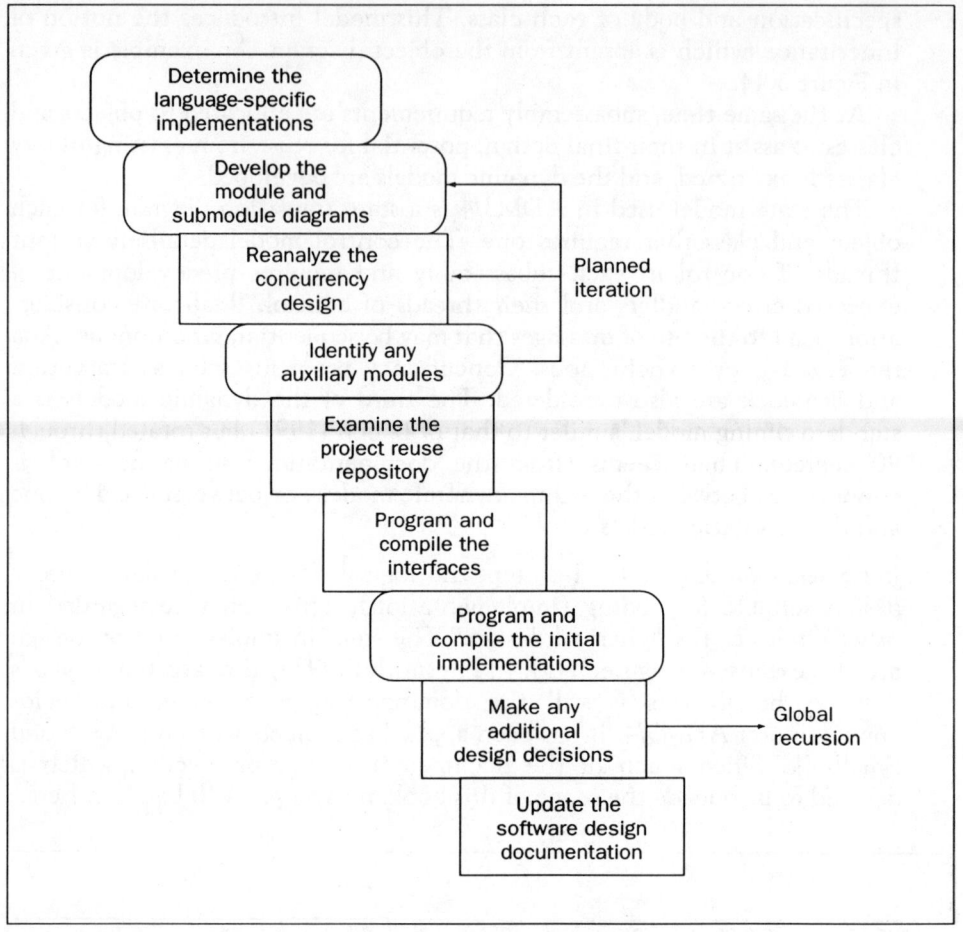

Figure 3.45 *Overview of implementation design (Firesmith, 1994)*

3. *Coding and unit testing.* Firesmith (1992a, 1993) gives one figure for this phase, portraying five steps:

- Program and compile all operations not requiring recursion.
- Informally debug all operations not requiring recursion.
- Examine the project reuse repository.
- Design, program, and compile all the unit-level test software and test cases.
- Perform initial subassembly unit-level blackbox and whitebox testing.

4. *Subassembly integration and testing.* Firesmith (1992a, 1993) gives one figure for this phase, portraying eight steps:

Object-oriented Development 175

- Place the subassembly in a library.
- Plan subassembly testing.
- Examine project reuse repository.
- Design and code subassembly test software.
- Integrate the subassembly software.
- Perform initial subassembly testing.
- Perform assembly integration readiness inspection.
- Place subassembly under configuration control.

5. *Assembly integration and integration testing.* Firesmith (1992a) gives one figure for this phase, portraying eight steps:

- Place the subassembly into the assembly library.
- Plan assembly testing.
- Examine project reuse repository.
- Design and code assembly integration test software.
- Integrate the subassembly into the growing assembly.
- Perform the initial assembly integration testing.
- Update the assembly diagram (AD).
- Add the subassembly software and documentation to the reuse repository.

Firesmith (1993) additionally stresses the importance of the AD in documenting the static architecture as well as providing a management tool.

Weaknesses of the approach include a lack of emphasis on reuse and perhaps an excessively complex model. Overall, though, the approach would appear to be particularly applicable to large-scale development projects oriented toward real-time problems. This is seen especially in the ubiquitous distinction between objects and classes throughout the lifecycle, leading to a proliferation of diagram suites.

Finally, it should be noted that ADM3/4 and OOSDL are supported by the CASE tools ObjectMaker and Paradigm Plus (see Section 9.1.5).

3.3.8 Shlaer and Mellor

One of the earliest OO methodologies, and one used by a number of organizations, especially in the United States (Firesmith, pers. com., 1992), is documented in two books by Shlaer and Mellor (1988, 1991). Their approach once again concentrates on the information model as the central feature of the model. In traditional information modeling (Shlaer and Mellor, 1988) services, messages, and classification structure (entity types and subtypes) are essentially missing (Coad and Yourdon, 1990, p28), which leads Graham (1991, p224) to conclude that this approach cannot be regarded as object-oriented. Nevertheless, some of the ideas and notational constructs from information modeling can make a significant contribution to object modeling.

The dynamic aspect is modeled by a combination of state transition diagrams and object lifecycles, which has been significantly expanded in more recent work (Shlaer and Mellor, 1991). DFDs are also used to describe the functional behavior of objects. The method includes a comprehensive, if verbose, notation (see below) and a significant amount of guidelines and heuristics. The method is strong as an OOA method and for data intensive applications but currently provides little OOD support. Major elements of the OO paradigm such as reuse and reengineering are little mentioned in Shlaer and Mellor's work. Once again, this work is largely an extended information modeling approach to OT that does not really consider the more detailed aspects of class design and reuse. The process is also not well defined in the literature, and documentation for the method seems to rely on the models themselves.

Shlaer et al.'s (1991) notation—the Object-Oriented Design LanguagE, or OODLE for short—is designed either to support the Shlaer and Mellor (1988, 1991) methodology or to coexist with other available methodologies. The notation consists of four diagram types: class diagram, class structure chart, dependency diagram, and inheritance diagram (Figure 3.46). Layering and navigation are also stated to be available in the notation, but this seems limited to a standard interrelationship between the four diagrams rather than addressing the complexity management issue, as is done in, for example, the MOSES notation (see Chapter 5).

The suite of diagrams are designed to be drawable by hand or supportable by a CASE tool; to be as similar to existing notations as feasible in order to be able to use existing CASE tool support; to provide multiple views in a comprehensible fashion with respect to icon density; and to be flexible with respect to symbol and label placements.

The class diagram (Figure 3.47) depicts the external view of an individual class. The icon is a rectangle labeled with the class name, surrounded by divided hexagons, known as "woks," to represent "logical components." The upper half is labeled with the meaning, the lower with its type. Internal rectangles abutting the class box boundary are "published operations," viz., the services externally available. Shlaer et al. (1991) differentiate here between "instance-based operations," which access the hidden data and are placed to the left of the class box, and "class-based operations" (to the right) "for which the caller does not supply a particular instance of the underlying data structure." (This differentiation also maps closely on to the Smalltalk OOPL.) The external woks provide input and output parameters (input above the line, output below). Virtual operations are indicated by a double bar (Figure 3.47). Exception handling is also included. As can be seen, the class diagram provides a detailed design level of information.

The class structure chart shows the *internal* structure, including data flows and control structures, based on traditional structured charts, but using woks to represent (typed) data items. Friends are also included, thus giving the class structure chart a strong language bias.

The third diagram is focused at the higher abstraction level of system-level

Object-oriented Development 177

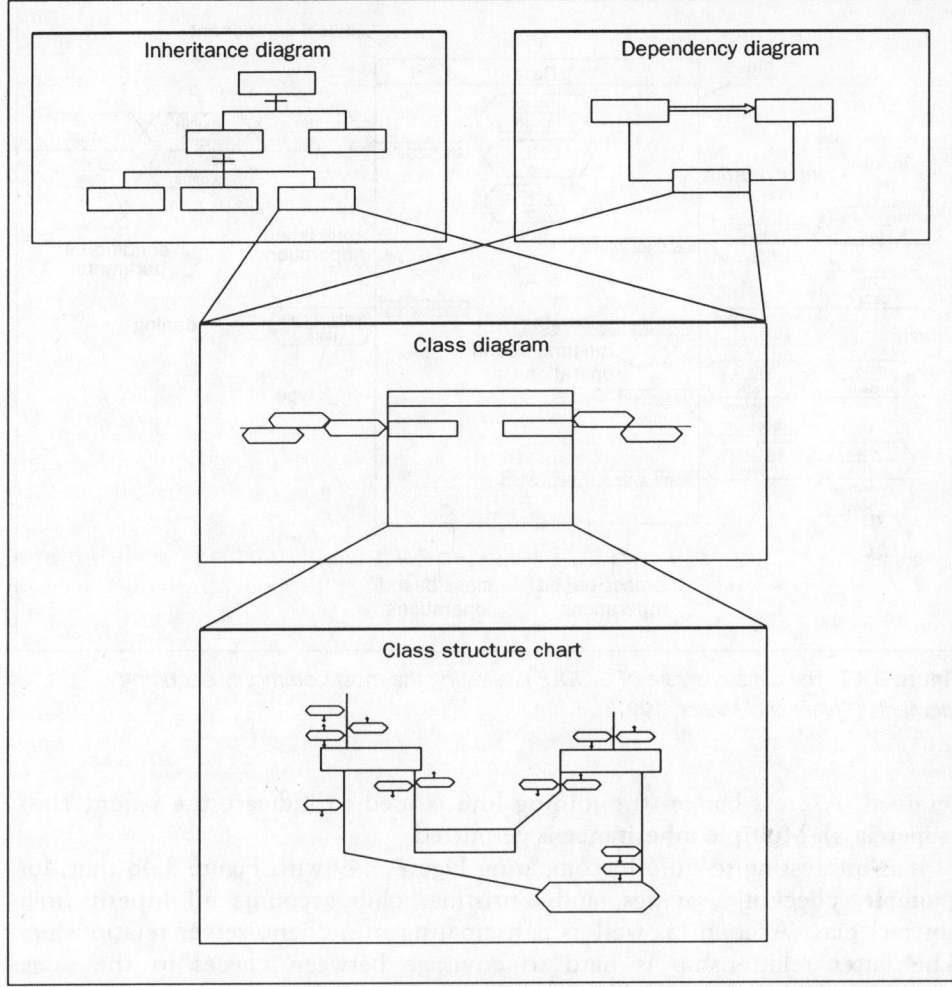

Figure 3.46 *The suite of OODLE diagrams of Shlaer and Mellor (Shlaer and Mellor, 1991)*

inter-class dependencies to describe coupling, in terms of (i) client–server and (ii) friends (again language-dependent). Client–server is shown as a directed arrow from client to server and the friend relationship as a double arrow from invoking class ("client") to the invoked class containing the "friend module." The notation also permits nonclass friend modules (see Figure 3.48), which violates the basic tenets of the object paradigm. In the figure, `Make mailing labels` is a stand-alone function.

The fourth diagram represents the inheritance hierarchy based on information modeling notations (Shlaer and Mellor, 1988). Figure 3.49 shows that in this fourth diagram type, external woks are omitted but internal details

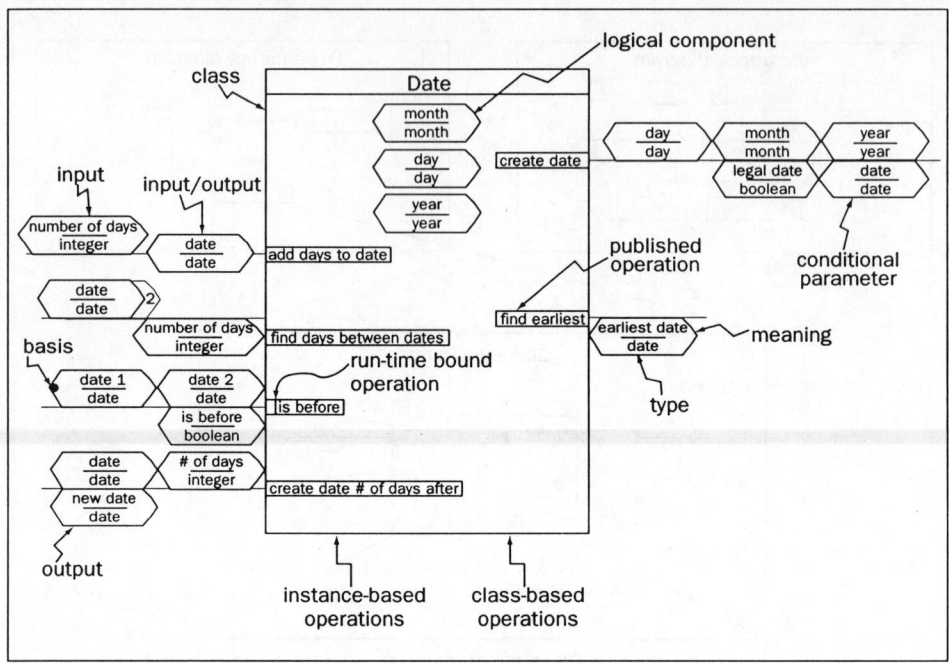

Figure 3.47 *The class diagram of OODLE illustrating the most commonly occurring elements (Shlaer and Mellor, 1991)*

retained. A cross bar on the joining line is used to indicate the parent class (superclass). Multiple inheritance is permitted.

It is interesting to note in comparing Figure 3.49 with Figure 3.48 that, for example, checking, savings, and Christmas club accounts all inherit from abstract class Account as well as participating in a client–server relationship. The latter relationship is hard to envisage between classes in the same hierarchy (but not impossible); compounded with this is the fact that class Account is noninstantiable, being an abstract class.

In summary, the method is a well-tried approach to developing OO systems. It supports a fully object-oriented model and has a comprehensive supporting notation. It is most applicable to data-intensive applications requiring, as it does, third normal form, or to organizations that wish to evolve from a more traditional structured background.

3.3.9 Berard

The highly iterative nature of the OO development lifecycle is stressed by many authors, and Berard (1990a, b) compares sequential, iterative, and recursive lifecycle approaches. He and others use the description "analyze a little, design

Object-oriented Development

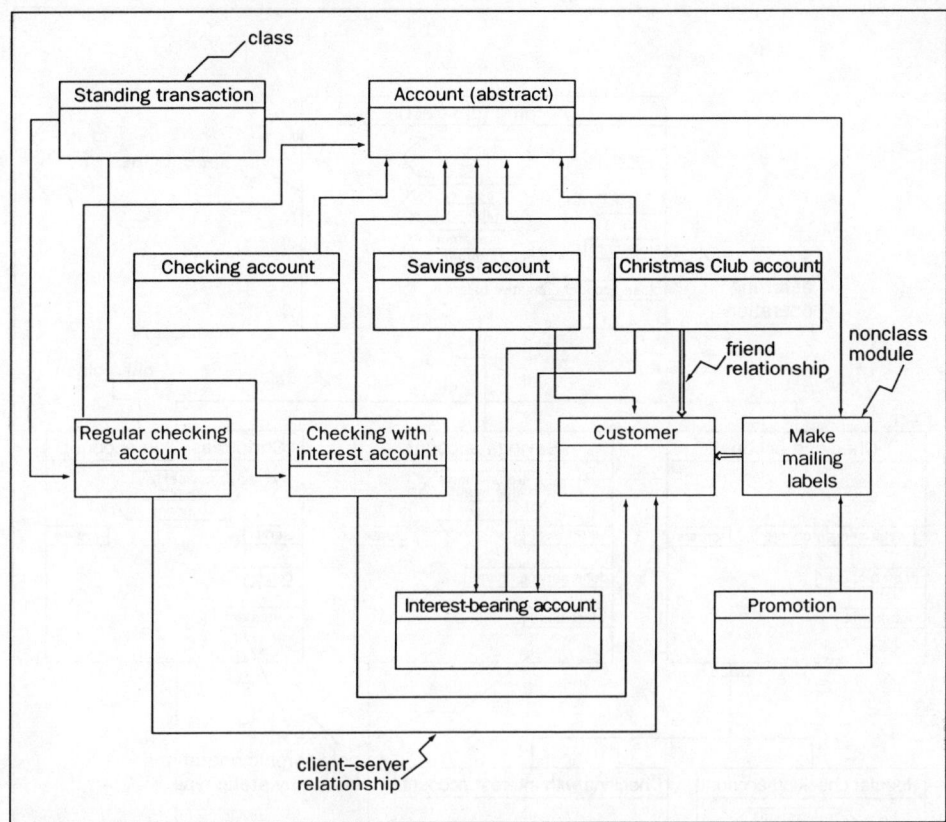

Figure 3.48 *The dependency diagram of OODLE. In this diagram Christmas Club account is a friend class of the Customer class, while Make mailing labels is a friend module of Customer. (Shlaer and Mellor, 1991)*

a little, implement a little, test a little" to capture an OO SDLC. This recursive/parallel model is highly analogous to the O-O-O methodological framework of Henderson-Sellers and Edwards (1990), discussed above.

There are seven steps (Table 3.8). Although presented sequentially, "some of them may be re-ordered, and some may even be accomplished in parallel" (Berard, 1992b, p258). The first stages are object identification and evaluation of object–object interactions. The software engineer is encouraged to construct an OO model or strategy of the proposed solution—models that include graphical, textual, or executable approaches.

In the second step, the designer identifies operations suffered by each object. Berard (1992b) differentiates between primitive methods (which require implementation knowledge) and composite methods, which are composed of two or more primitive methods, possibly from more than one object. At this point, library classes may be identifiable and retrieved and/or existing objects may be

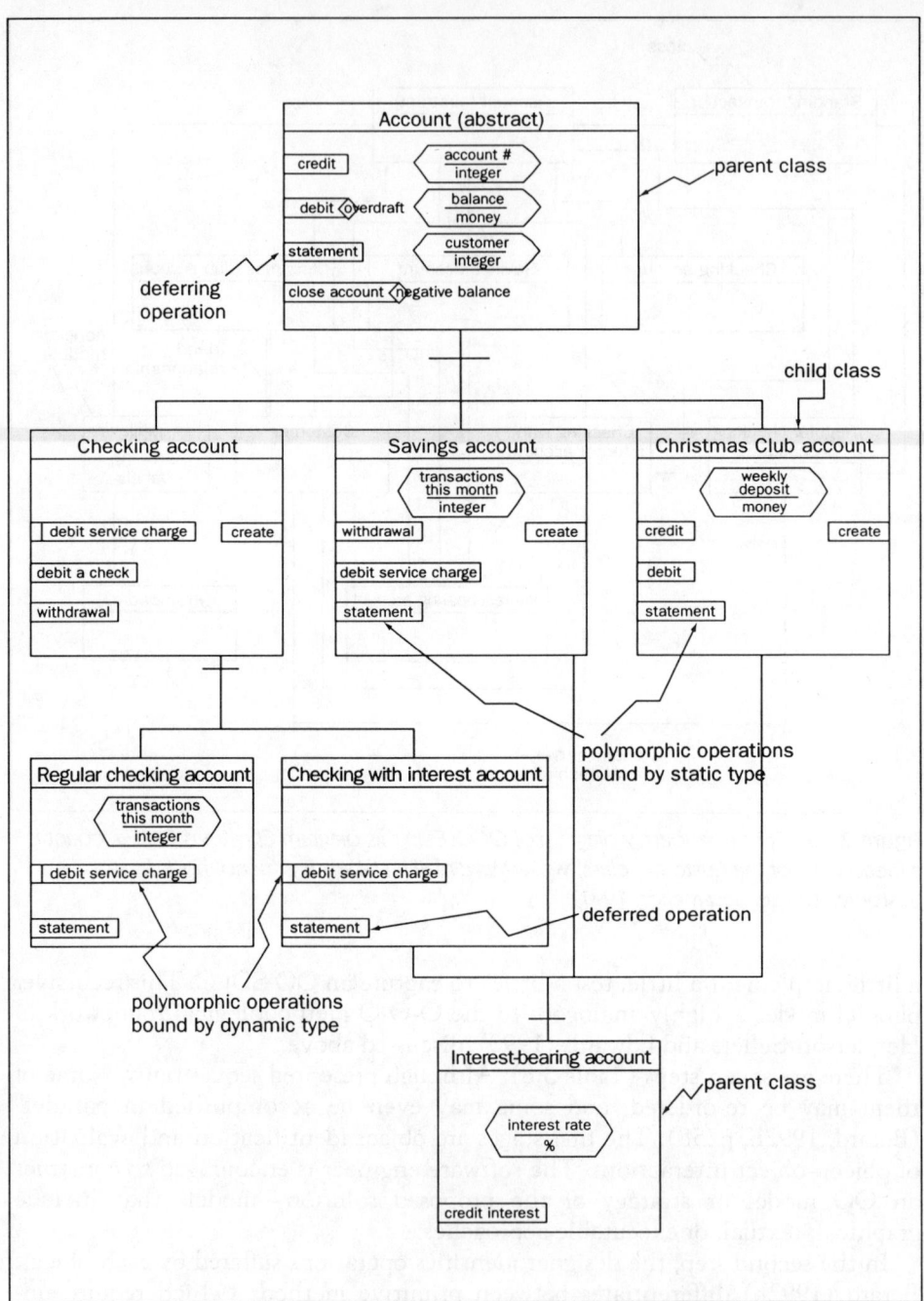

Figure 3.49 *Inheritance diagram of OODLE. Account is the parent class of Checking account, Savings account, and Christmas Club account. (Shlaer and Mellor, 1991)*

Object-oriented Development

Table 3.8 *Seven steps of recursive/parallel lifecycle methodology (Berard, 1992b)*

1.0 Identifying candidate objects
    1.1 Developing an object-oriented model of the solution
    1.2 Identifying objects of interest from the model
    1.3 Associating attributes with the objects of interest
2.0 Identifying operations suffered by, and required of, candidate objects
    2.1 Identifying operations of interest
    2.2 Associating attributes with operations of interest
    2.3 Handling composite operations
        2.3.1 Decomposition into primitive operations
        2.3.2 Decoupling of objects
3.0 Selecting, creating, and verifying objects for design
    3.1 Binding objects and operations
    3.2 Examining objects for completeness
4.0 Deciding on programming language implementations for objects
    4.1 Objects identified during analysis
    4.2 Objects identified during design
5.0 Creating object-oriented graphical models
6.0 Establishing the interface for each object-oriented item
7.0 Implementing each object-oriented item
    7.1 Refinement of the interface objects
    7.2 Refinement of the other objects
    7.3 Recursive application of the object-oriented development process

found reusable by incremental modification. (These are the three options of McGregor and Sykes (1992), discussed in Section 3.1.5.)

In the fourth step, language decisions are made and the choice of language is permitted to be reflected in the design. At this stage, then, language features would be incorporated.

Berard notes that at this stage there are two alternatives: (i) to switch to the chosen OOPL and finalize the coding of the object internals, or (ii) to iterate back to the products of the first design effort.

A useful contribution notationally are the "object and class specification" (OCS—pronounced "ox") diagrams (Berard, 1992b, p145 *et seq.*). They are intended not only to be useful in documenting the completed design but also in capturing design dynamically. Initially, OCSs (pronounced "oxen" according to Berard!) were textual descriptions plus graphical notations using semantic networks. These have now evolved to a five-part structure:

- precise and concise description—an "executive summary" that may be graphical or textual, or both;
- graphical representations—both static and dynamic;

- operations—listed per object plus brief description;
- state information—description;
- constants and exceptions—description of those found in public interfaces.

An OCS is found typically to be five to six pages in length and has been found useful not only by the author (Berard), but also by, for example, Murphy (1991) in her extension to the Coad and Yourdon methodology.

3.3.10 Nerson

The approach of Nerson (1991, 1992a) is one that has developed from the area of OOPL and OOD. In this methodology, the OOPL Eiffel has been extended to cover the OOD and OOA phases of a development (Nerson, 1991). The rich object model of Eiffel and its ability to be applied to analysis and implementation provide this approach with a powerful object model from which to work. The main advantages of this approach are that the language is formal and precise and allows models to be progressively refined to the level of code. This reduces the impedance mismatch between OOA, OOD, and OOP stages. The method also includes a significant amount of advice on reengineering and reuse, with the use of deferred classes playing a central role in the method. Class design is the major focus of the activities of the method, although the work has extended the idea of clusters to support higher-level systems architecturing. Scalability is also addressed (Nerson, 1992a).

Nerson's analysis ideas, first presented in late 1990, identify five phases:

1. Partition the problem.
2. Identify classes from specifications.
3. Merge, separate, add, and remove classes.
4. Identify responsibilities, relations, visibility, and constraints.
5. Work on inheritance; keep system open and flexible.

Although presented as analysis techniques, many of Nerson's ideas are more relevant to design. Indeed, his initial notation contained significant detail regarding detailed design and implementation design—for example, persistence, whether a class contains a deferred method, whether a class redefines a method, etc. The methodology was revised (Nerson, 1992a) as nine activities that are undertaken iteratively. These are shown in Table 3.9.

The heuristics and guidelines of the approach are limited, especially for the early stages of OOA. Instead the method is more applicable to design and software specification, although a great deal of work is currently being undertaken to develop the approach to the earlier stage of the lifecycle (Nerson, 1991, 1992a). Other problems with the approach are that it is to a large extent specific to the OOPL Eiffel and does not as yet have a stable notation for high-level models, although recent work has extended this aspect with the Better Object Notation (BON) (Nerson, 1991, 1992a). In early analysis, BON uses class and cluster charts. These two levels of support (class

Object-oriented Development

Table 3.9 *Outline of BON methodology (Nerson, 1992a)*

- Delineate the system borderline
- List candidate classes observed in the problem space
- Group classes into clusters
- Define candidate classes in terms of questions/commands/constraints
- Define behaviors: events, object communication protocols, object creation chart
- Define class features, invariants, and contracting conditions
- Refine class descriptions
- Work on generalization
- Complete and review architecture

and cluster) form the framework in which classes, relationships, and constraints are described. A range of relationships is included in the semantics of BON. Relationships between clusters are viewed purely as structural aids to assist with scaling problems. The notational constructs are shown in Figure 3.50. Class

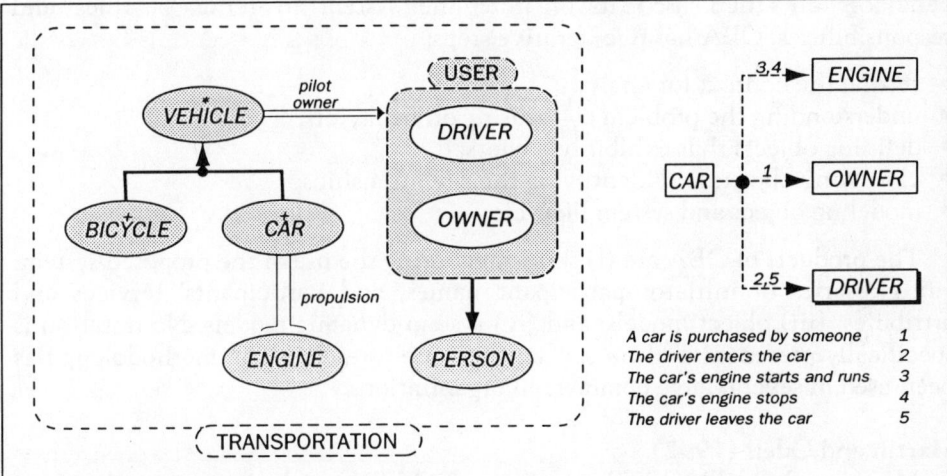

Static model (left side):
- Clusters are represented with rounded corner rectangles drawn with dashed lines and are tagged with a name.
- Classes are represented as a name inside an ellipse, with optional annotations: deferred classes are topped with a star sign, nondeferred descendant classes are topped with a plus sign, reused classes have an underlined name.
- Inheritance relationships are represented with a single line ending by an arrowhead oriented from the descendant to the parent. Client–supplier relationships are represented with a double line ending by an arrowhead in case of association and with an open curly bracket in case of aggregation. The double line may be tagged with class feature names involved in the client–supplier relationship. Relationships are defined between classes and can be extended to clusters.

Dynamic model (right side):
- Objects are represented inside rectangles. A shadowed rectangle denotes multiple instances.
- Communication protocols are represented with dash lines, labeled with numbers. These numbers are then referred to in commented scenarios.

Figure 3.50 *BON notation (Nerson, 1992a)*

charts (inspired by CRC cards), used to capture the requirements, are translated into clusters and dynamic aspects of the system. Design decisions are captured in class specifications as programming begins.

Business Class
Business Class is a three-year ESPRIT-funded project involving nine major European industries and research organizations, which began in early 1991. The aim of the project is to develop an Eiffel-based, CASE-tool-supported, MIS environment based on BON. A major item in the project is the development of an Analyst Workbench, the initial outcome being the EiffelCase product. The project's first technical review in September 1991 showed all tasks to be on time or ahead of schedule (Tenderich, 1992).

3.3.11 Other methods and notations
Object Behavioral Analysis
In contrast to searching for tangible objects, Object Behavioral Analysis (OBA) (Rubin and Goldberg, 1992) focuses on the analysis of behaviors. These behaviors are then used to organize the system in terms of roles and responsibilities. OBA has five iterative steps:

- setting the context for analysis;
- understanding the problem by focusing on behaviors;
- defining objects that exhibit behaviors;
- classifying objects and identifying their relationships;
- modeling object and system lifecycles.

The products of OBA are (i) scripts recording the use of the proposed system; (ii) glossaries of initiator–participant names, and participants' services and attributes; (iii) object models; and (iv) system dynamic models. No notation is specifically presented and no special tools are foreseen. The methodology has been used in several large commercial organizations.

Martin and Odell (1992)
In Martin and Odell's (1992) treatise on OOA/D, a tight integration between class structure analysis and class behavior analysis is achieved. The underlying rationale is that of information engineering together with clearly discussed and defined concepts. Their approach is one of presenting well-thought-out tools and their relationships, with less emphasis being placed on the process aspects of the software development lifecycle (SDLC). No complete full lifecycle methodology is presented, the discussion focusing rather on the nature of OO analysis and OO design and the seamless transition between them.

Document-Driven Analysis
In Document-Driven Analysis (DDA) (Drake *et al.*, 1992a) the focus is on customer-supplied documents. It combines an object model and a state model

Object-oriented Development

that are consistently cross-referenced. It is currently focused strongly on analysis, while the authors note it is still evolving. The notation is a rounded rectangle with three sections for (i) name, (ii) attributes, and (iii) methods.

DDA supports message passing, data relationships, and inheritance relationships, using single and double arrows as well as cardinalities (Figure 3.51). Object data dictionaries are used and the dynamics are captured using finite-state machine concepts and notation. The DDA approach has been compared with the approaches of Shlaer and Mellor (1988) and Coad and Yourdon (1990) in a case study of a hospital management system (Drake et al., 1992b).

de Champeaux

The de Champeaux method is one that has been developed within Hewlett Packard (HP) for a number of years. It initially arose on the basis of the work of Shlaer and Mellor and later Rumbaugh et al. (1991). It has a number of interesting features that are worthy of mention. Firstly, the approach aims to bring a "top-down" flavor, particularly to the analysis phase. The reason for this is that large systems require a "divide and conquer" approach to begin with, which is something the "analyst gets for free when working within the structured paradigm" (de Champeaux, 1991). This top-down approach is supported by the notion of ensembles. These are abstract objects that are essentially a tightly coupled collection of objects. They are therefore similar to subsystems or clusters. The difference is that they are a formal mechanism that may exist in the execution environment in a manner similar to that of classes.

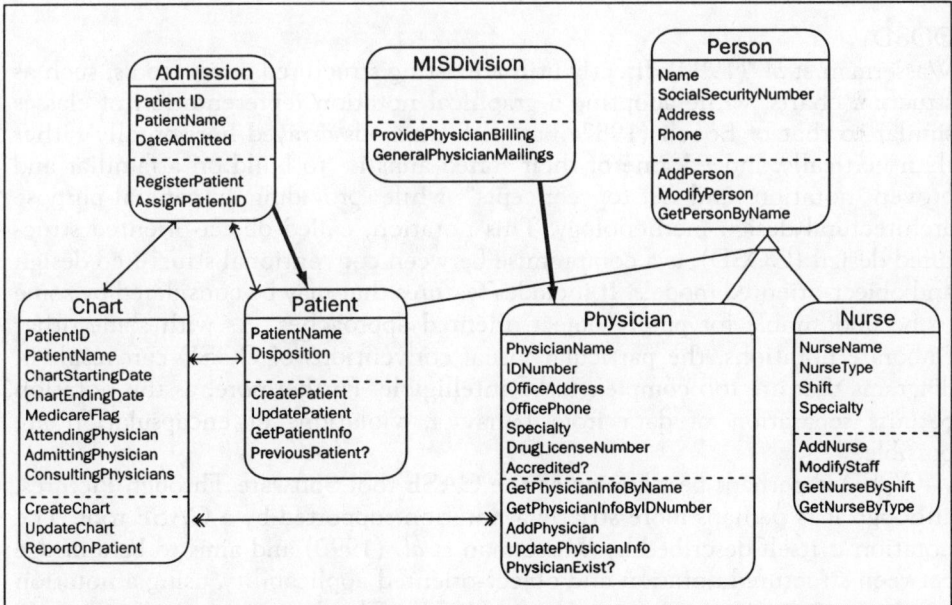

Figure 3.51 DDA notation—hospital example (Drake et al., © copyright SIGS Publications, 1992a)

The method is based on three models: an information model, a state model, and a process model. These models are similar to those of Rumbaugh *et al.* and Shlaer and Mellor, reflecting the ancestry of this approach.

The method is supported by a relatively informal notation and as yet there has been no detailed discussion of the process of OO development. It is therefore in the early stages of development but promises some interesting results, particularly with regard to OOA.

FUSION

Another HP methodology is known as FUSION (Coleman *et al.*, 1993). Its name derives from the authors' aim of integrating the existing methods of Booch, OMT, and CRC. The methodology has three stages: analysis, design, and implementation. From the requirements analysis, an object model (an ERD, since no operations are described) and a separate functional model are built. In design, object interaction graphs, visibility graphs, class descriptions, and inheritance graphs are constructed before programming. The static object model only supports specialization/generalization and aggregation (*not* association), aggregation being shown by nested icons. The functional model describes the specification of the system operations, including a postcondition. FUSION also adopts use cases and mixed graphical and textual documentation. Consistency and completeness are stressed. The inheritance notation has an arrow direction that is the opposite of most others, directed from superclass to subclass. Concurrency is not yet supported. CASE tool support is to be based on ObjectMaker (see Section 9.1.5).

OOSD

Wasserman *et al.* (1990) directly utilize existing structured design tools, such as structure charts, while adopting a graphical notation representation of classes similar to that of Booch (1987) but with methods arrayed horizontally rather than vertically. Indeed, one of their stated aims is "to build on a familiar and proven notation and set of concepts" while providing a general-purpose architectural design methodology. This notation, called object-oriented structured design (OOSD), is a compromise between conventional structured design and object-oriented models. It includes features that may be considered by some to be undesirable for purely object-oriented approaches. As with some other elaborate notations, the particular visual conventions of OOSD can result in diagrams that are too complex to be intelligible. Furthermore, as the notation permits separation of data from behavior, violations of encapsulation are possible.

OOSD is perhaps best known as the CASE tool Software Through Pictures, although it is perhaps more strictly a notation supported by a CASE tool. The notation is itself described by Wasserman *et al.* (1990) and aims to be a bridge between structured notation and object-oriented applicability, using a notation for concurrency derived from Hoare (1974). The basic icon is a rectangle (Figure 3.52). Visible methods are denoted by extruding rectangles: a

Object-oriented Development

visualization reminiscent of Booch's (1986) notation. Messages and their arguments take a very structured appearance by using "a notation familiar to most software engineers." Indeed, the authors describe it as a superset of structure charts and Booch's notation. Thick arrows are used to indicate an "instantiation from a generic class," although the use of the term "genericity" appears to merge the terms "abstract/deferred class" and "generic class" as used by, e.g., Meyer (1988a) and elsewhere in the present text. One feature of this notation and few others is that there is an explicit exception handling mechanism (Figure 3.53). Inheritance relationships are shown by a dotted arrow and MI is allowed. Concurrent processes (again the Ada influence is strongly felt here) are shown as parallelograms that represent Hoare's monitors. Private operations are just shown as internal boxes within the class icon. Relationships and cardinalities seem not to be considered and, overall, there is perhaps too much obeisance to structured notations to permit a truly object-oriented mindset to be supported. The full set of OOSD symbols is given in Figure 3.54.

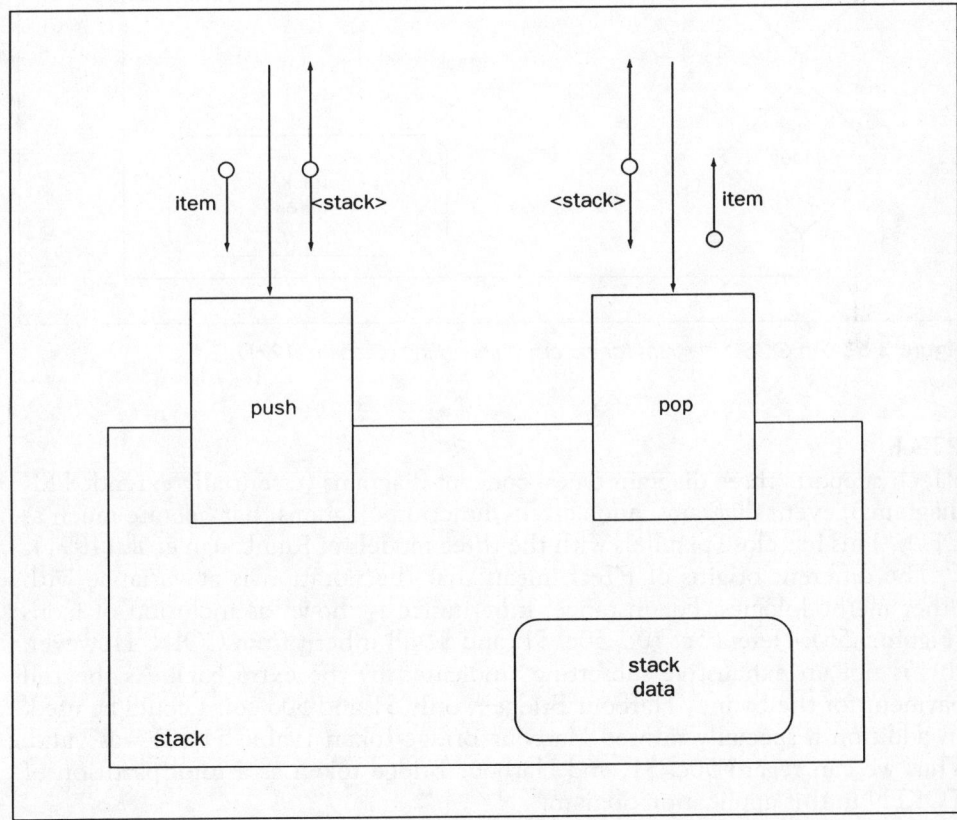

Figure 3.52 *An OOSD object representing a stack (Graham, 1991)*

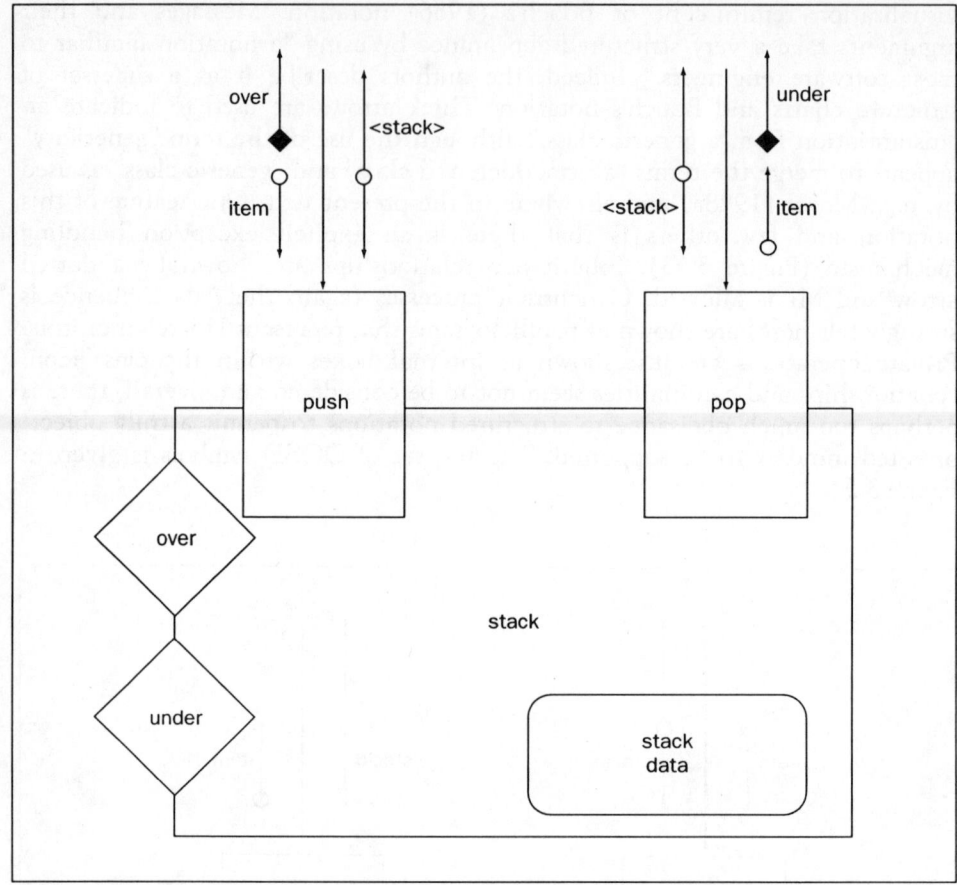

Figure 3.53 *An OOSD diagram for exception handling (Graham, 1991)*

PTech

PTech supports three diagram types: concept diagrams (essentially extended ER diagrams), event diagrams, and activity/function diagrams that operate much as DFDs. This has close parallels with the three models of Rumbaugh *et al.* (1991).

The different origins of PTech mean that the notation is at variance with other methodologies. For instance, inheritance is shown as inclusion of icons (Figure 3.55). Here a 5c, 10c, 50c, $1, and $2 all inherit from COIN. However, this is not an exhaustive subsetting (indicated by the extra bar). As the toll payment for the Sydney Harbour Bridge[16], only $1 and 50c coins could be used. In addition a specially minted Harbour Bridge token (value $1.50) was valid. Thus we can regard 50c, $1, and Harbour Bridge token as a total partition of TOKEN in this application domain.

---

16. At least, until the toll went up to $2 in August 1992!

Object-oriented Development

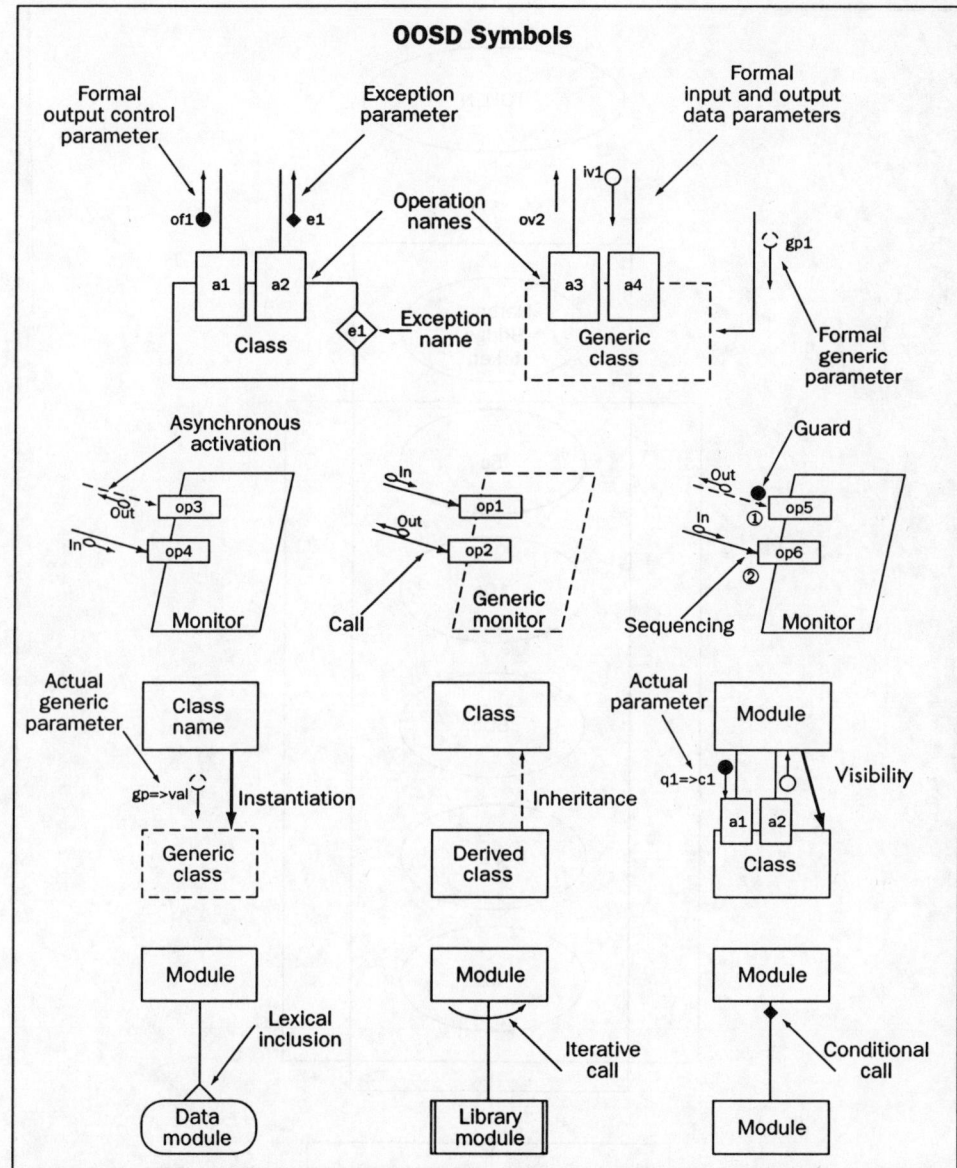

Figure 3.54 *The symbol set for OOSD/Software through Pictures (Wasserman et al., © 1990 IEEE)*

The model supports a novel view of states as subtypes and has a strong emphasis on event mechanisms for modeling the dynamics of the model. Dynamic classification is also a major part of this method (Martin and Odell, 1992). The model does not support multiple inheritance (de Champeaux, 1991) and is not behavior encapsulated.

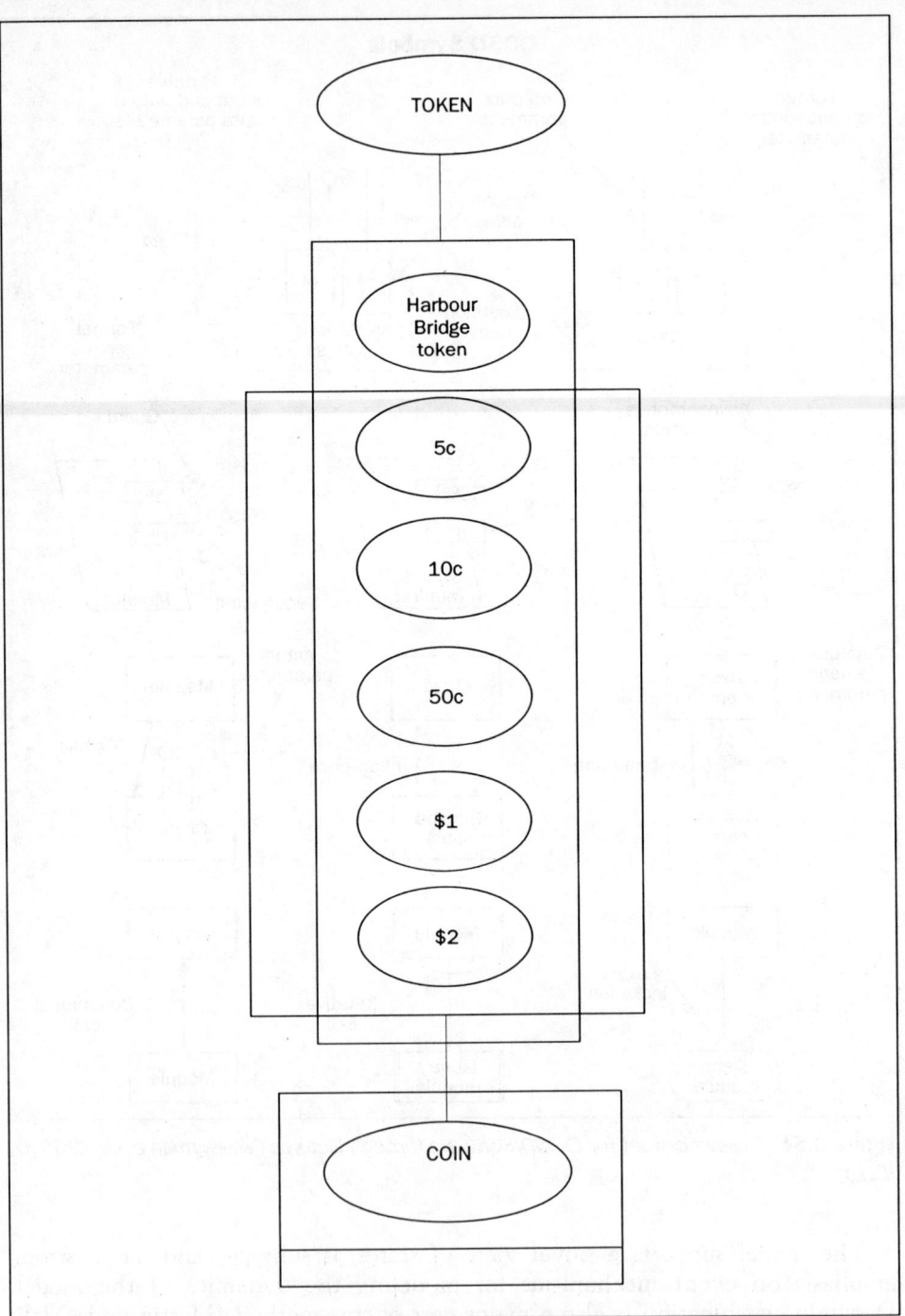

Figure 3.55 *Harbour Bridge tokens using PTech notation (Adapted from Graham, 1991)*

Object-oriented Development 191

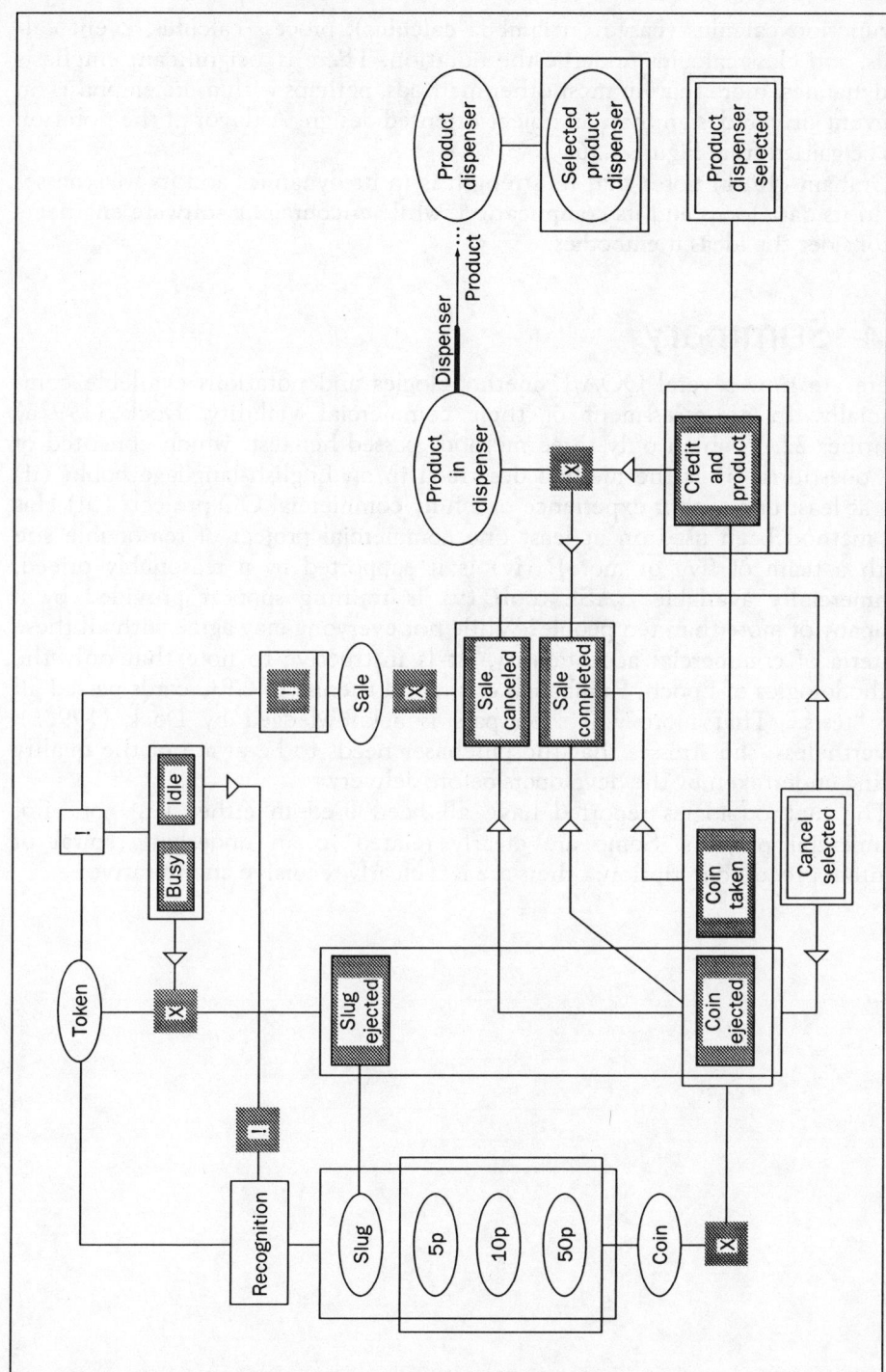

Figure 3.56 Combined concept and event schema for a vending machine example using PTech notation (Graham, 1991)

Function calculus (based on lambda calculus), process calculus, event calculus, and class calculus underlie the notation. There is a significant emphasis on dynamics, more than in most other methods, perhaps with more emphasis on an event-driven design than an object-oriented design. A flavor of the notation can be gained from Figure 3.56.

Graham (1991) notes that its strength is in its dynamics and its weaknesses are in its data focus and its complication, while encouraging software engineers to consider the ideas it embodies.

3.4 Summary

There are now several OOA/D methodologies and notations available commercially. In an assessment of their commercial viability, Dock (1992a) identifies 22 of which only three methods passed her test, which consisted of five questions: (i) Is the method described in an English-language book? (ii) Has at least one author experience of a fully commercial OO project? (iii) Has the method been used on at least one commercial project of reasonable size (with a team of five or more)? (iv) Is it supported by a reasonably priced, commercially available CASE tool? (v) Is training support provided by a company of more than ten people? While not everyone may agree with all these "criteria of commercial acceptability," it is instructive to note that only the methodologies of Booch, Rumbaugh et al., and the use of CRC cards passed all five "tests." That more will soon pass is acknowledged by Dock (1992a). Nevertheless, she stresses that the purchaser needs to be aware of the quality testing undertaken by the developers before delivery.

The methodologies reported have all been used in either large or pilot commercial projects. Some are clearly related to an underlying spiral or fountain process description; others are less clearly recursive and iterative.

CHAPTER 4

An Overview of MOSES

4.1 Introduction

The aim of this chapter is to present an overview of the Methodology for Object-oriented Software Engineering of Systems (MOSES), to be discussed in full detail in Chapters 5, 6, and 7.

MOSES is a complete lifecycle methodology that has evolved from and refined the work reported in Henderson-Sellers and Edwards (1990, 1993a, b), Henderson-Sellers (1992a), and Edwards (1992). MOSES, as well as its earlier versions, has been tested in both academic projects and commercial organizations and is being increasingly adopted for object-oriented software developments.

MOSES provides activities, guidelines, and deliverables for all aspects of an OO project. It delineates phases of the development process and is supported by a set of graphical and textual notations (Chapter 5). It utilizes graphical models throughout the development. There are five such graphical deliverables, supported by eight textual deliverables covering all phases of the lifecycle (Table 4.1).

One of the prime advantages of object-oriented development is that the use of a single object model throughout the product lifecycle permits significantly

Table 4.1 *The Deliverables of MOSES*

Textual Deliverables	Graphical Deliverables
Iteration Plan	O/C Model
User Requirements Specification (URS)	Event Model
Scenarios/Actor Glossary	Objectchart
Class Specification (CS)	Inheritance Model
Subsystem Responsibility Specification (SRS)	Service Structure Model (SSM)
Source Code	
Test Report	
Review Report	

smoother transitions between all stages of product development than is possible in a traditional structured development environment. Indeed, in MOSES many traditional phases (e.g., analysis and design) are able to be merged, supporting "seamless" development. This encourages rapid iterations and recursions between problem space and solution space, utilizing a single description, both conceptually and graphically, of O/Cs in a truly seamless fashion. True seamlessness requires the resulting object-oriented design to be executable, thus removing the need for a separate Implementation Phase. This is possible if the design is expressed in a current OOPL or if the methodology has an associated executable language. Without an associated executable language, a methodology requires some mapping to a particular implementation language. In its process lifecycle, MOSES differentiates between the conceptual Specification Phase that ignores constructs specific to programming languages and an Implementation Phase in which final design details and coding take into account the specific characteristics of the OOPL chosen for the implementation.

With respect to the issue of programming language independence, there are essentially four approaches that OO methodologies can take. First, a methodology can be targeted at one specific programming language. This results in a somewhat limited applicability for the methodology and one in which the models developed are constrained by the OOPL constructs, despite being ideally suited to the *current* version of that particular language.

Second, the methodology could support only those characteristics common to *all* OOPLs. Thus the methodology is a "common denominator" approach. This results in a widely applicable methodology but one that is constrained by a lack of expressiveness in having to support only the commonality of *present-day* programming languages; for example, using this approach would lead to the nonsupport of multiple inheritance.

The third approach is for a methodology to support all concepts found in the full range of current OOPLs and for the developer to ignore those that are not appropriate in the chosen language domain. The result is a complex (possibly unwieldy) but widely applicable methodology.

The final approach is to support an expressive object model but one that may not necessarily correspond to a particular OOPL. This results in an expressive and widely applicable method but one in which some individualized mapping to the final OOPL will probably be required.

This fourth approach is essentially that adopted in MOSES. We do, however, explicitly identify a number of constructs as "add-ons" to the object model. These "add-ons" tend to relate to a particular programming language.

The overall framework within which MOSES operates is shown in Figure 4.1. Essentially, we recognize (i) a product lifecycle that represents the complete history of a product (or a system) and (ii) a process lifecycle that represents the iterative development process (IDP) (Lorenz, 1993).

4.1.1 Product lifecycle

Within the product lifecycle, two major periods are evident: the Growth Period and the Maturity Period. The Growth Period is the one that over the years has occupied the mind of developers and methodologists more. However, it is the Maturity Period that has been identified as being the more costly in the complete product lifecycle. Maturity is often termed maintenance and simply added to the end of the process lifecycle. This view of maintenance is simply not appropriate within an OO project. Instead, maintenance, or more correctly enhancement, is a reapplication of the process lifecycle at a later point in the product lifecycle. The Growth Period of the product lifecycle is probably the single most significant period of activity. The Growth Period and successive Enhancement Periods may be decomposed into three stages. These are the Business Planning Stage, the Build Stage, and the Delivery Stage. The Business Planning Stage is where feasibility studies, strategic planning, risk analysis, and cost-benefit analysis (CBA) are undertaken to ascertain the necessity of the proposed system and its impact on the business. These activities are documented in a Business Planning Report, which is the major deliverable of this stage (Figure 4.2). This stage occurs at the start of the project and at the start of enhancement projects to varying degrees, leading to the inception or termination of the proposed product or enhancement. It is not discussed in detail within MOSES, since its relation to object technology (OT) is little different from its relationship to any other technology, e.g., packages and 4GLs, that may be used to solve a business problem. After the Business Planning Stage, the Build Stage begins if approval is given. This involves the application of the process lifecycle within the overall product lifecycle (Figure 4.1). It is this Build Stage on which methodologies (both traditional and OO) have tended to focus. Deliverables from the Build Stage are the sum of the process lifecycle deliverables as shown in Figure 4.2 and discussed in detail below.

Following the Build Stage is the Delivery Stage, where installation of the full system and site testing occur and the new system is reviewed. This review is

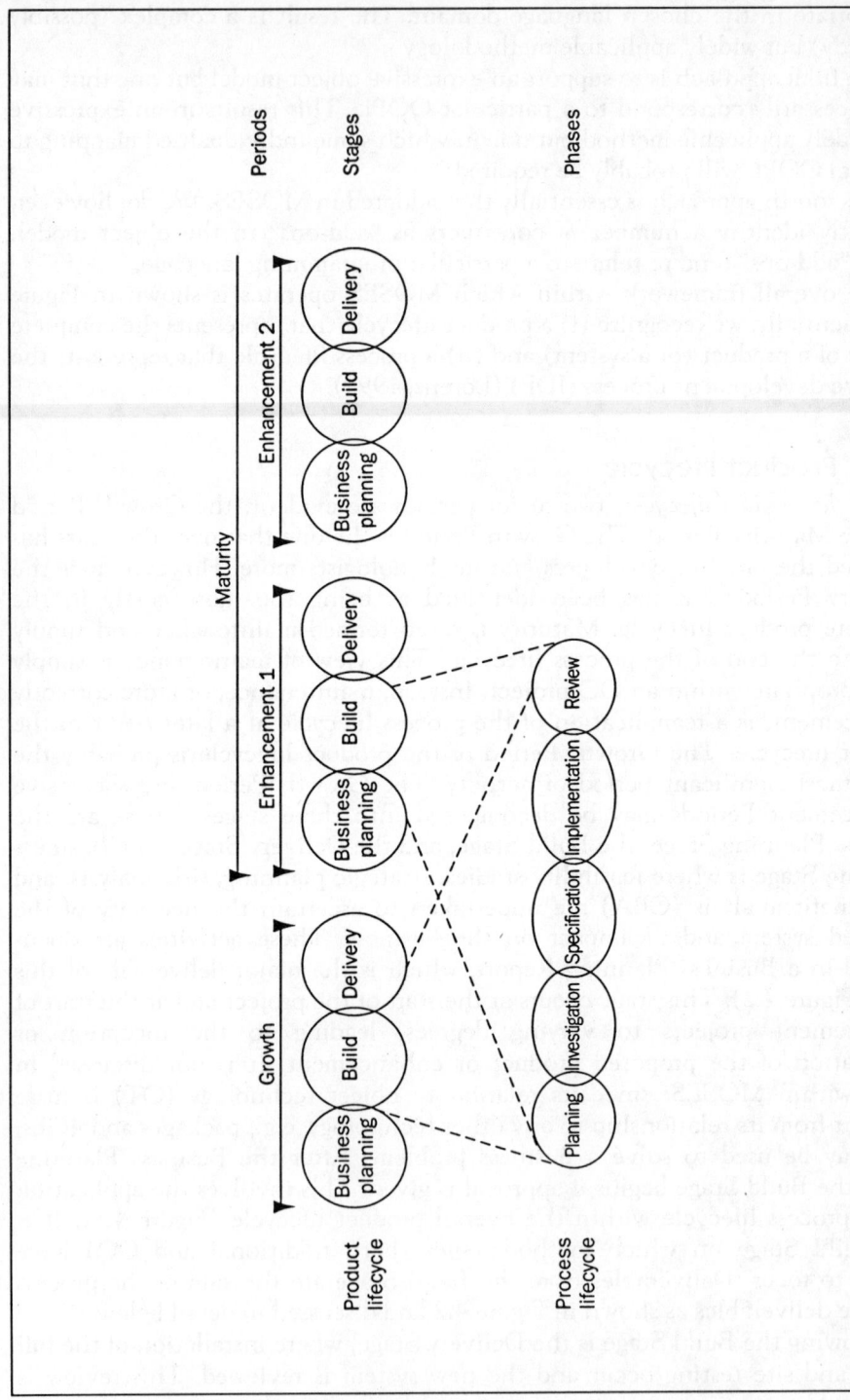

Figure 4.1 *The overall framework of MOSES, showing the relationship between the periods and the stages of the product lifecycle and the phases of the process lifecycle*

An Overview of MOSES

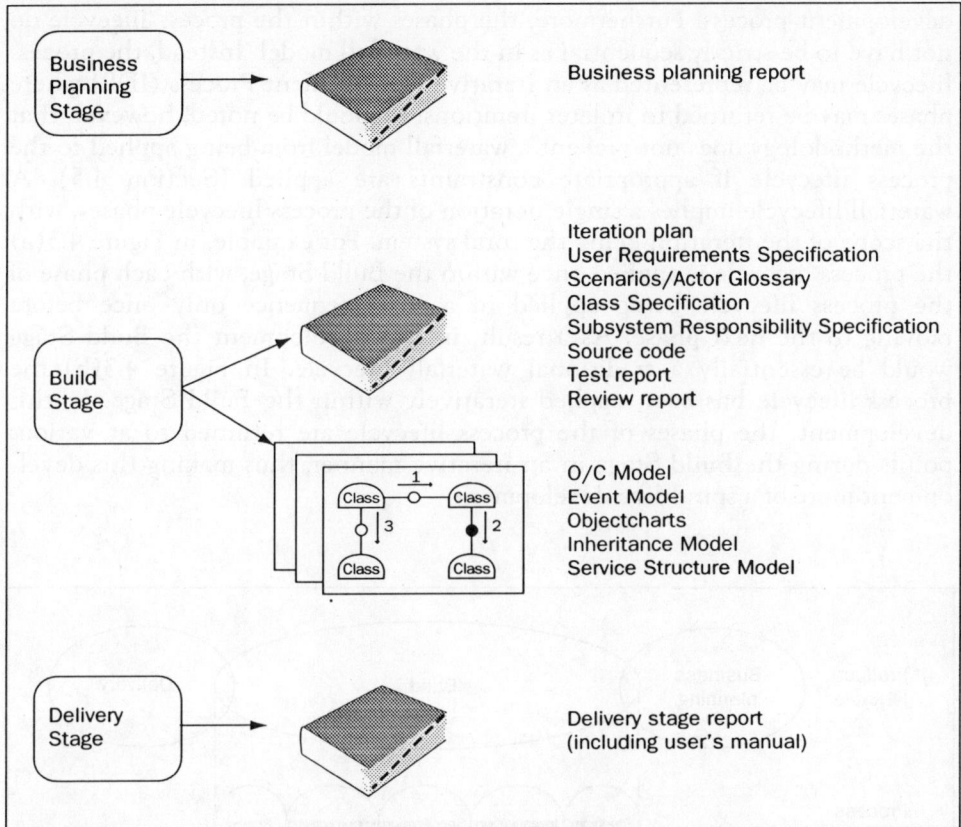

Figure 4.2 *Major deliverables of the three stages of the product lifecycle*

documented in a Delivery Stage Report (Figure 4.2). Together, these three stages make up the Growth Period and Enhancement Periods of the product lifecycle.

The Maturity Period of the product lifecycle is composed of a number of Enhancement Periods, each of which requires the reapplication of the process lifecycle, albeit on a smaller scale than in the initial Growth Period. In this period the software system grows, its quality being continually improved.

The process lifecycle, which most current methodologies address, is therefore viewed in MOSES as a recurring part of the overall product lifecycle rather than as being synonymous with it.

4.1.2 Process lifecycle

The *phases of the process lifecycle* are significantly simplified in an OO development because of the applicability of the object model *throughout* the development process. Furthermore, the phases within the process lifecycle do not have to be strictly sequential as in the waterfall model. Instead, the process lifecycle may be represented as an Iterative Development Process (IDP) where phases may be returned to in later iterations. It should be noted, however, that the methodology does not prevent a waterfall model from being applied to the process lifecycle if appropriate constraints are applied (Section 4.5). A waterfall lifecycle implies a single iteration of the process lifecycle phases, with the scope of the iteration being the total system. For example, in Figure 4.3(a) the process lifecycle is applied once within the Build Stage, with each phase of the process lifecycle being applied in a strict sequence only once before moving to the next phase. As a result, in this development the Build Stage would be essentially a traditional waterfall lifecycle. In Figure 4.3(b) the process lifecycle has been applied iteratively within the Build Stage. In this development, the phases of the process lifecycle are returned to at various points during the Build Stage in an iterative manner, thus making this development more of a spiral-like development.

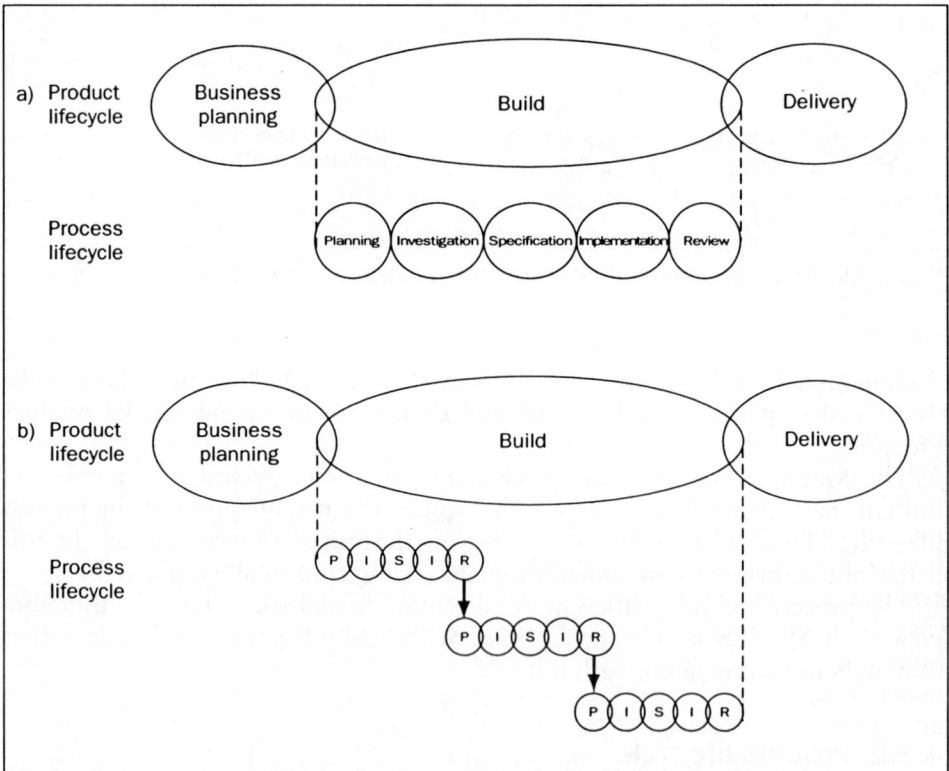

Figure 4.3 *The use of the process and product lifecycle in (a) a waterfall and (b) an iterative development environment*

The process lifecycle is therefore able to be tailored to the particular needs of a specific project or corporate development environment. This means that parallel development and iteration in the process can be managed on a per project basis, taking into account specific project resources and constraints.

Within an iterative lifecycle, a key concept in MOSES, no longer does the complete design have to be constrained by the first, and usually least well informed, decisions. Design decisions taken early are easily modified in light of feedback from users obtained during incremental delivery of systems and demonstrations of prototypes resulting from the iterations. Designs and systems can now evolve in the ethos of synergism between developer and user. Flexibility and product quality are thus readily enhanced.

4.2 MOSES: both a product and process lifecycle methodology

This book largely concentrates on the process lifecycle, although there is some discussion of the product lifecycle. Within this product lifecycle/process lifecycle context, the goals of MOSES include:

- provision of software engineering support for both large and small object-oriented systems development;
- provision of a development process that supports a smooth transition from initial modeling through to implementation;
- provision of a development approach for flexible and extensible systems;
- provision of guidelines for project and product management;
- support for development of highly reusable classes, systems, and designs;
- underpinning of the software development with a quality objective.

MOSES is applicable to projects of any size and for many types of applications, although the present version (2.1) does not yet fully support real-time or distributed systems in which concurrency plays a major role (limited concurrent behavior *can* be supported through the use of objectcharts—see Section 7.10).

MOSES is also an adaptable methodology in the sense that it does not impose a rigid sequence of steps on the developer during the process lifecycle. Instead, it recognizes the diversity of software projects and the realities of practical systems development where rigid methodologies often hinder rather than help developers. MOSES does, however, provide a framework, albeit a tailorable one, that guides the process lifecycle. It achieves this balance between flexibility and control by dividing the development process methodology into three components: phases, activities, and the lifecycle model (Figure 4.4).

Phases are the major structural units of the process lifecycle. MOSES recognizes five phases: Planning, Investigation, Specification, Implementation, and Review (Figure 4.1).

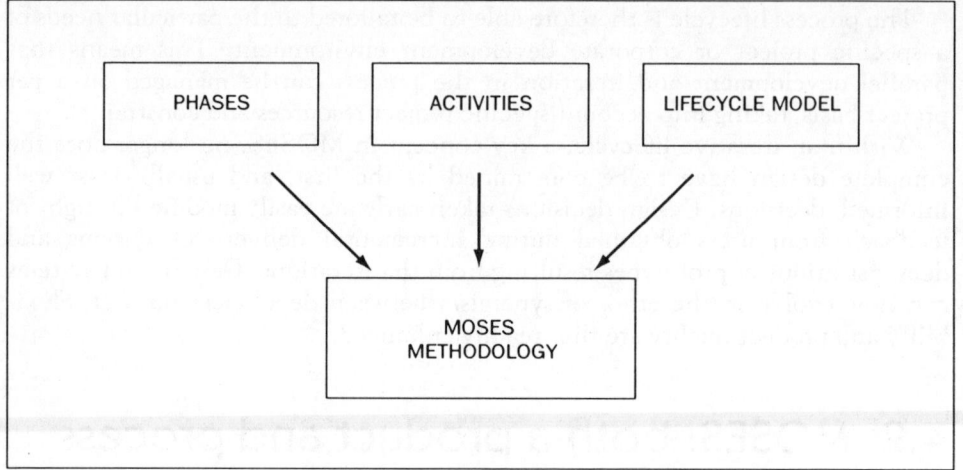

Figure 4.4 *The interaction of phases, activities, and lifecycle model in MOSES*

Activities are individual tasks that must be undertaken during the development process. Activities (Chapter 7) are discussed separately from phases, as each activity may occur in many phases.

The *lifecycle model* is a framework for the sequencing and interaction of the phases of the process lifecycle within the Build Stage. The same five phases may interact in quite different ways in different lifecycles (see Figure 4.3).

These three components, when integrated, provide a complete methodology for the process lifecycle to be applied in the Build Stage of the product lifecycle. Each component and their interactions are now discussed in more detail.

4.3 Phases and deliverables of MOSES

As noted above, within MOSES we identify five phases in the process lifecycle: Planning, Investigation, Specification, Implementation, and Review (Table 4.2). Deliverables are associated with each phase, as detailed below.

Deliverables of MOSES come in graphical and textual forms and are specified as being the outcome of a phase. They are prepared incrementally as a consequence of one or more activities. Some relate specifically to the system, some to individual O/Cs. A deliverable may be a final document if the iteration is the final one or if a waterfall model is adopted, or it may be an interim management deliverable produced during the iteration to ensure conformance to the overall plan.

The main textual deliverables (Figure 4.5) produced during MOSES are (i) an Iteration Plan, (ii) a formal User Requirements Specification (URS), (iii) Scenarios and an Actor Glossary, (iv) a Class Specification, (v) a Subsystem Responsibility Specification (SRS), (vi) Source Code, (vii) a Test

An Overview of MOSES

Table 4.2 *Five Lifecycle Phases of the MOSES Methodology*

Phase	Incorporating
Planning	scheduling, setting objectives
Investigation	user requirements capture, problem understanding
Specification	analysis, high-level (system) design
Implementation	detailed design, coding, class and service testing
Review	quality assessment, project plan assessment, scenario testing

Report, and (viii) a Review Report. Each of these deliverables is discussed in more detail in Chapters 6 and 7.

MOSES is complemented by a number of graphical notations described in detail in Chapter 5. The main graphical deliverables of MOSES (Figure 4.6) are (i) an O/C Model, (ii) an Event Model (EM), (iii) Objectcharts, (iv) an Inheritance Model, and (v) a Service Structure Model (SSM), although not all of these will necessarily be required on every project.

The Planning Phase is where work schedules, resources estimates, work

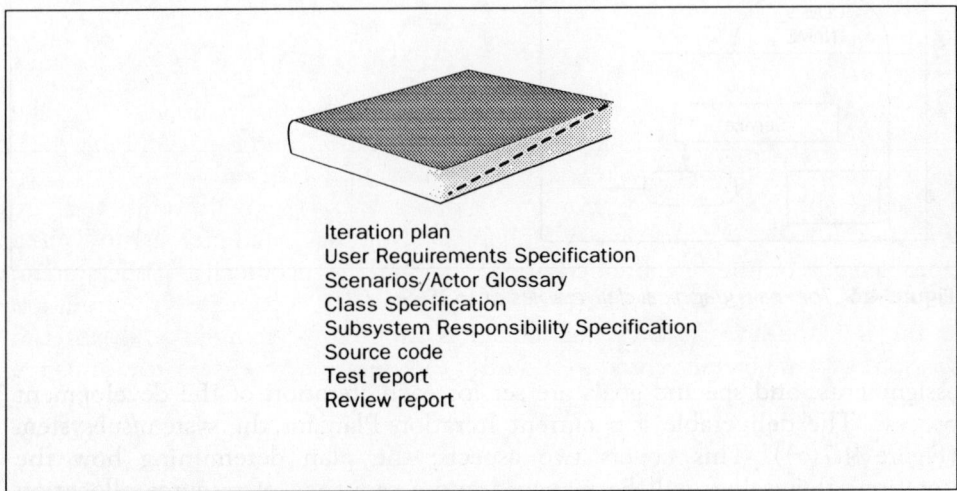

Iteration plan
User Requirements Specification
Scenarios/Actor Glossary
Class Specification
Subsystem Responsibility Specification
Source code
Test report
Review report

Figure 4.5 *The main textual deliverables of MOSES*

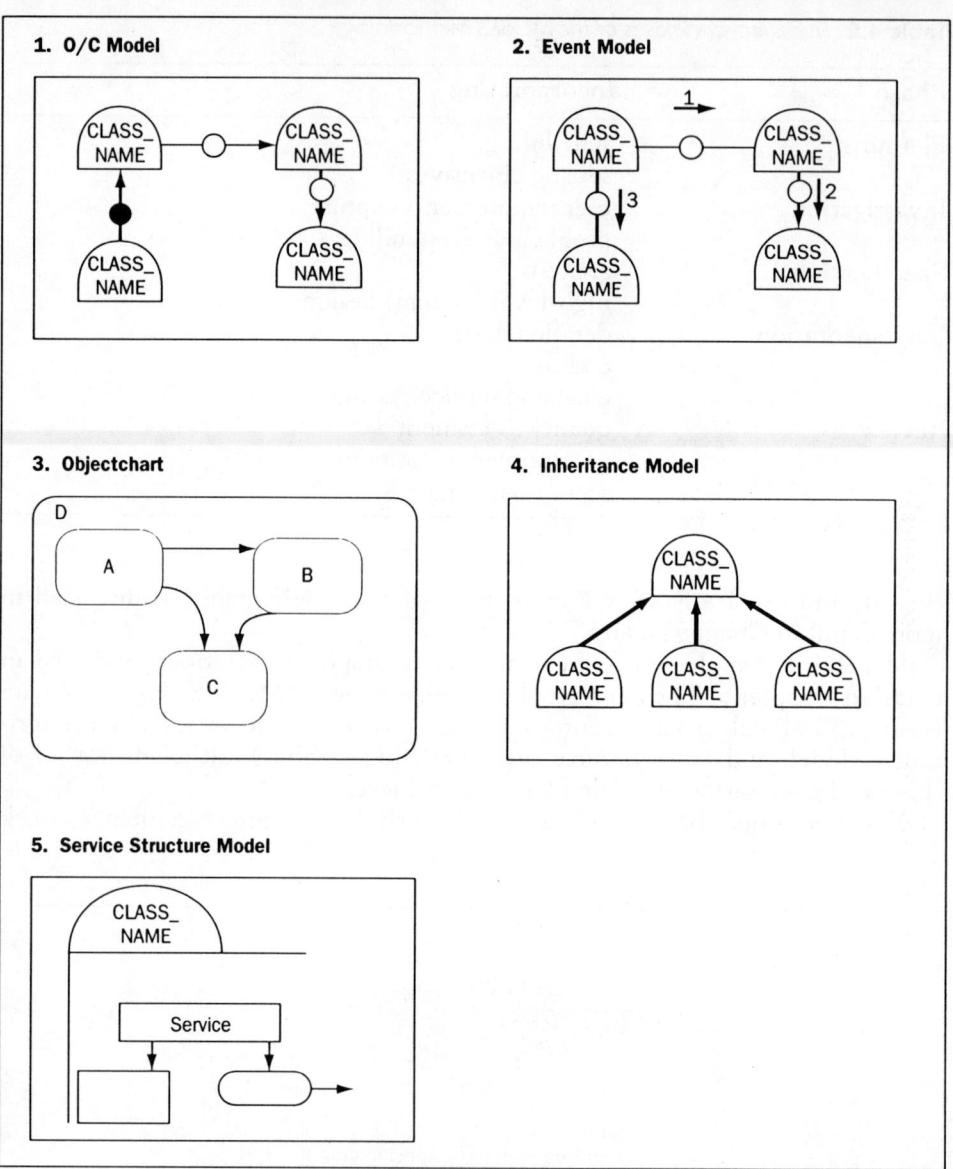

Figure 4.6 *The main graphical deliverables of MOSES*

assignments, and specific goals are set for each iteration of the development process. The deliverable is a current Iteration Plan for the system/subsystem (Figure 4.7(a)). This covers two aspects: the plan determining how the iterations themselves will be managed and a sequence of resource allocation plans, one for each iteration.

An Overview of MOSES

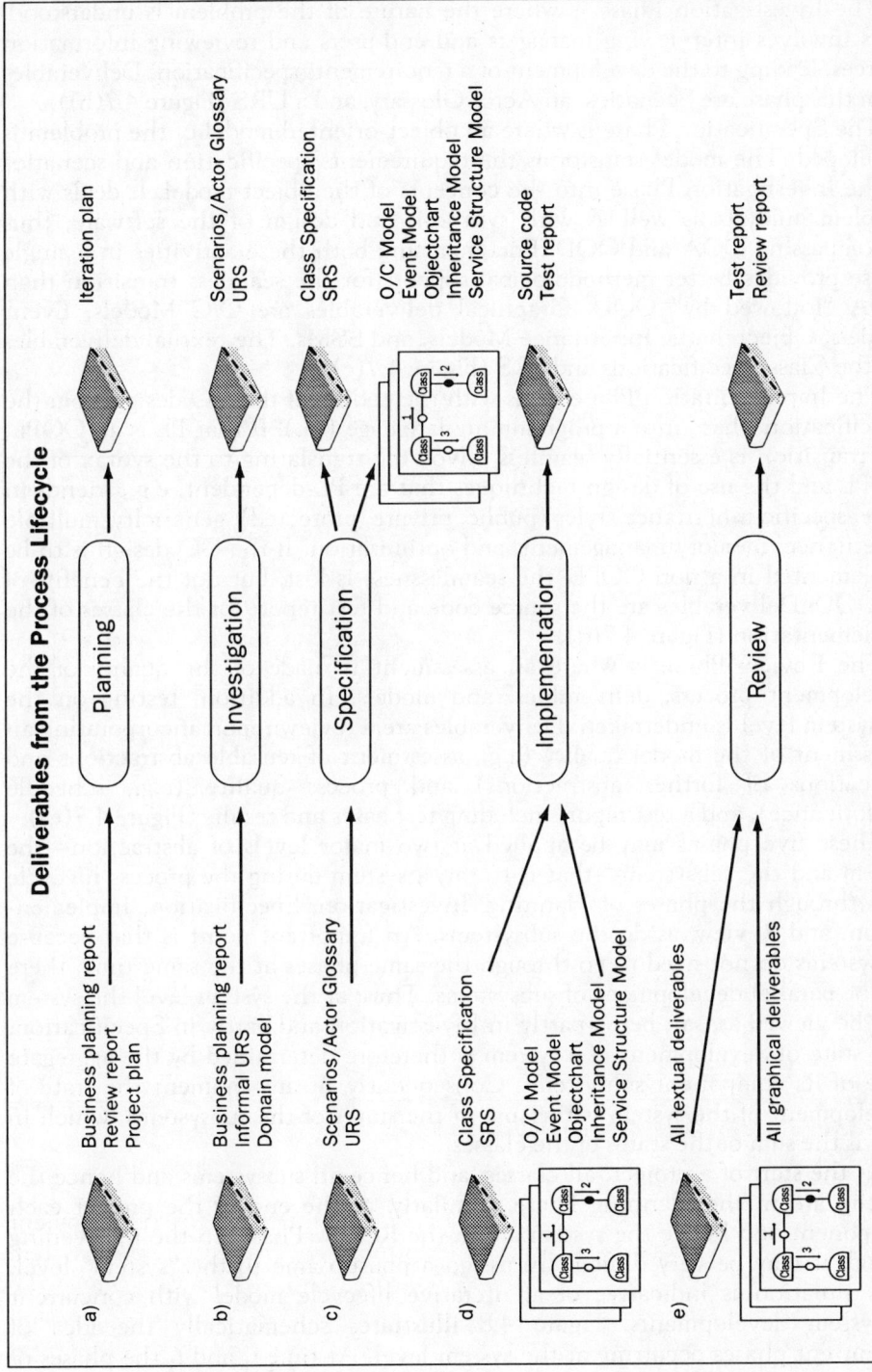

Figure 4.7 The deliverables from the five phases of the process lifecycle of MOSES

The Investigation Phase is where the nature of the problem is understood. This involves interviewing managers and end-users and reviewing information sources, leading to the development of a requirements specification. Deliverables from this phase are Scenarios, an Actor Glossary, and a URS (Figure 4.7(b)).

The Specification Phase is where an object-oriented model of the problem is developed. The model transforms the requirements specification and scenarios of the Investigation Phase into the concepts of the object model. It deals with problem analysis as well as with synthesis and design of the software, thus encompassing OOA and OOD. Encompassing both these activities in a single phase provides better methodological support for the seamless transition than OOA "followed by" OOD. Graphical deliverables are O/C Models, Event Models, Objectcharts, Inheritance Models, and SSMs. The textual deliverables are the Class Specifications and SRS (Figure 4.7(c)).

The Implementation Phase deals with the coding of the OO design from the Specification Phase into a programming language (PL). If that PL is an OOPL, the transition is essentially seamless, involving translating to the syntax of the OOPL and the use of design techniques that are PL-dependent, e.g., friends in C++, specific inheritance styles (public, private, protected), genericity, multiple inheritance, memory management, and optimization. If the OO design is to be implemented in a non-OOPL, the seamlessness is lost, but not the benefits of an OOD. Deliverables are the source code and test report for the classes of the implementation (Figure 4.7(d)).

The Review Phase is where an assessment is made of the quality of the development process, deliverables, and models. In addition, testing on the subsystem level is undertaken. Deliverables are a review report incorporating an assessment of the model quality (e.g., assessment of reusable abstractions and indications of further abstractions) and process quality (e.g., schedule conformance), and a test report including test cases and results (Figure 4.7(e)).

These five phases may be applied at two major levels of abstraction—the system and the subsystem—that is to say, a system during the process lifecycle goes through the phases of Planning, Investigation, Specification, Implementation, and Review, as do the subsystems. An important point is that because subsystems do not need to go through the same phases at the same time, there can be parallel development of subsystems. Thus, at the system level the system may be viewed as, say, being partly in Investigation and partly in Specification. The state of development of a system is therefore determined by the aggregate state of its component subsystems. Consequently, at any moment the state of development of the system is the sum of the states of the subsystems, which in turn is the sum of the states of the classes.

At the start of a project, all classes, and hence all subsystems and hence the system, are in the Planning Phase. Similarly, at the end of the project each component and hence the system are in the Review Phase. In the intervening period, it may be very difficult to assign a phase name to the "system" level. This situation is indicative of an iterative lifecycle model with concurrent subsystem developments. Figure 4.8 illustrates schematically the idea of concurrent phases occurring at the system level. At time t_1 and t_2 the phases of

An Overview of MOSES

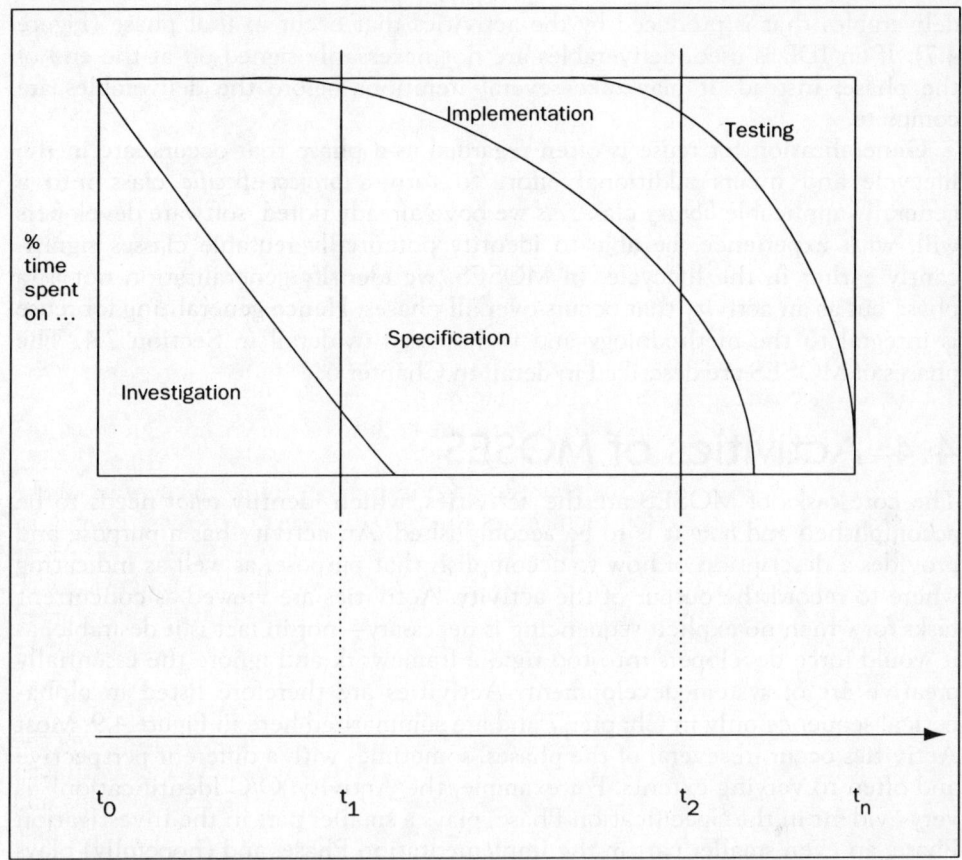

Figure 4.8 *A schematic diagram to show the distribution of effort between phases as time progresses through the project*

Investigation, Specification, and Implementation are all being undertaken, reflecting the different subsystems. However, the percentage of time spent on each phase changes over time, reflecting the sequence of the phases in the process lifecycle. At only a very few points, e.g., t_0 and t_n, is the system in only one phase.

This IDP is not necessarily the only possible solution. Indeed, a waterfall model would mandate that all Investigation be completed before Specification. The implication is that each component of the system is also in the Investigation Phase and may not move to the Specification Phase until such time as all the Investigation is deemed complete.

This separation of the lifecycle approach and the phases adds an important element to MOSES and is discussed further in Section 4.5. The phases also form the basis of the deliverables of the methodology. Each phase has a set of deliverables that is produced by the activities that occur in that phase (Figure 4.7). If an IDP is used, deliverables are not necessarily signed off at the end of the phase; instead, it may take several iterations before the deliverables are complete.

Generalization for reuse is often regarded as a phase that occurs late in the lifecycle and incurs additional effort to turn a *project-specific* class into a generally applicable *library* class. As we have already noted, software developers will, with experience, be able to identify potentially reusable classes significantly earlier in the lifecycle. In MOSES, we identify generalization not as a phase but as an activity that occurs over all phases. Hence generalizing for reuse is integral to the methodology and is discussed in detail in Section 7.4. The phases of MOSES are described in detail in Chapter 6.

4.4 Activities of MOSES

The core tasks of MOSES are the activities, which identify *what* needs to be accomplished and *how* it is to be accomplished. An activity has a purpose and provides a description of how to accomplish that purpose, as well as indicating where to record the output of the activity. Activities are viewed as concurrent tasks for which no explicit sequencing is necessary—nor in fact is it desirable, as it would force developers into too rigid a framework and ignore the essentially creative art of system development. Activities are therefore listed in alphabetical sequence only in Chapter 7 and are summarized here in Figure 4.9. Most Activities occur in several of the phases, sometimes with a different perspective and often to varying extents. For example, the Activity: O/C Identification[17] is very evident in the Specification Phase, plays a smaller part in the Investigation Phase, an even smaller part in the Implementation Phase, and (hopefully) plays no part at all in the Review Phase. On the other hand, the Activity: Testing occurs in all phases except the Planning and Investigation Phases and the Activity: Quality Evaluation (Metrics) in all five phases. We can thus identify phases in which an activity is largely concentrated, as illustrated by a cross in the chart shown in Figure 4.9.

The outputs of an activity do NOT constitute a deliverable package produced at some milestone. Deliverables are a collection of documentation from a *number* of Activities and are specified as being produced at the end of a phase (Figure 4.7). Such deliverables were discussed in Section 4.3 and will be examined further in Chapter 6 in relation to the five phases of the process lifecycle.

4.5 Lifecycle model of MOSES

MOSES does not impose a particular lifecycle. Instead, a developer is free to choose the appropriate lifecycle approach for the Build Stage of the project: the

---

17. We identify activities of the methodology using the convention of "Activity: Activity_name," as in "Activity: O/C Identification."

OO approach is able to support a number of lifecycle descriptors, varying from waterfall to an iterative development process (IDP).

For example, if a waterfall lifecycle is mandated, meaning that each phase must be "signed off" before the next phase can begin, this simply implies that each phase for each subsystem must be completed before the next phase begins (Figure 4.3(a)). Thus subsystems, while being developed in parallel, progress through the process at the same rate. Although such an approach does not maximize the usefulness of OT, it is nevertheless one that many companies may need or wish to adopt and they should not be prevented from doing so by the methodology.

The preferable approach is an iterative development model where subsystems and classes progress through the process at differing rates and hence may be in different phases at a particular time.

The MOSES methodology strongly supports this iterative approach and is compatible with the fountain lifecycle model discussed in Chapter 3.1.2. In terms of project management, an iterative model requires the identification of chronological "breakpoints" at which documentation can be usefully delivered, walkthroughs undertaken, etc. The "breakpoints" are defined to be at the end of each phase of an iteration.[18] These deliverables are built, in the main, from the information developed and recorded during specific individual Activities. Hence, in the framework of Figure 4.9, information recorded from given Activities will contribute to deliverables of more than one phase. Finally, each organization should consider how, when using this necessarily iterative and recursive lifecycle model, document "version control" is to be handled. For example, cluster "n" may undergo a total of three iterations and hence documents may undergo at least three major revisions. Final "signing off" may wait until the end of the last iteration.

This flexible interaction of lifecycle models and phases results from the OO approach (seamlessness) and the separation of concerns within MOSES. In Chapter 6, we discuss in more detail an *iterative* model, as this is the most appropriate, yet least known, lifecycle model, focusing, as it does, on *incremental deliveries* to the user/customer.

4.6 Summary

MOSES, as a methodology for object-oriented software engineering, provides a framework within which industrial-strength software development can be conducted. Its 20 major activities are overlain by a set of five phases (Figure 4.9) applied to the system and subsystem levels during the IDP (process lifecycle), which corresponds to the Build Stage of the product lifecycle (Figure 4.1). MOSES covers the process lifecycle from requirements analysis to product delivery and identifies a product lifecycle within which subsequent maintenance and extension simply involve the reapplication of the process lifecycle.

---

18. Alternatively, Firesmith (pers. com., 1992) suggests that reviews should be scheduled on a time basis, *not* by lifecycle phases.

Activities and Deliverables

ACTIVITY	Plan	Invest	Spec	Impl	Review
Contract specification			X	X	
Documentation review	X	X	X	X	X
Event Model construction			X		
Generalization for reuse – completion of abstractions – optimization – refinement of class hierarchies			X	X	
Genericity specification				X	
Inheritance identification – generalization hierarchy – identification – implementation inheritance – hierarchy identification			X	X	
Interaction specification – aggregation specification – association specification – invariant specification			X	X	
Iteration plan development	X				
Library class incorporation			X	X	
Objectchart construction			X	X	
O/C identification – refine initial class list – identify persistent class		X	X		
Optimization			X	X	
Quality evaluation (metrics)	X	X	X	X	X
Scenario development		X			
Service identification – operations – properties			X	X	
Subsystem identification	X		X		X
Subsystem coordination	X				
Testing – integration testing – subsystem testing – unit testing			X	X	X
Translation to OOPL – implementation of services – implementation of structure				X	
User requirements elicitation		X			X

Figure 4.9 *Activities and deliverables and their relationship to the phases of the MOSES process lifecycle*

	Plan	Invest	Spec	Impl	Review
DELIVERABLES					
Iteration plan	X				
Requirement specification		X			
Scenarios/Actor Glossary		X			
Class Specification			X	X	
Subsystem Responsibility Specification	X		X	X	
O/C Model			X	X	
Event Model			X	X	
Objectchart			X	X	
Inheritance Model			X	X	
Service Structure Model			X	X	
Source code				X	
Test case			X	X	X
Test report			X	X	X
Review report					X

Figure 4.9 *continued*

In the next three chapters, the notation is described (Chapter 5) and then, in Chapters 6 and 7, the phases and activities of the iterative development process lifecycle (Figure 4.1) are described in sufficient detail for *direct utilization* on an object-oriented software development project, including indication of project management guidelines/documentation/deliverables resulting from each activity and phase. In Chapter 8, an illustrative case study of the application of MOSES to the development of a decision support system (DSS) in a technical management area is presented.

• CHAPTER 5 •

The MOSES Notation

5.1 Introduction

In this chapter we discuss the representations (graphical and textual) for expressing and documenting OO designs in MOSES. The MOSES notation integrates a number of other notations, including refined versions of the notations proposed by Edwards and Henderson-Sellers (1993a), the Uniform Object Notation of Page-Jones *et al.* (1990), and objectcharts proposed by Coleman *et al.* (1992). It is a general and simple, non-language-specific (both natural and programming languages) notation reflecting the current object-oriented philosophy (rather than currently available languages). It provides a minimalist set of constructs required to support the basic agreed object-oriented concepts while leaving language-dependent features (such as friends in C++) as "optional extras," available within MOSES as secondary-level, add-on features. The MOSES notation reflects and supports the methodology at all stages of the lifecycle.

The MOSES notation includes:

- a graphical notation for the static aspect of an object-oriented system;
- a graphical notation for the dynamic aspect of an object-oriented system;
- a representation for complete documentation of classes;
- a suite of notations for managing large-scale complexity.

Any system, whether object-oriented or not, can be viewed at different levels of abstraction and from different perspectives (Shlaer et al., 1991; Edwards and Henderson-Sellers, 1991; Monarchi and Puhr, 1992); that is, we see only parts of a system at a time, at varying levels of detail. These perspectives are important at different times in promoting an understanding of the different aspects of a system. In the MOSES notation, several graphical and textual models are used. These are complemented by a number of complexity management techniques.

Each of these views describes some particular aspect of the system. The views are not mutually exclusive in the information they display. For example, an O/C Model of the system will also contain some, but not all, of the class hierarchy information. Similarly, not all the models are of equal importance in a project. For example, Service Structure Models may only be used in particularly complex services. Also important are the representations used in managing complexity in a model that, in MOSES, consist of mechanisms for physically dividing up diagrams, mechanisms for viewing the model at different levels of abstraction, such as subsystems, and mechanisms for layering a model (Table 5.1). Full documentation of a system is achieved by combining graphical models (e.g., the O/C Model) with textual documentation (e.g., Class Specification). Each of these views, and the appropriate graphics, will be described in detail in the sections below.

Table 5.1 *The graphical and textual models supported in the MOSES notation*

Name of model
O/C Model
Event Model
Objectchart
Inheritance Model
Service Structure Model

Complexity management techniques
Sheets
Subsystems
Layered Models
Selective Visibility

5.2 O/C Model

The O/C Model represents the structure of the application. This view contains the O/Cs, subsystems and their various relationships. An O/C Model that shows only classes may be viewed as the schema of the application, while if it shows only objects, it is representing a particular configuration of objects. The O/C Model is the dominant view of the system under development.

5.2.1 Classes

Classes are represented diagrammatically by a rectangle topped with a dome.[19] This shape, termed a tablet, is used to represent the encapsulation of data (rounded shapes) with functions (rectangles) in one icon—thus giving inbuilt meaning to the distinctive icon shape. The word "tablet" is used to reinforce the idea of important information being held within an O/C Model by classes. Tablets possess the following characteristics: (i) class name, (ii) public services, and (iii) private services, organised in a clearly specified manner. The box containing the public services protrudes slightly outside the class border (Figure 5.1(a)). This maintains the representation of the external interface visible to the object modeler, while permitting other internal characteristics, which are not discernible during the early Specification Phase, to be represented later. This discrimination between visible/concealed O/C details (i) is strongly influenced by modeling, and especially the notions of abstraction, and (ii) links smoothly with the software-domain concepts of information hiding, discussed further below with respect to the Implementation Phase.

It is also important to note that neither properties nor operations are isomorphically mapped to data in the software. This external view describes only the interface and is totally consistent with the principle of uniform reference and the concept of information hiding. In the Specification Phase, O/Cs are investigated "without prejudice toward what is going to be data or not" (Odell, 1991)—i.e., the modeling viewpoint is retained. In the Implementation Phase, however, concerns about data and data hiding provide a different viewpoint. Within the tablet, properties and operations should be grouped together. A dividing line (dotted) may be used to indicate such groupings (Figure 5.1(b)), although if the methodological distinction between properties and operations is not enforced during Implementation, this line may be removed. Figure 5.1(c) shows a variation where services protrude from both sides of the tablet. The dotted tablet shown in Figure 5.2 shows an abstract (or deferred) class.

As designs require more and more detail, it may be necessary to show services that are secret, being available to other services of the class but not to other classes. In the MOSES notation, the service name can be placed within the tablet yet not in the interface portion, graphically implying that the service is not visible from outside the class (Figure 5.3). In addition, decisions may be taken that specific services need to be implemented as attributes, i.e., data. These can be shown in a separate rounded "data box."

Persistence is shown by means of a round circle above the class name, representing a secondary storage disk (Figure 5.4), and is drawn from the work of Nerson (1991).

A *library class* is shown in bold outline to represent a more robust class from

---

19. You can blame Meilir Page-Jones for the shape of this icon. After three days of wrangling with colleagues over its shape, he saw the symbol in a dream that he had in July 1990 and drew it on his notepad by his bed.

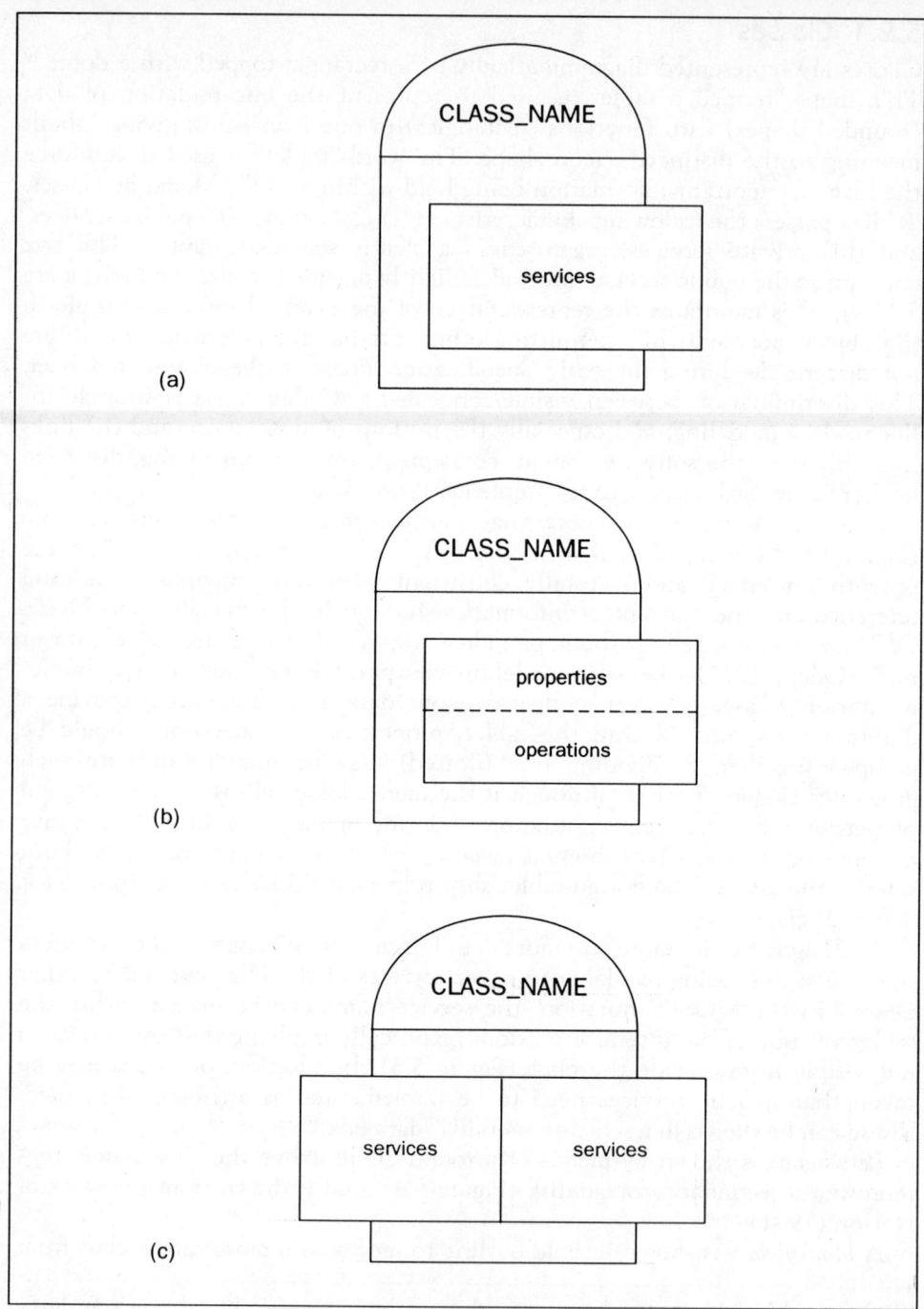

Figure 5.1 *(a) Class icon: the MOSES "tablet"; (b) class icon with dividing line between properties and operations; (c) services may overlap both sides*

The MOSES Notation

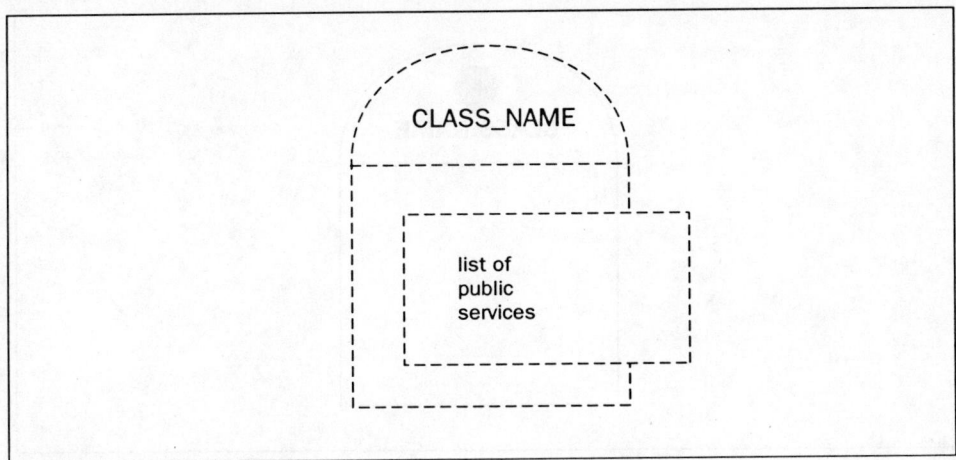

Figure 5.2 *Abstract class tablet*

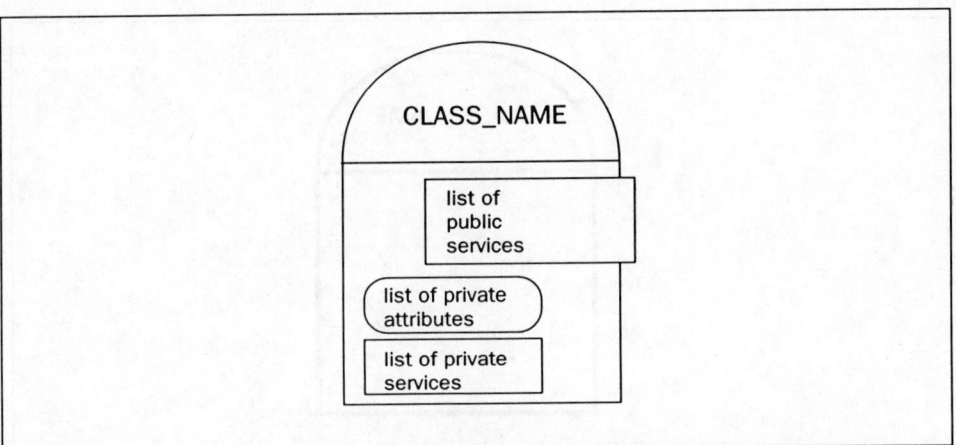

Figure 5.3 *Recommended notation for a class when internal (secret) services need to be represented*

the class library (Figure 5.5). Essentially a library class is closed from direct modification, although open to modification by inheritance. The thick border represents the closed nature of the module.

Generic classes as found in some languages (e.g., C++ Ver. 3, and Eiffel) are indicated by a formal parameter in the class name portion. The class name is separated from the generic parameters by (square) brackets and generic parameters are separated by commas, as shown below:

CLASS_NAME [GCLASS_1, GCLASS_2]

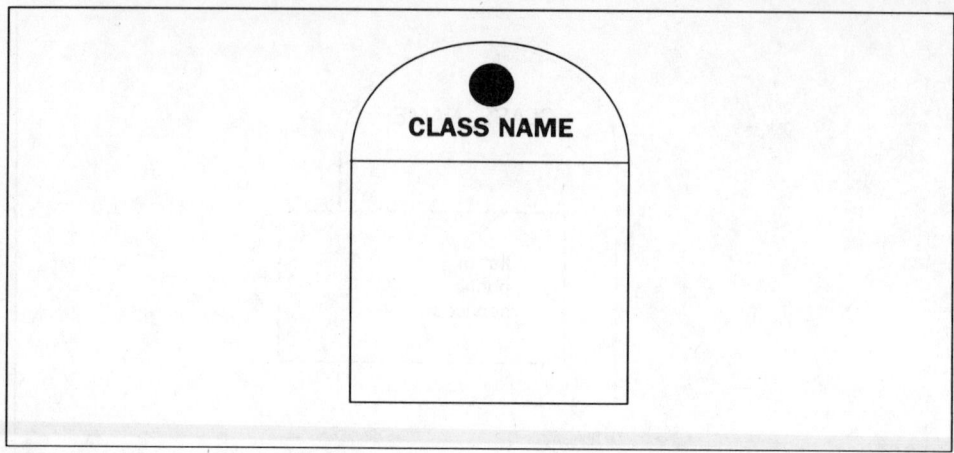

Figure 5.4 *MOSES notation for persistence*

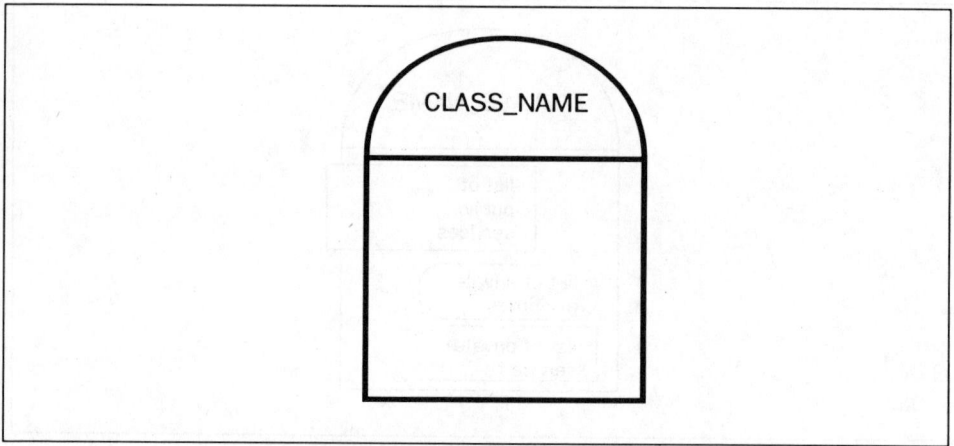

Figure 5.5 *MOSES notation for library class*

As the generic parameters are "used by" the class in some sense, the notation provides a means of visualizing this. This is shown in Figure 5.6.

A further notational concept is that of selective visibility, which is simply the removal of all interface details useful when it is necessary to take a higher-level (viz., more abstract) view of a large system (see Section 5.8.4).

Specification of services in the O/C Model is done using a formal syntax that is defined in Figure 5.7. This English-like syntax clearly indicates the inputs and outputs of a service. For example, an operation with one input and one output can be represented as:

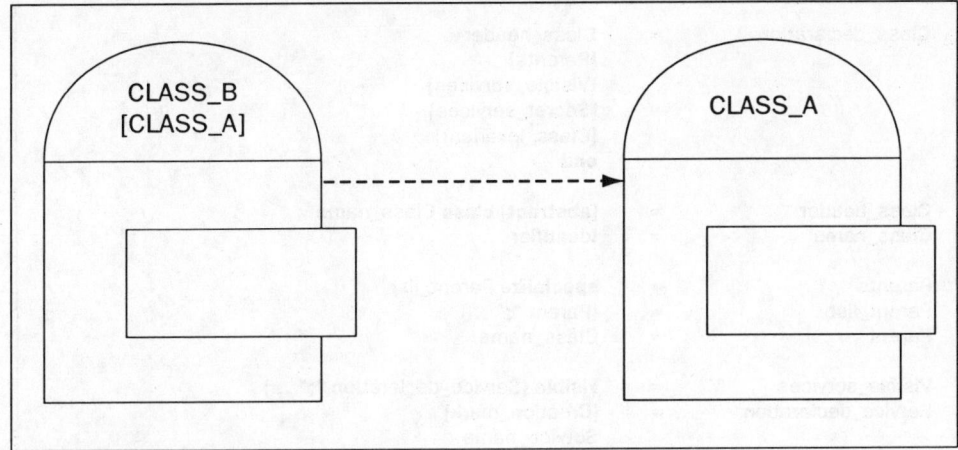

Figure 5.6 *MOSES notation for genericity*

<u>name</u>   <u>input</u>   <u>output</u>
operation (*arg*: CLASS): CLASS

This notation can be used in the graphical model and in the class specification. Graphical notation for a deferred, abstract, or virtual service is shown by placing the complete service specification in parentheses, for example (*operation*(*arg*:CLASS):CLASS), rather than by adding the keyword abstract. If a class contains even one abstract service, then the whole class must, by definition, be abstract (and therefore the tablet is dotted). Conversely, if an abstract class occurs in the system design, then at least one of the services *must* itself be abstract and indicated as such.

Services that are applicable to a class rather than to an object are termed class services. For example, a create service is a class service. A class may have many class services that are simply shown by placing a "$" in front of the appropriate services, as below:

$*service* (*arg*: CLASS_A)

It is unlikely that assertions will need to be shown directly on the tablet in the O/C Model. Rather, this detailed information is shown in the associated Class Specification, although, if needed, an optional box at the bottom can be used for invariant information[20] (Figure 5.8).

---

20. Graham (1991) also proffers an additional box (in his notation a fourth partition to the icon). With a similar intent in mind, he recommends using it for business rules, conflict rules (to resolve clashes introduced in multiple inheritance (MI) networks), and exception handling.

Class_declaration	=	Class_header [Parents] [Visible_services] [Secret_services] [Class_invariant] **end**
Class_header Class_name	= =	[**abstract**] **class** Class_name Identifier
Parents Parent_list Parent	= = =	**specialize** Parent_list {Parent ";" ...} Class_name
Visible_services Service_declaration	= =	**visible** {Service_declaration ";" ...} [Creation_mark] Service_name [Input_declaration] [Output_declaration] [Comment] [Specification] **end**
Creation_mark	=	"$"
Service_name	=	Identifier
Input_declaration Input_declaration_list Input_declaration_group Type_mark	= = = =	"("Input_declaration_list")" {Input_declaration_group ";" ...} {Input_label "," ...}+ Type_mark ":" Type
Output_declaration Service_output Component_output Association_output Symmetric_property Constraints Lower Upper	= = = = = = = =	Service_output I Component_output I Association_output Type_mark ":" **component** Type Constraints Type_mark "." Symmetric_property Constraints Identifier "(" Lower ".." Upper ")" +Integer +Integer I "m"
Comment	=	"- -" String
Specification Precondition Postcondition Assertion Assertion_clause	= = = = =	[Preconditions] [Postconditions] **precondition** Assertion **postcondition** Assertion {Assertion_clause ";" ...} Boolean_expression I Comment
Secret_services	=	**secret** {Service_declaration ";" ...}
Class_invariant	=	**invariant** Assertion

Figure 5.7 *BNF description of the Class Specification syntax*

The MOSES Notation

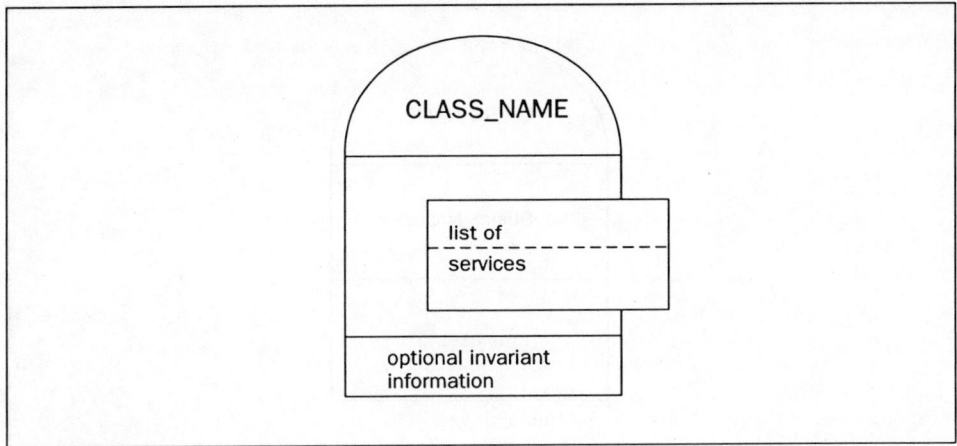

Figure 5.8 *Class showing optional constraint box*

5.2.2 Objects

Showing objects, rather than classes, in an O/C Model is useful when a particular configuration of objects needs to be explained or documented. O/C Models showing only objects are similar to Booch's (1991) object diagrams. They should be used sparingly within the documentation and reserved primarily for explaining particular situations. One problem with showing objects is that object names are in fact aliases (Coleman *et al.*, 1992). Aliasing implies that there may be many actual names for one object. Actual names are therefore correct only within the context of a client object. For example, an object may be referred to by the actual name "a" in object 1 and the actual name "b" in object 2. The server object therefore has actual names "a" and "b," which are aliases. The use of aliasing can significantly increase the complexity of the dynamic configuration diagrams. In order to overcome this problem of context-sensitive names, the object needs to show aliases and to provide a unique actual name. This unique actual name is equivalent to the object identifier. A name is used for comprehensibility reasons. Thus an object has three types of names in an O/C Model: a class name, a unique object name, and aliases. Only aliases from objects shown in the O/C Model are necessary. An object (as opposed to a class) is shown notationally the same as a class, but with two extra boxes below the dome (Figure 5.9). The dome still contains the class name, while the next box contains the unique object name and the lower portion contains the aliases. An alias for the object is a unique name of the referencing object, followed by the name of the object as used within the referencing object.

5.2.3 Relationships

In this section we present the notation for relationships between O/Cs: inheritance, aggregation, and association.

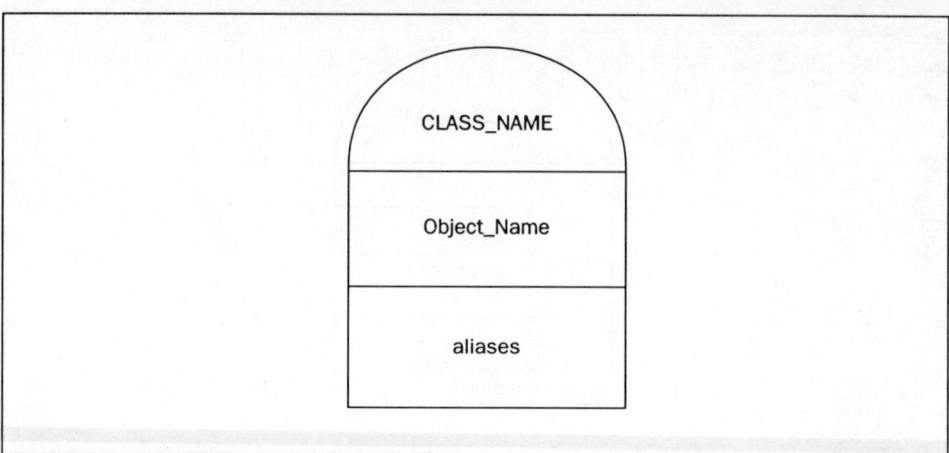

Figure 5.9 *MOSES notation for an object*

5.2.3.1 Inheritance
Inheritance within MOSES is subdivided into generalization (which is deemed to include both specification inheritance and specialization inheritance) and implementation inheritance. In order to show the similarities of these relationships we use the same basic graphic, differentiated slightly for each type.

Generalization
The MOSES notation uses a thick arrow to represent generalization (see Figure 5.10(a)), where the arrow points from the subclass to the superclass. Multiple parents are easily accommodated either by a fork notation (Figure 5.10(b)) or by two arrows (Figure 5.10(c)), and multiple specializations similarly (Figure 5.10(d)). When necessary, subclasses may be discriminated in the specialization hierarchy by addition of a label on the generalization line (Figure 5.10(e)) to indicate the property being used in the (sub-)classification, e.g., vehicles being discriminated on the basis of purpose between trucks (to carry goods) and cars (to carry people) (McGregor and Korson, 1992).

It should be noted that by specializing an ancestor, the descendant gains all the relationships of the ancestor. In the notation, this means that relationships of the ancestor need not be repeated for the descendant icon. Thus in Figure 5.11, the class PRIVATE_COMPANY, which specializes the class COMPANY, gains the relationship to DIRECTOR even though this connection is not shown explicitly. Thus the diagram need not show any redundant or duplicate information.

Implementation inheritance
Implementation inheritance is shown by a thick arrow that is from the subclass directed toward the superclass (Figure 5.12(a)). This reflects the generalization notation. This time, however, the arrow has a lexical "hat" to represent the

The MOSES Notation

module inclusion aspect implying implementation inheritance of code at the language level. For example, a class STACK may inherit the class ARRAY in order to use the implementation of ARRAY. An ARRAY and STACK, however, do not conform to the **is-a** relationship, as would be implied by specialization inheritance, and the relationship is termed implementation inheritance (see also Chapter 2). Multiple subclasses and multiple implementation inheritance are shown in a manner similar to that for generalization, with the arrows pointing from the one subclass to the two superclasses (Figure 5.12(b) and (c) respectively).

One problem with implementation inheritance, as opposed to specialization or specification inheritance, is that it does not imply a subtype relationship. Therefore, although in the generalization notation of Figure 5.11 the descendant could assume that the relationships of the ancestor were also applicable to it, this is not necessarily true for implementation inheritance. However, the notation makes the assumption that inherited relationships and services are exported by the subclass, and this must be checked for correctness in the class specification.

5.2.3.2 Association

The most basic notation for association (Figure 5.13) is a line with a circle on it joining the two collaborating classes. The relationship may be labeled.

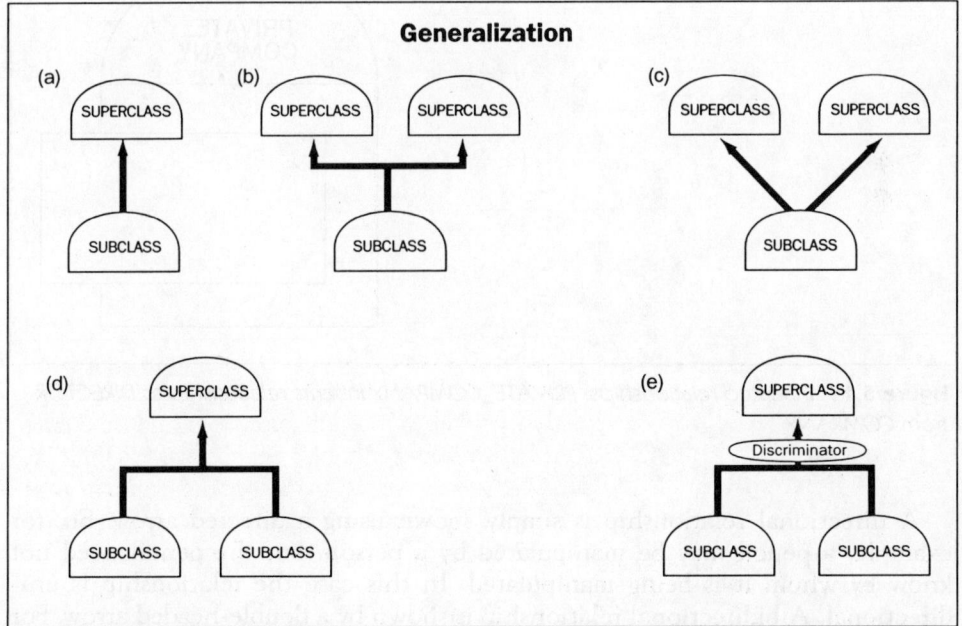

Figure 5.10 *MOSES notation for generalization: (a) single generalization; (b) fork notation for multiple parents; (c) alternative form for multiple parents; (d) disjoint multiple subtypes; (e) discriminator property for subtypes*

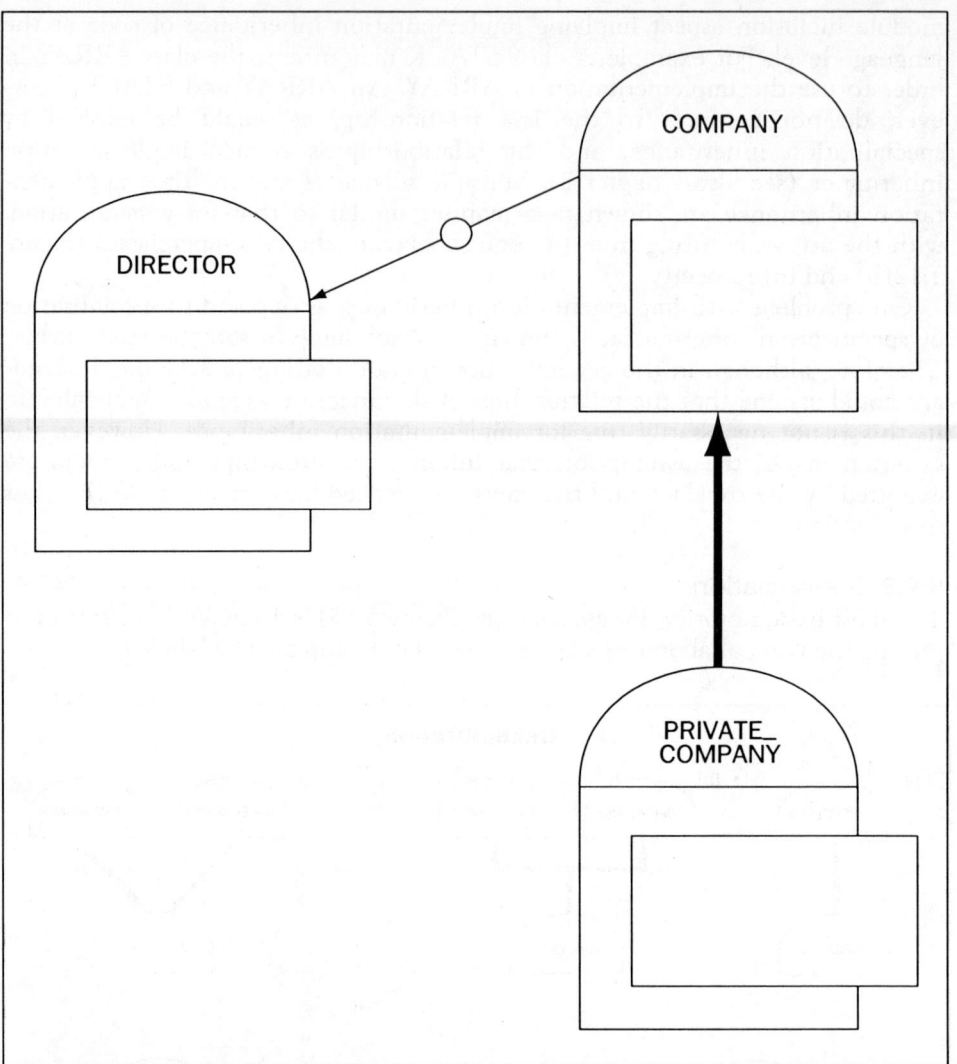

Figure 5.11 *Inherited relationships: PRIVATE_COMPANY inherits relationship to DIRECTOR from COMPANY*

A directional relationship is simply shown using a directed arrow. So, for example, a pencil may be manipulated by a person, but the pencil need not know by whom it is being manipulated. In this case the relationship is unidirectional. A bidirectional relationship is shown by a double-headed arrow. For example, it might be expected that a man and woman know of each other in a marriage and hence this relationship can be represented as a bidirectional relationship between a class MAN and a class WOMAN. If the unidirectional/

The MOSES Notation

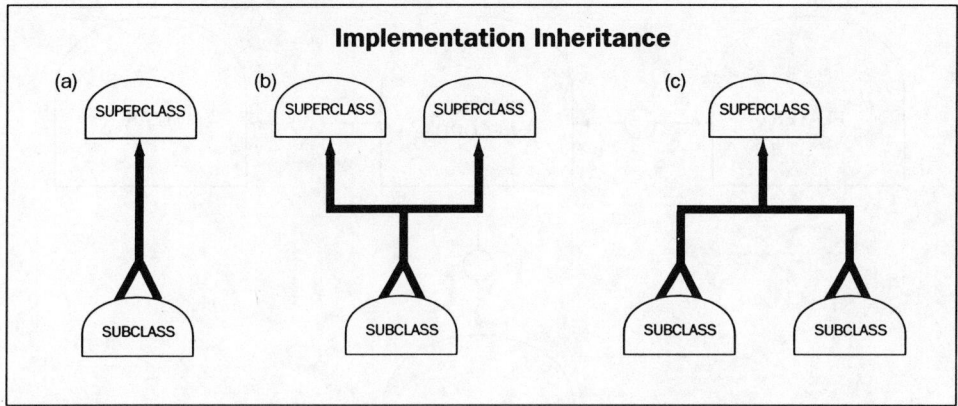

Figure 5.12 *MOSES notation for implementation inheritance: (a) single implementation inheritance; (b) multiple implementation inheritance; (c) multiple subclasses*

bidirectional nature of the relationship is not immediately determinable, an undirected line can be used and the arrowheads added later. Ternary relationships as found in ER models should be modeled as a class with binary relationships. So, for example, a ternary relationship between PLAYER, CLUB, and YEAR should be modeled as a class PLAYING_RECORD with binary relationships to each class (Figure 5.14).

Cardinalities and existence constraints of associations are discussed below (Section 5.2.3.4).

5.2.3.3 Aggregation

The notation for aggregations is a directed arrow that points from the aggregate (composite object) to the component (Figure 5.15(a)). Since aggregations are

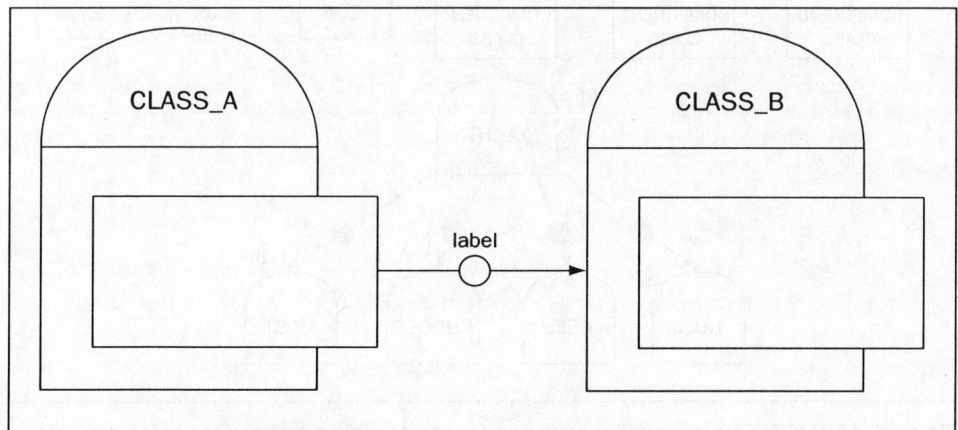

Figure 5.13 *MOSES notation for association (see text for discussion)*

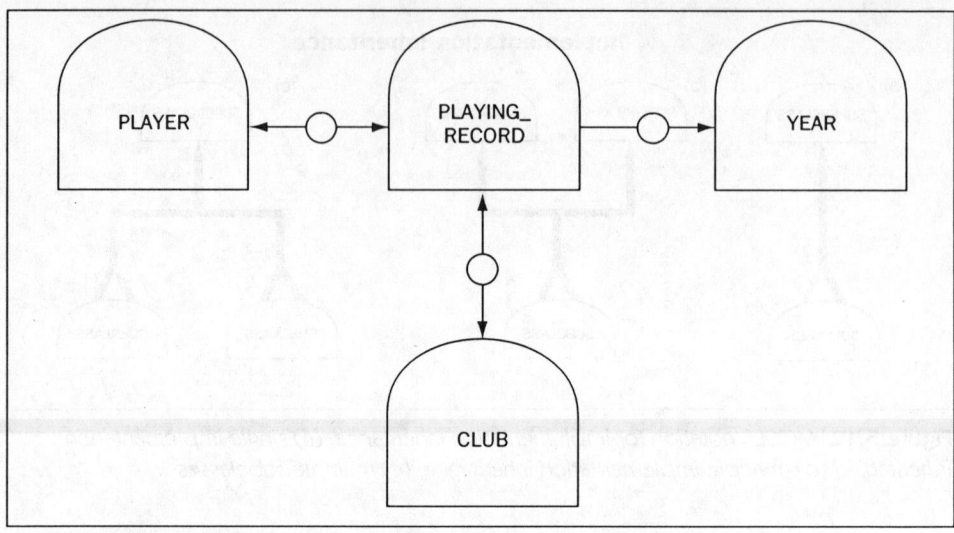

Figure 5.14 *Ternary relationships are modeled as a class with many binary relationships. In this example the class PLAYING_RECORD models a ternary relationship.*

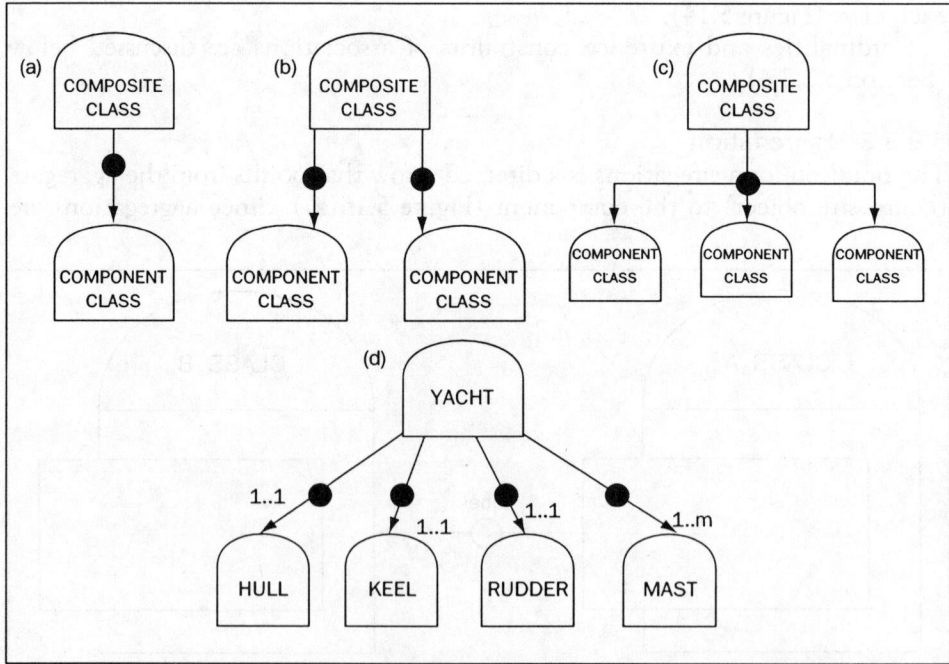

Figure 5.15 *MOSES notation for aggregation (see text for discussion): (a) single part; (b) multiple parts; (c) alternative notation for multiple parts; (d) example of composite object*

specialized forms of association (Rumbaugh et al., 1991), structural consistency is retained by labeling the connection with a circle, here filled in to represent aggregation. Multiple aggregates of different types can be shown using the notation of Figure 5.15(b) or the space saving notation of Figure 5.15(c). So, for example, a YACHT may be composed of a HULL, a KEEL, a RUDDER, and several MASTS (Figure 5.15(d)). Aggregation relationships may require the use of layering diagrams to simplify the presentation of the class (see Section 5.8.3). Cardinalities and existence constraints are also useful when specifying aggregation relationships.

5.2.3.4 Cardinality and existence constraints

Cardinalities are likely to be associated with aggregation and association relationships as well as various client–server relationships. The notation used here is a pair of numbers (arithmetic or algebraic, separated by two dots) representing the minimum and maximum numbers of participating classes at either end of the connection. These can be separated by a comma if the range is discontinuous, e.g., 1,3,5..7. This simple representation can show both optional and mandatory constraints (using 0 or 1 as the lower bound respectively) as well as cardinalities. The numbers relate to the O/C to which they are closest. For example, an optional one-to-many aggregation relationship may be expressed as shown in Figure 5.16(a). The relationship can be read as "class A is composed of zero or many class Bs." A mandatory one-to-many relationship may be expressed as shown in Figure 5.16(b) and read as "class A is composed of one or many class Bs." We suggest that the lower bound, often of zero or one, need not necessarily be clarified too early; rather, it is better to sketch the overall picture at a high level of abstraction before finally fixing the detailed constraints.

This notation can also be applied to association. For example, Figure 5.16(c) can be read as "class A has a relationship with zero or many class Bs and class B has a relationship with one or many class As."

5.2.4 OOPL-specific notations

Constructs specific to individual object-based or object-oriented languages may be useful in tailoring MOSES to specific implementation environments. We do not attempt to develop these in detail here. Rather, we note briefly that friends in C++, selective exports (in, e.g., Eiffel), and multithread tasks in Ada fall into this category. The MOSES notation currently supports "friends" (Section 5.2.4.3) as a consequence of its ancestry of the Uniform Object Notation (UON) of Page-Jones et al. (1990) but does not support concurrency specifically (other than in the dynamic model description using objectcharts).

5.2.4.1 Embedded structures (composite classes)

A structure that may be useful in Implementation is that of the composite class (Figure 5.17): a class defined with internal classes whose definitions are local and are not externally visible, i.e., lexically included classes.

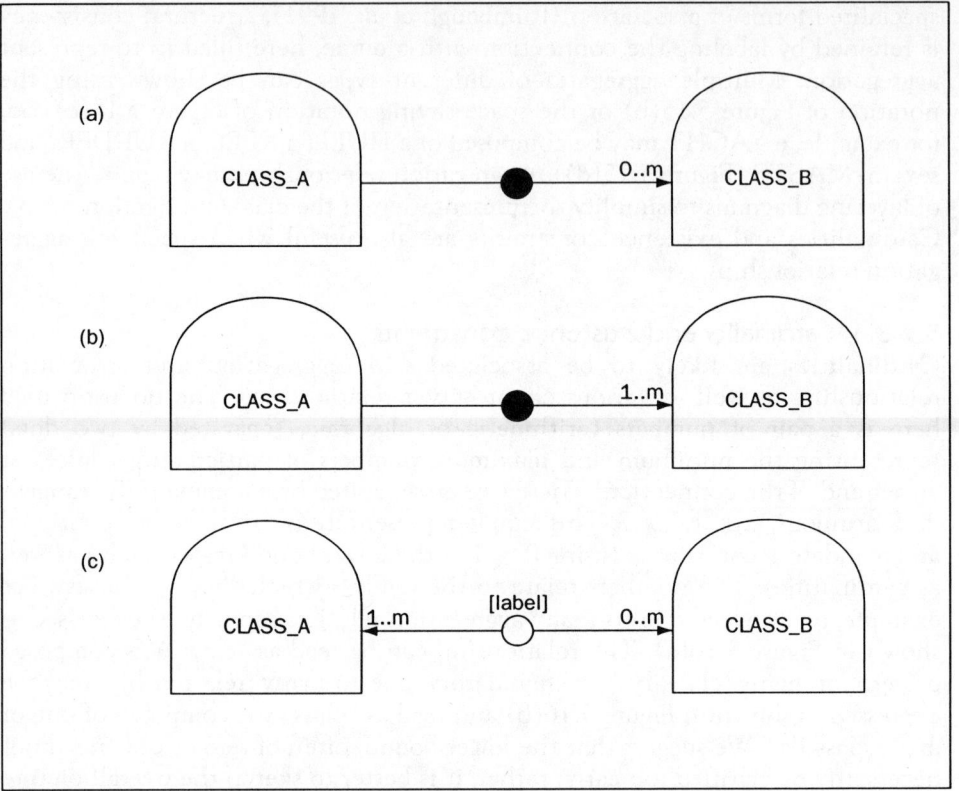

Figure 5.16 *MOSES notation for cardinalities: (a) optional one to many; (b) mandatory one to many; (c) association cardinality*

5.2.4.2 Client–server relationships

There are a number of OOPL constructs that are used to implement the basic relationships between classes. These language-specific constructs in some sense represent a client–server relationship between classes. Hence a notation is supplied to represent these different language constructs during the Implementation Phase of MOSES. These can form the basis of language-specific extensions, as discussed here. The basic notation, in which a class requires a service from another class, is a thin, directed arrow from the client O/C to the server O/C. However, since at this stage a specific OOPL will have already been chosen, in the Implementation Phase we can specify the type of client–server relationship. If this is to be implemented by reference, as in Eiffel or Smalltalk, a white circle is placed at the beginning of the arrow (the client end) (Figure 5.18(a)). In contrast, a C++ pointer, for example, is shown as a directed arrow with an asterisk (*) at the end (Figure 5.18(b)). This notation retains consistency with C++ syntax. Overall, the client–server notation retains flexibility for

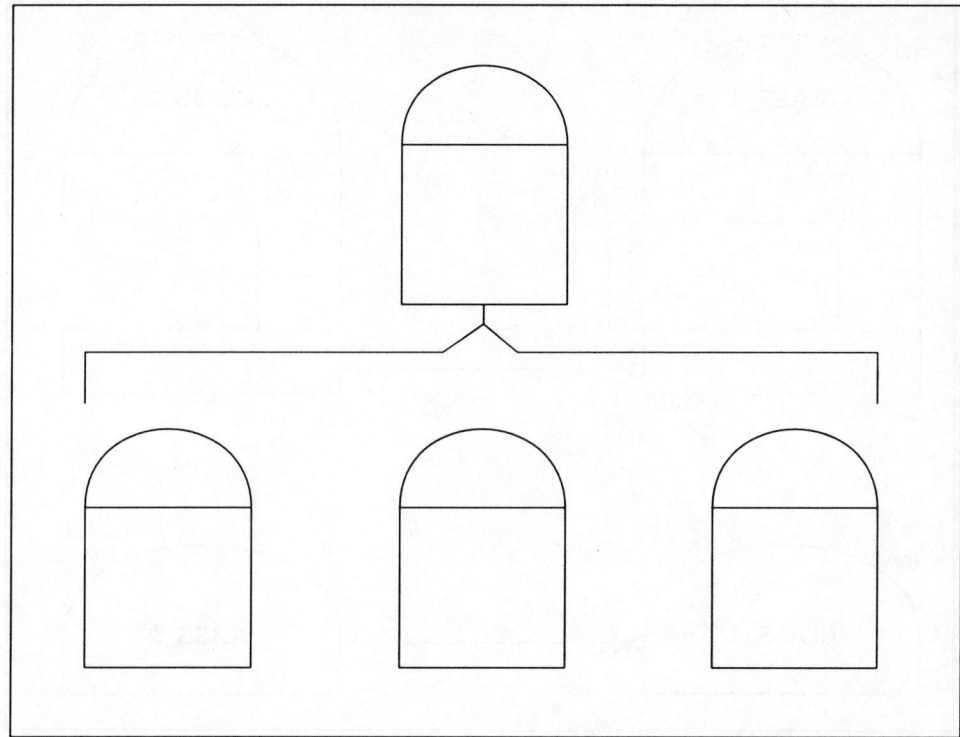

Figure 5.17 *Notation for contained classes. This combines aggregation structures with concerns of visibility.*

a wide range of current languages as well as forming the basis for future language implementations.

5.2.4.3 Friends
The MOSES notation for "friends" is that taken directly from UON and is an arrow pointing to the friend class that has a module inclusion symbol before it (Figure 5.19). This represents the fact that a class module uses another class module but via module inclusion rather than client–server. This allows access to the private part as well as the public part of the class module, including variables.

5.2.4.4 Exception handling
Exceptions are error conditions that are identified within objects and must be dealt with in a controlled fashion, either by stopping the system gracefully or by permitting second chances (cf. the RETRY mechanism in Eiffel). The MOSES notation for exception services essentially follows that for regular services except that an additional boundary symbol (a large diamond) is added to the class icon (Figure 5.20), following Wasserman *et al.* (1990).

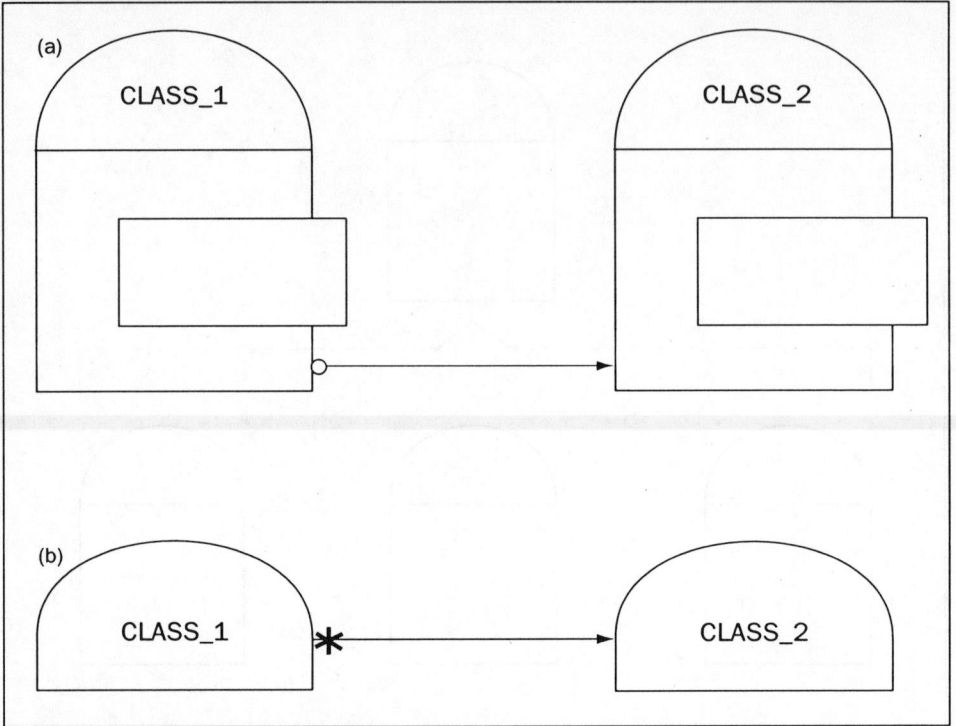

Figure 5.18 *Client–server (a) logical reference and (b) pointer relationship in a detailed Implementation Phase O/C Model*

5.2.5 Summary

The static notation detailed above is used to describe the components of the O/C Model (Table 5.1). No extra notation for instances of relationships is used; instead, the notation assumes that in instance models the relationships are actual instances.

O/C Models form a major part of the documentation once the system is complete. Figure 5.21 shows an example of an O/C Model for a wastewater plant, showing the class structure and relationships. Figure 5.22 shows the corresponding O/C Model, now showing the *objects* of the wastewater treatment plant. In this model there is only one instance of the class PRIMARY_SETTLER. This instance is being referred to by an instance of the class AERATOR and two instances of the class WATER_PACKET. The instance of AERATOR has a unique name "ar" and the instances of WATER_PACKET have unique names "w1" and "w2." The alias section of the PRIMARY_SETTLER instance shows that the instance is known as "psettler" by "ar" (the instance of AERATOR), and as "process" in "w1" and "w2" (both instances of WATER_PACKET). The instance of PRIMARY_SETTLER is

The MOSES Notation

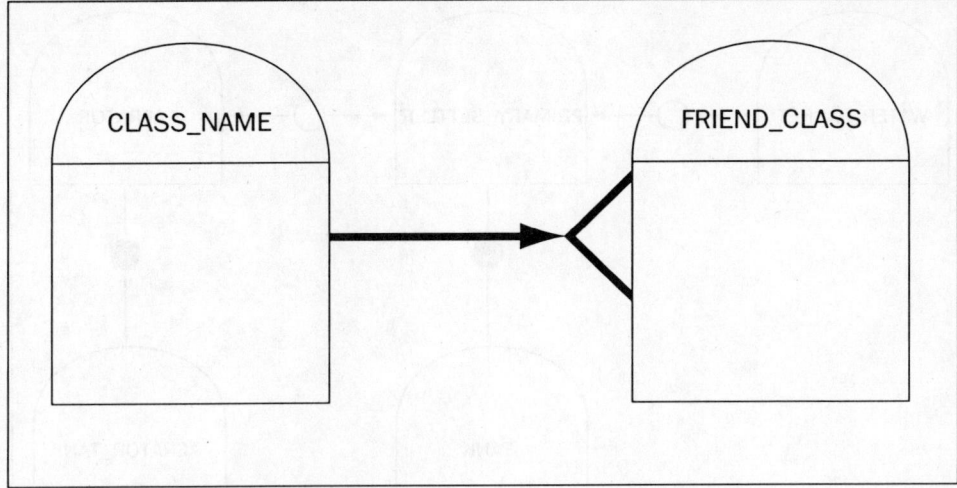

Figure 5.19 Notation for friends in C++

given the unique name "ps" and refers to the TANK instances as "t1", "t2," and "t3" respectively. This can be deduced from the alias section of each tank.

5.3 Class Specification (CS)

It is likely that once a detailed model has been developed, graphical notation will become too unwieldy to specify the class easily. Therefore, a textual class

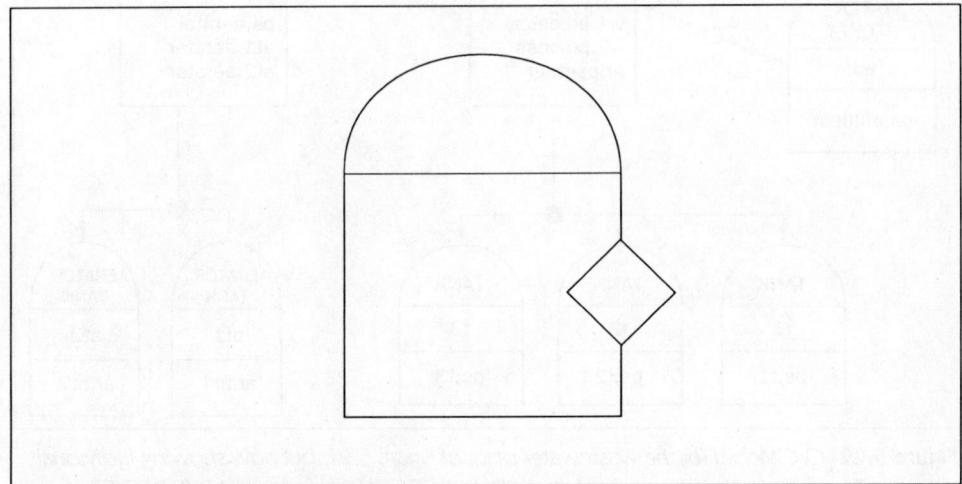

Figure 5.20 MOSES notation for exceptions

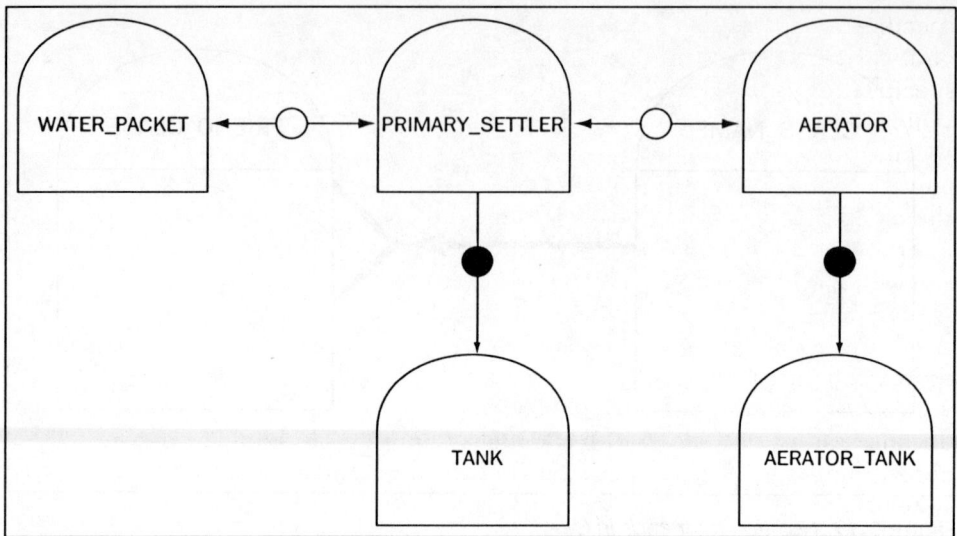

Figure 5.21 *Example O/C Model for a PRIMARY_SETTLER of a wastewater plant. The PRIMARY_SETTLER is composed of a TANK and has relationships with an AERATOR and WATER_PACKET.*

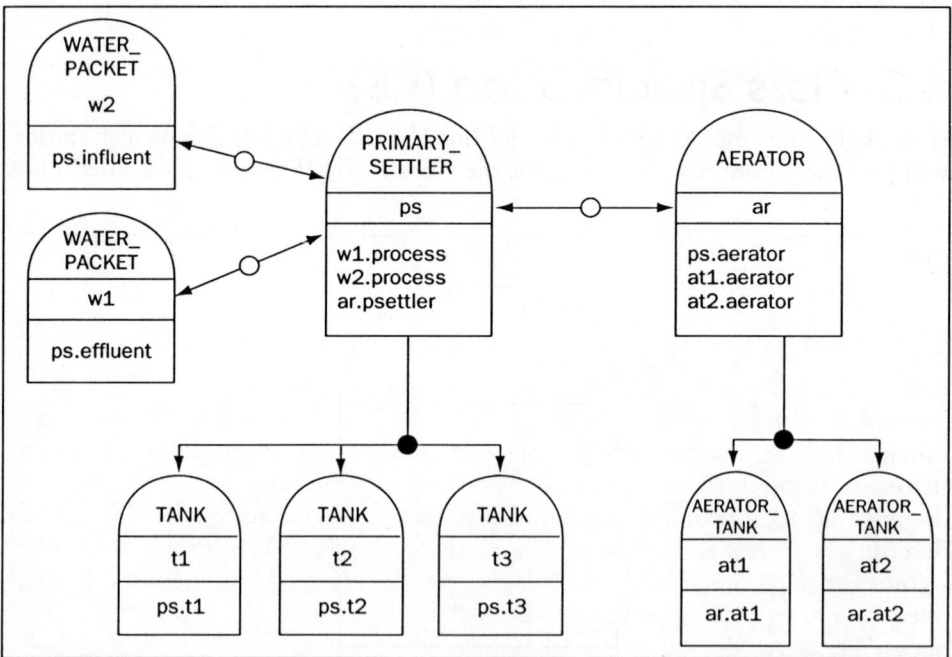

Figure 5.22 *O/C Model for the wastewater plant of Figure 5.21, but now showing individual objects. For example, the object ps of class PRIMARY_SETTLER has two WATER_PACKET objects—influent and effluent.*

specification is necessary. A Class Specification (CS) may be formal or informal and MOSES provides templates for both approaches. The formal class specification is developed using a structured syntax defined in Figure 5.7. The syntax is based on that of Eiffel (version 2) (Meyer, 1988a). The informal class specification is a template similar to that defined by Booch (1991). Which approach is adopted will depend on the organizational environment in which the modeler is operating. A class specification details the properties, operations, assertions, and relationships of a class. It does not need to show inherited services. Thus only new services or those that have been changed need to be specified in the class. The class specification is the primary source of (text) documentation on a class and can easily be refined to, or generated from, the source code. In some languages such as Eiffel the class specification is simply a view of the source code itself. The class specification provides the formal documentation of a class, which is then refined to an implementation in the chosen language. A class specification should be produced for all classes of the system.

A formal version of a class specification is shown in Figure 5.23 using the formal syntax of Figure 5.7. This document shows the name of the class; the generalization, association, and aggregation relationships of the class together with their cardinalities and existence constraints; the services of the class and their contracts; the visibility of the services; and finally the invariant(s) of the class. Creation operations can also be shown.

An informal version is shown in Figure 5.24. This shows the same information but in a more English-like form. It is possible to generate skeleton code in various OOPLs based on this formal syntax and in an appropriate CASE tool this could easily be automated. Without such support it may be more appropriate to translate the class specification into the OOPL syntax, with additional comments for those aspects of the CS not supported by the OOPL.

This CS is the specification of those features introduced in this class or those features changed in this class. Other diagrams, for example, objectcharts, are used to derive this information and to record certain interesting aspects; but basically the CS is the primary means of documenting the classes for coding. These CSs can be given directly to the programmer, who then has the capability of making implementation decisions about the class internals. However, in reality these implementation decisions are more likely to be made by both designer and programmer in collaboration. In some instances, the service description of the CS may be sufficient (for a simple algorithm) for no further significant decisions to be required. In other cases, the class specification will need to be supplemented by a detailed design of the algorithm itself. This occurs whenever the algorithm is large enough for it to need to be described by structured techniques. In that case, the programmer will require further documentation from the designer, possibly in the form of a Service Structure Model (SSM) (Section 5.4.2).

```
                abstract class CLASS NAME
                    -- description of class responsibility
                specialize
                    CNAME_A
                visible
                    service1: CNAME_B
                        -- description of property
                        -- (i.e. service which returns an object)
                        precondition
                        postcondition
                        end
                    service2: (a:CNAME_C)
                        -- description of operation
                        precondition
                        postcondition
                        end
                secret
                    service3: CNAME_D
                        -- description of property
                        precondition
                        postcondition
                        end
                    service4: (a:CNAME_E)
                        -- description of operation
                        precondition
                        postcondition
                        end
                    label_a: component CNAME (0..m)
                    label_b: CNAME.symmetric (0..m)
                invariant
                    invariant clause
                end
```

Figure 5.23 *Example of a Class Specification for documenting classes using the structured syntax defined in Figure 5.7*

5.3.1 Class Specification diagrams

The graphical form of a class specification is the class specification diagram, sometimes called a "pin-out" diagram (Figure 5.25). Each of the services offered is now represented by an individual bar. The pin-out diagram permits display of dynamic (message-passing) information so that the individual signatures (input and output arguments) can be attached unambiguously. For example, the class service, *new*, receives no argument to its incoming message and sends back to the client an object of class BANK_ACCOUNT. The second service, *make_deposit*, on the other hand, requires the incoming message to contain an object *deposit* of class DOLLAR. The service, which is obviously procedural in nature, undertakes the required adjustments to the internal attribute *balance*.

An inquiry about this balance (third service) sends back a copy of the object *balance* of class DOLLAR.

Class Specification diagrams may be used as supplements to class specifications. However, it is likely that such a documentation technique would quickly become unwieldy if every class were to be documented in this way.

```
Class Name: CNAME
Abstract: Abstract/Concrete
Description: Text
Specializes:    CNAME_A
                CNAME_B

Visible
  Services
    Name: Label
    Inputs:  arg_label_1: CNAME_A
             arg_label_2: CNAME_B
    Output: CNAME_C
    Description: Text
    Abstract: Abstract/Concrete
    Pre: Precondition_clause
    Post: Postcondition_clause

Secret
  Services
    Name: Label
    Inputs:  arg_label: CNAME_A
    Output: CNAME_B
    Description: Text
    Abstract: Abstract/Concrete
    Pre: Precondition_clause
    Post: Postcondition_clause

Components
  Name: Label
  Class: CNAME_D
  Constraints: (0..m)
  Description: Text

Associations:
  Name: Label
  Class: CNAME_E
  Constraints: (0..m)
  Description: Text

Invariants: Invariant Clause
```

Figure 5.24 *Informal Class Specification that records the same information as Figure 5.23, but using more natural English*

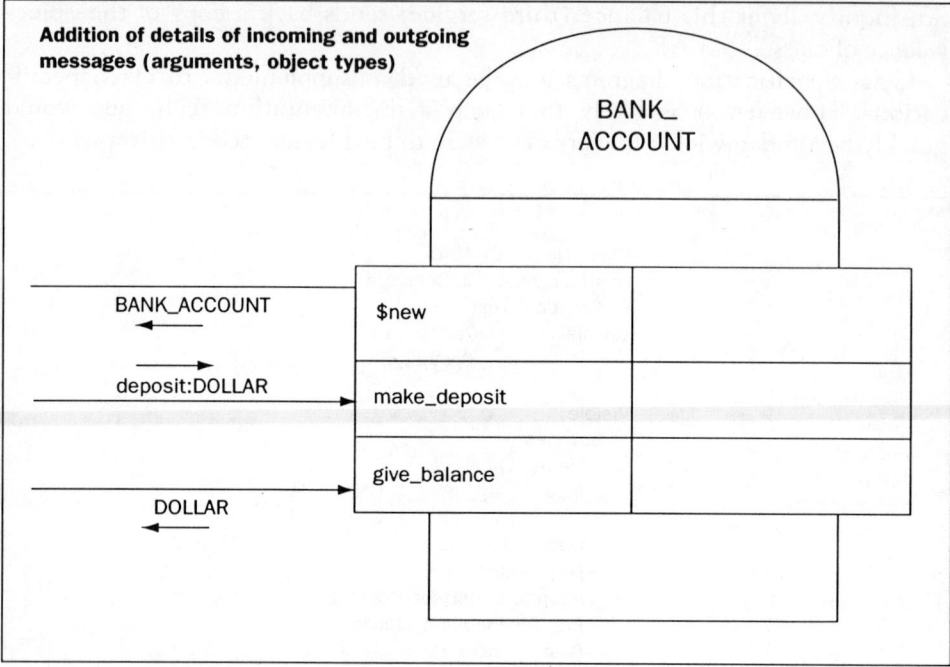

Figure 5.25 *Class definition (or "pin-out") diagram showing details of the messages and their arguments*

5.4 Service specifications

Services as shown on the O/C Model simply give the name, inputs, and outputs of a service. The detailed definition or specification of a service is recorded as a contract.

5.4.1 Contracts

A contract should be applied to each and every service. Information on an operation's contract is specified in the Class Specification (CS).

Meyer (1988a, 1992b) depicts the terms of these contractual obligations/benefits in a 2 × 2 matrix referred to as a Contract Matrix (CM) in Henderson-Sellers and Edwards (1993b). In MOSES we specify the contract in the Class Specification, which shows the complete pre- and postconditions for each service, including those inherited from ancestors. This implies that for any service the complete contract is specified in one place.

The contract essentially asserts a number of conditions under which the service will perform its function and the result of requesting that service. The contract is best expressed using a formal assertion language. In MOSES we use an assertion language derived from Eiffel (Figure 5.26). A contract specification is shown in Figure 5.27.

The MOSES Notation

```
Boolean_expression    =   Expression
Expression            =   {unqualified_expression "." ...}
Unqualified_expression =  Constant I Entity I Unqualified_call I Old_value I Nochange
                          I Operator_expression
Old_value             =   old expression
Nochange              =   nochange
Operator_expression   =   Unary_expression I Binary_expression
                          I Multiary_expression I Parenthesized
Unary_expression      =   not I "+" I "–"
Binary_expression     =   Expression Binary Expression
Binary                =   = I /=I<I>I>= I<=
Multiary_expression   =   {Expression Multiary ...}+
Multiary              =   "=" I "–" I "*" I "/" I and I and then I or I or else I implies
Parenthesized         =   "("Expression")"
Entity                =   Identifier I Result
Unqualified_call      =   Feature_name [Actuals]
Actuals               =   "("Expression_list")"
Expression_list       =   {Expression Separator ..}
Separator             =   "," I ";"
```

Figure 5.26 *BNF of MOSES assertion language based on the Eiffel language*

In some situations it may not be possible to express the effect of an operation easily by using assertions. In these cases the action to be performed may be expressed in a procedural form such as Structured English or pseudocode (Hawryszkiewycz, 1988). In this case the contract is simply a process specification similar to that found in Structured Analysis and Design (SA/SD). Indeed, a Service Structure Model (SSM) may be developed for services. This model is similar to a mini-structure chart for a service. SSMs are discussed below (Section 5.4.2).

In some languages, contracts may be inherited such that only the locally introduced assertions are placed in the class specification. In such languages the

```
              Services Specified by Contracts

service_name
    -- comments
    Precondition
        -- Boolean Expression or English Text
    Postcondition
        -- Boolean Expression or English Text
end
```

Figure 5.27 *Typical contract that specifies the complete contract for an operation*

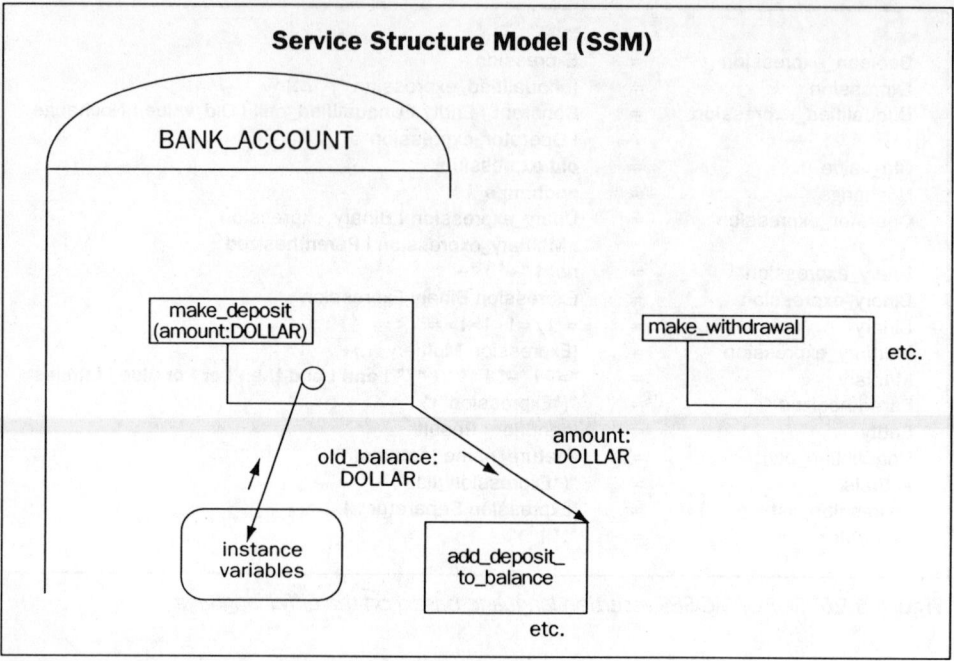

Figure 5.28 *Example of a Service Structure Model*

complete contract can be generated automatically using a "short" and "flat" tool (Meyer, 1988a, 1992b). However, this approach may not be possible in complex cases or where formal reasoning is required with regard to the service specification.

Contracts and/or pseudocode are therefore used to detail the semantics of the services either declaratively or procedurally, respectively. The emphasis in specifying contracts/pseudocode is on defining the behavior of the class's services.

5.4.2 Service Structure Model (SSM)

In some circumstances, it may be more appropriate to specify the semantics of a service using a graphical technique. In this case, a Service Structure Model (based on the Method Structure Diagram of Page-Jones *et al.*, 1990) may be used to specify a service (Figure 5.28). An SSM is used to show the logical structure of the internal algorithm for a single service. It can show control flows within the service itself or uses of services from other classes. At this detailed algorithmic level, any type of standard structured notation may be used. This approach may thus be more appropriate for some developers, particularly those familiar with functional decomposition methodologies.

Once again, such detailed graphical representations of the algorithm are not appropriate for every service; rather, they may be used to elucidate a particular service.

5.5 Event Models (EMs)

Contracts and SSMs are a means of representing the behavior of a class. However, functions are achieved by the collaboration of classes. This collaboration is specified using an Event Model. The purpose of the Event Model is to show graphically the messages that occur as a result of calling a service on an object. An Event Model shows objects or classes and a particular message-passing sequence between them. Event Models are therefore annotated O/C Models, usually shown for a small part of the system. Arrows annotate the relationships of the O/C Model, indicating a message name, a direction, and a sequence number (Figure 5.29). Simple timing of messages is shown using the sequence number. In more complex cases it may be necessary to use traces (see below).

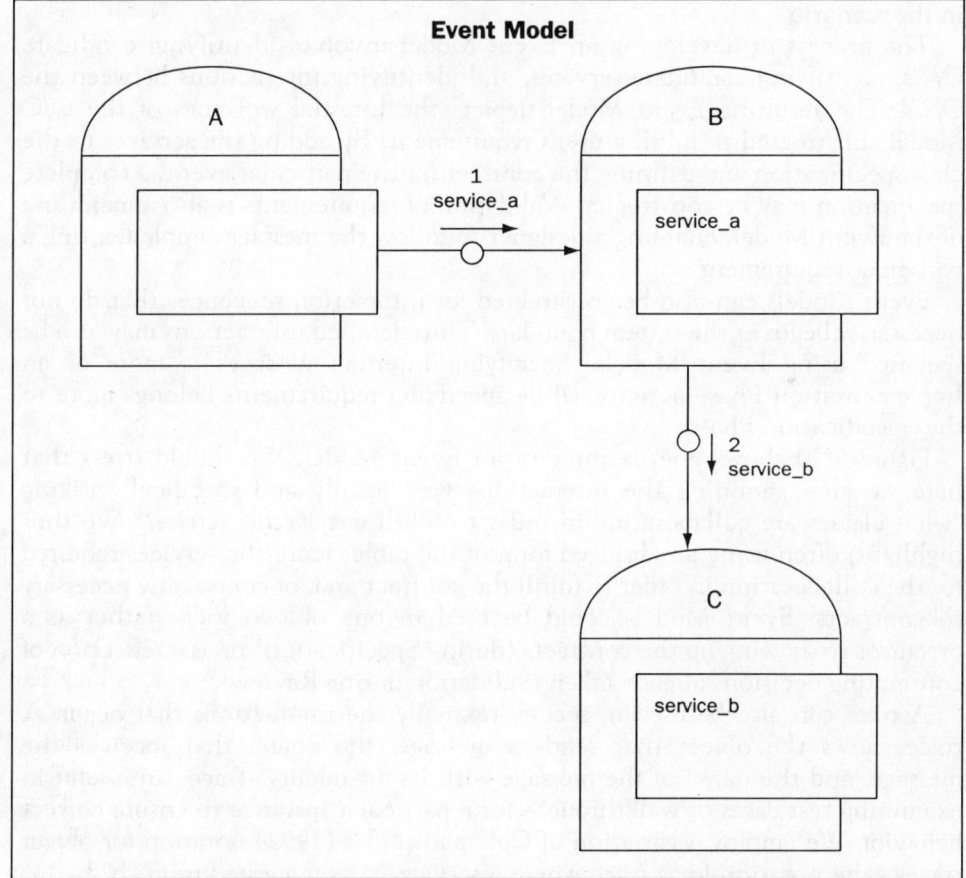

Figure 5.29 *MOSES notation for the Event Model. The ordering of messages is shown by the number on the message name. Thus class A sends a message "service_a" to class B, which then calls "service_b" on class C.*

Event Models are useful for showing how certain actions defined in a functional specification are achieved in the O/C Model. In particular, an Event Model may be defined for a scenario. A scenario is simply a natural-language description of a sequence of interactions with a system. Each scenario should be labeled and indexed. Associated with each typical scenario should be a list of exceptional scenarios. The scenario represents events that are identified as services, as discussed in Section 7.15.1. For example, a graphical output subsystem may have services for collecting parameters from the user, including datafile names and scaling ratios, and for displaying the output. A scenario can be developed indicating the dialogue between the user and the subsystem, and the events that the subsystem undertakes in response to this dialogue. (Rubin and Goldberg (1992) document such interactions as "scripts.") These events can be abstracted as services on classes of the subsystem. EMs are then developed from scenarios and show the major classes and interactions involved in the scenario.

The process of developing an Event Model involves identifying candidate O/Cs, identifying candidate services, and identifying interactions between the O/Cs. The resulting Event Model depicts the internal workings of the O/C Model constructed to fulfill a user's requirement. By adding the services to the class specification and defining the contract for the particular event, a complete specification may be constructed. Validation of requirements is also a major use of the Event Model, enabling a designer to follow the messages implementing a particular requirement.

Event Models can also be constructed for interaction sequences that do not necessarily begin at the system boundary. Thus detailed interactions may also be specified using Event Models. Specifying internal messages is more of an Implementation Phase activity, while specifying requirements belongs more to the Specification Phase.

Figure 5.30 shows one example of an Event Model. We should stress that here we are examining the interactions very locally and specifically asking "what classes are collaborating in order to fulfill *one specific service?*" We thus highlight, often using an abridged form of the tablet icon, the services required for the collaboration in order to fulfill the contract and, of course, any necessary subcontracts. Event Models could be used in one of two ways: either as a precursor to drawing up the contracts (during Specification) or as a reflection of contracting decisions already taken (validation during Review).

A *trace* can also be used to specify textually the interactions that occur. A trace shows the object that sends a message, the object that receives the message, and the name of the message with its arguments. Traces are useful in examining test cases or walkthroughs for a particular instance to ensure correct behavior. We employ a variation of Coleman *et al.*'s (1992) notation for object traces. The notation for a trace where a service "s" is requested from "b" by "a" is the triplet:

<a, s, b>

The MOSES Notation

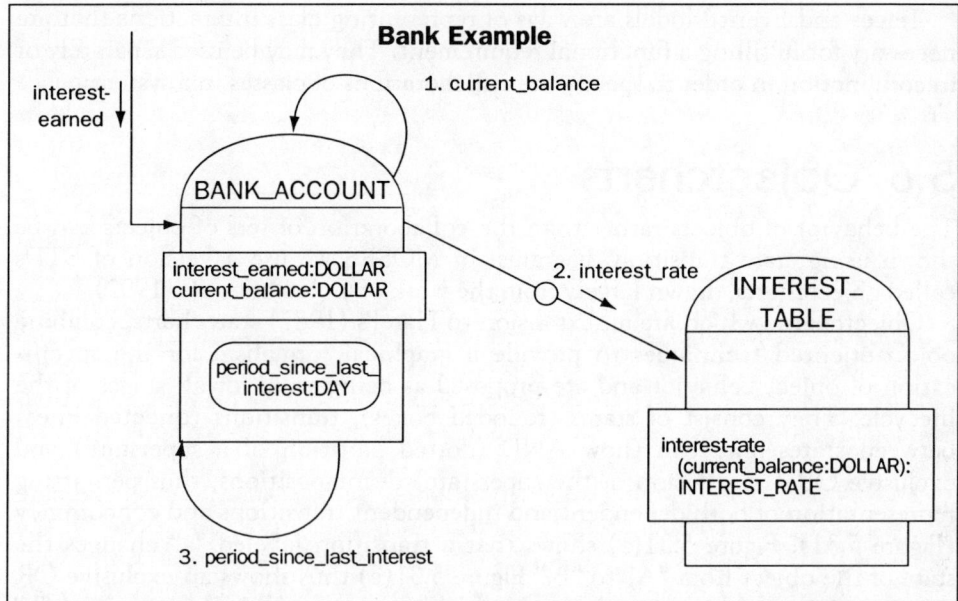

Figure 5.30 *Typical Event Model showing the timing sequence*

An example object trace using the actual names from the O/C Model of Figure 5.22 may be:

<ps, fill (w1), t1>

This specifies that the actual object "ps" of class PRIMARY_SETTLER (the class of the object can be determined from the instance model) sends a message "fill" with argument "w1" to the object "t1" of class TANK. A complete object trace can be developed for any particular set of messages and object configurations. For example, the trace:

<ps, is_empty: True, t1>
<ps, fill (w1), t1>
<ps, discharge (50), t1>

specifies that "ps" sends the query "is_empty" to "t1," which replies (instantly) "True"; "ps" then sends the message "fill" with argument "w1" to "t1" followed by the message "discharge."

In this notation the predefined symbol * is used to indicate a service request that is from an unknown source and "self" is used to define the object itself. Conditional results and branching need to be shown using separate traces for each condition. Traces are thus similar to scenarios in this respect, although at a lower level of detail.

Traces and Event Models are ways of representing class interactions that are necessary for fulfilling a functional requirement. They may be used separately or in conjunction in order to specify the collaborations of classes in a system.

5.6 Objectcharts

The behavior of objects rather than the collaboration of sets of objects can be shown using state transition diagrams. In MOSES we use a version of STDs called objectcharts, drawn largely from the work of Coleman et al. (1992).

Objectcharts, which are an extension to Harel's (1987) statecharts, combine object-oriented techniques to provide a graphical formalism for the specification of object behavior and are proposed as being valid for all stages of the lifecycle. They consist of states (rounded boxes), transitions (directed lines) between states, and can show AND (dotted partition of a superstate) and exclusive OR (no division of the superstate) decompositions, thus permitting representation of both dependent and independent transitions and concurrency (Figure 5.31). Figure 5.31(a) shows that a transition labeled "a" changes the state of the object from "A" to "B." Figure 5.31(a) thus shows an exclusive OR situation, i.e., the object is either in state "A" or in state "B." The transition "b" is one that can occur on state "A" or state "B" and as such can be viewed as a transition on the superstate "D." Transitions to initial states are indicated by a small arrow with no source state (Figure 5.31(b)) and the AND state is shown by a dotted line between states (e.g., between state "E" and state "D" in Figure 5.31(b)). Objectcharts extend statecharts by adding attribute information, and a communication protocol that is a direct request to an object rather than a

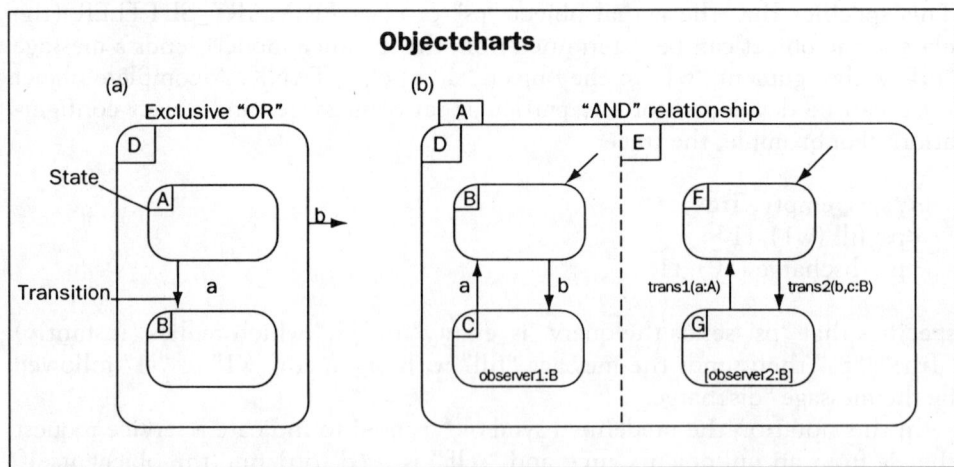

Figure 5.31 *Objectchart notation: (a) exclusive OR such that the object is either in state A or state B; (b) AND relationship such that the object can be, for instance, in state B and state G and observers, e.g., state G (Adapted from Coleman et al., © 1992 IEEE)*

broadcast model. Transitions between states are labeled with a service of the class and possibly services required from other classes. Thus a transition with one input would be defined simply as:

transition_name (in: INPUT)

In Figure 5.31(b) the transition "trans1" takes one input argument and the transition "trans2" takes two. An event may involve subevents, or services that are required from other objects. Required services can only be those that are available to the object from its clients; that is to say, the object has a relationship with another object that offers the service. The way to show such a required service is to prefix the service name with the formal class name and place the request after a transition name. A forward slash (/) is used to indicate the service required. A requested service on a transition looks like:

Transition_name / FORMAL_NAME.service_name (in: INPUT)

Coleman *et al.* (1992) distinguish observer services that only report the state of an object. Observer services are essentially properties of a class. Objectcharts extend statecharts by providing a notation to specify which properties can be called in various states (Figure 5.31(b)). Explicitly naming the property in a state makes the property visible in the state, as in state "C" of Figure 5.31(b). Properties that are secret are also treated as observers but their names are shown in square brackets, as in state "G" of Figure 5.31(b).

For all transitions, a transition specification should be developed. This transition specification should be recorded in a transition specification table. Each objectchart should have an associated transition specification table. The document template for the transition specification table is shown in Figure 5.32. Combining the different transition specifications for a particular type of transition forms the complete contract for the operation. So, for example, a transition "trans1" that changes the state to "B" if in state "A" or to "C" if in state "D" implies that the complete specification of an operation to achieve these changes is the combined transition specifications for "trans1." Such state-reliant operations should be minimized and often can be made into two separate operations, thus reducing the complexity of operations.

An important use of objectcharts is in checking for the correct semantics of generalization. Remembering that a generalization relationship implies that an instance of the descendant can be substituted for an instance of the ancestor; then the transition specifications of the ancestor should also hold for the descendant. This implies that generalization of an objectchart can only occur through the addition of a transition and/or the strengthening of the transition specification by weakening the firing condition (precondition), by strengthening the postcondition, or by strengthening the invariant (Meyer, 1988a, 1992a,b). Unfortunately, these rules do not always hold and it is argued that objectcharts would need to be extended with failure sets, as in communicating

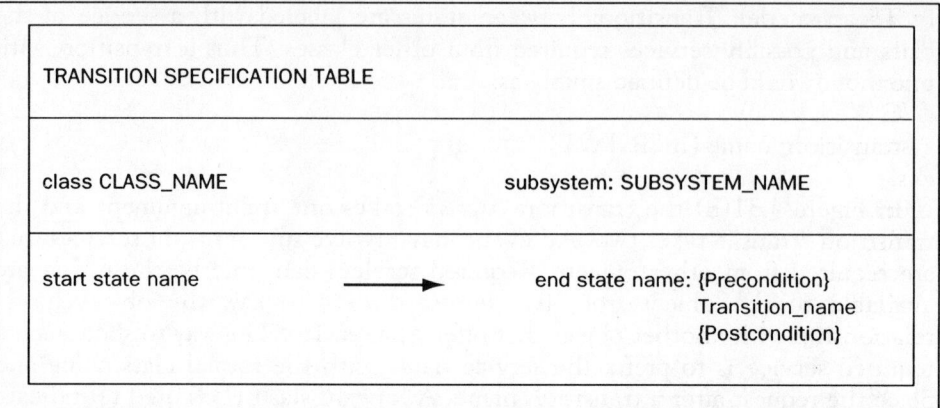

Figure 5.32 *A Transition Specification Table documenting the transition name, start state, end state, and pre- and postconditions for the transition*

sequential processes (CSP), to deal with the associated problems. They do, however, provide a basis for generalization.

Documenting the behavior of systems is a nontrivial task that is further complicated by the aliasing that occurs in object-oriented systems (Coleman *et al.*, 1992). Objectcharts provide the basic mechanism for graphically documenting the behavioral aspects of the object model, showing how a class responds to events. An objectchart should be produced for all non-trivial classes. The complete documentation of the operations that result from events is achieved through the use of assertions recorded as a contract in the CS.

5.7 Inheritance Model

The final view to be discussed is that of the class hierarchy. As discussed earlier, class hierarchies may either be generalization or implementation inheritance hierarchies. The amount of information shown about the ancestors in a class hierarchy may also vary. In Figure 5.33 only class names are shown, although this could be just one view of a set of increasingly detailed Inheritance Models. At a more detailed level of resolution, information on services is required. In general, only those services introduced or redefined by the class are shown, since inherited services are assumed to be available. However, this is not true for implementation inheritance, where it may be necessary to explicitly identify those services inherited and visible. If it is necessary to collect together in one subclass a clear indication of all applicable features, then a class "flattener" (either graphically or as a software tool) can be used. This extracts all inherited features (from all superclasses) and places them together so that they can be examined and/or printed. Thus the inheritance hierarchy is effectively "flattened" to only one level.

The class hierarchy should be documented separately from the class model using a class Inheritance Model (IM) either graphically (Figure 5.33) or textually (Figure 5.34). Separating the inheritance hierarchy structure from the O/C Model allows a class to be placed within the structure from any part of the system specification. This localizes information, making it more readable and easier to locate within a large system. In this representation only a single hierarchy needs to be drawn for the multiple uses of classes from anywhere within this hierarchy. It is generally necessary to show only the class name, since the class specification provides the more detailed information about the class's services.

5.8 Complexity management techniques

Small systems can be designed by simply building up a single diagram showing the relationships between all the classes. However, it is evident that in any real application, a full systems diagram is likely to rapidly become highly complex. Large graphical models quickly lead to reduced understandability and information

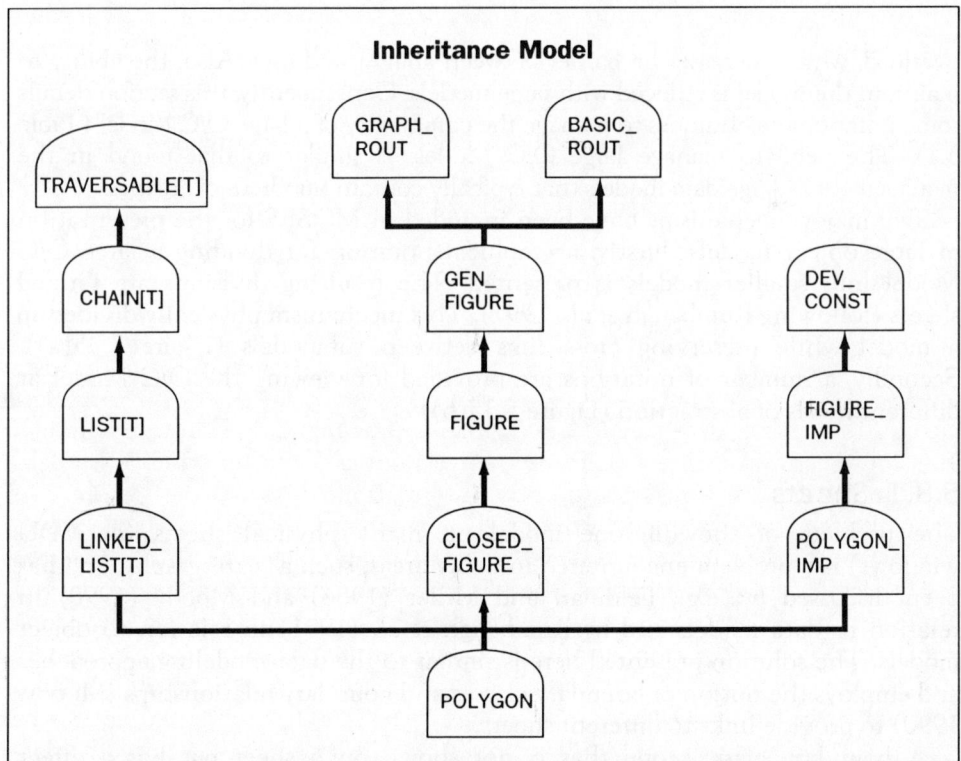

Figure 5.33 *Inheritance Model showing generalization hierarchy for POLYGON*

```
                    TRAVERSABLE[T]
                      CHAIN[T]
                       LIST[T]
                        LINKED_LIST[T]
                         POLYGON

                    GRAPH_ROUT
                     GEN_FIGURE
                    BASIC_ROUT
                     GEN_FIGURE
                      FIGURE
                       CLOSED_FIGURE
                        POLYGON

                    DEV_CONST
                     FIGURE_IMP
                      POLYGON_IMP
                       POLYGON
```

Figure 5.34 *A textual means of representing class hierarchies. Classes at an equal depth represent multiple generalizations.*

overload, which increase the barrier between analyst and user. Also, the ability to maintain the model is reduced with large models. Consequently, this section details some notational techniques to manage the complexity of a large O/C Model (Table 5.1). The need to manage large O/C Models is similar to that found in the management of large data models that typically contain hundreds of entities.

Two major mechanisms have been included in MOSES for the presentation of large object models. Firstly, a graphical notation for dividing a large O/C Model into smaller models is presented. The resulting divisions are termed sheets (following Rumbaugh et al., 1991). This mechanism physically divides up a model while preserving cross-links between submodels (Figure 5.35(a)). Secondly, a number of notations are provided for viewing the O/C Model at different levels of abstraction (Figure 5.35(b)).

5.8.1 Sheets

The problem of showing one model on many physical sheets (or VDU windows) is a problem encountered in many areas, such as cartography, and has been discussed by, e.g., Feldman and Miller (1986) and Moody (1990) in relation to data models and by Rumbaugh et al. (1991) in relation to object models. The solution presented here is similar to the data-modeling approaches and employs the notion of boundary classes and boundary relationships (Moody, 1990) to provide links to different sheets.

A boundary class is one that is not shown on a sheet but has a direct relationship to a class that is shown on the sheet. A boundary relationship is a

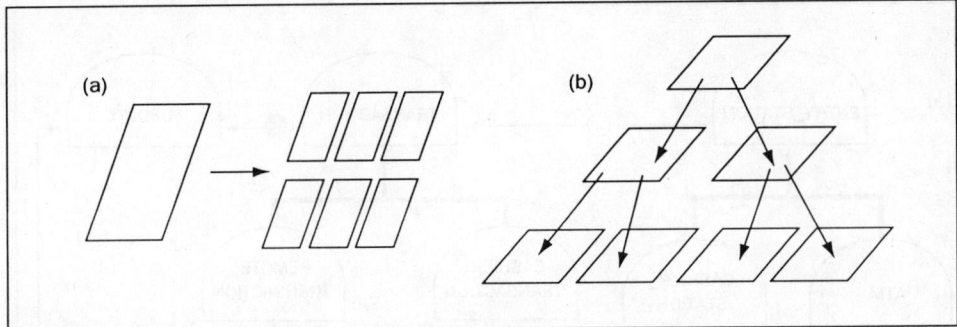

Figure 5.35 *Two dimensions to managing complexity: (a) dividing one sheet into many and (b) abstracting/layering one model*

relationship between a class on the sheet and a boundary class (Figure 5.36); it should not be an inheritance relationship.

Essentially, after the model has been partitioned, boundary classes and relationships are removed and replaced by small connector lines labeled with the boundary class and relationship name. Figure 5.37(a) shows an object model that is divided into two sheets (Figure 5.37(b) and (c)). This provides a means of navigating between sheets if navigation is not supported by an automated tool. Class hierarchies should be placed within the one sheet, although as discussed below a complete hierarchy is also shown in a separate Inheritance Model (see Section 5.7).

This approach is an effective means of managing the physical size of models without loss of information. However, it provides no means of viewing the model at varying resolutions (abstraction levels), which is often needed. A number of mechanisms required to achieve this are discussed below.

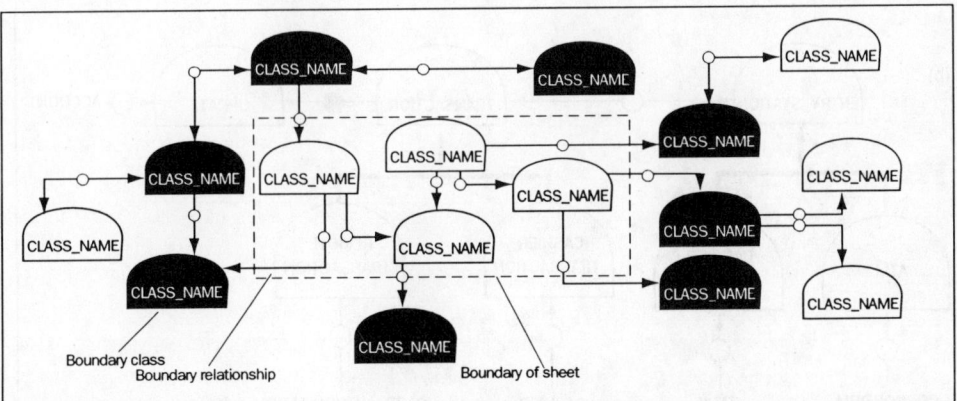

Figure 5.36 *Diagram to show boundary classes and boundary relationships when dividing a large O/C Model*

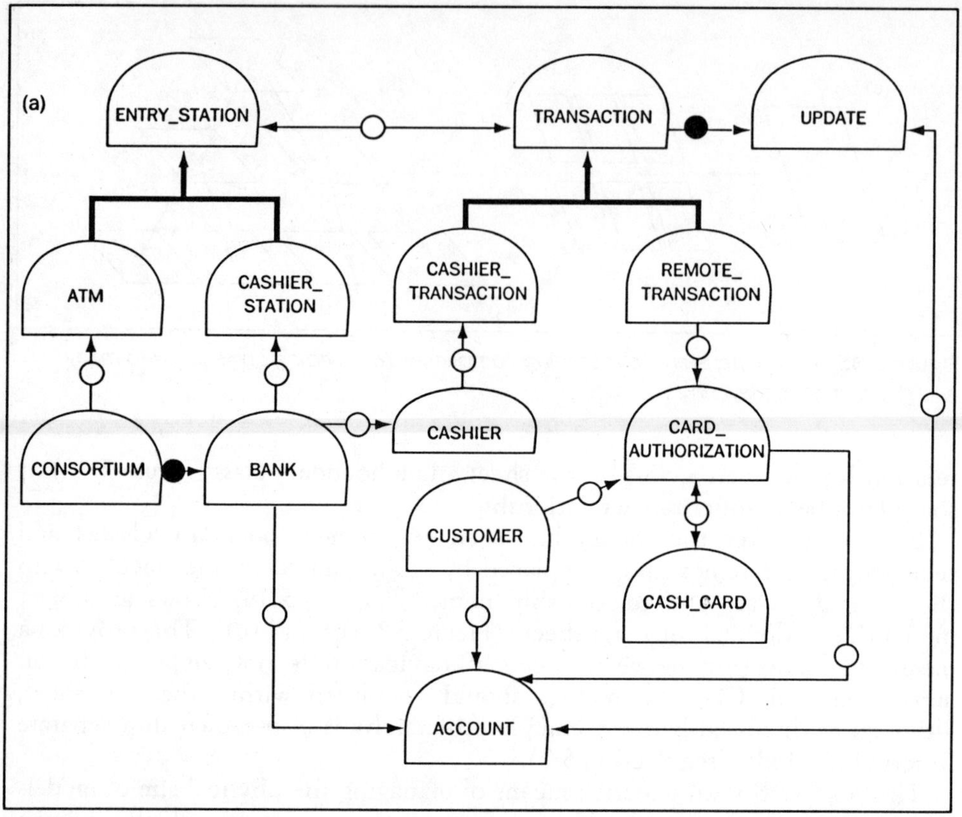

246 — Chapter 5

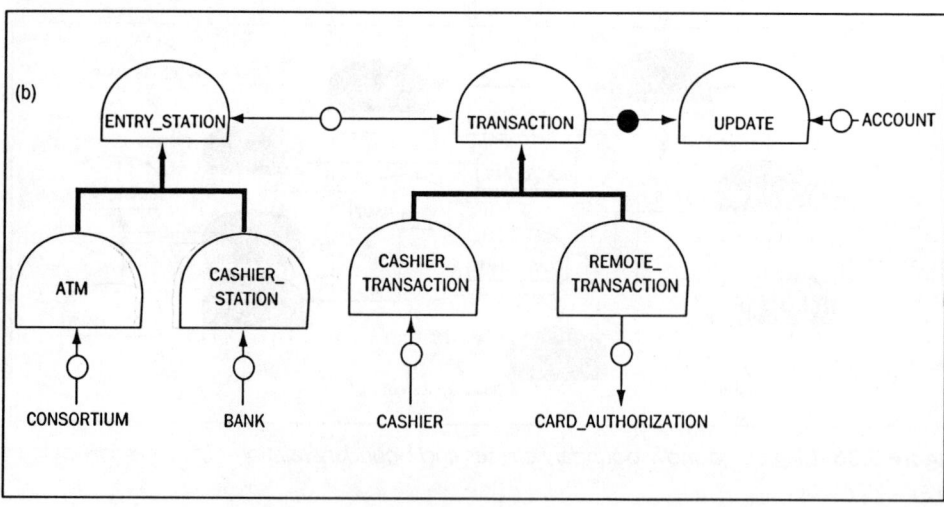

Figure 5.37 *Dividing an O/C Model using boundary classes: (above) a large O/C Model before division (adapted from Rumbaugh et al., 1991); (below) Sheet 1 after division; (opposite page) Sheet 2 after division*

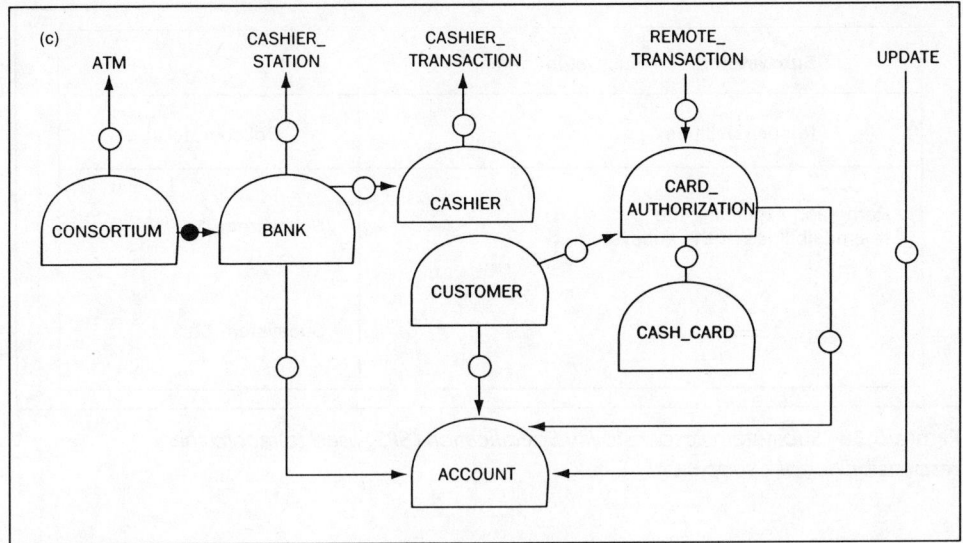

5.8.2 Subsystems

Subsystems are a mechanism for abstracting a set of classes into a single higher-level module and are simply a tool for managing the complexity of O/C Models, although they can also be used to manage the process of development using the subsystem fountain models. In this section we discuss them simply as a means of rationalizing diagrammatic complexity. Subsystems are depicted on the O/C diagrams.

Subsystems, while not enjoying the same level of conceptual rigor as a class, are vital for managing complexity in large systems. The aim of subsystems is to abstract out the major services of a group of related classes so as to hide details yet retain a coherent overall view of the system design. The decision to employ a subsystem rather than develop another class should take into account the abstraction represented by the subsystem, efficiency and information hiding requirements, as well as the need to manage complexity.

The documentation templates used for subsystems are similar to Class, Responsibility, and Collaboration (CRC) cards (Wirfs-Brock et al., 1990) and are shown in Figure 5.38. The Subsystem Responsibility Specification (SRS) template details the name of the subsystem, the responsibilities or services, and the collaborators of the subsystem. Responsibilities/services are achieved by hidden collaborating classes of the subsystem.

Diagrammatically, a subsystem is represented as a rectangular box with a section for a name (Figure 5.39). This icon may be reduced for space saving or when "exploding" a subsystem. Connections between subsystems are denoted by a hollow, thick arrow to represent the (possibly multiple) individual relationships that actually exist between the two subsystems. If one subsystem is subservient to another, i.e., if one client uses any of the responsibilities of the

Subsystem:	Subsystem name
Responsibilities	Collaborators
Paragraph explaining the responsibilities of the subsystem	Subsystem 1 Subsystem 2

Figure 5.38 *Subsystem Responsibility Specification (SRS) used to record the responsibilities of a subsystem*

other, the arrow is one way. Communicating subsystems, where the services of the one subsystem are used by the other, are shown by a two-way arrow (Figure 5.39).

By "exploding" a subsystem to its component classes, the collaborations that implement the responsibility may be traced. To permit ease of scalability only two of the "walls" of the subsystem are shown when "exploding." Class relationships across the boundary of a subsystem should be shown by a small-lined arrow from the class labeled with the name of the related class. This allows navigation between different subsystems. In a large system this expansion may actually contain a nested subsystem (Figure 5.40—Layer 1), which can be viewed as layers (Figure 5.40—Layers 2 and 3) (see also Section 5.8.3), thus providing a simple means of managing complexity in class models.

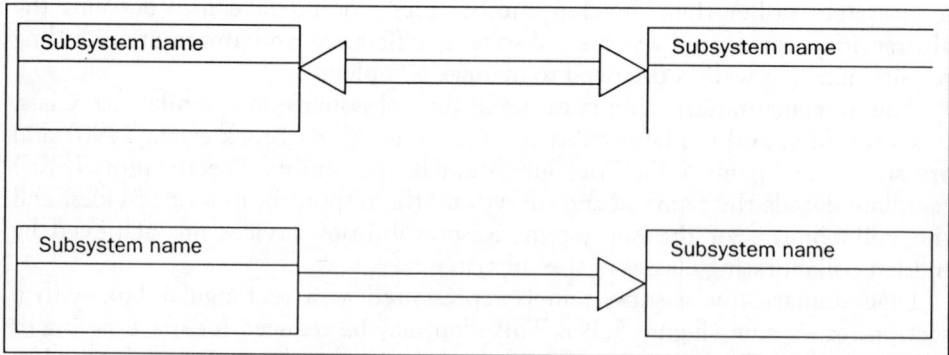

Figure 5.39 *MOSES notation for subsystem representing high-level abstraction of the system with low coupling and high cohesion composed of classes that collaborate closely and represent some identifiable logical subdivisions of the total system*

The MOSES Notation

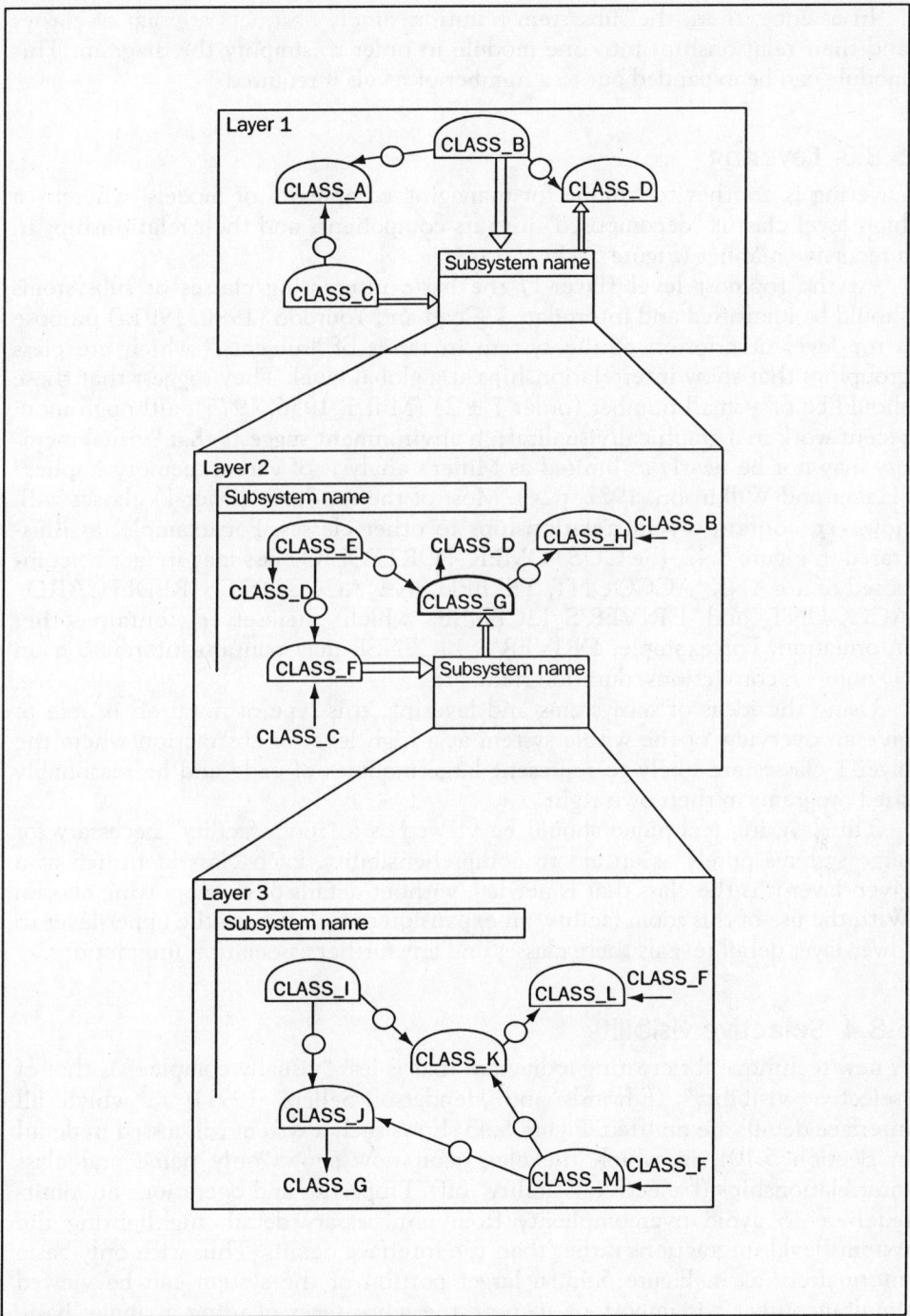

Figure 5.40 *Exploding subsystems to different layers*

In essence, then, the subsystem notation simply abstracts a group of classes and their relationships into one module in order to simplify the diagram. This module can be expanded out to a number of levels if required.

5.8.3 Layering

Layering is another technique for managing complexity of models, whereby a high level class is "decomposed" into its components and their relationships in a recursive manner (Figure 5.41).

At the topmost level (layer-1) the basic interacting classes or subsystems should be identified and interrelated. Coad and Yourdon (1990, 1991a) propose a top-level description of the system in terms of "subjects," which are class groupings that show interrelationships at a global level. They suggest that these should be of a small number (order 7 ± 2) (Miller, 1956, 1975), although more recent work in a graphical/visualization environment suggests that "visual memory may not be nearly as limited as Miller's analysis of verbal memory implies" (Haber and Wilkinson, 1982, p24). Most of the top-layer (layer-1) classes will, however, contain several relationships to other classes. For example, as illustrated in Figure 5.42, the CUSTOMER_PORTFOLIO class may in fact be composed of a BANK_ACCOUNT, TELEPHONE_ACCOUNT, CREDITCARD_ACCOUNT and DRIVER'S_LICENSE, which themselves contain other information. For example, DRIVER'S_LICENSE may contain information on ID number, convictions, duration held, etc.

Using the ideas of subsystems and layering, this type of notation is able to give an overview of the whole system at a high level of abstraction where the layer-1 classes are likely to represent large modules of code and be reasonably sized programs in their own right.

This layering technique should be viewed as a "zoom facility" necessary for large systems purely as an aid to comprehensibility. Each class identified at a given layer-n is the class that is needed, without details of its supporting classes. With the use of this zoom facility, an expansion of a class from the upper-layer to lower-layer detail reveals these classes and any further association interactions.

5.8.4 Selective visibility

A new technique for creating a diagram that is less "visually complex" is that of "selective visibility" (Edwards and Henderson-Sellers, 1991), in which all interface details are omitted. Figure 5.43 shows such a system (discussed in detail in Section 5.10), in which the class icon now shows only name and class interrelationships ("selective visibility" off). Properties and operations are omitted here to avoid overcomplexity from unnecessary detail, highlighting the systems-level interactions rather than the interface details. Thus with only basic information, as in Figure 5.43, a larger portion of the system can be viewed simultaneously. It is important to note the advantages of using a single, basic notation, yet omitting some information dependent on the resolution required.

The MOSES Notation

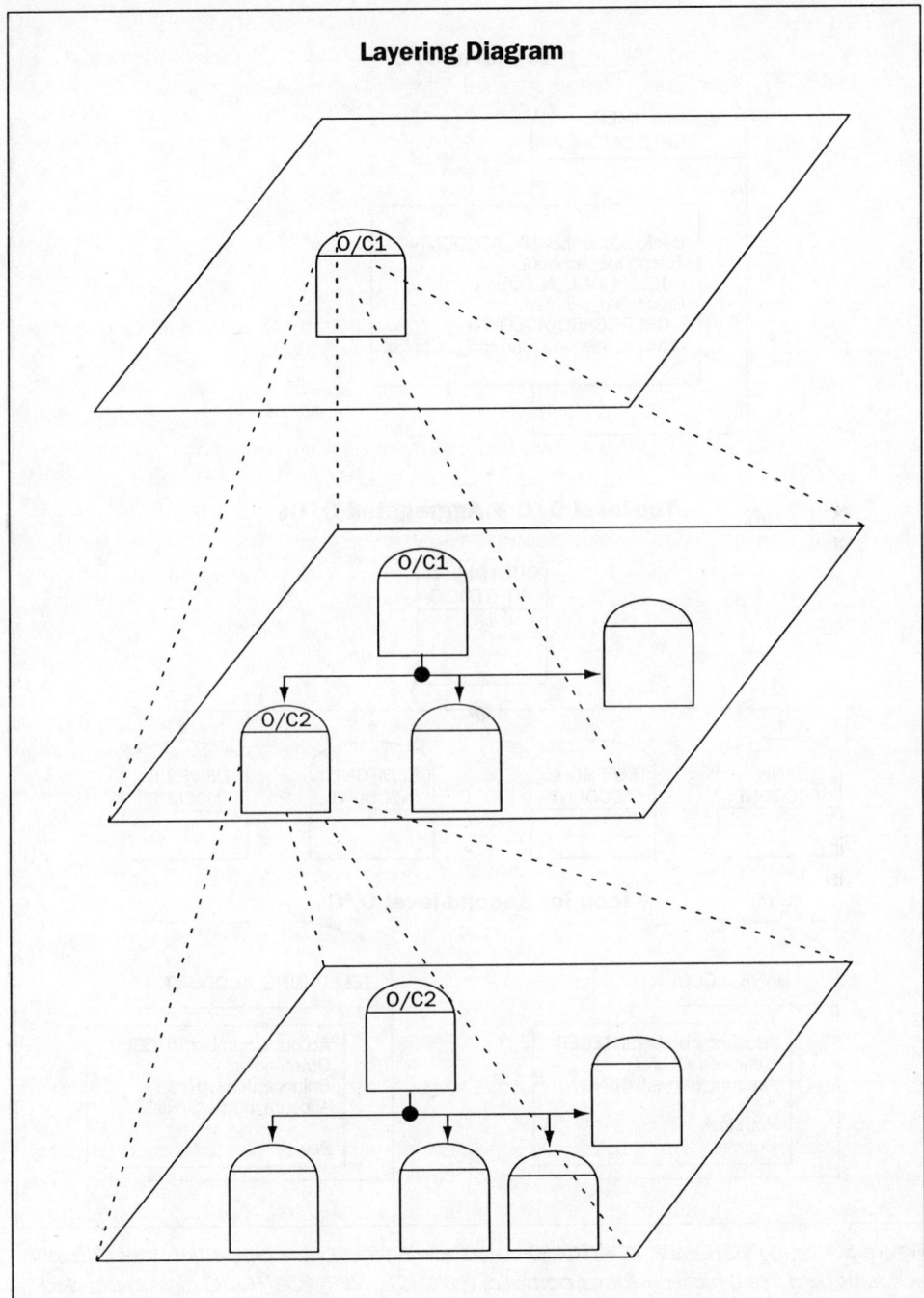

Figure 5.41 *Layering is recursive. Here aggregations in the second-layer diagram are expanded to a third layer of detail.*

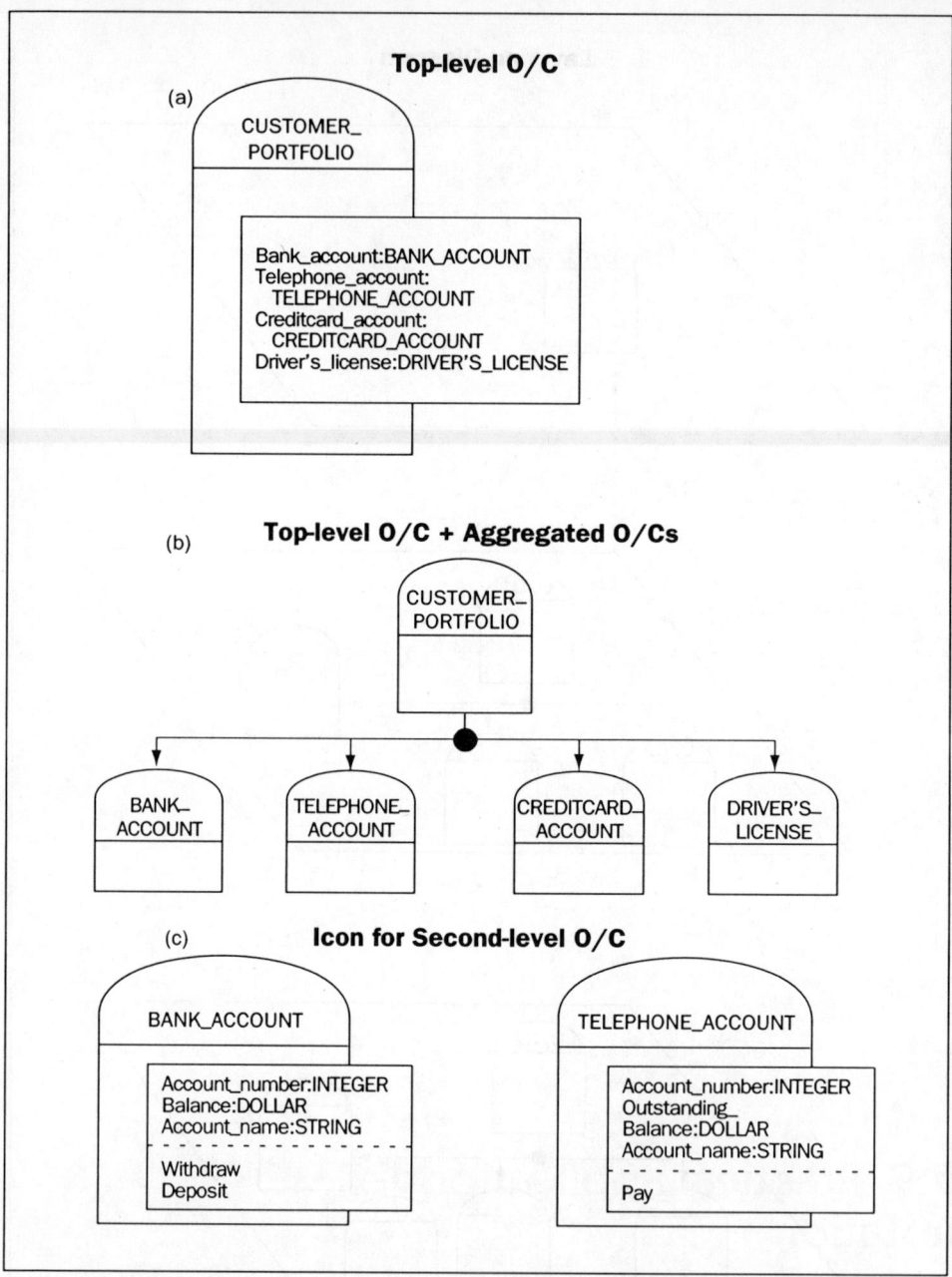

Figure 5.42 *(a) CUSTOMER_PORTFOLIO class showing four of the properties: four different accounts held in a typical customer portfolio; (b) CUSTOMER_PORTFOLIO class expanded explicitly in terms of relationships between customer and the various account and license classes possessed/used; (c) detail of two of these server classes: BANK_ACCOUNT and TELEPHONE_ACCOUNT, illustrating properties and operations*

The MOSES Notation

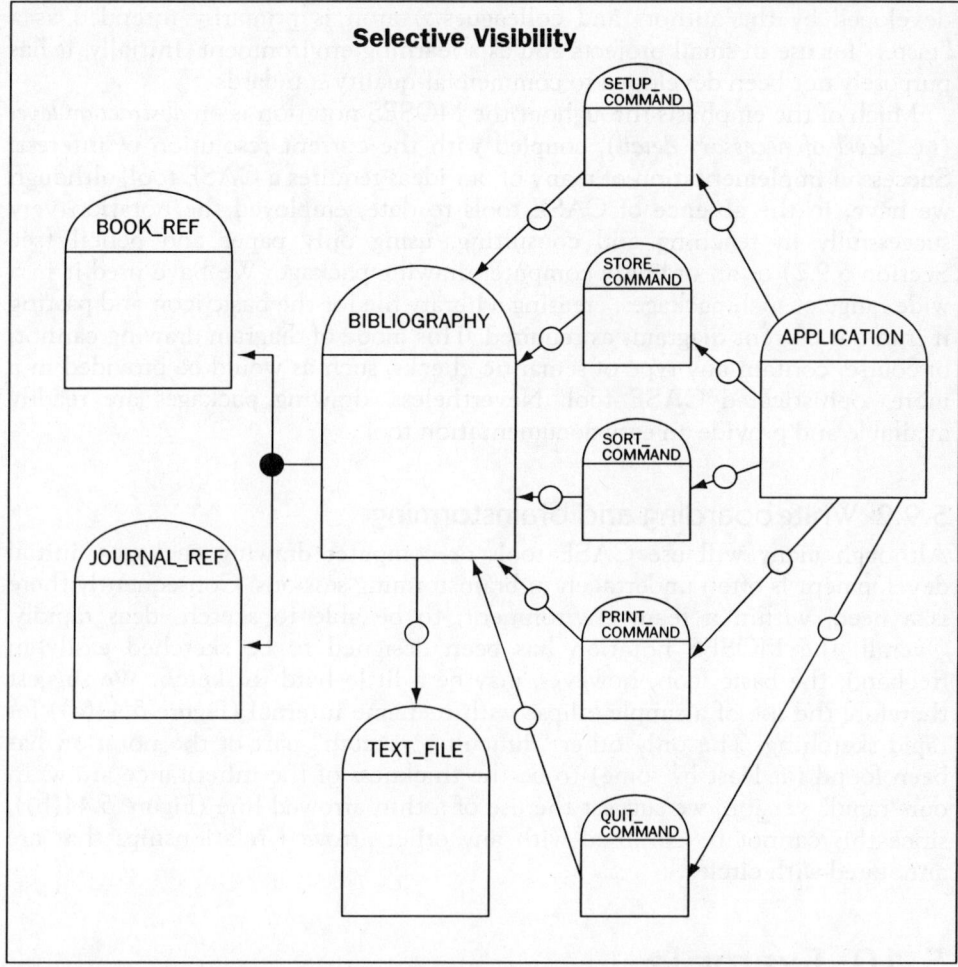

Figure 5.43 O/C Model for the bibliography system discussed in Section 5.10, showing relationships between classes. Properties and operations are omitted for clarity (selective visibility off).

5.9 Practical applications of MOSES notation

5.9.1 CASE tool support

In our design of the MOSES notation, we have borne in mind a final goal of CASE tool support. It is expected that parts of the notation, particularly the O/C Model, will soon be supported in a number of CASE tools, including ObjectMaker, Meta Edit, and Aaron, the teaching/learning tool being developed by the authors and colleagues. Aaron is primarily intended as a "taster" for use in small projects and as a learning environment. Initially, it has purposely not been developed to commercial-quality standards.

Much of the emphasis throughout the MOSES notation is on *abstraction level* (i.e., *level of necessary detail*), coupled with the current resolution of interest. Successful implementation of many of our ideas requires a CASE tool, although we have, in the absence of CASE tools to date, employed the notation very successfully in teaching and consulting, using only paper and pencil (see Section 5.9.2) or an ordinary computer drawing package. We have used it in a wide range of such packages, creating a library file for the basic icon and pasting it into our current diagrams as required. This mode of diagram drawing cannot, of course, contain any type of semantic checks, such as would be provided in a more sophisticated CASE tool. Nevertheless, drawing packages are readily available and provide an easy documentation tool.

5.9.2 Whiteboarding and brainstorming

Although many will use CASE tools or computer drawing packages, initial development is often undertaken in brainstorming sessions. Consequently there is a need, within a team environment, to be able to sketch ideas rapidly. Overall, the MOSES notation has been designed to be sketched easily in freehand; the basic icon, however, may be a little hard to sketch. We suggest therefore the use of a simple ellipse with its name internal (Figure 5.44(a)) for rapid sketching. The only other "difficult to sketch" part of the notation has been found (at least by some) to be the thickness of the inheritance arrow. In our "rapid" version, we suggest the use of a thin arrowed line (Figure 5.44(b)), since this cannot be confused with any other arrowed relationships that are annotated with circles.

5.10 Example

Trivially small systems can be documented by simply starting with a single O/C Model showing the relationships between the top-layer O/Cs (cf. Figure 5.45). For a large system, each of these models is likely to be represented as subsystems and "exploded" to lower-layer diagrams. For example, Figure 5.46 shows details "inside" class BIBLIOGRAPHY. Such addition of detail thus often requires scrutiny of smaller portions of the system with higher resolution (see Sections 5.8.3 and 5.8.4 on layering and selective visibility). On the other hand, for smaller systems, little use of layering may be needed. In Figure 5.47 is shown an association between the BIBLIOGRAPHY and the APPLICATION (i.e., the user in the domain), the former being an aggregate of BOOK_REF and JOURNAL_REF. As the Specification Phase proceeds, more computer-domain-specific classes are included—here the class TEXT_FILE (Figure 5.48).

Other relationships (possibly related to the aggregation structures identified

The MOSES Notation 255

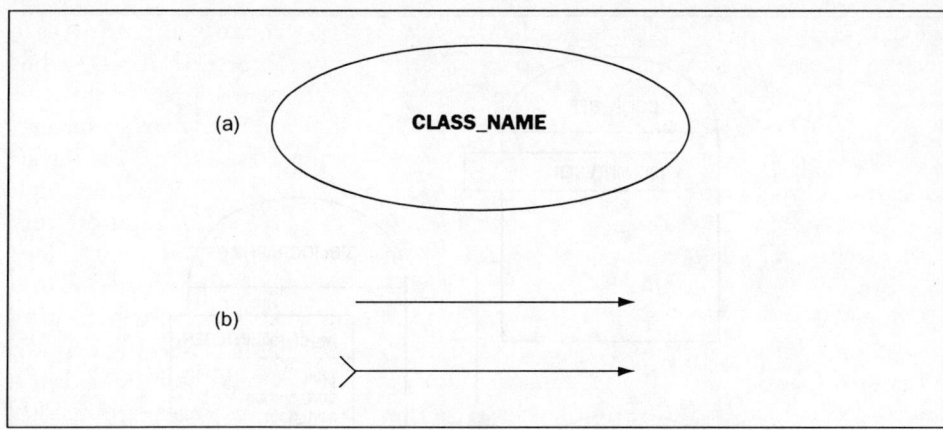

Figure 5.44 *MOSES sketching notation for (a) O/C icon and (b) inheritance*

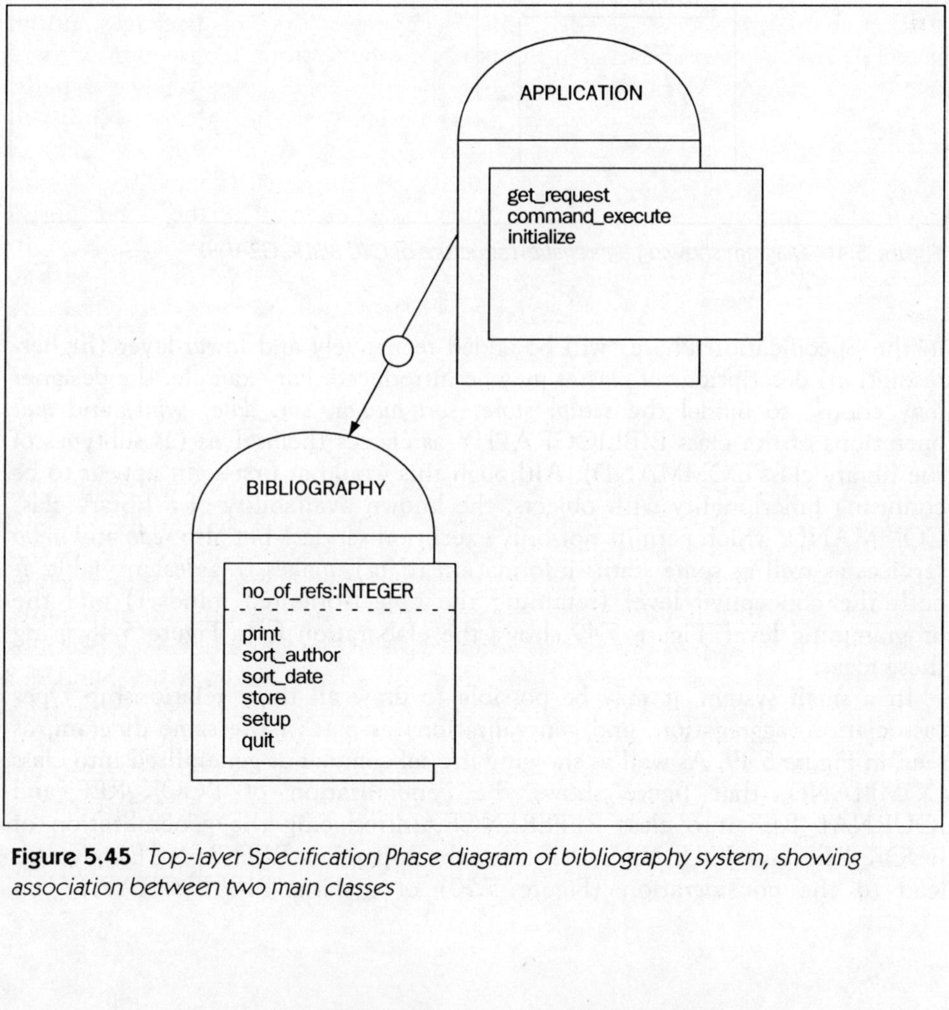

Figure 5.45 *Top-layer Specification Phase diagram of bibliography system, showing association between two main classes*

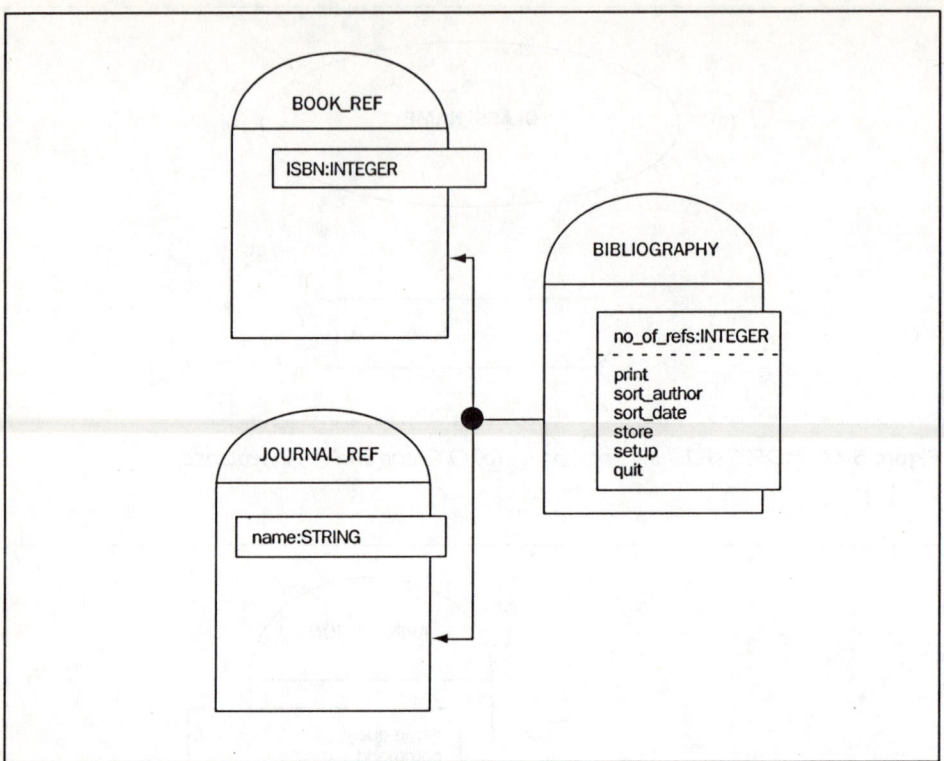

Figure 5.46 *Diagram showing aggregation structure of O/C BIBLIOGRAPHY*

in the Specification Phase) will be added recursively and lower-layer (higher-resolution) descriptions of classes may be introduced. For example, the designer may choose to model the *setup, store, sort_author, sort_date, print,* and *quit* operations of the class BIBLIOGRAPHY as classes themselves (as subtypes of the library class COMMAND). Although this would at first sight appear to be confusing functionality with objects, the known availability of a library class COMMAND, which permits not only execution services but also *redo* and *undo* services as well as some status information (data), makes this design viable at both the conceptual level (retaining the object-oriented mindset) and the programming level. Figure 5.49 shows the elaboration from Figure 5.48 using these ideas.

In a small system, it may be possible to draw all three relationship types (association, aggregation, and generalization) as part of the same diagram, as seen in Figure 5.49. As well as showing the subcommands generalized into class COMMAND, that figure shows the generalization of BOOK_REF and JOURNAL_REF into class REFERENCE. Introducing the generalization of BOOK_REF and JOURNAL_REF into the superclass REFERENCE may also lead to the consideration (Figure 5.50) of making BIBLIOGRAPHY an

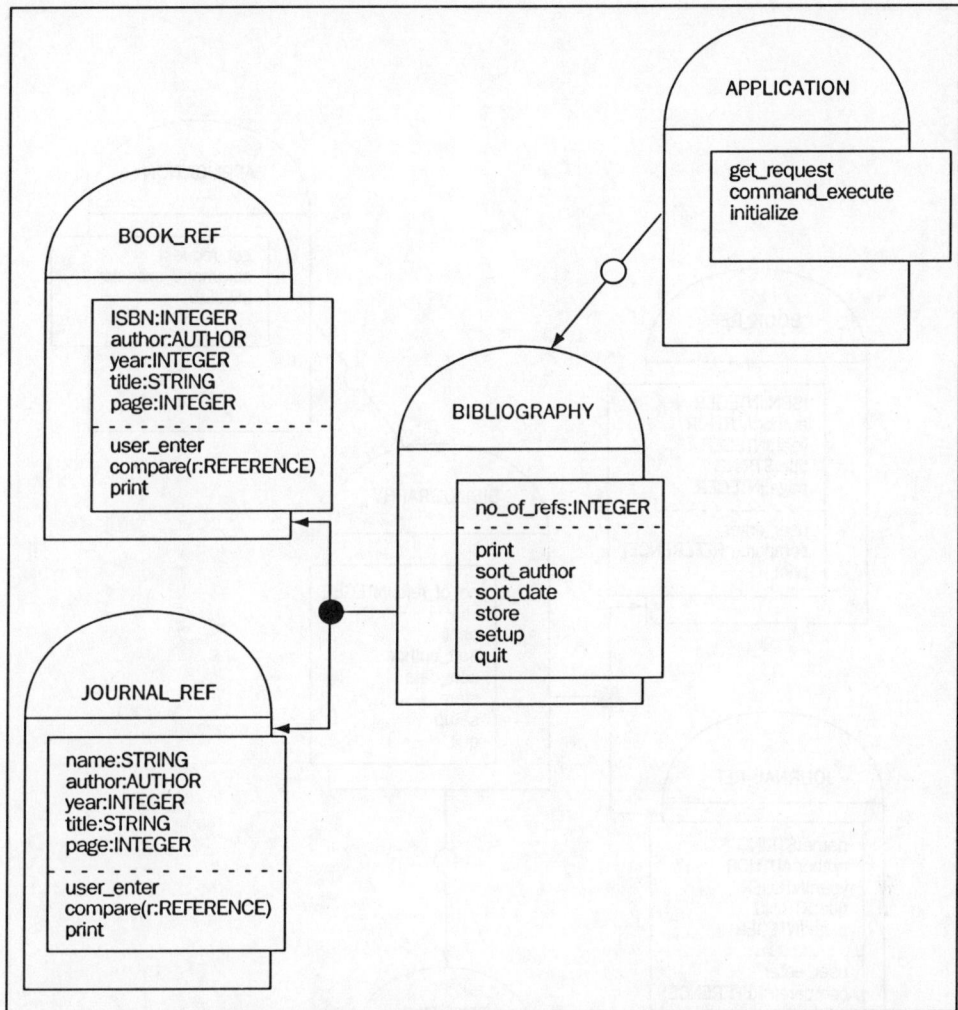

Figure 5.47 *Combination of Figures 5.45 and 5.46 to create a diagram showing high-level O/Cs related through association and aggregation*

aggregate of REFERENCE rather than BOOK_REF plus JOURNAL_REF. This would have the advantage of providing a structure that would assist polymorphic usage, in the same way that the APPLICATION class accesses the COMMAND class in Figure 5.49 rather than the various subclasses.

However, as more detail is added, especially when moving toward the Implementation Phase, this amount of detail on one page becomes untenable. Consequently, we use the suite of complementary diagraming notations described in this chapter, in which concepts of "selective visibility," "layering," and subsystems feature strongly as aids to comprehension. This suite of diagrams

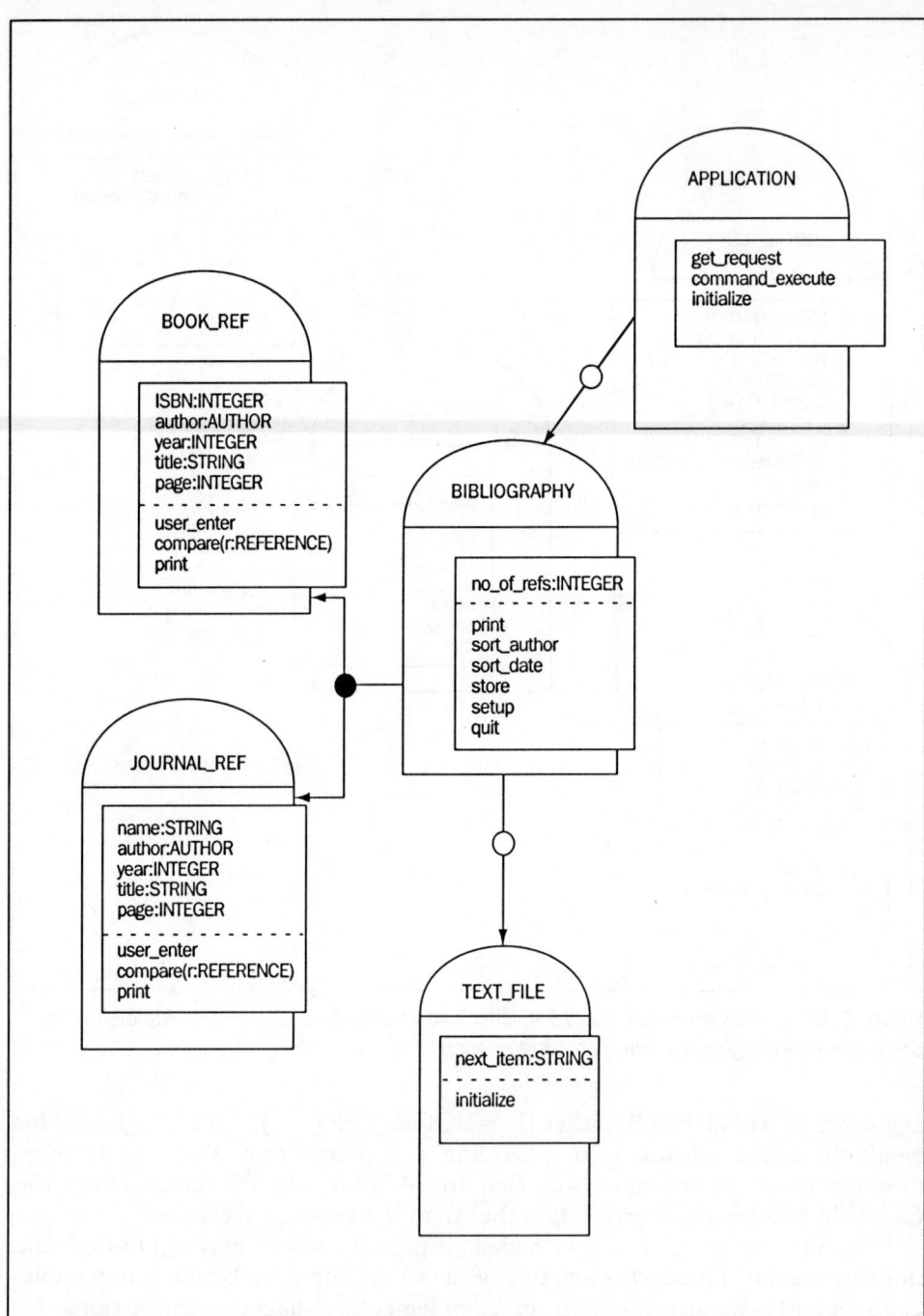

Figure 5.48 *As specification continues, more computer-specific O/Cs may be identified and added to the O/C Model*

The MOSES Notation

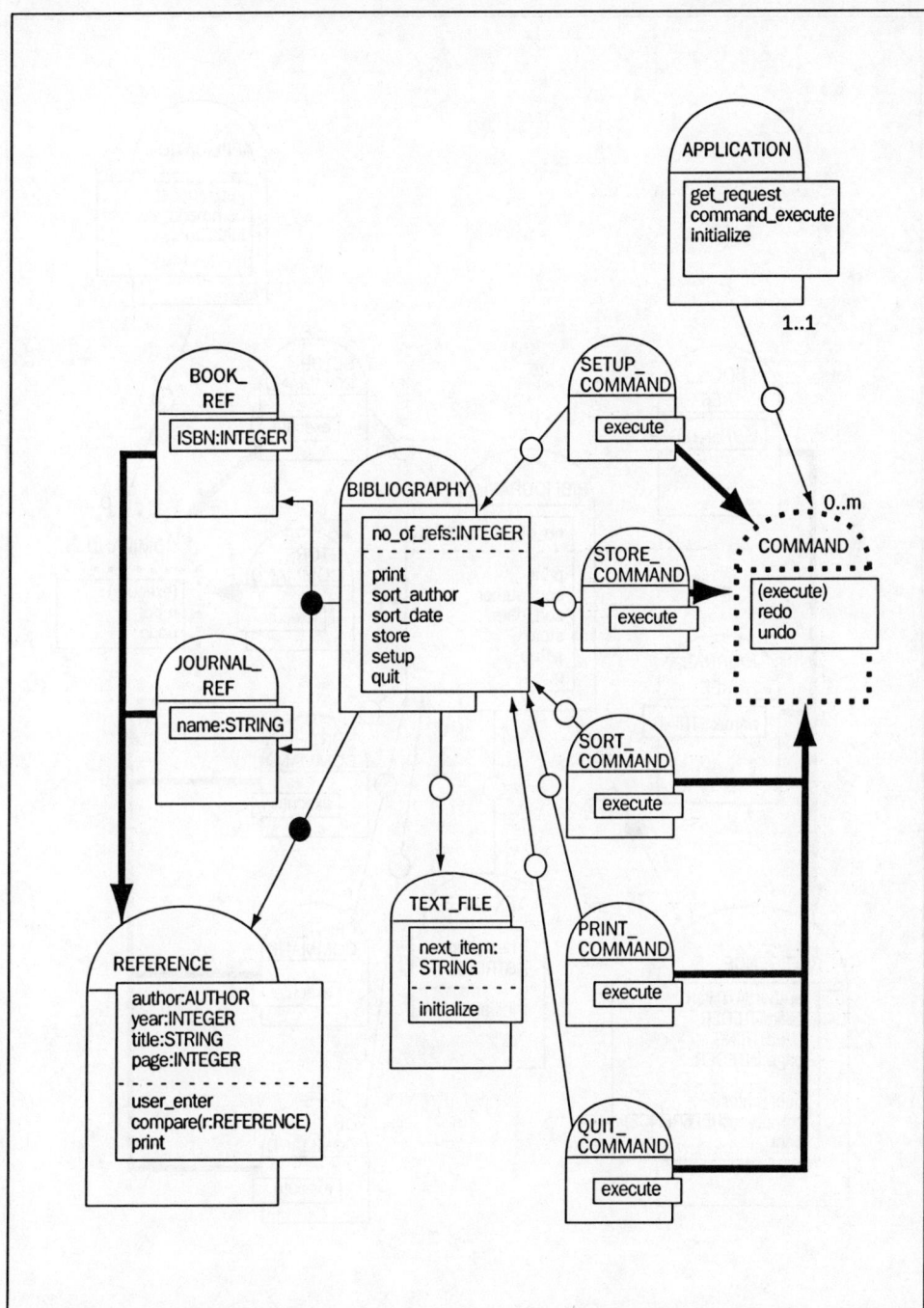

Figure 5.49 *Top-layer O/C Model showing associations, aggregations, and, now, inheritance relationships*

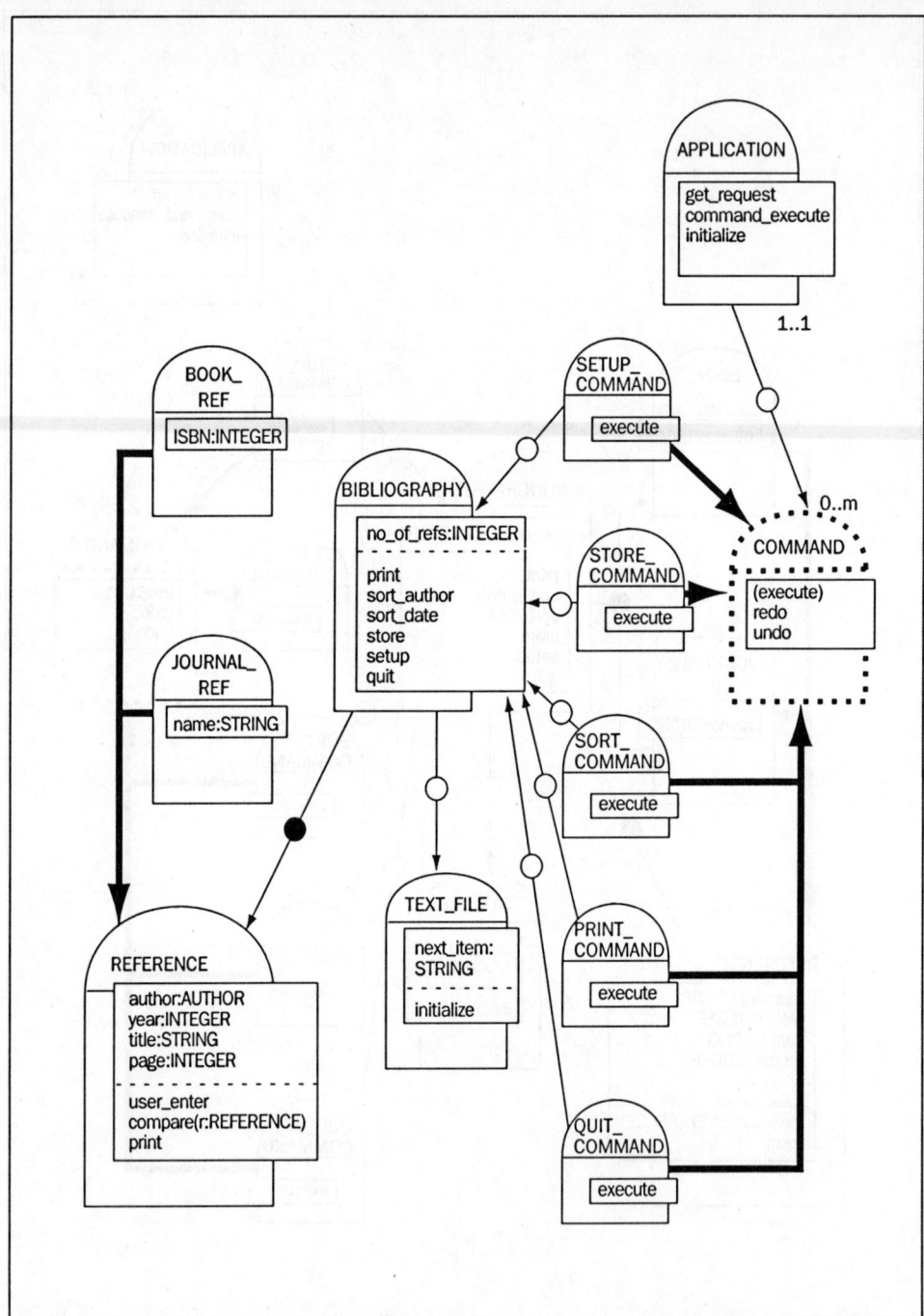

Figure 5.50 *As Figure 5.49, but with the polymorphic nature of the REFERENCE hierarchy made more explicit*

encourages separate presentation of association charts, aggregation "hierarchies" (expressed using "layering"), and generalization networks.

The O/C Model diagrams of the Specification Phase (for a small system) shown in Figure 5.50 translate readily into O/C Model diagrams of the Implementation Phase (Figure 5.51).

However, once again, for most systems such detail on one diagram becomes impossibly complex, and normally layering (Section 5.8.3) and selective visibility (Section 5.8.4) will be much-used techniques for mastering the design complexity. In addition, we recommend that the inheritance hierarchies be shown separately from the client–server relationships. For example, Figure 5.52 depicts the O/C Model of Figure 5.50 by two diagrams: one for the client–server relationships (Figure 5.52(a)) and a second (Figure 5.52(b)) for the inheritance hierarchy (in fact, one diagram for each inheritance hierarchy). The two versions here ((i) and (ii)) are alternatives, largely determined by the geometric layout of the "tablets" in the design representation document. Straight lines, as in part (ii), are not always possible, although if they can be used they often save space.

5.11 Summary and conclusions

Graphical notations have an important place within methodologies as a means of communication and documentation. However, graphical representation can easily hinder both activities if they become too unwieldy or complex. Finding a balance between expressiveness and conciseness is an important objective in any notation. The approach to the development of the graphics for MOSES has been a minimalist one, preferring to use textual notations when appropriate, rather than provide a symbol for all constructs. However, if the methodology is to be applicable to a wide range of system development projects of varying sizes, it is also important to provide a comprehensive suite of tools sufficient for the rationalization and documentation of large systems.

In this chapter, we have presented a complete and comprehensive set of complementary graphics and documentation tools for expressing clearly and concisely all aspects of a system at a number of resolutions, related to the levels of abstraction. The representations are programming-language-independent and do not include a number of language-specific features, preferring instead to view these as "add-ons" to the methodology that may be used if required, or desired, by the developer. The notation also includes a number of constructs that, although not in the object model proper, are useful for rationalizing the complexity of large-scale developments. Scalability has been a major concern in the development of this notation.

The discussion identified the graphical representation of an OO development, not all components of which are necessarily of equal importance in every project, as well as a number of complexity management techniques. In summary, we believe that the MOSES notation provides one of the most usable and complete sets of representations yet developed for OO software engineering and development.

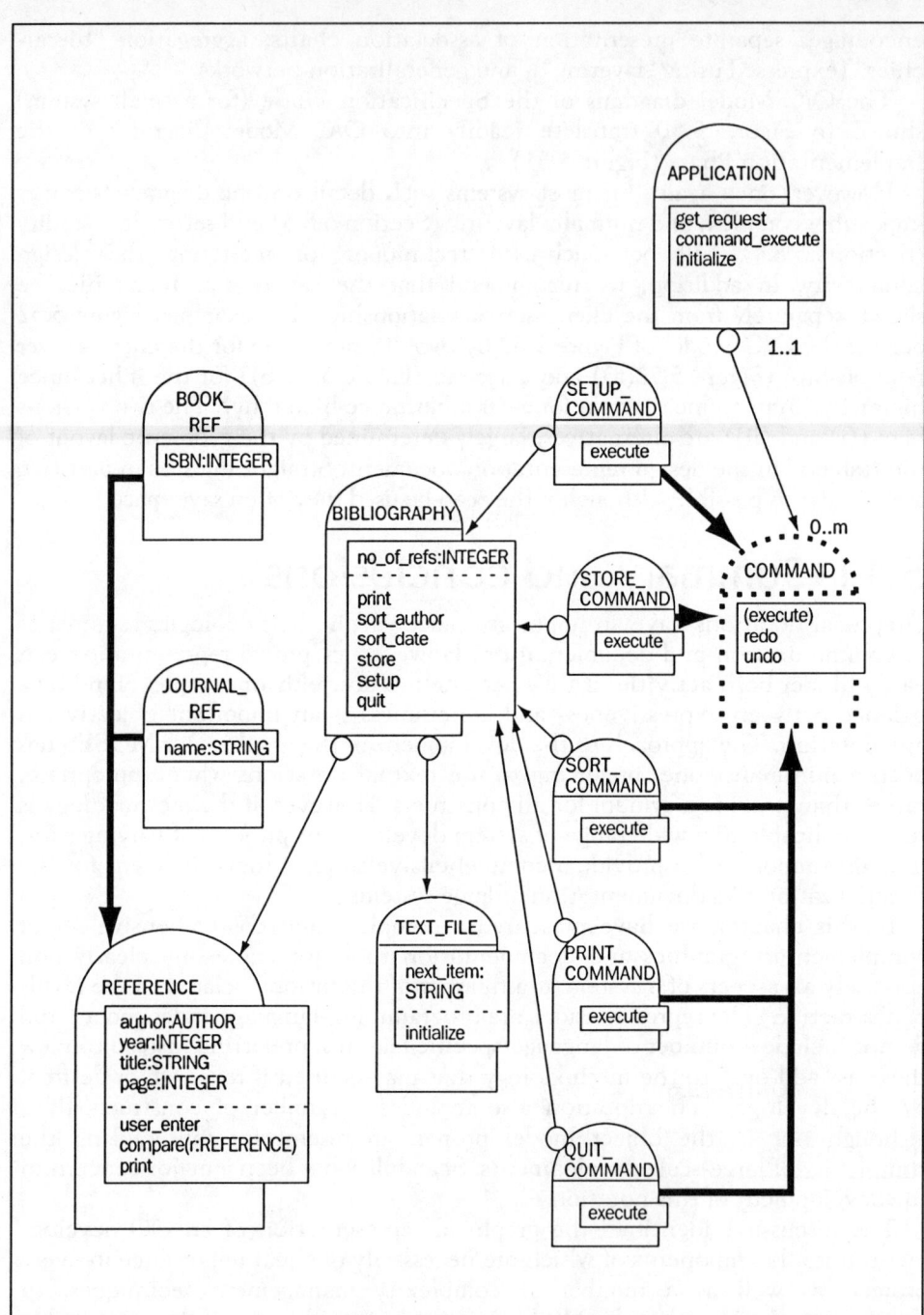

Figure 5.51 O/C Model of Figure 5.50 translated to an Implementation Phase diagram using logical references as in Eiffel and Smalltalk

The MOSES Notation

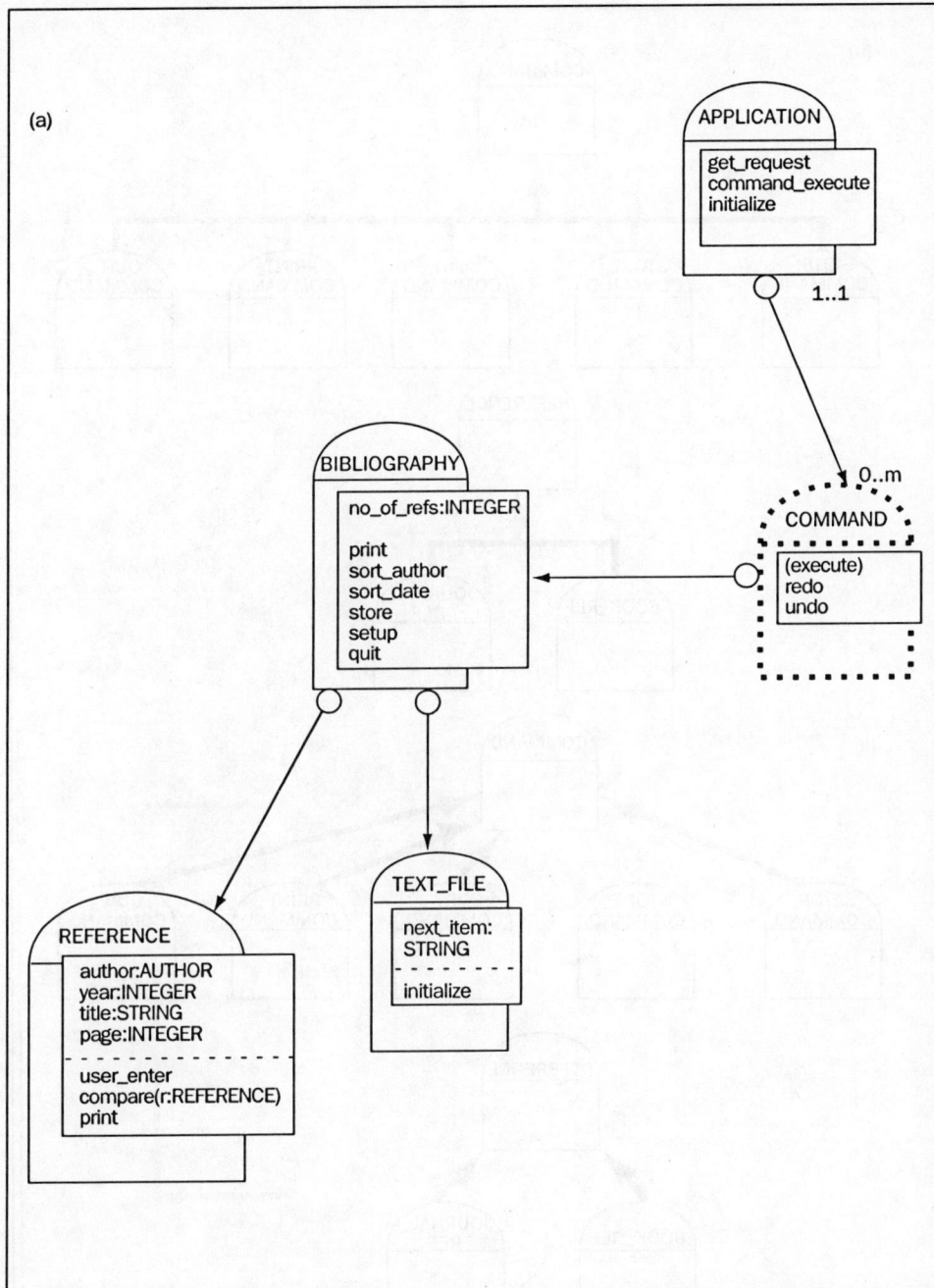

Figure 5.52 *In the Implementation Phase (above), it may be more appropriate to show only client–server and not inheritance (as compared to both being depicted in Figure 5.51). The inheritance relationships are shown overleaf.*

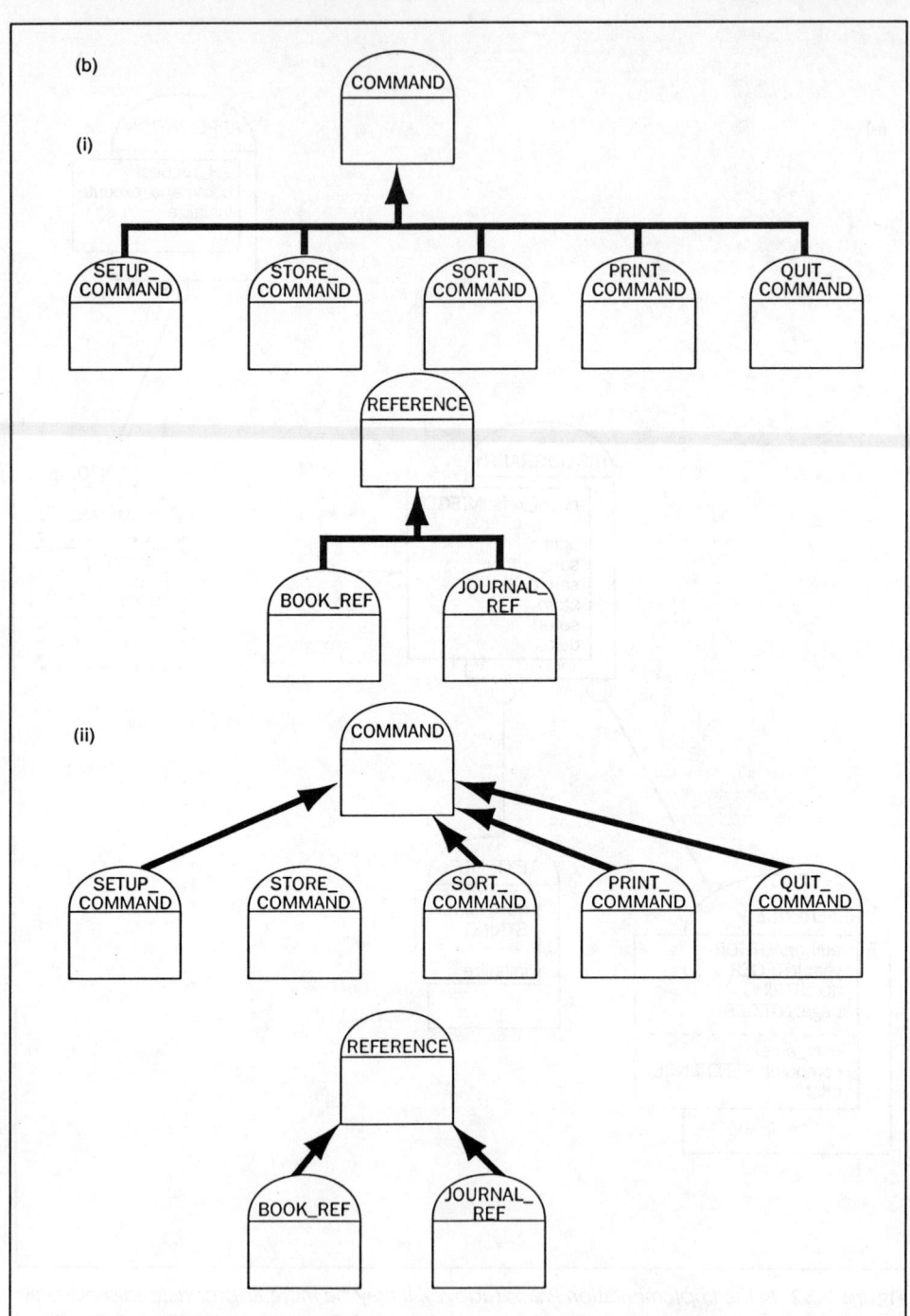

Figure 5.52 *continued*

5.12 Study examples

Exercise 2 In classical music, a musical composition consists of several movements, each of which is built up of chords or individual notes, grouped in bars with a given time signature and key signature. The music is scored on one or more staves.

In the specific context of building software designed to produce a printed score, identify the relationships and depict them using the MOSES notation.

• CHAPTER 6 •

The MOSES Product and Process Lifecycles

This chapter discusses the stages of the product lifecycle and the phases of the process lifecycle within MOSES. In particular, we concentrate on the phases of the process lifecycle, as this is the area of most significant difference between an OO approach and a traditional approach. For each phase, we detail the objective, the typical activities, the deliverables, and the interactions with other phases. The techniques and methods associated with a particular Activity are discussed in detail in Chapter 7. The present chapter, therefore, details "what" is to be done and "what" is to be produced, while Chapter 7 details "how" the activities are carried out, detailing the pragmatics and heuristics of each one. As discussed in Chapters 3 and 4, the preferred process lifecycle is an iterative development process (IDP). However, as discussed in Chapter 4, this does not prevent the methodology from being used within a spiral lifecycle, or even with a more traditional waterfall lifecycle. When describing the phases within this chapter, we will discuss them as applied within an IDP.

MOSES describes the product lifecycle in terms of a Growth Period and a number of subsequent Enhancement Periods, collectively termed the Maturity Period. Each Period is composed of three stages (Business Planning, Build, Delivery)—see Figure 6.1. The IDP applies in the Build Stage of each Growth Period and Enhancement Period and is composed of five phases: Planning,

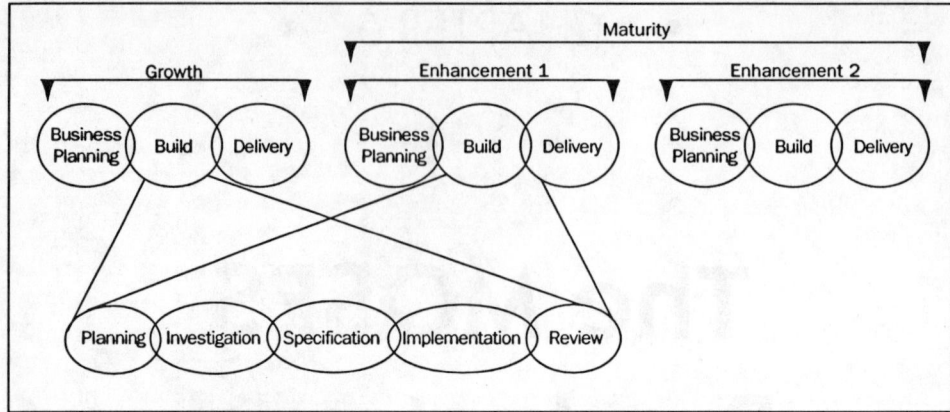

Figure 6.1 *The overall framework of MOSES showing the relationship between the periods and the stages of the product lifecycle and the phases of the process lifecycle*

Investigation, Specification, Implementation, and Review. Before we examine the process lifecycle in detail we will discuss the major stages of the product lifecycle, the activities involved, and the deliverables produced. Figure 6.2 is a summary of those stages and the associated deliverables.

6.1 Growth Period

A new system development project may be initiated by a number of means, including Strategic Information Systems Planning (SISP), or as a result of demand from users, or even from political pressures. Once the need for a new system has been identified, the product lifecycle enters the Growth Period (Figure 6.1).

6.1.1 Business Planning Stage

The first stage of the Growth Period or subsequent Enhancement Periods is the Business Planning Stage. This stage may appear only in truncated form in the Enhancement Periods, since the activities involved tend to address whether a *new* system is needed. However, Enhancement Periods often require some degree of business planning, although in most cases a full feasibility study or cost–benefit analysis is not required.

The Business Planning Stage involves a number of activities. These will be briefly discussed here, rather than separately in Chapter 7, as they are essentially unaffected by OT and there are many other texts covering this area.

The first such activity is to obtain a statement of the business requirements specification. User requirements may be quite general. For example, the desire may be as broad as "automate the accounting system at a cost of less than

The MOSES Product and Process Lifecycles

$200,000 using existing PCs and workstations." In other words, it is a statement of a problem and some notion of constraints that apply, usually derived from external-world budgetary consideration. For example, client–server architectures are currently gaining popularity. In such a distributed system, where several machines are networked together such that the processing is distributed across several CPUs (several machines or one multiprocessor machine), determining the appropriate configuration may be a Business Planning constraint. In this case, evaluation of the impact of such a choice may be important. At this stage, a software solution may or may not be indicated. Alternatives are evaluated in the Feasibility Study (see below).

As part of the business plan evaluation, critical success factors (CSFs) for the organization should be considered. These form the basis against which the options evaluated in the Feasibility Study can be measured. A CSF is simply a

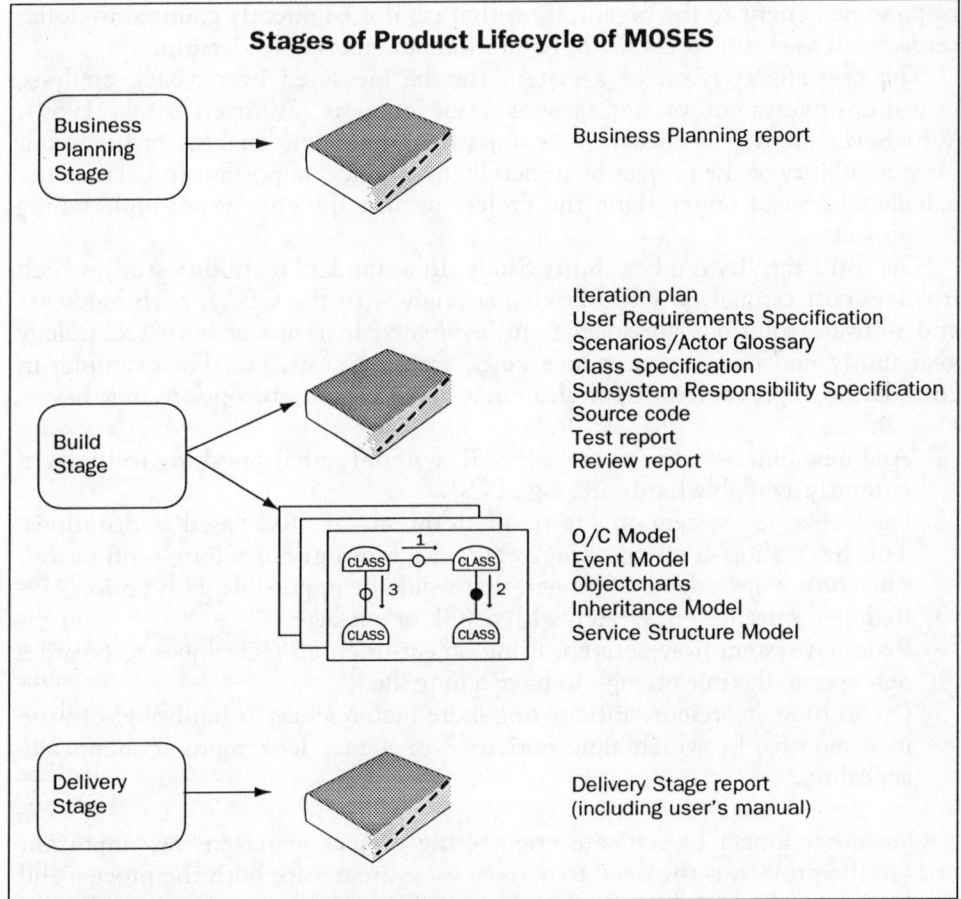

Figure 6.2 *Major deliverables of the three stages of the Growth Period*

factor that, if not optimized, could be critical to the success of the company. A typical CSF may be the delivery time for a company that promises speedy deliveries (e.g., Domino's Pizza).

The second activity is a cost-benefit analysis (CBA). A preliminary cost-benefit analysis should be undertaken in this stage in order to determine whether the business benefits likely to be achieved outweigh the cost of the project. It will be preliminary in the sense that it is hard to estimate likely costs when the solution has not been developed. However, it should be possible to indicate a net benefit or net loss from the project and hence permit an informed decision to be made.

Costs within a CBA should include personnel costs, computer usage costs, training costs, supply and equipment costs, as well as running costs. Running costs include both fixed and variable costs of usage and should be estimated as carefully as possible. Benefits cover tangible and intangible benefits—that is to say, those benefits on which a dollar figure can be placed and those that may bring some benefit to the organization that cannot be directly counted in dollar terms, such as customer goodwill, reputation, and market leadership.

The cost-effectiveness of a system can be measured by payback analysis, return-on-investment or net present value analysis (Whitten *et al.*, 1989). Whichever method is chosen, it is important that some analysis of the economic feasibility of the project be undertaken. It is also important to balance the calculated cost of undertaking the project against the cost of *not* undertaking the project.

The third activity is a Feasibility Study. In a standard feasibility study, which involves cost estimation (thus linking strongly with the CBA), both hardware and software solutions are sought and evaluated in terms of both technology availability and cost, maintenance costs, training costs, etc. For example, in considering improvements to an insurance claim system, the options may be:

1. Add new functionality to current 3GL system (perhaps pushing to limits of currently available hardware, e.g., PCs).
2. Develop a new system on a faster platform, say SPARC-based workstations. This has a short-term cost (hardware and training) but a long-term payoff, since future upgrades are foreseen that would be impossible with option 1.
3. Redesign system from scratch with a 4GL or package.
4. Redesign system from scratch, using object-oriented techniques to create a new system flexible enough to have a long life.
5. Do nothing at present, anticipating more mature/cheaper hardware/software in n months, by which time options 2 or 4 may look more economically appealing.

One other aspect of software engineering project management, important early in the project, is the need to derive cost estimates for both the process and the products, which is difficult if not impossible to achieve with any precision or accuracy. Graham (1991) suggests that only function points might be useful from a standard cost estimation toolbox. In an object-oriented development, reuse and generalization costs need also to be considered (e.g., Henderson-Sellers, 1992b). At the time of writing, unfortunately, no reliable cost estimation techniques have been developed and verified in an object-oriented environment, although progress is being made for object-oriented maintenance metrics (Chapter 10).

The outcome of this stage is a Business Planning Report that details the business case for a number of alternative solutions to the business problem identified. These solutions may involve package solutions, developing software, or simply "doing nothing." The outcome of the stage may lead to termination of the product lifecycle before the process lifecycle has even begun. A recommendation, derived from the Feasibility Study of the available options, is a key part of the deliverables. The recommendations should be reviewed by a number of peers before presentation to senior managers and business users.

Assuming a software solution is sought that requires some development work, the Build Stage (Section 6.1.2) of the product lifecycle is begun.

The deliverable produced at the end of the Business Planning Stage is termed the Business Planning Report (Figure 6.2). This should be structured as follows:

- statement of business requirements and external constraints;
- critical success factors;
- feasibility study (of options available);
- economic and technical evaluation and costing;
- cost–benefit analysis;
- recommendation of strategy (choice based on above analysis).

In addition to documentation the following activities are suggested:

- presentation by the developers of the documentation to software engineers, senior management, and users;
- peer review of the documentation (including users and developers), which can be critical.

6.1.2 Build Stage

The Build Stage of the product lifecycle is where the process lifecycle is entered. It may therefore be regarded as a high-level abstraction of the process lifecycle.

The actual process lifecycle chosen in this Build Stage may be a spiral, fountain, or waterfall approach. Whichever approach is taken is to a large extent independent of the subsequent Delivery Stage (Section 6.1.3).

We discuss the Build Stage further in the section on the process lifecycle (Section 6.3). The deliverables from this stage are essentially the final versions of the deliverables produced during the process lifecycle. These are shown in Figure 6.2.

6.1.3 Delivery Stage

The Delivery Stage is the last stage of the Growth Period and the Enhancement Periods and is where the system is tested and installed and users educated. This stage may be a "big bang" if a waterfall approach has been adopted for representing the process lifecycle. Alternatively, and preferably, it is of a smaller scale as a result of incremental delivery and an incremental development process lifecycle (e.g., Goldberg, 1993).

In either scenario, it is likely that the first version or delivery of the full system will require significant activities to be undertaken. Once again, it is not our intention to discuss the activities of this stage in detail, as they are to a large extent independent of OT. Thus only a brief description of the type of activities that occur is given below.

Once the product is complete, it is delivered to the customer's site and installed on their machines, where on-site testing follows. On-site testing includes preparing test databases and test data and determining and setting up on-site monitoring procedures.

Once the developers have site-tested the software, the customer will have a period of time (several weeks) in which to evaluate whether it meets their expectations and requirements (as spelled out in their contract with the software developer). These final checks will be less traumatic than in a traditional development, since in this incremental delivery environment, each incremental product will already have been exposed to user criticism and assessment. However, especially when a significant period of time has elapsed between order and delivery, it is more than likely that the business requirements of the customer may have evolved beyond their original specification so that the first iteration through the Enhancement Period may begin almost immediately.

Once the software has received official approval, the wider body of users will (usually) require some in-house training, probably supplied by the developer or associated company. This will be a combination of hands-on training and documentation evaluation/learning. Feedback on both the user feel of the software and its associated manuals will be given freely at this stage and should be incorporated by the developer into any later releases following a TQM approach to software development (Section 7.13). Assessment of all aspects of the development is important in this stage, including the system, the process, the documentation, and the project management components. The result of the Delivery Stage is the installation and acceptance of the initial version of the product.

Since historically most software developed has been found to be unusable without immediate modification or in fact is never used, acceptance testing within the object-oriented environment will be a crucial hurdle for more widespread acceptance and utilization of this new technology.

The deliverable produced at the end of the Delivery Phase is termed the Delivery Stage Report (Figure 6.2). This is a report structured as follows:

- assessment of implementation process;
- assessment of systems acceptance test;
- post-implementation review.

6.2 Enhancement Period

Subsequent work on the system may involve minor changes or addition of major new requirements. Either way, enhancements should involve the three stages of Business Planning, Build, and Delivery, although, as mentioned, in small enhancements the Business Planning Stage and the Delivery Stage may be nonexistent. Enhancement Periods will involve the reapplication of the process lifecycle, involving all the phases to be discussed below (Section 6.3). The number of subsystems impacted and the number of iterations involved will be a function of the size and complexity of the changes required. This view of enhancement as simply a reapplication of the process lifecycle is also applicable in an incremental delivery approach and as such is a view more in line with an OO development environment.

It is important to recognize the difference between error correction and evolution activities. The former are fixes to the system, while the latter are a natural part of the development process and essentially involve iteration back to lower levels in the fountain lifecycle model. New requirements lead to reconfiguration and extension of specific classes and subsystems. Changes can be made more easily by the use of inheritance and the use of a single object model throughout the process.

Errors should be fixed in the appropriate class and the subclasses corrected as necessary. Opening modules is generally against the OO approach, but not if the classes contain errors. The cost of opening modules for correction is likely to be significantly smaller than the effect of correcting software errors later in the project or in subsequent projects. The quality of the software should increase with reuse and, consequently, error correction should be a diminishing part of maintenance as more components are reused in later projects.

During operation, the developers will maintain a relationship with the customer so that any enhancements can be supplied quickly (cf. McCullough and Deshler, 1990). Metrics must be collected throughout the development process; also, it is crucial that metrics regarding the flexibility of software evolution be collected, since one of the strategic advantages promised by object technology is a faster response to user requests for software enhancements.

Maintenance involves error correction (bug fixes) and the collection of maintenance metrics (Wilde and Huitt, 1992). Note that both evolution and maintenance are initially focused at the systems level rather than the subsystem or class level, although changes required are likely to affect only small portions of the system, effectively returning that class/those classes to an earlier lifecycle activity in the iterative and recursive manner supported by MOSES.

6.3 Process lifecycle

The Build Stage of the Growth Period and the subsequent Enhancement Periods of the product lifecycle involve the application of a process lifecycle. The process lifecycle of MOSES identifies five phases: Planning, Investigation, Specification, Implementation, and Review. In the following subsections, we describe the process lifecycle and phase interactions in terms of an IDP based on the fountain lifecycle (see Figure 6.3 and Chapter 3). This does not preclude the use of the methodology in more traditional waterfall environments where essentially there is only *one* iteration of the phases, if such an environment is

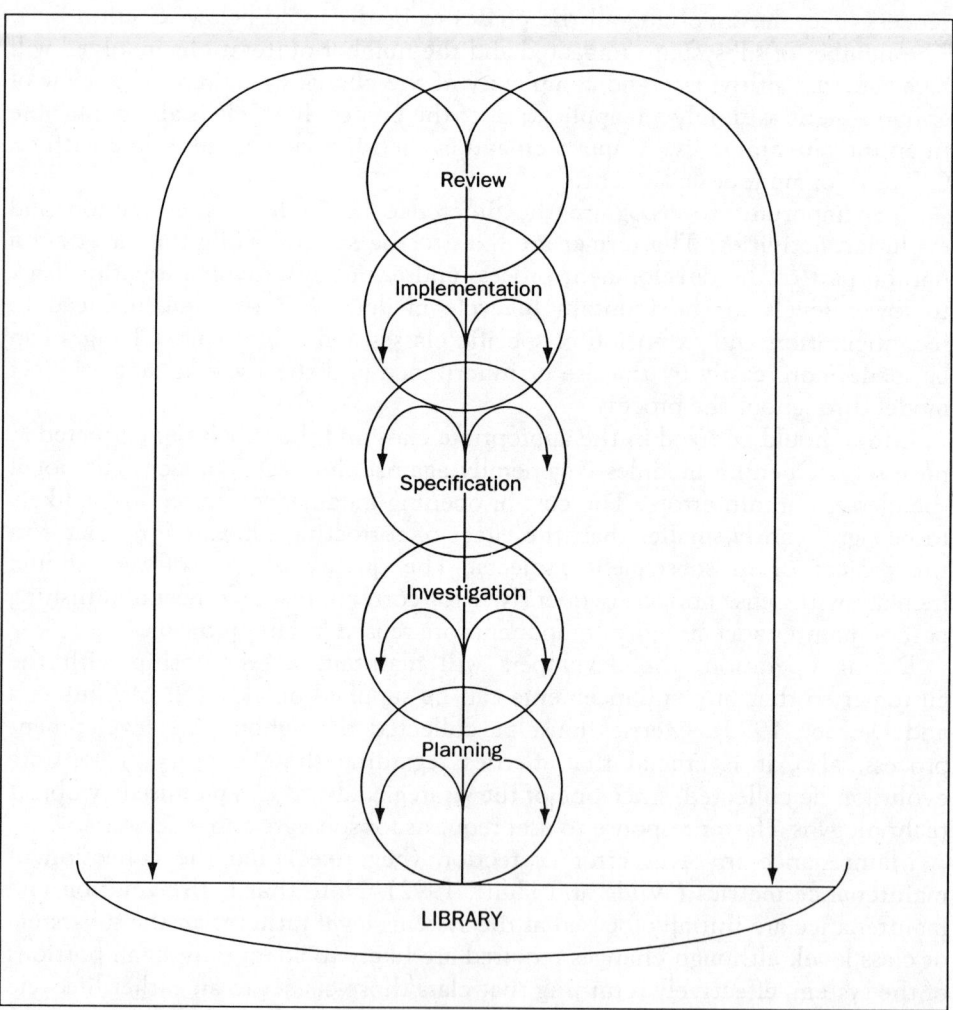

Figure 6.3 *The fountain (meta)model underlying MOSES*

mandated in the organization. Using a fountain lifecycle permits iteration to "earlier" phases, even from the Review Phase to the Investigation Phase, for instance, if serious problems are identified in that phase.

In an IDP, the number of iterations required is essentially a function of size and complexity. Lorenz (1993) suggests that a rule of thumb is three to six iterations on a system of 200 classes, with each iteration taking about three months. Once a more stable model has emerged from the process, the activities should begin to concentrate on generalization and verification and validation of the classes.

During the iteration and refinement process, the model should be completed for the subsystem, thus ensuring that it describes all the required services of the subsystem; this will lead to a restatement of the initial requirements if they are ill defined or fuzzy. Such a restatement can be used as a sign-off point for the next stage if this type of development process is being applied.

6.3.1 Planning Phase

The first phase of an iteration involves constructing first an overall plan and then a plan for each consecutive iteration. Planning involves estimation, resourcing, and setting objectives. During the early stages of the development process, before the system has really been decomposed into subsystems and work groups, planning will be done by the senior project leader. The major task in this phase is to estimate system-wide resourcing and strategies and to schedule the project. Scheduling may involve the use of standard project management tools such as PERT or Gantt charts.

The main difference between this phase and the Business Planning Stage is that in the Planning Phase, the outlook is shorter term and focuses on resources to be made available for the next iteration. These resources include, for example, people, workstations, technical backup, and desktop publishing (DTP) support. Goals and objectives are set over a period of a few days or weeks and personnel allocated such that these goals and objectives can be met successfully. As each plan is iterated, a risk analysis should be undertaken so that if the project appears to be encountering insurmountable difficulties, it can be curtailed before it expends enormous amounts of unrecoverable resources.

During later iterations of the IDP, the project leader can make decisions on high-level decompositions of the system and assignment of tasks to work groups. Decomposing a system into subsystems (Activity: Subsystem Identification) or composing classes into subsystems is the responsibility of the project leader. Guidelines for such decompositions are discussed in Chapter 7. Once these decisions have been made, further planning can be undertaken by team leaders, whose planning emphasis is that of the individual subsystems.

System-wide coordination of the iterative development plans of multiple teams is obviously an important task and regular team-leader reviews will be required. These reviews are, however, more coordination meetings than system-wide planning meetings. This decentralized approach is reflected in Meyer's

(1988a) cluster model and the subsystem fountain model of Henderson-Sellers and Edwards (1993a).

During the Planning Phase, the classes of other subsystems should be examined. If other subsystems are at a similar stage, yet being designed separately, review meetings should be held to ensure that classes are not duplicated between models and that complete abstractions are developed for each class. Classes should be allocated to one subsystem and all the services placed in this one class. If the subsystem is to use the services of other subsystems, then it must be ensured that the appropriate relationships exist. Parallel development of collaborating subsystems should involve regular reviews.

Figure 6.4 shows graphically how planning begins as a system-wide function but soon decomposes into a subsystem-level function. Subsystem planning therefore involves tasks similar to those of system-wide planning but on a smaller scale.

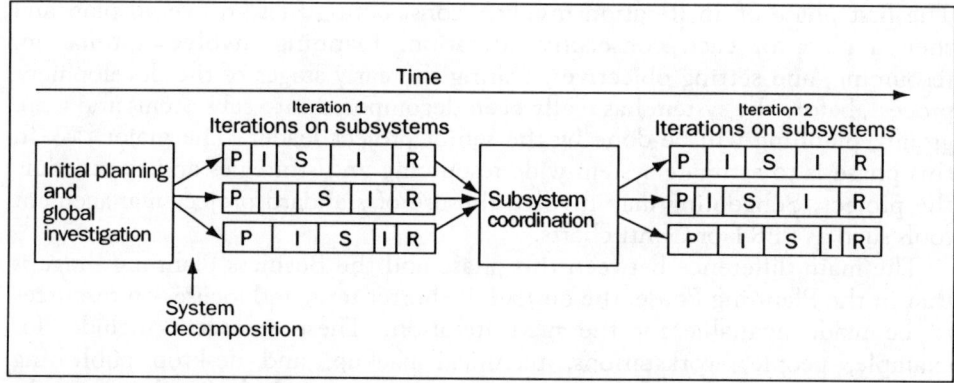

Figure 6.4 *At the start of the project the task is to decompose the problem into smaller, more manageable subsystems. From then on each subsytem can undergo the MOSES lifecycle phases independently. The subsystems should be coordinated at the end of each iteration to ensure that the O/C Model is consistent and redundancy is minimized. Following this reevaluation each undergoes another iteration.*

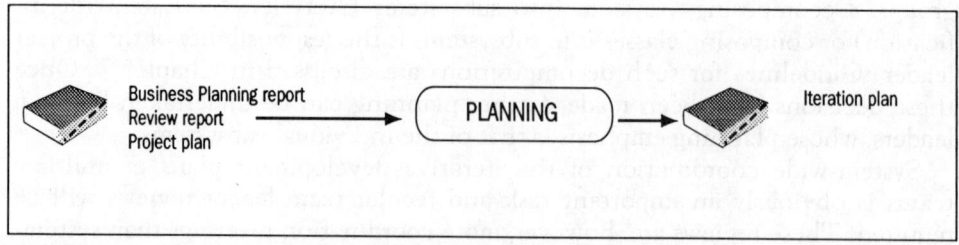

Figure 6.5 *Planning Phase deliverables*

The MOSES Product and Process Lifecycles

The deliverable from this phase is an Iteration Plan, which should be formally reviewed before delivery (Activity: Documentation Review) (Figure 6.5). A typical Iteration Plan may include:

Iteration Plan: XXXX   Date: mm/dd/yy

Team Leader:

Subsystem Name:

Start Date:

End Date:

Description:

Phase:

Investigation

- Gantt charts
- Activity
- Resources
- Time

Specification

Implementation

Review

6.3.2 Investigation Phase

The Investigation Phase of an iteration is where the developer gains a detailed understanding of a part of the user requirements. This phase involves the Activity: User Requirements Elicitation and the Activity: Scenario Development. Inputs into this phase are the informal statement of business requirements from the Business Planning Stage, other models such as data models, previously developed O/C Models, process models, and numerous other sources of informal and formal information about the system and its context.

User Requirements Elicitation

The Activity: User Requirement Elicitation is detailed in Chapter 7 but essentially involves structured interviews with business users and domain experts. The analyst should identify the potential end users, including those who may be affected by the system even if they are not actually using it. The analyst should then investigate the current system, if one exists, and the required functionality, initially by interview and discussion. Questions such as: What led to the request for a system? What are the expectations of the system? What is the scope? Who is involved? What are the constraints? are all important in gaining an understanding of the project.

Initially, the requirements may describe only fairly high-level objectives. These requirements can be used to form the basis of a decomposition of the system into manageable areas of functionality. These areas can then be allocated a priority and, on the basis of available resources, be investigated further, either in parallel with other areas or sequentially. Decomposition of the system into subsystems, which are then allocated to different teams, is principally the responsibility of the overall project manager. The output of this activity is a textual document detailing the functionality and constraints of the required system, called the User Requirements Specification (URS). Initially, the URS may be quite informal. It will be formalized once further investigation is undertaken during the development of scenarios.

Scenario development

Once the scope of the requirements has been defined, a second activity—scenario development—is undertaken for each functional area. This activity, which is discussed in detail in Chapter 7 and is based on the requirements model of Jacobson *et al.* (1992), leads to a scenario description that details the way in which a user interacts or wishes to interact with a system. Scenarios are developed by consultation and discussion with users and are recorded as simple narratives, indexed for easy reference. This index is also recorded in the Actor Glossary for traceability purposes. Developing scenarios is an effective means of communicating with business users, as it is essentially a description of what they do with the system, leading to a detailed description of the requirements of a functional area. The result of the activity is a collection of scenarios detailing both the normal and the exceptional cases during system operation, together with an associated Actor Glossary. The scenario model may also include screens showing the external interface with which the user interacts. The screens may be developed using screen painters, exploratory prototyping, or simple sketching. The objective is not to implement the system or screen, but to tease the requirements from the user, by means of a visual representation of the system. Scenarios and screen mock-ups can therefore be developed in conjunction with an exploratory prototyping technique. Through the techniques discussed in the Activity: User Requirements Elicitation and Activity: Scenario Development, a formal document representing the requirements emerges.

During later iterations, the Investigation Phase may simply be a refinement

The MOSES Product and Process Lifecycles

of the URS and scenario development. Indeed, it is important that change requests are not allowed to continue *ad hoc* during the development; otherwise budgets and initial planning estimates will be overrun. During later iterations, the period of activity spent on Investigation should diminish as the users' requirements are refined.

The deliverables of this phase are a URS and a scenario model (Figure 6.6).

Document Type	Information Generated and Recorded
User Requirements Specification	Required functionality Resource constraints—manpower Resource constraints—hardware/software Specification of problem domain Sufficiently detailed contractual documentation Cost estimation
Actor Glossary	Actor name user representative contact address scenarios
Scenario	Narrative Interface

6.3.3 Specification Phase

After a period of Investigation, the Specification Phase can begin. The objective during this phase is to develop the object-oriented model needed to support the URS and scenarios that were developed during the Investigation Phase. The inputs to this phase are therefore an Actor Glossary, scenarios with appropriate interface models, and the User Requirements Specification.

Early iterations of this phase are oriented toward the problem space. Little cognizance should be taken of the possible computer constraints of the model.

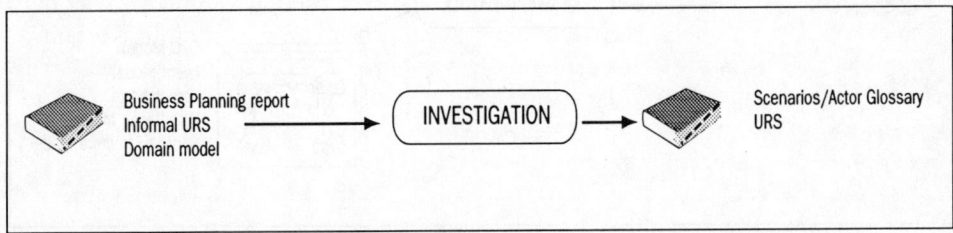

Figure 6.6 *Investigation Phase deliverables*

During later iterations, the focus/mindset switches from problem domain to solution domain. The design is now influenced by computer constraints. These later parts of the Specification Phase still detail the construction of a conceptual model, but one that includes computer-oriented, or solution domain, classes. A strong concentration on library integration activities is important during these later iterations.

The Specification Phase leads to a detailed object-oriented model of the problem domain that, in a complex problem, may involve a number of layers and subsystems. The O/Cs and their specification should be as independent of a particular implementation environment as possible, reflecting the focus of the development activity.

The output from this phase is a detailed specification of the OO model, which is captured in a series of graphical and textual representations (Figure 6.7) and detailed at the end of the section. This phase involves a large number of activities for which techniques and heuristics are detailed in Chapter 7. While it is not possible to detail a sequence of activities within this phase, it is possible to describe a general approach to the construction of an object-oriented model. This general approach is discussed below.

Identify structure

The scenarios developed during the Investigation Phase are input to the first set of activities that lead to the development of the O/C Model, which details the structure of the model. Candidate classes are identified from the scenarios and URS using the Activity: O/C Identification. This activity, which is discussed in detail in Chapter 7, indicates sources of possible O/Cs leading to the identification of candidate O/Cs and their basic properties. The initial list can be refined immediately using the guidelines in Section 7.11.

During the early iterations, the O/Cs and their interactions may deal at a high level of abstraction only. In particular, early iterations should concentrate on the O/Cs representing the business knowledge. These will tend to be

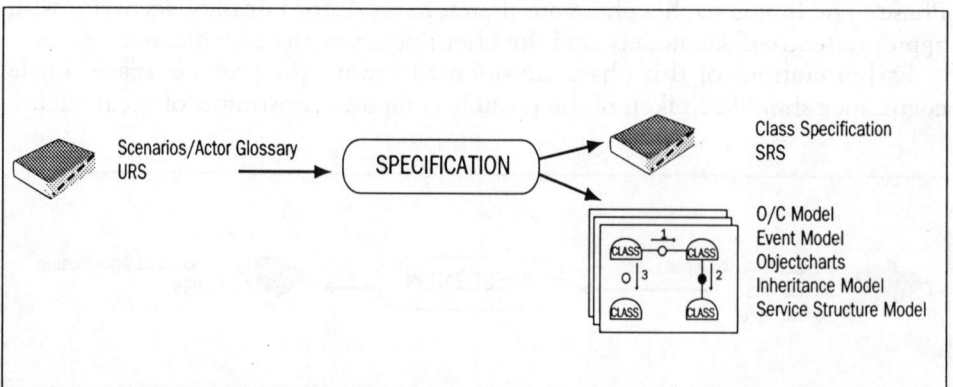

Figure 6.7 *Specification Phase deliverables*

"discovered" from the scenarios and URS. Detailed implementation of O/Cs need not be included. As iterations proceed and the business classes stabilize, a direct consequence of the increasing stability of the URS and scenarios, the developer can concentrate more on the design-oriented classes that will not have a direct counterpart in the "real world" and hence will tend to be "invented." Classes such as queues, lists, and database classes, which are not necessary for validating user requests, are now refined and specified.

Early iterations of this phase are therefore characterized by identification of real-world O/Cs (Section 7.11), concentrating on identifying those that are likely to provide good user-defined types (i.e., abstract data types, or ADTs). Good ADTs possess both state and functionality and offer a range of services to other O/Cs. The first priority therefore is to ask of a class, "What services does it offer/what collaborations does it enter into?" If the answer is none, then it is unlikely that this is a good abstraction. A poor class may be simply a data structure or be one that offers only a single piece of functionality. At the other end of the scale, a class that is overly complicated probably mixes two or more abstractions and should be rationalized into several classes.

From this point it is generally easiest to define O/C structures in terms of associations and aggregations (Section 7.7) as defined in the Activity: Interaction Specification, although it may be best to start with relationships that are not fully defined (e.g., with respect to cardinalities). These relationships can then be refined later.

Three relationships are useful for object modeling: association (roughly a **uses-the-services-of**), aggregation (an **is-part-of** aggregate–component relationship), and generalization/specialization (the **is-a-kind-of** relationship between classes). Again, these are relationships that are identifiable in the real world/problem space as well as in the solution space. Hints on identification of relationships are given in Chapter 7 in Activity: Interaction Specification.

Identify behavior
Once initial structures have been defined using the Activity: O/C Identification and the Activity: Interaction Specification, the initial behavior of the system can be modeled.

During early iterations, development of Event Models, as discussed in Activity: Event Model Construction, will be particularly important. Event Models, developed from scenarios, will detail the classes and interactions required to support the business knowledge and lead to the identification of events that are modeled as operations defined on classes. The operations should be recorded with a unique name on the class specification and the O/C Model, as detailed in Activity: Service Identification.

Once a number of operations have been defined from the scenarios, their effects can be modeled as postconditions (Section 7.1). The full specification of an operation is detailed in a contract. Techniques for identifying and specifying contracts are discussed in detail in Chapter 7 under Activity: Contract Specification. The effect of an event should be determined from the requirements, the scenario, or the user and recorded as functions on the values of the properties of the class. The postconditions simply specify the "what" of an operation, not the "how."

After a number of behaviors have been identified, objectcharts (Section 7.10) can be constructed for those O/Cs that appear to have interesting dynamic behavior. They should include the events identified from the scenarios (Section 7.14) and will lead to the identification of services required from other collaborating objects. These events are operations on the supplier object. There needs to be a relationship between the two objects that should be checked in the O/C Model. For each transition, a transition specification should be developed, leading to the development of the preconditions and postconditions for the operations. This should complete the contract for each operation (Activity: Contract Specification). If the contract is particularly complex, it may be preferable to develop a Service Structure Model (SSM). This graphically portrays the service using traditional structure chart techniques.

During later iterations, the model will be iterated and refined. During these iterations, O/Cs should be amalgamated or split as required and properties removed, added, or reorganized (Section 7.4); the same should happen with operations (Section 7.15.1) and objectcharts (Section 7.10). Reorganizing and refining the model require a good deal of skill, the essence of a good model being its simplicity.

Identify generalization
Generalization hierarchies can be defined on the basis of commonality of properties and operations (Activity: Inheritance Identification). The objectcharts of each class can be used to check the generalization relationship on the basis of the operations' contracts. Hierarchies can be developed in two ways. The first approach is to generalize a class, that is, to recognize commonality and create a general class that is possibly a deferred class. The second approach is to create more specialized classes from more general classes. This may help to find exceptional cases or special cases of more general situations in the model. The newly created classes should be abstractions in their own right and not simply collections of services common to a number of classes. Leaving generalization until after an initial pass means that the modeler has a good feel for the abstraction before generalizing classes. The existence of properties, operations, and contracts means that commonality is more obvious than if generalization is done too early on the basis of class name alone. The identified hierarchies are recorded either graphically or textually in an inheritance model.

Integrate library classes
During the iterations, the O/C Model should begin to stabilize. Once this happens, the developer can examine the class library for similar abstractions in order to reuse them in this problem (Activity: Library Class Incorporation). Looking for abstractions in libraries too early may involve too wide a search

initially. Therefore, it is best to leave an evaluation of the class library until after an initial pass. This reduces the search and enables the developer to match the required and available abstractions better.

When a class is integrated into a system from a library, its ancestors should also be examined carefully, as the class should not be "opened" in any way within the new model. Integrating library classes with the conceptual model is something that few people have yet examined in detail and really requires a formal description of the class. Much more class library integration will occur during the late Specification Phase and the Implementation Phase. Nevertheless, if classes can be integrated at this level of abstraction early in the Specification Phase and it is beneficial to integrate them, then such decisions, if taken wisely, may well reduce the Implementation Phase load significantly.

Refine the model
During later iterations, the object-oriented models are developed in increasingly more detail. Essentially, this process involves the identification of solution space classes and their addition to the O/C Model. Subsystems such as utilities and interfaces are identified, as are candidate O/Cs for these subsystems. Further solution-space-specific O/Cs will be created that have no immediate traceback to external-world objects. These are described as "non-essential objects" by Firesmith (1992a) (as opposed to "essential objects," which are the software analogs of the external world entities). They relate to resource and efficiency constraints and introduce "software and hardware world" O/Cs. The introduction of computer-related classes will often raise questions regarding the user requirements and business model. Such questions are addressed in the next iteration through the Investigation Phase.

One important difference between the earlier and later iterations of the development process is the amount of library reuse (Activity: Library Class Incorporation in Section 7.9) and the concentration on refinement and optimization (Activity: Generalization for Reuse and Activity: Optimization in Sections 7.4.3 and 7.12 respectively). Currently, significantly more computer-oriented classes are available in class libraries and these should be integrated into the design early on. Indeed, in some cases, such as the user interface, whole class libraries are available, thus making the subsystem essentially a refinement of the class library.

Testing
Testing the model during the Specification Phase is essentially a walkthrough process of evaluating scenarios and the URS against the Event Models (Activity: Testing). For each scenario, it should be possible to trace the messages and objects involved in fulfilling the scenario. Missing or incomplete message traces imply an error in design. Regular walkthroughs of this nature are essential for ensuring that the design is meeting the original specification. Testing of code and subsystems occurs during the Implementation Phase once a subsystem has been implemented in an OOPL.

Subsystem evaluation
The time designated for the phase having been completed, it may be necessary to decompose the area of work further into other subsystems. This should be the responsibility of the project manager and be incorporated into the Planning Phase of the next iteration.

Nested subsystems beyond two or three should be examined carefully to ensure that they correspond to one high-level set of services. Too much nesting leads to relationships that are hard to understand. The identification of subsystems should be separate from the layering of the O/C Model, which is a presentation and notation issue. Subsystem identification should be based on the requirements and services and be a coherent decomposition unit, while the layering mechanism is more a way of managing the complexity of the representation and presentation of the O/C Model in a logical way.

General discussion
Although iteration and recursion are good techniques for developing a system, they should not be allowed to continue indefinitely, and it is up to the designer to recognize the point at which further iterations are producing diminishing returns for the project. It is possible to use scenarios as a measure of completeness of the model and hence control the iterative process. Scenarios clarify the required extent of the business functionality and can be used as a means of determining what has, and has not, been completed. Thus the model is driven by the business needs as defined by the functionality specified in scenarios. This provides a coarse-grained measure of completeness and a yardstick for the project manager in determining when sufficient iterations have occurred.

A further issue is that design of one subsystem may require that another subsystem has already been designed. This interaction of subsystems should be minimized and the interaction that does occur should be explicit in the services requested by classes. As yet unimplemented services required by one class from another subsystem should be noted in the appropriate subsystem and a protocol agreed. This allows a more refined subsystem to continue being developed and identifies services to be specified in other subsystem(s).

The model that finally emerges from the IDP is a design describing a number of subsystems and classes, such as windowing, dialogue management, and the business model. The design aims at the executable as opposed to the purely conceptual model. Other decisions relating to design will also need to be made—for example, the overall architecture, the use of databases, and the allocation of subsystems to processors (Rumbaugh et al., 1991). We do not specifically consider concurrency issues or distributed systems in this methodology at the present time. These will be added to the methodology as specific activities when adequate quality information becomes available.

The Specification Phase is, therefore, where most of the activities discussed in Chapter 7 are applied. The phase leads to the development of an object-oriented model that is refined from and refines the URS. The initial iterations concentrate on the business components of the problem, while later iterations address the implementation of the model and hence introduce computer-related classes not part of the URS.

This approach provides for a simple methodology. There is no sharp break between analysis and design, as in some methodologies—the approach is one of continual refinement and iteration.

Deliverables from this phase, which should also undergo formal review (Activity: Documentation Review), are (Figure 6.7):

Document Type	Information Generated and Recorded
Class Specification	Completed design of all interfaces
Subsystem Responsibility Specification (SRS)	
O/C Model	
Event Models	
Objectcharts	
Inheritance Model	
Service Structure Model (SSM)	

6.3.4 Implementation Phase

As we enter the Implementation Phase we focus on the final algorithmic design and coding of each class and its internal structure. This phase leads either to a language-independent implementation design (Firesmith, 1992b) or to a language-specific design and hence to source code. If source code is not the result, the design should be sufficiently detailed for the programmer, who needs to know exactly what services are required in order to "cut the code."

This Implementation Phase is introduced for three reasons: (i) there can often be a change of perspective from the external view to the internal view; (ii) especially on large projects, it makes project management more easily defined in the sense that deliverables and documentation (to an organizationally defined level of abstraction) can be highlighted; and (iii) it permits acknowledgement of language influences on design—since the design is to be finally implemented in a chosen PL, the mapping from design to this selected PL must be accomplished smoothly. Implementation is the phase in which language constructs should be acknowledged and utilized. However, in some situations, for example where the design has been targeted at a particular language, the distinction between Specification and Implementation can be completely eliminated.

The Implementation Phase thus takes as input the object-oriented model from the Specification Phase; maps class details to the chosen language; rationalizes relationships, especially clarifying the inheritance hierarchy and choosing an implementation strategy for the system; and, finally, describes the classes' internal structure in terms of algorithms and data structures.

The focus now is on the class as a coded module—both its interface details (external view) and its internal workings.

Implementation of structure

The first aspect of the construction process is to translate the relationships of the Specification Phase model into those of the implementation language. This is discussed in Activity: Translation to the OOPL (Section 7.19) and essentially involves both association and aggregation being modeled as a client–server relationship as supported by the OOPL. Thus, if implementation-level notation is used (Section 5.2.4), it needs to support the relationship of client–server rather than association and aggregation directly. This translation process may also involve the introduction of new classes in the software implementation to model association classes. Other class relationships may also be added during more detailed design of the class implementation, for example, to particular data structure classes. Many of these decisions will reflect trade-offs in efficiency, space, and reusability in the final software model.

In most OOPLs, the relationships between classes do not imply a sequential model of communication where the calling object must wait for the server object to return control. Instead, relationships are a structuring mechanism between O/Cs, modeling the dependency between O/Cs. In addition, a number of other forms of communication protocol can be supported. These must be modeled using an extended set of constructs (see e.g., Booch, 1991; Firesmith, 1992b). A design model for parallel communication between objects is not yet fully integrated into the object model, although the approach appears to be very supportive of a parallel communication mechanism.

Other important decisions are those regarding physically stored data and derived, or calculated, data. Until this point all the properties have been logical only. Within the Implementation Phase, O/Cs should export only services, not internal attributes, thus hiding from clients how a message result is implemented. The developer therefore needs to allocate attributes to store the necessary information in a class. Physical attributes should still be hidden at this stage, the class interface being an abstract specification of the logical behavior.

Implementation of behavior

Another activity that occurs in construction is the implementation of the operations' algorithms (SubActivity: Service Identification (operations)). Algorithm design can be recorded using pseudocode/structured English or flow charts. This design process is quite traditional, dealing with individual functions. Each service should generally be small—approximately 10–20 SLOCs is usual (although these size heuristics are OOPL-dependent). Larger services often imply too much control in one service and are an indication of poor design.

Inheritance

A further important characteristic of this phase is that bottom-up activities should be realized even more strongly than in previous phases. As the degree of resolution increases and more implementation decisions are made, library classes are identified and implementation decisions may be made on data structure and module inclusion approaches, that is, using the language inheritance mechanism as module inclusion providing subclasses rather than subtypes (Activity: Inheritance Identification)—often termed implementation inheritance.

Other design decisions
Other design decisions include detailed evaluation of exception mechanisms and optimization of access paths and service utilization. At this stage it is also necessary to detail secret services (e.g., Figure 5.3), that is, those that are available to other services of the O/C but not to other O/Cs—since algorithmic details need to be specified before the programmer can code. Language-specific constructs are now selected. These might include friends, selective exports, and embedded classes (Section 5.2.4).

Testing
Once a class has been implemented, it should undergo the Activity: Unit Testing. Unit testing is performed by the developer of the class, the objective being to ensure that the class services meet the specified contracts. Test cases and test results should be recorded on a per class basis and automated for regression testing purposes if possible.

The result of the Implementation Phase is that the interface and relationships between O/Cs are fully specified and tested, as are a number of other detailed implementation decisions, such as algorithmic definitions and data structures.

The type of documentation derived from this phase will vary with the project. If an object-oriented programming language (OOPL) is used in this phase, no other textual documentation may be needed. If, however, a language-independent implementation design has been developed, documentation similar to that of the Specification Phase will be required.

The Implementation Phase can occur early in the iterations, leading to incremental delivery of functionality. Alternatively, little construction may occur until late in the iterations. Thus coding is not necessarily relegated to the final stages of the lifecycle. Other activities of this process are language-specific and we do not intend to discuss them here, although they include language coding conventions, naming conventions, "good" programming practice, and commenting (McDowell, 1992). Numerous books and articles are available on specific languages and the reader is referred to these for further information (e.g., Booch, 1991; Lippman, 1989; Winder, 1991; Meyer, 1992a; Switzer, 1993).

Implementation thus follows naturally from Specification when using an OOPL. With a pure OOPL, such as Eiffel or Smalltalk, and with a design targeted to that language, this phase may be almost nonexistent—again since the underlying model is almost transparently identical. Some organizations may prefer to leave algorithmic decisions to the jurisdiction of the implementor rather than the designer; in others, coding is a relatively mechanistic procedure, given the detailed design.

Deliverables for the Implementation Phase are (Figure 6.8):

Document Type	Information Generated and Recorded
Option (A) Classes in the OOPL Test cases Test report	Fully completed and coded classes

Option (B) "Generic" Implementation
    Phase design
Class Specification/"pin-out" diagram
    if required
Service Structure Model diagram/
    pseudocode as required
Event Models
Objectcharts
Inheritance Models
	Fully completed detailed design

6.3.5 Review Phase

The final phase of an iteration is the Review Phase. This involves subsystem testing, evaluation of the documentation, assessment of progress toward the objectives, and assessment of the quality of the models. It is basically an opportunity to compare what has been achieved with what was intended to be achieved in all aspects of the product development. It focuses on quality and performance checks, together with an evaluation of the degree of reuse achieved and remaining to be achieved and the usability of the (possibly embryonic) system.

The Review Phase should involve not only peer review but also evaluation by management and assessment by customers/users of the product and process.

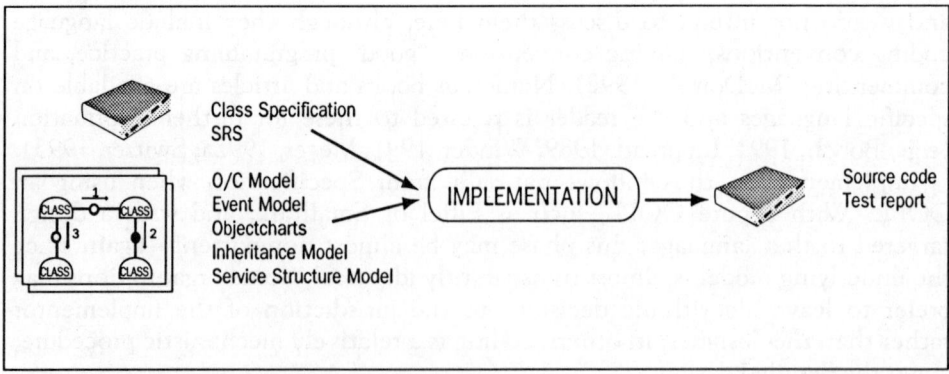

Figure 6.8 *Implementation Phase deliverables*

It is vital that customers be involved in validating and possibly updating requirements. Customers should be involved in the Review Phase of each major iteration (Lorenz, 1993).

Assessment can be undertaken at all stages of the project, including assessment of design documents, code, metrics, and quality. However, this explicit phase provides an opportunity to allocate time to the process of assessing the whole iteration.

Subsystem testing
Once the classes in the subsystem have been coded, they need to be thoroughly tested, initially by class and then by subsystem, since the subsystem represents the set of collaborating classes (Activity: Testing). The subsystem has a high cohesion and low coupling to the rest of the system, while typically there will be a higher coupling *between* the classes *within* the subsystem. Fiedler (1989) advocates both blackbox and whitebox testing as valuable. Blackbox testing effectively checks the services (i.e., it is interface- or specification-focused), while whitebox testing evaluates the accuracy of the hidden algorithms supporting the specification. Subsystems are tested using the scenarios developed in the Investigation Phase. Scenarios act as a test case in that they will often exercise a number of classes, unlike unit testing, which exercises only a single class. This subject is discussed further in Activity: Subsystem Testing (Section 7.18).

Subsystems integration and system testing
When an individual subsystem has been tested, the classes are stored in the project library. In a medium-to-large development, there will be a need for subsystem integration (SubActivity: Subsystem testing). Subsystem integration ensures that the subsystems have the correct protocol for message passing and that the pre- and postconditions have been adhered to by the different classes. In environments where assertions are used, they should be activated for this phase, allowing the developer to trap errors in assumptions made of the services. Such errors should be rectified and recorded in the design and in the contract diagrams for the service, and may involve some iteration back to the Specification Phase.

When all subsystems are complete, system testing can be undertaken (SubActivity: Integration testing). This is, in some ways, the phase most nearly equivalent to the testing phase in a structured development, in that the full system capabilities are checked. In a structured environment, this "big bang" testing was often the first time that requirements were tested, i.e., the first test of the program logic as opposed to the syntax checking/debugging always necessary before this real test. In an object-oriented environment, the system's "alpha test" (i.e., testing by the developers) is less traumatic, since all the class services have been checked out at the class and subsystem levels. Testing at the system level should reveal very few adverse synergistic interactions, *assuming* that the design was good and earlier testing thorough. This phase should then be followed by β testing of the embryonic product in which external teams, other than the developers, assess the system capabilities against the published requirements specification.

Once subsystems are operational, they may be incrementally delivered, thus providing the opportunity for constructive feedback from the potential users.

Product quality

Product quality assessment is made of the model deliverables and source generated during the iteration. This involves the activities of Activity: Documentation Review, Activity: Quality Evaluation, and Activity: Generalization for Reuse.

Documentation Review assesses the quality of the deliverables in terms of completeness, consistency, and presentation. It results in a report recommending required updates and work necessary before sign-off of the deliverables.

Quality Evaluation is an assessment of the quality of the models developed in terms of robustness, stability, and "object-orientedness." This activity may involve design reviews by independent consultants or other internal groups. A metrics program should be developed (Pfleeger, 1993) to provide empirical support for any recommendations made regarding the models.

Generalization for Reuse is an assessment of the models with regard to reuse, both reuse of components and the ability to develop reusable components from the model. Once again, recommendations should be made to encourage reuse and generalization.

Process quality

Finally, an assessment should be made of the process, that is to say, an assessment of the project plan, the resources allocated versus those needed, and the development environment in which the process operates. The results of assessing the project plan can be fed back into the Planning Phase for the next Iteration Plan.

The deliverables produced at the end of the Review Phase include (Figure 6.9):

Document Type	Information Generated and Recorded
Test report	Class test results
	Subsystem test results
Review report	Process assessment
	Model assessment
	Documentation assessment

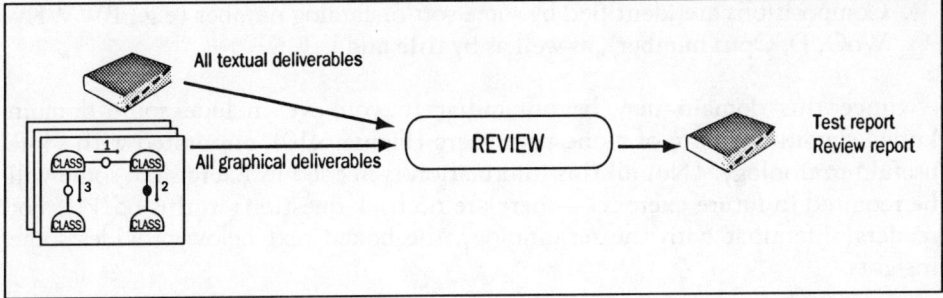

Figure 6.9 Review Phase deliverables

6.4 Summary

The MOSES phases of the process lifecycle complement and expand the Build Stage of the product lifecycle. Within the MOSES iterative development process (IDP), five phases are identified: Planning, Investigation, Specification, Implementation, and Review. Although all are crucial, Planning and Review have a more "management flavor" and Specification is frequently the most time-consuming. Each phase is evaluated in terms of deliverables, although it may take a small number of iterations before these are of acceptable quality.

Documentation ranges from a number of business/planning reports through to highly detailed and technical descriptions (textual and graphical) of the O/C Model and its supporting details (CS, EM, etc.). The MOSES notation is focused on these technical descriptors, providing a seamless transition from the Planning Phase and the Investigation Phase through to Implementation and subsequent Review. OOPL-specific concerns are the domain of the Implementation Phase, while graphical constructs in the Specification Phase focus on describing the semantics of the O/Cs and their interactions.

Reuse permeates the lifecycle and is described in this cross-lifecycle sense with other similarly focused activities in the next chapter.

6.5 Study examples

Exercise 3 Consider again the example you undertook in Exercise 2. In this exercise, we suggest that you translate that example into a simple initial O/C Model, using the MOSES notation given in Chapter 5. As you do this, begin to add more detail (iteratively added by the user!). As well as information on compositions and movements, please consider the following:

1. A note has a pitch and duration.
2. Compositions are written by a composer.
3. A composer has a year of birth and (sometimes/often) a year of death and a nationality.

4. Compositions are identified by some sort of catalog number (e.g., BWV, Kv, WoO, D, Opus number), as well as by title and key.

Since this domain may be unfamiliar to you, we include some domain knowledge in the form of a one-page score (Figure 6.10), annotated with some useful terminology. (Not all this information is needed in Exercise 3; some will be required in future exercises—there are no trick questions in this book!). For readers unfamiliar with the terminology, the boxed text below provides some insights.

> We are considering in these examples "regular" music that can be represented by notes drawn on a stave. This includes so-called classical music and much of modern popular music. Each note is placed on one of the five lines of the stave. This gives the relative pitch. The absolute pitch is determined by inspecting the clef sign. This is placed at the beginning of each line of music and can change at intermediate stages (although we won't consider that here). In the example, the clef sign used indicates the treble clef that defines the bottom line to be the E just above middle C. On the last line of the music, the second of the two staves has a bass clef sign that determines that the top line is the A just below middle C. This happens to be a piano piece, so that the staves are laid out in pairs: ostensibly the upper stave for the right hand and the lower for the left. Other "global" information is found at the beginning of the piece. Here we find the key signature that dictates how many and which note names (A through G) will always be played either sharp or flat. Again, this is repeated at the beginning of each line, but also may change during the piece (a sophistication not considered here). Occasional changes to the key signature are shown as accidentals (naturals, sharps, flats, double sharps, or double flats).
>
> The other piece of initial information on the stave is the time signature, which gives the number of beats per bar (upper figure) and the length of each of those beats (lower figure). Thus $\frac{6}{8}$ means six beats and each of those beats are one-eighth beats. A quarter beat is a crotchet, so a one-eighth beat is a quaver. Crotchets have a stem and quavers have a stem and a tail. The following music is then divided up into bars or measures (divided by bar lines) with 6 quaver beats per bar (the first bar is allowed to be an anomaly as here). A dot after a note multiplies the normal note length by 50%. Thus a dotted crotchet (e.g., left hand of bar 6) is equal in length to three quavers. The dot above the note indicates the note is to be played staccato rather than legato (smoothly). This effectively shortens the note length in performance. When no notes are to be played, rests are used to indicate silence. These are of different shapes to indicate the length of silence (e.g., bar 22).
>
> Other marked notation in Figure 6.10 relates more to performance than to the structure of the music. The dynamics include a range of markings that

The MOSES Product and Process Lifecycles 293

Figure 6.10 *Manuscript version of a piece of music illustrating some musical terminology useful for the exercises (see also boxed information)*

are occasionally added to the score. These include indications of loudness or softness (p = soft, f = loud, and a preceding m moderates those sound levels so that, for instance, mf is moderately loud). A "hairpin", as in bar 8/9, indicates that the sound level decreases over that distance: a diminuendo or decrescendo. If the gradients are opposite, it would indicate a crescendo (i.e., gradually getting louder). Marks such as rall(entando) or rit(enuto) indicate a gradual slowing down, which is canceled by the marking of "a tempo."

The other features of interest in this piece are the textual annotations at the top and bottom. All pieces (well, almost all) have a title: here "Seven Dances" (this is just the first of the seven). They often have a tempo marking to indicate to the performer whether this is to be a quiet, slow piece, and what mood it is to be played in (e.g., bright, melancholy). This textual annotation can be in virtually any language, but is often in Italian, French, German, or English (roughly in that order of frequency of occurrence in classical music). Just to make sure, some composers add a metronome mark. Here the composer indicates that the speed is such that 160 crotchets are to be played each minute. This would be the value to which you would set your metronome for practice. The composer's name is also likely to appear somewhere on the piece, either at the top, the bottom (as here), or on a cover. The date of composition may also appear.

The end of the piece is indicated by a double bar line. Double bar lines can also be used in repeats and sometimes at key changes in the middle of pieces.

• CHAPTER 7 •

The MOSES Lifecycle Activities

Of the three components of MOSES introduced in Chapter 4, namely, the activities, phases, and lifecycle, two have been discussed so far. Chapter 5 described the MOSES notation and Chapter 6 described the phases of the process lifecycle. In this chapter, we discuss the activities of MOSES, detailing for each their purpose, process, and output. This chapter therefore deals with the *techniques* of the methodology. We should note that the output of an activity does not necessarily constitute a deliverable provided to management, but rather may simply be a part of a deliverable package provided at the end of a phase (Table 7.1). This is one of the reasons we prefer the term "output of an activity" rather than "deliverable."

We have arranged the activities in alphabetical order so that no time sequence is implied by the presentation. Sequencing and interaction of activities was discussed in Chapter 6. In contrast, this chapter, and the subsections it contains, can be used as a reference guide on any particular activity. This chapter is therefore more of a repository of techniques indexed by activity than a linear development of ideas.

7.1 Activity: Contract Specification

The objective of this activity is to document the meaning of a service. O/C services need to be specified in some manner, preferably one that does not impose an implementation, i.e., in a way that specifies the "what," not the "how," of the service. The most effective approach is to utilize a declarative notation using assertions (preconditions, postconditions, and class invariants). Such an approach integrates well with the notion of design by contract (Meyer, 1992f), whereby a client and a supplier formalize a contract that specifies under what conditions a service is available and what the result of the service will be. A contract is detailed by one or more assertions.

Table 7.1 *Deliverables for the various phases and stages of MOSES*

Phase/Stage	Deliverable
Business Planning Stage	Business planning report
Build Stage	
Planning Phase	Iteration plan
Investigation Phase	Scenarios/Actor Glossary
	URS
Specification Phase	Class Specification
	Subsystem Responsibility Specification
	O/C Model
	Event Model
	Objectchart
	Inheritance Model
	Service Structure Model
Implementation Phase	Source code
	Test report
Review Phase	Test report
	Review report
Delivery Stage	Delivery stage report

Contracts can be applied at various levels of abstraction, thus making them applicable throughout the development process. They are continually updated and revised during the development process as the behavior of an O/C becomes clear from an examination of the scenarios, user requirements, and objectcharts.

When developing contracts, a number of guidelines are useful. Those services that occur in all states and that may occur for all values of any of the arguments require no precondition. Strictly, the precondition is true. However, those services that require an object to be in a certain state before a service is called, or may require the arguments to be of a certain value before the service is valid, will require a precondition. Preconditions are used to specify the conditions under which the service is valid. If, during a service call, the precondition is evaluated as false, the service should fail. Such a failure represents an error either in the model specification or in the model implementation. The use of preconditions at all stages of the development is an important approach to the development of high-quality, correct software.

An operation (as opposed to a property) is a service that may change the values of an object; that is, it changes some or all of the object's properties. The effect of an operation on the object state should be specified in a postcondition. A postcondition describes the effect of the operation on the state; it is the "what" of the operation. An operation must not only satisfy the postcondition but also leave the object in a valid and stable state as defined by the class invariant (see below). If an operation does not satisfy both the postcondition and the invariant, there has been an error in the operation specification or implementation. Once again the use of postconditions throughout the development process is an important means of ensuring software correctness.

A complete operation specification consists of pre- and postconditions that describe the object's state before and after the operation occurs. Both are Boolean expressions. The means of expressing pre- and postconditions vary from formal specification languages such as Object-Z (Duke et al., 1991) to informal English statements. Which approach is used will vary with the domain in which the model is developed and the experience of the modeler. The use of formal specification languages in the specification of operations is one area of work that is extremely useful in the development of correct software (Jones, 1991). Indeed, the use of pre- and postconditions in the specification of operations can be seen to have influenced practical methods for the construction of production software systems today.

Contracts can be found by examining the business rules of the domain as specified in the URS or embedded in scenarios. Business rules about one object will be spread among many scenarios, and it is important to ensure consistency of the business rules between scenarios. Indeed, the explicit specification of contracts often leads to the discovery of ambiguous business procedures and policies that will need to be addressed.

Contracts are documented as part of the class specification and will be refined throughout the different phases. For example, an initial contract may be for an operation to permit the withdrawal of money from an ACCOUNT. The initial contract may be:

    class ACCOUNT
        withdrawal(amount: REAL)
            postcondition
                balance = **old** balance − amount

This contract may be refined when extra information is identified which states that the operation is only valid if the balance − amount ≥ overdraft limit. Hence the contract is refined to:

```
class ACCOUNT
    overdraft_limit: REAL
    withdrawal(amount: REAL)
        precondition
            balance − amount ≥ overdraft_limit
        postcondition
            balance = old balance − amount
            balance ≥ overdraft_limit
```

Such a refinement process will occur throughout the Specification Phase.

Contracts also help ensure a disciplined use of inheritance. A class that inherits from a superclass may redefine a service of the superclass. However, this redefined service should have the same essential semantics, that is, the same contract. The principle of subcontracting permits the precondition to be weakened and/or the postcondition strengthened, thus ensuring the correct usage of inheritance.

Design by contract and the use of contracts are an important mechanism within MOSES for developing quality software.

7.1.1 Subactivity: Invariant specification

Invariants may be specified at any time in the Specification Phase. Quite often they are application-specific and are clarified late in the SDLC; sometimes they are the most obviously identified characteristics and provide the nucleus for the O/C derivation. Sometimes they will be appropriate for general O/Cs, but it is important for the designer to question the specificity of the constraint at all times. One technique is to develop an abstract class, with more general invariants, and a subclass for the more specific application invariants. In this way, the general pattern of O/C relationships is available for reuse in other applications.

Invariants may appear directly in the requirements document where property values are limited to certain ranges or as invariants on relationships. Alternatively, the use of objectcharts (Section 7.10) may highlight further invariants, especially on the operations. Invariants are useful for ensuring that parameter values in a model are reasonable and that relationships are realistic—further support for ensuring the production of high-quality software.

Invariants can thus be viewed as postconditions of all services of an O/C. A request for a value of a property must occur when the invariant is satisfied, and as properties do not change the state of an object, only report it, the invariant must also be satisfied after the request. During implementation, properties may be viewed as queries on the state that simply report the value of the physical attributes. They do not, therefore, change the state of the O/C.

The invariants constrain the O/C properties. Constraints on the properties can always be modeled by defining a separate O/C that constrains all its instances to be in the defined state. For example, a property that returns an INTEGER value may be constrained to values between 10 and 20. This constraint could be modeled by a separate O/C called, for example, CONSTRAINED_INTEGER, which only returned values of between 10 and 20. The property of the original O/C could, instead of being modeled as an O/C INTEGER, be modeled as an O/C CONSTRAINED_INTEGER. The decision on whether to introduce a separate O/C to describe this constraint is in the hands of the modeler and will depend on issues such as understandability and complexity. Constraints on the properties, although redundant in some sense, are useful elements that can be employed effectively in modeling O/Cs.

Although the idea of an invariant was originally introduced into the OO community by Meyer (1988a) in his description of the language Eiffel, it provides significantly more than a language feature, being an important way of specifying constraints on classes rather than individual operations (e.g., Masotti, 1991; Kilov, 1992). Invariants should therefore be declared explicitly rather than hidden within operation definitions. The constraint clause may become quite large and may be hidden at various resolutions by a suitable tool for simplicity of presentation. Its presence, however, is important in that it provides a way of specifying important semantic constraints on the class.

Output

Deliverable Impacted	Information Generated and Recorded
Class Specification	Contracts
Objectcharts	Transition Specification

7.2 Activity: Documentation Review

The purpose of this activity is to ensure that the current design is being adequately documented in the various deliverables.

Documentation review should be carried out at regular intervals (i.e., weekly, monthly) or at predetermined "breakpoints" in the development process (see Chapter 6)—for example, at the end of an Implementation Phase of an Iteration. In particular, the Review Phase should have as one of its activities an evaluation of the documentation developed so far.

All documents must be reviewed in the contexts of:

1. *Existence.* A check can be made for mandatory and optional documents. These could be mandatory because of the lifecycle being used or mandated by the organization.
2. *Accuracy and consistency checks of the models used.* For example, all O/Cs shown in inheritance diagrams must have a class specification and should appear in one of the layered class diagrams. CASE tools, as they become increasingly available, can be useful here.

This activity is essentially a check on the deliverables before final presentation.

Output

The output of the phase is the particular deliverables, with some confidence that they contain no errors.

7.3 Activity: Event Model Construction

The purpose of an Event Model (EM) is to show graphically the messages that are sent between objects as a result of a service call. An Event Model shows O/Cs and a particular message-passing sequence between them. Arrows annotate the relationships with a message name, a direction showing called services and a sequence number. EMs are useful in the process of confirming that certain required functionality can be achieved. Figure 5.30 shows one such example. We should stress that here we are examining the O/C interactions very locally and specifically asking, "What O/Cs are collaborating in order to fulfill *one specific service*." We thus highlight, often using an abridged form of the basic icon, the services required for the collaboration in order to fulfill the contract and, of course, any necessary subcontracts. Event Models can be used in one of two ways: either as a precursor to drawing up the contracts or as a reflection of contracting decisions already taken.

Event Models are particularly useful in specifying the interactions involved in scenarios (Section 7.14). A scenario is a textual description of an interaction between a user and a system. During the Specification Phase this textual description will be transformed to a set of objects and their interactions in an Event Model. The result of this transformation process is an object-oriented model and the necessary sequencing of operations to support a user-defined scenario. Later in the Review Phase, these same scenarios will be tested out against the O/C Model to ensure that they can be fulfilled by the services defined for the operations. If the Specification Phase has been completed successfully, the Review Phase will lead to all scenarios being accomplished successfully.

The work involved in developing Event Models is focused firstly on supporting the scenario by services on O/Cs and secondly on allocating services to O/Cs that will lead to a robust, stable, and extensible architecture. Scenarios may be implemented by many Event Models, and it is the job of the designer to allocate services to O/Cs as discussed in the Activity: Service Identification. An example of two Event Models for a single scenario is given below.

The process of developing an Event Model is broadly the following. Firstly, the classes should be identified from the scenario (Activity: O/C Identification) or if classes have already been defined from a domain analysis they should be included in the Event Model. Secondly, services should be identified from the scenarios (Activity: Service Identification), which usually represent the verbs of the scenario. Interactions will also indicate services on objects. Thirdly, messages should be defined in order to fulfill the scenario requirements and then labeled in a numerical sequence. The resulting Event Model depicts the internal workings of an object-oriented model constructed to fulfill a user's

The MOSES Lifecycle Activities — **301**

requirement. The services thus identified should be added to the class specification and the contract defined for the particular Event Model interaction, leading to a complete specification of the class.

Event Models can also be constructed for interaction sequences that don't necessarily begin at the system boundary. Thus detailed interactions may also be specified using Event Models.

An example of two Event Models developed from a single scenario is shown in Figure 7.1. The scenario that describes a document scanning manager is as follows. In order to scan a set of documents into digital storage, the operator places the documents on a feeder tray. The system senses the documents, enabling the operator to start the scanning process. This process begins with the operator telling the system to scan through a scanner menu. The system scans each document, recording the image in a queue of scanned articles with a number and a date.

In the first Event Model, the SCAN_DEVICE is responsible for scanning a

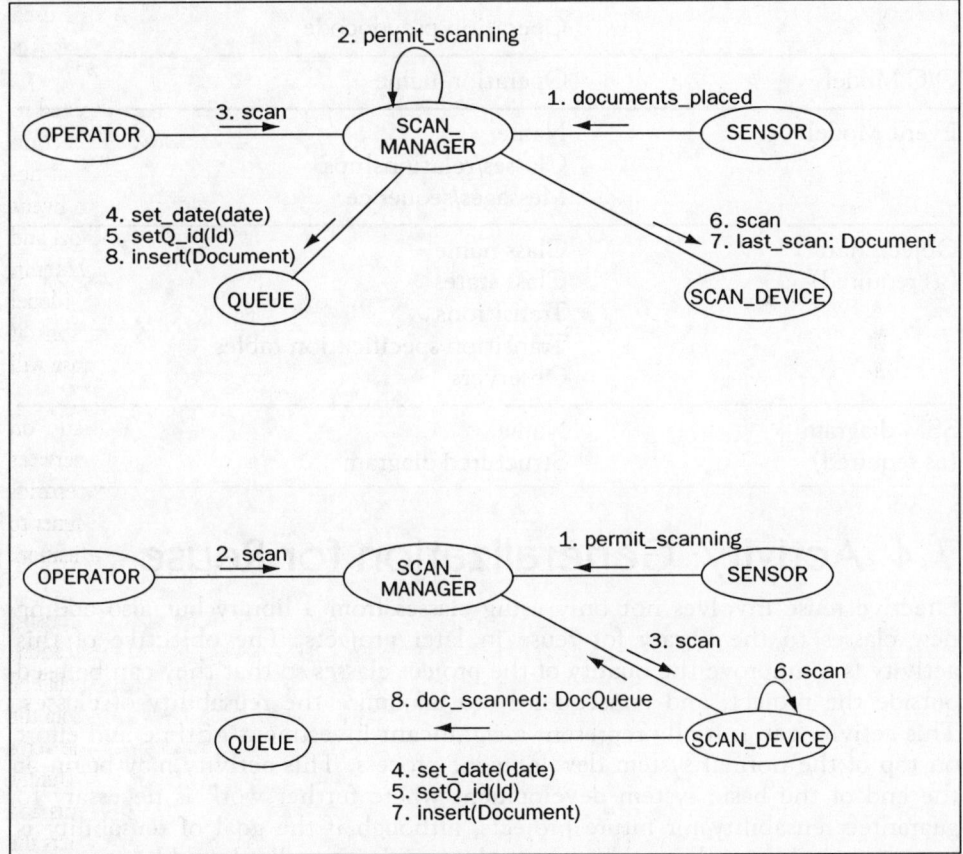

Figure 7.1 *An example of two alternative Event Models developed from a single scenario*

document and returning the scanned image to the SCAN_MANAGER, who allocates the document to a QUEUE. In the second Event Model, the SCAN_DEVICE returns a complete QUEUE of scanned documents to the SCAN_MANAGER. Both Event Models implement the scenario but by allocating different responsibilities to different objects. The pros and cons of each approach need to be weighed up, taking into account factors such as flexibility, robustness, and extensions.

Output

Deliverable Impacted	Information Generated and Recorded
Class Specification	Operation name Operation signature Operation preconditions local to class Operation postcondition local to class OR Operation pseudocode
O/C Model	Operation name
Event Model	Name Classes/relationships Messages/sequence
Objectchart (as required)	Class name Class states Transitions Transition specification tables Observers
SSM diagram (as required)	Name Structured diagram

7.4 Activity: Generalization for Reuse

Effective reuse involves not only using classes from a library but also adding new classes to the library for reuse in later projects. The objective of this activity is to improve the quality of the project classes so that they can be used outside the project, and consequently to maximize the reusability of classes. This activity can initially represent a significant investment of time and effort on top of the normal system development process. This activity may begin at the end of the basic system development where further work is necessary to guarantee reusability for future projects, although if the goal of reusability is borne in mind throughout the process, the activity actually should be occurring throughout all the phases. This is unlikely in the first few OO projects, but as more OT skills are acquired so generalization will become integrated into the overall development process.

While one good approach is to plan to add quality and reusability to designs and classes after successful implementation in the current project, other organizations might prefer to defer incurring this cost until a future project so that classes created in project n are not generalized until it is seen that they are to be useful for project n+1 (or even n+m). Such a strategy might, at the same time, reflect less of a commitment to reuse but also take the pragmatic view that, at least in the early years of using object technology, inexperience might lead to the generalization of classes that really should have been left as project-specific and not migrated beyond the project library to the organizational library. Empirical evaluation of these two strategies is currently lacking. This view of possible management strategies for reuse is supported by the discussion of Menzies et al. (1992), who propose that generalization *must* be undertaken before the first release of the product. Henderson-Sellers and Pant (1993) propose two further alternative reuse models: (i) a two-library model of potentially reusable components (PRC) and a library of generalized components (LGC), and (ii) an alternative cost-center model based on an emerging technology group (see Section 9.1.4).

As part of quality assurance (QA), measurements are needed in order to effect maximal control. These measurements need to be able to assess costs of (i) changing the internal implementation of classes; (ii) adding new classes; (iii) modifying inheritance hierarchies; (iv) changing a class interface; and (v) changing aggregation structures (Graham, 1991, p306).

From a management point of view, software developers are required to fill the roles associated with quality assurance and class library manager.

The additional work during generalization may be simply a "honing" or refinement of existing classes, or it may require the introduction of additional classes (possibly of a deferred or abstract nature, viz., ones that cannot be instantiated) at intermediate levels in the inheritance hierarchy. Furthermore, overly complex classes may require splitting into a larger number of smaller classes. The underlying guideline here is to consider whether a class developed in the current project really represents a single concept of the domain (an abstract data type) or whether it encompasses two (or more) concepts. This refinement work is needed to ensure that classes are really reusable and augments any project-specific refinement of the inheritance hierarchy (Section 7.6). Such refinements may, of course, lead to iteration and a reconsideration of the O/C Model describing the system.

It should also be remembered that increasing refinement of inheritance hierarchies is likely to lead not only to deeper hierarchies and more multiple inheritance but also to the introduction of abstract (or deferred) classes. It is generally advised that abstract classes should not inherit from concrete classes (de Paula and Nelson, 1991), although exceptions to this rule do exist. Another heuristic (Grosberg, 1993) is to construct an inheritance hierarchy using the rule that no concrete classes should have subclasses. With this strategy, for example, the hierarchy of Figure 7.2 would be revised to that shown in Figure 7.3.

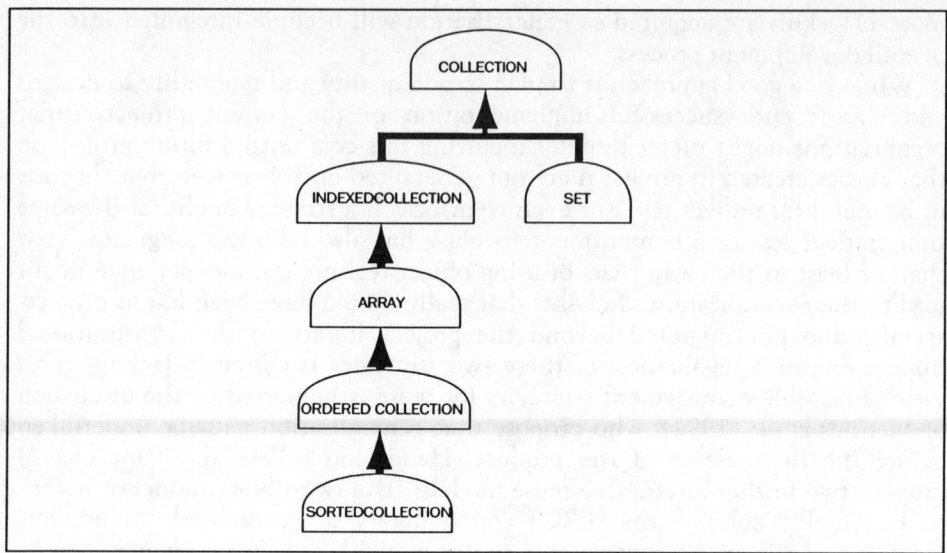

Figure 7.2 *Simple inheritance hierarchy in which each subclass is instantiable*

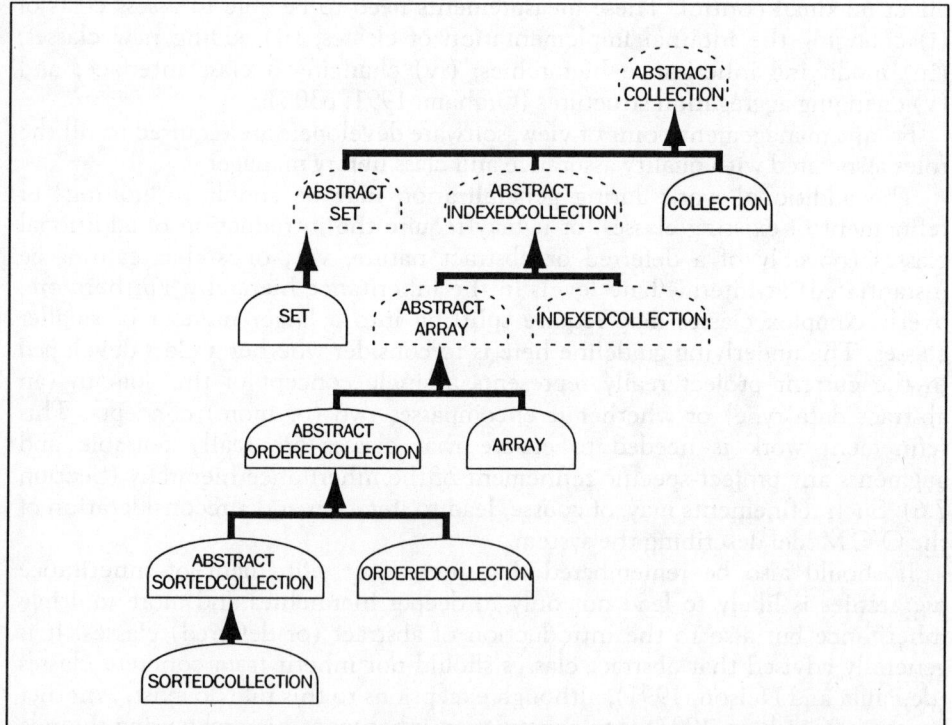

Figure 7.3 *Revised hierarchy (from Figure 7.2) in which classes are either instantiable or inheritable from, but never both*

7.4.1 Subactivity: Completion of abstractions

As part of the process of making a class more general, the class should represent a complete abstraction. This activity is therefore focused specifically on the class and involves refinement of a Class Specification. This may involve the addition of services that are not explicitly required by the current subsystem specification. A "shopping list" approach is recommended by Meyer (1988a) and McGregor and Sykes (1992), which could easily involve adding large numbers of services to the class. This should lead to the definition of further services to complete the abstraction. The activity requires the designer to step back from the particular role that the class plays in the system and to examine other services that could/should be provided by the class. Here the metric of semantic cohesion is useful (Chapter 10).

For example, a class that models a pen may have the services of writing and indicating the current level of ink. To complete the abstraction, it may be useful to add capabilities to refill the pen, or even empty it. Although completing an abstraction is useful, it should not be taken to extremes. For example, a CALCULATOR class that has services of add and subtract can add the services of divide, multiply, and percentages. However, the services can continue to be added almost *ad infinitum*—tangent, sine, cosine, reciprocal, and so on. Thus completing an abstraction is relative to the understanding of the concept within the context of an application domain.

Another activity is the refinement of services, that is, either dividing up services to provide more specific functionality per service, or amalgamating services to provide a shorthand for a frequently used combination of services (Firesmith, 1993). The O/C should have its functionality "walked through" in order to consider the different ways in which the O/C may be used to identify these types of operations.

7.4.2 Subactivity: Optimization

Optimizing the implementation of an O/C is another important activity. Particularly important are the algorithms used, the use of extra variables to store calculated data so that they need not be recomputed, optimizing access paths, designing associations, and possibly adding redundant associations for efficiency. Guidelines for these activities are discussed in Rumbaugh *et al.* (1991). These activities should not, in general, impact on the interface of the class, but be internal optimizations for the particular implementation of the abstraction. This activity is therefore targeted largely at the Implementation Phase. However, it may be that the O/C Model resulting from the Specification Phase is not efficient in its architecture and that internal optimizations are not sufficient. In this case, the O/C Model will need to be revisited during another iteration, this time with an optimization/design focus. Such design-oriented work should occur in later iterations once the business model has been captured.

7.4.3 Subactivity: Refinement of inheritance hierarchies

As a separate subactivity, one should refine the hierarchies of the O/C Model. This involves examining the hierarchy somewhat apart from the systems within which it is being designed. The designer is thus able to attempt to "fill gaps" in the generalization hierarchy and to try to develop a more abstract and semantically sound hierarchy. Abstract classes are especially useful in filling these gaps, as they provide places from which the hierarchy may branch in currently unforeseen ways (Figure 7.3).

Refinement of hierarchies should be an ongoing activity during the development process, and its inclusion as a separate subactivity is a reminder that in developing inheritance hierarchies the developer should be thinking of other situations in which a hierarchy might be applied. This leads to a more robust and reusable hierarchy.

This additional work includes reevaluation of the total set of O/Cs, requiring an iterative analysis of whether new superclasses (parents) or new subclasses (children) will be useful. For example, we may find that within the system we have created three classes for TRAIN, BICYCLE, and TRACTOR (Figure 7.4), all of which have the behavior of motion. These are obvious candidates for restructuring because not only do they have the same behavior (*moves*)[21] but also they are semantically linkable as three specializations of a new abstract class VEHICLE (Figure 7.5). The functionality of "moves" is itself moved to the higher level and becomes attached to class VEHICLE. In this case, part of the functionality may be implemented in VEHICLE and part specialized in the subclasses. The class VEHICLE is abstract because (i) it has no instantiations

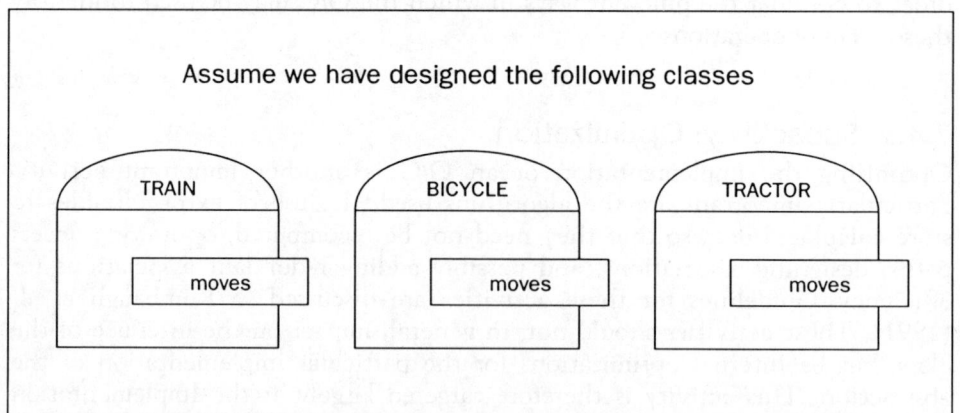

Figure 7.4 *Three classes designed independently (Adapted from Henderson-Sellers, 1992a)*

---

21. An example of the same behavior in semantically unrelated classes would be classes AIRCRAFT and BIRD, which both have the behavior of *flight*.

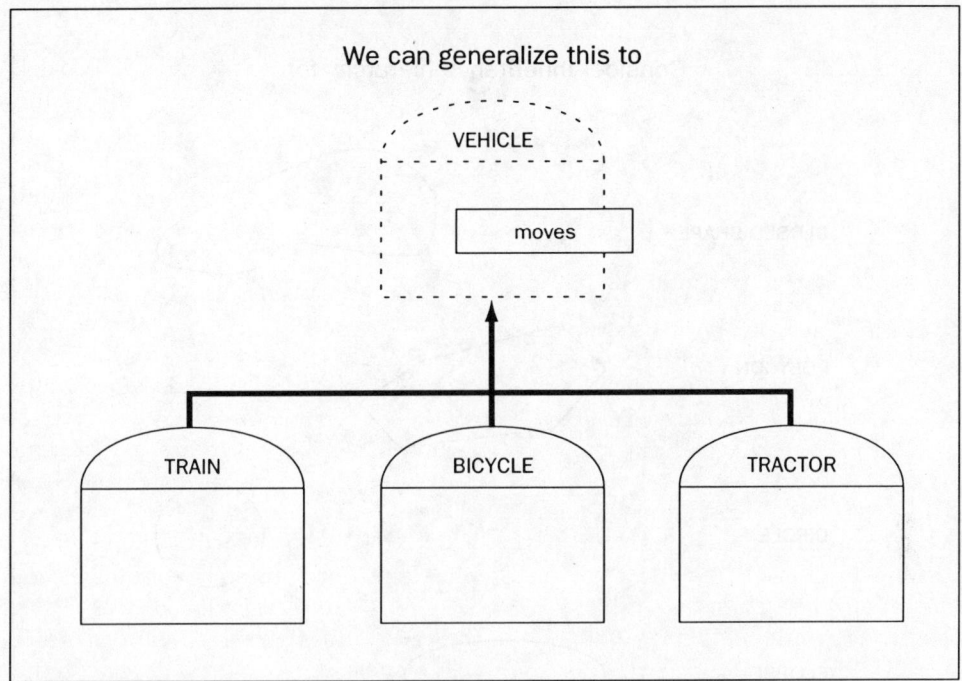

Figure 7.5 *Reassessment of three classes of Figure 7.4 in which the generalization class VEHICLE is identified as potentially useful (Adapted from Henderson-Sellers, 1992a)*

and (ii) it contains (at least) one deferred service. However, the abstraction of "vehicle," quite correctly, has the capability of "moving" so that the hierarchy of Figure 7.5 shows a set of subtypes. Polymorphic substitutions then become possible, since all subclasses possess a consistent interpretation of *move*.

Let us consider a more extended example. Figure 7.6 illustrates a commonly posed problem—that of constructing an hierarchy for geometric shapes. The initial hierarchy probably reflects a single application and will be hard to extend (Figure 7.7). At a later phase of the development process and/or when generalization is considered, questions arise out of the simple answer of Figure 7.7. For example, RECTANGLE inherits from POLYGON in that a rectangle is defined geometrically as a polygon with four sides and four right angles. However, a polygon (a closed shape with n straight edges) would have a service of *add_a_side/vertex*. RECTANGLE inherits from POLYGON and thus inherits *add_a_side*. However, we *cannot* add a side to a rectangle since this destroys its very nature *as* a rectangle.

Two possible solutions spring to mind. The first, that of negating the *add_a_side* service, has been shown (e.g., Brachman, 1985) to lead to confusion in interpreting hierarchies, and it is now generally considered that canceling or negating services in class hierarchies is ill-advised. The second (the topic of this

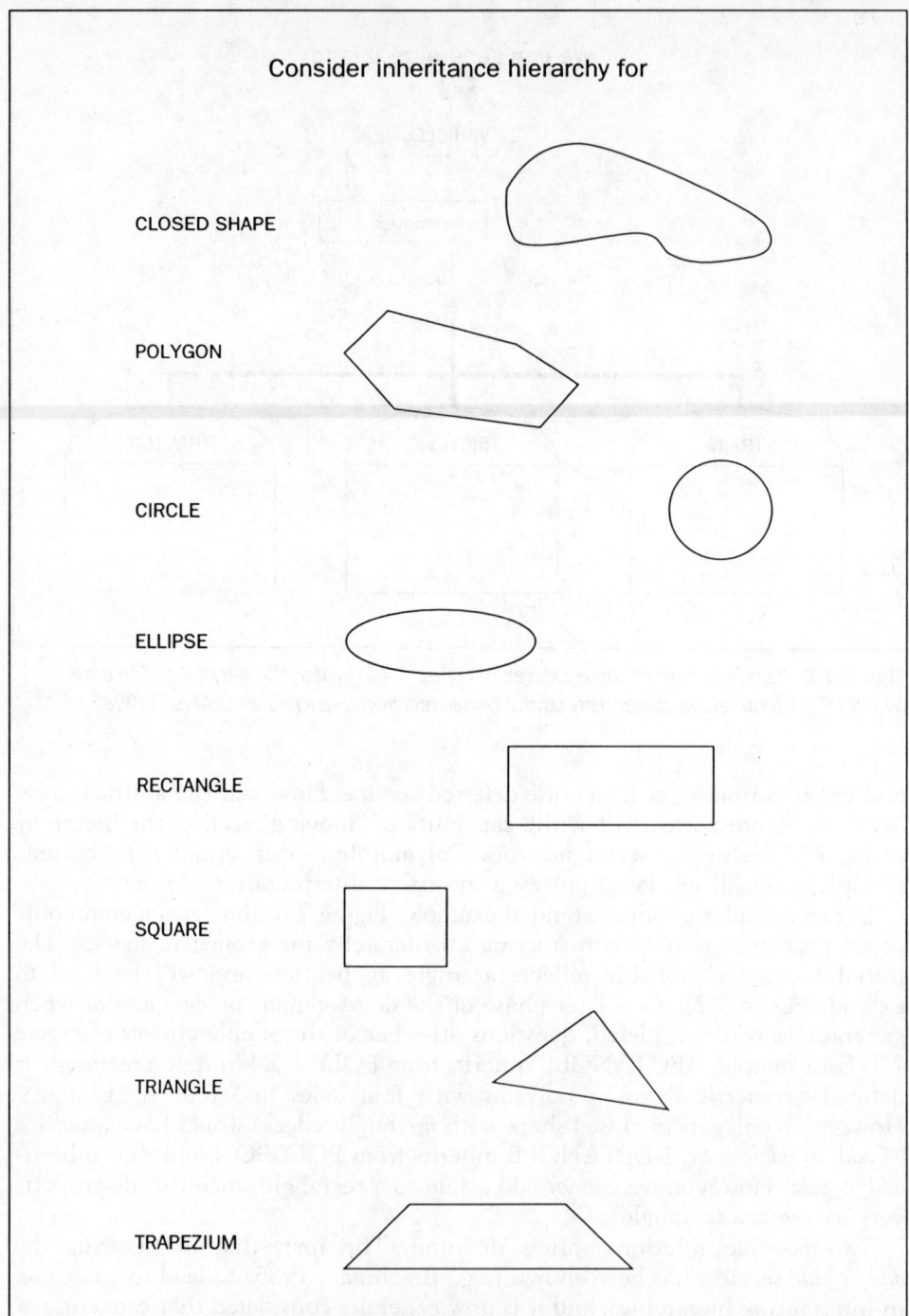

Figure 7.6 *Consider an inheritance hierarchy for these shapes*

The MOSES Lifecycle Activities

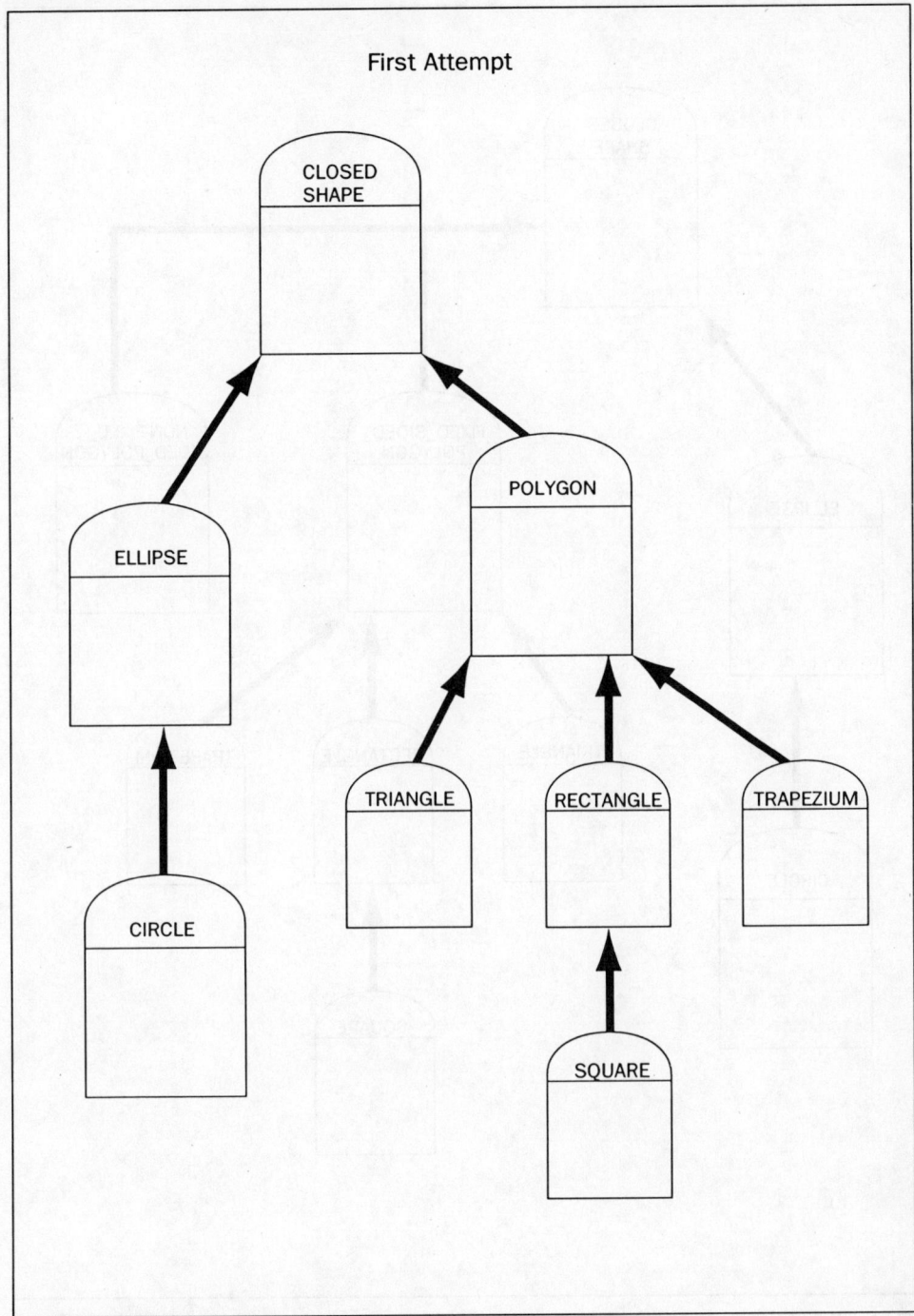

Figure 7.7 *The first attempt might link all the shapes (and no others)*

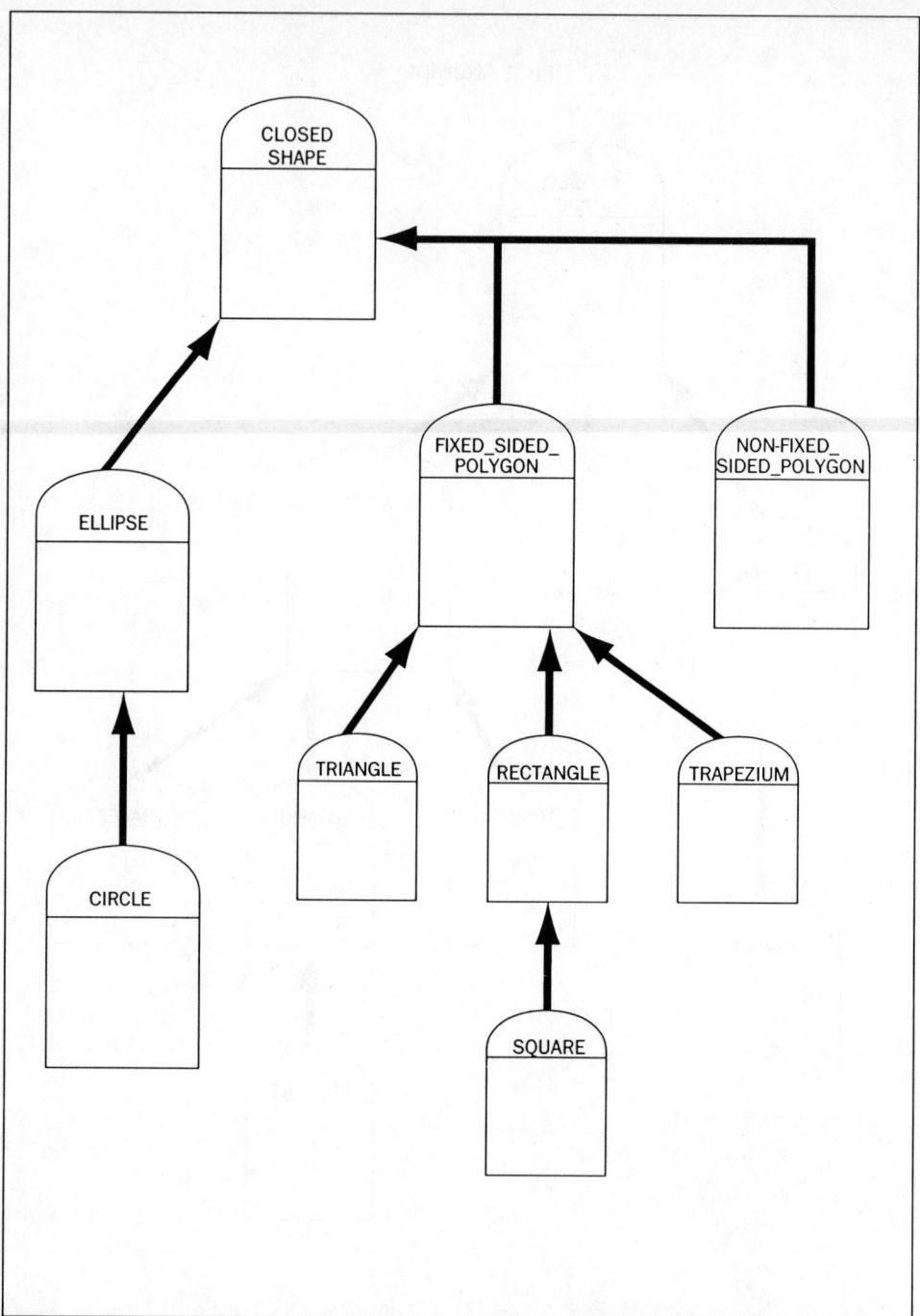

Figure 7.8 *In a second iteration, the problem of rectangle and square inheriting a feature "add_side" is obviated by the introduction of a class FIXED_SIDED_POLYGON*

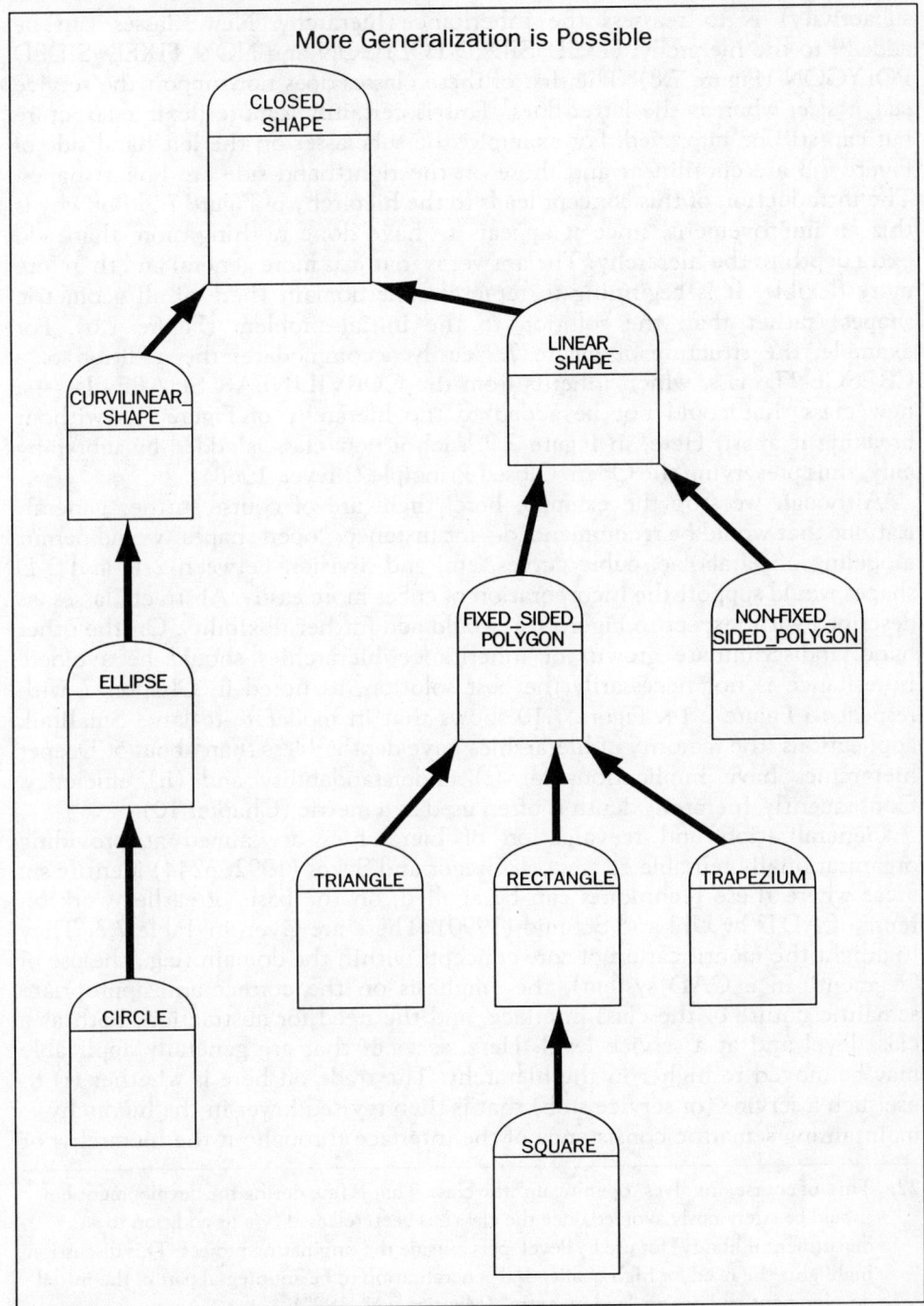

Figure 7.9 *Further generalization is aimed at future reuse. Here a class CURVILINEAR_SHAPE is introduced that does not represent an application class but rather a domain-specific class.*

subactivity) is to reassess the inheritance hierarchy. New classes can be added[22] to the hierarchy: FIXED_SIDED POLYGON and NON_FIXED_SIDED POLYGON (Figure 7.8). The first of these classes does not support the service *add_a_side*, whereas the latter does. This is certainly a more flexible structure but can still be improved. For example, the subclasses on the left-hand side of Figure 7.8 are curvilinear and those on the right-hand side are linear shapes. The introduction of this concept leads to the hierarchy of Figure 7.9. But why is this an improvement, since it appears to have done nothing more than add extra depth to the hierarchy? The answer is that it is more general and therefore more flexible. It is beginning to represent the domain (here of all geometric shapes) rather than the solution to the initial problem (Figure 7.6). For example, the structure of Figure 7.9 easily accommodates the addition of a CRESCENT class, which inherits from the CURVILINEAR SHAPE class—a new class that could not be added to the hierarchy of Figure 7.8 without breaking it apart. Here, in Figure 7.9, such a new class is added by subtyping *only*, thus preserving the Open–Closed Principle (Meyer, 1988a).

Although we stop the example here, there are of course further generalizations that would be recommended—for instance, "open shapes" would permit modeling of parabolae, cubic curves, etc, and division between 2-D and 3-D shapes would support the incorporation of cubes more easily. Abstract classes, as described with respect to Figure 7.3, would add further flexibility. On the other hand, indiscriminate growth of inheritance hierarchies should be avoided. Inheritance is not necessarily the best solution, as noted in Chapter 2 with respect to Figure 2.14. Figure 7.10 shows that in moderate-to-large Smalltalk applications, the majority of hierarchies have depths[23] less than about 5. Deeper hierarchies have implications for (i) understandability and (ii) efficiency. Consequently, hierarchy depth is often used as a metric (Chapter 10).

Generalization and reevaluation of hierarchies are aimed at providing organizationally reusable classes. McGregor and Sykes (1992, p244) identify six areas where these techniques can be applied, on the basis of earlier work on reuse of ADTs by Uhl and Schmid (1990). These are given in Table 7.2. They highlight the identification of core concepts within the domain (e.g., the use of "segment" in a CAD system), the emphasis on the correct and appropriate semantic nature of the class interface, and the need for abstraction, both at a class level and at a service level. Here, services that are generally applicable may be moved to higher in the hierarchy. The trade-off here is whether (i) to use such a service (or service stub) that is then revised lower in the hierarchy— maintaining semantic consistency of the interface throughout the hierarchy; or

---

22. This, of course, involves "opening up" the class. That is fine during the development but should be strenuously avoided once the class has been released (via its addition to a departmental library) for use by developers outside the originating project. This discussion highlights the need for high quality and generalization to be an integral part of the initial development and not an "add-on extra" (Menzies *et al.*, 1992).
23. As Smalltalk only uses single inheritance, transferring these figures unreservedly to languages supporting multiple inheritance is not advisable.

The MOSES Lifecycle Activities

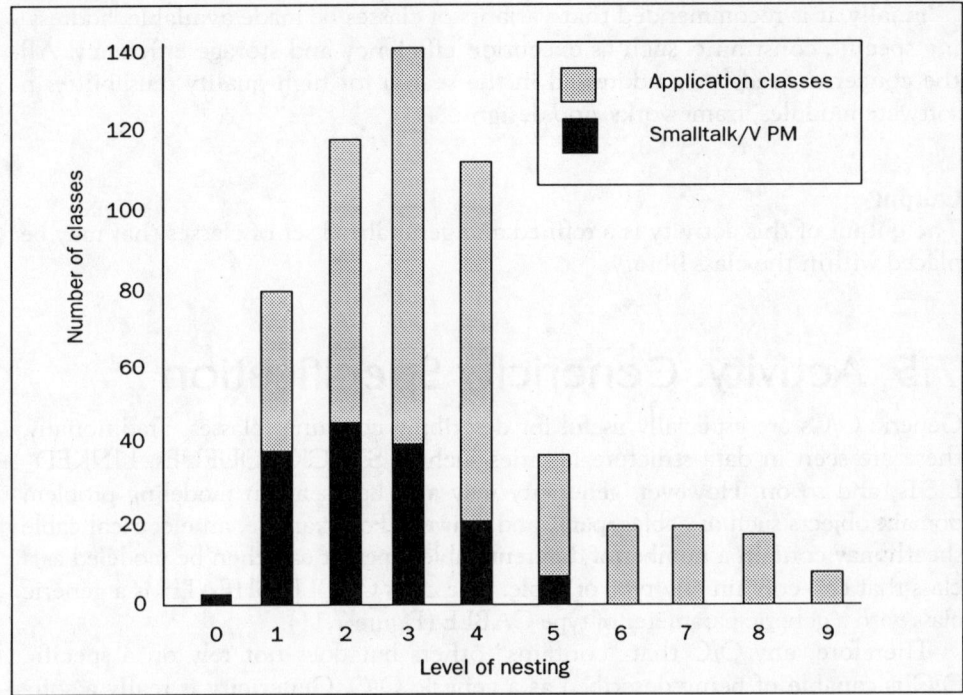

Figure 7.10 *Inheritance hierarchy depths for Smalltalk applications (Lorenz, 1991)*

(ii) to implement multiply at a low level if the service is semantically similar but needs to be implemented differently from an algorithmic standpoint.

McGregor and Sykes (1992) extend Uhl and Schmid's (1990) work and recommend careful selection of the most appropriate subclasses. These may be most difficult when several similar classes are available, such as in container classes. Although this recommendation is given by McGregor and Sykes in terms of the reuse of existing classes, we can easily invert it so that it becomes a guideline for *creating* reusable classes. In other words, the careful design (and iterative redesign) of inheritance hierarchies is of crucial importance for ensuring a high-quality, reusable hierarchy (or network) of classes.

Table 7.2 *Reuse guidelines (Adapted from McGregor and Sykes, 1992)*

- Identify the classes required for an application
- Determine the behavior needs from this class in this application
- Abstract these behaviors from the application domain to a more general domain
- Select the abstract class with matching behavior
- Select the appropriate subclass
- During the application's lifetime, tune the performance of the component, perhaps by choosing or developing different implementations

Finally, it is recommended that variants of classes be made available, addressing specific constraints such as execution efficiency and storage efficiency. All the concerns need to be addressed in the search for high-quality reusability in software modules, frameworks, and designs.

Output
The output of this activity is a refined and generalized set of classes that may be placed within the class library.

7.5 Activity: Genericity Specification

Generic O/Cs are especially useful for describing container classes. Traditionally, these are seen in data structure libraries such as STACKs, QUEUEs, LINKED_LISTs, and so on. However, genericity may also be useful in modeling problem domain objects such as cables, pans, and drawers. For example, an electrical cable sheath may contain a number of different cable types. It can then be modeled as a class that can contain any type of cable. The class CABLE_SHEATH is a generic class with a generic parameter of type CABLE (Figure 7.11).

Therefore, any O/C that "contains" others but does not rely on a specific O/C is capable of being described as a generic O/C. Genericity is really a software engineering technique for modeling aggregation or association relationships in the O/C Model. Quite often those relationships may be transformed into a generic parameter in the Implementation Phase. If constrained genericity is supported by the OOPL, a particular O/C may be specified as the parameter. This permits an increasing number of operations to be called on the parameter and hence on the generic class. Generic O/Cs are particularly reusable structures and their specification should therefore be encouraged (where supported by the OOPL). Genericity is, however, really applicable only to strongly typed languages such as Eiffel and C++ Version 3. If the target language supports genericity, this may be introduced into the design process as soon as the target OOPL has been selected. The decision to use genericity will therefore tend to be project-specific.

Output
The output of this activity is an identification of generic classes and the genericity relationship. The impacted deliverables are:

Deliverable Impacted	Information Generated and Recorded
O/C Models	Generic parameters
Class Specification	Generic parameters

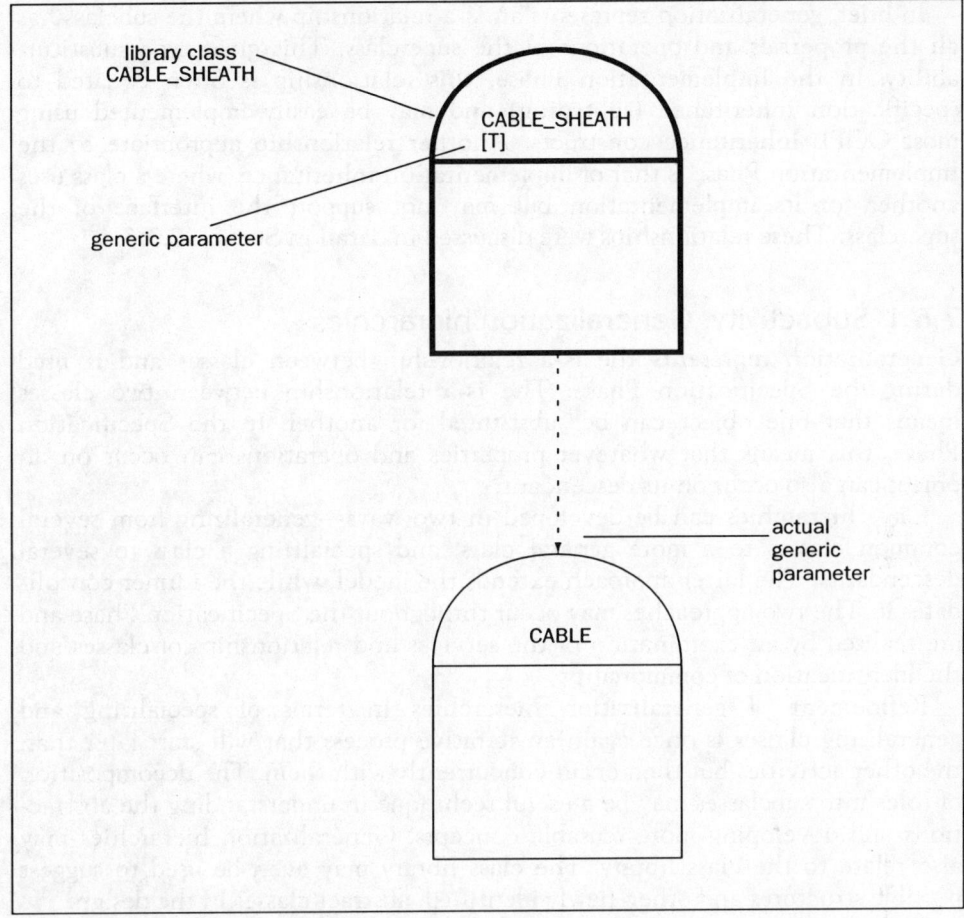

Figure 7.11 *Notation for genericity. Here CABLE_SHEATH is a generic "container class" for objects from the class CABLE (see Section 7.6 for further details on inheritance notation).*

7.6 Activity: Inheritance Identification

The purpose of this activity is to identify hierarchies, or inheritance, between classes.

MOSES refines the general notion of inheritance into two concepts: generalization (which subsumes both specialization and specification inheritance—see Chapter 2) and implementation inheritance. The former is appropriate for the Specification Phase, the latter for the Implementation Phase. The discussion of the two types of hierarchy within the one activity reflects the incremental refinement process of OO design as we move from the Specification Phase (Section 7.6.1) to the Implementation Phase (Section 7.6.2).

In brief, generalization represents an **is-a** relationship where the subclass has all the properties and operations of the superclass. This gives type substitutability. In the Implementation Phase, this relationship is often equated to specification inheritance (subtyping) and may be easily implemented using most OOPL inheritance constructs. Another relationship appropriate to the Implementation Phase is that of implementation inheritance, where a class uses another for its implementation but may not support the interface of the superclass. These relationships were discussed in detail in Section 2.3.6.

7.6.1 Subactivity: Generalization hierarchies

Generalization represents the **is-a** relationship between classes and is used during the Specification Phase. The **is-a** relationship between two classes means that one object can be substituted for another. In the Specification Phase, this means that whatever properties and operations can occur on an object can also occur on its descendant.

Class hierarchies can be developed in two ways—generalizing from several common classes to a more general class, and specializing a class to several descendants. The latter approach extends the model, while the former consolidates it. The two approaches may occur throughout the Specification Phase and are realized by an examination of the services and relationships of classes and the identification of commonality.

Refinement of generalization hierarchies in terms of specializing and generalizing classes is once again an iterative process that will start later than the other activities but then occur concurrently with them. The decomposition of roles into subclasses may be a useful technique in understanding the abstractions and developing more reusable concepts. Generalization hierarchies may also relate to the class library. The class library may even be used to suggest possible structures and other, newly identified, abstract classes in the design.

The generalization of services encourages services of classes to be abstracted to higher levels in the hierarchy, and descendants to be defined as specializations of the ancestor. The result is a reduction in redundancy of service specification. A newly identified class can be declared to be a specialization of an existing class if it has all the services of the ancestor. This reduces the amount of specification that needs to be undertaken and uses abstraction to reduce conceptual complexity and effort in the Specification Phase.

For example, consider three types of bank account: CHECKING, PASSBOOK, and SAVINGS_INVESTMENT (Figure 7.12). All three have common operations of *withdraw*, *deposit*, and *transfer*, and common properties of *account_number* and *balance*. However, it is known that the *withdrawal* algorithm depends on the current value of *balance* in different ways for the three accounts. In addition, CHECKING does not possess feature *interest_rate*. An obvious grouping gives us the generalization hierarchy of Figure 7.13. The abstract nature of *withdrawal* means that SAVINGS_ACCOUNT is an abstract class.

Still further refinement is possible, since portions of the interfaces of

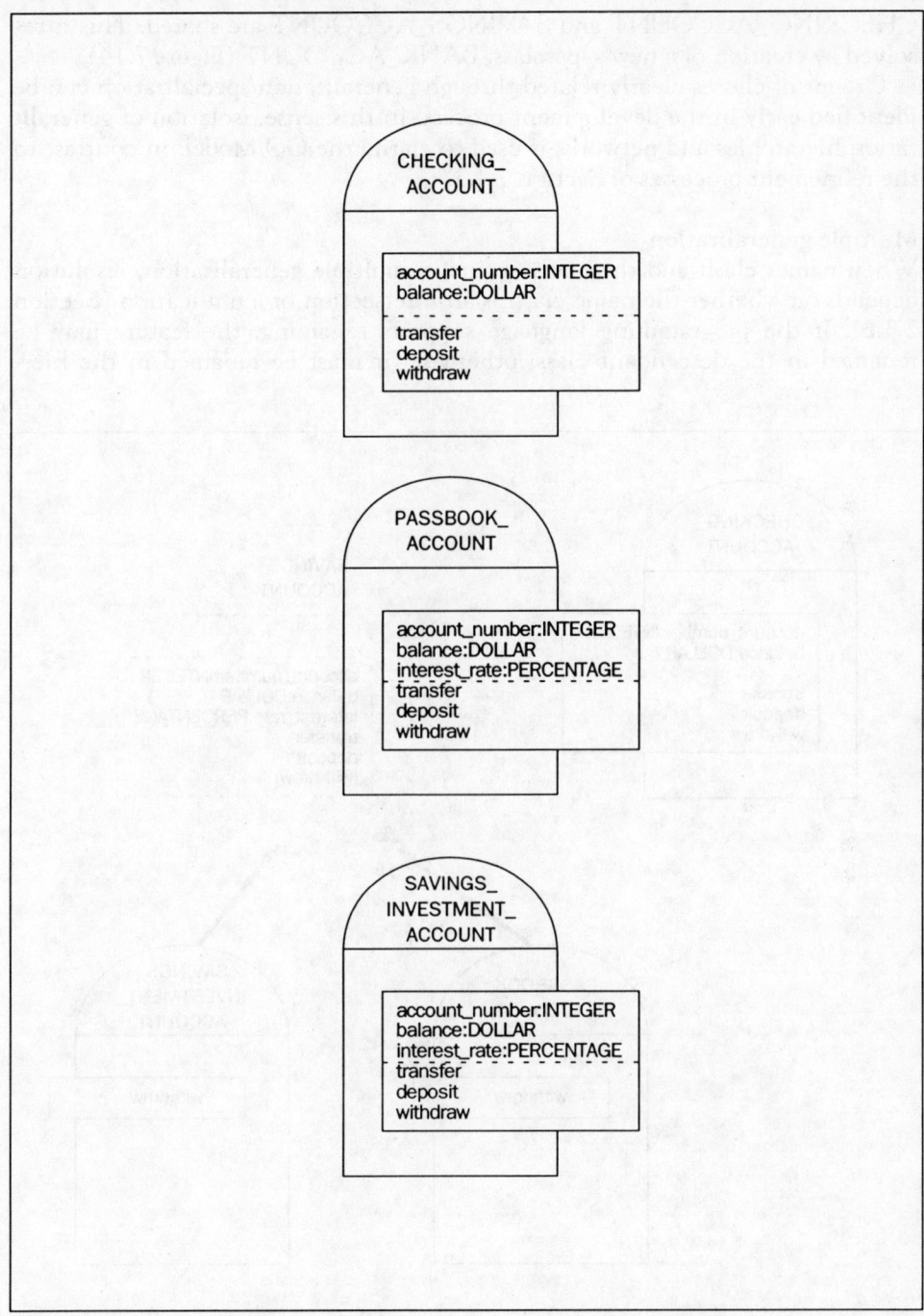

Figure 7.12 *In a development, three classes are identified independently, perhaps by different teams*

CHECKING_ACCOUNT and SAVINGS_ACCOUNT are shared. This is resolved by creation of a new superclass, BANK_ACCOUNT (Figure 7.14).

Groups of classes clearly related through generalization/specialization can be identified early in the development process. In this sense, isolation of generalization hierarchies and networks is used to clarify the OO Model, in contrast to the refinement processes of Section 7.4.3.

Multiple generalization

When names clash and the clash occurs in multiple generalization, resolution depends on whether the name clash is an intersection or a unification (Section 2.3.6). If the programming language supports renaming, the feature may be renamed in the descendant class; otherwise, it must be renamed in the hier-

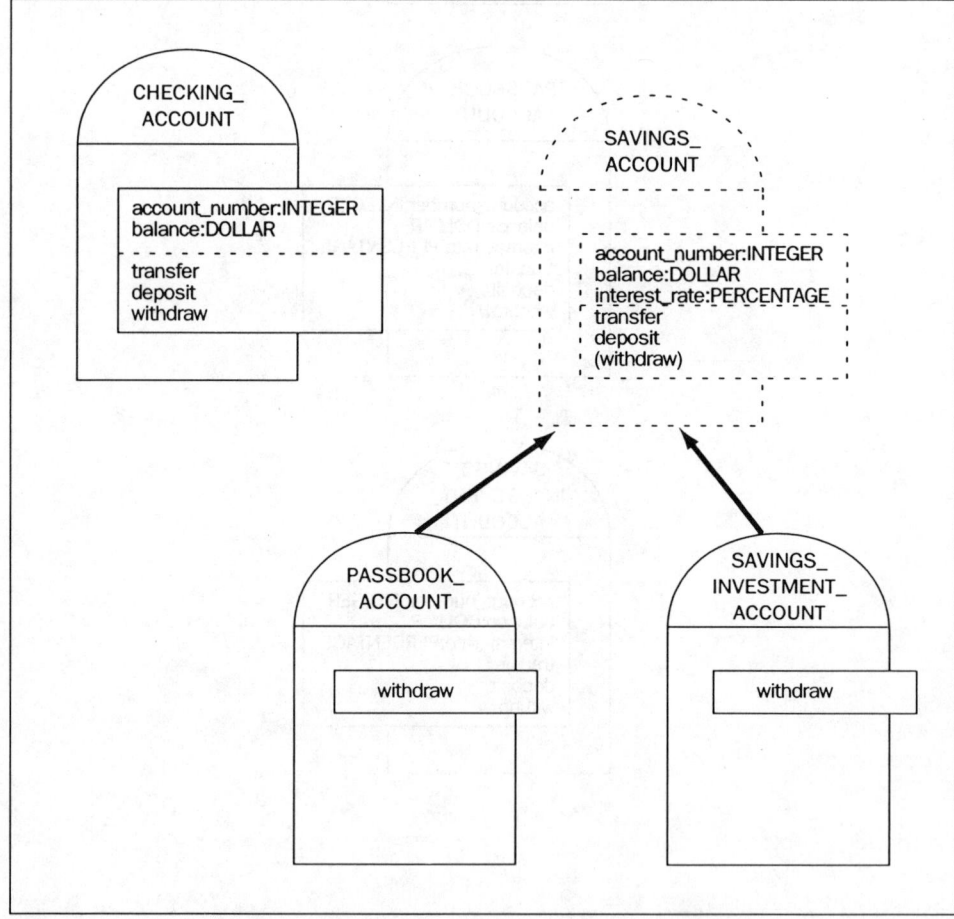

Figure 7.13 *Consideration of the three classes of Figure 7.12 identifies some obvious commonalities based on business rules*

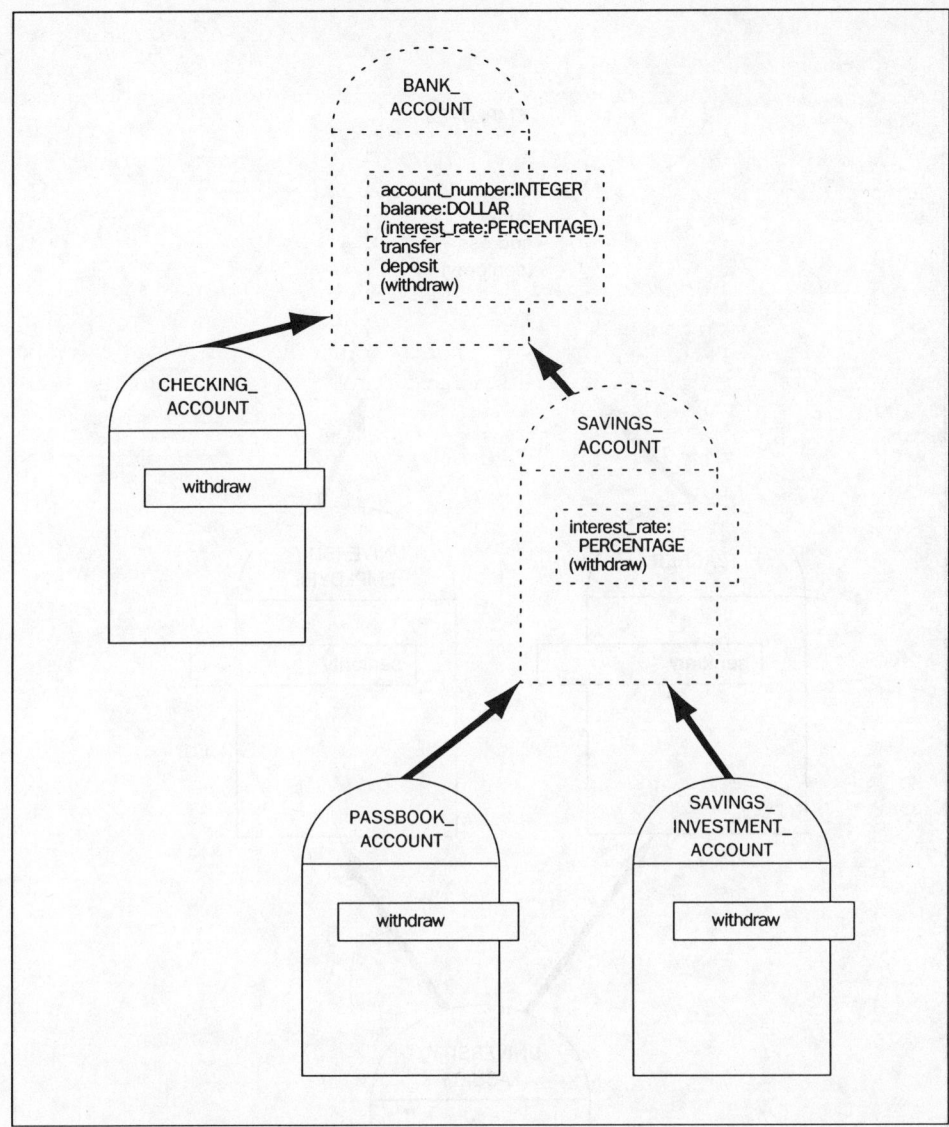

Figure 7.14 *Further generalization (from Figure 7.13) leads to the invention of a new O/C BANK_ACCOUNT, which did not figure in the original specification and is noninstantiable (i.e., abstract)*

archy before implementation. Where service name clashes are intended, that is, where service names model the same thing, the service must be unified into one property or operation. In this case, the classes returned by a property must be compatible. Thus, they must be either the same class or related in the abstraction hierarchy. In the former case no further specification is required,

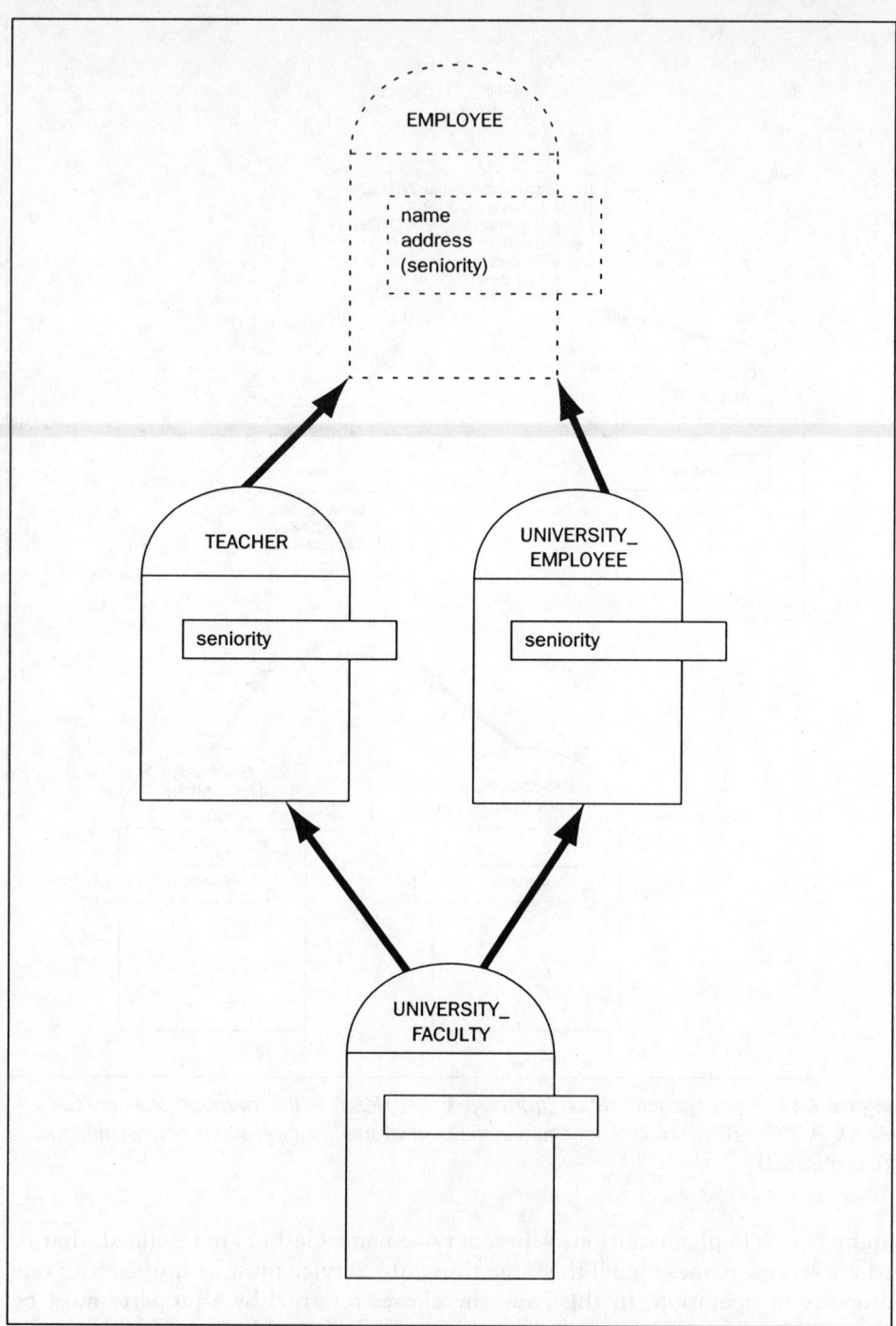

Figure 7.15 *Multiple specialization hierarchy requiring renaming*

while in the latter case the class of the property must be specified in the new class, and it must be a common subclass or the more specialized class of the two.

For example, Figure 7.15 shows a multiple specialization hierarchy where renaming is necessary. The renaming for the class TEACHER and UNIVERSITY_ EMPLOYEE is such that the descendant class has two separate "seniority" properties as shown below:

```
class UNIVERSITY_FACULTY
specialize
   TEACHER
      rename
         seniority as teacher_seniority;
   UNIVERSITY_EMPLOYEE
      rename
         seniority as university_employee_seniority;
end
```

If renaming is not supported, it will be necessary to change the names of the properties in the classes from which they originated. This is not a problem during the Specification Phase before the classes have stabilized and before they have been reused, but it is a significant problem once the classes have been placed in a library.

Following Meyer (1988a), an operation should require a precondition no stronger than the inherited operation and a postcondition no weaker than the inherited operation. Logically, this implies an "and" to the postcondition of the inherited operation. Deciding on the behavior specification of operations specialized from several ancestors is a nontrivial task for modelers.

Multiple specialization therefore leads to a descendant with all the properties and operations defined for all ancestors, and possibly more. The properties of each can be redefined in a covariant way so that a descendant is a subtype of the ancestors.

Repeated specializations are also permissible in the model (see Figure 7.15). As with multiple specialization, this raises the issue of name clashes, which are dealt with in the same manner as discussed previously. With repeated specializations, the behavioral semantics must be examined very carefully to ensure compatible behavior.

7.6.2 Subactivity: Implementation inheritance hierarchies

The objective of this subactivity is to maximize reuse of code in the software development. The developer should be examining the available library of components in order to maximize reuse of already existing classes. A significant part of this activity comes with the "reuse mindset," that is, the motivation to search libraries of classes and to look for redundancy in the hierarchy.

"Implementation inheritance" is used in the Implementation Phase for reuse of code from one class in another, but not for supporting the notion of the **is-a** relationship. This means that one class may use the services of another in its internal implementation but not support the semantics of the interface of the inherited class. In this case, substitutability of objects is *not* possible. Instead, the technique allows code to be used and modified quickly in a design without reworking the entire inheritance hierarchy of which the class is a member. In addition, code reuse may lead the designer to consider the use of "mixins" (Booch and Vilot, 1990a,b). This mechanism is a technique to produce designs and systems in the least time and with the least effort. The relationship is often termed the "is-implemented-in-terms-of" relationship between classes, as it specifies that one class is-implemented-in-terms-of another. It is solely an implementation concern, when the internals of classes are being developed and the library is being reused to its full extent. For example, a STACK may be implemented in terms of an ARRAY such that a STACK inherits an ARRAY. The STACK class therefore has access to all the services of array and may implement STACK-specific services using these inherited services. However, this use of inheritance is not strictly correct semantically, as elements of a STACK should not be indexable directly, but only through certain services such as *pop* and *push*. Hence a STACK is not an ARRAY even though it may be implemented by inheriting an ARRAY. This is therefore an example of implementation inheritance, which, although useful, is not to be overused or encouraged, particularly in the Specification Phase. Nonetheless, it is an important yet potentially dangerous use that many designers employ, but it is one that should be clearly identified as being an implementation decision rather than part of the conceptual model. In the Implementation Phase, therefore, it is possible that both types of inheritance may be employed, using the one language construct.

Multiple inheritance

The use of multiple inheritance (MI) networks is OOPL-dependent, but again involves name clashes and feature redefinition. Cancellation of services is also possible, but a technique we would strongly discourage. Brachman (1985) points out that negating features opens up the floodgates to many nonsensical relationships, e.g., a mouse inherits from elephant, but we cancel or change the size, the tusks, and the habitat, and simply retain the "grayness" attribute.

Output

Deliverable Impacted	Information Generated and Recorded
Class Specification	Updated as necessary
O/C Model	Generalization hierarchies
	Implementation inheritance
Inheritance Model	Generalization hierarchies
	Implementation inheritance hierarchies

7.7 Activity: Interaction Specification

The objective of this activity is to identify and define relationships between O/Cs. These can take a number of forms. During the Specification Phase, relationships are association, aggregation, and generalization. In the Implementation Phase, O/C relationships are language-dependent, where the concept of client–server is the generally applicable relationship, supplementing inheritance structures. The process of translation to particular OOPL constructs will be discussed in Section 7.19, which recognizes the practicalities of today's OOPLs. The interactions inherent in inheritance hierarchies were discussed separately in Section 7.6.

Candidate O/Cs should be structured in some sort of object-oriented model as early as possible. It is not necessary to define relationships fully or be accurate in the cardinality, etc.; rather, it is better to draw informal connections between O/Cs than none at all. In this way redundant O/Cs can be identified and removed more effectively. Indeed, even an unnamed association may be suitable at this early stage. Mandatory constraints and cardinalities should not be enforced too soon, as they are likely to change as the Specification Phase model is continually refined. Once the initial relationships have been identified, they should be depicted in the object-oriented models and documented in the class specifications.

Class relationships in the problem domain can be identified from the scenarios and the URS. Whenever a class requires the services of another class, some relationship should exist. Hence relationships may also be identified from EMs and objectcharts.

7.7.1 Subactivity: Aggregation specification

Aggregation structures represent the **is-part-of** relationship. Hence once a relationship has been identified, the developer should ask: "Could I use the phrase 'is-part-of' to describe the relationship?"; "Is the relationship one-way, i.e., is there some inherent antisymmetry?"; "Does the relationship model a parts hierarchy?"

You are quite likely to identify aggregate relationships through identifying the constituent parts of another object through complex properties (Section 7.15.2). In many aggregates the components may finally be placed in the private part, not the public part, of the O/C, representing internal, rather than visible, structuring. Later, the structure of these aggregate classes in terms of their properties and operations will be made more explicit. This requires the use of layering diagrams (see Section 5.8.3), although for a simple system or for an initial foray into the object-oriented model description you may wish to show aggregate classes in a less complicated way (Figure 7.16). When examining an aggregation relationship, question what happens during destruction of the composite object. If the component object is not destroyed also, then it is likely that association is the appropriate relationship rather than aggregation.

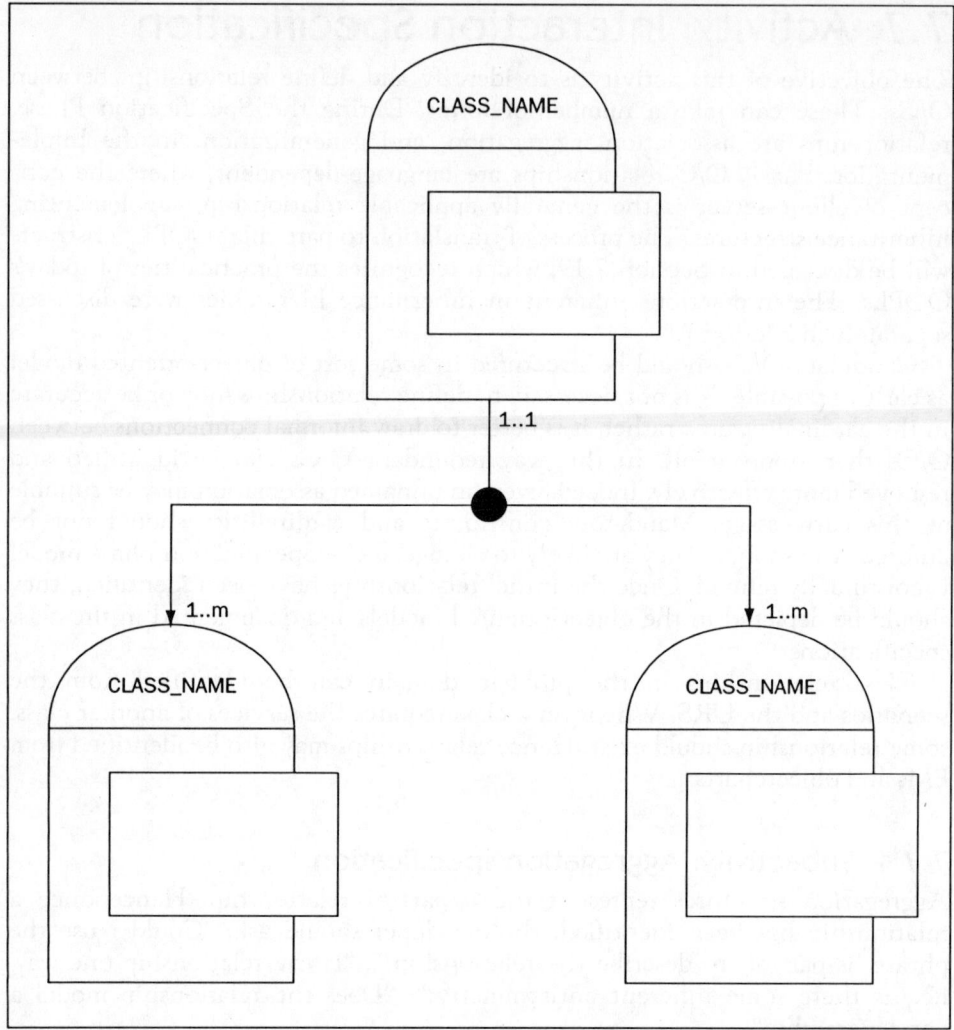

Figure 7.16 *Notation for the aggregation relationship between classes, with cardinalities*

7.7.2 Subactivity: Association specification

An association is a named relationship between one O/C and another (e.g., a CUSTOMER uses the services of a BANK). Cardinalities are likely to be associated with these connections, although details of the constraints is a concern of the late Specification Phase.

Associations should first be given a name and, if necessary, a direction. Association is a relationship between two "equal" objects, although the simplest approach to modeling this relationship is as a unidirectional connection between two O/Cs. Directionality often requires a statement of the semantics of the relationship; in other words, as noted in Chapter 5, such directed relationships need to be labeled with a descriptive name.

In some cases, bidirectional relationships are required, especially for database applications (although this provides a much tighter binding between O/Cs, which tends to destroy class autonomy and encapsulation, possibly thwarting reuse). In this case, a symmetric property or inverse function approach is useful. In this approach, the relationship is modeled as a property of the O/C, with the related inverse function available on the related O/C. For example, an EMPLOYEE might *work_for* a COMPANY. This may be represented as a property of EMPLOYEE called *employer* and as a property of COMPANY called *employee*. These two properties can be defined as the inverse of one another, hence modeling the same relationship. They relate the two O/Cs of COMPANY and EMPLOYEE in a bidirectional manner. Martin and Odell (1992, p264) note that association relationships and functions are two views of the same conceptual notion.

The identification of problem domain associations will primarily occur for the scenarios and the URS. Any interaction or relationship between classes specified in the URS or the scenarios should at first be modeled as an association. Only upon refinement should some of the relationships be refined to aggregation using the guidelines defined earlier.

The identification of associations may also arise from the dynamic model where the need of one O/C for information requires a connection to another. Unless the relationship fits the semantics of aggregation, it is likely that this will require the identification of a further association relationship. Association relationships, as with all other features of an O/C, should be moved as far up the inheritance hierarchy (Section 7.6.1) as possible. Useful guidelines for modeling associations are given in Rumbaugh (1992a) and Kilian (1991), including:

- Ensure that associations are structural properties, not simply transient events or actions.
- Check that ternary associations are really necessary to describe the problem domain. Quite often they can be decomposed into binary associations without loss of information. Note that in MOSES we advocate the total avoidance of ternary relationships.
- Remove redundant associations, especially in the late Specification Phase. However, note that earlier in this phase, redundant information may actually be useful in understanding the problem.
- Add a role name on associations that may be useful for clarifying the O/C Model.
- Be aware of eliminated associations as the candidate class list is refined and classes are removed from the model.

In identifying associations, a large number of traditional data modeling techniques can be reapplied as well as a number of more refined techniques such as "fact analysis" (Ratjens, 1991). The techniques aim to transform a requirement into a collection of facts such that a fact relates two or more concepts. This fact can then be modeled as a relationship between O/Cs. For example, in a system to be designed for a local golf club the following facts apply:

- A player may be a member, associate, or public.
- A player may only play one game per day.
- A game may be 9 or 18 holes.
- A player may hire clubs and carts/trolleys.

From these facts, a number of relationships can be defined. For example, a player may be one of three types; this makes player a superclass of member, associate, and public. A player has a relationship with game and with clubs and carts. This relationship is an association, as the semantics of generalization do not apply (a player is not a club or cart). Nor are the semantics of aggregation appropriate (the player is not composed-of a cart or clubs). Instead the player may hire clubs and carts. Facts should be clarified with the clients and formalized into an O/C Model.

Output
Information produced will be used to update the O/C Model and class specification.

Deliverable Impacted	Information Generated and Recorded
Class Specification	Aggregations
	Associations
	Cardinality/existence constraints
O/C Model	Associations
	Aggregations
	Cardinality/existence constraints
	Layering as required

7.8 Activity: Iteration Plan Development

The iteration plan development activity is the primary activity involved in the Planning Phase. The purpose of this activity is to develop a project plan detailing the required resources, objectives, and time frame for the next iteration. Lorenz (1993) has defined a number of tasks that make up this activity, including:

1. *Identify and prioritize system requirements.* It is important to understand the objectives of the iteration, even if this is at a fairly high level of abstraction. This understanding can be gained from the Business Statement and initial investigation undertaken to scope the project. The objective should be

specified in terms of functionality required by the customer/business user. By specifying the functionality to be delivered, the project manager has a means of satisfying the customer with continual delivery and of managing scope.
2. *Document external dependencies and deliverables.* This activity records those resources and dependencies of the iteration that may have an impact on the project schedule if they are not delivered or slip. Making such dependencies explicit permits a degree of risk management to be undertaken within the iteration.
3. *Establish a schedule.* The iteration should be decomposed into the phases, with particular schedules assigned to each phase. Such scheduling requires effective estimation techniques. Unfortunately, such techniques are not yet mature within the OO area and it is important to build in a significant estimation error into the schedule during the early stages of the project.

Tasks in developing a schedule include listing all project tasks, determining intertask dependencies, estimating the duration of a task, and defining the earliest and latest completion dates for a task. On the basis of these tasks, a PERT or Gantt chart should be developed for the iteration.

7.9 Activity: Library Class Incorporation

The objective of this activity is to maximize the reuse of library components that already exist. OO development emphasizes the importance of reuse in the development process and, as we have already discussed, the successful outcome of this methodology is a software base of reusable components. The fountain model in Figure 3.7 graphically represents this.

Integrating and reusing the corporate class library in a new development is an important part of the process. During Specification and Implementation the developer should be examining the library of components in order to maximize reuse of already existing classes. A significant part of this activity comes with the "reuse mindset," that is, the motivation to search libraries of classes and to look for redundancy in the inheritance hierarchy. This reuse mindset encourages a bottom-up approach, particularly useful during Implementation, whereas in Specification there is initially an emphasis on a top-down refinement process. This mixing of approaches appears "fuzzy" and undisciplined but in fact more closely reflects the way many designers operate (Turner, 1987).

It is perhaps worth noting here some of the possible library sources for this activity. McGregor and Sykes (1992) categorize five types of libraries: (i) team-specific components (classes developed by a team for their own later use); (ii) project-specific components (classes developed as part of a team's project for their own use; these may be found to be more widely useful later and are those for which reuse may be a secondary impetus); (iii) problem domain-specific components available from a third party vendor (such vendors are likely to develop classes for resale in specialized domains such as banking, finance, and insurance); (iv) general components from a components vendor (libraries, such as the NIH libraries (Gorlen et al., 1990) or the Booch C++ libraries (Booch and Vilot, 1990c), are low-level widely applicable classes written in a specific language); and (v) language-specific primitives obtainable from a compiler vendor, possibly bundled with the language (as in some versions of Eiffel) or available separately.

When considering any of these later categorized libraries (iii–v) for possible purchase, McGregor and Sykes (1992) introduce some guidelines, derived from Korson and McGregor (1992). They provide the following checklist—the library should:

- give a complete general model (classes and their interrelationship are logical);
- be designed around a few key abstractions;
- model standard knowledge in the domain;
- use inheritance;
- be designed as networks of classes without freestanding data or procedural items (avoid hybrid styles);
- be designed with a low level of coupling between classes;
- provide a consistent and easily understood approach to error handling;
- provide "inspector" functions to check preconditions;
- make it impossible for users to violate abstractions represented;
- conform to a minimal set of standards;
- have maximum efficiency;
- provide a consistent naming scheme;
- provide generic classes;
- provide full documentation as specified in Table 7.3;
- provide commercial-strength support (from vendor).

In addition, a good library should include good examples of class usage (Nerson, 1993). The above guidelines are also useful for classes you build yourself (Ratjens, pers. com., 1993).

Table 7.3 *Documentation required for library classes (Adapted from Korson and McGregor, 1992)*

- Documentation on state of completeness of each class implementation
- Documentation reflecting structure of library
- Documentation containing overview of library, including contents and structure
- Different documentation for different levels of user
- Documentation accessible by a minimum of 3 methods:
    alphabetic by class name
    hierarchical via inheritance structure
    keyword facility

Reuse of classes can be achieved in a number of ways: instantiation, composition, use of class hierarchies, and abstract-level reuse (McGregor and Sykes, 1992, p242). An important point is that reuse can occur at all levels of the development process, it is not confined to the Implementation Phase. The reuse of specifications from previous development phases is an important element.

Generalization hierarchies, for example, may be reused from a domain analysis activity (e.g., McGregor and Sykes, 1992). For this type of reuse to be successful, a proper domain analysis activity, as well as an adherence to complete specification and generalization hierarchies, needs to be a part of the development environment. Thus specification of generalization hierarchies (Section 7.6.1) should involve the examination of the class library and its hierarchy, which is the repository of considerable domain knowledge. Similarly, a powerful library tool, as well as incentives for developers to reuse classes, needs to be part of the process. Without this infrastructure support, reuse will not be effective even in an OO project.

Reuse by composition will lead to new aggregation, association, and client–server relationships in the Specification Phase and the Implementation Phase.

The extent to which classes from a library have been incorporated into the design can be judged within the Review Phase, where the development team can stand back from the design and undertake a design review. Design reviews should aim to be critical and try to identify classes that can be reused from the corporate library.

The outcome of this activity is a refinement of the O/C Model such that as many classes as possible are reused. For example, there is a requirement for a Rolladex application where cards are sorted alphabetically such that each card can contain information and be viewed by "flipping" to the appropriate card. In the initial design, a number of "problem domain" classes can be identified, as can a number of generalization relationships. Thus, we may identify a CARD, with attributes of title and notes and with a relationship with a Rolladex. Figure 7.17 shows the O/C Model for this small problem. However, on reflection and examination of the class library, this O/C Model can be viewed at a higher level of abstraction reusing a number of classes. For example, CARD is the Smalltalk DICTIONARY class and the ROLLADEX is like a SORTED_COLLECTION. Thus, a ROLLADEX can be viewed as a SORTED_COLLECTION of DICTIONARYs. In the new design, more classes are used but only one new class is required, all the others being used directly from the Smalltalk library. Figure 7.18 shows the new O/C Model.

This small example shows that by examining class libraries a problem domain model can be reassessed to maximize reuse. The reevaluation process may lead to significant savings in development and testing time and even to the identification of frameworks for designs based on library class structures.

Output

The output from the activity is a refined O/C Model and a number of classes identified as being able to be reused in the design.

Deliverable Impacted	Information Generated and Recorded
O/C Models	Library classes/relationships

7.10 Activity: Objectchart Construction

The purpose of this activity is to fully specify the behavior of objects of the class and to identify missing behavior. This is achieved by developing objectcharts, a graphical tool for representing object behavior (Section 5.6). Objectcharts are an elaboration of Harel's (1987) statecharts, as presented by Coleman *et al.* (1992). They are valid throughout the lifecycle and thus provide an ideal tool to represent state changes (behavior) of classes. They will tend to be developed only after a first pass at the static structure and after scenarios have been developed for the subsystem that have led to the identification of some initial operations.

An objectchart specifies the state transition diagram (STD) for an object of a class together with a set of transition specifications and a set of invariant specifications that record the effect of a message on the object.

The process of developing an objectchart begins with identifying states applicable to an object. Transitions between these states are then identified on the basis of services that are offered by the object. States should be "interesting" from the point of view of having some effect on the object behavior. In this sense, objectcharts are no different from statecharts. Statecharts should then be refined to an objectchart by:

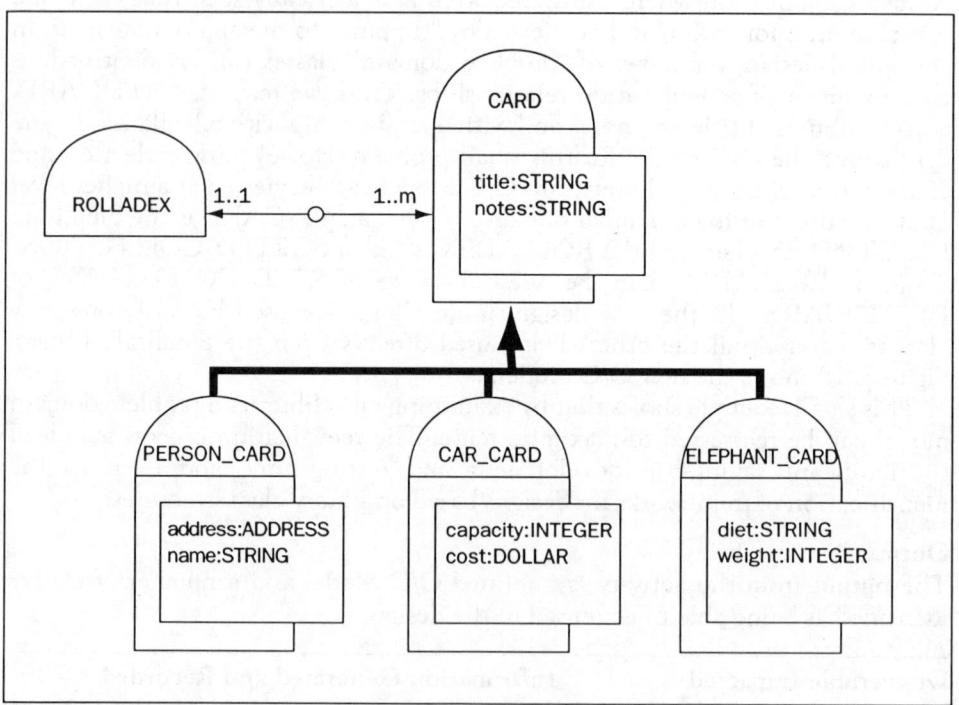

Figure 7.17 *First draft of an O/C Model for the Rolladex problem*

The MOSES Lifecycle Activities

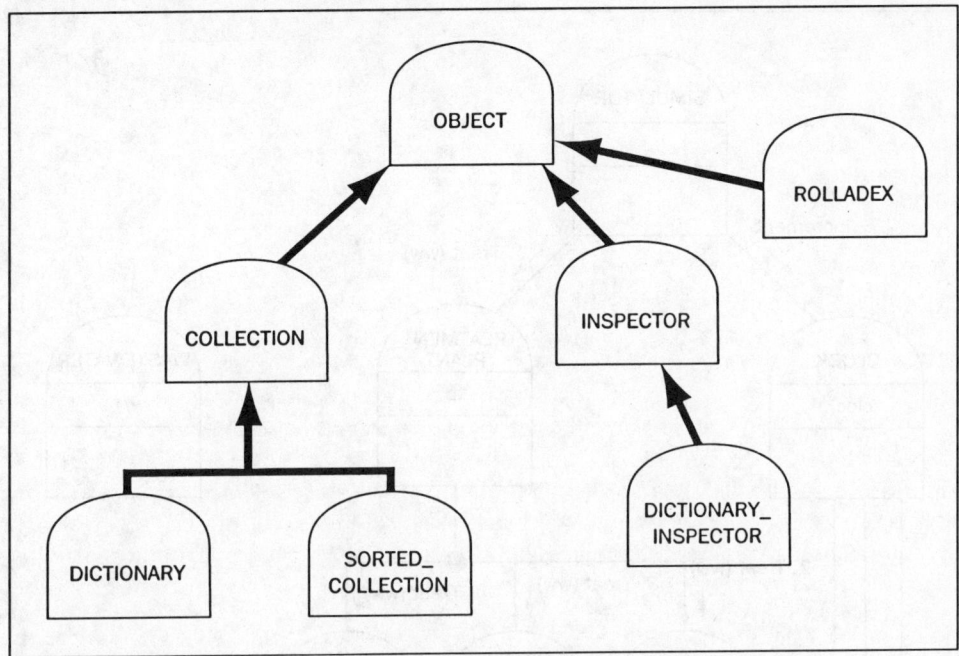

Figure 7.18 *Second draft of the Rolladex problem following evaluation of available classes from the Smalltalk library*

- annotating states with properties (observers and attributes in Coleman *et al.*'s terminology);
- defining firing postcondition specifications for all state transitions;
- defining invariant specifications for the derived properties.

Coleman *et al.* (1992) then suggest techniques for grossing up the objectcharts to the system behavior level. These are diagrams that show the actual system configuration of objects and, as such, use actual object names. These diagrams are similar to O/C Models except that they are used with objects rather than class notations and are called configuration diagrams by Coleman *et al.* (1992) (Figure 7.19). An object (as opposed to a class) is represented by an icon similar to the class icon except that it has two extra sections—one for the object name that is unique to the model and one for the aliases of the object (see Section 5.2.2).

An example of an objectchart is shown in Figure 7.20. This describes an ALARMCLOCK class that describes the state changes for a computer alarm clock using a window system. When the alarm "rings," it opens a window, which is otherwise iconized. An alarm (of class ALARMCLOCK) is in one "anded" state of time polling and alarm on/off. In other words, time polling happens concurrently with (and therefore independently of) the alarm being on

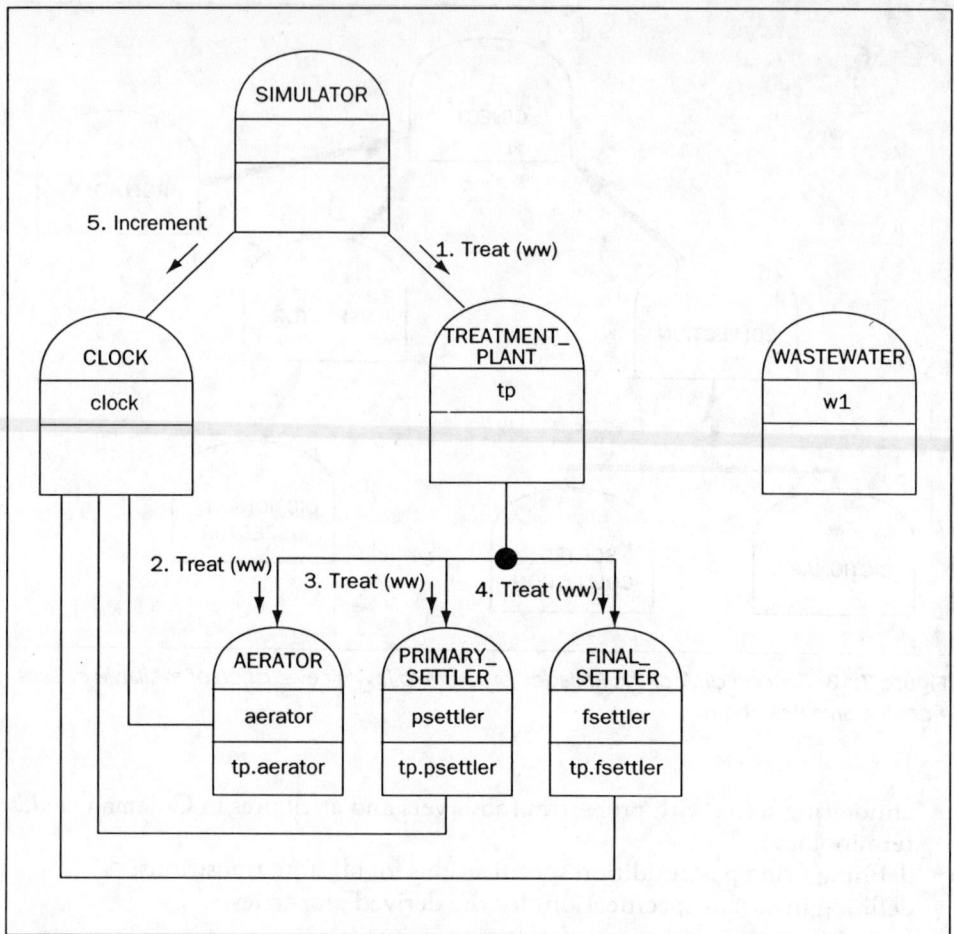

Figure 7.19 *O/C Model showing objects and their relationships (based in part on Coleman et al., 1992). The MOSES tablets are the truncated versions augmented to show not only class name (top portion) but also unique object name (second portion) and its alias(es) (third portion). Arrows indicate direction of message passing. This model has strong similarities with the event-neighborhood diagram of Page-Jones et al. (1990) and the object scenario diagram of Booch (1992).*

or off. The alarmon state is then defined as being either "quiet" or "ringing." Transitions are indicated on the arcs, where a solidus, "/", indicates a requested service. In this example, *W.service* indicates an external call to an object of class WINDOW. Hence Figure 7.20 indicates that when in the ringing state, the alarm window may be closed either after a fixed duration (indicated by the condition on the transition) or as a result of cancellation by the user (*alarm.stop*).

The MOSES Lifecycle Activities

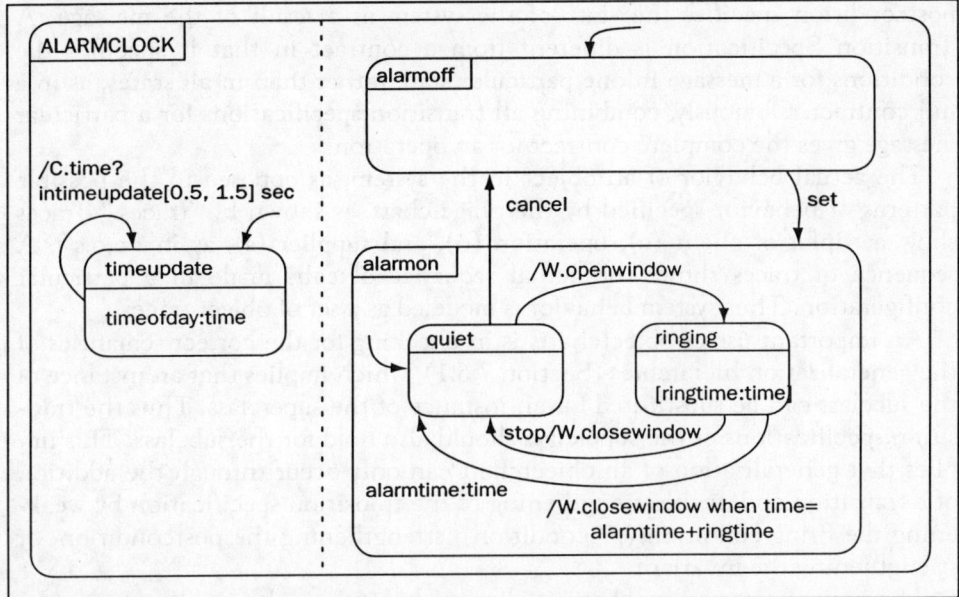

Figure 7.20 *Objectchart illustrating the recursive state transitions, here of an ALARM_CLOCK class (Coleman et al., © 1992 IEEE)*

For all transitions on the objectchart, a transition specification should be developed. This transition specification should be recorded in the Transition Specification Table (Figure 7.21). The transition specification details the pre- and postconditions of a particular stage. The precondition specifies what must be true about the system in order for the message to be valid, while the

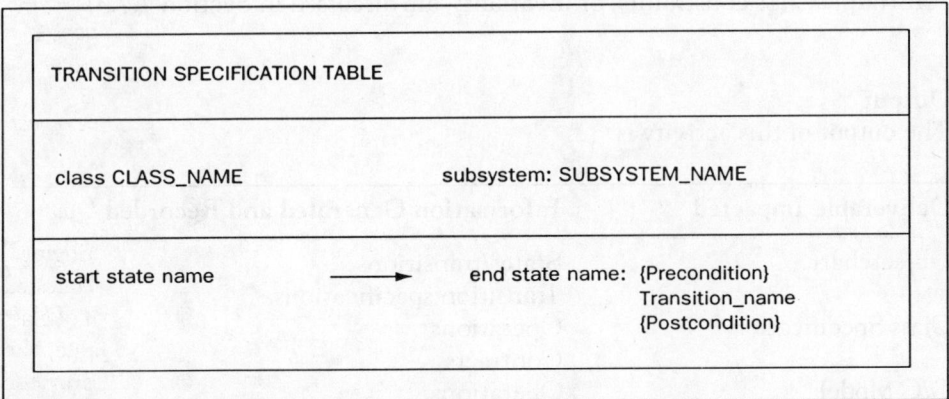

Figure 7.21 *A Transition Specification Table documenting the transition name, start state, and pre- and postconditions for the transition*

postcondition specifies the state of the system as a result of the message. A Transition Specification is different from a contract in that it specifies the conditions for a message in one particular state rather than in all states, as in a full contract. Obviously, combining all transition specifications for a particular message gives the complete contract for an operation.

The actual behavior of an object in the system, as opposed to the possible patterns of behavior specified by the objectchart, is shown by "traces." Traces show a triplet of client (c), operation (o), and supplier (s), as in <c,o,s>. A sequence of traces shows the actual sequence of calls made in a particular configuration. Thus system behavior is modeled as a set of object traces.

An important use of objectcharts is in checking for the correct semantics of the generalization hierarchies (Section 7.6.1), which implies that an instance of the subclass can be substituted for an instance of the superclass. Thus the transition specifications of the superclass should also hold for the subclass. This implies that generalization of an objectchart can only occur through the addition of a transition and/or the strengthening of the transition specification by weakening the firing condition (precondition), strengthening the postcondition, or strengthening the invariant.

The communication mechanism discussed above results in changes to the state of an object. The new state must be a valid one. Valid states are specified by invariants. Invariants can be placed on the values of properties or on the relationship between property values. In fact, class constraints may be viewed as being logically "anded" to the precondition and postcondition of all class operations. The reason is that an object may have an operation called on it only when it is in a stable state. A stable state is when all the class invariants are met. Thus, it is a precondition of calling an operation that the class invariants are true. Similarly, an operation must ensure that the object is in a stable state after it has been called, thus ensuring that the class invariants are true. This is equivalent to the operation having a postcondition that includes the class constraint. Class constraints, or invariants, are discussed in Section 7.7.3.

Output
The output of this activity is:

Deliverable Impacted	Information Generated and Recorded
Objectchart	States/transitions
	Transition specifications
Class Specification	Operations
	Contracts
O/C Model	Operations
Event Model	Updated for new operations

7.11 Activity: O/C Identification

The core activity of object modeling is the identification and specification of O/Cs. Early in the process of deriving a model, the activity will essentially be one of discovery, whereas later in the process it will be more one of refinement and invention. The refinement activity will never result in a "perfect" model but will, after a few iterations, lead to a stable model. Newly discovered O/Cs should be documented in the O/C Model and in the Class Specification (see discussion in Section 5.4), and will be refined as the development proceeds.

7.11.1 Subactivity: Determine initial class list and refine

Identification of O/Cs is at the same time both easy and hard. Meyer argues that "objects are just there for the picking" (Meyer, 1988a, p51). However, while this may be true in a well-understood and defined domain such as data structures, well-defined business objects are significantly harder to find.

A number of techniques are available for identifying O/Cs. Firstly, objects (or more rightly classes) are easily identifiable through nouns in the requirements document (Abbott, 1983). These can be both concrete nouns (things) and abstract nouns (concepts and other abstractions). Unfortunately, this approach often leads to too many classes and it is necessary to reevaluate the list of classes a number of times as the analysis is refined. Wirfs-Brock *et al.* (1990) suggest looking for two O/Cs with names that are essentially synonyms, to be wary of the use of adjectives as qualifiers that may or may not identify different O/Cs, and to be wary of sentences in the specification with missing or misleading subjects.

Candidate classes in the model will be those entities that the modeler deems primary within the model boundaries. For example, Coad and Yourdon (1991a) recommend looking for events, roles played, location, and organization. Jacobson *et al.* (1992) divide their classes into those representing things, software interface classes, and classes used for control within the system.

Graham (1991, p18) notes that real-world objects (also called "entities") are not only concrete occurrences but also arise out of social and professional relationships. While some O/Cs relate to real-world things, such as employees and banks, others reflect anthropogenic abstractions such as stacks—although many such O/Cs would be more likely to be identified in the Specification Phase as software domain artifacts. Iivari (1991) suggests five categories of classes: (i) user classes; (ii) classes of the Universe of Discourse (UoD) (e.g., entities and events); (iii) information-type classes (e.g., I/O documents, databases); (iv) user interface classes (e.g., windows, menus, icons); and (v) classes of abstract technology (i.e., those required solely for technical reasons demanded by implementation decisions).

Firesmith (1992a) suggests using the following list: (i) nouns; (ii) DFDs; (iii) recursion; (iv) ADTs and abstract state machines; (v) states; (vi) attributes, operations, and exceptions; (vii) requirements; (viii) CRC cards; (ix) OO diagrams; (x) object abstraction; (xi) personal experience; (xii) OO domain analysis; (xiii) previously developed software; and (xiv) repositories. Noting that identification of O/Cs is a difficult step, he offers a wide selection of techniques and a variety of conceptual abstraction levels. In a later publication (Firesmith, 1993) he groups these into recommended, traditional, and miscellaneous approaches (Table 7.4) together with additional elaboration.

Table 7.4 *Suggestions for identification of O/Cs (Firesmith, 1993)*

- *Recommended Approaches*
    - Using object abstraction
        - using the types of the modeled entities
        - using the definitions of objects and classes
        - using object decomposition
    - Using inheritance
        - using generalization
        - using subclasses
    - Using object-oriented domain analysis
    - Using repositories of previously developed software
        - reusing application frameworks
        - reusing class hierarchies
        - reusing individual objects and classes
    - Using specification and design languages
    - Using personal experience
- *Traditional Approaches*
    - Using nouns
    - Using traditional data flow diagrams (DFDs)
        - using terminators on context diagrams
        - using data stores on DFDs
        - using complex data flows on DFDs
- *Miscellaneous Approaches*
    - Using abstract data types and abstract state machines
    - Using states
    - Using resources
        - using attributes
        - using operations
        - using exceptions
    - Using requirements
    - Using CRC cards
    - Using entities on Entity-Relationship Attribute (ERA) diagrams
    - Using object-oriented diagrams
        - using nodes on semantic nets
        - using nodes on interaction diagrams

Possible candidate classes thus include:

- real-world objects of the model, e.g., tanks, pipes, chairs;
- abstract concepts of the model, e.g., a race, a demand curve, a maintenance schedule, an asset;
- abstract or real processes (Arnold and Early, 1988; Gomaa, 1990), e.g., a wastewater process, a cruise control process;
- roles (Wieringa, 1991, Coad and Yourdon, 1991a), e.g., a manager, a student, an employer, a threat;
- events in a system (Meyer, 1988a; Coad and Yourdon, 1991a), e.g., commands in a user interface;
- events to be remembered (Gomaa, 1990; Coad and Yourdon, 1991a), e.g., ATM transactions, overflow events in a tank;
- physical devices (Sommerville, 1989; Gomaa, 1990; Coad and Yourdon, 1991a), e.g., sensors and printers.

Classes should typically represent a large collection of actual objects. If there is only a single object (single instance) within one specific class, it is unlikely (though not impossible) that this class will remain in the system.

Identity is the fundamental notion of objects. If objects of a class cannot be counted, that is, if they do not have identity in their own right, then they are not true objects and the classes from which they are derived are probably not good ones.

Each class should immediately be given a unique name that is concise yet informative. A description of the meaning of each class should also be given. Classes may also be identified from scenarios. Once again, nouns within the scenario are candidate classes. Other sources of classes are class libraries or already specified components. Also, data models or database schemes provide indications of classes useful in the domain.

7.11.2 Subactivity: Identify persistent classes

Specification of persistence should generally be undertaken during the Implementation Phase, although it may be possible to indicate it during the Specification Phase. Persistent O/Cs are the results of a particular program execution—for example, a simulation run's results, or information that outlasts the program execution, such as configuration information. This information may be read from a file or stored as a persistent O/C, depending on the nature of the storage environment (e.g., relational database, objectbase, or operating system files). Unless persistence is a major part of the application, e.g., a database system, specifying O/Cs that are to be saved to secondary storage can be left until quite late in the development process.

Output
Information produced during Activity: O/C Identification:

Deliverable Impacted	Information Generated and Recorded
Class Specification	Name
	Persistent or not
	Brief description
O/C Model	Name

7.12 Activity: Optimization

When computing resources are scarce and/or the problem demands are great, the design may require optimizing. This is an activity that occurs in the process after the basic business model has been defined. Unlike the optimization activity as part of generalization for reuse, this activity changes class structures and interfaces. The changes are due to a redesign/optimization of the design rather than individual algorithms.

Optimization requires a detailed knowledge of physical information storage and processing. Optimized code may avoid excessive paging in the machine and may minimize loops, excessive resetting of attribute values, etc.

Optimizations take place at two levels. The first is that of redesign of the O/C Model developed during the Specification Phase and the Implementation Phase to optimize the time/space parameters of the system. Such redesign may involve removing classes and relationships or adding design classes to store information. Rumbaugh *et al.* (1991) suggest a number of guidelines for optimizing the O/C Model based on the "hit" rate of queries in the search for objects. They suggest the use of indexes to reduce the search and traversal requirements of the model. Alternatively, redundant relationships may be added to reduce traversal paths and message sends. Reevaluation and optimization of the O/C Model are best undertaken during late stages of Specification when certain "hot spots" can be identified.

The second level is that of breaking the O/C Model to optimize a solution. For example, violating encapsulation or the use of friend mechanisms can lead to reduced overhead, albeit at the expense of flexibility and reuse. Such optimizations and redesign are largely system-specific, including a reworking and prototyping iteration to ensure the performance criteria are met. Quite often the designer may be able to identify critical optimization points during the Specification Phase. In these circumstances the developer may undertake a prototyping exercise to provide a proof of concept. Such prototypes can be incorporated as short iterations at the start of the project to minimize the risk that the development will fail on the basis of performance criteria.

7.13 Activity: Quality Evaluation (Metrics)

A prime focus is quality, since it is imperative that any classes generalized for future addition to the company's library of classes be of guaranteed quality. This involves not only code testing (Section 7.18) but also an assessment of the

The MOSES Lifecycle Activities

compatibility of the class with other library classes (in other words, the class library structure); its potential usefulness in the company's specific business domain; its potential usefulness in other business domains so that profits can be reaped by resale; and, perhaps most important, the standard of its documentation. Continuous monitoring of classes during development, using quality mechanisms such as assertions, assists here.

Quality is more than end-phase testing. Testing identifies "OK" or "needing rework" (Zultner, 1989, as quoted in Adams, 1992b). Quality is built in *throughout* the development process, not as a one-off quality assessment test of the final product. Thus this activity spans the whole lifecycle—see also Figure 4.9. Adams (1992b) advocates short cycle times in a "constant quality management" framework (Figure 7.22). Metrics (Chapter 10) provide the tool to accomplish this quality goal.

Evaluating quality is difficult and seldom quantitative. Heuristics do, however, exist for "good design." McGregor and Sykes (1992) present ten design guidelines for creation of object-oriented modules, based in part on the work of Johnson and Foote (1988). These guidelines, shown in Table 7.5, express the following concerns:

1. & 2. Information hiding is maintained in such a way that the only access point is through the interface. This is supported by the recommendations of Wirfs-Brock and Wilkerson (1989a).
3. & 6. Only services required to be publicly available should be included in the interface and information exchange should be kept explicit—in other words, no global access "just in case."

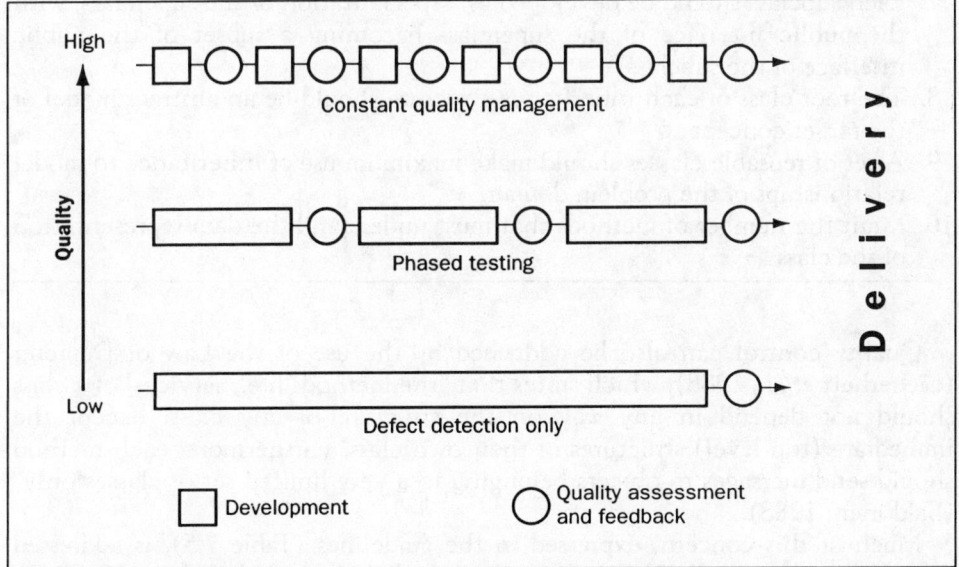

Figure 7.22 *The evolution toward constant quality management (Adams, © copyright SIGS Publications, 1992b)*

4. Classes should be ADTs with high semantic cohesion.
5. Weak coupling is a goal. Modularity and coupling tend to work in opposition such that the use of metrics (see below) is needed to evaluate these trade-offs.
7. Inheritance should be used primarily/only for the inheritance of the interface (specification inheritance or subtyping).
8. The "top" or root class in an inheritance hierarchy is generally an abstract class, containing all common services (or stubs thereof).
9. & 10. Good design of reusable components requires further quantification using metrics.

Table 7.5 *Design guidelines (Modified from McGregor and Sykes, 1992)*

1. The only members of the public interface of a class should be methods of the class
2. A class should not expose its implementation details, even through public accessor operations
3. An operator should be a member of the public class interface if and only if it is to be available to users of instances of the class
4. Each operator that belongs to a class either accesses or modifies some of the data of a class
5. A class should be dependent on as few other classes as possible
6. The interaction between two classes should involve only explicit information passing
7. Each subclass should be developed as a specialization of the superclass, with the public interface of the superclass becoming a subset of the public interface of the subclass
8. The root class of each inheritance structure should be an abstract model of the target concept
9. A set of reusable classes should make maximum use of inheritance to model relationships of the problem domain
10. Limit the number of methods that must understand the data representation of the class

Quality control can also be addressed by the use of the Law of Demeter (Lieberherr *et al.*, 1988), which states that "the methods [i.e., services] of a class should not depend in any way on the structure of any class, except the immediate (top-level) structures of their own class. Furthermore, each method should send messages to objects belonging to a very limited set of classes only" (Sakkinen, 1988).

Much of this concern, expressed in the guidelines (Table 7.5), is addressed directly by the rapidly developing area of object-oriented metrics. Software metrics or software measures (Chapter 10) attempt to quantify either (i) the software product or (ii) the software process. Product metrics are typically code-oriented, measuring parameters such as module size or the complexity of the intramodule logical structure. Process metrics typically attempt to relate estimates of the product metrics, made relatively early in the lifecycle, to overall effort required in order to produce costing estimates (e.g., Verner and Tate, 1992).

The application of metrics to object-oriented systems is very much in its infancy (see Chapter 10), and it is probably this activity, most of all in MOSES, that will evolve as new ideas are found and testing in this new area of object-oriented metrics is undertaken. Current MOSES metrics are thus tentative. They can be divided into three areas: intraclass metrics (size and logical complexity), interclass (or systems) metrics (coupling), and cognitive metrics (e.g., based on the cognitive complexity model (CCM) of Cant *et al.*, 1992).

Intraclass metrics
Lines of code (LOC) is probably the most widely used intraclass metric for size. However, the size of an object-oriented code module benefits from reuse as well as newly written LOC (Jacobson *et al.*, 1992, p460) so that any LOC-type measure for classes must take this into account. On the basis of initial work by Thomas and Jacobson (1989), Henderson-Sellers (1991a) suggests using a first-estimate size metric, s, for classes of:

$$s = (AW_A + MW_M) \tag{7.1}$$

where the class has A attributes and M operations. The values of the weighting coefficients W_A and W_M have yet to be determined empirically but are likely to be in the range of $W_A \sim 1$ and $W_M \sim 5\text{--}20$. Another version of this, proposed by Chidamber and Kemerer (1991), is the simpler weighted methods/operations per class (for further details see Chapter 10). Other code metrics worth collecting (Lorenz, 1993) are average method/operation size and average number of methods/operations per class, although there is yet no definitive work on whether or how these numbers can be related to concepts such as understandability, maintenance and cost estimation.

Logic structure metrics focus on variants of the McCabe (1976) cyclomatic complexity. Since this measures complexity associated with a DAG (directed acyclic graph) drawn to visualize control flow structures, it is more clearly applicable to control-independent chunks within the class. For some classes this would entail the metric's being applied to each individual service; for others containing both public and private services a more extensive control structure may be realized. Overly complex services can thus be readily identified. No empirical relationship between this measure and, say, effort has yet been attempted in an object-oriented environment.

Interclass metrics
Details of intermodule metrics are to be found in Section 10.3. The application of cyclomatic complexity to object-oriented *systems* to describe class–class

connections is not a simple adaptation of McCabe and Butler's (1989) structured system metric, since this requires a DAG to be drawn to represent the system. In an object-oriented system, connections (cf. Figure 7.23) no longer represent flow of control (except when developing Jacobson et al.'s (1992) "use cases," called scenarios here).

System-level (interclass) coupling can, however, be measured simply by the mean fan-out number (Henry and Kafura, 1981; Card and Glass, 1990), which gives the average system fan-out, $\overline{S_C}$, as:

$$\overline{S_C} = \frac{\sum^n (\text{fan-out})^2}{n} \quad (7.2)$$

Fan-out measures the amount of dependence on other classes—a measure of subcontracting. High fan-out indicates a high degree of interclass dependency and is thus to be avoided. On the other hand, high fan-in values show the extent of reuse and are thus good. This contrasts with a traditional environment where fan-in and fan-out contribute equally and large values in both are regarded as indicating poor design.

Note that Card and Glass's metric, $\overline{S_C}$, can be applied in design (Figure 7.23), whereas Henry and Kafura's family of metrics (see Chapter 10) require code size and are thus restricted to code-level applications (viz., implementation and maintenance). Again, empirical evaluation of these metrics in an object-oriented environment has not yet been undertaken.

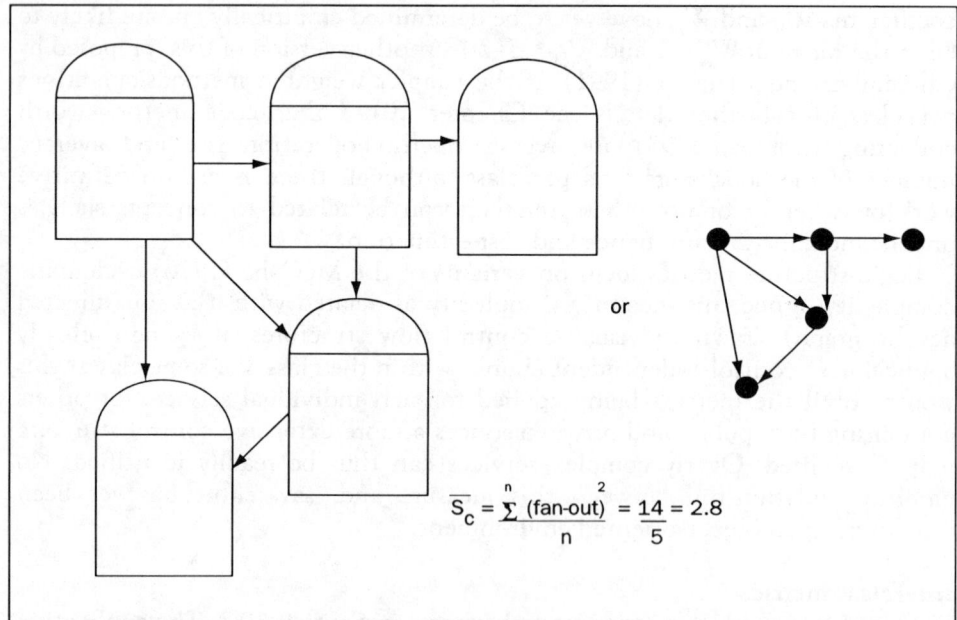

Figure 7.23 *Complexity represented by either fan-in/fan-out or a directed graph*

An important interclass metric is the depth of the inheritance hierarchies. Guidelines for acceptable maximum depths are often given as around 7—perhaps influenced by the "Miller limit" (Miller, 1956). As well as maximum depth and average depth of inheritance hierarchies, reuse and specialization ratios may be useful. The reuse ratio is the ratio of the number of superclasses to the total number of classes and is a measure of the reuse by the developers of hierarchies. The specialization ratio is the number of subclasses to the number of superclasses and characterizes the extent to which the superclass represents a useful abstract data type (Yap and Henderson-Sellers, 1993a). However, new metrics for inheritance are still required, especially to discriminate between specification and implementation inheritance. External semantic cohesion, vital for OT, remains a subjective assessment (Section 10.3.2), although internal cohesion can be addressed in part by considering the overlapping of methods/accessed data structures within the class (Chidamber and Kemerer, 1991—see Chapter 10).

Cognitive complexity model metrics

The cognitive complexity model of Cant *et al.* (1992) has been applied by Cant *et al.* (1994) to an object-oriented environment in which a pilot empirical evaluation of part of the model was undertaken. Although the initial findings are promising, further development, object-oriented application, and empirical evaluation are needed before the metric can be recommended for application in commercial projects.

Output

Information produced during Activity: Quality Evaluation (Metrics) is as follows:

Deliverable Impacted	Information Generated and Recorded
Size values	Sizes on a per class basis
	Average module size per system/subsystem
Complexity	Cyclomatic complexity per class operation
System complexity	Fan-in/fan-out values of each class (unnecessarily high values highlighted)
	Average fan-out per system
Inheritance complexity	Depths of hierarchies (with numbers of overridden features indicated)

7.14 Activity: Scenario Development

The purpose of scenarios is to describe in natural language an interaction sequence with a system from which O/Cs, events, and interactions can be identified. Scenarios also lead to a formalization of user requirements.

The process of developing scenarios is essentially one of interviewing the business user to identify possible interactions. Initially, scenarios should be developed for a "typical" interaction and only later extended to cover abnormal or error conditions. Each scenario should be significantly different; minor differences may be recorded within the same scenario.

The first activity is to identify the actors in the system. These may be human users or other systems that are external to the system and need to exchange information with the system being developed. Actors help delineate the boundary of the system.

Actors can be recorded in a simple glossary format as follows:

Name: Name of the actor
Description: Purpose and function of the actor
Scenarios: Names of the scenarios performed by the actor
Contact: Person to contact for further information on the actor

A starting point for finding actors is to ask, "Who are the people that this system is supposed to help?" Finding human actors is often relatively simple. It is, however, relatively more difficult to identify machines or other systems. Identifying actors leads to a model of the external influences on the system and hence the boundary of the system to be developed.

Once actors have been identified, scenarios can be described for each actor. Scenarios are specific ways of using a system. They represent a complete sequence of events that can occur in the application as part of the functionality of the system. A complete collection of scenarios specifies all the ways in which the system can be used. Scenarios should be recorded as a simple narrative.

Actors perform scenarios. Hence by examining each role of each actor in turn and identifying ways in which each actor interacts with the system (the different scenarios that the actor performs) it is possible to define the complete functionality of the system. Scenarios can be identified from the requirements specification by reading the specification from a user's perspective. Jacobson et al. (1992) list the following questions as an aid in the identification of scenarios:

- What are the main tasks of each user?
- Will the user have to read/write/change any of the system information?
- Will the user have to inform the system about outside changes?
- Does the user wish to be informed about unexpected changes?

Several scenarios may be very similar in their description, varying only in some small way, while others may describe completely different functionality and be very different. Whether a scenario is a variant of an existing scenario or a different scenario can be hard to decide. Essentially, a "basic course" and "alternative courses" should be identified. A basic course is that scenario that best describes the normal course of operation and gives the best understanding of the user's requirements. Variants or error conditions are alternatives of this basic course.

The MOSES Lifecycle Activities

Detailing scenarios and identifying alternative courses will lead to unclear points in the User Requirements Specification being uncovered. These points will need to be clarified with the business user. Scenario development can occur in separate functional areas at the same time, possibly leading to parallel development. Parallel development requires sound project management plans.

Jacobson *et al.* (1992) discuss how scenarios may be structured using an "extend" mechanism. This mechanism indicates how one scenario may be inserted into another, thus extending the original scenario. Each scenario should be independent of the others and should be able to be developed without recourse to another scenario. The extend mechanism can be used:

- to model optional parts of a scenario;
- to model complex and alternative courses that seldom occur;
- to model the fact that several different scenarios can be inserted into a special scenario.

The extending scenario describes where in the original scenario it is to be inserted by specifying a location in the original. When a new scenario is inserted, the original scenario runs as normal until the new scenario location is reached. At this point the new scenario starts and runs to completion. On completion the original scenario runs as if there had been no interruption.

Refining a scenario model is done to maximize reuse and reduce redundancy. The main activity is identifying similar parts of a scenario and extracting them from the scenarios in which they occur. The objective is to describe a scenario or part of a scenario only once. This refinement process is essentially only of interest to the developers of a system and may be regarded as an reengineering function of the requirements model. A further refinement activity that may occur is specifying the scenarios from an internal perspective, that is, as a logical description of the business function. Essentially, this activity is a refinement of the user requirements specification document on the basis of the scenario.

An example of a scenario is shown in Figure 7.24. In this scenario, the user has entered the "Create Model" command, resulting in the display of a window. The user then enters data into fields that are validated and stored, resulting in a model being created in the modelbase. Such a scenario is a typical interaction for this functionality.

Scenarios are a useful mechanism for identifying operations (Section 7.15.1) (Rumbaugh *et al.*, 1991; Jacobson *et al.*, 1992). They show a trace of events and the response by the supplier. These traces should show the interactions involved in fulfilling the responsibilities of the subsystem, leading to a detailed examination of how the system behaves. This activity will lead to a more detailed understanding of the system and its requirements.

Scenarios are thus useful for identifying operations and can be developed for different subsystem responsibilities (Rumbaugh *et al.*, 1991; Jacobson *et al.*, 1992). They should be developed for different situations that the system is to

> User enters "Create Model" menu item
> Entry window for the class is displayed
> User enters data into entry fields that are validated as they are entered
> After final field is entered and validated the screen disappears and an object is created in modelbase with the appropriate parameters

Figure 7.24 *Scenario for Create Model command*

handle, concentrating on those "typical" for the system. Such scenarios are useful in identifying external events and how they are handled by the system.

Output
Information generated during this activity is as follows:

Deliverable Impacted	Information Generated and Recorded
Scenario model	Scenarios
	Actor Glossary

7.15 Activity: Service Identification

The purpose of this activity is to develop an understanding of object behavior (i.e., functionality) by specifying the services applicable to an O/C. Services are specified at the class level, although they actually act on individual objects. The exception to this is creation operations, which act at the class level and create new objects of the appropriate class. Services may be either operations, which describe a resulting action, or properties, which describe the current state of an object. Services are simply procedures or functions as found in normal procedural design, although the terminology is OOPL-dependent. One common term is "method"; others include features and member functions.

7.15.1 Subactivity: Operations

Operations describe the response of an object to a command. They can be identified from scenarios and are loosely connected with the verbs of the requirements specification. In a detailed requirements document, this approach may be able to provide a number of operations, although it may result in too many operations. Such an approach is useful for an initial foray into the requirements document.

Initial operations may also be derived from the general subsystems' responsibilities (Section 7.17). These do not have to be implemented by a single class; they can be divided up between a number of classes if necessary. It is important to try to take on the role of a class and continually ask oneself, "Can I suffer this operation?" This anthropomorphic view allows the designer to visualize what does and does not belong to a particular class of objects (Wirfs-Brock *et al.*, 1990).

Operations may also be found by examining other classes and seeing what operations they may need to request. If, for example, a class A requires class B to be in some state before it can execute an operation, there should be some way for that class A to operate on class B to change its state. In other words, class B should provide that operation in its interface. Operations may therefore affect the state of other objects by sending them messages as part of the operation (see below).

In identifying relationships and services, some comments are needed. "Services offered" are the descriptors of the functionality *offered* by an O/C, *not* the actions undertaken by the O/C. It is quite easy to place services (incorrectly) in the client rather than the server. A simple example will help to illustrate what we find to be a common mistake[24] in OOA/D (Figure 7.25). A TELLER wishes to deposit an amount of money into an ACCOUNT. Where should the deposit operation be placed? We have noted, along with Drake *et al.* (1992b), that there can be a temptation to draw it as in Figure 7.25(a) on the grounds that it is the teller who is doing the depositing. However, *deposit* is an intrinsic part of the specification of what an ACCOUNT is and can do. The correct location for the *deposit* operation is in fact in ACCOUNT (Figure 7.25(b)). Further confirmation can be seen in the corresponding code: the TELLER object sends the message *account1.deposit(amount)*. It is useful to differentiate between services offered and collaborations required—in the sense of CRC cards (see, e.g., Wirfs-Brock *et al.*, 1990). An object of class ACCOUNT therefore offers the service of *deposit*. Objects of a TELLER class may utilize this service. However, TELLER has need of collaboration from the ACCOUNT class in order to do this and the ACCOUNT class has a responsibility to provide the *deposit* service. In other words, responsibilities from a CRC card translate into services offered and appear in the interface, while collaborations *do not* appear in any interface, but rather are indicated by relationships (Figure 7.25(b)).

During the Activity: Generalization for Reuse (Section 7.4) further operations are likely to be identified that are required to complete the behavior of the abstraction without allowing a client to break that abstraction.

Objectcharts (Section 7.10) may also provide other operations. By analyzing the events that may occur on a class, and by taking a class-centered view of the event, the designer can determine what operation is required in response to the event and what parameters the operation may require. Parameters may appear as conditions on the state transition diagram (objectchart).

---

24. A mistake we note, from our experience, in teaching OOA/D and one also stressed by Drake *et al.* (1992b).

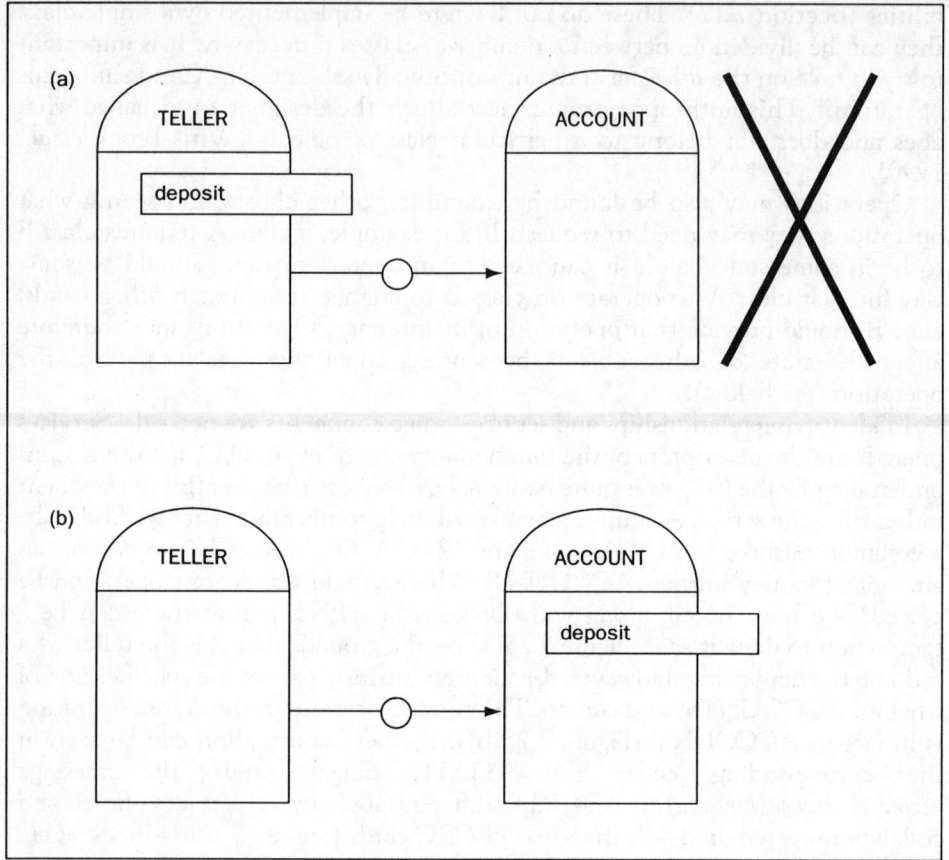

Figure 7.25 *Location of individual services can be difficult. They should be identified with the O/C to which they have the closest affinity on the basis of a semantic analysis.*

7.15.2 Subactivity: Properties

Properties are services that return information about the object. That information may be a value such as an INTEGER, REAL, or CHARACTER or it may be an object such as ENGINE or WING. Properties that return values tend to be the easiest to find in the requirements document, e.g., representing data on entry forms or possibly in tables. This information can be thought of as services provided by the O/C, which represent the information that needs to be known about an O/C in the system. Properties do not imply a particular physically stored data structure; decisions on data storage may be deferred right up to the Implementation Phase if necessary.

Properties are often directly associated with an O/C in the requirements document. For example, "the volume of the tank is to be recorded every ten minutes" shows that "volume" is a property of tank. If no information is associated with "volume" other than a value of a basic property, then "volume" can be placed as a property of TANK, with a type REAL. Some properties may at first appear to be O/Cs with a relationship to other O/Cs, but later be turned into properties of an O/C. This is a perfectly valid part of the Specification Phase. For example, an O/C ACTIVATED_SLUDGE may have a relationship to an O/C TANK that has a property *volume* of type REAL. If the tank has no other properties or operations and no other O/C is related to it, the property *volume* may be moved to the O/C ACTIVATED_SLUDGE and the O/C TANK dispensed with.

Placing of properties and reevaluation of properties are part of the refinement process of OO development. Refining the O/Cs of the object-oriented model is an iterative process, although the model should begin to stabilize after a small number of iterations. Many of the candidate O/Cs will model the same concept, but will have different names or slightly varying properties. For example, in an air traffic control system the candidate O/Cs may include AIRCRAFT and AIRPLANE. If these O/Cs have the same properties, they may in fact be synonyms for the same concept and should be amalgamated. Similarities in their properties (and operations) provide the most effective means of identifying such synonyms.

Therefore, as O/Cs become evident, the object modeler will label them with obvious properties and operations. These two activities can occur in either order—or more likely concurrently across the subsystem. This is the beginning of the Class Specification (CS), which will be slowly "fleshed out," finally to form a complete description of the class interface.

Output
Output for this activity is as follows:

Deliverable Impacted	Information Generated and Recorded
Class Specification	Property
	Operation
O/C Model	Property
	Operation

7.16 Activity: Subsystem Coordination

Subsystem coordination is essentially a project management task and involves the coordination of teams of developers who are working on separate subsystems. The objective of this activity is to ensure that redundancy is not occurring in the development effort by virtue of the fact that different teams are developing similar abstractions in isolation. The task should identify such potential redundancy and allocate responsibility for a class to one team. Inter-team collaboration may be facilitated by a linchpin person (see Section 9.1.1).

Other teams that require services from this class will therefore subcontract the work to the team responsible for that class.

In essence, the task is concerned with managing a global O/C Model for the application by coordinating at certain points the O/C Model of each subsystem. Team responsibility for a class is an important concept and one that should be encouraged.

The output of this activity is a list of "duplicate" classes and the teams to be responsible for them.

7.17 Activity: Subsystem Identification

The objective of this activity is to identify a number of subsystems that can be used to manage complexity in large projects.

The initial use of a top-down approach is an important "divide and conquer" technique that has been discussed in an OO context by de Champeaux (1991), who introduces "ensembles." Typically, this would be a task undertaken by the project manager or software architect responsible for the overall direction of the software development (Meyer, 1992c). Subsystems abstract out the major characteristics, or responsibilities, of a group of related classes so as to hide detail, yet retain a coherent overall view of the system design. For example, a decision support system would require modelbase, database, user interface, and systems manager subsystems (Guariso and Werthner, 1989).

The division of a system into large-scale subsystems should be done on the basis of high-level responsibilities (Wirfs-Brock et al., 1990) or overall services. Responsibilities are an informal specification of the tasks of a particular subsystem. Identification of responsibilities can be top-down, decomposing the requirements document or other, higher-level responsibilities in a manner similar to that for functional decomposition. Responsibilities can also be identified later by bottom-up analysis by forming an abstraction of the services of a set of collaborating classes to form a subsystem.

As these subsystems are identified their responsibilities can be defined on SRS cards (Figure 5.38). It is certainly possible that a subsystem will be identified before all the system requirements have been defined. If a particular subsystem is clearly delineated from the others and well understood, it may move into the first iteration of the Specification Phase before other subsystems have even been clearly identified or specified.

Top-down identification of responsibilities involves the project manager or analyst decomposing the requirements/responsibilities into groups that act upon similar abstractions, or are recognizable as a coherent subsystem of the problem. For example, high-level requirements may include the ability to browse models and data, manage models and data, and print data files and documentation relating to models. These requirements should be decomposed around the abstractions they act upon, resulting in two sets of services: one to manage models involving printing, editing, creating, and browsing models, and one to manage data involving printing, editing, creating, and browsing data (Figure 7.26(a)). In contrast, functional decomposition would have been to group the services around similar functionality.

Bottom-up identification of subsystem services involves abstracting the overall objectives of a group of collaborating O/Cs. This approach is useful in managing the complexity of a large system. Using the same example, we may have O/Cs for the database and modelbase subsystems that provide services to edit, print, create, and browse. These services can be abstracted as a subsystem responsible for managing data and models respectively (Figure 7.26(b)).

In MOSES, subsystems are not conceptual entities in the same way as classes, but act as a grouping mechanism. They are used primarily as a means of managing complexity. Subsystem identification can occur at any stage of the Specification Phase. Once again, this is not a one-off process but may involve a number of iterations as user requirements are specified in more detail. Subsystems are not formally part of the object model and they are not supported by any major OOPLs, although similar concepts may be managed by the software environment.[25] It should be noted that a number of other methodologies have also found the need to include a unit of decomposition greater than that of a class (e.g., Wirfs-Brock *et al.*, 1990; Booch, 1991; Rumbaugh *et al.*, 1991; de Champeaux, 1991; Coad and Yourdon, 1991a; Nerson, 1992a; Firesmith, 1993).

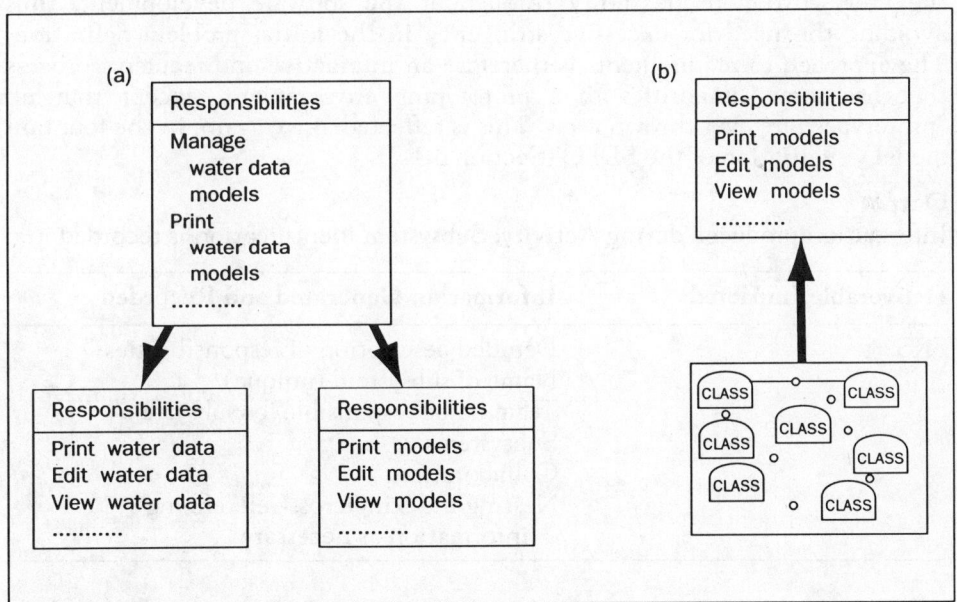

Figure 7.26 *Using a subsystem as a means of decomposition and a means of abstraction: (a) decomposing subsystems to classes and other subsystems; (b) abstraction of subsystems from classes and other subsystems*

---

25. For example, Rational's CASE tool, ROSE™, supports categories and subsystems.

When a subsystem is simply an abstraction or decomposition mechanism, it has very little effect upon the architecture, although it may be used as a unit of work to which people and resources may be allocated. Communication can occur between any subsystems, although, in general, intersubsystem communication should be minimized as much as possible. This can be measured by the number of boundary relationships between subsystems that act as a measure of subsystem coupling.

However, subsystems can also be used to represent virtual machines. This has implications for the architecture and for intersubsystem communication. Essentially, a virtual machine implies that the subsystem can interact only with lower-level virtual machines. This use of subsystems is a significantly "stronger" design decision than for normal subsystems (Seidewitz and Stark, 1987; Rumbaugh et al., 1991).

This activity leads from the evolution of an informal problem statement derived during the earliest phases of the development process to a more detailed requirements specification over time (Booch, 1991; Coad and Yourdon, 1991a). At each stage the developer should ensure that the requirements are met by at least one set of services. Similarly, new services should be recorded in the restatement of requirements.

The lifecycle approach and the methodology to be employed ensure that changes, especially the provision of additional functionality, can be offered to the user with more flexibility throughout the software development, thus avoiding the need for excessive stringency in the initial problem definition. The approach to requirements is therefore an interactive and recursive process that has some similarities to a prototyping environment, except that no "prototypes" are ever thrown away. This is reflected, once again, in the fountain model visualization of the SDLC (Section 3.1.2).

Output
Information produced during Activity: Subsystem Identification is recorded in:

Deliverable Impacted	Information Generated and Recorded
SRS	Detailed description of responsibilities
	Name of subsystem (unique)
	Team name responsible for subsystem
	Subsystems
	Collaborations
	Nesting/indexing/cross-referencing information as necessary

7.18 Activity: Testing

Designs must undergo testing (verification and validation). However, testing and quality assessment (Section 7.13) must be distributed across the whole lifecycle with short cycle times between tests (Adams, 1992b).

In software engineering, the term "verification" is summarized by the question "Is the system being built correctly?"; whereas validation relates to the question "Is the correct system being built?" Complete object-oriented testing methodologies are currently under development (Perry and Kaiser, 1990; Harrold and McGregor, 1992; Smith and Robson, 1992; Turner and Robson, 1992). Testing can be either specification-based (or "blackbox") or program-based (or "whitebox"). In the former the behavioral specification is tested, in the latter the implementation of each class. Berard (1992b, p292) also differentiates between static testing and dynamic testing. In static testing, the software is evaluated without executing on a processor, whereas dynamic testing involves actual execution of the code.

It also needs to be remembered (Berard, 1992b, p306) that without a "control" set of results to provide a baseline against which test results are to be compared, any testing program is virtually useless. A list of test cases, and their expected outcomes, needs to be prepared. Scenarios form a useful basis for blackbox testing of components.

Smith and Robson (1992) note that since object systems have no explicit threads of control, traditional testing techniques, which attempt to examine all routes through the system, are not directly applicable. Nevertheless, the ideas of "walkthroughs"—in which the author explains their analysis/design/code to peers under the control of an impartial moderator who schedules and runs the meeting—are still valuable. Only a small number of people should be involved in such inspections.

7.18.1 Integration testing

System-level integration testing takes classes that are internally checked, both semantically and syntactically, and evaluates their "correctness" when part of the whole system. Essentially, integration testing involves seeing whether the classes have been developed in a coordinated manner to fulfill the systems requirements. Scenarios by their nature involve many classes and hence form the basis of the integration testing procedure. The success of a scenario is indicated by the ability of the class model to support the required functionality and fulfill the contracts of the classes. Jacobson *et al.* (1992) use a decision table to record the success of testing scenarios.

Integration testing is generally less traumatic than a system test in a structured system. Integration/system testing is the final validation of the system before delivery. System testing is really an external test of the system and should be performed by a separate testing team. The role of this team is to assess the functionality of the system with regard to the URS and scenarios. The results of the test should be fed back to the developers for correction before further (unit) integration and finally system testing is undertaken. System testing is therefore no different from traditional methodologies except that it can be based on the scenarios of the Investigation Phase.

7.18.2 Subsystem testing

Subsystem-level testing focuses on the interactions of groups of collaborating classes (Smith and Robson, 1992). Scenarios form the basis of the testing strategy at this stage. Jacobson et al. (1992) discuss the testing process using scenarios in some detail. Essentially, it involves "driving" a scenario through the O/C Model in a similar way to that for walkthroughs. The results of the execution are recorded in a testing table. Basic and alternative courses should all be tested.

7.18.3 Unit testing

The smallest unit of testing for OO systems is the class rather than the individual service (Turner and Robson, 1992). These authors recommend the testing of classes with zero fan-out first, then recursively testing the O/Cs that use their services. This testing approach comes close to merging unit testing with integration testing (Section 7.18.1). Although strictly it is the objects that are tested, not the classes, more important is the effect of the ability of an O/C to retain state information between accesses. Repeatability in testing is thus less guaranteed than in a traditional testing program. Therefore, Turner and Robson (1992) advocate a "state-based testing" strategy, which they acknowledge is still under development (at the time of writing).

Validation of new classes and revalidation of modified classes are considered explicitly in the developing testing methodology of Harrold and McGregor (1992). They aim to minimize testing based on the inheritance hierarchy and the existence of well-tested classes in the higher levels of the hierarchy, although Perry and Kaiser (1990) warn that reliance on the "well-testedness" of superclasses does not necessarily obviate the need for retesting of the same services in derived subclasses. Lorenz (1993) notes the need to test superclasses before subclasses.

Operations must be tested individually and also with respect to their interactions with (i) other services within the same class and (ii) other classes (McGregor and Sykes, 1992, p207). Unit testing is usually performed by the developers themselves. It involves developing a test bed for the class that sets up a simulated environment around the class to be tested (Jacobson et al., 1992). The class is then sent messages and the results are analyzed according to a set of expected criteria. Specification, or blackbox testing, can be recorded in a matrix where messages, the state of the object, and the expected response are recorded. Objectcharts provide a useful means of constructing these matrices, as each state will be associated with messages to which it can respond in that state. These messages and states can be displayed in the testing matrix. The expected result of the message is based on the contract for the service that is called as a result of receiving the message. As the contract is declarative, it integrates well with the specification testing employed here.

Unit testing strategies for OO remain immature at this stage, although many of the traditional testing procedures can readily be applied.

Output
Information produced during Activity: Testing is as follows:

Deliverable Impacted	Information Generated and Recorded
Testing Specification	
Test results	Comparison of trial results with testing specification
	Whitebox/blackbox testing results

7.19 Activity: Translation to the OOPL

7.19.1 Subactivity: Implementation of services

During the Implementation Phase, actual code is written for each service. At this stage, the design of algorithms is paramount. Implementations can be recorded in the PL, as a mini-structure chart, pseudocode, or structured English. We do not intend to discuss the details of translating to an implementation, as these are well covered elsewhere (e.g., Meyer, 1988a, 1992a; Lippman, 1989; Winder, 1991). Suffice it to say that detailed implementation decisions can be left until relatively late in the development process. This is particularly true if the design by contract idea has been adhered to throughout the development, since the operation specification will be in a declarative format that can be implemented in a number of procedural ways.

7.19.2 Subactivity: Implementation of structure

When this activity occurs during the development of the software model, a number of decisions need to be made with regard to the final implementation. Associations may be implemented using pointers or references, or classes. The need for two-way relationships will be determined by the application requirements. In most cases, bidirectionality will not be required and the more efficient unidirectional client–server relationship can be implemented as a pointer (Rumbaugh *et al.*, 1991). In some cases, however, this translation process may require bidirectionality to remain. Therefore, the association may be implemented either using an O/C, or by two pointers whose relationships are managed within the two O/Cs. These decisions depend on trade-offs in efficiency, reusability, and the need for a smooth transition between phases. Services of an O/C, say B, can be used in a unidirectional manner by an O/C, say A, by declaring an instance of class B within the body of class A. Associations and aggregations using a "many" relationship cardinality require the use of container O/Cs.

O/C interactions at all phases should be minimized (McGregor and Sykes, 1992) reflecting the principle of loose coupling. Loose and explicit coupling of classes are important for reusability and are quantified using OO metrics

(Henderson-Sellers, 1991a; Chidamber and Kemerer, 1991). Once again, it is not our intention to discuss the detailed implementation techniques of a particular OOPL, as these are well covered in other texts, as noted earlier.

Output
The output from this activity is as follows:

Deliverable Impacted	Information Generated and Recorded
Source code	OOPL statements to implement design

7.20 Activity: User Requirements Elicitation

The purpose of this activity is to develop and refine a formal and stable user requirements specification. The *systems requirements documents* are prepared in the language of the user, as normal, and include timing details, hardware usage, cost constraints as well as problem specification and functional user requirements.

The process of user requirements elicitation involves interviews, scenarios, and possibly prototyping effort. Graham (1991, Section 8.2.2) gives useful guidelines on conducting interviews in an object-oriented development environment. He advocates the use of a trained interviewer, if possible two: one to talk and listen and one to take notes. If feasible, interviews should be taped for later analysis. Interviewers should be trained both in interview techniques and in object technology (Graham, 1991, p299). Interviews should be arranged with the end users regarding business requirements. However, it is important to note that the user/customer is not interested in the use/nonuse of object technology in providing them with their demanded quality product. The final product will be independent of its method of production. Quality and maintainability will be the only manifestations of OT that the end user will ever perceive. The commitment of top executives is particularly needed for the successful adoption of new technologies—and object technology (OT) is no exception. Hence interviews with senior management may also be useful.

After initial interviews with business users, the user requirements can be refined and formalized through the use of scenarios. Scenarios may form the basis of a prototyping effort that results in a clearer understanding of the requirements. This iteration and refinement of the user requirements can occur independently of the object-oriented model being constructed, although it is more likely that Event Models (Section 7.3) and object-oriented diagrams are being developed simultaneously.

In summary, user requirements elicitation involves initial interviews with business users, followed by the development of scenarios that should be validated either by a prototyping effort or by walking through the scenarios with the users.

The MOSES Lifecycle Activities 357

Output
Information produced during Activity: User Requirements Elicitation is as follows:

Deliverable Impacted	Information Generated and Recorded
Requirements Specification	Identification of required responsibilities and real-world constraints
	Full specification of problem
	Sufficiently detailed documentation to form a contractual specification for the software analyst(s)

7.21 Summary

This chapter has defined a number of activities that need to occur during the MOSES development process. For each activity, a series of techniques has been discussed or referenced. It is not possible within one text to encapsulate all the guidelines, ideas, and techniques that go to make OOA/D. Therefore, this chapter should be viewed as a repository of approaches that can grow over time. This repository is, however, a structured repository in the sense that the techniques are discussed within a framework of 20 activities. It should be possible that the techniques for each activity will grow, and indeed this should be encouraged. Hence, the activities described here provide "hooks" around which to hang new ideas and other techniques. As such, this chapter provides a checklist of activities and techniques rather than a mandatory and comprehensive set of steps for OOA/D.

7.22 Study examples

Exercise 4 On the next iteration, consider more user requests to enhance the O/C Model done for Exercise 3 (perhaps supplemented by a sneak look at our answers to Exercise 3 in the back). Consider (and incorporate) the following additional detail:

1. Each movement has a tempo marking, possibly indicated by a metronome marking.
2. Add phrases, tied notes, and dynamics.

Create two O/C diagrams, to represent:

(a) associations
(b) aggregations

Exercise 5 We can now use layering concepts and subsystems to revise our music printing system in Exercise 4. For this system, start by drawing a layer-1 O/C Model. Identify which classes need expanding to layer-2 and draw these more detailed diagrams. Continue to "zoom in" on these classes until you get to the "bottom layer" where library classes become evident.

Complement these stacked O/C diagrams by inheritance hierarchy diagrams and, if possible, by class specifications (CSs) and/or contracts.

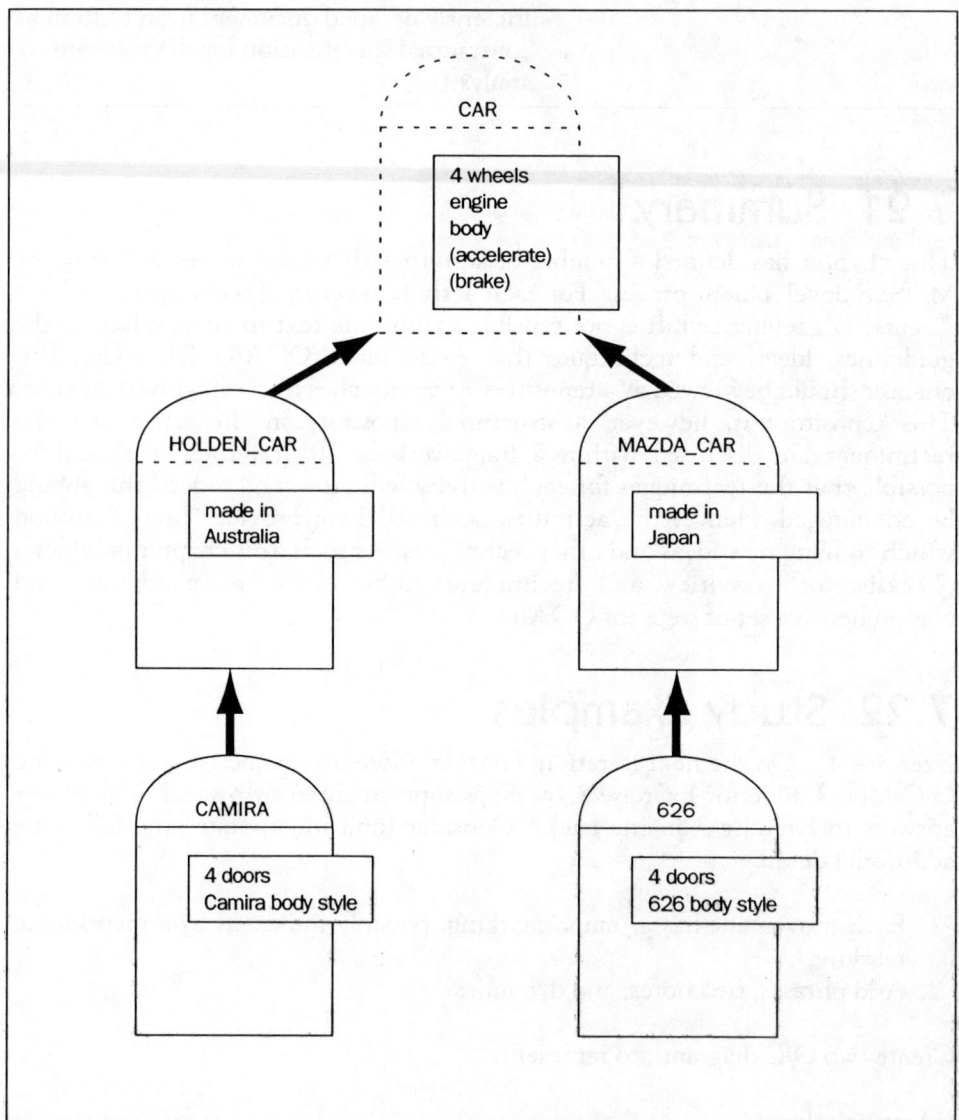

Figure 7.27 *Inheritance hierarchy of a subset of the car problem*

The MOSES Lifecycle Activities

Exercise 6 Consider the problem statement of Exercise 3 (at the end of Chapter 6) and its solution as an O/C Model derived in that exercise. Construct an appropriate *Implementation Phase diagram* that will also include the following information:

(a) A note may be a semibreve, a minim, a crotchet, or a quaver.
(b) A piece may be played by a soloist or by an orchestra.

Also consider separate inheritance diagram(s) that would complement the client–server diagrams corresponding to the O/C Model derived in Exercise 3. Are the identified inheritance relationships for specification or for implementation?

Exercise 7 As a little digression from music, this exercise considers buying a new car—well, not actually buying, more modeling a small number of makes and models to illustrate some object-oriented concepts discussed in this chapter.

In our simplified global market for cars there are but two manufacturers: in Australia there is Holden and in Japan there is Mazda. Holden's first model is a sedan/wagon known as the Camira, very standard in all its features. Mazda makes a competitor, the 626. Different stylistically, it has the same basic function and mechanical features.

Mazda now introduces a revolutionary new engine. This rotary engine, used in the RX7, makes for a very different type of car. How does this sports car fit into the class hierarchy shown in Figure 7.27?

• CHAPTER 8 •

A Case Study Using MOSES

Chapters 4–7 have presented a methodology for object-oriented software development, named MOSES. This methodology builds on a number of other approaches and extends their capabilities. It has been applied to a number of projects of varying size both in commercial and academic contexts. This chapter aims to provide an example of how MOSES is applied to real system development projects by discussing a particular case study in more depth. As always in situations where one is trying to describe the events of a project in a case study, the text cannot capture the development process in detail. Instead, our aim is to provide the flavor of development using MOSES and, in so doing, to discuss some further details of the approach.

8.1 Evaluating MOSES for completeness

Before moving to the case study we provide an evaluation of MOSES based on a framework for assessing OO methodologies developed by Walker (1992). The framework is essentially a matrix of desired or required criteria for object-oriented methodologies. This approach to evaluating methodologies has been taken in the OO literature and in the wider methodology literature, e.g., Olle *et al.* (1982) and Sutcliffe (1991). Such a comparison cannot easily evaluate the practical aspects of the methodology, nor is it able to evaluate the quality of the products of the process. It is, however, able to provide a comparison of the *potential* strengths and weaknesses of the methodology as compared with other OO methodologies and to provide some indication of the completeness of the methodology. MOSES is therefore assessed within this framework, with its strengths and weaknesses highlighted.

Walker recognizes two dimensions in the assessment of an object-oriented method. The first dimension relates to the support for the object model throughout design and implementation, while the second dimension relates to mechanisms for increasing the effectiveness of the method (e.g., notation, heuristics, and pragmatics). Table 8.1 presents an evaluation of MOSES alongside a number of other OO methodologies as they were evaluated by Walker.

The general conclusion from this comparison is that MOSES does provide all the necessary components of an OO analysis and design methodology, although its support for the later stages of the lifecycle is not quite so comprehensive. The emphasis on the earlier stages of the lifecycle is a clear reflection of the objective of the methodology in providing solid MIS, rather than coding, support. A second conclusion is that MOSES is somewhat stronger in the management dimension, that is, in the definition of metrics and management checkpoints, than are a number of other leading approaches.

8.2 Case study: Decision support system for wastewater management

In this section a partial solution to a wastewater resources problem is presented using MOSES. The problem described is adapted from a real development project in the Australian water industry. The result of the project was a design for a decision support system called ECWAT: an EConomic decision-aid for WATer managers.

The general problem statement is to provide wastewater managers with information on the costs of wastewater treatment facilities within a flexible, interactive decision-aid environment. This requirement has grown out of important changes to the business environment within which water agencies operate. In particular, water agencies are being required to be more focused on the economic and environmental costs of providing services. The result has been a dramatic change in the information requirements of water managers. Essentially, these new requirements center on establishing linkages between demand, costs, environmental impact, and pricing mechanisms in order to provide managers with information about operation and maintenance costs of wastewater treatment facilities. Thus the primary goal of the project was to develop a decision support system (DSS) to support operations managers of wastewater treatment plants in running those plants in a more cost-effective manner.

Table 8.1 Criteria for an OO method (Modified from Walker, 1992)

	Booch	OMT*	OOSD†	MOSES
Abstraction				
Support for aggregation	Y	Y	N	Y
Support for generalization‡	NE	Y	N	Y
Support for implementation inheritance	Y	N	Y	Y
Support for functional abstraction	Y	Y	Y	Y
Methods for identifying state, services and interfaces, and encapsulation	Y	Y	P	Y
Support for abstracting commonality into abstract superclasses or mixins	Y	Y	N	Y
Notation				
Notation for aggregation	Y	Y	Y	Y
Notation for generalization	N	Y	N	Y
Notation for inheritance	Y	Y	Y	Y
Notation for "uses" relations	Y	Y	Y	Y
Notation for message sending within aggregation	Y	P	Y	Y
Notation for message sending within inheritance	Y	P	P	P
Notation for message sending between autonomous objects	Y	P	Y	P
Support for constraints representation	N	Y	N	Y
Validity of Design				
Explicit transformation rules between alternative representation	Y	Y	Y	Y
Clear set of design metrics	P	P	P	Y
Support for test generation	N	N	N	N
Reuse				
Heuristics for identifying parent classes from which to subclass (for reuse)	P	P	AFM	Y
Heuristics for identifying classes within a class library‡ (with reuse)	P	P	N	Y

Y = Yes; N = No; AFM = Automated Formal Method; NE = Not Explicit; P = Partial
* OMT = Object Modeling Technique, Rumbaugh et al. (1991)
† OOSD = Object-Oriented Structured Design, Wasserman et al. (1989)
‡ Criteria added to Walker's originals

In developing a solution to this problem the theoretical approach to the treatment plant models and the approach to constructing the DSS needed to be addressed. A number of engineering production process functions were used as the basis of the treatment plant models. These engineering models give the production surface for a particular technology and can be used to derive economic production functions for use in economic planning. The models can then be used to simulate different scenarios for cost management. With regard to developing the DSS, an object-oriented approach employing MOSES was selected.

A secondary, although no less important, goal of the project was to maximize the comprehensibility, flexibility, extensibility, and reusability of the system and its components. Up to this time, the major deficiency in the modeling process of the water industry has been its case-specific nature. The traditional approach has been firstly to focus on the underlying model and then to add extra features for easy manipulation. The problem is that most of these models are one-off projects that are often poorly documented, of limited generality and not designed to be integrated into larger modeling environments such as DSSs. Friedman et al. (1984), in a survey for the United States Congress, found that the major barrier to the use of models in the water resources sector was the lack of an integrated approach to model use, communication, and training.

A question that was identified as vital to the future of water resource planning and policy modeling was "How can we develop and apply our models in a manner that will increase their utility to planners and policy makers?" (Fedra and Loucks, 1985, p114). Fedra and Loucks identified the need for interactive computer systems with a range of models that were well structured, modularized, easily maintainable, and extensible, since with current system development approaches model management and reuse were not being attained. The lack of an effective component-driven design was a significant cost factor, particularly in maintenance, although poor utilization of models due to a general lack of comprehensibility and reusability was also an important factor. The goal of reusability and comprehensibility was based on an attempt to rectify these problems.

The sections below describe in some detail the process, the phases, and the activities of the development as they occurred when using MOSES. The objective of this discussion is to provide an understanding of the process of development as it occurs in a "real-world" problem. Any such description of the process cannot give a complete picture of the methodology or of all the design decisions that occurred during the development. However, it can show how certain activities occur and how different activities and phases interact within MOSES.

8.2.1 Investigation Phase
8.2.1.1 Initial requirements
An initial set of requirements was derived from an investigation into the field of wastewater resources together with a number of interviews with wastewater managers. The requirements solicitation process essentially involved inter-

views and research (Activity: User Requirements Elicitation). The first set of requirements was extremely fuzzy, representing a high-level statement of general objectives rather than a detailed specification of the system. Such a situation is not unusual because of the exploratory nature of a DSS. A summary of the "requirements" statement was developed by Edwards (1992) as follows:

> The system is to provide the manager with a means of planning operations of a wastewater treatment system in order to minimize costs, minimize the environmental impact, achieve the discharge license requirements, and react to varying demand.
>
> The system should be interactive and menu-driven with a graphical display.
>
> The system should enable the manager to configure, create, edit, and view models of the treatment processes. The primary function of the system is to be able to simulate a sewage treatment system and examine the implications of changing operational strategies. The results should include engineering variables and economic variables.
>
> The variables of the system should be manipulated by the manager in response to changing conditions in the treatment system; for example, new licensing regulations, new management directives regarding number of breaches of the license, changes in demand, and the effect of different pricing structures on the demand and thus on the system operations. The interaction of economic and engineering variables is of primary importance to the system's effectiveness.

These requirements include some design constraints, e.g., GUI-based and PC-based, as well as actual system requirements. These constraints may be imposed because of cost, current resources, or availability of tools. Initially, we try to focus on the logical aspects of the requirements; that is, we examine what the objective of the system is without thinking too deeply about the solution.

Initially, these broad requirements can be decomposed into a number of more manageable subsystems (Activity: Subsystem Identification) (Figure 8.1(a)). This is both part of the Investigation Phase and the beginning of the Specification Phase involving the construction of a conceptual model of the problem domain.

8.2.1.2 Identify subsystems and responsibilities

From the initial requirements document a set of responsibilities for the system can be developed and recorded using Subsystem Responsibility Specifications (SRSs). For the treatment plant subsystem these responsibilities may be as follows:

Subsystem 1: Wastewater Treatment System
Responsibilities

Create, view, edit, and configure pumping system models.
Simulate pumping system.
Report costs for pumping stations.
Create, view, edit, and configure conveyance models.
Simulate conveyance system.
Report conveyance system costs.
Create, view, edit, and configure treatment plant models.
Simulate treatment plant models.
Report costs for each process unit.
Report water quality for each process.
Store models and output for each model run.

Further investigation revealed that the treatment system could be subdivided into three major components (Activity: Subsystem Identification). These components, viewed as subsystems, are:

1.1 Treatment Plant System
1.2 Collection System
1.3 Pumping System

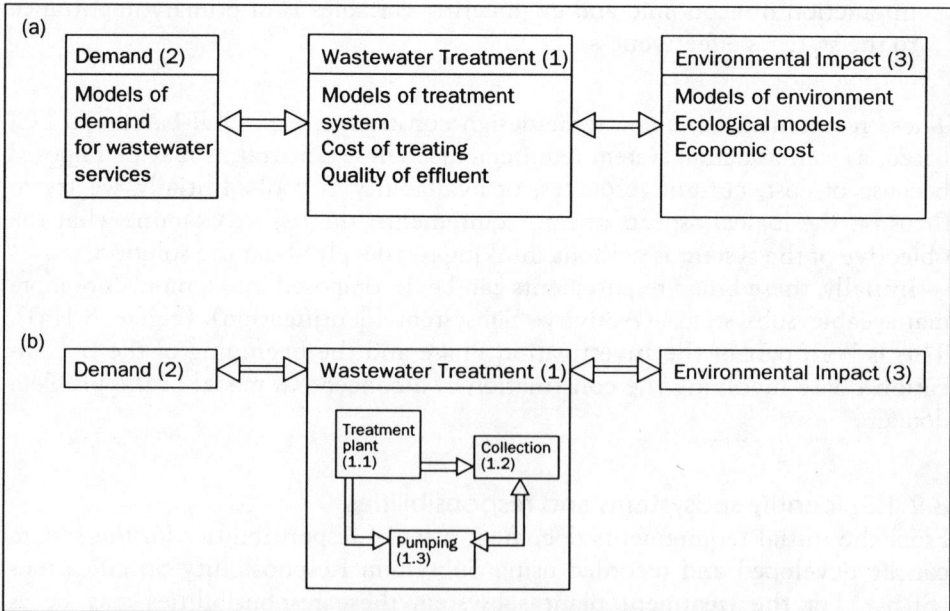

Figure 8.1 *First pass subsystem diagram of ECWAT*

A Case Study Using MOSES

These subsystems may or may not become actual subsystems in the final system, but at this stage they provide a useful framework for further analysis. The numbering used is similar to levels in dataflow diagrams and represents a hierarchical decomposition allowing subsystems to be traced to their "parent." Responsibilities should be documented for each subsystem and fulfill some responsibility of the "parent" system. The responsibilities of the treatment plant subsystem are shown below and act as mini-requirements. Thus we have begun to enter the first phase of the subsystem fountain model. Figure 8.1(b) shows an overview of the hierarchically decomposed subsystems using the notation of subsystems (Chapter 5).

Subsystem 1.1: Treatment Plant Subsystem
Responsibilities

To model a wastewater treatment plant at the process level and possibly below in terms of the water quality and the costs of production.

To model water quality factors including: Volume, Suspended Degradable Load, Suspended Nondegradable Load, Dissolved Degradable Load, and Active Biomass.

To model cost factors including: Fixed Capital Cost, Variable Capital Cost, Fixed Operating Cost, Labor Cost, Maintenance Cost, Variable Operating Cost, Power Cost, and Chemical Cost.

Create, edit, view, and configure wastewater treatment system models.

Simulate models for periods of months to decades.

Report costs of operation (operational and capital) for components of the system.

Report effluent output and impact on water quality.

Store models and output for each model run.

The hierarchical decomposition of Figure 8.1(b) is important to managing the complexity of large systems and provides a framework for further analysis of classes and relationships. Without it one must move straight into classes and interactions that can overwhelm a project very quickly. The subsystems may be decomposed into further subsystems if necessary, but discussions revealed the next stage to be the objects of the treatment plant, which appear to be better represented as classes. The depth of subsystem decomposition is a function of the system complexity and as such is a design decision.

Up to this point the activities have been restricted to Activity: User Requirements Elicitation and Activity: Subsystem Identification, since essentially we are in the Investigation Phase of the development. As yet, no computer-oriented constructs have entered the analysis. Although they existed as part of the initial requirements, they should not be part of the initial O/C Model.

Rather than trying to present a discussion of all the subsystems, we intend to discuss one particular subsystem, namely, the wastewater treatment plant (subsystem 1.1). A brief description of the treatment plant, its purpose, and its operation is given below.

8.2.1.3 Description of treatment plant subsystem

There are a number of types of wastewater treatment plant and, to begin with, we concentrate on the most common—an activated sludge plant. The conceptual model can be extended with other processes to model different types of plant in later models. These extensions should be kept in mind during the development in order to allow flexibility of the system.

An activated sludge treatment plant consists of six basic units: the screening unit, the primary settlement unit, the aeration unit, the final settling unit, the thickeners, and the digestor. The combination of aeration unit and final settlement unit, which provides "seed" sludge to the aeration unit, is often referred to as the activated sludge (AS) unit and is unique to this type of wastewater treatment plant (Figure 8.2).

The screening unit removes the larger debris and solid matter by means of screens or meshes at the entrance to the treatment plant. These screens are periodically scraped either manually or by automatic scrapers. The material is collected and eventually disposed of by incineration or landfill.

The primary settler removes a significant proportion (50–70%) of the suspended load of the wastewater (Barnes *et al.*, 1981) by slowing the influent velocity to the point where particles of a certain size are able to settle out of suspension. These particles form a sludge layer at the bottom of the tank, which is regularly scraped by automatic scrapers. The sludge is then piped to a dewatering unit and finally piped to the digestors.

The activated sludge process consists of two subprocesses: the aeration unit and the final settling unit. The purpose of the aeration unit is to reduce the biochemical oxygen demand of the wastewater to an acceptable level by mixing mixed liquor (also known as the activated sludge) with the wastewater. The mixed liquor contains a large number of biological organisms. The activated sludge is aerated with oxygen, which allows the organisms to grow rapidly and

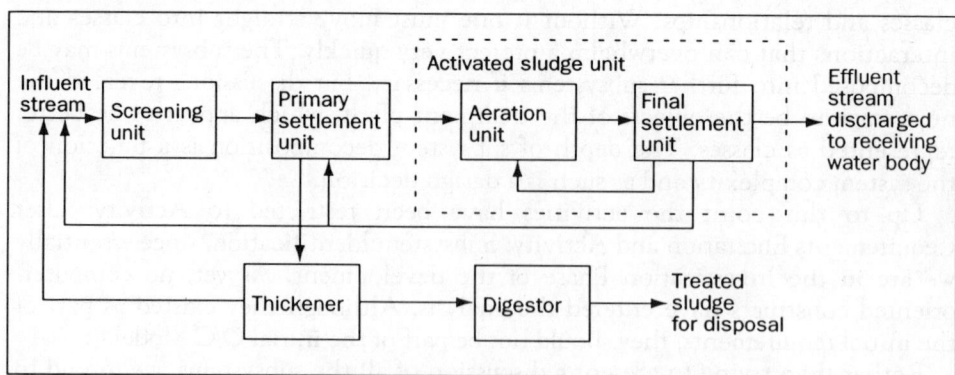

Figure 8.2 *Schematic of an activated sludge treatment plant*

digest, and hence remove, the suspended degradable load. The material is then piped to the final settling unit, where the velocity of the wastewater is once again reduced to the point where the suspended solids are settled out and scraped from the surface and bottom of the tank. This material is then recycled back to the aerator while the resulting effluent is discharged into the ocean or river. Excess sludge is periodically removed by recycling it to the primary settling unit, which separates it out and pumps it to the digestors. The rest of the sludge is then sent back to the activated sludge process to "reseed" the process.

The digestors degrade the separated solids further. The resulting sludge is then used as landfill or in some cases sold as fertilizer to city councils. The digestor produces methane that can be sold, burnt off, used to heat the digestors, or used to power the plant.

The system requires large amounts of electricity and oxygen to operate, and a significant amount of maintenance is needed for each process. Chemicals are sometimes added to the settling process to increase its efficiency, and chlorine or ozone may be used to treat the water further for discharge into relatively unpolluted environments.

The responsibilities identified indicate that the basic requirement of the system is to aid the wastewater agency in achieving productive efficiency, that is, becoming fully aware of the costs of production and what factors can be adjusted to ensure least-cost operation of all activities. Such information is essential for enhanced managerial operations and meeting of performance targets. Therefore, it is necessary first to examine the nature of the operational models of the DSS (Edwards *et al.*, 1991). It was decided to model the processes using a *production process model* approach (Marsden *et al.*, 1972, 1974; Edwards *et al.*, 1991) that integrates economic and engineering information.

This approach builds on the existing information base containing engineering design and operating data, and provides the conceptual basis for the simulation model. Tackling the problem from a detailed microengineering specification shifts the basis of the functional forms from desirable economic properties to physical aspects of the process under consideration. The parameters of the production function, rather than being estimated from historical data, are based on engineering representations of the process. The focus of attention is moved, initially, from the factors of production (energy, materials, labor, etc.) to the underlying chemical and biological processes.

Consider, for example, a treatment plant that is concerned with producing treated water with a biochemical oxygen demand (BOD) concentration, m_1, at a rate that is a function of the BOD concentration and the microorganism concentration, m_2. The reaction rate is expressed (Marsden *et al.* 1974) as:

$$r_1 = k_1 C_1^a C_2^b \tag{8.1}$$

where r_1 is the reaction rate, k_1 is the "rate constant" as a function of temperature and pressure, C_1, C_2 are components of the reaction, and a, b are constants.

Integrating the differential form of this equation over the "holding time" t_H, assuming that the reaction component C_2 remains roughly constant over the holding time, gives the following:

$$C_1 = [k_1 t_H (1-a) C_{20}^b + C_{10}^{1-a}]^{1/(1-a)} \qquad (8.2)$$

This equation is a variable elasticity of substitution production function, where C_{10} and C_{20}, the initial concentrations of BOD and microorganisms, are the inputs, and C_1, the final concentration of BOD, is the output of the production process.

A significant point to note is that this production function expression does not have marketable inputs as variables. The output is, however, a direct result of decisions taken by the water agency. The water agency determines the output level of BOD required, or a BOD standard is imposed by a regulatory body, and the agency then selects the least-cost set of inputs that enables the agency to achieve its target BOD concentration output. Marsden *et al.* (1972) initiate the decision process by selection of the plant size—the investment decision. The plant volume and volumetric flow, together with the initial concentrations and a rate constant that is dependent on temperature and pressure, appear in the above production function expression. Once the desired output has been chosen, the plant size is limited to a certain set of feasible plants. The selected plant provides engineering feasibility constraints in relation to the volumetric flow that, in turn, determine the purchases of raw materials and energy and the employment of labor. The agency searches for the least-cost production process to meet the selected output level. Operating costs of plants depend on use of energy and labor, which tend to have time-specific pricing schedules; raw materials, which tend to have time-invariant prices; and plant capacity, which has duration-specific costs. (See Winston (1982) for a discussion of factors associated with least-cost production in a time-specific framework.) Operations research procedures can be added to this process to estimate the production surface and the cost functions that are necessary for achieving productive and allocative efficiency.

8.2.1.4 Scenarios

Having examined the nature of the mathematical models and subdivided the requirements into subsystems, we can develop the requirements for each subsystem in more detail using the concept of scenarios (Activity: Scenario Development). To begin, we identify the actors of the system. These are the plant manager, the system administrator, and the operator. The plant manager is able to operate the modelbase component and develop operating scenarios for planning purposes. The system administration is able to do this as well as perform system maintenance activities, while the operator is able to examine the scenarios but not create them. These actors should be recorded in the Actor Glossary (Figure 8.3). Looking at the treatment plant subsystem, we can identify a number of scenarios:

A Case Study Using MOSES 371

Actor Glossary

Actor name:	System Administrator
Description:	Has access to all functions of the system for operation and maintenance purposes
Contact:	K. Hemings
Contact details:	STP 101, x9892
Actor name:	Plant Manager
Description:	Has access to operational functions for performing scenario analysis of the different treatment plant configurations
Contact:	M. Clayton
Contact details:	STP 221, x9282
Actor name:	Operator
Description:	Has access to database and scenario representation functions
Contact:	S. Lewis
Contact details:	STP 221, x9332

Figure 8.3 *Actor Glossary for ECWAT*

- initializing a new model
- configuring a new model
- reconfiguring a saved model
- executing a simulation
- creating new model components.

Two initial scenarios for initialization and execution are described below.

Initial Scenario for Initialization
Having informed the system that the user wishes to initialize a model, the user selects a preconfigured model from a list presented to him or her. The user chooses a model, which then becomes the active model. The user then asks for a list of initialization files to be displayed. One initialization file is chosen. The user asks for the file to be displayed to check that the values

are appropriate. The user then tells the system to initialize the active model with the data in the initialization file. The model is now active and initialized.

Initial Scenario for Execution
The user selects the execution option. The user enters the name of the output file in which the output data are to be stored. This name is checked for validity. The system accepts the name and the user enters the start command. The active model is executed with the data being entered from the input file and output data going to the output file. The system displays a message to indicate the estimated percentage time complete. On completion of the execution, a message is displayed informing the user that the execution has ended.

For each scenario a screen is developed. The objective is not to design the screen but to use it as a mechanism for teasing out the user requirements (Figure 8.4).

These initial scenarios are what Jacobson *et al.* (1992) refer to as the basic course for a scenario; that is, they include no exceptional circumstances or error processing. Also, these are very much initial scenarios defining input screens and output formats only in very limited detail. They are easy to construct and yet because of their logical nature and simplicity are easy to

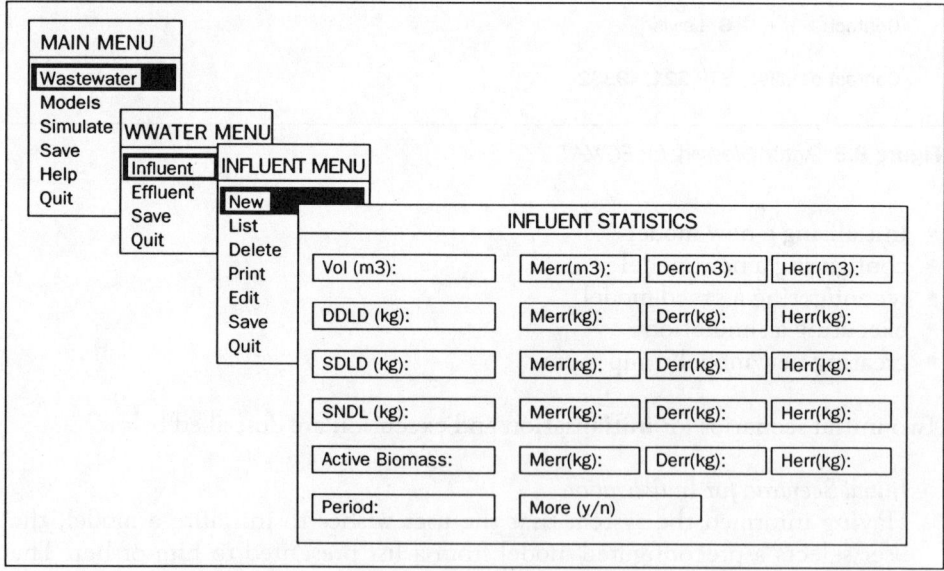

Figure 8.4 *The wastewater scenario entry screen of ECWAT. The fields Merr, Derr, and Herr are the monthly, daily, and hourly maximum random error from the chosen predefined distribution. The figure also shows the menu structure to this point.*

change. Later in the development process these scenarios will be refined to include exceptional conditions and more detail, and to be associated with screens.

8.2.2 Specification Phase

We now examine how an object model is developed for this system using MOSES. The object model can be developed for each subsystem independently and later integrated to give a comprehensive and complete object model for the system. This decomposition of the system, based on scenarios, is very much a business-driven approach in that it permits business functionality to be developed as prioritized by the user. This approach, however, requires careful coordination of the O/C Models developed for each scenario to ensure that O/Cs are not duplicated between scenarios.

In this example, we examine the scenarios associated with the treatment plant subsystem. Basically, the underlying function of this subsystem is to simulate a treatment plant. Since we are trying to simulate a real-world set of interacting objects, object identification and structuring of the model are relatively straightforward. We have not detailed the scenarios for configuring the treatment plant model owing to limitations of space. However, these would normally provide the major input into the object identification phase.

8.2.2.1 Initial class structure

We begin by identifying and specifying a number of candidate classes (Activity: O/C Identification). As we are simulating a real-world physical system, identifying an initial set of classes is relatively straightforward. Candidate classes include the physical entities of a wastewater treatment plant, the wastewater processes (themselves composite entities of the physical entities), and entities such as influent and effluent. These entities, represented as classes, should initially be simply listed or diagramed (e.g., Figure 8.5). Many of these objects are derived from a model of a treatment plant and from on-site investigations of actual treatment plant designs. By examining a number of different designs, the model does not represent one particular configuration of one actual plant but the general characteristics of activated sludge plants.

One of the responsibilities identified for the treatment plant model is to provide cost information at the level of individual processes of a plant. The production process models, taken from Smeers and Tyteca (1984a, b), and the system requirements do not require information on the physical objects. However, this may change and much of the process-level information can be viewed as emergent properties from an aggregation of lower-level physical classes; that is, they emerge from the component parts of the class. These factors, combined with the desire to develop a number of reusable components, led to the decision to retain the physical objects of the processes, at least as candidate objects, at this stage.

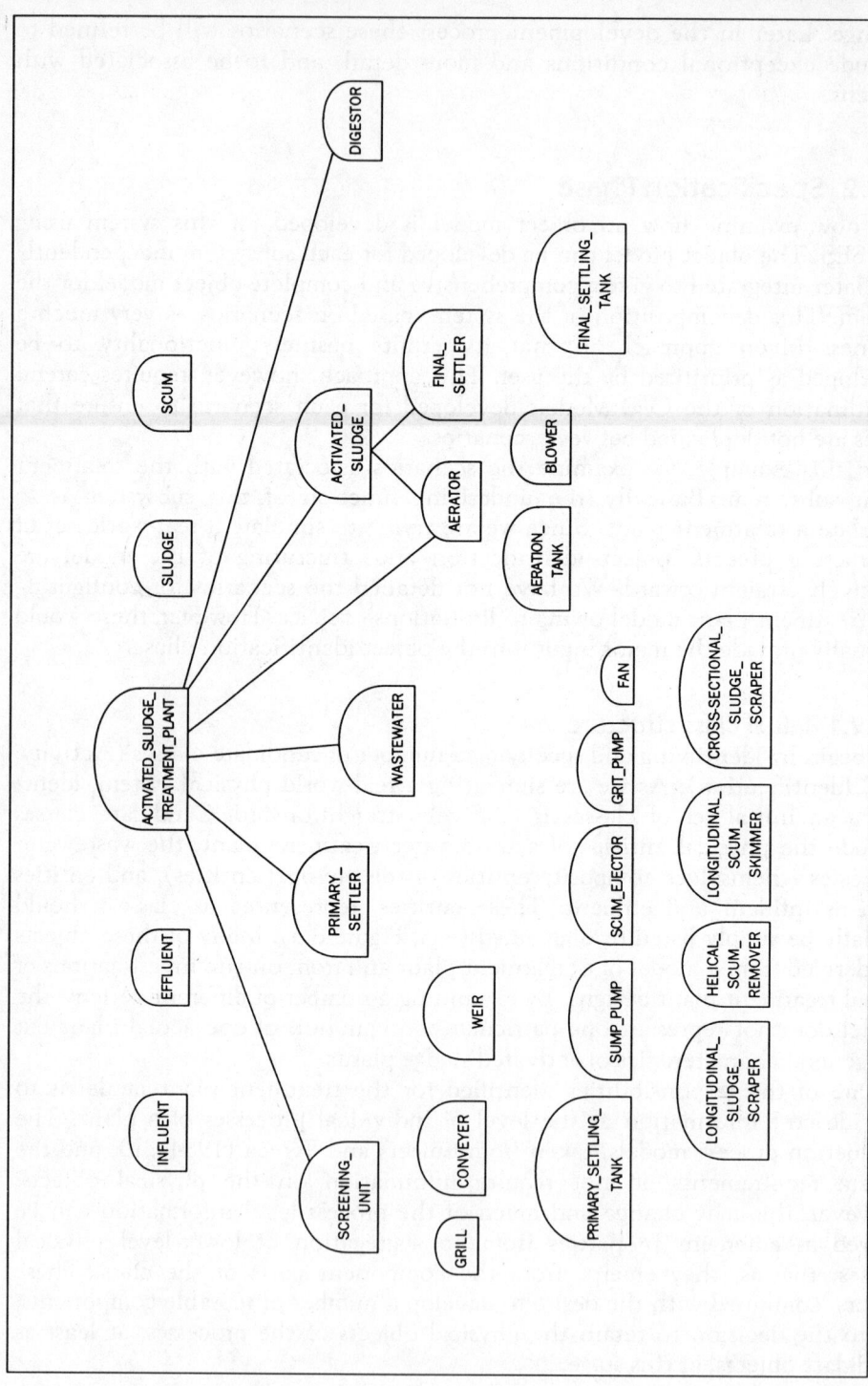

Figure 8.5 Candidate classes as an initial object collaboration diagram

A Case Study Using MOSES

Another important decision taken was about the way in which wastewater was to be modeled in the system. Wastewater is a mass that, as Wieringa (1991) discusses, is not an object. In order to model a mass as an object it is necessary to convert to a measurement unit. In this case, wastewater has a number of characteristics, e.g., suspended solid load, density, and temperature. Each of these characteristics is associated with a "package" of wastewater. In this model the properties are represented by basic types, although a better representation would be to develop a class for each general notion of a measure rather than for each unit (e.g., classes for AREA, MASS, etc.). The wastewater package can be modeled as a class with properties where "sdl" is suspended degradable load, "sndl" is suspended nondegradable load, "ddl" is dissolved degradable load, "ab" is active biomass, "bod" is biochemical oxygen demand, "ss" is suspended solids, and "omega" is a conversion factor "ss" to "bod." The functional relationship between properties can be defined as invariants of the class (Subactivity: Invariant specification) (see below).

```
class WASTEWATER
visible
    sdl: REAL;
    sndl: REAL;
    ddl: REAL;
    ab: REAL;
    ss: REAL;
    bod: REAL;
    omega: REAL;
    volume: REAL;
invariant
    bod = ddl + omega * sdl;
    ss = sdl + sndl + ab;
    sdl >= 0.0; ddl >= 0.0; sndl >= 0.0;
    ab >= 0.0; ss >= 0.0; bod >= 0.0;
    volume >= 0.0;
end
```

This view of a wastewater package and process units raises an interesting problem. It is possible to model the plant as three lots of wastewater, one for each of the process units. These three wastewater packages would then have the ability to "treat" themselves on the basis of operations that model the treatment processes. In this approach, a wastewater class has significant knowledge of how to treat water. This may be termed a "strict" OO design, that is to say, the operations that act on the data are encapsulated with those data in a strict fashion giving rise to an "intelligent" class WASTEWATER. Such a class may look something like that shown below.

```
class WASTEWATER
visible
  primary_settle
  - - operation based on primary settler
  aerate
  - - operation based on aerator
  final_settle
  - - operations based on final settler
end
```

The alternative, termed "reality" OO design, tries to model the way the real situation appears to be most "naturally" modeled. In this case, wastewater is passed from one process to another and each process changes properties of the wastewater packages on the basis of the equations of the process. This model appears more "natural" even though it is more data-flow-oriented. This poses something of a dilemma for the modeler: to be faithful to what appears to be the "strict" OO design or to model the world as it appears. In this situation it is argued that the comprehensibility is the important factor and that the "reality" OO design should take precedence in this architecture. This type of discussion about various architectures is an extremely important part of the early design process (Wirfs-Brock et al., 1990).

This discussion raises the issue of classes as processes. The discussion above identifies the process view of classes (Arnold and Early, 1988). Classes, therefore, present a unifying theme to conceptual models where processes, relationships, and entities are all classes that have different dynamic and static emphases (Martin and Odell, 1992).

Having decided that the processes are still candidate classes, we continue to identify the structural aspects of the model. At the early stages of development the O/C Model documents possible relationships (Figure 8.5) that should be refined during the analysis. It is possible to identify a number of relationships (Activity: Interaction Specification), reflecting the physical structure of the treatment plant, before identifying properties. Figure 8.6 shows an O/C Model of an activated sludge treatment plant.

The next stage is to identify the properties of the candidate classes (Subactivity: Property Identification). A useful source of information comes from engineering specification documents that detail numerous properties of each class. These specification documents provide a wealth of information, not all of which will be necessary or appropriate for the model's objective. The primary properties are the variables and parameters of the model, which should be recorded (with a unique name and signature) in the O/C Model and in more detail in the class specification. Understanding the model relationships leads to the identification of a number of other classes, such as a global clock, as well as some association relationships (e.g., *held_water*).

A Case Study Using MOSES   377

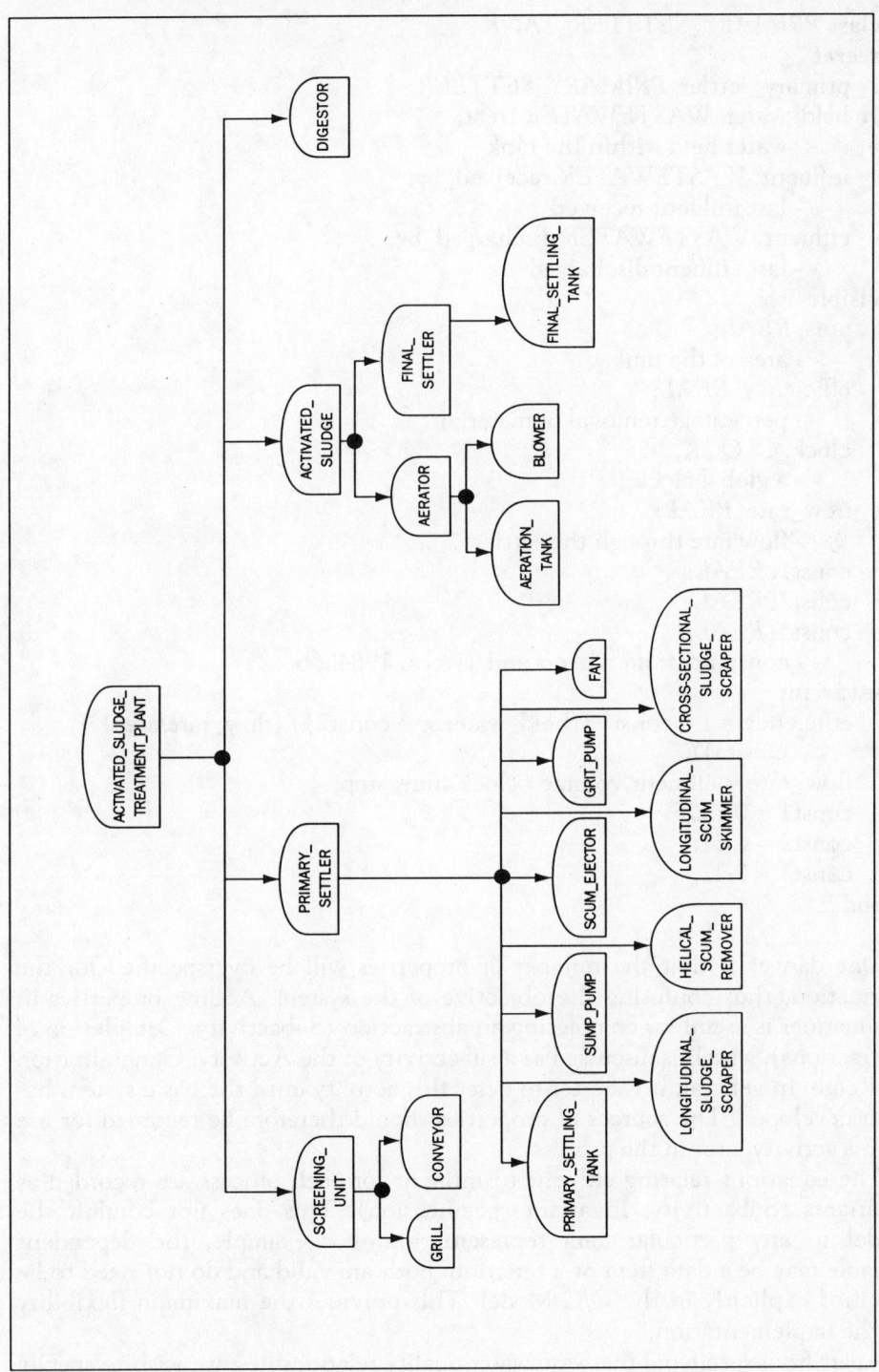

Figure 8.6 Aggregation relationships for the treatment plant model

```
class PRIMARY_SETTLER_TANK
secret
    primary_settler: PRIMARY_SETTLER
    held_water: WASTEWATER.treat;
        -- water held within the tank
    influent: WASTEWATER.received_by;
        -- last influent received
    effluent: WASTEWATER.discharged_by;
        -- last effluent discharged
visible
    area: REAL;
        -- area of the tank
    efficiency: REAL;
        -- percentage removal of material
    clock: CLOCK;
        -- a global clock
    flow_rate: REAL;
        -- flow rate through the settler
    const1: REAL;
    const2: REAL;
    const3: REAL;
        -- constants from Smeers and Tyteca, 1984a, b
invariant
    efficiency = 1 – const1 ((held_water.ss ^ const2) / (flow_rate/area) ^
        const3));
    flow_rate = effluent.volume / clock.time_step;
    const1 = 0.1395;
    const2 = 0.27;
    const3 = 0.22;
end
```

One danger is that the number of properties will be overspecified for the abstraction, thus confusing the objective of the system. Adding properties in this manner is useful for completing an abstraction (Subactivity: Completion of abstractions), which is discussed as a subactivity of the Activity: Generalization for Reuse. In general, it is better to defer this activity until the basic system has been developed. The sources of properties should therefore be recorded for use in this activity later in the process.

The equations relating effluent to influent for each process are recorded as invariants (Subactivity: Invariant specification). This does not commit the model to any particular data representation. For example, the dependent variable may be a data item or a function: both are valid and do not need to be specified explicitly in the O/C Model. This provides the maximum flexibility for the implementation.

Apart from specifying the wastewater quality relationships, we wish to specify a number of economic properties and relationships for each process. Economic properties are a function of the throughflow of wastewater, the quality of the effluent, e.g., electricity cost, or simply a function of time, e.g., depreciation. The properties and relationships are determined from interviews with water managers and the requirements of economic models. The following economic-oriented properties are identified as important for the PRIMARY_ SETTLER_ TANK.

```
class PRIMARY_SETTLER_TANK
   ... as before
visible
   capital_cost: DOLLAR;
   operating_cost: DOLLAR;
   maintenance_cost: DOLLAR;
   fixed_maintenance_cost: DOLLAR;
   variable_maintenance_cost: DOLLAR;
   historic_cost: DOLLAR;
      - - the original (actual) cost of the asset
   depreciation: DOLLAR;
      - - depreciation charge paid for last full year
   residual_value: DOLLAR;
      - - expected value of the asset after the useful life has expired
   actual_age: HOUR;
      - - measured in hours
   useful_life: HOUR;
      - - measured in hours
invariant
   total_depreciation = annual_depreciation * (age/8760);
   annual_depreciation = historic_cost - residual_value / (useful_life /8760);
   historic_cost >= 0.0; total_depreciation >= 0.0; residual_value >= 0.0;
   actual_age >= 0.0; useful_life >= 0.0
end
```

For the processes, which are abstractions of a number of physical devices, many of these properties are emergent. For example, the operating cost of a process is the sum of the physical device operating costs plus other costs assigned to the process that are not modeled by actual classes.

Together, the engineering and economic properties and invariants specify the dependent and independent variables of the model. Encapsulating and localizing these properties has been relatively straightforward in the object model, and no implementation representation has yet been necessary. Placing these properties in an O/C Model will often make it too big for one sheet of paper and the model should therefore be divided up into *sheets*, as discussed in Chapter 5. The most obvious division in this model is based on the process units of the plant. This division into sheets does not represent a design decision of the model, but merely an easier way of representing the model, and may be changed later. Figure 8.7 shows diagrammatically properties specified for the primary settler sheet.

So far, we have developed an understanding of the basic classes of the systems (Activity: O/C Identification), some of their properties (Subactivity:

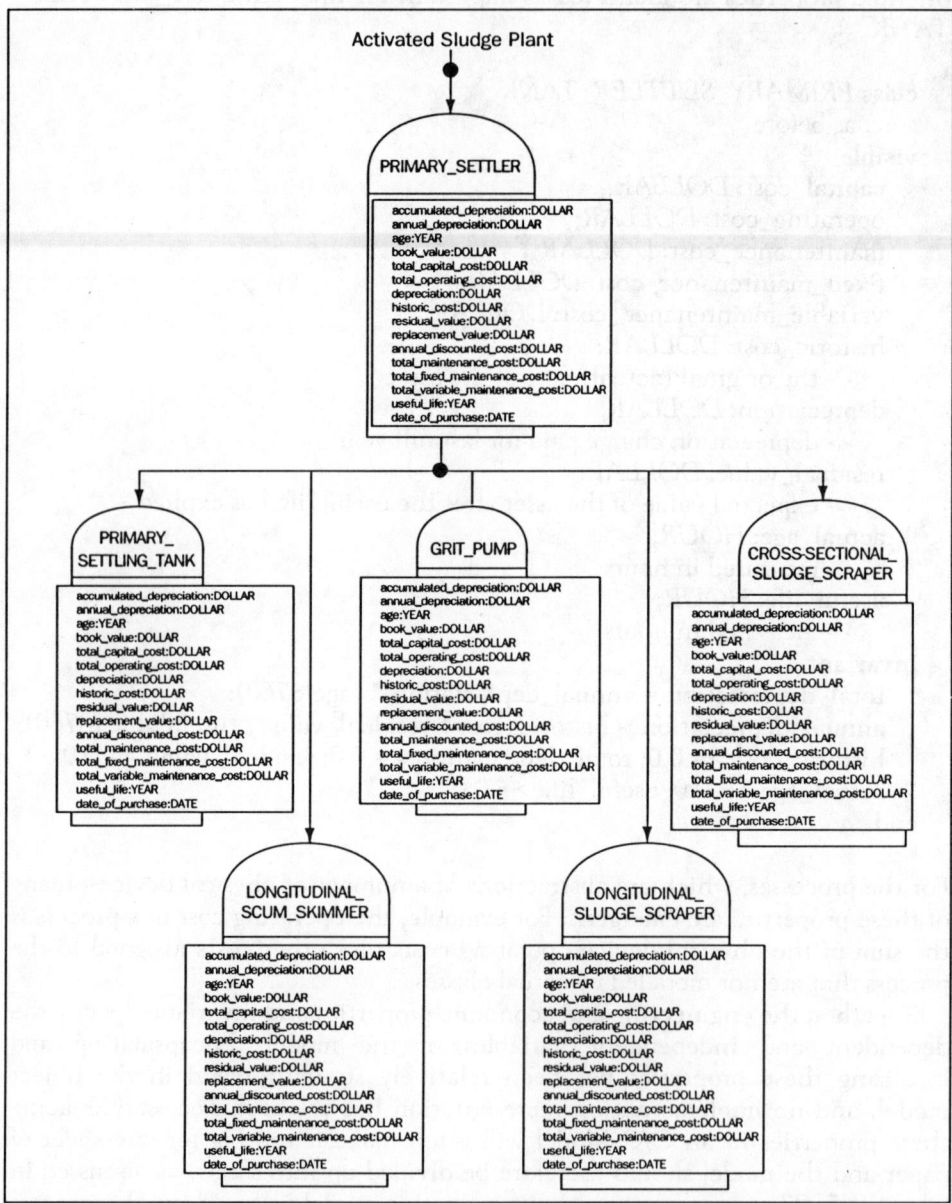

Figure 8.7 *O/C Model of the primary settler sheet showing properties for each class*

A Case Study Using MOSES

Property identification), invariants (Subactivity: Invariant specification), and their aggregation relationships (Activity: Interaction Specification). To complete our initial structural model, we need to identify the relationship of association (Subactivity: Association identification). A number of associations have already been identified in the model, such as the *is discharged by* and *is received by* relationship between the INFLUENT and EFFLUENT and the classes of processes. These were given their role names of "influent" and "effluent" in the PRIMARY_SETTLER_TANK model. One other association relationship to be identified is between MAINTENANCE_SCHEDULE and physical devices. A MAINTENANCE_SCHEDULE is really a specification of costs with relation to time and it was identified during an analysis of economic properties. This is a class that was not originally identified as a candidate class. All classes of the model should be related to each other in some way, otherwise there is no way in which the class could be used within the system. Figure 8.8 shows association and aggregation relationships for the primary settler sheet.

8.2.2.2 Refined scenarios

The above activities have provided us with a basic structure for the O/C Model and the relationships between properties of the model. The model currently lacks operations to change the state of the wastewater processes as they treat wastewater over time. That is to say, we do not have an understanding of the

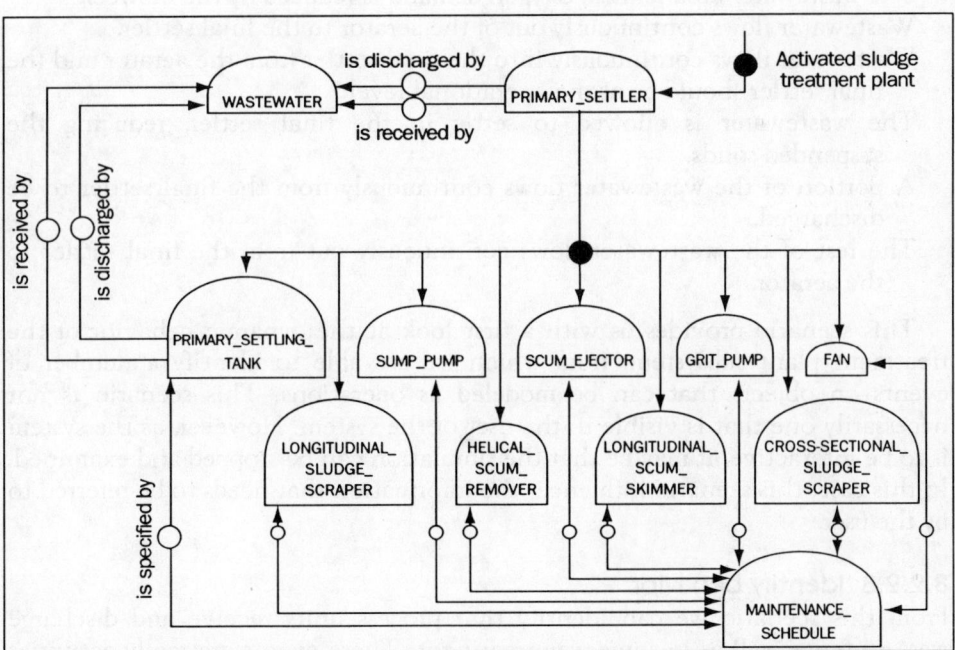

Figure 8.8 *O/C Model for the primary settler sheet showing association and aggregation relationships only*

dynamics or the behavior of the objects of the model. The first step is to work through and refine the initial scenarios developed for the treatment plant model.

The scenario we will examine for this subsystem describes the way in which the process units and tanks operate in a treatment plant. It is developed in conjunction with the domain expert. A scenario for the treatment plant is given below. Notice that this is for the "normal" operation of the process only. Exceptional scenarios can be developed later in the process if they need to be modeled.

Scenario for Treatment Plant

Wastewater flows continuously into the plant through the screening process, after which the larger material has been removed.

Wastewater flows continuously into the primary settler from the screening process. The primary settler is at the operational level.

Wastewater flows continuously out of the primary settler. The level of sludge should increase over time and the level of suspended solids should be reduced.

Wastewater flows continuously into the aerator from the primary settler and the aerator is at the operational level.

Wastewater flows continuously into the aerator from the final settler in a recycle loop.

The wastewater is continuously aerated in the tanks by the blowers.

The wastewater biochemical oxygen demand is reduced by the blowers.

Wastewater flows continuously out of the aerator to the final settler.

Wastewater flows continuously into the final settler from the aerator and the final settler should be at the operational level.

The wastewater is allowed to settle in the final settler, reducing the suspended solids.

A portion of the wastewater flows continuously from the final settler to be discharged.

The rest of the wastewater flows continuously out from the final settler to the aerator.

This scenario provides us with a first look at the dynamic behavior of the treatment plant subsystem, from which we are able to identify a number of events on objects that can be modeled as operations. This scenario is not necessarily one that is visible to the user of the system. However, as the system is to be interactive, it may be that the simulation can be stopped and examined. In this case, this scenario influences the information that needs to be referred to by the user.

8.2.2.3 Identify behavior

From this scenario we can identify that process units receive and discharge wastewater as well as in some way treating it. These events are really activities that occur continuously, but as we are dealing with a discrete model they will be viewed as events in time. Thus *receive* and *discharge* are two operations on the process units that occur at an instant. The dissection of time into discrete events or operations on objects is a standard approach to modeling continuous systems (Neelamkavil, 1987).

The first thing we can do is to develop an Event Model (Activity: Event Model Construction) and identify those objects and events that need to be sent to fulfill the scenario. Part of an Event Model for this scenario is shown in Figure 8.9.

In developing the Event Model the first thing to do is to identify the objects involved in the event. These may be "typical instances" of a class or specifically identified instances. In this example we can identify the typical instances. Examining the O/C Model gives us objects for an AERATION_PROCESS, PRIMARY_SETTLER, TANK, etc. The relationships of the O/C Model show possible connections between objects. Thus there may be a relationship between PRIMARY_SETTLERs and TANKs and there may be many TANKs for each instance of a PRIMARY_SETTLER. On the basis of this configuration we can walk through the scenario and identify messages and services to fulfill those messages. For example:

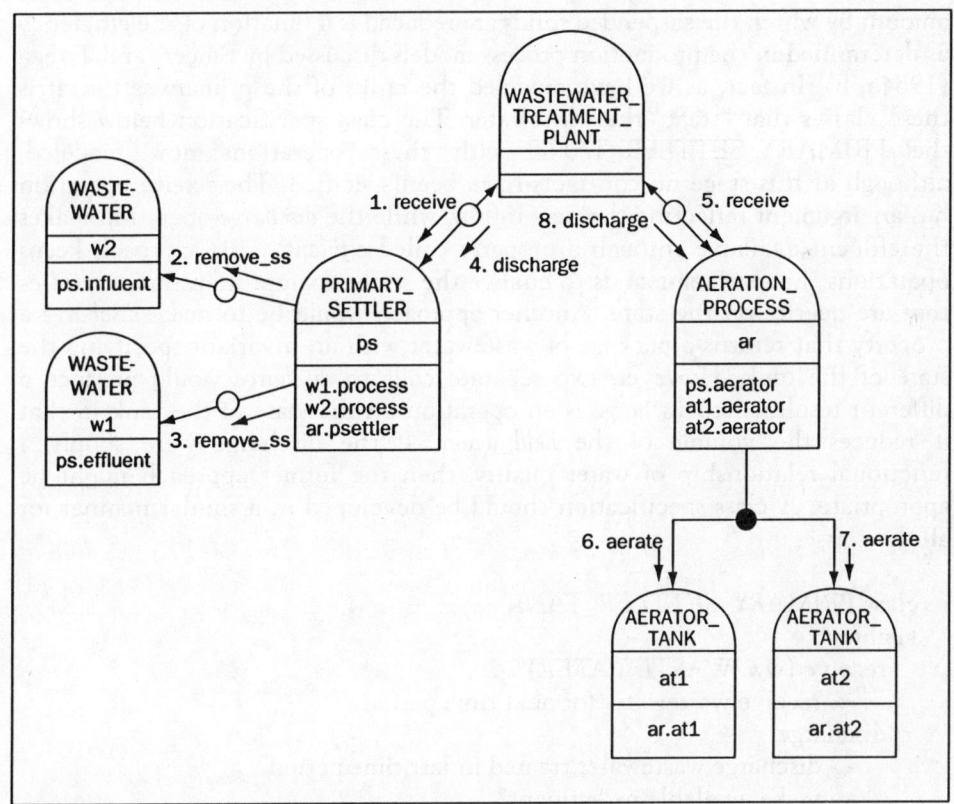

Figure 8.9 *Event Model for normal wastewater treatment plant operation*

Wastewater flows continuously into the plant through the screening process, after which the larger material has been removed.

indicates that wastewater enters the screening process where it acts upon the wastewater values, specifically removing the larger debris. Thus we can identify a service on a SCREENING_PROCESS of *receive* wastewater. This message is sent by some CONTROLLER class, which in this case we can model as the PLANT itself. Thus a message is sent from the PLANT to SCREENING_PROCESS. The screening process then treats the wastewater in some way. The details of this treatment service must wait for further investigation, but we can identify a *treat* service. Thus the Event Model continues to be built from the scenarios.

The scenario does not detail the effect of the events on the state of the objects; that is, it does not detail the contract of the operation (Activity: Contract Specification). This must be discovered from the requirements or by further investigation. For example, the result of receiving and discharging wastewater through a primary settler is that the wastewater's suspended solid content is reduced and the sludge quantity of the primary settler increased. The amount by which the suspended solids are reduced is a function of the efficiency as determined in the production process models discussed by Smeers and Tyteca (1984a, b). In fact, as we have modeled the tanks of the primary settler, it is these classes that "treat" the wastewater. The class specification below shows the PRIMARY_SETTLER_TANK with these operations now modeled, although at this stage no contracts have been specified. The *receive* operation has an argument reflecting the new inflow, while the *discharge* operation makes the effluent available through a property called *effluent*. This approach keeps operations that are commands to change the state separate from the properties that are queries on the state. Another approach would be to make *discharge* a property that returns a package of wastewater with an invariant specifying the state of the tank. However, two separate calls to *discharge* would produce a different result, since *discharge* is an operation on the state of the tank in that it reduces the volume of the *held_water*. If the discharge were simply a functional relationship of water quality, then the former approach might be appropriate. A class specification should be developed in a similar manner for all the classes.

```
class PRIMARY_SETTLER_TANK
visible
   receive (ww: WASTEWATER)
      - - receive wastewater for next time period
   discharge
      - - discharge wastewater treated in last time period
      - - make available in "effluent"
end
```

These operations, identified from the scenario (Activity: Service Identification), fulfill some of the responsibilities of the treatment plant subsystem. These responsibilities state that the effects of the processes on the wastewater over time have to be modeled, that is to say, how each process treats the wastewater. The wastewater quality aspects are specified by the effluent as generated by the discharge operation, and the cost outputs are functions of the time and the throughflow. These are modeled by the economic properties and invariants.

The development of the system behavior raises the issue of the level of abstraction at which the plant should be modeled, in much the same way as was discussed for the static model. In identifying behavior, the issue is whether the behavior of the physical classes should be modeled and the processes seen as an aggregation of this behavior, or whether the behavior should be at the level of the process only. The decision was taken to model the behavior of the physical classes and to aggregate this to the level of the process. This was based on a number of factors:

- the reality of the model;
- the desire to develop a set of reusable classes for further developments;
- the recognition that the model may be used for operational planning at the physical device level.

The behavior of the processes will therefore involve emergent operations of the physical devices. For example, a *receive* operation of the primary settler will involve receive operations on the various tanks of the process, with the PRIMARY_SETTLER acting as a controller.

Once various operations have been identified, it is necessary to determine their effect on the class and to document this as a contract (Activity: Contract Specification). In many cases, such as *receive*, the contract is quite simple, but in other cases, such as *discharge*, the contract can be quite complex (see below). A contract specifying the meaning of the operation should be developed for each operation of the class. This contract essentially will be the postcondition at this stage, although some preconditions may be identifiable, as with *receive*.

```
class PRIMARY_SETTLER_TANK
visible
   volume: REAL;
      - - volume of the tank
   receive (ww: WASTEWATER)
      - - receive wastewater for next time period
      precondition
      ww =/ Void
      postcondition
      influent.equal (ww);
```

```
                held_water.volume = old held_water.volume + ww.volume;
                held_water.ss = old held_water.ss + ww.ss;
                held_water.bod = old held_water.bod + ww.bod;
                held_water.sdl = old held_water.sdl + ww.sdl;
                held_water.sndl = old held_water.sndl + ww.sndl;
                held_water.ddl = old held_water.ddl + ww.ddl;
                held_water.ab = old held_water.ab + ww.ab
            end
        discharge
            - - discharge wastewater treated in last time period
            - - make available in "effluent"
            postcondition
                effluent.ddl = old held_water.ddl * efficiency;
                effluent.sdl = old held_water.sdl * efficiency;
                effluent.ab = old held_water.ab * efficiency;
                effluent.sndl = old held_water.sndl * efficiency;
                effluent.volume = old held_water.volume – volume
                held_water.volume—volume
        end
    end
```

8.2.2.4 Dynamic model

Having identified a number of operations and their contracts, we can begin to examine the dynamic model for the classes (Activity: Objectchart Construction). The dynamic model is represented by objectcharts. Figure 8.10 shows a basic objectchart for a TANK class. This objectchart identifies a number of states relating to whether the tank is "full," "overflowing," "empty," or "partially full." It shows that in order for a tank to *receive* and *discharge* wastewater it may be "full," "empty," "exactly full," or "partially full." Events are restricted to certain states in the model. So, for example, when a tank is "overflowing" it may not *receive* further wastewater. Objectcharts should be developed for each class of the model that appears to have interesting behavior; however, many classes, such as MAINTENANCE_SCHEDULE, will not so appear.

For each event on the objectchart, a transition specification is developed (Activity: Objectchart Construction), detailing the effect of the transition on the properties of the class and the conditions under which the transition may occur. The preconditions of the transition specification are sometimes called guards (Rumbaugh *et al.*, 1991). In the notation of Rumbaugh *et al.* (1991), these are shown on the statechart. However, this was found to become too cumbersome for real systems and instead a transition specification table is used. Below is a selection of the transition specifications for the tank object. In these specifications a number of operations on WASTEWATER are discovered that reduce the redundancy of specifications for the TANK class. For example, rather than the effect on the properties of the wastewater being specified separately for every *receive* event, the

A Case Study Using MOSES

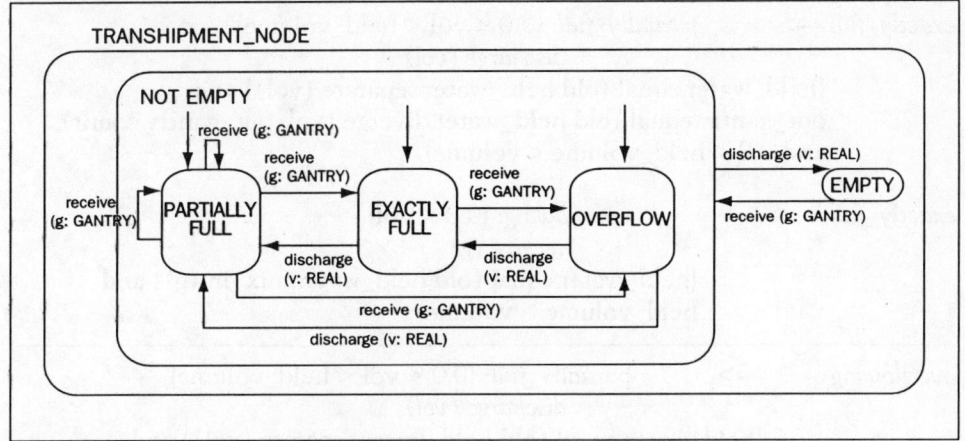

Figure 8.10 *Objectchart for the class TANK*

event *mix_in* is specified once for the WASTEWATER class. The specification of *mix_in* can then be implied for every receive operation. This reduces the need for redundancy of the specification.

class TANK		subsystem: Treatment Plant
empty	—>	*not_empty*: {ww.volume > 0.0} *receive* (g) {held_water.equal (**old** held_water.mix_in (g)) **and** held_volume = ww.volume}
empty	—>	*overflowing*: {ww.volume > volume} *receive* (g) {held_water.equal (**old** held_water.mix (g)) **and** held_volume = ww.volume **and** held_volume > volume}
not_empty	—>	*empty*: {vol = held_water.volume} *discharge* (*vol*) {out_gantry.equal (**old** held_water.diverge (vol, out_gantry.count)) **and** held_water.equal (**old** held_water.separate (vol))}
partially_full	—>	*exactly_full*: {held_volume + ww.volume = volume} *receive* (*ww*) {held_water.equal (**old** held_water.mix (ww)) **and** held_volume = volume}

exactly_full —>	*partially_full*: {0.0 < vol < held_volume} *discharge (vol)* {held_water.equal (**old** held_water.separate (vol)) **and** out_gantry.equal (**old** held_water.diverge (vol, out_gantry.count) **and** 0.0 < held_volume < volume}	
exactly_full —>	*overflowing*: {0.0 < vol} *receive (g)* {held_water.equal (**old** held_water.mix_in (g)) **and** held_volume > volume}	
overflowing —>	*partially_full*: {0.0 < vol < held_volume} *discharge (vol)* {held_water.equal (**old** held_water.separate (vol)) **and** out_gantry.equal (**old** held_water.diverge (vol, out_gantry.count) **and** 0.0 < held_volume < volume}	
overflowing —>	*exactly_full*: {vol = held_volume − volume} *discharge (vol)* {held_water.equal (**old** held_water.separate (vol)) **and** out_gantry.equal (**old** held_water.diverge (vol, out_gantry.count) **and** held_volume = volume}	

Events and their transition specifications are then modeled as operations on the class in the Class Specification. As we have already identified many of the operations, we can simply complete the contracts of the operations in the class specification (Activity: Contract Specification). The completed contract thoroughly specifies the conditions under which the operation is able to be called by a client object and what the result of the call will be.

The way we have modeled the tank raises an important issue of the lifecycle and time dimension of the model. The two events *receive* and *discharge* occur instantaneously and therefore do not model the passing of time. Time can be modeled simply as an INTEGER in the model representing the smallest time step (e.g., seconds, hours). The question is how to model the passing of time for each class. One possibility is to add an operation to each class so that it can simulate itself for one time step. Another is to have the processes act as controllers for their components and drive the time sequence of events for them. More generally, the question is whether the events that model the lifecycle of the object be controlled by the process itself, or by another object. For example, a *receive* event adds water to the tank, but in a full tank it also results in a *discharge* event. This can be modeled by two separate events, *receive* and *discharge*, controlled by a second class that only calls the *discharge* events when the tank is overflowing. This approach allows the tank to be examined at many different time intervals.

Alternatively, a single event that combines the specification of the two events may be specified for the class. In this approach the lifecycle becomes another operation on the object that aggregates the two different events. In the first case an intelligent driver object is required to drive the object's lifecycle on the basis of certain conditions, whereas in the second case the dynamics of the lifecycle are specified within the class. Thus, in this example, an operation *cycle* would receive water and discharge water if the tank was overflowing. This would amalgamate the different events into one event. This lifecycle can be thought of as an "activity," since it models something that takes time to complete.

From this discussion we decide to model the time-dependent events in the process as an operation called *cycle* on the object. The *cycle* operation specifies the dynamics in one place, calling the operations *receive* and *discharge*. This approach models time yet keeps the time-independent operations for use in other modeling situations. The TANK class now has three operations: *receive*, *discharge*, and *cycle*. The *receive* operation models the instant in time when the tank has received a new package of water. This event may result in the tank overflowing, which is feasible at an instant in time. The *discharge* operation simply discharges a package of wastewater representing the overflowing volume and makes it available in effluent. However, one simulation cycle should *not* leave the tank in an overflowing state and, therefore, the simulation model uses the *cycle* operation that simulates one time step. (This assumes that all the overflowing wastewater can leave the tank in the time interval. This is a reasonable assumption under most circumstances.) During the *cycle* the *receive* and *discharge* operations will be called as necessary, on the basis of the state (overflowing or not) of the tank. This *cycle* event models a lifecycle of the object that is a sequence of events. This sequence can be viewed as a trace, as below.

Common Trace for TANK class
    < *, time: 00, CLOCK >
    < *, increment, CLOCK >
    < *, time: 01, CLOCK >
    < *, receive (WASTEWATER), TANK >
    < *, discharge, TANK >   One time step
    < *, time: 01, CLOCK >
    < *, increment, CLOCK >
    < *, time: 02, CLOCK >
    < *, receive (WASTEWATER), TANK >
    < *, discharge, TANK >
    < *, time: 02, CLOCK >

< *, increment, CLOCK >
< *, time: 03, CLOCK >
< *, receive (WASTEWATER), TANK >
< *, discharge, TANK >
< *, time: 03, CLOCK >

This sequence of behavior, or lifecycle, represents one time step through the model that is modeled more effectively as *cycle* with the trace:

< *, time: 00, CLOCK >
< *, increment, CLOCK >
< *, time: 01, CLOCK >
< *, cycle (WASTEWATER), TANK >   ⎫
< *, increment, CLOCK >   ⎬ One time step
< *, time: 02, CLOCK >   ⎭
< *, cycle (WASTEWATER), TANK >
< *, increment, CLOCK >
< *, time: 03, CLOCK >

where the specification of cycle is given as:

class PRIMARY_SETTLER_TANK
visible
   cycle (ww: WASTEWATER)
   -- simulate treating the next hour's wastewater
    postcondition
    receive (ww) **and**
    ww.volume + held_water.volume > volume **implies**
    discharge
   end
end

The sequence of events that make up one time step can be amalgamated into a *cycle* operation for each class that is to be simulated. The processes, for example, will have a *cycle* operation that will decide how to distribute water to the different tanks of the process and how to trigger the cycle event for the tanks.

The basic simulation loop of the system is very similar to this *cycle* operation in that it involves subevents on the processes called from the treatment plant class.

class TREATMENT_PLANT
visible
   primary_settler: **component** PRIMARY_SETTLER;
   aerator: **component** AERATOR;
   final_settler: **component** FINAL_SETTLER;

cycle (ww: *WASTEWATER*)
   -- simulate treating the next hour's wastewater
      postcondition
      primary_settler.cycle (ww);
      aerator.cycle (**old** primary_settler.effluent, **old** final_settler.effluent);
      final_settler.cycle (**old** aerator.effluent);
      effluent = **old** final_settler.effluent;
   end
end

Figure 8.11(a) shows an Event Model of a plant with a primary settler, aerator, and final settler process, as well as a clock. Part of the dynamic model for the plant is shown, as is part of the dynamic models for the other processes (Figure 8.11(b) and (c)). The objectchart of the plant shows the events on other objects as a result of the *cycle* event.

8.2.2.5 Refinement

We have now defined the structure, behavior, and dynamics of the basic classes involved in the conceptual model of the treatment plant subsystem. Basically, we have a TREATMENT_PLANT composed of processes (e.g., PRIMARY_SETTLER) that are composed of devices (e.g., PRIMARY_SETTLER_TANK). Each level of abstraction can be simulated by operating on the composing classes. For example, the TREATMENT_PLANT drives the simulation loop by calling operations on the processes. The processes make available the effluent after each iteration of the treatment process and record the changes in state in the processes with regard to cost factors, such as power used and maintenance cost. At any time during the simulation run these results are available from each process and can be reported to the user.

We have not, at this stage, looked at particular implementation mechanisms in detail, although a number of possibilities have been raised. The model at this stage is oriented purely toward modeling the UoD and is specified in a declarative fashion. So far we have undertaken a first iteration of the model, although a number of iterations have already occurred within the different activities. The model should now be validated to see whether the responsibilities of this subsystem are met by the model, and whether any reorganization of the classes is required. This can be done by other scenarios or following through each responsibility for the model. In this case we have validated the model by examining one scenario of a simulation and looked at the traces that result.

We should also reevaluate the classes of the model by examining their properties and operations (Activity: O/C Identification). For example, in the model of Figure 8.8 the different scrapers and fans can be replaced by a single class called MECHANICAL_EQUIPMENT, because the various scraper classes have no extra or different properties and, in fact, represent instances of a more general class. The reevaluated model is shown in Figure 8.12.

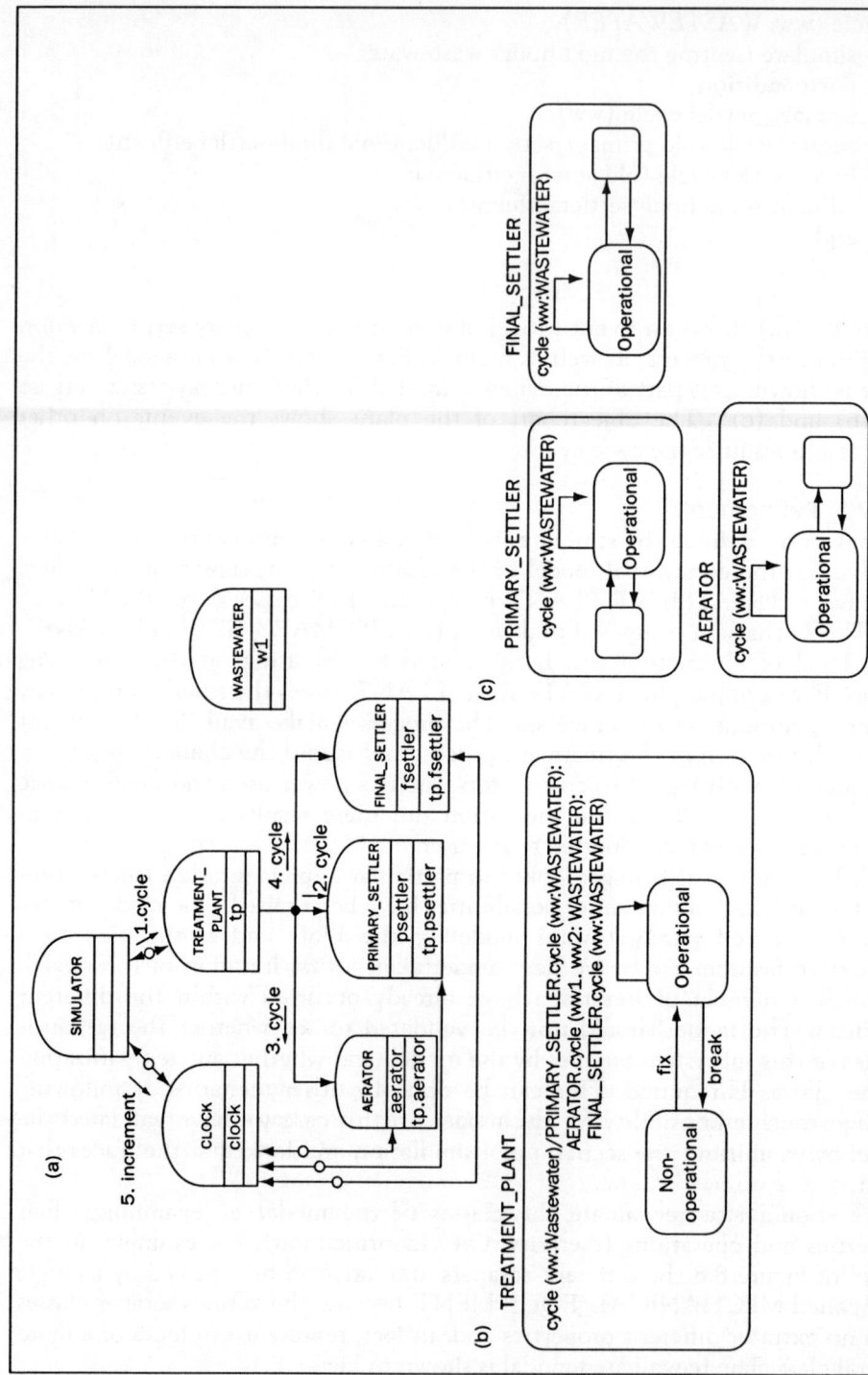

Figure 8.11 (a) Event Model; (b) and (c) objectcharts

A Case Study Using MOSES

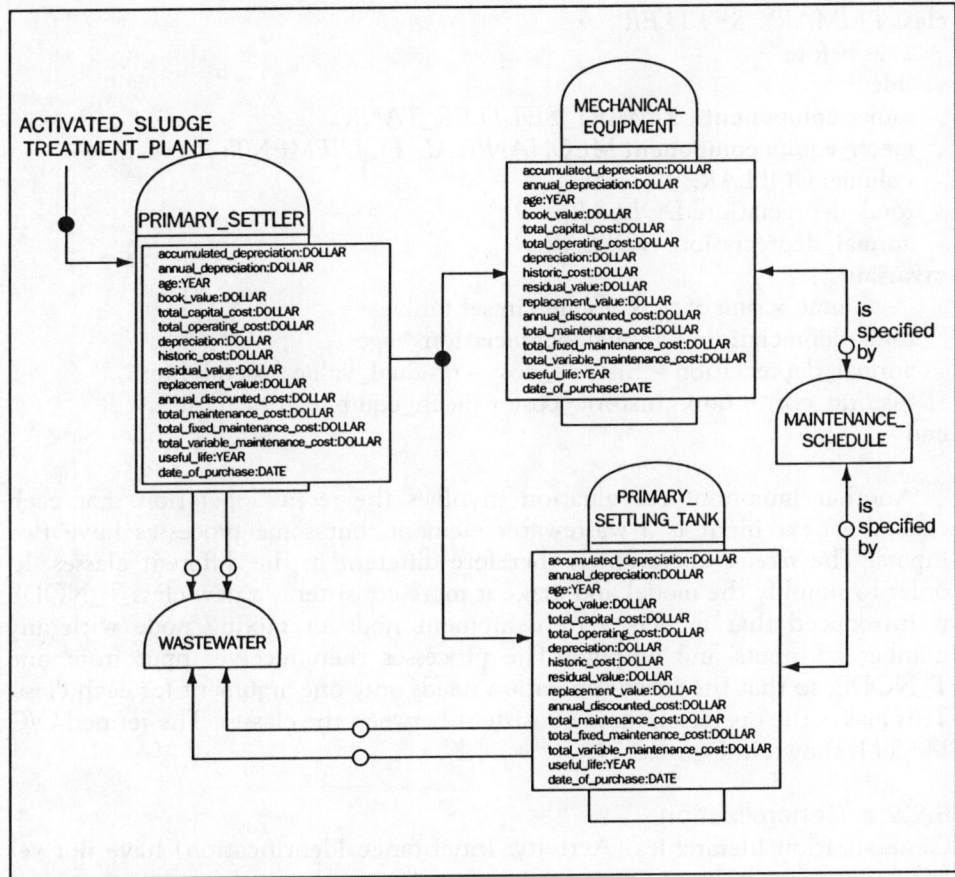

Figure 8.12 *Refined O/C Model for the primary settler sheet*

Other classes that can be removed from the initial model are the INFLUENT and EFFLUENT classes that are replaced by a single WASTEWATER class, together with many other detailed components of the processes. The physical classes remaining are the major components of the process rather than the more detailed parts. This reevaluation of classes is an important part of the initial analysis and should be done for each class to ensure that it represents a clear and concise abstraction of the problem domain. Classes that are, in fact, instances add no new information to the model and, importantly, classes at too low a level of abstraction for the model should be removed.

We can also clarify the role of the process units and the properties of the units. Many of the properties of the process units are, in fact, emergent properties. For example, the volume of a process unit is the sum of the volume of the tanks, and the depreciation includes the physical component values. These can be modeled as follows:

class PRIMARY_SETTLER
   ... as before
visible
   tanks: **component** PRIMARY_SETTLER_TANK;
   mech_equip: **component** MECHANICAL_EQUIPMENT;
   volume: DOLLAR;
   total_depreciation: DOLLAR;
   annual_depreciation: DOLLAR;
invariant
   - - volume = sum of tank.volume in set tanks;
   total_depreciation = annual_depreciation * age
   annual_depreciation = historic_cost − residual_value / useful_life;
   historic_cost = tanks.historic_cost + mech_equip.historic_cost
end

Another important reevaluation involves the *receive* operation. For each class the next input is a wastewater element, but some processes have two inputs. The *receive* operation is therefore different in the different classes. In order to simplify the model and make it more consistent, a new class T_NODE is introduced that models a transshipment node or mixing node with any number of inputs and outputs. The processes then receive input from one T_NODE, so that the *receive* operation needs only one argument for each class. This makes the operation more consistent between the classes. The refined O/C Model is shown in Figure 8.13.

8.2.2.6 Generalization

Generalization hierarchies (Activity: Inheritance Identification) have not yet been considered, since we prefer to defer a thorough examination of generalization until a sufficiently rich O/C Model has been developed. This is because until a rich enough model (including properties and operations) has been developed, generalizations must be identified on the basis of the name of the abstraction alone. Relying on names of abstractions too early in the development may lead to a misrepresentation of an abstraction and its relationship. Generalizations will therefore need to be continually reevaluated as more properties are identified. Furthermore, once a relationship has been defined, it tends to have an inertia that may be hard to overcome later in the design.

For example, the classes SEWAGE_TREATMENT_PROCESS and PRIMARY_SETTLER_PROCESS may be identified during a high-level analysis and related by generalization on the basis of name early in the process. Only after further analysis does it become clear that SEWAGE_TREATMENT_PROCESS is in fact a SEWAGE_TREATMENT_PLANT and "contains" a PRIMARY_SETTLER_PROCESS. Thus the relationship is aggregation rather than generalization. Although change and reevaluation are all part of the process of model construction, it is better to change the model infrequently if

A Case Study Using MOSES

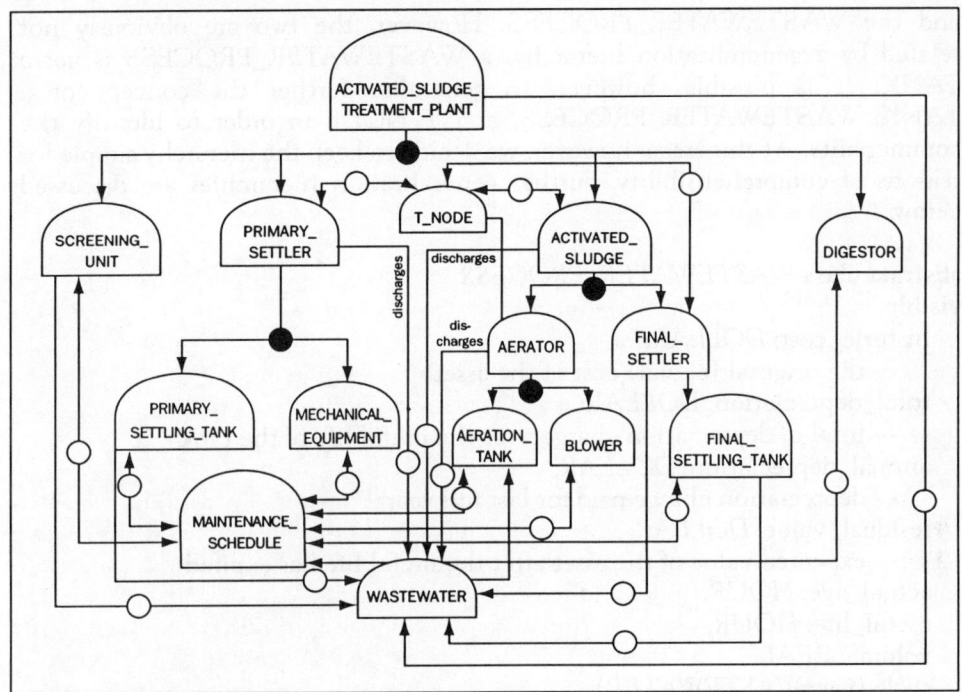

Figure 8.13 O/C Model for the treatment plant showing association and aggregation relationships only

possible. Names of classes can be misleading, particularly in the early stages of the process, and we therefore argue that it is better to leave generalization until an initial model has been defined. Then, once the relationship is defined, it will tend to be more stable, although not completely immutable.

Therefore, having developed an initial O/C Model, we identify a number of generalizations. Firstly, we generalize the classes that model the treatment plant processes to one class, WASTEWATER_PROCESS. This abstraction models a number of common characteristics, such as the *receive*, *cycle*, and *discharge* behaviors and the *influent*, *effluent*, and *volume* properties. The class is a deferred class, as it is not possible to specify fully a number of the services of the class. The class does, however, reduce a significant amount of specification in the descendant wastewater processes. A partial class specification is given below.

A second generalization is between different tanks. These can be abstracted to the more general notion of a TANK class. The different tanks are not simply instances of a general TANK class, as was the case with the scrapers and MECHANICAL_EQUIPMENT, because the behavior of the tanks, in terms of specifying the effect on the wastewater, is different between different tanks. There is a significant amount of overlap between the specification of TANK and the WASTEWATER_PROCESS. However, the two are obviously not related by a generalization hierarchy: a WASTEWATER_PROCESS is *not* a TANK. It is possible, however, to generalize further the concept of a TANK, WASTEWATER_PROCESS, and T_NODE in order to identify the commonality. At this stage, however, we decide to keep the hierarchy simple for reasons of comprehensibility. Further generalization hierarchies are discussed below.

abstract class WASTEWATER_PROCESS
visible
    historic_cost: DOLLAR;
      -- the original (actual) cost of the asset
    total_depreciation: DOLLAR;
      -- total of depreciation charge over the useful life of the tank
    annual_depreciation: DOLLAR;
      -- depreciation charge paid for last full year
    residual_value: DOLLAR;
      -- expected value of the asset after the useful life has expired
    actual_age: HOUR;
    useful_life: HOUR;
    volume: REAL;
    cycle (ww: WASTEWATER)
      precondition
      ww ≠ Void
      postcondition
      ww.volume + held_volume > volume implies discharge
    end
    receive (ww: WASTEWATER)
      -- receive wastewater for next time period
      precondition
      ww ≠ Void
      postcondition
      influent.equal (ww);
      held_water.volume = **old** held_water.volume;
    end
    discharge
      -- discharge wastewater treated in last time period.
      -- make available in "effluent"
      postcondition
      effluent.volume = **old** held_water.volume – volume
      held_water.volume = volume
    end
invariant
    total_depreciation = annual_depreciation * age;
    annual_depreciation = historic_cost – residual_value / useful_life;

A Case Study Using MOSES

        historic_cost >= 0.0; total_depreciation >= 0.0; residual_value >= 0.0;
        actual_age >= 0.0; useful_life >= 0.0;
        volume = sum of tank.volume in set tanks;
end

A third generalization is an ASSET. Nearly all the classes of the model represent either an asset or an asset group, that is, an asset that is composed of other assets that reflect the parts hierarchy of the model. Therefore, ASSET can be abstracted out as an abstract class. For example, the *historic_cost* of an asset may be an emergent property (a sum of its components) or be specified for the class. The use of a deferred class permits all possibilities to be specified in the descendants. The deferred class WASTEWATER_PROCESS can also be viewed as an ASSET and can therefore be generalized further. This results in the generalization hierarchy in Figure 8.14. The reevaluated and reorganized classes, together with the class hierarchies, give the O/C Model of Figure 8.15 (shown as one diagram here).

8.2.2.7 Dividing into sheets

The O/C Model, even having been reorganized, with redundancy removed by generalization and selective visibility, is still quite complex (Figure 8.15). Therefore, it is useful to show the model in sheets. Dividing the model was started in the initial class structure phase (Section 8.2.2.1), where two sheets are shown—Sheet 1 and Sheet 2—modeling the primary settler and the activated sludge process (Figure 8.16(a) and (b) respectively). A number of the classes are repeated between the different sheets, aiding readability of the different models in isolation. A CASE tool should be able to identify logical inconsistencies between the sheets easily and ensure they are updated between the different sheets.

8.2.2.8 Class Specifications

The classes should now be documented in the Class Specification. Once again, a CASE tool should have the ability to ensure that the information between

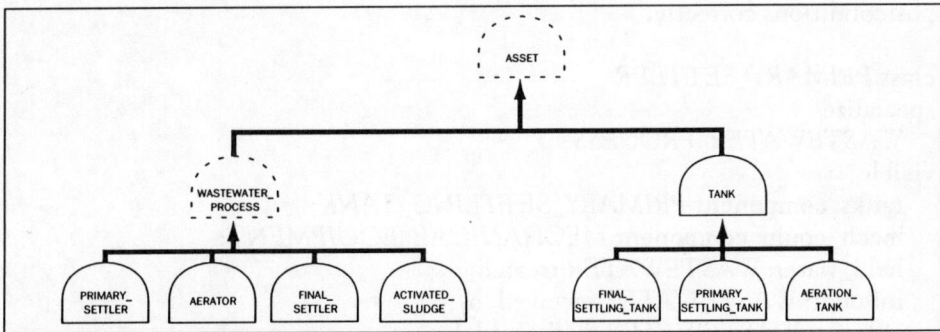

Figure 8.14 *Generalization structure for the treatment plant model*

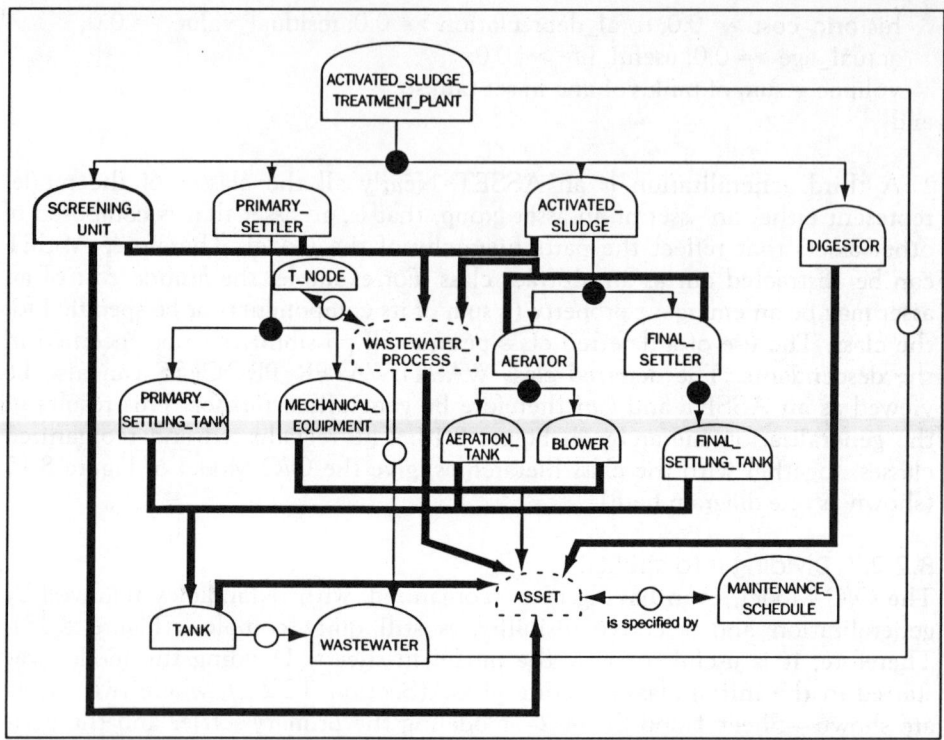

Figure 8.15 *O/C Model for the treatment plant showing all relationships and classes*

the different sources is correct, thus making the generation of the Class Specification almost automatic from the diagrams (and vice versa). Below is the complete Class Specification for the PRIMARY_SETTLER, and one of these should be produced for each class of the model. The major activity here is translating into the syntax of the Class Specification and ensuring that the objectchart transition specifications are developed into operation pre- and postconditions correctly.

class PRIMARY_SETTLER
specialize
   WASTEWATER_PROCESS
visible
   tanks: **component** PRIMARY_SETTLING_TANK;
   mech_equip: **component** MECHANICAL_EQUIPMENT;
   held_water: *WASTEWATER*.treated_by;
   influent: *WASTEWATER*.received_by;
   effluent: *WASTEWATER*.discharged_by;
   maint_sch: *MAINTENANCE_SCHEDULE*.specifies;

A Case Study Using MOSES

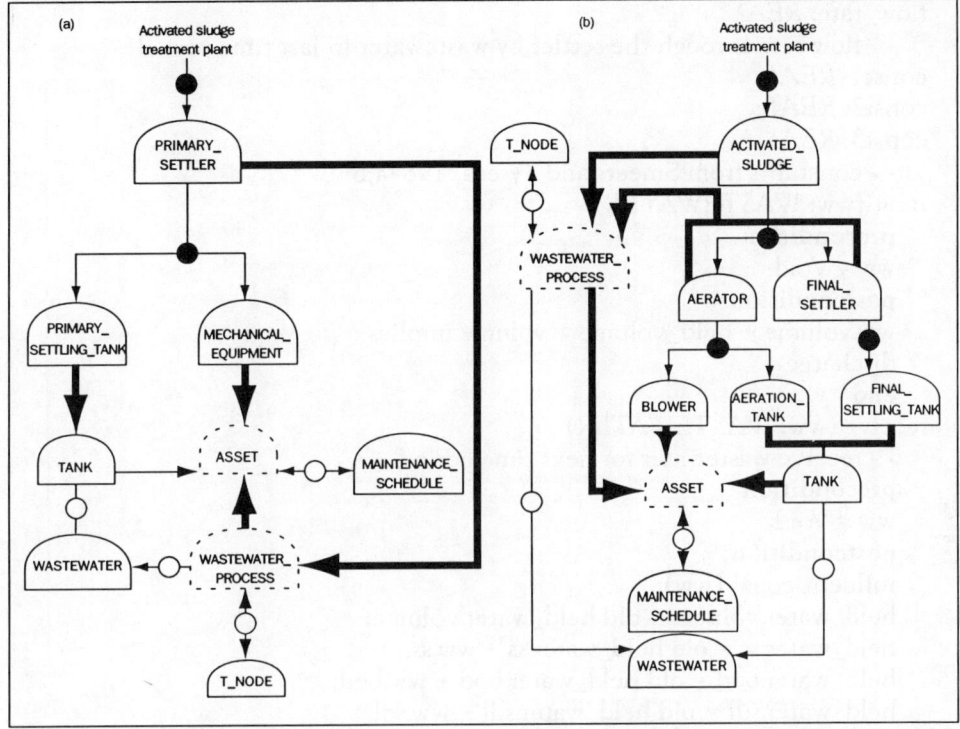

Figure 8.16 *Refined O/C Models for the two sheets: (a) activated sludge sheet; (b) primary settler sheet*

historic_cost: *DOLLAR*;
  -- the original (actual) cost of the asset
total_depreciation: *DOLLAR*;
  -- total of depreciation charge over the useful life of the tank
annual_depreciation: *DOLLAR*;
  -- depreciation charge paid for last full year
residual_value: *DOLLAR*;
  -- expected value of the asset after the useful life has expired
actual_age: *HOUR*;
useful_life: *HOUR*;
volume: *REAL*;
area: *REAL*;
  -- area of the tank
efficiency: *REAL*;
  -- percentage removal of material
clock: *CLOCK*;
  -- a global clock

flow_rate: *REAL*;
  -- flow rate through the settler by wastewater in last time period
const1: *REAL*;
const2: *REAL*;
const3: *REAL*;
  -- constants from Smeers and Tyteca, 1984a,b
treat (ww: *WASTEWATER*)
  precondition
  ww ≠ Void
  postcondition
  ww.volume + held_volume > volume implies
  discharge
  end
receive (ww: *WASTEWATER*)
  -- receive wastewater for next time period
  precondition
  ww ≠ Void
  postcondition
  influent.equal (ww);
  held_water.volume = **old** held_water.volume;
  held_water.ss = **old** held_water.ss + ww.ss;
  held_water.bod = **old** held_water.bod + ww.bod;
  held_water.sdl = **old** held_water.sdl + ww.sdl;
  held_water.sndl = **old** held_water.sndl + ww.sndl;
  held_water.ddl = **old** held_water.ddl + ww.ddl;
  held_water.ab = **old** held_water.ab + ww.ab
  end
discharge
  -- discharge wastewater treated in last time period. Make
  -- available in "effluent"
  postcondition
  effluent.ddl = **old** held_water.ddl * efficiency;
  effluent.sdl = **old** held_water.sdl * efficiency;
  effluent.ab = **old** held_water.ab * efficiency;
  effluent.sndl = **old** held_water.sndl * efficiency;
  effluent.volume = **old** held_water.volume − volume
  held_water.volume = volume
  end
invariant
  total_depreciation = annual_depreciation * (age/8760);
  annual_depreciation = historic_cost − residual_value / (useful_life /8760);
  historic_cost >= 0.0; total_depreciation >= 0.0; residual_value >= 0.0;
  actual_age >= 0.0; useful_life >= 0.0
  volume = sum tank.volume in set tanks;
  efficiency = 1 − const1 ((held_water.ss^const2) / (flow_rate/area)^const3));

```
        flow_rate = effluent.volume / clock.time_step;
        const1 = 0.1395;
        const2 = 0.27;
        const3 = 0.22;
end
```

8.2.2.9 Iteration

The activities to this point have led to a first draft of the specification model comprising the O/C Model, objectcharts, and Event Models for subsystem 1.1. The next step is an iteration of these activities concentrating on making complete abstractions for each class (Activity: Generalization for Reuse), detailing the contracts of each operation, including the specifications of cardinality and existence constraints, and ensuring that the responsibilities of the subsystem can be satisfied by the model. These later activities involve further verification and validation of the classes by traces, and evaluation of the model for its flexibility and potential reusability. For example, many of the classes such as TANKs, MECHANICAL_EQUIPMENT, and WASTEWATER are not unique to the wastewater application and are applicable to many other similar systems.

WASTEWATER, for example, can be found to occur in every subsystem, which raises the question of which subsystem it actually belongs to. There is no clear-cut answer: either the class can be assigned to one subsystem and other subsystems request that services be developed for this class, or it can be assigned to a separate subsystem. In this case we assign WASTEWATER to the subsystem *Liquid*, where a number of high-level abstractions are developed using a shopping-list approach (Meyer, 1988a), independent of any one actual system.

8.2.2.10 Discussion

The process described above has involved the application of all the activities of the MOSES methodology. The process of developing a model and its documentation using O/C Models, objectcharts, Event Models, and Class Specifications has been examined. A number of decisions that needed to be made during a development, particularly the reality versus strict OOA/D, and the modeling of lifecycle behavior, were also discussed. The use of generalization came later in the process, once a first pass at the O/C Model had been undertaken. This model was validated by the use of object traces and scenarios for the "normal" cases to ensure that the model satisfies the major responsibilities.

The process also involved thinking about reuse early. For example, a number of components were modeled that, although not strictly necessary for this system, will be useful to other systems. Reevaluation and iteration were also important aspects of refining the model. Further refinements may be expected as we move to implementation.

The methodology has been presented for only one subsystem (subsystem 1.1), that is, only one cluster. Other teams may be dealing with other subsystems. The communication between groups is important in order to identify reusable classes, or classes developed in both subsystems. A review should identify which classes should be assigned to which subsystem if similar classes are found in two or more subsystems. Similarly, generalization hierarchies may cross subsystems and the control of hierarchies should be a project-wide issue. The coordination of subsystems and O/C Models is defined in Activity: Subsystem Coordination. This activity needs to be explicitly planned for during the project and is particularly important on a large project. An example of this cross-subsystem development is the class WASTEWATER mentioned above, which appeared in a number of subsystems.

The outcome of this phase of the methodology is a set of classes that model the economic costs of wastewater treatment plant operations at the time scale of hours. They provide the ability to simulate a wastewater plant at the level of the processes and therefore enable the water manager to manage variable costs more effectively and understand the possible impact of different operational strategies.

With the basic O/C Model now in place, we now move on to develop the specification model for the more design-oriented subsystems. This involves developing new classes and refining already specified classes by adding detail to the static and dynamic models. However, before continuing we should seek feedback from the users regarding the high-level O/C Model we have created. The use of an iterative development approach here is thus aimed at better defining the user requirements rather than incrementally delivering system functionality. This distinction between incremental delivery and iterative development or prototyping is an important aspect for project management.

8.2.3 Specification of the GUI model

We now begin to add classes which emphasize the computer domain, including the graphical user interface (GUI) (see below). By examining the responsibilities of the system, a number of more detailed requirements can be identified. For example, the system is to be interactive and menu-driven. For the overall architecture of the system it was decided to use the Sprague and Carlson (1982) DSS framework. Hence there are three basic components of the application: the interface, the modelbase, and the database. In the following sections we concentrate on the models of the modelbase and the interface components. We now refine the O/C Model developed so far by adding more "design-level" O/Cs and relationships, including the menu and command structure of the application. Data entry and validity checking operations will also need to be developed. Once again, identification of these operations will be based on the responsibilities of the subsystem.

The requirements and subsystem responsibilities identify the need for configuring models, storing and retrieving models, editing and creating models, and simulating models. Also, facilities for viewing and printing the results of the models are required. Analysis of this functionality is a detailed process, again requiring interviews and possibly prototyping the interface with interface builder tools.

A Case Study Using MOSES

We begin with a detailed list of the menu structure and commands of the application. Figure 8.17 shows the menu structure that was developed.

For each menu item it is possible to develop a scenario and thereby define how the functionality is to be seen by the user. This leads to the identification of required events (Activity: Service Identification) from a number of objects. For example, the "create model" scenario is shown below:

Scenario for Create Model Command
User enters "Create Model" menu item.
Data Entry window for the model is displayed.
User enters data into entry fields, which are validated on a per field basis.
After the final field is entered and validated the screen is closed and an object is created in modelbase with the appropriate parameters.

This scenario identifies a number of new classes, including data ENTRY_WINDOWs and ENTRY_FIELDs, which provide services to display and enter data for the different objects of the system. A number of new services on existing classes are also identified, such as requests to create a class and store objects in the modelbase.

An Event Model can be developed (Activity: Event Model Construction) for this scenario, showing the new classes and the new messages needed on the classes already specified. One Event Model is shown in Figure 8.18.

Scenarios for other functionality identified in the responsibilities, such as the ability to create, modify, delete, and configure models, should also be developed, and traced to services on classes through the use of Event Models.

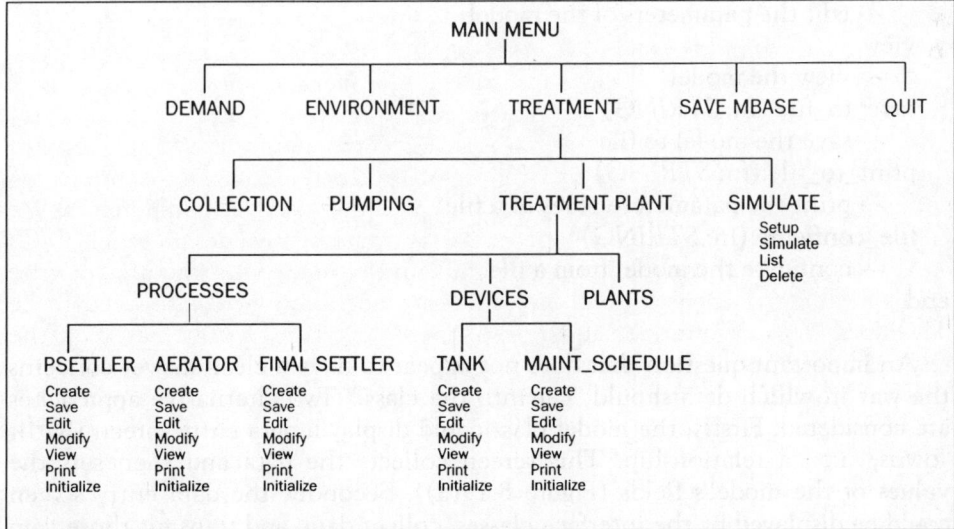

Figure 8.17 *Menu and command structure for ECWAT decision-aid*

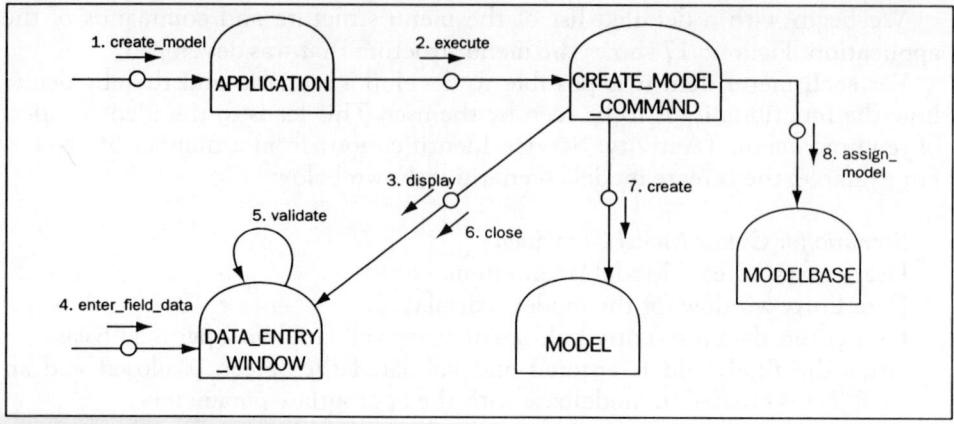

Figure 8.18 *Event Model for Create model scenario*

The definition of each message identified should be recorded in the class specification. The class specification below shows the basic functionality required for each class of the model and represents the available menu options for the class.

class PRIMARY_SETTLER
visible
    new
        - - create a new valid model
    edit
        - - edit the parameters of the model
    view
        - - view the model
    save_to_file (fn: *STRING*)
        - - save the model to file
    print_to_file (fn: *STRING*)
        - - print the parameter values to a file
    file_configure (fn: *STRING*)
        - - configure the model from a file
end

An important question that does not appear to have a clear answer concerns the way in which data should "get into the class." Two alternative approaches are considered. Firstly, the model class could display a data entry screen that it "owns," i.e., a relationship. This screen collects the data and then sets the values of the model's fields (Figure 8.19(a)). Secondly, the data entry screen could be displayed by the interface classes, collect data, and transmit those data to the model class (Figure 8.19(b)). The first approach involves the model

A Case Study Using MOSES

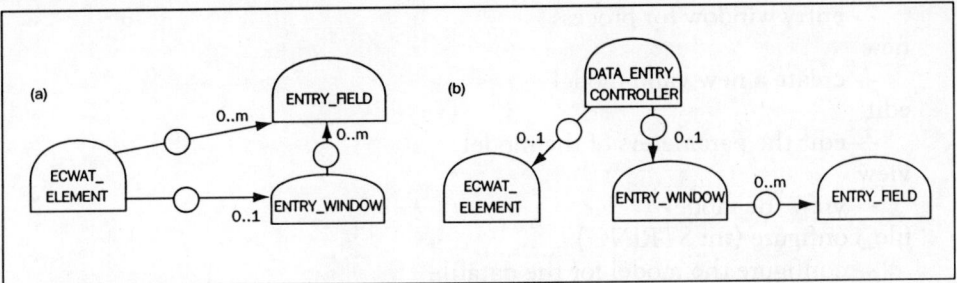

Figure 8.19 *Two options for the relationships between ENTRY_WINDOW and ECWAT_ELEMENT*

being involved to some extent in the user interface, while the second approach involves information on the model being split between two classes, the model and the entry screen. The solution adopted is to have each class of the model use the services of a data ENTRY_WINDOW class. Instances of a data ENTRY_WINDOW class would be configured for the individual classes of the model by services provided by the ENTRY_WINDOW. So, for example, a PRIMARY_SETTLER class has a relationship with an ENTRY_WINDOW class that it configures from services provided by the ENTRY_WINDOW. This approach requires less data transmission between classes and a localization of knowledge about the model. However, it does tend to blur the pure "model" versus "interface" abstractions that have been developed. This is deemed acceptable, since the user interface can rarely be completely separate from the model. The classes associated with the user interface are discussed further below.

As most of the additional services discovered on the classes of the model are applicable to all the classes of the treatment plant, an abstract class ECWAT_ELEMENT was abstracted out. A significant amount of the specification for entering and validating the data entered into a class is generic and could therefore be specified for the class of ECWAT_ELEMENT. For example, *new* builds an ENTRY_WINDOW whose characteristics are specified by a *build_entry_window* service. This service will need to be redefined for each class. This means that many of the services related to the interface can operate on any class that is a descendant of ECWAT_ELEMENT rather than having to discriminate between the different types of models. The result of this decision is a more flexible interface that allows other models of the treatment plant to be added with little trouble by specializing ECWAT_ELEMENT.

abstract class ECWAT_ELEMENT
visible
   identifier: STRING;
     - - name of model
   interface: ENTRY_WINDOW

```
        - - entry window for process
    new
        - - create a new valid model
    edit
        - - edit the parameters of the model
    view
        - - view the model
    file_configure (fn: STRING)
        - - configure the model for the datafile
    print_in_file (fn: STRING)
        - - print the parameters to the file "fn"
    save_to_file (fn: STRING)
        - - save parameters to file "fn"
    set_values_of_entry_fields
        - - set the values of the entry fields of the "interface"
    set_values_from_entry_fields
        - - set values of parameters from entry fields of the
        - - "interface"
    build_entry_screen
        - - build the characteristics of the entry screen
end
```

Responsibilities of the subsystem should be validated against the menu, which in turn should be validated by walking through the object services and object traces. For example, one responsibility is to be able to edit the model. This is provided for by the command that involves the service *edit* on ECWAT_ELEMENT. This service calls the *build_entry_screen* service, which builds an instance of the appropriate data entry screen, and then the *entry_cycle* service which is responsible for validating the entered data. Once *entry_cycle* is complete, the data entry screen is closed and data are assigned to the model by the *set_values_from_entry_fields* service.

The requirements stated that the system was to be menu-driven. Within the Specification Phase, it was not possible to do any domain analysis or to investigate libraries for reuse, as no applications or classes have been developed for this domain. However, in the more general domain of user interface, a significant number of classes have been developed that can often be reused almost without modification. We therefore examined the applicability of a number of class libraries (Activity: Library Class Incorporation) that had already been developed for this type of application. We decided to use the Winpack library of Eiffel V2.3, which has a large number of reusable components for windows and user interface development. The library contains the classes POPUP_MENU, COMMAND, and WINDOW among others. Not only were the classes reused, but the architecture employed was based on this framework of reusable components. This reuse of components early is an important part of developing *with* reuse. In this case, although the language decision was apparently taken early, in many ways these library classes were considered simply prototypical of reusable library classes to be found in many different language domains.

Therefore, even though we did not have a specification O/C Model for this subsystem, there was very little need to identify classes, structure, and behavior in this subsystem, as a "framework" was already provided by the library. The classes did, however, require modification and extension for the purposes of the application. This subsystem therefore reflects the "modification" and "direct use" subsystem/cluster lifecycles. A number of "new" classes were developed as specializations of the more general classes of the library (Activity: Library Class Incorporation and Activity: Inheritance Identification).

The basic architecture adopted was to have a menu that contains either a popup menu or a command and to loop on the main menu until a command is found that can be executed. This approach maximizes the flexibility of the command structure by employing dynamic binding and polymorphism. For example, the service *execute* is applied to the appropriate instance of COMMAND, which is only known at run-time. New commands can be added to the system by generalizing the class COMMAND and defining the *execute* operation. No other services need be impacted by the change.

One class from which many extensions were developed was the class COMMAND. This class provides an abstraction of a basic menu command in an interactive system and is specialized to provide the necessary functionality for the different commands of the system. Initially, the class COMMAND appears to be a functional class and little else. However, its services include *execute*, *undo*, and *redo*, all of which require state information to be held in the class (Meyer, 1988b). Thus the class is a broader notion than simply a function that forgets its state upon completion. Each class COMMAND acts on some component of the model; for example, the edit COMMAND acts on ECWAT_ELEMENT instances that are stored in the modelbase. Requests are sent to the instances of ECWAT_ELEMENT services in order for the user to edit the class. These instances may, at run-time, be descendants of ECWAT_ELEMENT, e.g., PRIMARY_SETTLER.

For each COMMAND, a scenario is developed presenting a picture of how the system interacts with the user. These scenarios should be developed in a similar manner to the "create" scenario described earlier and include dialogue and error messages passed to the user via windows and dialogue boxes. Once again, windowing is a domain rich in reusable components and a further examination of the class library revealed a large number of window classes for user interface display. These classes were specialized further to provide a number of services that were to be used in the system, such as the different types of windows, including input, output, and help windows. Figure 8.20 shows the O/C Model for this aspect of the system. The important point is that much of the development occurred through specialization of an existing framework of classes and thus followed the "modification" cluster model of Figure 3.15.

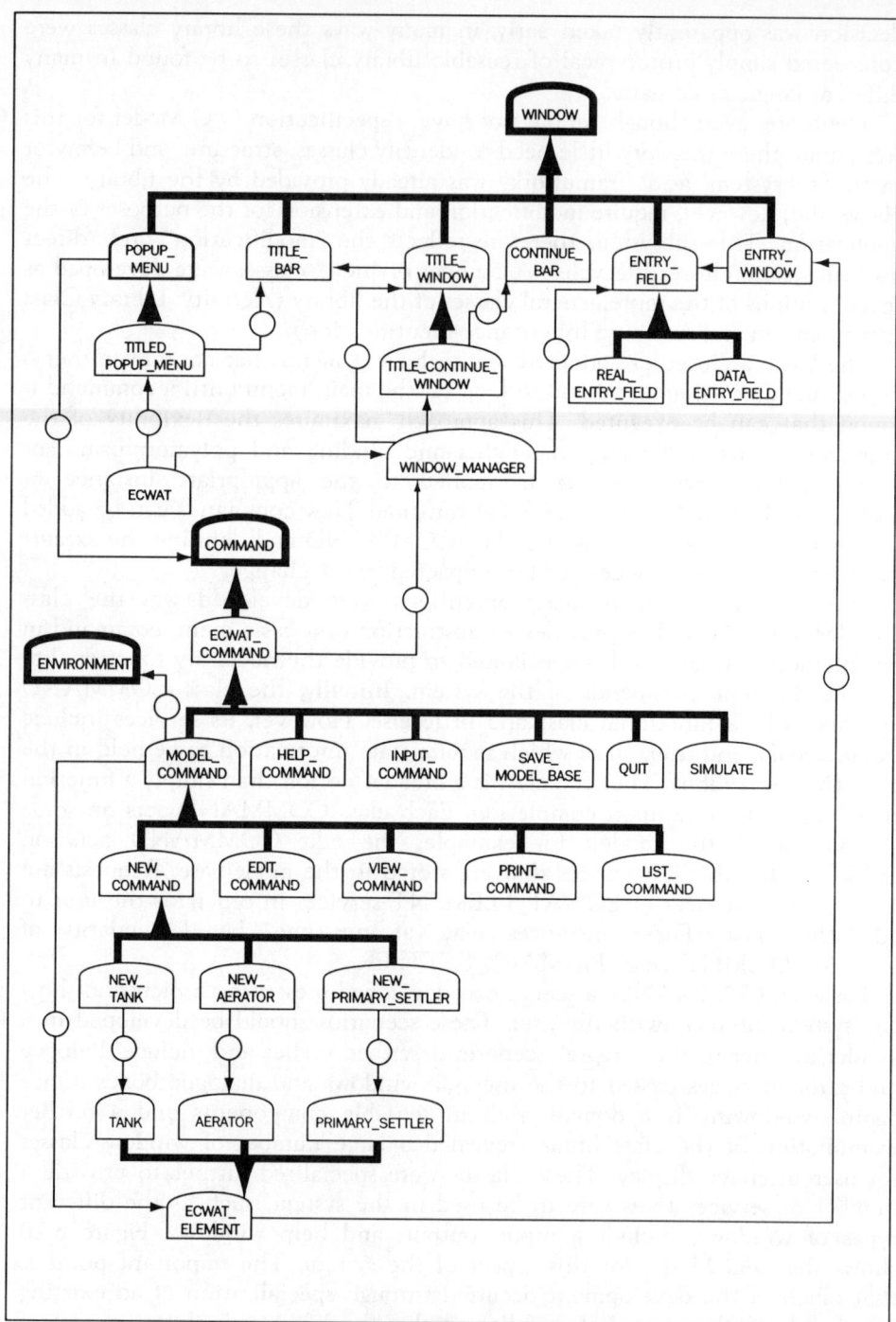

Figure 8.20 O/C Model for the menu and command structure

In this architecture the command classes control the scenario by coordinating the user interface classes with the model and database classes. In general, separating the interface, dialogue, and view components from the model is a useful approach to application design, and this approach has been adhered to in this design wherever possible. The COMMAND, model, and interface approach is similar to the model-view-controller model and leads to a fairly clear separation between the different aspects of the model. A class WINDOW_MANAGER was developed to encapsulate the responsibilities for the dialogue and presentation of the results, as well as to manage windows on the screen. We do not attempt a detailed description of the windowing aspect of the model.

Each class COMMAND therefore fulfills some of the functional requirements of the system. These requirements should be validated by walkthroughs of the functionality and class services and by checking that each piece of required functionality is provided by some class. For example, the major piece of functionality is to be able to simulate a treatment plant. This is provided by the class SIMULATE and other related classes (Figure 8.20). A scenario for the simulate command is as follows:

Simulate Scenario
User enters "Simulate" menu item.
Input window displayed prompting for the name of the model to run.
User enters model name, which is validated against the modelbase.
Model retrieved from database.
User asked to start simulation (y/n).
User enters "yes".
Simulation of model begins.
Message to tell user that model run is completed.

This scenario identifies a number of operations on the WINDOW_MANAGER, MODELBASE, and models that should be traced to objects and specified. The scenario above is controlled by the *execute* operation of the class SIMULATE, which is specified below.

class *SIMULATE*
visible
  sim_run: SIM_RUN
    - - template specifying the input, output, and model to be simulated
  modelbase: MODELBASE
    - - storage of models and simulation run information
  input_window: WINDOW
    - - window for inputting text
  simulate
    BEGIN
    get next_input from input_window;

```
            IF input_window.last_input exists in modelbase THEN
                sim_run = modelbase.sim_run where
                    sim_run.name = input_window.last_input;
                get next_input from input_window
                IF input_window.last_input = "yes" THEN
                    ask sim_run to simulate model;
                    IF simulation ok THEN
                        report "simulation run completed"
                    ELSE
                        report "error in simulation"
                    END
                ELSE
                    report "simulation canceled"
                END
            ELSE
                report "name does not exist"
            END
            END
        end
    end
```

The operation specification above has been developed using Structured English rather than the pre- and postconditions normally used (Hawryszkiewycz, 1988). It is possible to specify this type of operation using pre- and postconditions with the **implies** and **or** operators (see below). However, quite often the Structured English approach provides a specification that is more readable and understandable to users than Boolean assertions. Which approach is adopted is left to the developer. It is recommended, however, that in defining the specification model, the developer be as formal as possible in order to achieve a correct and rigorous specification for the core model, but that for the interface and user-oriented specifications a Structured English approach be adopted, since User Interface tends to be procedurally oriented. Each approach has advantages and disadvantages and these needed to be evaluated during the development. A pre- and postcondition specification of the above scenario may look as follows:

class *SIMULATE*
    ... as before
visible
    simulate
    postcondition
    exists n_1, n_2: *STRING*;
        n_1 = input_window.next_input;
        n_2 = input_window.next_input;

… [modelbase.item_exists (n_1) = False implies
      output_window.message = "No item exists"]
   or
   [modelbase.item_exists (n_1) = True and n_2 = "yes" and sim_run.simulated
      = True **implies** output_window.message = "Simulation Ok"]
   or
   [modelbase.item_exists (n_1) = True and n_2 /= "yes" **implies**
      output_window.message = "Simulation canceled"]
   or
   [modelbase.item_exists = True (n_1) and n_2 = "yes" and sim_run.simulated
      = False **implies** output_window.message = "Error in simulation"]
   end
end

The details of the functionality and COMMAND classes are now quite specific to the application and basically implement the scenario developed for that function.

This operation identification and specification and trace approach should be completed for all the functionality identified for the system. As the functionality is specified further it may require iteration to the design model of subsystem 1.1 in order to check invariants and constraints and addition of extra services.

8.2.3.1 Discussion

The refinement and elaboration processes as described above illustrates a number of interesting features of MOSES. Firstly, for subsystem 1.1, the process was a continuous *refinement* of the existing O/C Model, with very few new classes being required. Instead, a number of new services were identified from the scenarios, and a number of new generalizations were able to be developed. This subsystem reflects the "direct-use" cluster model (Figure 3.15).

On the other hand, the user interface and window management aspects were not developed until later in the Specification Phase. This subsystem involved a significant amount of reuse, not only of classes but also of larger "frameworks" of classes that provided the architecture for large portions of the system. In this subsystem, reuse and specialization were the major activities occurring. A number of new classes were identified that represented classes specific to the system, such as the classes ECWAT and WINDOW_MANAGER. Every system will need these system-specific classes.

This large-scale reuse in the subsystem negated almost completely the need to construct an O/C Model for the user interface. Instead, library integration allowed a modification process to occur that was also a refinement of the O/C Model (Activity: Library Class Incorporation). This subsystem therefore followed the "modification" cluster model (Figure 3.15).

The outcome of the Specification Phase is a design for ECWAT that should be easily implementable in an OOPL. The design describes the user interface and modelbase components, although at this stage the graphical output components specified initially have not been developed.

8.2.4 Implementation Phase

The next phase is the Implementation Phase. In this project, the OOPL Eiffel was used, which is a pure OOPL that supports the "programming by contract" ideas used in MOSES. As a result, very little translation is required to the target language and there is really no need to build a "generic" software model. The primary activities in this process therefore involve exploiting the language mechanisms to the full and are relatively language-dependent. However, a number of general tasks can be identified.

Firstly, it is necessary to decide on the implementation strategy for the remaining association and aggregation relationships (Subactivity: Implementation of Structure). The major decision when translating to the relationships of the OOPL is the direction of the relationship. For example, in the discharge relationship between WASTEWATER and WASTEWATER_PROCESS the relationship is made into a reference from the process to the wastewater. The wastewater does not need to know which process is treating it, and the system never requires such information. Therefore, many of the relationships identified can easily be modeled as (unidirectional) relationships and simply implemented using the client–server model of the OOPL.

Another Implementation Phase task is to identify and maximize genericity (Activity: Genericity Specification). In this model, genericity was identified for a class GANTRY that modeled a number of flows into a tank and wastewater process. Any liquid can flow in a GANTRY and so GANTRY is a constrained generic class, constrained by the class LIQUID. Once again, if the target language is known before the development begins, identification of genericity may be possible earlier in the development. This is a project-specific decision.

Thirdly, persistent classes should also be specified (Subactivity: Identify Persistent Classes). In this system, persistent classes are simply entered into an ENVIRONMENT, which is a secondary storage capability for objects from the Eiffel library. Persistency was a fairly straightforward matter using this approach.

A fourth, and major, implementation task is to implement the behavior specified in the contract table for each operation (Activity: Translation to OOPL; Subactivity: Implementation of Services). It is at this point that details of algorithms and internal optimization should be of prime concern (Activity: Optimization). In this example the implementation was a relatively straightforward matter of translating the contracts or Structured English descriptions into the implementation language.

Implementing generalization was also relatively easy, as Eiffel provides a powerful inheritance mechanism. The use of inheritance in the Implementation Phase was as near to a generalization hierarchy as possible using the language mechanism, although an implementation-inheritance-type hierarchy was applied in a few cases. This inheritance hierarchy was more of a "mixin" approach in some cases and provided access to some features of the system by means of inheritance rather than client–server. For example, many of the constants of the system were inherited into a class. This does not truly represent the **is-a** relationship but may sometimes be a useful implementation mechanism.

We do not intend to discuss this phase in any further detail, as it is really implementation-language-specific. However, an important point is that at this stage a significant amount of inheritance may occur that was not identified at the early Specification Phase. These inheritance relationships will be more like "mixins" that are oriented toward reuse of classes from the library that are not necessarily the subtype relationships. Nonetheless, they are useful relationships for efficiency and productivity, whose usefulness will depend on the language construct and its semantics for its application.

8.2.5 Generalizing the O/C Model

The activity we wish to discuss is that of generalization (Activity: Generalization for Reuse). Generalization involves a number of subactivities such as Subactivity: Completion of abstractions, Subactivity: Optimization, and Subactivity: Refinement of inheritance hierarchies. We view generalization as a separate activity in the development cycle, although the "reuse" mindset should pervade the development (Menzies et al., 1992; Henderson-Sellers and Pant, 1993). That is to say, during the development the developers have been consciously thinking of developing reusable abstraction and maximizing generalization. If this is the case, the generalization activity becomes less of a burden on the overall project and is likely to be better integrated within the overall development. Generalization is also a process that tends not to be complete until after a number of projects. This case study, being the first development of its kind, did not have a large generalization phase. A number of activities could, however, be identified.

Firstly, we aimed to complete the abstractions of a number of the treatment plant models (Subactivity: Completion of abstractions). In particular, a number of services were developed to provide easier reporting of information from the model for different time periods. These provide a number of short-cut services that make the abstraction easier to use.

Secondly, the refinement of the class hierarchies was a major undertaking in this phase (Subactivity: Refinement of inheritance hierarchies). The class hierarchy structure was abstracted even further than during the analysis, with the commonality between processes and tanks being noted. This led to the class TRANSSHIPMENT_NODE being developed, which is a more abstract notion of a node through which liquids flow. Also, classes such as TANK and ASSET are sufficiently abstract to be used in numerous different systems.

The third subactivity was to optimize the design (Subactivity: Optimization).

As the system was not thoroughly implemented, optimization was not a major problem, although a number of the classes for generating input to the simulation were optimized in terms of the data structures and algorithms used. This work did not impact on the class interface and therefore did not affect the structure of the model.

There was only one set of multiple implementations of an abstract class in this system, which was for the class LIQUID. The implementations allow for the different combinations of data and calculations used for the density, volume, and mass properties.

Much of the work of the generalization activity will continue after this system has been developed, as the further identification of services and generalization hierarchies only comes with extended domain knowledge and experience. Once a number of systems have been developed within this area, it will be easier to complete the abstraction.

8.3 Summary and conclusions

This chapter has given a flavor of the development process, activities, and deliverables using MOSES by applying the approach to development of a wastewater decision support system. The resulting design of ECWAT has been implemented as a prototype decision-aid offering the minimum required functionality. The prototype was developed in Eiffel (V2.3) and is approximately 150 classes and 15,000 lines of code.

The case study and checklist approach both provided a useful demonstration of how the methodology is applied in a practical situation.

8.4 Study example

Exercise 8 The car market (Exercise 7 in Chapter 7) is widening. Customers can make a free choice from among the Holden Camira, the Ford Falcon, the Mazda 626, and the Mazda RX7. Mechanics are needed to service the vehicles, but they need special training for the RX7. Further, there is rumored to be a new three-wheeler about to enter the market, but no one seems sure which manufacturer is producing it.

Develop an Implementation Phase O/C Model that will maintain sufficient flexibility and reusability to encompass these possible market directions.

• CHAPTER 9 •

Project Management and Commercial Adoption of OOSE

9.1 Project management

9.1.1 Managing the OO SDLC

The successful adoption, on a large scale, of object-oriented technology for information systems development depends not simply on the availability of object-oriented languages in a technically well-supported environment, but, as we have seen, on the adoption of the object-oriented *philosophy* or *mindset* by both technicians (programmers and analysts) and managers (project managers and higher-level executives) (cf. Henderson-Sellers, 1992a).

It is generally accepted that there is an urgent need for supporting tools, methodologies, and management structures (e.g., Page-Jones, 1991a). Such support has been rapidly developing over the last few years, both in the research and commercial contexts (some examples are given in Table 9.1). CASE tools are particularly highly sought after by the commercial and industrial sectors.

As noted in Section 1.2, the basic aims of all software developers, as outlined by Goldberg (1991a), are:

- to deliver the product on time (and within budget);
- to ensure that the product meets user requirements;

- to respond to user requests for changes;
- to offer increasingly sophisticated applications;
- to keep up with technological standards;
- to ensure that project teams feel well motivated and successful.

Table 9.1 Some examples of recent research on project management issues within OT adoption

Topic	Reference
Lifecycle methodologies	Henderson-Sellers and Edwards (1990a), Henderson-Sellers (1990)
Requirements analysis	Bailin (1989), Umphress and March (1991)
Libraries	Meyer (1990a), Price and Girardi (1990)
Databases	Premerlani et al. (1990)
Management implications	Thomsett (1990)
Metrics	Henderson-Sellers (1991a), Tegarden et al. (1992, 1993)
CASE tools	Korson and McGregor (1990)

In managing the object-oriented software development process, certain dissimilarities with standard structured systems development must be identified. Two of these crucial areas relate to the potential for reuse and the development of appropriate metrics as an additional tool to assist in project management. In Chapter 10, the use of metrics for project management and reuse is analyzed in terms of return on investment (ROI). An example simulation over a number of projects illustrates the potential savings of adopting a consistent reuse management strategy.

It should be noted that in an object-oriented development environment, not only is effort required to learn about the new technology but also, in a mature development team, the effort required in the Specification Phase (analysis and especially design) is significantly more than in a traditional development environment (Figures 9.1 and 9.2). OT resource expenditures are compared with the level required in a traditional development, as indicated by the horizontal line in Figure 9.1. Coding is less for a well-specified, bounded OO system; testing decreases as a result of incremental modifications of existing library classes, which are themselves well tested; and integration testing becomes in OT a natural component throughout a significant portion of the incremental delivery style of lifecycle (e.g., Goldberg, 1993). Overall, this can lead to increased costs for the first release (Figure 9.2) but lower maintenance costs and an overall decrease in total system costs.

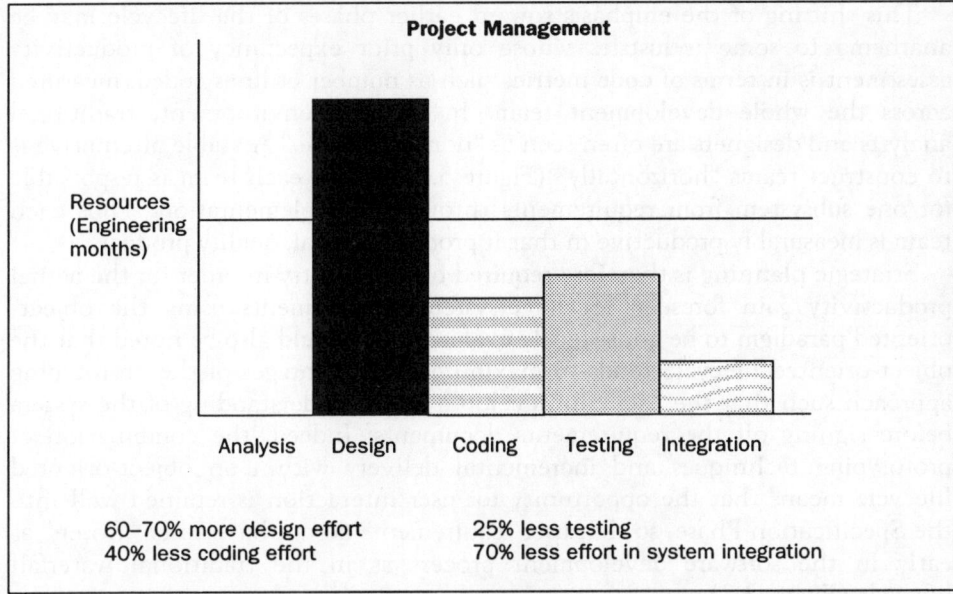

Figure 9.1 *Comparison of OO resources per lifecycle phase and non-OO environments (represented by the normalized horizontal line) (Booch, 1991)*

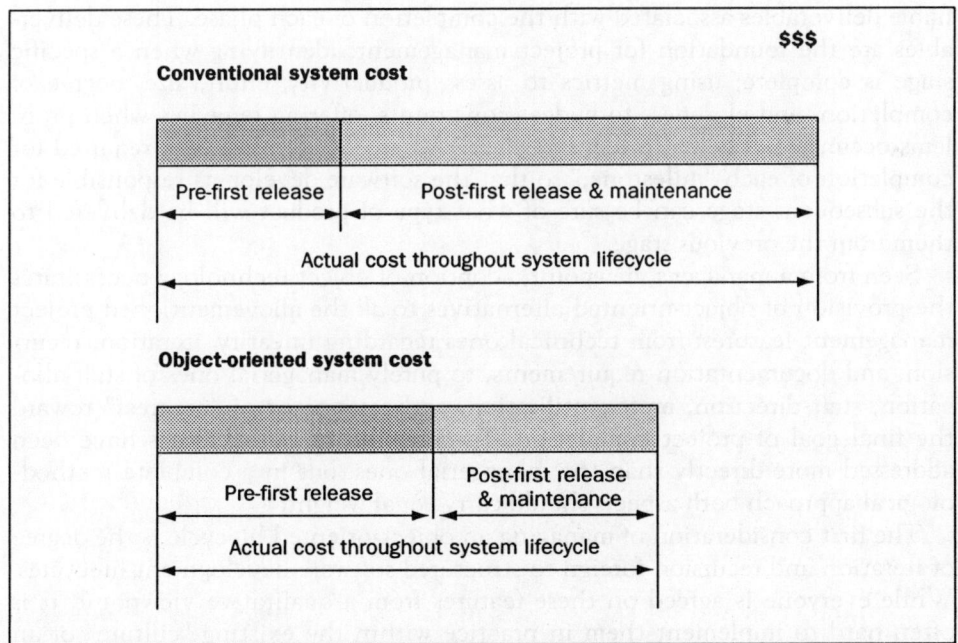

Figure 9.2 *Comparison of conventional and OO costs with respect to the first release data (Kandibur, © copyright SIGS Publications, 1992)*

This shifting of the emphasis toward earlier phases of the lifecycle may be anathema to some industries whose only prior expectancy of productivity assessment is in terms of code metrics such as number of lines coded, measured across the whole development team. In such an environment, traditional analysts and designers are often seen as "nonproductive." A viable alternative is to construct teams "horizontally" (Figure 3.5) so that each team is responsible for one subsystem from requirements through to implementation. Thus each team is measurably productive in that it produces a final, quality product.

Strategic planning is therefore required by an industry in order for the actual productivity gain foreseen for large-system developments using the object-oriented paradigm to be consistently evaluated. It should also be noted that the object-oriented lifecycle tends to maximize the advantages of the prototyping approach such that the user can develop a better understanding of the system before signing off the requirements documents. Indeed, the combination of prototyping techniques and incremental delivery within an object-oriented lifecycle means that the opportunity for user interaction is retained well into the Specification Phase, so that user requirements do not have to be "frozen" as early in the software development process as in the traditional waterfall lifecycle (Figure 3.2).

The primary focus of a methodology is "process" and process control. In the traditional "waterfall" model, this was reflected primarily in its identifiable stages, the linear progression throughout these stages, and the readily identifiable deliverables associated with the completion of each phase. These deliverables are the foundation for project management: identifying when a specific stage is complete; using metrics to assess productivity, effort, size, degree of completion, and closeness to budget constraints; offering remedies when problems occur, etc. They also identify clearly what documentation is required for completion of each "milestone," so that the software developers responsible for the subsequent stage can be sure of what type of product will be delivered to them from the previous stage.

Seen from a manager's viewpoint, adoption of object technology necessitates the provision of object-oriented alternatives to *all* the abovementioned project management features: from technical ones regarding linearity, iteration, recursion, and documentation requirements, to purely managerial ones of staff allocation, staff direction, metric utilization, and assessment of "progress" toward the final goal of project completion. To date, the technical issues have been addressed more directly than the managerial ones; but in a complete methodological approach both aspects should carry equal weight.

The first consideration of managing an object-oriented lifecycle is the degree of iteration and recursion foreign to structured software development lifecycles. While everyone is agreed on these features from a qualitative viewpoint, it is often hard to implement them in practice within the existing "culture" of an organization.

Of similar importance to project management is documentation and deliverables, within the context of the chosen methodology. It is crucial that some "milestones" can be identified and deliverables specified. This is also a weak feature of most current methodologies. For example, it should be feasible to specify deliverable documents at the end of the Specification Phase in the form of a design that acts as a blueprint for the subsequent implementation. Furthermore, because of the frequent use of recursion and iteration, the associated degree of granularity is critical. In other words, documentation should center on the subsystem level rather than the more traditional total system level.

Iteration and recursion, although desirable techniques from a user requirements specification perspective and from an incremental delivery perspective, require strong project management to ensure that objectives and budgets are met. In this regard, the scenarios of the MOSES Investigation Phase provide an important project management tool. A scenario is a defined piece of functionality as described and seen by a user of the system. Scenarios therefore describe the functionality of the system as perceived by the business. As such, scenarios can be prioritized by business users and management. High-priority scenarios are ones that are most important to the business and provide the core functions of the system. Once prioritized, scenarios, and the business functionality they represent, form the basis of the objectives of an iteration. Once the resources required to implement these scenarios have been estimated, the project manager has at his or her disposal a measure of completion and cost. Rather than trying to measure how complete the object model for the iteration is (an impossible task since the total size of the final object model is an unknown), the project manager can measure how many scenarios are completed and hence assess how far through the objectives the project currently is.

The focus on business functionality, as recorded in the scenarios, as a measure of completeness, is a more effective and meaningful measure to the business. This approach still suffers from problems such as (i) not all scenarios will be equally complex, thus taking different amounts of time to complete, and (ii) the early scenarios may take longer to implement owing to the need to build infrastructure classes. Despite these problems, scenarios provide a business-driven measure of the objectives of an iteration and the percentage of those objectives completed at any point in time.

Managing the MOSES process through scenarios means that traditional management milestones of "end-of-the-phase" and the associated deliverables have a reduced, although not totally absent, role in project management. End-of-phase milestones are replaced in MOSES by "end-of-iteration" milestones with the associated deliverables. With MOSES, end-of-phase milestones (within any one iteration) will tend to be of less significance, possibly acting as minor checkpoints throughout the development. End-of-iteration milestones are where the completed deliverables and current demo/delivery are produced. These iteration milestones should be about three months apart, interspersed with scenario-oriented milestones when major scenarios have been implemented. This approach to project management is very much a results-driven one, ensuring control over the iteration and recursion techniques of an OO SDLC.

Two other major responsibilities of a project manager in an object-oriented world are (i) the division of the project into subsystems that can then be assigned to individual project teams for development, and (ii) to be in charge of the latest demo (Meyer, 1992c). This is the working system *at the current stage of development*. Since the lifecycle model is highly iterative, iterations tend to correspond to incremental improvements to the system—though the system can remain operative, to different degrees of requirements satisfaction, *throughout* the development process, which is itself perhaps described as one providing incremental deliveries. The project manager's main responsibility is for this growing, embryonic product and to be able to demonstrate it to users/customers throughout its development.

One of the other major gains from OT is, as noted above, a decrease in testing and implementation costs and, more important, a significant decrease in maintenance costs. One management problem here is that often those costs are traditionally allocated to a division other than the developers. In other words, producing a product that requires less maintenance will not necessarily benefit the production team.

The United States Department of Defense estimates that corrections cost more than ten times as much as new developments (Graham, 1991). In a general environment where about 70% of programmers' efforts are devoted to maintenance of existing code, of which about 80% is spent on "bug fixes" (corrective maintenance) rather than enhancements (extensive maintenance), a new technology that is aimed primarily at a reduction in maintenance costs must be evaluated seriously.

In the increasingly competitive world within organizations, where internal cost accounting and cost and profit centers are the order of the day, managing the costs of object-oriented projects can cause a significant problem. On the one hand, they reduce costs to the organization in the long term, but these benefits may be accrued by a different department from the one that produced them. For example, if a business line pays for an initial development, the benefits from reduced testing through reuse may actually be felt by a competing business line in later projects. While the organization as a whole benefits, these benefits may not be evenly distributed throughout the business lines. A number of alternative business models may therefore be required to be implemented, depending on the internal accounting structure of an organization.

The incorporation of reuse into the business plan requires insight and a corporate policy to be developed. Four models have been proposed (Henderson-Sellers and Pant, 1993). Firstly, the "traditional" view is that generalization *for reuse* is an "add-on" to the lifecycle activities and occurs after the completion of the project (as implicit in the discussion above). Investment of additional effort to undertake the generalization activities necessary to create good, reusable classes has to be costed; but it is generally impossible to cost against the current project that, after all, is ostensibly finished. Building in reuse as an integral part of the lifecycle is discussed by Menzies *et al.* (1992). They propose that by bringing the generalization phase to earlier in the lifecycle, a "reuse mindset" can be created throughout the lifecycle. In this way, the generalization is undertaken *before* the finalization of the first product so that it is then available at no additional cost for future work. This means that the generalization costs are squarely laid on the customer for whose product the class was originally developed. Consequently, although such a refocusing should indeed encourage a full lifecycle reuse mindset, customers requesting products that have a significant component of already generalized classes are going to benefit, at the expense of the investment made by earlier customers.

The third model is that of a two-library model that may be useful in some industrial contexts. The first step is to put "on hold" project-specific classes from the current project by placing them in a library of potentially reusable components (LPRC) (Figure 9.3). The only additional project-specific effort is thus the identification of these classes. This adds basically nothing to the current costs. The second library is the high-quality company resource—the library of generalized components (LGC).

At the beginning of each future project, an early lifecycle activity is thus an assessment of classes currently residing in both the LPRC and the LGC databases as to their potential value in this new project. If so, then and only then is the additional spending on generalization made. Since this is to the benefit of the new project, it is perfectly reasonable to allocate the cost to this customer. It will still be a saving, and the developing company will then have a fully generalized class that can now undergo final quality checks and then be placed in the LGC for future reuse.

Henderson-Sellers and Pant (1993) also consider, as another option, the "alternative cost center" model in which the equivalent of an emerging technology group should be created. This would be an independent cost center that initially was funded solely to take those components of the LPRC and, in parallel and not customer-driven, invest in generalization. Their costs could be recovered on a longer time scale when these generalized costs were being used in projects that could therefore make a saving over a greenfield development. However, it is inevitable that such a group would run at a loss for a year or two, and this model is therefore only possible with those larger companies that are able to put aside this more strategic-type investment. Its operation is as an emerging technology group that acts as a facilitator rather than a profit center. The recognition of software, and especially library classes, as company assets may require a reevaluation of accounting practices within the company (Adams and Burbeck, 1992).

These business models and the accounting procedures surrounding OO projects are an important management aspect of introducing object technology into an organization.

As noted in Section 1.3.3, reuse is one of the major benefits of adopting object technology commercially. This requires detailed library management, which must be another concern of the project manager (Section 9.1.4). Gibbs

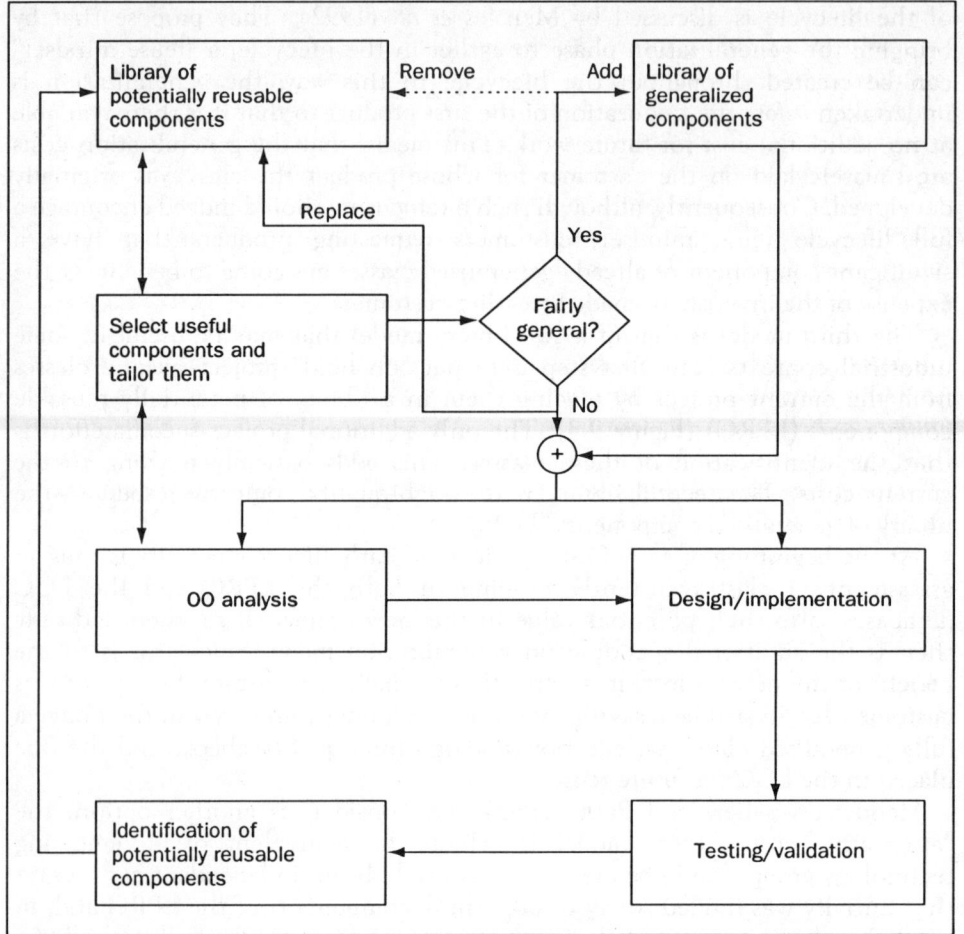

Figure 9.3 *A software reuse model using libraries of reusable and potentially reusable components (Henderson-Sellers and Pant, 1993)*

et al. (1990) describe class management in terms not only of database techniques but also of taking into account new concerns implicit in an object-oriented system. These relate to class evolution, class selection, and class packaging.

Apart from the mechanics of reuse, there are other management-oriented questions partly related to generalization that must be dealt with in an OO project. Not least of these is the issue of appropriate metrics to measure reuse (see Chapter 10). Other management questions arise regarding the interface between two project teams (cf. Constantine, 1990c). For example, if you are the project manager for one team, you presumably want your team to succeed, even perhaps at the expense of your colleague's team. Within such a competitive corporate culture, how is one team encouraged to build generalized classes useful not for its own future projects, but for an alternative team's next projects? Since generalization decreases your own productivity (with the currently available metrics) yet reuse of existing classes increases productivity, the "other team" will benefit from the first team's generalization efforts. Management will need to reassess how productivity, effort, and success are measured in an object-oriented software development environment (e.g., Hopkins and Warboys, 1990; Bollinger and Pfleeger, 1990). Thomsett (1990) evaluates such potential conflicts between two program development teams within the same organization. He recommends the institution of a linchpin role (Figure 9.4) between the two teams: someone who is responsible to both team leaders. This shared human resource will enhance the production and generalization of reusable library classes, as well as providing central support to both teams to avoid the conflict between class builders and class reusers identified above. Such a reporting structure is necessary if the quality of software is to be enhanced by the use of this new approach to software engineering: an approach for which traditional management structures are ill suited. Indeed, Thomsett (1990) stresses that we should regard the object-

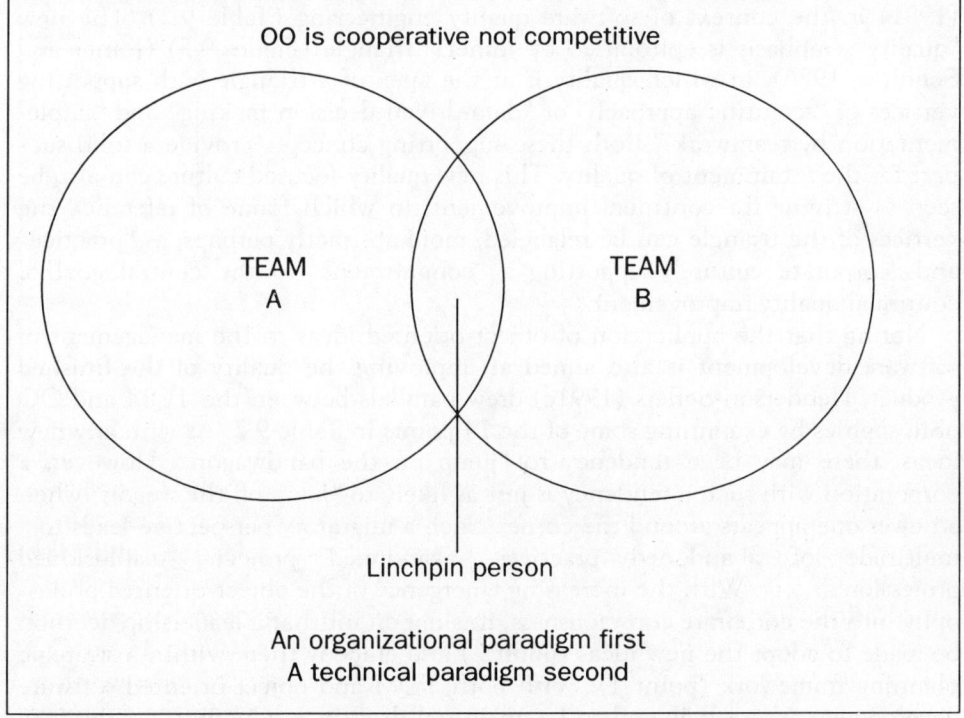

Figure 9.4 *The sphere of influence/responsibility of two object-oriented development teams overlaps. To avoid competition, a single person should belong to both teams in order to circumvent potential competition. (Thomsett, 1990)*

oriented development paradigm as an *organizational* paradigm first, and a technical development paradigm second.

Another of the prime motivations for management to adopt object technology could well be the search for quality improvement. Hence, identifiable similarities and synergies between object-oriented systems management and total quality management (Henderson-Sellers, 1991c; Howard, 1992a; Adams, 1992b) may facilitate an understanding of the use of object-oriented techniques in software engineering and the contribution that can be made in software quality assurance (SQA). SQA is designed to discover product defects. However, many problems occur because of defects in the *process* used to produce the products. Quality control (QC) introduces process modifications as a consequence of the identification of poor quality production.

Total quality management (TQM) is a modern management philosophy, developed essentially in industrial and commercial environments, which takes quality control even further. It focuses on the concept of quality, which it identifies as arising from the process central to the particular project/industry. A quantitative (statistical) study of this central process can highlight improvements that management, but not workers, can make to the system itself.

Zultner (1988) examines the interpretation of the 14 points of Deming (1981) in the context of software quality engineering (Table 9.2). The new "quality" emphasis is epitomized by Joiner's Triangle (Figure 9.5) (Joiner and Scholtes, 1986), in which quality is at the apex of a triangle with supporting vertices of "scientific approach" or "data-driven decision making" and "implementation by teamwork." Both these supporting concepts provide a solid support for the attainment of quality. This new quality-focused culture can also be seen as striving for continual improvement, in which frame of reference the vertices of the triangle can be relabeled, more abstractly perhaps, as "practice" and "corporate culture" supporting a "commitment" to the central goal of continual quality improvement.

Noting that the application of object-oriented ideas to the management of software development is also aimed at improving the quality of the finished product, Henderson-Sellers (1991c) drew parallels between the TQM and OO philosophies by examining some of the 14 points in Table 9.2. As with any new ideas, there may be a tendency to "jump on the bandwagon." However, a corporation with such a tendency is just as likely to "jump off the wagon" when a newer one appears around the corner. Such a migratory perspective leads to a multitude of abandoned practices, abandoned projects, disillusioned professionals, etc. With the increasing emergence of the object-oriented philosophy into the corporate consciousness, it is important that a leadership decision be made to adopt the new ideas (point 2) and embody them within a strategic planning framework (point 1). With both TQM and object-oriented software development, there is bound to be an initial drop in productivity as the new tools are learned. However, both are essentially *long-term investments* and the ultimate goal is that a *higher-quality product* (Table 1.3) will result that will take less time and cost less.

Project Management and Commercial Adoption of OOSE

Table 9.2 Deming's Fourteen Points

1. Create constancy of purpose
2. Adopt the new TQM philosophy
3. Evaluate the system objectively and quantitatively
4. Don't award business on price tag, rather on quality
5. Aim for constant improvement
6. Institute on-the-job training
7. Institute leadership rather than control
8. Drive out fear (of punishment)
9. Break down interdepartmental barriers (and rivalries)
10. Eliminate slogans (which are usually not achievable)
11. Eliminate numerical goals and objectives (including MBO)
12. Give workers pride in their work
13. Institute programs of self-improvement
14. Involve everyone

It is in the development of the library classes that quality can be built in. In developing object-oriented library classes (e.g., Meyer, 1990a), it is *vital* (and indeed perfectly feasible) that correctness, robustness, integrity, etc. (in other words, quality) (Meyer, 1989b) be built into each class before acceptance into the reuse library. Continuous monitoring of these classes during the development process, using safety mechanisms such as assertions (Meyer, 1989b), permits a continuous assessment (point 3) to be made. Since quality can now be built into the code modules, they will be purchased on an evaluation based on

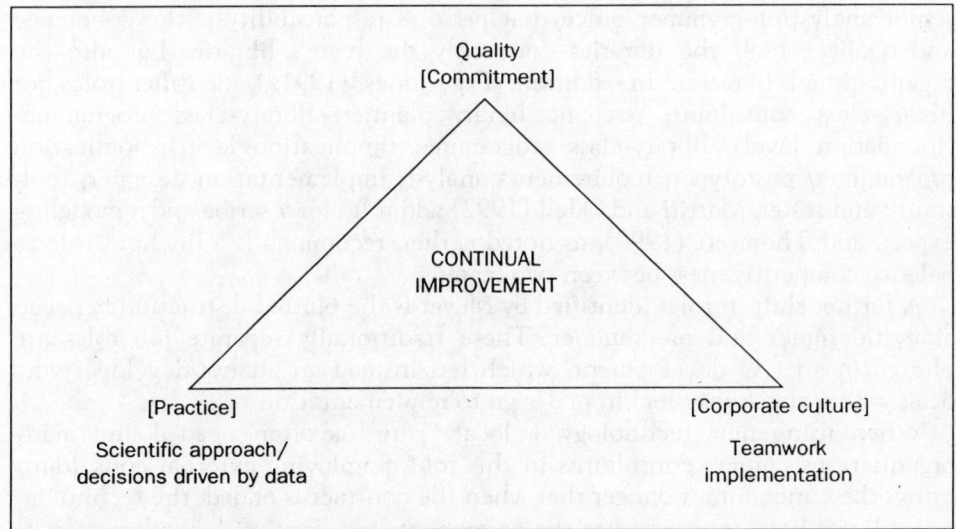

Figure 9.5 Joiner's Triangle (Henderson-Sellers, 1991c)

this stated quality, rather than on price (point 4). Additionally, it may be foreseen that software developers of truly generic and useful classes will indeed take pride in a job well done (point 12).

Quality and quality control are responsibilities of the project manager. Ensuring quality means holding regular design reviews, using a software engineering methodology, following standards and guidelines, and having skilled personnel. This last factor is probably the most crucial and probably the hardest to control, although it can be addressed by providing adequate training for the project team before and during the development. MOSES, as described in this book, is an important part of a project manager's tool kit for quality assurance. Its emphasis on contracts, rigorous software engineering techniques, process control, and design reviews aims to ensure that a quality product results. In particular, MOSES supports guidelines for reviews and assessment of the process and product throughout the process of development. Quality, an important management goal, is therefore supported by use of MOSES within an OO development project.

In this changing, quality-focused environment, organizational concerns are raised regarding the roles that need to be filled in an object-oriented development team. These are discussed in Section 9.1.2.

9.1.2 Organizational roles

Several observers of the object-oriented scene (e.g., Page-Jones, 1991a; Goldberg and Rubin, 1990; Urlocker, 1990; Thomsett, 1990; Lorenz, 1993) have noted that there are major organizational implications for the adoption of object technology. New professional positions need to be identified, clarified, and filled. Most notable here is the new role of "librarian." This should be a senior analyst/programmer, since that person's responsibility is the coherence and quality of all the libraries—not only the team's libraries but also the organizational libraries. In addition, Page-Jones (1991a) identifies roles for library-class consultant; strategic library planner; library-class programmer (foundation level); library-class programmer (application level); application programmer/ prototyper; requirements analyst; implementation designer; toolsmith; and tester. Martin and Odell (1992) add roles for a scribe and a modeling expert, and Thomsett (1990), as noted earlier, recommends a linchpin role to balance competitiveness between two teams.

A further shift in roles identified by Meyer is the blurred distinction between analyst/designer and programmer. These traditionally separate job roles are blurred in an OO development, which has instead an analyst/developer who deals with a class/subsystem from design to implementation.

When using new technology, a local "guru" is often needed and many organizations employ consultants in this role. Employing external consultants brings the concomitant danger that when the contract is ended, the technology has still not been transferred to the permanent staff. Part of this failure may be the pressure on the consultant to "get the job done"; part may be the resentment of the permanent staff at seeing a highly paid consultant being brought in effectively to "replace" them during the consultancy contract. What is needed is an in-house "object methodologist" (Jacobson et al., 1992, p454) who will first educate themselves, possibly in liaison with a more knowledgeable consultant, in identifying the most appropriate methodology and keeping up with its developments, both theoretical and empirical, and will then disseminate that knowledge to other team members. In addition to such an "object mentor," Goldberg (1991b; pers. com., 1993) identifies the need for an object administrator and an "object coach" to maintain consistency between implementation and design intent.

Other significant roles are those of people responsible for documentation and training and for quality assurance. There are probably two roles here in the overlap between quality assurance and librarian plus a technical writer. In a small organization these roles would probably be filled by the same person. Finally, with increased emphasis on incremental delivery and prototyping, a person with specific prototyping skills would be a welcome addition to the team.

In many projects, usually smaller ones, one person may play several roles. It is likely that a more "horizontal" stratification will be used where teams of people are allocated to individual subsystems (or clusters) and will follow their subsystem lifecycle all the way through from requirements specification to implementation.

It is likely (Urlocker, 1990) that software developers themselves will diverge to become either "builders" or "reusers." Builders operate in a more traditional environment; it is the skills of reusing existing code that are novel to OT and that have never performed more than a perfunctory role in software engineering curricula over the last few decades.

These new roles are best filled by people who have certain qualities (Meyer, 1992c). For example, a domain analyst is someone who has a good ability to abstract from the specific to the general. This is important if reusable classes are to be identified from the details of specific projects. Role changes will depend on the organization and its human resources. However, it is important to note that significant changes do occur in the organization's structure as a result.

9.1.3 Reuse

Reuse does not just "happen" (even using object technology!) but must be planned for and managed. Griss et al. (1991) suggest that one of the main inhibitors to reuse is the NIH[26] syndrome, which makes software developers unwilling to pay for good quality, third-party software. Learning how to optimize on reuse (Smart et al., 1988) is therefore not just a technical issue but also a management concern. For example, classes should conform strictly to the notion of being an implementation of an abstract data type and not simply a

---

26. NIH = not invented here.

collection of pieces of data and functionality in a single module "for convenience." Good metrics are also highly useful here. However, even perfectly designed and constructed classes and frameworks will need to be made readily available and "managed" (Meyer, 1990a; Gibbs et al., 1990). The granularity at which reuse is operated ranges across classes, frameworks, and subsystems.

When a new project is begun, commonalities with past projects are first identified and then the experience of those past projects is "reused" in terms of library classes either directly or in terms of slight modifications, usually through inheritance.

In procedural libraries, code modules are well tested and then frozen in libraries for future use by others (Section 9.1.4). Although this certainly provides some reuse, such modules are limited to highly specific applications areas insofar as the module has to be "perfect" as-is, or is essentially unreusable. However, in OO reuse the "Open–Closed Principle" (Figure 9.6) can be applied. This principle states that once a class has been tested and accepted into a library, it should *not* need to be "opened up" (the "Closed Principle"), although remaining "open" to further extension by inheritance (Meyer, 1988a). In other words, reuse is enhanced by the capability of building on and extending existing modules and "personalizing" them for the specific task in hand.

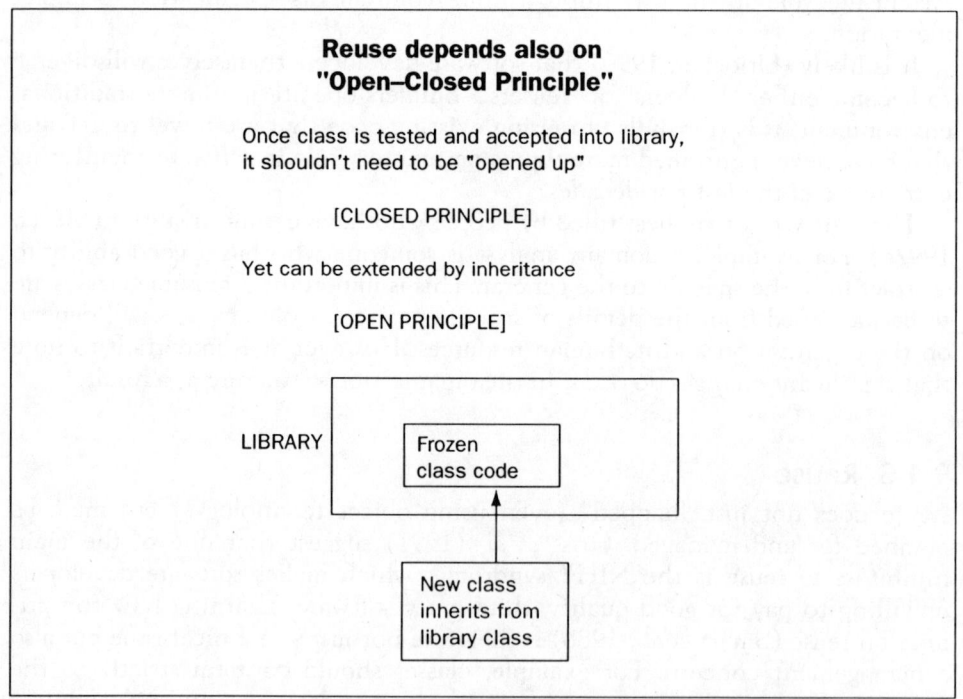

Figure 9.6 *Meyer's (1988) Open–Closed Principle for the creation and reuse of library classes (Henderson-Sellers, 1992a)*

Reusable classes are indeed seen as a major benefit of adopting the object-oriented paradigm in the commercial data processing and applications programming worlds (e.g., Humphrys, 1991; Lewis et al., 1992). However, without some efficient and effective method of locating previously written classes, this benefit could too easily be lost since the ease of reprogramming a class will discourage spending time in locating existing code (cf. Prieto-Diaz and Freeman, 1987; Page-Jones, 1991a). This code could be stored in libraries on an individual developer's workstation, in a divisional library, in an organizational library, or in a wholesaler's library, e.g., a global center for the resale of library classes in a given language environment (see the discussion of electronic markets in Baetjer and Tulloh (1992)). Some type of classification structure seems vital for navigating around the class libraries before selecting the class you want (see Section 9.1.4 for further details).

Reusability on a slightly larger spatial scale, that of program portions, occurs in the development of *frameworks*, such as MacApp, a framework for constructing Macintosh programs (Schmucker, 1986a, b), or zApp, a C++ application framework supporting several operating system/windowing environments (Anders, 1992). A framework is an application-specific class library (Winblad et al., 1990), in other words, a grouping of classes tuned specifically to a single applications-oriented environment, but still general enough to be widely reusable. Another way of viewing this is as reuse of design (Johnson and Foote, 1988; Wirfs-Brock and Johnson, 1990.) It should also be noted that to use a framework, you must accept its model of the problem solution; but hopefully it will provide so much functionality that you are happy to accept its "structure" (Wirfs-Brock, pers. com., 1991). Nevertheless, the development of more frameworks is seen by many as one of the most important practical requirements in the next few years.

Reuse of detailed design is also seen at the program level when classes written in one language are translated into another OO language. On an even larger scale, off-the-shelf software (including software operating systems) can be viewed as reuse by procurement (Bollinger and Pfleeger, 1990).

9.1.4 Library management

Technical issues relating to generalization of classes are raised by, e.g., Meyer (1990a). In terms of the fountain model of Henderson-Sellers and Edwards (1990, 1993a) (see Section 3.1.2) applied to classes or subsystems, generalization follows class development and testing before inclusion in a project (or other) library. Meyer (1990a) details the necessary steps and some of the pitfalls. He stresses that although "it is always preferable, of course, to get the inheritance right initially," in practice this is rarely achieved and should not be regarded as an indicator of a software engineer's ability. (This is supported directly by Meyer's own library development work.) The final product is seen as more important than the process, although of course an efficient process is also to be encouraged. This again reflects a shift from a process-oriented software culture to a product-oriented one (Cox, 1990b).

In terms of code and design elements there may now be two conceptual libraries to deal with: one for the project, storing revisions for the project under way, and one for components that are fully generalized. This product library would be where the components produced after generalization and acceptance testing would eventually reside, ready to be accessed for other developmental projects (Meyer, 1989c, 1990a). Indeed, several language environments currently include a number (usually no more than a couple of hundred) of prewritten and (as users we trust) well-validated classes (Auer, 1989). The availability of these library classes, once learned, makes building new software systems through specialization and using relationships significantly easier than in the domain of procedural programming.

Gibbs et al. (1990) describe class management not only in terms of database techniques, but also taking into account new concerns implicit in an object-oriented system. These relate to class evolution, class selection, and class packaging. In addition, there may be purely commercial concerns of pricing and licensing policies. There is a growing need, therefore, for the efficient management of class libraries for a number of reasons:

1. *To reduce redundancy*. In a multiuser object-oriented development environment, users will develop their own applications and application classes. If there is no centralized system for the management of these classes, it may lead to redundancy of class design.
2. *To avoid inconsistency*. Inconsistency may result from redundancy in a class library. If a number of different versions of a class are derived, and they are not managed properly, inconsistencies may arise when the same class is used by a number of different applications.
3. *To allow multiple users to share classes in the same class library*. In a distributed object-oriented environment, users at different sites may want to share classes for their applications. Thus a centralized system is needed for the management of those classes (Ma and Edwards, 1991).

As the repository of reusable classes grows, there is a need for communicating information about the availability and features of classes. On the interorganizational scales, this may result in software catalogs, analogous to the hardware catalogs, and the emergence of Software-IC™ catalogs (Cox, 1986) and a Software IC industry. On an intraorganizational scale, classes in a library will need to be documented, stored, and made available to other groups within the organization.

One of the problems associated with the supply of reusable components is highlighted by Cox (1992) as that of copyright and royalty payments. In a traditional manufacturing environment multiple copies are tangible and a sales policy is easy to implement and enforce. However, software is intangible and easily copied illegally. Cox (1992) proposes that instead of selling copies of software packages, royalties should be paid on a usage basis. He draws the succinct precedent of the broadcast of recorded music, which works very successfully in this framework. He also notes that a Japanese initiative (Mori, 1989; Mori and Kawahara, 1990) along these lines proposes a technique called "superdistribution," which allows free dissemination of software designed only to run on computers equipped with an appropriate hardware monitoring device. The software is thus paid for, by the user to the developer, on a "user-pays" principle analogous to that used for services such as water, electricity, gas, and telephone in many countries. Cox (1992) notes the potential importance of this idea, while noting its potential ramifications for information privacy—a political issue.

Currently, intraorganizational reuse is probably the more feasible option. Interorganizational reuse will require a great deal of work and coordination on the economic issues of reuse. Intraorganizational reuse of class libraries is already achieved to some extent through the use of object-oriented browsers and the directory structuring mechanisms of operating systems, as are implemented in OOPLs such as Smalltalk (Goldberg, 1985), C++ (Stroustrup, 1986), and Eiffel (Meyer, 1992a). These tools allow a developer to navigate through the class library, following various relationships among classes, such as the inheritance and association relationships. These techniques are appropriate while the class library contains only a few hundred classes. There are, however, several problems with browsers that make them of limited use in the management of large class libraries. Firstly, browsers tend to be navigationally oriented. They are poor at querying the whole library to look for specific features, class types, inheritance relations, and so on. Secondly, the techniques are procedure-oriented. Thus complex navigational paths need to be defined before retrieving a class. Finally, multiple names for features and classes are required to be stored in the class library, representing overloaded feature names and multiple vendor classes. Once the number of classes begins to reach thousands or tens of thousands, as is likely in corporate class libraries, the size and complexity of the class library are such that more sophisticated tools will be required. This storage/retrieval problem will be ameliorated to some degree by the fact that in such corporate resources, access will be at the subsystem, framework, or application level, not solely at the class level.

As a basic degree of functionality, what is required is a means of enabling the user to search the entire class library freely, looking for features, classes, and their relationships. The issues of class packaging and class organization are crucial to this requirement (Gibbs *et al.*, 1990). Class packaging and class organization need to take into account facilities such as multiple naming conventions in the library both for classes and features. Multiple feature names are required because feature name overloading is a common practice in object-oriented programming, and multiple class names are required because often a class name may be reused in a different cluster or application group, or indeed by different vendor libraries (e.g., Yap and Henderson-Sellers, 1993a). Other facilities that will eventually need to be incorporated into any class management system are related to class evolution. Gibbs *et al.* (1990) discussed requirements for class tailoring, class surgery, class versioning, and class reorganization in large-scale and comprehensive software information systems. Indeed, the management of class evolution is one of the most complex issues facing object technology, and the area is one of continuing research activity (e.g., Johnson and Foote, 1988).

The development of classes as modules of code and collaborating classes within clusters and subsystems requires those classes to be classified on the storage medium in such a way that they can be rapidly relocated. This is no minor problem. Documentation is a key here. The classes need to be identifiable by the services they offer; clear documentation is therefore required of the specification. Several methods are currently being investigated; but at the time of writing no methods have been advanced as far as widely available tools.

One obvious method is to use classification techniques based on library science. Classification systems attempt to categorize a domain of human knowledge at an abstract level and cataloging identifies specific items in terms of properties (e.g., size, author, content) in accordance with a set of predefined rules. Classification attempts to look for relationships between (sub)domains of interest and to formalize these, often in terms of a skeleton hierarchy, either in terms of an enumerated classification or a faceted classification (Prieto-Diaz and Freeman, 1987; Frakes and Gandel, 1990; Freeman and Henderson-Sellers, 1991).

In the object-oriented context, classification is a way of grouping object/classes into related categories so that any member of a group can be identified both in its natural position and in its relationship to other members. The second stage is locating an individual object/class in the appropriate location within the classification schema (cataloging).

Classification schemes have been created both for specific purposes, i.e., within discrete bodies of knowledge, as can be seen in the field of natural history, and for encyclopedic treatment of the total body of knowledge or for practical location of books. Some of the better-known classification schemes include those developed by Melvil Dewey (1876), Ranganathan (1958), Bliss (1940–1953), and the International Federation for Documentation (1943 to date), as well as by a corporate group within the Library of Congress. Each of these was intended to be a general-purpose classification scheme that would enable anyone to categorize a particular publication or some form of communication medium ranging from clay tablets to computer disks. Most of these classification schemes were developed from the top down, from the general to the specific in an hierarchical array, although attempts have been made, with varying success, to establish relationships across the "ends of the branches" (Needham, 1971).

Conventional wisdom within the classification (librarian/information science) community has recognized that the fundamental technique of classifying is to observe entities, abstracting various properties that they may possess and identifying characteristics that differentiate one from another. It is of little importance that in one situation the entities are books and in another situation groupings of program code and data—the principles of classification remain the same.

Foskett and Bury (1982) identified some major characteristics of a successful classification, including universality, adaptability, and orderliness. They also note that the patterns used should match those patterns by which the human mind works. There should be a capacity to combine terms from different parts of the classification scheme, relationships should be clear, and notation simple and expressive. Any proposed scheme should also be evaluated in terms of user friendliness. Are the index and instructions for cataloging (viz., using the classification scheme) clear? Will the scheme be maintained or will it date quickly? In the context of retrieval (especially important for object library management), is the scheme both effective and highly efficient?

At present, browsers are the only commercially available tools with which to manually search the archives. As a more powerful alternative, Henderson-Sellers and Freeman (1992) propose the use of natural language based on freetext storage and retrieval augmented by a set of cataloging rules. Their prototype tool, OLMS (Object Library Management System), utilizes a full text storage freetext retrieval software package (Freeman and Henderson-Sellers, 1991) and is currently being evaluated in terms of existing object-oriented software libraries as a prelude to potentially larger-scale use. Use of such off-the-shelf packages, already well developed for information retrieval, especially in the traditional library environment, makes it possible to obviate the need to use retrieval algorithms and software support mechanisms such as those evaluated by Price and Girardi (1990) and instead concentrate on designing a more abstract classification and cataloging methodology.

Within the framework of such a package, records are created for each class that are identified within an hierarchical structure of field names for Object Library Name/Cluster Name/Class Name/Superclass Name, and qualified with a subset of terms relating to the essential features of the object and other collaborations (Table 9.3). Provision is also made for short descriptive summaries or abstracts to be included in each record.

Using faceted classification (Vickery, 1975) the classes are documented internally in such a way that an automated tool (based on an inverted index and freetext retrieval) can locate required classes using an SQL-like interface.

Within any one record for a particular class, there is a physical linkage between feature, class, cluster, and library in that they exist as fields within the one record. Selecting all class records with specific or similar features is simply a matter of using a natural language query including Boolean logic, for example:

- Find (withdraw or open_account or display_balance) within FEATURE and Library = Banking.
- Find (sort or arrange or list) within FEATURE and Library = Inventory.

Class library management has also been discussed by Ma and Edwards (1991). They examined the role of a relational database management system in the management of class libraries and showed how current relational technology can be employed to solve some of the library management issues that arise with the application of object-oriented methods. The approach involved decomposing the information required for searching and querying classes into relational tables, thus providing all the benefits of a nonprocedural query language for the retrieval of information. It also helped to reduce redundancy and avoid inconsistency in a class library.

Table 9.3 *Description of class library database entry (Henderson-Sellers and Freeman, 1992)*

Database **Number**
Library name
Cluster or category name
    Class name
        Class **Services/Features**: state/data and behavior/functionality
    Superclass name(s)
    Classes required as **suppliers** of services to this class
    Related entries: **See-also**
    Synonyms:
Facet Category
Language
Date originated
Version (original unless modified)
Size (in bytes)
Source (viz., author)
Vendor
Cost: $
Notes: 1) Classes required as aggregate components (included with this class as part of cost)
          2) Other

The approach employed involved relational schemata for class specifications. Firstly, an entity relationship diagram (ERD) (Chen, 1976) is used to model the concepts of the class. Then the ERD is transformed into relational schemata that permit the implementation of the queries and manipulations over the class library. An example ERD for the concepts of the programming language Eiffel and the associated relational schema is shown in Table 9.4 and Figure 9.7. The proposed approach of Ma and Edwards (1991) is aimed at medium-scale multi-user environments that require efficient, well-tried technologies to support their object-oriented development needs. Indeed, this approach has already been used by a number of larger firms.

Ideally, many of the classes to be developed for a specific design will already exist as library classes before the beginning of the specific project (e.g., Meyer, 1990a). The management of such a class library is of current concern, since it needs to be addressed not only at a corporate level (e.g., Chan and Henderson-Sellers, 1990) but also at the national and international level (Gibbs *et al.*, 1990).

Project Management and Commercial Adoption of OOSE

Table 9.4 *Relational schemata for the representation of a class library (Ma and Edwards, 1991)*

(a) CLASS(CNO, CNAME, CSPEC)	(b) FEATURE (CNO, FNAME)
(c) INHRLT(SCNO, CNO)	(d) INVAR(CNO, FNAME, VAR, VARTYPE)
(e) PRECOND(CNO, FNAME, COND)	(f) POSTCOND(CNO, FNAME, COND)
(g) CLNTCLS(CNO, CCNAME)	(h) GNRCCLAS(CNO, GNAME)
(i) CLSINVR(CNO, INVARIANT)	

Project-specific classes are the first obvious step and should provide little trouble if good procedures are in place to control versioning, to ensure quality,

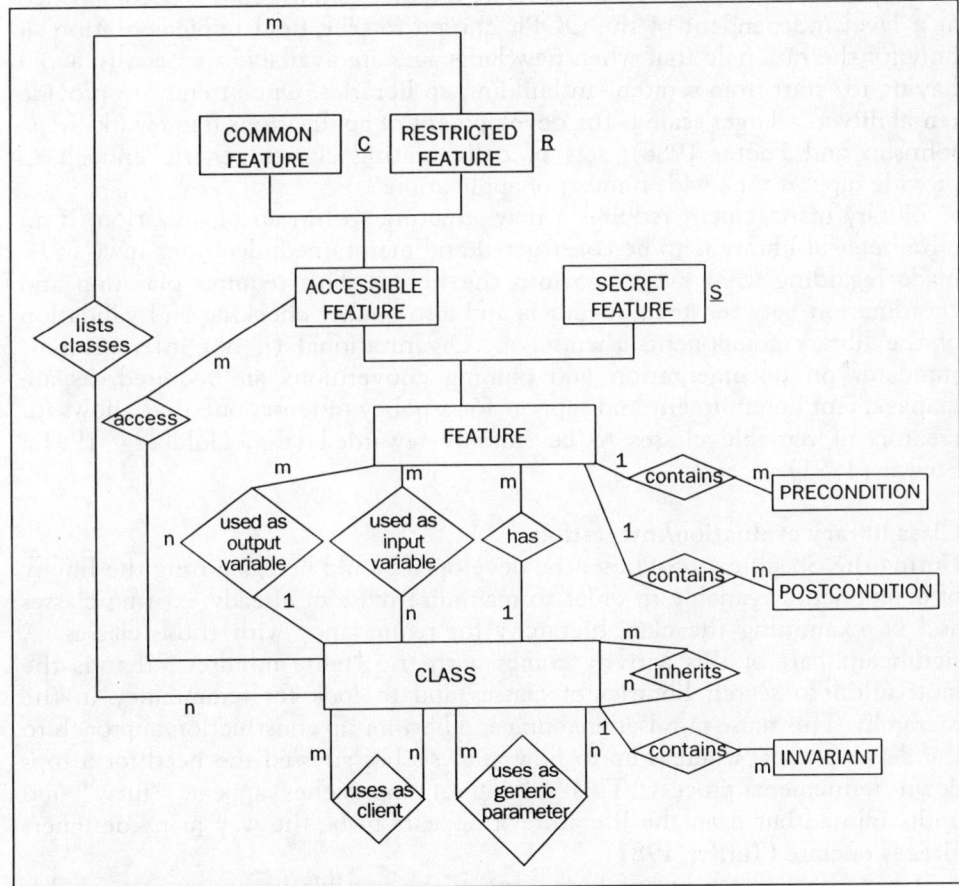

Figure 9.7 *Entity Relationship model of (restricted) Eiffel model for use in querying the repository of classes (Ma and Edwards, 1991)*

and to maintain the Open–Closed Principle (Figure 9.6). It is then a small step technologically (and probably one that should be considered early in an organization's adoption of object technology) to organize corporation-wide libraries, although, as discussed earlier, economic and political considerations may be a more important problem.

Industry-specific classes, say for the insurance industry or the banking industry, raise the question of competitiveness. However, this is really a win-win situation in that the use of already coded classes must improve productivity and permit the exploitation of creative ideas and niche marketing to create competitive advantage. Indeed, in several industries, for example, some United States banks, a trade in classes is already under way.

At the global scale, the only success to date is really the vending of low-level library classes to do routine jobs across a large number of problem domains, such as time classes (e.g., Nerson, 1992b), although other projects are developing to encompass wider domains. What is really required is reuse that is accomplished at a level independent of the OOPL chosen for the final implementation, if only for the rationale that when new languages are available we need to avoid having to "start from scratch" in building up libraries. One attempt to provide reusability at a larger scale is the development of applications frameworks (e.g., Johnson and Foote, 1988): sets of collaborating classes generic enough to provide support for a wide number of applications.

Library management requires a new structure within an organization. If an *organizational* library is to be constructed and maintained, decisions have to be made regarding what classes go into the library. This requires planning and coordination between team members and also quality checking and validation of the library components themselves. Organizational (if not international) standards on documentation and naming conventions are required, as are management commitment and support for a policy of reuse, one that allows for creators of reusable classes to be suitably rewarded (e.g., Goldberg, 1991a; Stewart, 1991).

Class library evaluation/integration
During the Specification Phase, the developer should be examining the library of components available in order to maximize reuse of already existing classes and be examining the class hierarchy for redundancy with those classes. A significant part of this activity comes with the "reuse mindset," that is the motivation to search libraries of classes and to look for redundancy in the hierarchy. This reuse mindset encourages a bottom-up construction approach to the development, whereas up to now analysis has stressed the need for a top-down refinement process. This mixing of approaches appears "fuzzy" and undisciplined but from the literature it appears to be the way many designers already operate (Turner, 1987).

It is perhaps worth noting here some of the possible library sources for this activity. McGregor and Sykes (1992) categorize five types of libraries: (i) team-specific components (classes developed by a team for its own later use); (ii) project-specific components (classes developed as part of a team's project for its own use; these may be found to be more widely useful later and are those for which reuse may be a secondary impetus); (iii) problem domain-specific components available from a third-party vendor (such vendors are likely to develop classes for resale in specialized domains such as banking, finance, and insurance); (iv) general components from a components vendor (such libraries, e.g., the NIH[27] libraries (Gorlen *et al.*, 1990) and the Booch C++ libraries (Booch and Vilot, 1990c), are low-level widely applicable classes written in a specific language); and (v) language-specific primitives obtainable from a compiler vendor, possibly bundled with the language (as in some versions of Eiffel) or available separately.

When considering any of these later categorized libraries (iii–v) for possible purchase, McGregor and Sykes (1992) introduce some guidelines. They provide the following checklist—the library should:

- give a complete general model (ensuring classes and their interrelationships are logical);
- be designed around a few key abstractions;
- model standard knowledge in the domain;
- use inheritance;
- be designed as networks of classes without freestanding data or procedural items (avoid hybrid styles);
- be designed with a low level of coupling between classes;
- provide a consistent and easily understood approach to error handling;
- provide "inspector" functions to check preconditions;
- make it impossible for users to violate abstractions represented;
- conform to a minimal set of standards;
- have maximum efficiency;
- provide a consistent naming scheme;
- provide generic classes;
- provide full documentation as specified in Table 9.5;
- provide commercial-strength support (from vendor).

Table 9.5 *Documentation required for library classes (Adapted from Korson and McGregor, 1992)*

Documentation on state of completeness of each class implementation
Documentation reflecting structure of library
Documentation containing overview of library, including contents and structure
Different documentation for different levels of user
Documentation accessible by a minimum of 3 methods:
- alphabetic by class name
- hierarchical via inheritance structure
- keyword facility

---

27. Now NIH = National Institutes of Health (cf. footnote 26).

9.1.5 Tool support

Although notations (Chapter 3) can be regarded as tools, they are increasingly being supported by software tools, notably drawing packages and CASE tools. In this section, we therefore look briefly at the types of products becoming increasingly available to provide automated support for the methodologies and notations described in Chapters 3 to 7. However, we should note Booch's (1991, p158) warning that "one of the things that [automated] tools can do is help bad designers create ghastly designs much more quickly than they ever would in the past."

The availability of good CASE support can swing a manager's decision in favor of adoption of that particular methodology/notation. In the current climate outside academe, the lack of a CASE tool is likely to be a major inhibitor for even the "perfect" methodology and notation. Certainly, those methodologies and notation that obtain *good* CASE support are likely to flourish, although currently there is little good support for large projects.

Three types of CASE tools are emerging: (i) extensions of structured tools (e.g., Software Through Pictures); (ii) brand new OO tools (e.g., OOATool); and (iii) CASE tools that support many methodologies and notations and possibly even different software development paradigms (e.g., ObjectMaker™, Paradigm Plus™, System Architect™, MetaEdit™. Once again, the more powerful desktop machines will provide good hardware support for these relatively complex software tools, although many of the tools are also available for high end (386 or better) DOS machines.

CASE tools differ in the functions they support and the degree of support for a methodology. All CASE tools offer drawing capabilities to some extent. Each OO CASE tool supports at least one OO notation. The tool needs to be able to represent that notation as envisaged by the notation originator and to do it in a manner flexible enough to suit human working styles. For example, if a basic class icon is selected from a menu and placed on the screen, is the user (i) forced to name it immediately, (ii) name it and be forced to specify at least one service, or (iii) be able to continue to draw icons without naming any? Each CASE tool follows one of these philosophies (see also Constantine, 1992). Studies are urgently needed (and indeed are under way) to evaluate how a person interacts with a piece of software that operates in each of these modes.

Other more advanced functions that are sometimes supported by these tools include the ability, for a large system, to "zoom in" on selected localities to examine the system in increasingly more detail. Furthermore, the tool should support indexing and consistency checking between different diagrams.

The tools also offer functions to permit focusing on a variety of features. For example, we might focus simply on properties in an O/C Model, or on one particular type of connection, say aggregation. In inheritance hierarchies, we might well wish to discriminate between inherited features and noninherited features. The user-friendliness of the tool is also important—for example, how easy it is to place, locate, and move classes, relationships, and services.

Most methodologies offer some means of coping with complexity—embedding classes, linking different diagrams, layering techniques, or selective visibility (see earlier chapters for details of these techniques). The tool should support these techniques as well as others such as removing and adding different features to a particular diagram, while the overall model remains consistent.

Other features of a tool, and ones that should be demanded before a drawing tool can really be called a CASE tool, are means of syntactic checking and preferably semantic checking, although currently available OO CASE tools fall far short of this goal. For example, if a relationship is drawn between two classes, A and B, to show that A inherits from B, then an attempt to link A and B with an inheritance line/arrow whereby B would inherit from A should give an error. In other words, the user must not be permitted to make such errors. If a tool shows objects, rather than or as well as classes, then if the cardinality has a value of 3 and the user attempts to link in four objects, an error message should be displayed. Similarly, relationship connections need to be connected at both ends, etc. Consistent use of names and operations as well as classes of features can all be checked (Wasserman et al., 1990).

Finally, most CASE tools tend to support a notation and its semantics rather than the methodology *per se*. Does the CASE tool support all phases of the lifecycle and the transitions between them? How easy is it to trace changes and return (iteratively or recursively) to an earlier phase and transform design diagrams back to analysis diagrams in cases where these notations differ? What facilities are there for printing graphical and other textual documentation from each of the phases? Is code generation supported? Can the tool be used for reverse engineering, by which technique changes made to the code itself can be reflected back in the design document?

Here, we do not consider it appropriate to evaluate the available CASE tools against this set of questions. Rather, we offer the questions as suggestions of what *you* might require in your particular organization. Remember that a positive initial evaluation does not necessarily prove that the tool can be used for large projects as well as for the small examples usually considered in evaluation exercises.

Of course, the cost of these tools must also be considered as well as the track record. Most vendors will supply an evaluation period before purchase and details of an existing customer who could give a developer's insight into the tool's use. Other factors important in any assessment of a tool include (i) its completeness in supporting a methodology/notation, (ii) the support facilities of the vendor, (iii) the update agreements, (iv) the ease of use, (v) the availability of training, and (vi) the tailorability of the tool to the organization.

In the following section, we examine a number of tools currently available. We begin with a "low-tech CASE tool"—CRC cards—and then examine why and how software tools can best support OO methodologies and notation. In so doing, we look at facilities available or demanded by object technology, and we then briefly consider some tools to assist in an OO SDLC, such as intelligent debuggers, inspectors, browsers and library managers, and associated CASE tools. Indeed, it has been suggested that we are moving rapidly from an era of "language wars" to one of "tools wars."

CRC cards

A method known as CRC cards, where CRC stands for "Class, Responsibility, and Collaboration," has been used in both teaching applications (Beck and Cunningham, 1989) and commercial environments (Wirfs-Brock et al., 1990). This is a "low-tech" tool in a high-tech arena. A CRC card (Figure 9.8) is simply a personal filing card or index card, approximately 10 cm × 15 cm (4" × 6"), on which class names, class responsibilities, and interacting or collaborating classes are named. A short description of the overall purpose is written

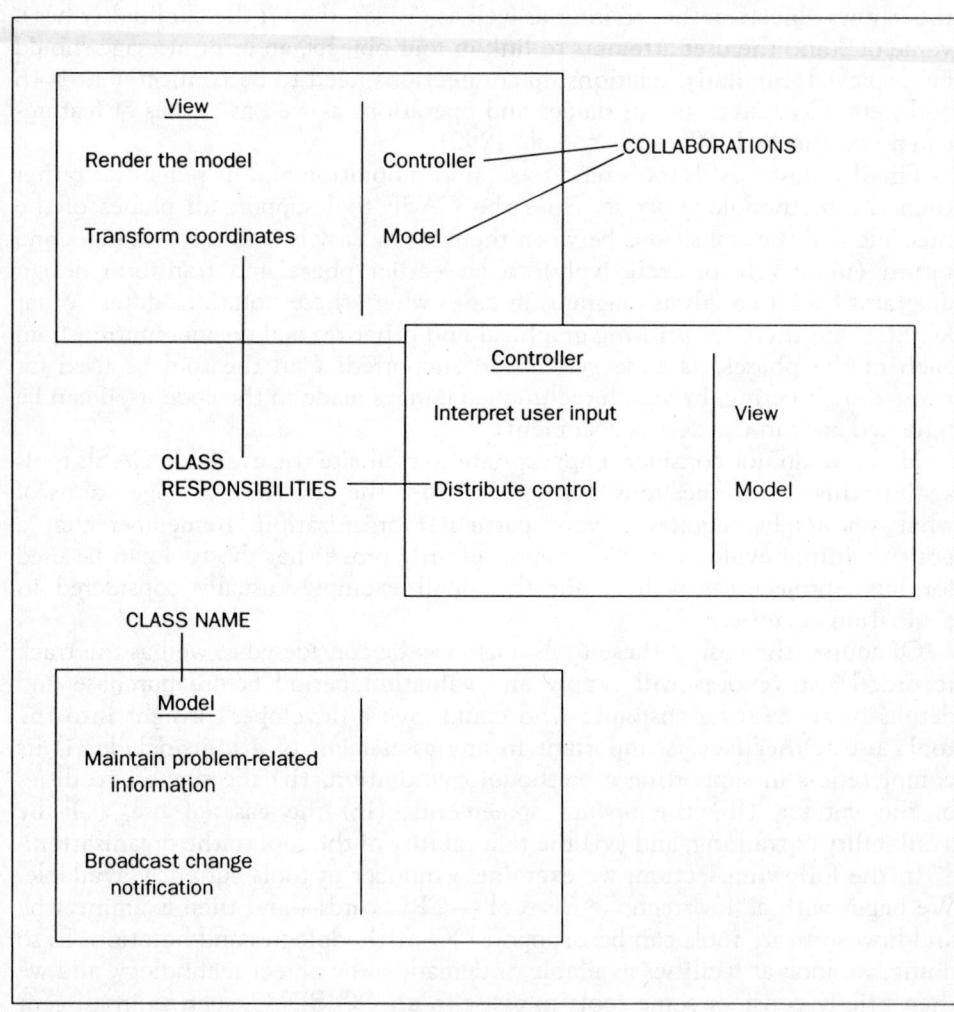

Figure 9.8 *CRC card (Beck and Cunningham, 1989)*

on the back. Advantages claimed for this technique are the easily flexible rearrangements (usually by spreading the cards on a desk or the floor) and the possibilities of assigning the card completion across a larger team than it would be possible to seat around a single VDU on which the project would be focused. Although hypermedia versions have been tested, the designers claim that users prefer the card variety. The use of CRC cards is seen as an early exploration tool in which key objects, key collaborations, and key subsystems can be identified in a highly interactive atmosphere, perhaps somewhat akin to "brainstorming." Disadvantages are that in the highly interactive nature of OOD, corrections and revisions to cards, possibly involving total rewrites as corrections to corrections to corrections become indecipherable, are finally harder than in a more flexible electronic-medium format. Final, agreed documentation would also be a problem if this technique were applied to later detailed design and implementation work. Even as an exploratory tool, returning a stack of cards to the user for verification may not be very successful (Booch, pers. com., 1991).

The following discussion briefly examines a number of available OO CASE tools and then examines a number of other OO tools.

It has been estimated that the total United States OO CASE tools market in 1991 was just over $90 million (9.3% of total OO market), and is projected to grow to $500 million in 1997 (17% of total market). The newsletter *Object-Oriented Strategies* (1992) expected "this market to grow very briskly in 1992." However, a survey of its readers undertaken in early 1992 by *Object Magazine* reported in the April 1992 issue that 0% of its respondents were using OO CASE tools. Partly this response may be a result of the lack of availability of CASE tools in the survey period of 1990–1991; partly it may be that developers are not to be seduced solely by notations and drawing support, but rather are awaiting CASE tools that support a total integrated environment of methodology and project management support as well as notation (Goldberg, pers. com., 1993).

ObjectMaker
ObjectMaker, from Mark V Systems in California, is a second-generation CASE tool supporting twin paradigms: structured and object-oriented. There are more than 20 notations available as well as a code generation capability for Ada, C, and C++. It can be further customized by the user with a rule-based language, available as an optional extra. It is support essentially for notation and not for the methodology itself. It has a set of menus that are tailored for each of the notations supported. Drawings can be linked to provide layering facilities by "spawning" additional windows. Method and process support can be added as desired using the metatool version.

Facilities to edit diagrams are extensive and the change in shape of the cursor is an ideal aid to navigating the diagrams and to permitting its precise location. Editing operations can be done either by selecting the menu operation and then clicking on the target item, or by the reverse: identifying the target item and then performing operations on it. This provides welcome flexibility. A significant number of the notations come with typical examples, although those most newly installed into ObjectMaker are less well represented. It is a stated aim of the vendor to try to support as many of the current OO methodologies/notations as possible. Consequently, ObjectMaker, and the other multinotational tools (see below) provide good experimental platforms for organizations preferring to evaluate several notations and perhaps (by the purchase of an additional piece of software) tailor the notation to suit company practice.

ObjectMaker has some nice technical features, including icons that can be drawn to any size, five magnification levels that can be centered on any portion of the diagram, and output not only graphically in PostScript format but also in other formats compatible with systems such as PageMaker, Word, Ventura, WordPerfect, Interleaf, and Troff. Code generation is currently for Ada, C++, and COBOL.

Many of the tool subsets are linked into a repository that provides a common base so that the model is independent of the notation in which it is currently represented. The repository isolation layer is designed for easy rehosting to various environments, such as PCTE (Portable Common Tool Environment), and objectbases, such as ObjectStore. Integration with PCTE and SoftBench is under way at the time of writing.

The product is still evolving, especially with the addition of new notations. It is available for DOS (WINDOWS), VMS, Macintosh, and Unix (X-windows) systems. The vendors offer support and training.

In addition to various structured notations, ObjectMaker currently supports (at the time of writing) the object-oriented methodologies/ notations of Shlaer and Mellor (1988, 1991), HOOD (1989), Colbert (1989), Bailin (1989), Wirfs-Brock et al. (1990), Coad and Yourdon (1990, 1991a,b) (OOA), Booch (1991), Rumbaugh et al. (1991) (OMT), and Firesmith (1993) (ADM3), as well as the MOSES notation described in this book (in preparation).

Paradigm Plus
Paradigm Plus, from Protosoft in Texas, is another CASE tool that supports multiple notations (called in this tool "paradigms"). The menus in this tool are identical across all paradigms except for one menu that has the title of the name of the paradigm. Using this menu one accesses the icons and relationships of that particular notation. With other menus it is possible to draw symbols such as lines, boxes, and ellipses. In other words, the paradigmatic notation and standard drawing package notation are accessible simultaneously in one diagram.

Several windows can be opened simultaneously and arranged in a cascade or as side-by-side "tiling" that permits multiple views. Sublevel diagrams can be attached to higher-level diagrams for layering purposes, although there is no syntactic or semantic checking.

There are three levels of magnification. Browsing facilities are extensive, including a "matrix" option to show, in spreadsheet style, how classes are connected. This matrix can then be edited "live" such that these changes are immediately reflected in the graphics. Users can also change the defaults for many of the settings and two options are often available for choosing commands: menus and a graphic toolbox. Paradigm Plus is aimed at multiple users, with locking mechanisms to prevent multiple (and contradictory) updating and to allow groups (à la Unix) to be formed under the control of a supervisor who can restrict access by the mandatory password on each project.

Code generation is currently available for C, C++, COBOL, SQL, and Ada. Interfaces are provided for several databases: Versant's OBMS, Objectivity, and ANSI SQL schema generation. Its Object Repository links the various views of the system (diagram, matrix, browser).

Paradigm Plus currently supports (at the time of writing) the methodologies/ notations of HOOD (1989); IDE OOSD (e.g., Wasserman et al., 1990); EVB methodology (e.g., Berard, 1992b); Booch (1991); Rumbaugh et al. (1991) (OMT); Protosoft's own OOA/D, which extends OMT; and Firesmith (1993) (ADM3).

System Architect

System Architect is a meta-CASE tool in the sense that it supports a number of different methodologies, both object-oriented and traditional structured approaches. The object-oriented methodologies currently supported are Booch 91 and Coad and Yourdon, with others likely to be added. The tool is highly configurable, allowing the developer to edit a file that configures the data dictionary for any element of the model. This provides for a very extensible tool and one that can be adapted to a particular project environment. The data dictionary and reporting facilities are both good, with a scripting language being available for report writing and configuration. The tool also provides a degree of rule checking for the models, ensuring consistency with the methodology. It is somewhat weak in its diagraming capability and does not provide full support for the lifecycle—since it is really an upper-CASE tool. It is, however, one of the most configurable tools on the market and hence is particularly appropriate for those organizations still examining and developing methodologies to suit their own particular requirements and environment.

MetaEdit

The MetaEdit™ tool has been developed as a consequence of a research project on metamodeling (Smolander et al., 1991b) and is available from the MetaCase Consulting Inc. in Jyväskylä in Finland. Academic and professional versions are available. Its meta-CASE nature is based on four domains of model information in which the meta-metamodel is based on the Object, Property, Role, Relationship (OPRR) model of Welke (1988). The tool supports a growing number of standard OO and traditional notations, while offering a changeable methodology modeling language and a generic graphical representation of a number of metatypes. Each notation is expressed by its own metamodel, written in OPRR. Addition of new notations is simple and the number of notations supported is growing rapidly (e.g., OMT, Booch, MOSES).

Software Through Pictures

The Software Through Pictures CASE tool itself supports drawing, consistency checking, design reuse, and comprehensibility based initially on the OOSD notation of Wasserman *et al.* (1990). Reuse is available through a controlled library of validated designs and code components and an associated browsing facility. Comprehensibility is incorporated in terms of options to hide parts of diagrams and levels of detail. Complementary analysis and programming environment tools are continuously being developed (Wasserman and Pircher, 1987).

PTech
PTech was originally available only on Silicon Graphics workstation and only recently became available on other platforms. Its author, John Edwards (1989), emphasizes prototyping and executable specifications. The tool, again supporting a single notation, probably has more semantic checking than other tools, being founded on process engineering principles. Graham (1991, p217) comments that this process orientation displaces it somewhat from object-orientation, yet the facilities provided have usefulness for object technologists sufficient to warrant inclusion here. It has certainly been used successfully in object-oriented projects (e.g., Fowler, 1991).

ObjectWorks
ObjectWorks™ is an environment available from ParcPlace for either C++ or Smalltalk. It is type-safe and supports MI. Included with the Smalltalk-80 version is a library of over 400 classes and several thousand services. It runs across a number of different hardware platforms.

ObjectWorks provides an environment and a set of tools. The initial "launcher" window provides tools for (i) system browser, (ii) system transcript, (iii) workspace, (iv) file list, (v) file editor, (vi) change list, (vii) inspector, (viii) debugger, and (ix) project. The principal tool, the system browser, permits examination of class definitions as well as providing facilities for editing, printing, and compilation (Figure 9.9). These browsing windows also provide access to code, as well as definitions.

The inspector tool permits closer examination of a class's internals. Both the inspector and the debugging tool are useful for error location. Execution can be stepped on slowly using these tools, so that values of objects (variables) can be examined carefully. ObjectWorks is a highly interactive environment that is highly applicable to a prototyping development approach. In an evaluation of ObjectWorks for C++, Rothe and Meyer (1990) advocate its use, especially for prototyping, for relatively small programs, for systems with intensive use of inheritance hierarchies, and where teams are small and no external tools are involved. These restrictions have been removed in later versions, which are open to access and reuse of external tools and thus are aimed directly at large systems developments.

These ideas have been extended in the VisualWorks™ environment, which offers a similar total environment, but visually-driven. It is centered on a Reusable Application Framework and offers a "Chameleon View" to conform to a range of look and feel GUIs.

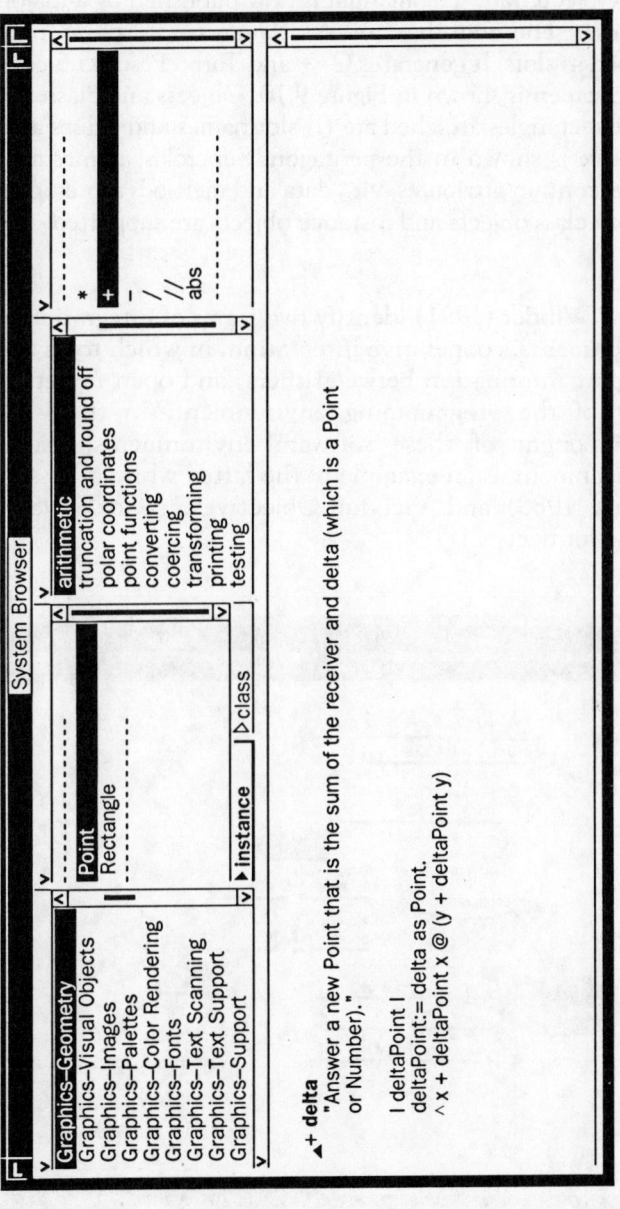

Figure 9.9 Example of the Objectworks/Smalltalk system browser window (McGregor and Sykes, 1992)

ObjectCraft

ObjectCraft (Harmon and Sawyer, 1991) was originally marketed as ObjectVision, until Borland bought the name and the original object-oriented CASE tool was remarketed as ObjectCraft. The manual is now published by a major international publishing house. The tool has an AI flavor to it, using nonstandard OO terminology such as slots. It generates C++ and Turbo Pascal 5.5 code.

An example screen is shown in Figure 9.10. Objects and classes are represented by ellipses. The rectangles attached are (i) slot names and values and (ii) methods. The method code is shown in the pentagon. Superclass names are stored within the ellipse; slots contain attributes, viz., data and methods represent the procedures of the O/C. Both class objects and instance objects are supported.

Purchase and Winder (1991) identify two forms of integration within current software environments: cooperative integration, in which tools are independent but import/export information between them; and open integration, where all tools are part of the programming environment. In their analysis of the debugging component of these software environments, they identify the Smalltalk environment as an example of the latter, while tools such as GDB for C++ (Stallman, 1988) and Vici for Objective-C (Cox, 1988) are seen as examples of the former.

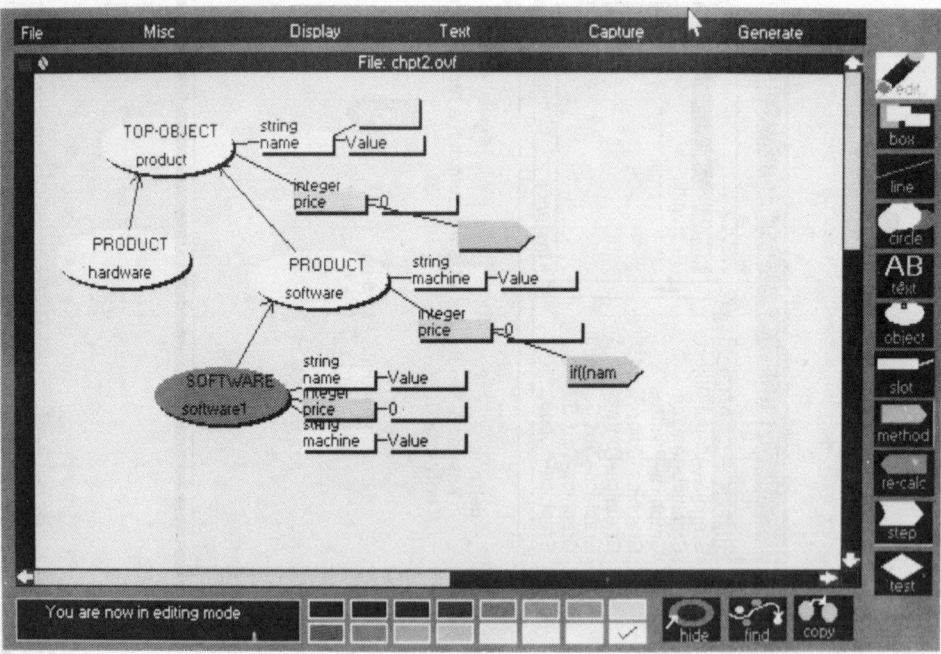

Figure 9.10 *Example of ObjectCraft interface (Harmon and Sawyer, 1991)*

9.2 Commercial adoption of OO

9.2.1 Migration paths

Choosing a migration path for a specific industry is not trivial. Factors affecting the choice will include availability of staff, training budgets, managerial enthusiasm and knowledge, investments in structured CASE technology, typical organizational project size, hardware platforms (cf. availability of OOPLs on that platform), the existing balance between strategic and operational planning, budgets, the company's culture (whether it regards itself as a "leader" or a "follower"), the company's position on the Nolan curve (Figure 9.11), and so forth. Connell (1991) urges that adoption policies be a mix of enthusiasm and caution, as with the adoption of any new technology.

Most guidelines on migration paths to date have been heuristics, that emphasize the safety in starting with a small project (see below) in an important yet not critical area, investing heavily in education and training, and deferring the language issue until after the mindset issues have been seriously addressed. From his experience at US West Advanced Technologies, Parkhill (1992) offers seven "critical principles" (Table 9.6) for use in accomplishing a successful transition to object technology, in addition to underlining the need for key people to understand the object paradigm. These key people should form a

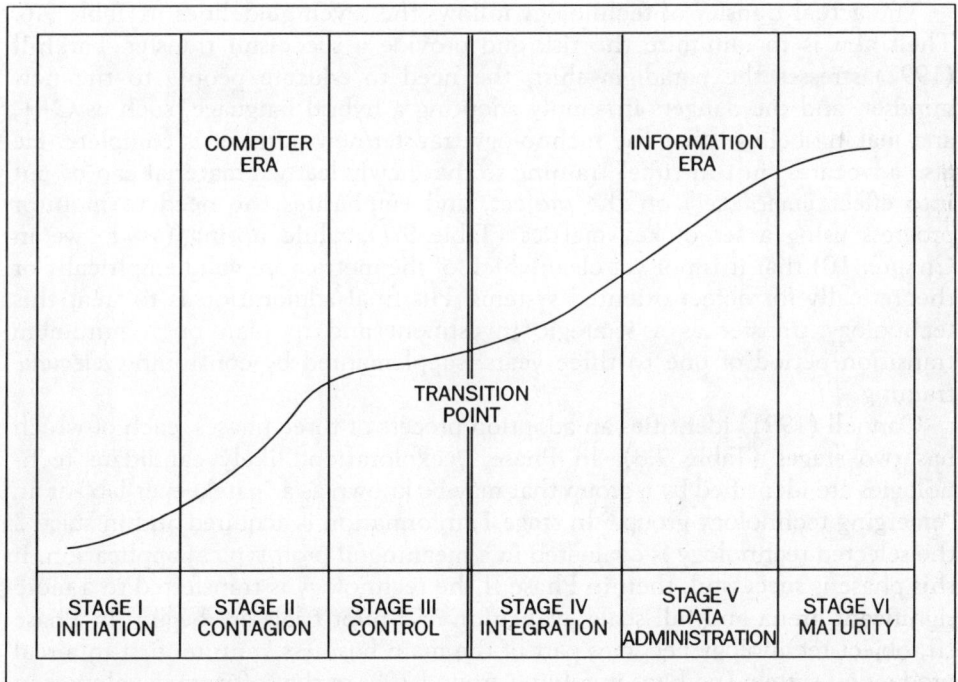

Figure 9.11 Nolan curve (Nolan, 1979)

small "receptor group" of at least three or four people (called a "SWAT" team by Bellin, 1992) and have a mandate to "pioneer" object technology in the organization or division. They should have at least six months to a year to become knowledgeable before the technology is introduced on a larger scale. Even after the transfer of technology to the wider organization begins, the receptor group needs to keep continually three to six months ahead of the rest of the organization.

Table 9.6 *Seven critical principles for successful adoption of object technology (Parkhill, 1992)*

1. Use only those portions of the technology that are ready
2. Use the technology in both design and implementation phases of the project
3. Target projects that can absorb additional risk
4. Transfer technology through people and mentors
5. Start small—don't be too ambitious
6. Utilize "just in time" training
7. Measure key process indicators

The actual transfer of technology follows the seven guidelines in Table 9.6. Their aim is to minimize the risk and provide a successful transfer. Parkhill (1992) stresses the paradigm shift, the need to educate people to the new mindset, and the dangers in simply adopting a hybrid language, such as C++, and making believe that the technology transfer/new mindset is complete. He also advocates "just-in-time" training so that newly learned material can be put into effect *immediately* on the project, and emphasizes the need to monitor progress using a set of key metrics (Table 9.7), while noting (as do we in Chapter 10) that it is not yet clear which of the metrics are valid empirically or theoretically for object-oriented systems. His final admonition is to treat this technology transfer as a strategic investment and to plan on a minimum transition period of one to three years, supplemented by continuing *adequate* training.

Connell (1991) identifies an adoption process of three phases, each of which has two stages (Table 9.8). In Phase I, exploration, likely candidate technologies are identified by a group that may be known as a "gatekeeper lab" or an "emerging technology group." In stage 1, information is acquired and in stage 2 the selected technology is evaluated in a meaningful prototypical application. If this phase is successful, then in Phase II the technology is transferred to a more significant arena and full-scale evaluation and pilot trials are begun. In Phase III, object technology becomes part of the main business venture, first in a real production system (perhaps involving around 20% of the software developers in the organization) and then the technology diffuses throughout the entire organization. Connell (1991) stresses the oft-stated need for the adoption of any new technology to be problem-driven, not technology-driven, while noting that a firm that lags behind the competition in adopting critical computing capability can suffer irreparable damage (as can too hasty a commitment to an innovative technology).

Table 9.7 *Set of key metrics for initially tracking an object-oriented pilot project (Parkhill, 1992)*

Design time (calendar and staff months)
Implementation time (calendar and staff months)
Resulting code size (function point and lines of code)
Cost per function point
Number of defects by severity by phase
Time to repair defects
Reuse of components from existing libraries
Reuse cost savings
Training cost (time and course fees)
Mentor costs
Code available for reuse on future projects

Table 9.8 *Three phase adoption process (Connell, 1991)*

Phase	Stage 1	Stage 2
I. Exploration	Prospecting	Proof of concept
II. Technology Transfer	Evaluation of alternatives	Pilot trial
III. Deployment	Initial production	Diffusion

"Wrapper" technology may provide a partial and temporary solution, although it has yet to be tested on industrial-strength projects. Here a large chunk of procedural (say COBOL) code is encased in an object "wrapper" so that to the outside it looks like a class and can thus interact with the remainder of the system, which is truly object-oriented. Then, the internals (in COBOL) can either be incrementally replaced by decomposition techniques or just allowed to wither away when a fully-fledged OO replacement becomes available (e.g., Graham, 1991, p85; Graham, 1992).

An initial object-oriented project should be chosen on the basis of the following criteria:

- The project should be a smaller rather than a larger one (e.g., Henderson-Sellers, 1992a; Leathers, 1992), but should be large enough to keep the attention of upper management (Love, 1993, p226). Management of projects

is often the stumbling block and it is much easier to manage a small project than a large one. In addition, it is easier for a small group to learn at the same rate and thus to add a coherency to the project team.
- It is important to prove to senior management that this new technology is viable. Consequently, choice of a small but "mickey-mouse" project will not impress them. The project chosen should be real and of recognizable worth to the company, while not being critical to the company's future viability. All new technologies have a risk attached that is greater than the status quo (see also Leathers, 1992)—but then the payoffs are greater. In the longer term, however, it may be more risky to stick with the current generation of software technology (Love, 1993, p96).

  Four groups of failures can be identified: technology deficiencies, technology–problem mismatch, technology–organization mismatch, and organizational deficiencies (Leathers, 1992). Although some failures may be technology-related, Leathers (1992) argues that this may be the easiest scapegoat since it is probably more likely that the faults are human-related—and thus more difficult to admit to!

  Jacobson et al. (1992, p435) differentiate between (i) risk identification, (ii) risk evaluation, and (iii) risk management. Risks identified relate to staff familiarity with the new (OO) paradigm and the urge to code too soon, corporate maturity and training practices, the availability of familiar and integrated tools, the application domain, and market pressures. Each project needs to be evaluated, with respect to likely risks as well as their probabilities of occurrence, on a project-specific basis. Identifying and evaluating risks leads to more successful management of them and to the success of early projects in your organization.
- The project should be measured as it progresses. The data thus obtained then provide a "baseline" for future projects against which their viability can be assessed in the context of the particular organizational culture.
- Deliverables should be clearly stated and incremental. Expectations for a first project must be *realistic*—for example, a rule of thumb (Graham, 1991) suggests that it takes about two months of person effort to build and test a good-quality class. Many existing methodologies do not address this issue, which is crucial to management. The lack of stated deliverables has been held responsible for many outstanding failures, both in object technology and standard structured technology.

Jacobson et al. (1992, p432) add the following recommendations:

- Select a well-understood problem domain.
- Select experienced people open to new ideas in whom management may place their confidence.
- Select a project manager interested in making a success of the project.
- Ensure that staff work solely on this pilot project and are not distracted by other commitments.

Finally, the evaluation method for the first object-oriented project must be clearly stated, essentially as part of the requirements rather than *ad hoc* or *post facto*. The deliverables, which form part of this assessment, should be made available *externally*, not simply to project team members and those "in the know."

Lorenz (1991) identifies several stages through which we all pass as we migrate to the new technology. As "novices," we have problems moving from function-oriented to object-oriented, often needing the help of a "guru." When we are "apprentices," the light begins to dawn (a stage Lorenz identifies as marked by lots of "ah-ha!"s and "I see!"s). Although a guru is still needed, some design work can be started. The period of apprenticeship may last three to six months. At the next stage, that of "journeyman," real work is accomplished by the individual, generally without external assistance except with the odd difficult problem and, of course, with design reviews. This period could last a year or more. The nirvana of this object road is being a guru, when "objects come naturally" (Lorenz, 1991). This role is one of knowledge repository and of catalyst (facilitator). Lorenz notes that there are only a handful of gurus to be found globally as yet! Meyer (1992c) advises that prospective employees be asked to supply a selection of their coding/designs, much as an artist or photographer would supply a portfolio, as part of any interview process for job selection, so that their credentials as novice, journeyman, etc., can be established.

Training is seen by Lorenz (1991) as essential, probably lasting several weeks in an overall learning curve spanning around six months (as noted above). He also reminds us of the need to include managers in that training schedule! Fully object-oriented methodologies, incremental delivery development processes, and appropriate tools are important. Reusable libraries must be seen as key assets of the company and accounted for as such (e.g., Adams, 1992a). Small teams and rapid build cycles are also encouraged. Lorenz's (1991) checklist is as follows:

1. Get management commitment for an important, pilot project with clear deliverables.
2. Get education/training for a small group (3–6 people) and outside consulting expertise.
3. Buy tools for methodology support and class library management.
4. Set organizational standards and hold design reviews. Look for good models, short and readable methods, and on-line design information.

In the spirit of passing on his teams' experiences, Lorenz (1991) notes that following these guidelines can offer "orders of magnitude of improvement in productivity."

Education, training, and reading are also emphasized by Bennett (1991). Small enthusiastic teams with the right tools and open minds are all seen as prerequisites to a successful migration. Berard (1992b, p323) notes that in reading about rapidly changing technology it is important to (i) read more than one source, looking for agreements, differences of opinion, and outright conflicts; (ii) discriminate between concepts and one particular implementation (viz., a biased view) of that concept (a confusion found in some texts); and (iii) be aware of new sources, since significant changes/new ideas can occur over time frames of less than a month.

9.2.2 Industry case studies

This section highlights a number of OO case studies that have been reported in the literature and discusses the advantages and problems in adopting OO technology.

Wyatt

Smalltalk/V was used by Wyatt Software for an implementation of an early and highly successful object-oriented software system to provide United States pension fund management (McCullough and Deshler, 1990). Flexibility was the key here in a rapidly changing business environment. In one case a client made some change requests that were satisfied within three days: difficult within a traditional (3GL) programming environment. The resulting system, WyCASH+, comprises 750 classes and was released in January 1990. It makes extensive use of class hierarchies and vendor-supplied window classes; and it was found that most classes could be implemented with a small number of methods (e.g., typically around two to six methods per class in the instrument hierarchy). The whole development took 5.5 person years using a prototyping lifecycle development style in which the prototype became the final product. McCullough and Deshler (1990) report the continuing success of this product, which lives up to all its expectations.

ACUS

The Australian Centre for Unisys Software (ACUS) has recently developed an OSI X.500 product using OOD and C++ (Malone, 1991). The project was begun in 1988, at which time there were few publications and training courses in OOD or OOPLs. The decision to adopt an object-oriented approach followed the completion of the analysis phase. It acknowledged a number of risks: (i) the design team had little experience in object technology; (ii) OOD and particularly CASE tool support was minimal at that time; (iii) the applicability of OOD or C++ to medium-size commercial projects had not been proven; (iv) it was not clear whether a language compiler would be portable to an appropriate (Unisys) platform; and (v) no training courses were available. Despite these risks, it was felt that the adoption of object technology would be beneficial, largely for the following reasons: (i) the underlying soundness of OO principles was appreciated; (ii) the X.500 application was particularly suitable; (iii) C++ provided adequate language support; (iv) the expertise in C gave the development team a migration path to C++; (v) the fact that C++ was a translator into C assisted future porting to other non-Unix platforms; and (vi) the entire development team gave its full support. Indeed, this last point was seen by Malone (1991) as perhaps the critical factor in the successful adoption of object technology.

As a consequence of ACUS's early adoption OT or in a climate where methodologies, notation, and CASE tools were inadequate, much of the methodological development had to be based on in-house innovations. The team's experiences reveal some useful heuristics.

1. *Design.* The incorporation of OOA as well as OOD and OOP was recommended in order to provide a smooth transition throughout the lifecycle. The learning curve should not be underestimated. It was observed to consist of two parts: learning OO concepts and putting them into design practice. The use of inheritance and polymorphism was found to be a powerful tool in achieving elegant solutions to complex problem areas. Assertions were identified as aiding clarification of the design. Finally, utility objects (reuse) were noted as an important benefit of an OO methodology.
2. *Implementation.* Assignment of tasks to different team members was aided by source code control mechanisms and object partitioning. Information hiding leading to object autonomy resulted in the possibility of transferring responsibility for particular classes from designer to designer if necessary. Interfaces between the chosen OOPL (here C++) and preexisting structural code in C were highlighted as being of relevance to many projects. The lack of an automatic garbage collection mechanism in C++ was identified as a potential source of memory management problems. Reuse of existing utility classes was a boon in saving time in recoding "standard" object structures, especially with respect to reliability of those previously written and well-tested classes. The role of unit testing (cf. system testing) was noted.
3. *C++ Considerations.* In-line methods were recommended for use whenever possible to save run-time overheads. However, when virtual functions were used, this resulted in major overheads. The developers' final recommendation was that in-line functions not be used for virtual methods. Other overheads identified for virtual methods were the costs of initialized static data (largely a consequence of the early version of C++ utilized at that time). Task classes were found especially useful, while debugging operations were found difficult.
4. *Extensibility.* Changes to the system were found to be relatively simple, as a result of (i) information hiding, (ii) inheritance, and (iii) dynamic binding.

Some metrics were also collected as part of the project. The X.500 project members identified a division of their effort between Analysis+Design, Implementation, and System Test to be in the ratio 1.6:2.9:1. The project was 70,820 lines of code supplemented by 159,083 comments. This was encapsulated in 412 classes, which were coded at an average rate of 36 lines of tested code per day. The average number of methods per class was 6.8. Development defects (those detected throughout all stages of development in code placed under source code control) were identified at 3.4 per 100 lines of code, while qualification defects (those problems detected in the two-month period subsequent to development when full tests are undertaken) were only 0.04 per 1000 lines of code.

This very successful project was an endorsement of ACUS's decision to adopt object technology, and the organization continues to develop and adopt OOA and OOD methodologies as they emerge, supplemented by investigations into new CASE tools and metrics standards. (Other ACUS experiences are also related by Taylor (1992).)

NCR

In a three-year project involving over 100 software engineers in which over 350,000 lines of object-oriented code were developed, NCR were able to produce a sophisticated key commercial product named COOPERATION for integrated office automation running across enterprise configurations of PCs, servers, LANs, and WANs, and on a variety of platforms (Guttman and Matthews, 1992). Initialized using Actor, giving a sound approach to OO programming, and later transferred to C++, the product engendered enthusiasm and commitment from developers to senior managers.

The existing management structure was initially very traditional with an hierarchical reporting structure. To provide more flexibility, as required for OO development, a second, more informal and collaborative management structure was superimposed. This new structuring focused on task teams, mentors, and review teams, which facilitated communication across traditional roles, e.g., analyst versus designer, manager versus developer. In addition, a consequence of the seamless transition was the recognition, for instance, by the tester/quality assurance team that a class identified by the analyst was likely, eventually, to require the construction of a good testing strategy *based on the same abstraction*.

Consultants were used as mentors and facilitators of technology transfer to the NCR staff; this worked well, leaving behind a significant cadre of knowledgeable object-oriented software engineers.

Class reviews and code reviews were both undertaken. Class reviews were undertaken at regular time intervals rather than at specific lifecycle stages. They were largely informal so as to encourage occasional participation by senior managers. The meetings were found to be productive and many serious flaws were easily identified in this way. Later, code reviews were conducted separately from the class reviews and temptations to hack around a design problem were thus easily thwarted. The voluntary nature of these reviews also led to less ego-dominated discussion. Moreover, absence from a given meeting was not detrimental to the managerial assessment of an individual's productivity or capabilities.

The product itself was only a few months late; it met and often exceeded its original specifications and had many other positive spin-offs. Reuse was found to be high; portability to other platforms was easy; the experience left over 100 highly skilled OO developers and managers; productivity was estimated at 200% higher overall than in traditional environments; and, perhaps most importantly, a new and solid organizational culture for software development had been established.

The downside included the initial lack of expertise, which led to frequent mistakes and necessary revisions; some hesitation by both developers and managers in coming to grips with the new paradigm/mindset; and the loss to the organization of those individuals unwilling or unable to make the transition.

Automated Research Systems
Martin and Odell (1992, p446 et seq.) report on a successful project utilizing their OOA/D approach. The lessons learned by the company were fourfold:

1. *Enterprise project definition*. Overenthusiastic developers might start coding too early. Project planning is crucial.
2. *Methodology*. This should include environment, objectives, people, and the organization.
3. *Tools*. CASE tools are essential for quality and timely development and for identifying automatically inconsistencies in the developers' models. Code generation by CASE tools is also highly beneficial.
4. *Training*. Methods and tools are only as good as the developer's skill in using them.

In this first project the company, Automation Research Systems, Limited, estimated that 50–70% of code was reusable (cf. 5–10% in its previously utilized traditional development environment). It envisages savings also in future maintenance as well as in the evident enhanced quality of its software product.

Cadre
A redesign and reimplementation of a CASE tool is described by Wybolt (1990). Here Cadre Technologies Inc.'s Teamwork®, which supports multiple methodologies, mostly based on traditional techniques, was rewritten in C++. The product size was immediately reduced by a factor of around 8, although navigation through the code proved difficult. Wybolt (1990) notes that the development team quickly came to realize the need for object-oriented analysis—they used Shlaer and Mellor (1988). He also notes the need for adequate training, tool selection, and good migration paths.

NAPS
Another C++ product redevelopment is reported by Berman and Gur (1988). This Network Application Programming System (NAPS) was written to support 40 programmers writing large applications. At that time little literature was available on OO design such that the hybrid nature of C++ probably offered a needed link back to a known environment (C). At the time of this report by Berman and Gur (1988), the system consisted of around 350 classes with an average size of 300 (noncommented) lines of code per class. They note

the need for more design-level effort and less programming effort, although they were unable to produce any statistics to show whether the new, OO system was any smaller than it would have been if written in, say, C.

Winston
Winston (1990) reports on a number of projects successfully using object technology. These include a project to build an expert system using fuzzy logic and C++, the development of telecommunications management software using Eiffel, and a real-time distributed switching system for Wall Street traders using Objective C. In all cases, extensibility, maintainability, modularity, inheritance, and reuse are cited as major advantages.

Apple
The success of Apple in reusing object-oriented code from the Lisa in newer versions of the Macintosh series is well known. System 7.0 Finder is written in C++.

KPMG Peat Marwick
After seven years of programming in Pascal, an international software and development group within KPMG Peat Marwick, the international accounting and consulting firm, decided to move from Pascal to C++ (Sollisch, 1991). Since they were working in a Macintosh™ environment, the applications programmers received enthusiastically the decision to use C++. Initially, the work was done in a mixed environment, which allowed the developers to "put off the laborious task of converting the KPMG Peat Marwick Toolbox" (written in Pascal). Learning was done at the language level using standard C++ programming texts (first in C, then in C++).

The advantages and disadvantages of C++, as uncovered in this project, are outlined by Keller (1991). The major advantages identified were the availability of inheritance (especially multiple inheritance), virtual member functions, strong modularity (easing debugging and testing), and code reusability. On the other hand, it was noted that "One potential disadvantage results from the C++ language being less structured than Pascal, allowing obscure code to be written." Keller (1991) also stresses the need to ensure that data can only be manipulated by operations, i.e., never directly, which is anathema to procedural programmers. The learning curve was also seen as a disadvantage of adopting an OOPL. In addition, although the decision was a language one, it soon became evident that OO design issues must be considered. Part of this realization was caused by the decision to retain Pascal code and work in a mixed environment and part was that design heuristics at the class level were required. The design process for classes was essentially bottom-up.

Gole (1991) assesses the costs and benefits of this KPMG group's transition to C++ and especially the costs of retaining a mixed C++/Pascal environment. He notes, however, that "The cost of the change will be outweighed by a more powerful and robust language and development environment." He reports that initially a procedural design methodology was applied to OOP, which resulted (not surprisingly) in almost no use of inheritance. Thus "the greatest benefit was the move from Pascal to C, not Pascal to C++." A second project tried to address the perceived problem. Programmers were trained specifically in C++ and object-oriented design concepts before the implementation phase of this follow-on project, although a bottom-up approach was retained. The organization is now rapidly building up a useful, reusable class library in C++. There is less maintenance and the development team has found a new focus on class design guidelines.

CAT
Graham (1991, p86) reports on existing OO systems of 100,000 lines of code, or 2,200 classes, and on object technology being used successfully on real-time control systems, container tracking in docks, and Computer-Assisted Tomography (CAT) scanner software, the latter being an example of objects used in a safety-critical domain.

HP
Hewlett-Packard (HP) has made a significant resource input to object technology, both in the United States and in the United Kingdom. Its experiences are related by Coleman and Hayes (1991a, b). In 1989–90, a total of 11% of all HP projects were being undertaken using object technology, a figure that had grown rapidly over the preceding two years. Perceived benefits are reuse, modularity, and prototyping. HP has succeeded by using small project teams, champions who act as "internal consultants" (see Section 9.2.1), and good software engineering. Incremental product development is used, as are analysis and design techniques (generally developed in-house), although Coleman and Hayes note the lack of a complete notation set (as of August 1991). They also stress the need to manage the transition to object technology, and not just "jump on the object bandwagon and hope for the best."

Rational
In their report on the "benefits of OOD on large systems" Bachman and Marasco (1992) recount some of the experiences of projects undertaken by Rational using Booch's OOD methodology. They describe three projects. In the first of these, a developer of real-time systems in the defense environment undertook a 1.5 million LOC project running in a distributed environment on board ships. The company used OOD and implemented the design in Ada. Even with only the first product delivery (out of five), the productivity had more than doubled, compared with the company's historical average productivity value. On subsequent ships this rose by a further factor of 3, resulting from a significant amount of reuse (around 70%).

The second project reported by Bachman and Marasco (1992) was in the MIS environment. Here a financial accounting system was developed, again in Ada. The system consisted of almost two million lines of code. Work began in

1987 and the system was delivered in 1989. Productivity was approximately twice as great as in the company's traditional (COBOL) environment. This in itself saved the company around US$24.2 million. In the third project, a telecommunications system of four million LOC of C code required reengineering into C++.

The conclusions from these three projects were that a significant increase in productivity was easily achievable, resulting directly in dollar savings; that complexity management must be considered; that an incremental development can reduce risks and shorten schedules; and that investment in tools and training is necessary and can provide one of the most significant savings in using object technology. Perhaps more important, a new mindset and new corporate culture are required by business, planning is vital, and the use of pilot projects and external consultants is highly recommended.

Bytex
The Bytex product "Series 7700 Intelligent Switching System" provides sophisticated software to allow users to set up multiple virtual LANs within a single hub with per port switching (Howard, 1992b). Bytex's use of object technology is clearly identified as having given the company a competitive advantage and a unique selling position in this technologically rapidly expanding area of networking. The need for OO training was clearly identified and iteration became evident early in the production cycle. The usefulness of language vendor library support was also highlighted, leading to a choice of Eiffel as the implementation language. Roger Osmond, software development leader for this project, identified the key correct decision as being that of decoupling the project into a number of communicating subsystems (Howard, 1992b). Extensibility was also proven when significant new features were added to the delivered product in four to six week cycles, and customer acceptance has been high. This rapid response to new requirements has been identified as providing a major competitive advantage.

IBM
In a report by IBM Ireland Information Services (IISL), Humphrys (1991) describes the development by the same team of a project using both structured and object-oriented techniques. The original software was written using C and a total rewrite using C++ was undertaken to provide comparative metrics. Humphrys concluded that "the claims of OO regarding dramatic new forms of reuse and flexibility are totally substantiated." The OO program was 1,059 LOC, compared with the procedural program of 5,827 LOC, and the time taken was about half. For this international company (IBM), Humphrys (1991) recommends the development of corporate-wide business objects. He notes the need to be aware of the learning curve, which must be approached with an open mind and a capability to deal with different levels of abstraction. "This is a long term investment and will demand a proper investment in education" (Humphrys, 1991)—sentiments echoed earlier in this book.

Cognos

It should be noted that there is no guarantee that an OO project will succeed. While the chances are extremely good, realization requires commitment and an awareness of the potential risks involved (Leathers, 1992). Object technology is innovative and the introduction of any new technology into an organization brings with it risks of failure. Leathers (1992) notes that probably the most important area for assessing likely success/failure is not the technology, but the organization and management structure—perhaps a lesson learned from the earlier failure of the Cognos project (Leathers, 1990a). Management prudence is also advocated by Coleman and Hayes (1991b).

9.2.3 The OMG

The Object Management Group (OMG) is a consortium of influential hardware and software companies dedicated to establishing standards for open computing in the object-oriented arena and to promoting the use of object technology to the software engineering community. The OMG is dedicated to maximizing portability and interoperability in a multivendor, heterogeneous environment (Barber, 1991). It aims to bring about agreements between vendors on OO terminology, models, and style. It is also dedicated to producing a framework and specifications for commercially available object environments.

The OMG was founded in April 1989 and has over 340 members worldwide—drawn from vendors, researchers, and users alike. It has a 23-member Board of Directors, drawn from corporate members, and a Technical Committee consisting of all corporate, university, and end-user members. The latter oversees technical product evaluation using a basic sequence of model development, requests for information relating to this developed model, requests for proposals (RFP), and technical evaluation of RFPs.

In October 1991, the OMG announced the adoption of the Common Object Request Broker Architecture (CORBA) for objects in a distributed environment (Figure 9.12), which is supported by 45 companies (Stone, 1992). The OMG is currently working on the development of a standard Object Model and an Object Services Architecture. Other current projects include a study of portability and interoperability of class libraries. The OMG also has a number of special interest groups. The first of these deals with objectbases, languages, end-user requirements, parallel processing, analysis and design methodologies, Smalltalk, and class libraries. The OMG also runs the series of international ObjectWorld conferences as the showcase for object technology.

9.3 Summary

Project management is of crucial concern in the commercial adoption of OT. The recursive and iterative nature of the OO SDLC introduces new concerns into an organization. New roles for software developers can be identified, including those of librarian and quality manager. Breakpoints are perhaps harder to define, and the need for support tools is often seen as critical.

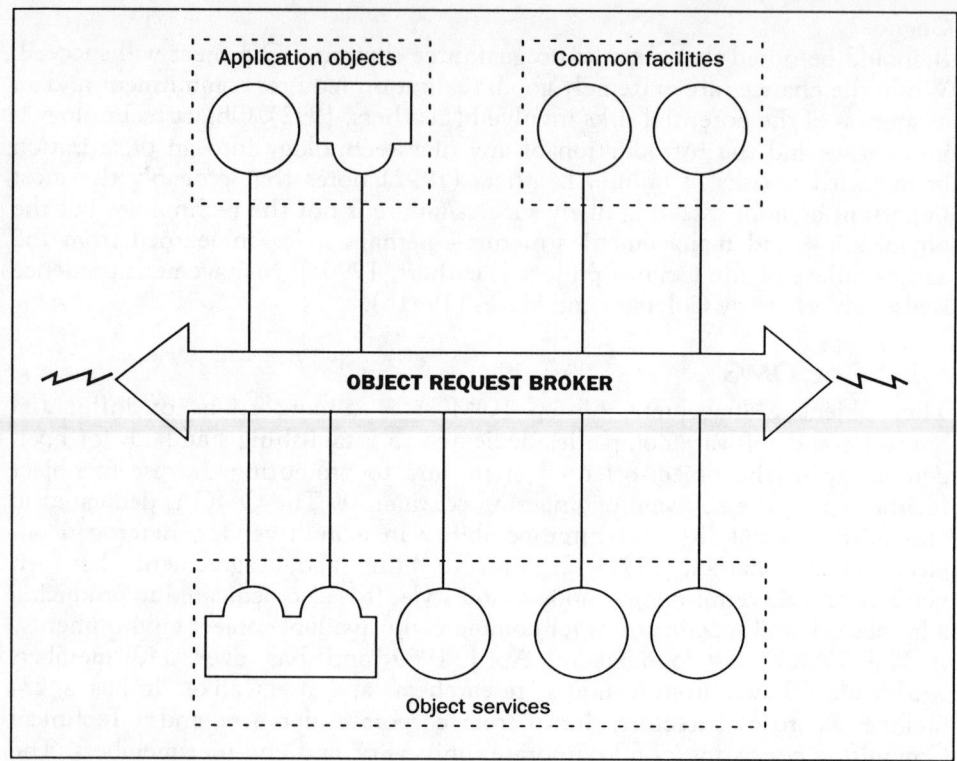

Figure 9.12 *The Object Request Broker architecture (Barber, © copyright SIGS Publications, 1991)*

A major commercial advantage to the adoption of OT is seen to be the reuse potential. Reuse can occur on a variety of time and space scales, yet once again the management of reusable libraries of code and design needs to be addressed seriously within the organizational culture.

A significant number of case studies are emerging from the commercial world, from which others entering the field can learn. The infusion of the new technological and project management ideas needs to be seen to be true "technology transfer" and is unlikely to be ultimately successful by simply hiring in industry "experts" for short periods.

The worldwide computer industry is certainly embracing OT as a significant advance toward high-quality software engineering. The creation of the Object Management Group (OMG) and other standards bodies, such as the ANSI Accredited Standards Committee (ASC) X3H7 and International Organization for Standardization (ISO) committees, as well as standards committees for most languages, is seen to be a highly supportive move toward establishing OT as a viable alternative to traditional software development methods within an organization.

CHAPTER 10

Object-oriented "Metrics"

Management of any production process is simplified if some measures of progress toward a quality product are collected and analyzed. In manufacturing, tolerance limits are prescribed and individual components evaluated as to their acceptable quality (and therefore the quality of the process producing them) against these "standards." Costs are tracked during the process and compared with estimates made initially.

Software development shares with manufacturing industry the need to measure costs, productivity, and quality. The main difference lies in the "one-off" nature of software.

Nevertheless, quality can be evaluated against prespecified criteria, progress toward the goal evaluated on a temporal basis and final costs compared with estimated costs. Specific goals are (i) to be able to do cost estimation from the requirements analysis; (ii) to estimate maintenance costs from the code; (iii) to evaluate the reusability of designs, frameworks, and code; and (iv) to allocate resources most wisely. Such goals require collection of data on the process, effort expended (often measured in time resources × people resources), and objective measures of the code itself.

In a study of Contel, Pfleeger (1993) describes the introduction of a metrics program to that organization. She links the appropriateness of the metrics to the

Software Engineering Institute (SEI) maturity level (Humphrey, 1989). She identifies several common themes that contributed to the project's success in Contel and that should be equally important in an object-oriented environment:

- Beginning by focusing on the process.
- Keeping the metrics close to the developers.
- Focusing initially on those who need help—they will then "spread the good word."
- Automating data collection as far as possible.
- Keeping things simple to understand.
- Capturing whatever information is possible but without burdening developers.
- Not forcing the developers to implement a metrics program against their will.
- Using some metrics is better than using no metrics.
- Tailoring the metrics used to the individuals responsible.
- Criticizing the process and the product, but *not* the people.

In this chapter we discuss traditional metrics, their application or potential application to object-oriented systems, and necessary object-oriented extensions. Although the focus is currently at the code level, since it is the simplest and most concrete to measure, it is vital that lifecycle concerns be incorporated. This is especially true for OT as a result of the incremental delivery style of the lifecycle model—a topic that is not addressed by any traditional metrics set. The subject of OO metrics is in its infancy. We hope that this chapter both offers guidelines for setting up a metrics program and stimulates researchers to investigate this challenging area of OT.

10.1 Metrics and measures

Over the last few years, several authors have focused on the distinction between a "metric," which strictly is a function with two arguments (for example, the distance between two points), and a "measure," which is a numerical value for an attribute assessed for magnitude against an agreed scale (for example, the length of a piece of string). Although this is strictly correct, many authors nevertheless continue to use the terms "measure" and "metric" interchangeably unless they wish to be very specific. Another interpretation (Fenton, 1991) is that metrics characterize simple attributes, whereas measures are functions of metrics (Côté and St-Denis, 1992) to assess more complex attributes such as quality or complexity. Whichever definition/rationale you prefer, it must be clearly stated that the modern trend is toward the development and use of metrics/measures[28] that can be underpinned by measurement theory. This laudable trend leads to the identification of scales for the measures (and hence

---

28. We will not be pedantic and will use these terms loosely and, effectively, interchangeably unless specified otherwise.

Object-oriented "Metrics"

Admissible transformations	Scale types	Examples
$M' = F(M)$ (F 1–1 mapping)	Nominal	Labeling/classifying entities
$M' = F(M)$ (F monotonic increasing i.e. $M(x) \geq M(y)$ $\Rightarrow M'(x) \geq M'(y)$)	Ordinal	Preference, hardness, air quality intelligence test (raw scores)
$M' = \alpha M + \beta \quad (\alpha > 0)$	Interval	Time (Calendar) Temperature (Fahrenheit, Celsius) Intelligence tests ("standard scores")
$M' = aM \quad (a > 0)$	Ratio	Time interval, length, temperature (absolute)
$M' = M$	Absolute	Counting entities

Figure 10.1 *Nominal, ordinal, interval, ratio, and absolute scales of measurement (Fenton, 1991)*

consideration of dimensions and units becomes paramount—a woefully neglected area in software metrics as well as in some other areas of engineering and science). These scales can be of five types (Figure 10.1): nominal, ordinal, interval, ratio, and absolute. A nominal scale is a simple labeling (e.g., the numbers on municipal bus fleets); an ordinal scale implies ordering only; and an interval scale is used for ordered data such that the same interval between two pieces of data at different parts of the scale has the same meaning. Ratio scales are like interval scales except that, as well as addition and averaging which are possible with data measured on an interval scale, the data have a zero point and can thus be ratioed. Hence we can say that datum A is n times as big as datum B. (This is not possible on an interval scale, as can readily be seen from consideration of two different temperatures on the Celsius scale. Not until the ratio Kelvin scale is used can such statements be made.) Finally, an absolute scale is one used for simple counts. Ideally, we would wish our software measures to be ratio or interval scale measures so that means, standard deviations, and correlation coefficients are meaningful; sadly, however, this is not always true in the software metrics research literature.

Another point seldom made is that when arithmetical manipulations are done with different measures, it is crucial that dimensional analysis arguments are applied. Adding a metric measured on an ordinal scale to one measured on a ratio scale is nonsensical—yet all too frequently seen in the literature. Secondly, even when each datum is on the same scale and the operation is valid on that scale, it is important to check that we are (say) adding apples to apples and not apples to oranges. For example, if we add 100 lines of code to 13 decision points to get a value of 113, are these 113 lines of code, 113 decision points, or 113 of some other unit? Of course, the answer is that the arithmetic sum of LOC and decision points is meaningless. Yet once again, many published metrics papers can be criticized strongly on these grounds alone. There are similar concerns when one considers "complex" metrics: vectors of a number of metrics, e.g., the (cyclomatic number, operator count) pair of Hansen (1978). If the individual metrics are not orthogonal, then once again vector arithmetic is inapplicable. Care is demanded!

Metrics, or rather measures, thus measure something. They are the software equivalent of length or mass measures in the physical (i.e., nonsoftware) world. Unfortunately, as noted by Fenton (1991, p21), such software metrics have been "used" for many other applications. Fenton describes the use by various authors of the term "software metrics" to describe, variously:

- a number derived from product, process, or resource (e.g., LOC, effort, personnel experience);
- a scale of measurement (e.g., a proposed nominal scale for, e.g., software failure);
- an identifiable attribute (e.g., "portability" or "coupling");
- a theoretical or empirical model (e.g., "the COCOMO metric" of Boehm, 1981).

The confusion between a measure and a model is certainly widespread. Description of a software product or process using an appropriate measure *does not* and *cannot* predict anything. Indeed, Fenton's illustrative example of the use of a person's height (a measure) as a predictor of, say, intelligence (Fenton, 1991, p156), which is clearly, he notes, nonsensical, is illuminating. A measurement of LOC should not be used to predict, say, quality unless intervening causality can be identified. Furthermore, an extensive data collection program of values for LOC and quality, commonly expressed as a correlation, can be at best suggestive. Correlations only indicate the possibility of *interpolation* within the same data set or possibly another data set from an identical environment. They cannot be extrapolated to other domains *unless a causal link is sought*. Perhaps the most useful role of correlations is to suggest to the researcher *possible* causal links. At present, there are insufficient data for those causal links to be identified. Within your own organization, however, you may be able to use in-house correlations for prediction purposes, although always with caution.

In the remainder of this chapter we will retain the (perhaps inaccurate) term "metrics" in describing the state-of-the-art application of traditional quantitative characterization of software—first, briefly in the traditional structured environment, and then, second, in the object-oriented environment.

10.2 Product and process metrics

Software measures aim to quantify some characteristic of either (i) a software product, which could be the analysis, the design, or the code; or (ii) the dynamics of the software development, including variables such as staffing levels as a function of time, effort as a function of time, overall effort, and overall cost. These measures may be used directly, for instance, as part of an evaluation of the complexity of a design or piece of code. Alternatively, they may be included in prognostic models to forecast other characteristics. In this context, the complexity of a piece of code might be used to give a forecast of likely maintenance costs.

The desire to forecast costs (of production or maintenance usually) is a major driving force in the derivation of a model useful for cost estimation, although frequently the emphasis in cost estimation is on production rather than maintenance costs, i.e., the Growth Period rather than the Maturity Period of the product lifecycle. Since

$$\text{Total costs} = \text{``Tool-up'' costs} + \text{production costs} + \text{maintenance costs} (+ \text{running costs}) \qquad (10.1)$$

where

$$\text{Production costs} = \text{Investigation costs} + \text{Specification costs} + \text{Implementation costs} + \text{Integration costs} + \text{Testing costs} \qquad (10.2)$$

it is possible to evaluate the likely trade-offs. For example, skimping on production costs almost inevitably leads to an increase in maintenance costs. Equation 10.1 could thus be used as a predictor of total costs for various scenarios of decreased production/increased maintenance costs or, alternatively, be used in the context of fixed total budgets to allocate costs between production and maintenance.

Furthermore, it is generally accepted that the unit costs for fixing an error in maintenance are significantly larger than those for correction at earlier lifecycle phases. Running costs are related to the costs incurred by the user in utilizing the software (i.e., not borne by the developer). However, they are included in Equation 10.1 since it is frequently the case that software is developed for in-house use, so that the same organization is billed for all component costs.

This use of process metrics not merely to *measure* the software process but to extrapolate it to being a predictor of cost (but cf. comments in Section 10.1) has led to the development of "cost estimation" techniques based on models such as COCOMO (Boehm, 1981), SLIM (Putnam, 1978); and PAMELA (Jeffery, 1987a). Other process metrics focus on performance and state of completion.

Although being able to cost projects at their inception might be highly desirable, it is dubious whether there are currently *any* widely applicable and reasonably accurate cost estimation models available. Indeed, seeking such models may turn out to be an impossible quest, or certainly at least until more work on the psychological characteristics of the staff involved is taken into account more realistically (see the discussion in Section 10.4 regarding initial steps for assessing psychological complexity of programs with respect to maintenance). A further complicating factor is that since no two software projects are identical, it is inevitable that in each new project there is an element of "research" embedded within the software "engineering" process (Meyer, 1992d)—effort associated with the research process being notoriously difficult to forecast.

Assessing production costs becomes easier the later it is in the production process, since the project is finally ended and the costs are known accurately. In other words, any cost/size estimate made early in the lifecycle must have significant error bars, which should gradually decrease as the point of completion approaches (Figure 10.2) (see further details in Section 10.5).

Process measures thus cover the whole lifecycle, either by describing the temporal (dynamic) variation of properties (e.g., staff allocation) or by integrating (summing) over the lifecycle phases. In contrast, a "snapshot" taken of the process at a given instant can be used to describe the static characteristics. The static properties, usually referred to as product metrics (e.g., Rombach, 1990; Ince, 1990), should be for a specific lifecycle phase. Different individual measures are appropriate for design (e.g., intermodule complexity) and code (e.g., lines of code), for example. These different measures are detailed in Section 10.3.

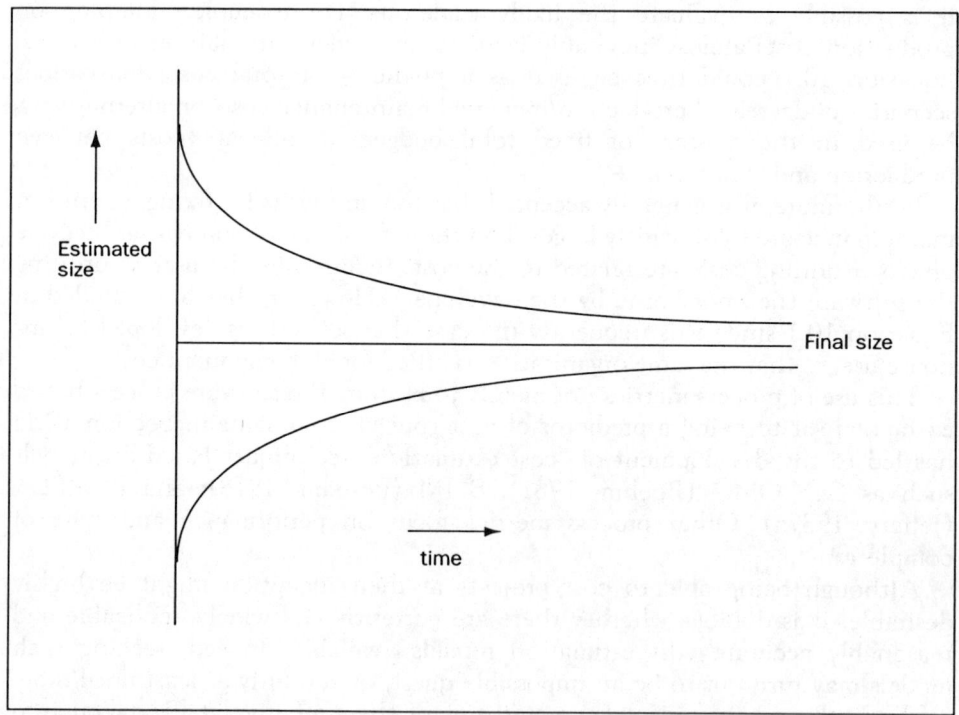

Figure 10.2 *Error bars on size estimates are initially large, but gradually decrease as the system development proceeds (Adapted from Laranjeira, © 1990 IEEE)*

Object-oriented "Metrics"

In order to estimate effort (process[29] metric), a connection has traditionally been made to the overall "size" (product metric) of the system being developed, by means of an organization-specific value of team productivity. The use of size from the many product metrics available as input to the process model equation should not suggest that size is the "best" product measure, but rather that it is one of the most obvious and easiest to measure, although unfortunately only available toward the end of the lifecycle. Consequently, this has fed back to a focus in *product metrics* on estimating or measuring size, viewing it as in some way influenced by program modularity and structure (Figure 10.3). However, a more thorough analysis of the product metric domain suggests that "complexity," and not size, is more relevant to modern software systems. Here complexity can be loosely defined as that characteristic of software that requires effort

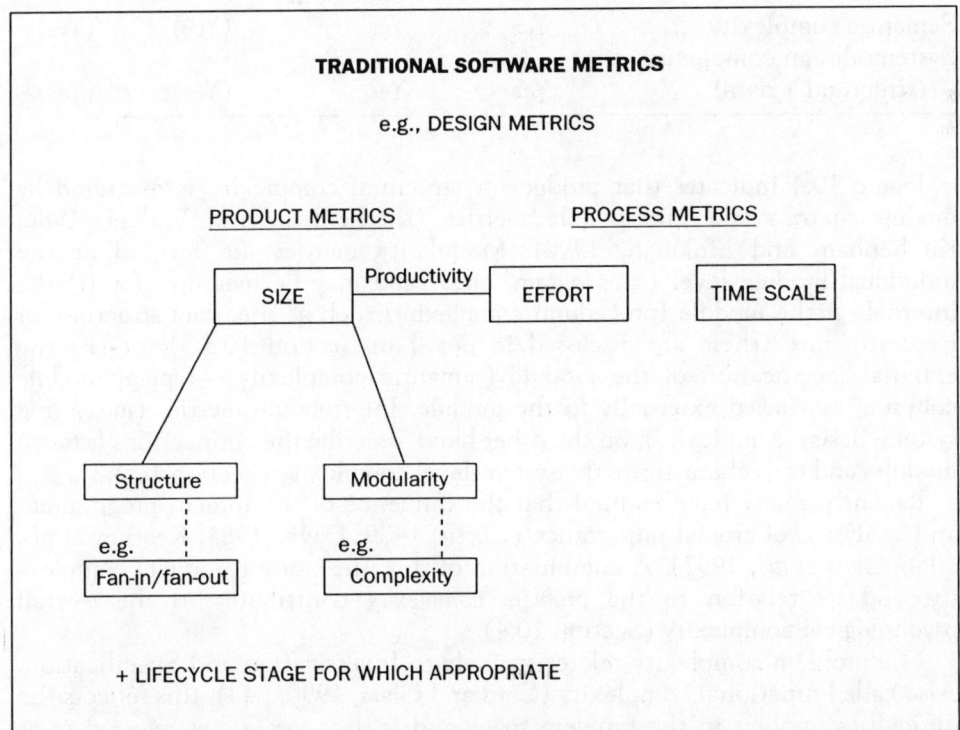

Figure 10.3 *Product and process metrics. Product metrics relate essentially to product size, which can be measured either in terms of its structure or of its modularity. Process metrics measure effort as a function of time. Size and effort are related in terms of productivity, either as a function of time or averaged over the whole lifecycle of the project.*

---

29. Note that this traditional metrics use of the words "process" and "product" is not identical to the use of the same words in describing the MOSES lifecycle in Chapters 4–7. Here "product" is essentially a static concept focused at the (usually) code level.

(resources) to design, understand, or code. In Figure 10.4, a composite picture is shown of the various components of software complexity (a product measure). It should be noted that not all these facets relate to all lifecycle stages (this is indicated in Table 10.1).

Table 10.1 *Appropriate measures of complexity at different lifeycle stages*

	Analysis	Systems design	Unit design	Code level
Problem/functional complexity	Yes	No	No	No
Product/document complexity	Yes	Yes	Yes	Yes
Procedural complexity	No	Function points only	Yes	Yes
Semantic complexity	Yes	Yes	(Yes)	(Yes)
Systems design complexity (structural + data)	Yes	Yes	(Yes)	(Yes)

Figure 10.4 indicates that product or structural complexity is measured by module metrics and intermodule metrics (Kitchenham and Walker, 1986; Kitchenham and Linkman, 1990). Modularity metrics are focused at the individual module level (subprogram, class) and may be measures for (i) the internals of the module (procedural complexity) such as size, data structure, or logic structure (these are discussed in detail in Section 10.3.3); or (ii) the external specification of the module (semantic complexity)—typical module cohesion as viewed externally to the module. Intermodule metrics (measuring systems design complexity), on the other hand, describe the connections *between* modules and thus characterize the system-level complexity (Section 10.3.2).

Recently, many have realized that the influence of the human programmer and analyst is of crucial importance (Curtis, 1979; Davis, 1984; Kearney *et al.*, 1986; Cant *et al.*, 1992). A combination of this, the static (product) complexity, and its relation to the *problem complexity* contributes to the overall psychological complexity (Section 10.4).

The problem complexity relates strongly to Investigation and Specification. Also called functional complexity (Card and Glass, 1990, p44), this reflects the difficulties implicit in the problem space and is thus sometimes referred to as "difficulty" (Meyer, 1992d). The only measures are ordinal and subjective (e.g., Fenton, 1991, p166). It is often argued (e.g., Card and Glass, 1990, p46) that problem complexity cannot be controlled and it is therefore frequently dismissed from consideration. However, it is important to realize that it should figure in terms of a comparison with design measures. In other words, the design and code complexity measures described above *do not* provide an absolute rating; rather, they should be evaluated as relative to the problem complexity. For example, a problem with a complexity of 1 unit (if we could measure this!)

Object-oriented "Metrics"

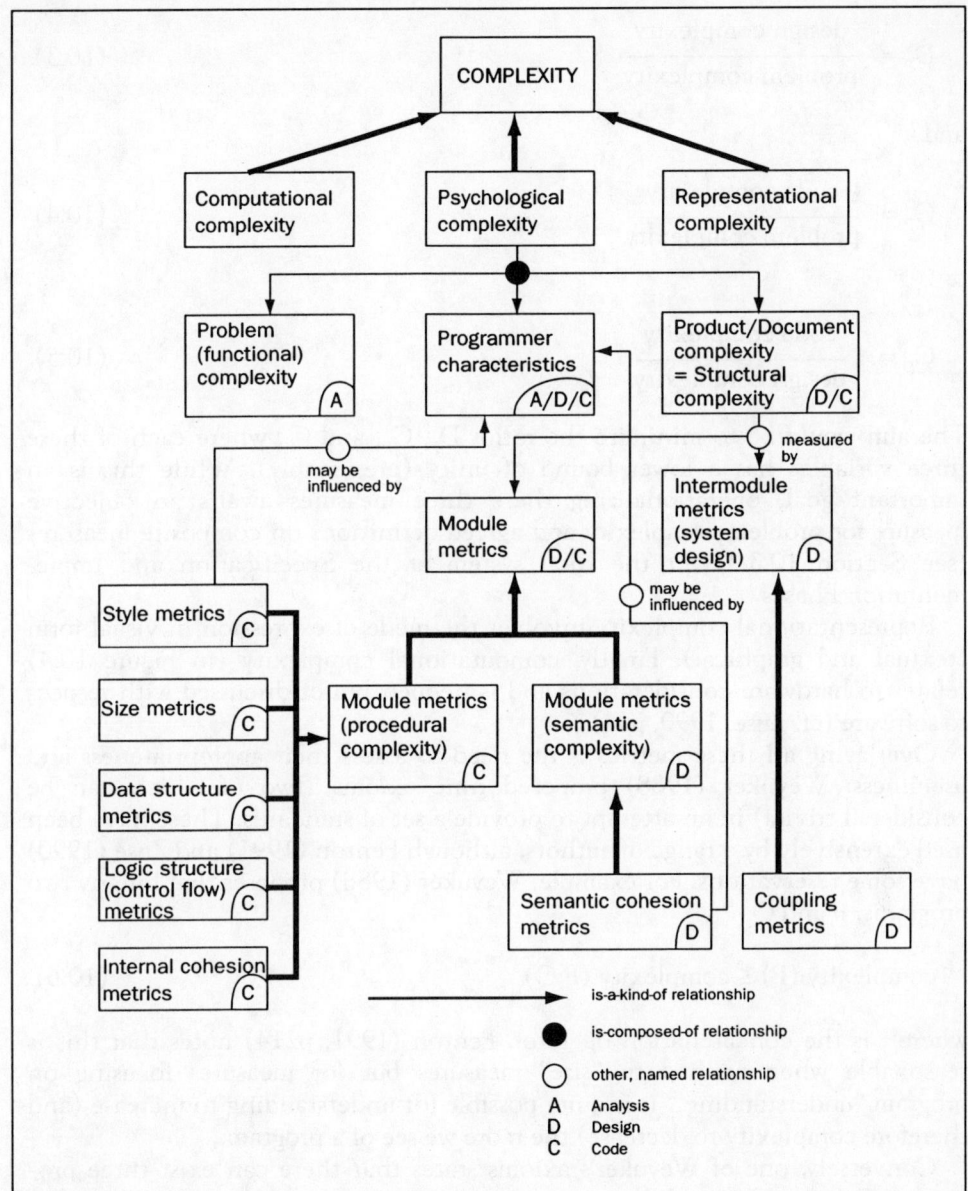

Figure 10.4 *Classification of complexity metrics*

that gives rise to a design of a complexity of 100 units leads us to believe that this is a bad design. However, if a design of 100 units complexity models a problem of 100 units complexity, we perceive this as a good design. The most appropriate measures are therefore the ratios:

$$D_P = \frac{\text{design complexity}}{\text{problem complexity}} \quad (10.3)$$

and

$$C_P = \frac{\text{code complexity}}{\text{problem complexity}} \quad (10.4)$$

or

$$C_D = \frac{\text{code complexity}}{\text{design complexity}} \quad (10.5)$$

The aim would be to minimize the ratios D_P, C_P, and C_D where each of these three variables has a lower bound of unity (presumably). While this is an important goal, operationalizing these three measures awaits an objective measure for problem complexity and agreed definitions on composite measures (see Section 10.3.4) for the total system at the Specification and Implementation Phases.

Representational complexity involves the mode of expression in visual form (textual and graphical). Finally, computational complexity (in Figure 10.4) relates to hardware considerations and is frequently not discussed with respect to software (cf. Zuse, 1990, p31).

Overlaying all these metrics is the need to assess their appropriateness and usefulness. Weyuker (1988) proposed nine axioms (two of which can be considered trivial) in an attempt to provide a set of standards. These have been used extensively by a range of authors, although Fenton (1991) and Zuse (1990) have some reservations. For example, Weyuker (1988) proposes that for any two programs, P and Q,

$$\text{complexity (P)} \leq \text{complexity (P;Q)} \quad (10.6)$$

where ; is the concatenation operator. Fenton (1991, p214) notes that this is reasonable when applied to "size" measures but for measures focusing on program "understanding," it is quite possible for understanding to increase (and therefore complexity to decrease) the more we see of a program.

Conversely, one of Weyuker's axioms states that there can exist three programs—P, Q, and R—such that

$$\text{complexity (P)} = \text{complexity (Q)}$$
$$\text{and complexity (P;R)} \neq \text{complexity (Q;R)} \quad (10.7)$$

In this case, no size measures can satisfy the axiom, but complexity measures may. In other words, at least two of Weyuker's axioms are self-inconsistent in that they cannot all be applied to all types of measures.

Object-oriented "Metrics"

Before proceeding with the discussion of product and process metrics, it is appropriate to note that there are other applications of metrics, notably to quality assessment. Arthur (1985) describes the application of metrics to assess correctness, efficiency, flexibility, integrity, interoperability, maintainability, portability, reliability, testability, usability, and reusability.

10.3 Product metrics (or structural complexity)

Some measure of the interactions between classes is perhaps a more important concept. It certainly is in terms of a well-constructed object-oriented system in which only good-quality ADTs are used; i.e., the system is a pure OO system and is not a hybrid of OO and traditional functional modules. Traditionally, the term "coupling" relates to the strength of the data coupling, D_C, and to the structural intermodule coupling, S_C. The former relates to the number of I/O variables entering or leaving a module and the latter to control coupling in the form of subroutine CALLs or message passing. Card and Glass (1990) argue that the "system complexity," C_S, is the arithmetic sum of these two:

$$C_S = S_C + D_C \tag{10.8}$$

It should be noted that these authors equate data coupling to cohesion, as defined by Stevens et al. (1974). We prefer to discriminate between (i) the objective (countable) measures such as the number of I/O variables and the number of control flow connections, and (ii) the semantic measures needed to assess the cohesiveness of a module via the interface it presents to the rest of the system.

We therefore need to modify Equation 10.8 explicitly to take into account semantic cohesion, C_h. Noting that increasing cohesion leads to a lower system complexity, we propose, initially, that

$$C_S = S_C + D_C + (C_{hmax} - C_h) \tag{10.9}$$

although this depends greatly on the scale used for C_h. (C_{hmax} is the maximum cohesion possible for the module.)

Data Complexity, D_C
The contribution of data complexity to systems design complexity in Equation 10.8 or 10.9 is derived from the I/O variable list. This is given as

$$\overline{D_C} = \frac{\sum^n \frac{I_0}{(\text{fan-out} + 1)}}{n} \tag{10.10}$$

where fan-out is defined below. It can be seen that this is a totally objective measure and bears no relationship to the semantic cohesion of the module as discussed in Section 10.3.2. Rather, it is qualitatively suggestive that a module with excessive I/O is one with low cohesion. While this is roughly acceptable, it does not translate well into the object paradigm where cohesion is high, yet interconnections, via messages and services, can also be high. Indeed, it could be argued that in object-oriented systems, there is minimal data connectivity such that this notation of data complexity at the intermodule level is virtually redundant.

Card and Glass (1990) then propose that a better comparative measure is the relative (per module) system complexity ($\bar{C}_S = C_S/n$ where n is the number of modules in the system). This normalization allows us to compare systems of contrasting sizes. Since it gives a mean module value, it offers potential applicability to object-oriented systems as an average class metric.

10.3.1 Intermodule metrics (for system design complexity)

Sheetz et al. (1991) summarize the recommendations of Tsai et al. (1986) and Zuse (1990) for properties of system design complexity metrics. They suggest that:

1. A measure of both the structure of the data and of the process must be included.
2. The measures must demonstrate consistency (i.e., if a structure is contained within another structure, the containing structure is computed to be at least as complex as the contained structure).
3. The measures must be capable of representing at least a weak order (i.e., they must be at least on an ordinal scale).
4. Measures must be additive (i.e., if two independent structures are put into sequence, then the total complexity of the combined structures is simply the sum of the complexities of the independent structures).
5. It must be possible to automate the measures.

Sheetz et al. (1991) suggest that coupling and cohesion metrics (generalized by Page-Jones (1992b) into a single measure of "connascence") may be appropriate in this context (see discussion below), although the abstraction level(s) at which these might apply needs to be carefully delineated.

Structural intermodule coupling, S_C

An easy measure of intermodule coupling is the fan-in/fan-out metric (Henry and Kafura, 1981). Fan-in refers to the number of locations from which control is passed *into* the module (e.g., CALLs to the module being studied) plus the number of (global) data; and, conversely, fan-out measures the number of other modules required plus the number of data structures that are updated by the module being studied. Since these couplings are determined in the Specification Phase, such intermodule metrics are generally applicable across the lifecycle.

Object-oriented "Metrics"

Although there are many measures incorporating both fan-in and fan-out (see below), Card and Glass (1990) present evidence that only fan-out and its distribution between modules contribute significantly to systems design complexity. Thus they propose:

$$\overline{S_C} \equiv \frac{S_C}{n} = \frac{\sum^n (\text{fan-out})^2}{n} \qquad (10.11)$$

Henry and Kafura (1981) propose a family of *information flow metrics*:

1. fan-in × fan-out
2. (fan-in × fan-out)^2
3. S_S × (fan-in × fan-out)^2

where S_S is the module size in LOC. These metrics of Henry and Kafura have been widely utilized and were thoroughly tested by their developers with data from the UNIX™ operating system.

Minimizing module complexity

Finally, it is interesting to note that for a single module, a minimum complexity can be determined. From Equation 10.8 (ignoring semantic concerns for the present), and paralleling the argument of Card and Glass (1990, pp60–1), we can substitute for S_C and D_C to give:

$$C_S = (\text{fan-out})^2 + \frac{I_0}{(\text{fan-out} + 1)} \qquad (10.12)$$

Values for C_S are tabulated in Table 10.2 for reasonable ranges of fan-out and I_O. Since Equation 10.12 is nondifferentiable we have to resort to tabulation and derive results that are similar to, but more correct than, Card and Glass' (1990) Figure 5.10, which is incorrectly derived by assuming Equation 10.12 to be differentiable. Since 100–200 is a large number of I/O variables for many systems, it suggests that low fan-outs are generally highly preferable.

Page-Jones (1992b) recommends as follows: "eliminate any unnecessary connascence and then minimize connascence across encapsulation boundaries by maximizing connascence within encapsulation boundaries." This is good advice for minimizing module complexity, since (i) it acknowledges that some complexity is necessary; (ii) it focuses on self-contained, semantically cohesive modules; and (iii) it reflects the need for low fan-out.

Object-oriented applications and extensions

The concern of software quality, described in the MOSES methodology in Chapters 4–8, is highly relevant here. The design guidelines of Table 7.5

expressed, as an objective, the need to minimize coupling and maximize cohesion. To some extent, this should indeed follow accepted structured heuristics. However, accepting that classes are autonomous modules with well-defined interfaces and responsibilities, in one sense the complexity added to the system by incurring an additional service connection (message passing) is likely to be less than adding a subroutine call in a procedural programming paradigm, which tends to have less well-defined responsibilities.

Table 10.2 *Values for C_s as a function of fan-out and number of I/O variables*

Fan-out	Number of I/O variables					
	0	10	20	50	100	200
0	0	10	20	50	100	200
1	1	6	11	26	51	101
2	4	7.3	10.7	20.7	37.3	70.7
3	9	11.5	14	21.5	34	59
4	16	18.0	20	26.0	36	56
5	25	26.7	28.3	33.3	42	59
6	36	37.4	38.8	43.1	50	64

During the Specification Phase, and indeed in any code evaluation undertaken at the module level, intermodule coupling is measured by the number of relationships between classes or between subsystems (Lorenz, 1993). In OO systems, connectivity between classes is usually a binary state for any pair of classes. This contrasts with the later, more detailed Implementation Phase where a single connection of the Specification Phase may be expanded to show multiple message paths when several services of an O/C are used by the same "client" O/C.

Class coupling should be minimized, in the sense of constructing autonomous modules; yet a tension exists between this aim of a weakly coupled system and the very close coupling evident in the class/superclass relationship (Booch, 1991). Berard (1992b, p102) differentiates between necessary and unnecessary coupling. The rationale is that without any coupling (viz., minimization of coupling) the system is useless. Consequently, for any given software solution there is a baseline or necessary coupling level—it is elimination of extraneous coupling that is the developer's goal. Such unnecessary couplings needlessly decrease the reusability of the classes, a fact again underlined by Page-Jones' (1992b) introduction of the term "connascence" and its associated guidelines (discussed above).

Interestingly, Sharble and Cohen (1993) showed that using a responsibility-driven methodology (e.g., Wirfs-Brock *et al.*, 1990), as opposed to an OO, yet data-driven, methodology (e.g., Coad, 1991) produces lower values of coupling and higher values of cohesion.

Booch (1991, p124) also notes that coupling occurs (i) on a peer-to-peer basis or (ii) within a generalization/specialization hierarchy. The former should exhibit low coupling; of necessity, classes in a generalization hierarchy are more closely related. Wild (1991) discriminates between these as "interface coupling" and "internal coupling." Internal coupling occurs both as "inside internal coupling," which describes the coupling of methods to their data (an intramodule metric—see Section 10.3.3) and the coupling of a composite class to its parts; and "outside internal coupling," which relates to relationships exemplified by the "friend" construct of C++.

Coupling as a result of inheritance and/or polymorphism is original to object systems. While Sharble and Cohen (1993) advocate the increase of polymorphism to reduce complexity and Tegarden et al. (1992) show that the use of either inheritance or polymorphism reduces the counts of standard metrics, it remains true that the tight coupling of inheritance provides a potential complexity (especially in maintenance) not foreseen in the development of traditional metrics. Subclasses can essentially access their superclass's internal data and methods—a form of violation of information hiding (Wild, 1991) and a high value of connascence (Page-Jones, 1992b). Complexity is also added as a result of excessive hierarchy depths, compounded when methods are overridden in descendant subclasses. Sheetz et al. (1991) thus define a "fan-down" metric as the number of subclasses that redefine any feature.

During Specification, the number of association and aggregation relationships and the argument lists can be counted. However, early in the process these will be scantily defined. In other words, if two classes are coupled in early Specification, it is highly likely that in late Specification and Implementation this will expand to several connections as well as the addition of message arguments that would not be expected to be shown earlier. With those caveats we can certainly evaluate the fan-in and fan-out of classes. With an analysis such as that shown in Figure 10.5, we would say that the analysis fan-out of class A is 3, of class B 1 and of classes C, D, and E zero, whereas the fan-in numbers are 0, 1, and 1 respectively. Berard (1992b, Chapter 7) confirms Card and Glass' (1990) suggestion that a low fan-out is desirable, since a high fan-out is characteristic of the large number of classes needed by the particular class in question. On the other hand, high fan-ins represent good object designs and a high level of reuse. Since these two are compensatory, it would not appear to be possible to maintain a high fan-in *and* a low fan-out across the whole system, as the cumulative values must be equal. More research is clearly needed in this crucial area.

A similar connectivity count can be done at various stages in the design. However, unlike in the structured paradigm when it is clear when the end of an activity has occurred, in the "seamless" transition of object technology it is harder to define the completion of phases until the Implementation is complete. This makes analysis metrics even harder to define than previously, since each analyst will tend to end the analysis at a different abstraction level,

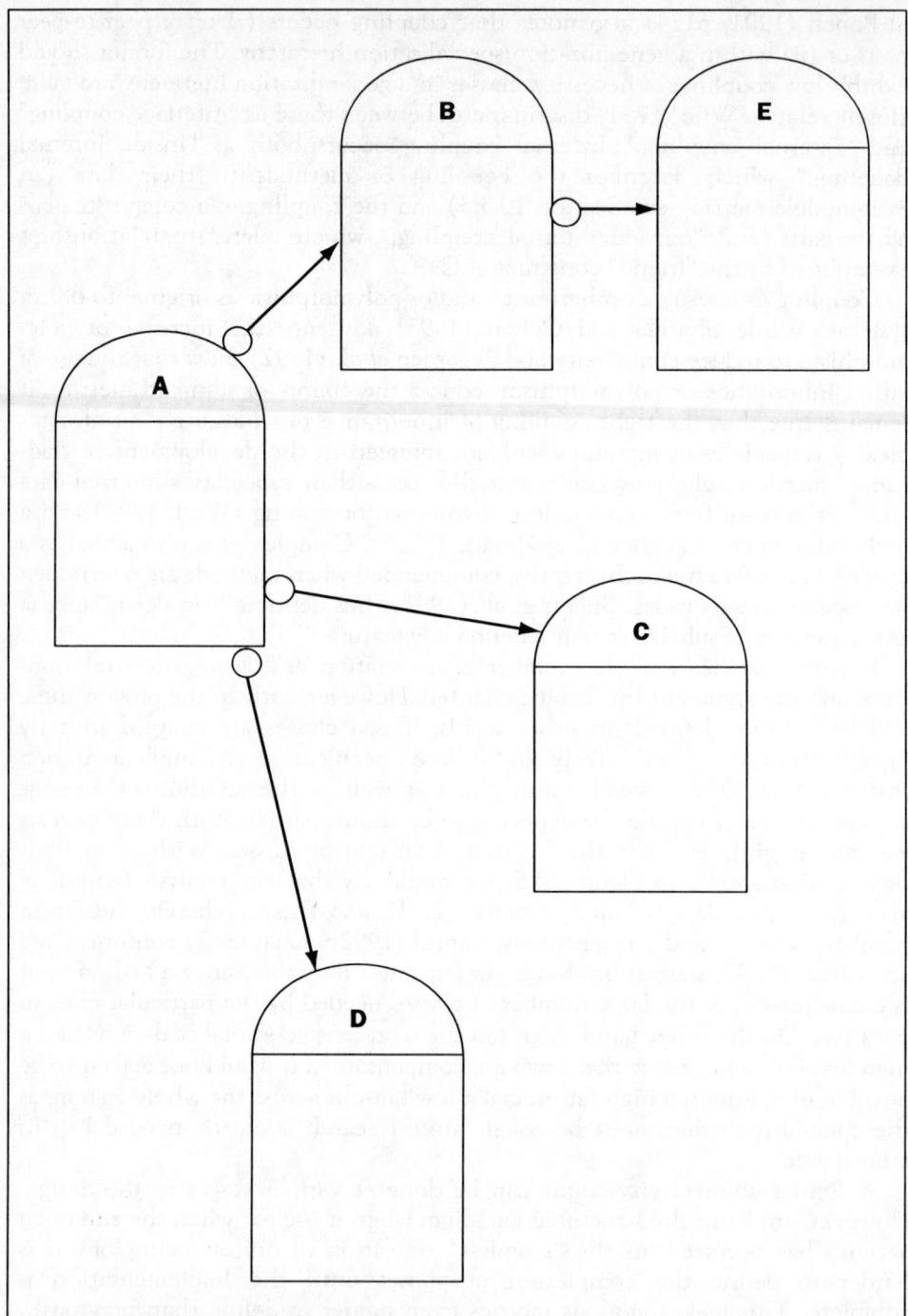

Figure 10.5 Fan-in/fan-out of five classes

although using a Specification Phase rather than explicit analysis and design phases can obviate this problem.

Laranjeira (1990) depicts this uncertainty in terms of a set of error bars (Figure 10.6) that become smaller as a function of the lifecycle phase. He then develops this idea to assess to what degree of granularity a system must be decomposed in order to gain a required (prestated) accuracy in estimates. Although his goal is cost estimation (dynamics) rather than the product metrics addressed here, and despite the fact that the mathematics in that paper are flawed, Laranjeira's (1990) underlying ideas are worth investigating further.

The curves shown in Laranjeira's paper are described as exponentials, but they are plotted on log axes. Figure 10.6 actually shows that the error bars are multiplicative. In other words, if the upper curve has a value of qA, then the lower curve will have a value of A/q—the errors are the true value multiplied or divided by the same value. It is not surprising, therefore, that the additive confidence intervals (described as negative and positive deviations), *which are linear in nature*, are not equal. If we follow Laranjeira (1990) by assuming that the error bars are multiplicative in this sense, then we can deduce that we might increase *n* sufficiently, where *n* is the number of levels to which we decompose the classes, so that these multiplicative error bars (confidence interval) are smaller than some predetermined level. That level could be stated

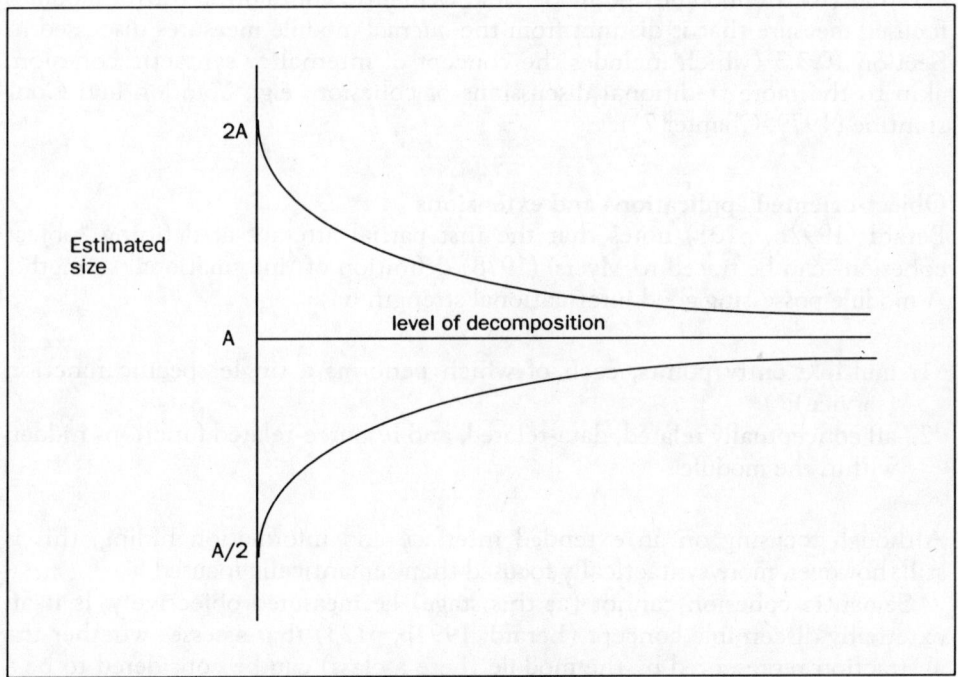

Figure 10.6 *Estimated size ranges can be decreased in an object-oriented environment by increasing the level of decomposition (Adapted from Laranjeira, © 1990 IEEE)*

either as some absolute value (linear, additive) or as some percentage error (logarithmic, multiplicative). Laranjeira quotes a value of 25%, which suggests a multiplicative value. In this case, his values of d_1 and d_2 do not apply since they give the additive error bars.

Qualitatively, this approach is appealing in its applicability to object-oriented systems. However, further research is needed (i) to establish the curves themselves (since the algebraic descriptions of Laranjeira are clearly flawed); (ii) to establish the value of the coefficient that determines the rate of convergence of the assumed decaying exponential functions; and (iii) to develop criteria to establish appropriate values of acceptable accuracies, from which we can determine N, the level of necessary decomposition.

10.3.2 Module metrics (for semantic complexity)

Intermodule metrics (Section 10.3.1) were originally characterized by Stevens *et al.* (1974) and Yourdon and Constantine (1979) as "cohesion" and "coupling," which Card and Glass (1990, p31) use to provide the concept of "modularity." Cohesion or module "strength" refers to the notion of a module-level "togetherness" viewed at the system abstraction level. Thus, although in one sense it can be regarded as a system design concept, we can more properly regard cohesion as a semantic concern expressed *of* a module evaluated from an external (to the module) point of view. Semantic cohesion is thus a module-focused measure that is distinct from the *internal* module measures discussed in Section 10.3.3 (which includes the concept of internal or syntactic cohesion, akin to the more traditional discussions of cohesion, e.g., Yourdon and Constantine (1979, Chapter 7)).

Object-oriented applications and extensions
Berard (1992b, p101) notes that the first partial attempt at defining "object cohesion" can be traced to Myers' (1978) definition of "informational strength." A module possessing good informational strength has:

1. multiple entry points, each of which performs a single specific function (service);
2. all conceptually related, data-related, and resource-related functions hidden within the module.

Although focusing on an extended interface and information hiding, this is still, however, more syntactically focused than semantically focused.

Semantic cohesion cannot (at this stage) be measured objectively. Is it an externally discernible concept (Berard, 1992b, p123) that assesses whether the abstraction represented by the module (here a class) can be considered to be a "whole," semantically. Booch (1991, p124) describes cohesion as embracing the behavior of this (external world) "concept," the whole concept and nothing but the concept—although his use of the term "functionally cohesive" (rather than "semantically cohesive") is perhaps misleading in light of the discussion here and in Berard (1992b). Booch (1991) also adds criteria of (i) sufficiency, (ii) completeness, and (iii) primitiveness. Sufficiency requires the abstraction (here class) to capture sufficient characteristics to be identifiable and meaningful. Completeness requires the class to capture *all* meaningful characteristics. A primitive operation is one that can be efficiently implemented only if given access to the underlying representation of the abstraction (e.g., adding an item to a set). Sufficiency is thus a minimalist view, probably rendering the abstraction useful for present purposes; completeness aims at reusability by supplying a *full* specification. Primitiveness is slightly different in that it describes operations for which knowledge of the underlying representation is needed.

It is after all possible to have a class with high internal, syntactic cohesion but little semantic cohesion. For example, imagine a class that includes features of both a person and the car that the person owns. Assuming that each person can own only one car and that each car can only be owned by one person (a one-to-one association), then *person_id* ↔ *vehicle_id* (which would be equivalent to data normalization). However, classes have not only data but also methods to perform various actions. They provide behavior patterns for (a) the person aspect and (b) the vehicle aspect of our proposed class. Assuming there is no intersecting behavior between PERSON and CAR, then what is the meaning of our class, presumably named CAR_PERSON (Figure 10.7)? Such a class could be internally highly cohesive, yet semantically *as a whole class seen from outside* the notion expressed (here of a thing known as a "car-person") could well be nonsensical. As a simple heuristic, consider the name of such classes and ask if they are meaningful within the UoD (Monarchi, pers. com., 1992).

10.3.3 Module metrics (for procedural complexity)

Of the five types of module metrics shown in Figure 10.4, size and logic structure account for the majority of the literature on metrics, perhaps because of their perceived relationship to cost estimation and to the difficulties of maintenance, respectively, and perhaps because of their ease of collection. However, it should be reiterated that these metrics can, in general, only be obtained from code and are inappropriate for the Specification Phase.

Size metrics (notably lines of code, LOC, Halstead's Software Science, Function Points, and their variants) will be discussed in Section 10.3.3.1 and their applicability to object-oriented systems evaluated. Logic structure metrics, especially McCabe's (1976) cyclomatic complexity, are discussed in Section 10.3.3.2. It should be noted that the use of the term "complexity metrics" in the literature tends to imply McCabe's metric and its variants (an overloading of the phrase "complexity metric"!). Data structure metrics, internal cohesion, and style metrics are discussed together in Section 10.3.3.3.

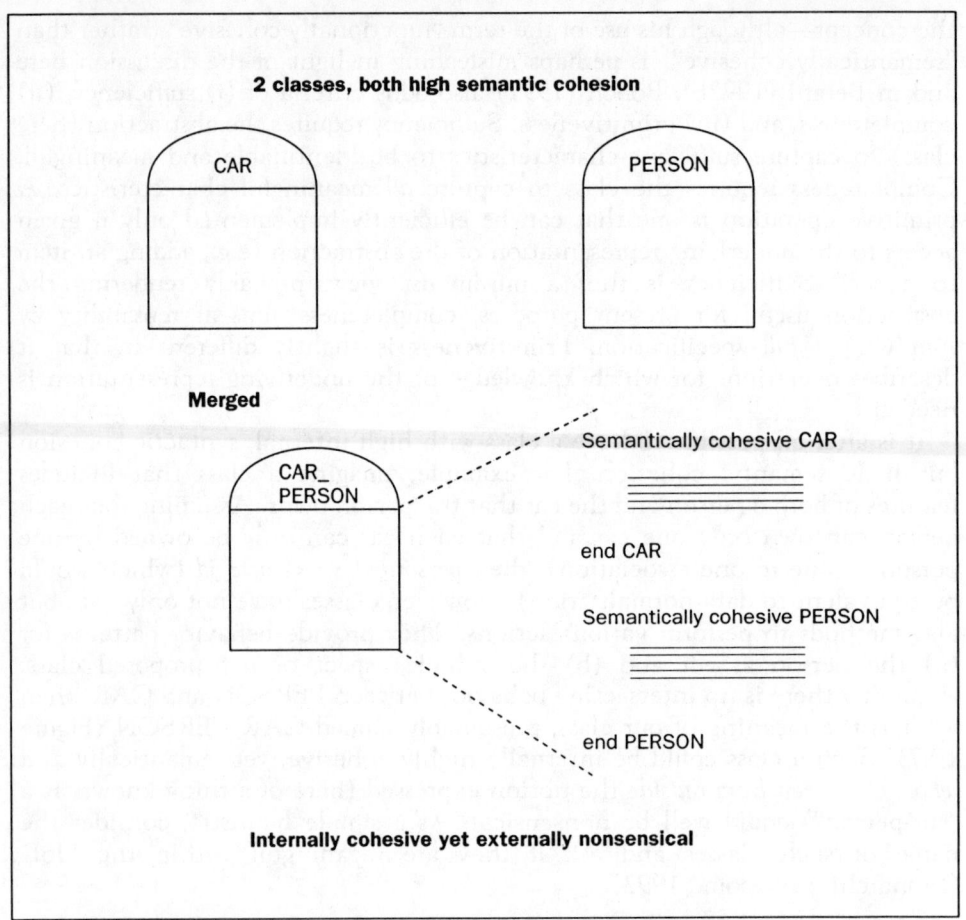

Figure 10.7 *Individually semantically cohesive classes may be merged to give an externally semantically nonsensical class, while retaining internal semantic cohesion*

10.3.3.1 Size metrics
Lines of code

The use of source lines of code (SLOC) as a measure of software size is one of the oldest methods of measuring software. It was first used to measure the size of programs written in fixed-format assembly languages. Its use as a metric began to be problematic when free-format assembly languages were introduced (Jones, 1986), since more than one logical statement could be written per line. The problems became greater with the advent of high-level languages that describe key abstractions in the problem domain (Booch, 1991), removing some accidental complexity (Brooks, 1975). Furthermore, lines of code can be interpreted differently for different programming languages. Jones (1986) lists eleven different counting methods, six at the program level and five at the project level.

With the introduction of fourth-generation languages, still more difficulties were experienced in counting source lines (Verner and Tate, 1988; Verner, 1991).

The currently most accepted definition of SLOC is given by Conte *et al.* (1986):

> A line of code is any line of program text that is not a comment or blank line, regardless of the number of statements or fragments of statements on the line. This specifically includes all lines containing program headers, declarations, and executable and non-executable statements.

Notwithstanding their many shortcomings, SLOC counts are still one of the major tools widely used today (Côté *et al.*, 1988; Bourque and Côté, 1991). The wide acceptance of SLOC as a size/complexity metric (Weyuker, 1988) is due to its simplicity, ease of application, inertia of tradition, absence of alternative size measures (Levitin, 1986), and its intuitive appeal (Dunsmore, 1984). In addition to these properties, many empirical results also have shown the usefulness of SLOC. For example, Basili (1980) found that effort correlated better with SLOC than with Halstead's metrics (Halstead, 1977) and was at least as good as McCabe's cyclomatic complexity metric (McCabe, 1976). Similar results were also reported by Evangelist (1983) and Weyuker (1988). These empirical findings indicate that for some of the attributes of software systems, SLOC is better or at least as good as any other metric. As a result, it has been used for a number of different software development activities, such as estimating, planning, tracking the progress of projects, normalizing measures of productivity and defect densities, and deriving measures and effectiveness of reuse strategies (Yu *et al.*, 1991; see also discussion in Section 10.1). As a consequence, SLOC counts have also been used as a baseline for the evaluation of almost all empirical studies of metrics, including function points (Albrecht and Gaffney, 1983).

One of the features lacking in SLOC counts, reducing its usefulness as an effective size measure for understanding a piece of code (for maintenance, debugging, testing, etc.), is the ability to account for complexity of a line of code. This ambiguity of complexity between different lines of code is addressed in the new metric of CL (complexity and lines of code), described by Pant *et al.* (1994). Although it provides a measure that satisfies Weyuker's (1988) seventh axiom (a property *not* possessed by Halstead's effort measure, McCabe's cyclomatic complexity, or statement counting), this metric remains to be fully tested empirically (having been tested so far only by Pant *et al.*, 1994).

Inclusion of reused code (e.g., code from previous projects, libraries, macros, other systems, etc.) in the SLOC measure also creates problems; for example, Jones (1986) counted all reused code modules each time they occurred in the system.

Tokens

Tokens are the basic lexical units out of which a program is synthesized. A lexical analyzer, the first phase of any compilation process, converts high-level statements to tokens for further processing. Tokens are similar to words in natural languages but the number of bytes that it takes to represent a token in one specific hardware implementation is always the same.

In order to solve some of the problems of SLOC measure, Halstead (1977) proposed a metric based on operator and operand as the fundamental counts. It is based on the following four counts:

η_1 = the number of unique operators
η_2 = the number of unique operands
N_1 = the total number of operators
N_2 = the total number of operands

In an algorithm or program, any symbol or keyword used to represent data is normally classified as an operand and a keyword that is used to specify an action is considered as an operator. Thus variable names and labels are operands, while most punctuation marks, arithmetic symbols (such as +, −, *, and /), keywords (such as **if**, **while**, **do**, etc.), special symbols (such as :=, braces, parentheses, = =, !=), function names, etc., are counted as operators. According to Halstead, operators and operands and their sum are the key concepts of software and can be used to measure (or estimate) size of programs or algorithms. Halstead applied these four parameters to get a synthetic metric for estimating software attributes such as program length, volume, level, purity, programming effort, language level, errors, modularity, etc., many of which, it should be noted, are ill defined.

The vocabulary of a program, η, is defined as the sum of operators and operands ($\eta = \eta_1 + \eta_2$) and the length of a program, N, is equal to the sum of the total number of operators and operands ($N_1 + N_2$). If each line of a machine language program consists of one operator and one operand, SLOC can be defined as equal to $N/2$ (Shen et al., 1983).

Software Science also defines program size in terms of volume (in bits) as $V = N \times \log_2 \eta$ (which, it should be noted, is dimensionally incorrect). Halstead mentioned that a reasonable size estimate can be made well before the program is written. The approximate size of a program, $N = \eta_1 \times \log_2 \eta_1 + \eta_2 \times \log_2 \eta_2$, is calculable from a knowledge of distinct operators and operands that are likely to be in the program. This may be converted to SLOC via the relationship $S = N/C$, where C is a language-dependent constant. Conte et al. (1986) have proposed that the value of C is equal to 2 for machine language (each line having one operator and one operand) and 7 for FORTRAN.

There have been many criticisms of Software Science (e.g., Lister, 1982; Shen et al., 1983; Levitin, 1986). For example, there are many variations in counting and classifying operators and operands, and there is no general agreement among researchers on what is the most meaningful way to classify and count operators and operands (Shen et al., 1983). Furthermore, the counting scheme is language-dependent and the Software Science counts are very sensitive (Elshoff, 1978). There is ambiguity in the counting of statement labels (Conte et al., 1986). Originally designed with languages such as

FORTRAN in mind, Software Science metrics are difficult to apply to more modern programming languages (Lister, 1982) that support advanced powerful concepts such as data abstraction, classes, hierarchy, etc., although some attempts have been made (e.g., Tegarden et al., 1992)—see further discussion below. Similar problems are also experienced in counting pairs such as opening and closing parentheses, "begin–end," and "if–then–else." Levitin (1986) suggests that counting rules for the above pairs as single operators or two operators will affect length and volume measure, since they are based on the sums of operators and operands.

Most of the Software Science formulae were derived for algorithms (not programs) (Halstead, 1977) and it is difficult to say whether these formulae are still applicable to real-life programs. Algorithms are generally independent of programming languages. In other words, a programming language is a specific notation in which an algorithm can be expressed. Although most of the formulae are derived algebraically, several assumptions are also made without any formal justification (Shen et al., 1983) and there are several errors in the derivation, especially in the use of logarithmic transformations (Card and Agresti, 1987; Shen et al., 1983; Zweben, 1990) and in application of the results of cognitive complexity, human memory models and searching strategies (Coulter, 1983; Card and Glass, 1990).

Finally, concerns have been voiced about the external validity of the experimental data used to "verify" the Software Science metrics (e.g., Lister, 1982; Hamer and Frewin, 1982; Shen, 1983). Card and Glass (1990, p27) voice these concerns in their recommendation that *"practitioners can safely ignore software science* at present."

Function points
Function point counting (Albrecht, 1979; Albrecht and Gaffney, 1983) is a technology-independent method of estimating system size without the use of lines of code. Function points have been found useful in estimating system size early in the development lifecycle and are used for measuring productivity trends (Jones, 1986) from a description of users' specifications and requirements. They are probably the sole representative of size metrics *not* restricted to code.

Albrecht argued that function points could be easily understood and evaluated even by nontechnical users. The concept has been extended more recently by Symons (1988) as the Mark II function point counting approach—a metric that the British government uses as the standard software productivity metric (Dreger, 1989).

In function point application, system size is based on the total amount of information that is processed, together with a complexity factor that influences the size of the final product. It is based on the following weighted items:

- number of external inputs
- number of external outputs

- number of external inquiries
- number of internal master files
- number of external interfaces

The weights assigned to each item depend on the characteristics of the system being developed. For example, the weights to the number of inputs can vary from 4 to 7, depending on the complexity of the system being developed, which is divided into low, medium, and high. The initial count is summed to get unadjusted function points that are later modified using 14 factors, including the use of structured programming, the use of high-level languages, the use of on-line development, the use of a software library, performance, ease of use, etc., in order to derive a value for "adjusted function points" (Albrecht and Gaffney, 1983; Jones, 1986; Verner, 1991).

Verner (1991) groups problems of function point analysis into the following three headings:

- problems in measuring unadjusted function point size;
- problems with the system adjustments;
- other general problems.

Feature points
Jones (1988) introduces the metric of feature points, which complements the functionality of Albrecht's (1979) function points by characterizing internal complexity in terms of a weighted algorithm count. Such a system is most useful in software containing a high degree of internal algorithmic complexity and permits the metric to be more widely applied, e.g., outside the commercial MIS environment.

Object-oriented applications and extensions
Thomas and Jacobson (1989) suggest some of the components required in moving toward object-oriented metrics. These include lines of code reused per programmer, number of methods per class, class coupling and cohesion, and amount of reuse possible. Jacobson et al. (1992, p460) point out that lines of code *per se* are not very elucidating, since the smaller the number of LOC written, the greater the likelihood that you have reused significant code chunks and (hopefully) the greater the quality of the final product.

At the detailed design stage, it would appear that a good estimate of size can be gained more simply, at least as a first-order estimate, from:

- number of attributes, A (low weighting, W_A)
- number of methods, M (weighting W_M)

Indeed, a simple count of the number of classes can be roughly indicative of system size. The number of methods could probably be related partly to function points, or a more recent modification thereof, such that the overall system "size" would be, for N object classes, each of size s_i (Henderson-Sellers, 1991a):

$$S = \sum_{i=1}^{n} s_i = \sum_{i=1}^{n} (AW_A + MW_M)_i \tag{10.13}$$

At this detailed design stage, the class–class interactions needed by utilizing an external class as an instance variable in the class code should have been taken into account using object-oriented cognitive complexity metrics (Cant, 1990). However, work is still needed to evaluate appropriate weights, W_A and W_M, which are likely to be language-dependent (Thomas, 1989a) but of the order of $W_M = 5\text{--}20$ where $W_A = 1$. Since object-oriented code strongly supports high modularization, both externally and internally, the variance of method lengths is likely to be lower than that for a function point implementation in a procedural programming language.

An object-oriented development environment supports design and code reuse, the most straightforward type of reuse being the use of a library class (of code) that perfectly suits the requirements. Perhaps more commonly, a new class will be constructed by using inheritance. In this case a fraction, I, of the old code is effectively reused and a fraction $(1 - I)$ written anew. If there are k classes reused "as-is," l classes partially reused, and m classes fully coded from scratch (where the total number of classes in the system is $N = k + l + m$), then formula 10.13 becomes

$$\sum_{i=1}^{k} W_{R_i} + \sum_{i=k+1}^{k+l} \left[(AW_A + MW_M)_i (1 - I)_i + W_{R_i} \right]$$

$$+ \sum_{i=k+l+1}^{k+l+m} (AW_A + MW_M)_i \tag{10.14}$$

where W_{R_i} is the (very small) weighting/cost of library reuse, viz., the cost of locating and obtaining a single library class, which is independent of whether all or only part of the code is to be reused.

Tegarden et al. (1992) consider the applicability of several traditional procedural complexity metrics to object-oriented systems. The use of LOC as a measure of the size of a class is questioned, not only on the basic definition of a line of code, but also in respect of whether an inherited method should be counted as a contributory LOC to every class that inherits it, or simply counted once in the defining class. They applied LOC, Halstead's Software Science, and McCabe's cyclomatic complexity (see next section) to four versions of a small accounts system. These four versions were with and without inheritance, together with and without the use of polymorphism. The results (Table 10.3), expressed for the overall system, showed that, as might be expected, the use of polymorphism and/or inheritance decreased the size measures of Total SLOC and Halstead's V. To some extent, this must reflect the elimination of duplicate code. These results were also corroborated at the class level (Tegarden et al., 1992). No comment was made by these authors regarding the additional "complexity" of an increased number of classes when using inheritance.

Table 10.3 Results of PC metrics for four versions at the system level (Tegarden et al. 1992)

Count or Metric	No Poly No Inher.	Poly No Inher.	No Poly Inher.	Poly Inher.
Number of classes	7	7	12	12
Members/class	7	7	2	2
Number of methods	42	42	30	30
η_1	75	53	58	53
η_2	58	56	56	56
N_1	955	735	541	521
N_2	453	259	254	245
N	1,408	1,094	795	766
V	9,934	7,404	5,432	5,184
V(G) Sum	95	71	57	55
File V(G)	54	30	28	26
Total SLOC	676	626	539	534
Exec. SLOC	202	181	126	124

In a commercial MIS study, Humphrys (1991) found that the use of object-oriented techniques resulted in an 80% reduction in code size. He suggested that a simple size decrease of this magnitude has immediate repercussions in terms of greater flexibility and a significant decrease in maintenance costs.

In addition to measures readily equivalent to standard metrics, there are some measures needed that are very specific to object-oriented systems. These include (Jacobson et al., 1992):

- width and height of inheritance hierarchies;
- number of classes inheriting a specific operation;
- number of collaborating classes (although this can be measured by an object fan-in/fan-out measure—see Section 10.3.1);
- a measure of the proportion of the system that consists of reused code.

Object-oriented "Metrics"

In a discussion of design metrics, Lorenz (1993) advocates measuring eleven items (Table 10.4). Some of these coincide with Jacobson et al.'s list and some with the six recommendations of Chidamber and Kemerer (1991) (Table 10.5). Here we discuss only those metrics appropriate as size metrics; the remainder have either already been discussed in Section 10.3.1 (coupling) or will be discussed later in Section 10.3.3 (cohesion).

Table 10.4 *Items recommended by Lorenz (1993) as useful design metrics*

Metric	Item being measured
1. Average method size	Size
2. Average number of methods per class	Size
3. Average number of instance variables per class	Coupling
4. Class hierarchy nesting level	Size
5. Number of subsystem–subsystem relationships	Coupling
6. Number of class–class relationships within each subsystem	Cohesion and coupling
7. Instance variable usage	Semantic complexity
8. Average number of comment lines	Cognitive complexity
9. Number of problem reports per class	Process
10. Number of times class is reused	Process
11. Number of classes and methods thrown away	Process

Table 10.5 *Six metrics of Chidamber and Kemerer (1991)*

Metric	Item being measured
1. Weighted methods per class	Size and complexity
2. Depth of inheritance tree	Size
3. Number of children	Size/coupling/cohesion
4. Coupling between objects	Coupling
5. Response for class	Communication/complexity
6. Lack of cohesion in methods	Internal cohesion

Average method size should be small—Lorenz suggests less than 8 SLOC for Smalltalk and less than 24 LOC for C++, illustrating the language dependency implicit in this measure. It is recommended that the average number of methods per class be less than 20, although this is perhaps better judged from a semantic cohesion viewpoint than a mere count. (Some typical values are given in Table 10.6, showing that only the NIH library exceeds this "threshold value.") Weighted methods per class (Table 10.5) focus at the class rather than the system level, and the weights used represent the static complexity of the methods (Chidamber and Kemerer, 1991) that these authors do not choose to define. This has some relationship to Equation 10.1, which essentially weights by a mean value for all methods rather than an individual method "complexity." It is probably also worth measuring the distribution of the values, say in terms of a standard deviation or range, as well as the mean.

Table 10.6 Summary of library characteristics (Yap and Henderson-Sellers, 1993a)

Library	Size (no. of classes)	Total no. features	Average no. features	Depth	Average depth
Actor 3.0	119	1579	13.27	8	3.07
Borland V2.0	30			6	2.10
Instantiation		228	7.60		
Derivation		244	8.13		
Borland V3.0	166			5	1.58
Instantiation					
Templates		1014	6.11		
Without templates		1087	6.55		
Derivation					
Templates		1098	6.61		
Without templates		1183	7.13		
Booch components	32	340	10.63	1	0.09
C++ Views	75			7	3.24
Instantiation		967	12.89		
Derivation		1035	13.80		
Eiffel/S	75			7	3.78
Unrestricted exports		475	6.33		
With restricted		572	7.63		
NIH C++	66			5	2.14
Instantiation					
Lower limit		1683	25.50		
Upper limit		1694	25.67		
Derivation					
Lower limit		1823	27.62		
Upper limit		1838	27.85		
Smalltalk/V—Windows	173	1825	10.55	7	2.54
Smalltalk/V for PM	139	1518	10.92	5	2.38
Zinc Interface	54			3	1.81
Instantiation		549	10.17		
Derivation		637	11.80		

Object-oriented "Metrics"

All authors note the need to measure inheritance structures: in terms of depths and node density. These can be measured by the maximum depth, since the depth is likely to affect the distribution of inherited features. A rough guideline of 6 or 7 is recommended for hierarchy depths. Data for ten libraries are given in Table 10.7, which support this heuristic.

Table 10.7 *Average depth of inheritance for 10 class libraries: histogram data (number of occurrences) (Yap and Henderson-Sellers, 1993a)*

Library	0	1	1.5	1.75	2	2.5	3	4	4.5	4.72*	5	5.5	6	7	8
Actor 3.0	1	29			17		27	22			11		7	4	1
Borland 2.0	4	8			7		6	3			1				
Borland 3.0	35	53	1		38		25	13			1				
Booch components[†]	30	3													
C++ Views	4	15			13		8	12			9		13	1	
Eiffel/S	1	1			1		33	21	4	1	7	1	4	1	
NIH C++	3	16			26		12	8			1				
Smalltalk/C (Windows)	1	39			57		38	21			14		2	1	
Smalltalk/V (PM)	1	35			42		37	19			5				
Zinc Interface	7	12	1	2	13	4	15								

*This is the depth calculated for the NONE class. Since NONE inherits from everything, its depth is the sum of all other classes' depths (275.5) divided by the number of all other classes (74), plus (1), as it descends from each of those classes (and should be one level deeper), i.e., (275.5 / 74) + 1 = 4.72.

†The Simple_Vector class was not described in the documentation. It will be assumed that it does not inherit from any class, and so has a depth of 0. The total number of classes (for calculating the average depth) will include Simple_Vector.

Another depth measure is the average inheritance depth, which is calculated by:

$$\frac{\Sigma \text{ Depth of each class}}{\text{Number of classes}} \qquad (10.15)$$

In the hierarchical fragment shown in Figure 10.8, the depth for Subclass 1 is 1, as it inherits from only one parent, which in turn does not inherit from anything else. The depth for Subclass 2 is $(2 + 1) / 2 = 1.5$, as it inherits from two parents, of which one (Superclass 3) inherits from another (Superclass 1) and the other (Superclass 2) inherits from nothing.

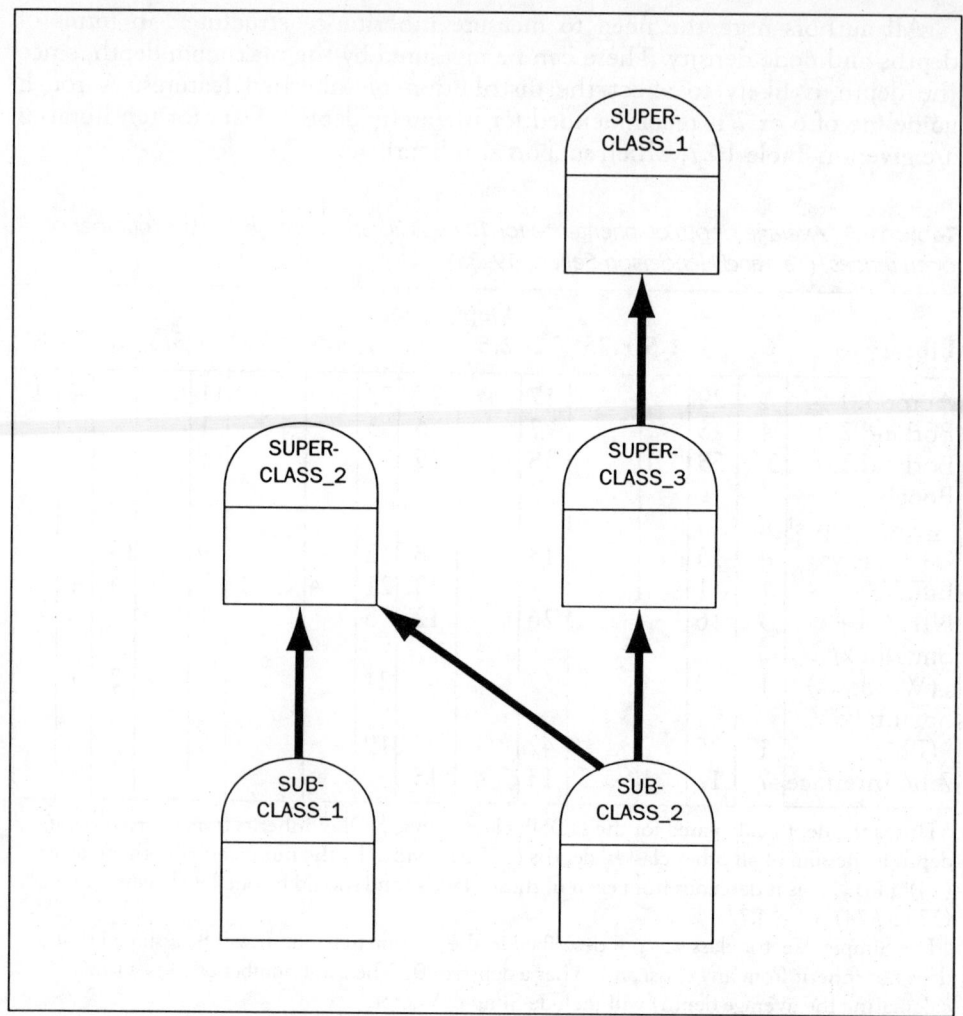

Figure 10.8 *Fragment of inheritance hierarchy to illustrate the calculation of reuse metrics (Yap and Henderson-Sellers, 1993a)*

The average depth of inheritance, overall, for this hierarchy is calculated as follows:

Sum of each depth is given as 0 (Superclass 1) + 0 (Superclass 2) + 1 (Superclass 3) + 1 (Subclass 1) + 1.5 (Subclass 2) = 3.5. Thus the average depth = 3.5/5 = 0.7. The average depth of inheritance indicates the general level of modeling or abstraction used in the hierarchy (Table 10.6).

Chidamber and Kemerer (1991) introduce NOC as the number of children, suggesting that classes high in the hierarchy should have more subclasses than those lower down. Yap and Henderson-Sellers (1993a) discuss two similarly focused measures designed to evaluate the level of reuse possible within hierarchies, especially those found in or destined to be part of a class library. The reuse ratio, U, is given by:

$$U = \frac{\text{Number of superclasses}}{\text{Total number of classes}} \qquad (10.16)$$

This ratio indicates the extent to which the implementors of the class library have been able to inherit from their own classes to create new classes.

Secondly, the specialization ratio, S, is given as:

$$S = \frac{\text{Number of subclasses}}{\text{Number of superclasses}} \qquad (10.17)$$

The specialization ratio measures the extent to which a superclass has captured the abstraction, since a large value of S indicates a high degree of reuse by subclassing. Table 10.8 summarizes values of U and S for ten class libraries.

Table 10.8 *Reusability statistics (Yap and Henderson-Sellers, 1993a)*

Library	No. of subclasses	No. of superclasses	Reuse ratio	Specialization ratio
Actor 3.0	118	45	0.38	2.62
Borland 2.0	11	27	0.37	2.45
Borland 3.0	67	131	0.40	1.96
Booch components*	4	3	0.12	0.75
C++ Views	30	71	0.40	2.37
Eiffel/S†	74‡	74§	0.99	1
NIH C++	16	63	0.24	3.94
Smalltalk/V—Windows	51	172	0.30	3.37
Smalltalk/V for PM	40	138	0.29	3.45
Zinc Interface	13	47	0.24	3.61

*Structures and Tools classes only. Note that Simple_Vector is included in these calculations, as classes inherit from it.
†The reuse and specialization ratios indicate the direct acyclic nature of the Eiffel/S hierarchy where everything inherits from ANY and NONE inherits from everything.
‡All except for NONE.
§All except for GENERAL.

10.3.3.2 Logic structure metrics

Zuse (1990) lists over a hundred "complexity measures." However, the best established measure of module complexity is probably the cyclomatic complexity introduced by McCabe (1976). Its basis is in graph theory (e.g., Berge, 1973; Bollobás, 1979), which states that for a *connected* graph the graph cyclomatic number[30], v, is given as

$$v = e - n + 1 \tag{10.18}$$

and for a graph with p components

$$v = e - n + p \tag{10.19}$$

(e.g., Harary, 1969, p39), where e is the number of edges and n the number of nodes. A connected graph (Equation 10.18) is a graph where *all* nodes are reachable from every other node. A disconnected graph is one with p components that are disjoint, but that could, with the addition of $(p - 1)$ additional edges, be turned into a connected graph (Figure 10.9). Since in a connected graph, a path from a to b is equivalently a path from b to a, there is no notion of "strongly connected" until the graph becomes directed, as in software representations. This means that for a single program or program module, the connected, directed acyclic graph (DAG) does not satisfy the definition of strong connectedness until an edge is added from the stop node to the start node. The resultant graph is thus known as a strongly connected graph and has one more edge than its corresponding undirected graph (or the regular DAG equivalent). Thus the cyclomatic complexity, or cycle rank, is given for a single, strongly connected DAG by

$$V(G) = e - n + 2 \tag{10.20}$$

—a form frequently quoted in the literature as representing the standard McCabe metric. McCabe's (1976) Theorem 1 states that in a strongly connected graph, $V(G)$ is equal to the maximum number of linearly independent circuits through the DAG and *not* the number of test paths, as it is frequently misquoted (e.g., Kearney et al., 1986; Nejmeh, 1988). As McCabe (1976) himself notes, "There are often additional (to those identified by $V(G)$) paths to test." These paths can be derived from the basis set identifiable by the use of $V(G)$ or directly using, for example, the NPATH metric of Nejmeh (1988).

Equation 10.20 is useful for the cyclomatic complexity of a single component DAG. However, with respect to the extension of $V(G)$ to more than one component, there appear to be two options. Assuming that we are trying to describe a measurement effectively for the connected graph of Figure 10.9(b)

---

30. Also called the first Betti number, the nullity, or the cycle rank.

Object-oriented "Metrics"

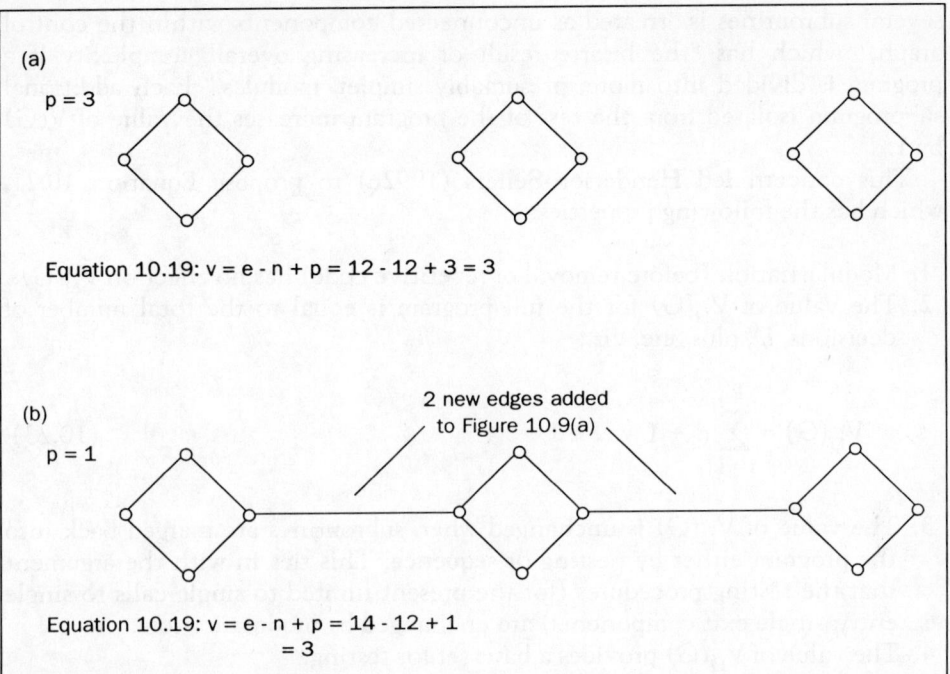

Figure 10.9 (a) Disconnected graph with three components; (b) connected graph constructed from three components by adding two edges

but expressed in terms of the three disjoint components of Figure 10.9(a), then the argument there is easily extended to give, inductively:

$$V_{LI}(G) = e - n + p + 1 \tag{10.21}$$

This is the form proposed by Henderson-Sellers (1992c) and relabeled here with a subscript LI (linearly independent) (Henderson-Sellers and Tegarden, 1994), as we will later show that this metric (Equation 10.21) is strongly related to the cycle rank of the graph.

Feghali and Watson (1994) point out that a different approach was taken by McCabe (1976); it was, however, apparently rescinded in McCabe and Butler (1989). He argued that *each* of the components needs to be converted into a strongly connected graph, thus giving:

$$V(G) = e - n + 2p \tag{10.22}$$

Thus each component is treated independently and the value given by Equation 10.22 is relevant to each component but not really to the integrated system. Indeed, Shepperd (1988) noted that this means that a program with several subroutines is "treated as unconnected components within the control graph," which has "the bizarre result of increasing overall complexity if a program is divided into more, presumably simpler, modules." Each additional subprogram isolated from the rest of the program increases the value of $V(G)$ by 1.

This concern led Henderson-Sellers (1992c) to propose Equation 10.21, which has the following properties:

1. Modularization (before removal of repetitive code) has no effect on $V_{LI}(G)$.
2. The value of $V_{LI}(G)$ for the full program is equal to the total number of decisions, D, plus one, viz.:

$$V_{LI}(G) = \sum_{i=1}^{p} d_i + 1 = D + 1 \tag{10.23}$$

3. The value of $V_{LI}(G)$ is unchanged when subroutines are merged back into the program either by nesting or sequence. This ties in with the argument that the testing procedures (for the present limited to single calls to single entry, single exit components) are unchanged by modularization.
4. The value of $V_{LI}(G)$ provides a basis set for testing.

A simple example will help here to illustrate the differences between $V(G)$ and $V_{LI}(G)$. In Figure 10.10 there is a main routine and two subroutines, A1 and A2. The values of $V(G)$ and $V_{LI}(G)$ are $19 - 18 + 2 * 3$ and $19 - 18 + 3 + 1$ respectively. Hence $V(G) = 7$ and $V_{LI}(G) = 5$. In terms of testing paths, these graphs are equivalent to a single DAG, using the node splitting technique of Henderson-Sellers (1992c), as shown in Figure 10.11, for which both $V(G)$ and $V_{LI}(G)$ have the same value, given by Equation 10.20, viz., $23 - 20 + 2 = 5$. In both figures, there are four decisions, while the basis set is more easily obtained from Figure 10.11. The (nonunique) basis set is:

1 6; 2 4 3 7; 2 5 3 6; 2 5 3 8; 1 7

All other paths (1 8; 2 4 3 6; 2 4 3 8; 2 5 3 7) are expressible as linear combinations of elements of the basis set. For example, (1 8) = (1 6) + (2 5 3 8) − (2 5 3 6). Finally, both Figures 10.10 and 10.11 depict the infinite 2-D plane divided into five regions. These results are summarized in Table 10.9.

The relationship between the whole and the sum of the parts is also different. McCabe (1976) shows that

$$V(G) = \sum V(G_i) \tag{10.24}$$

whereas Henderson-Sellers (1992c) deduces that

Object-oriented "Metrics"

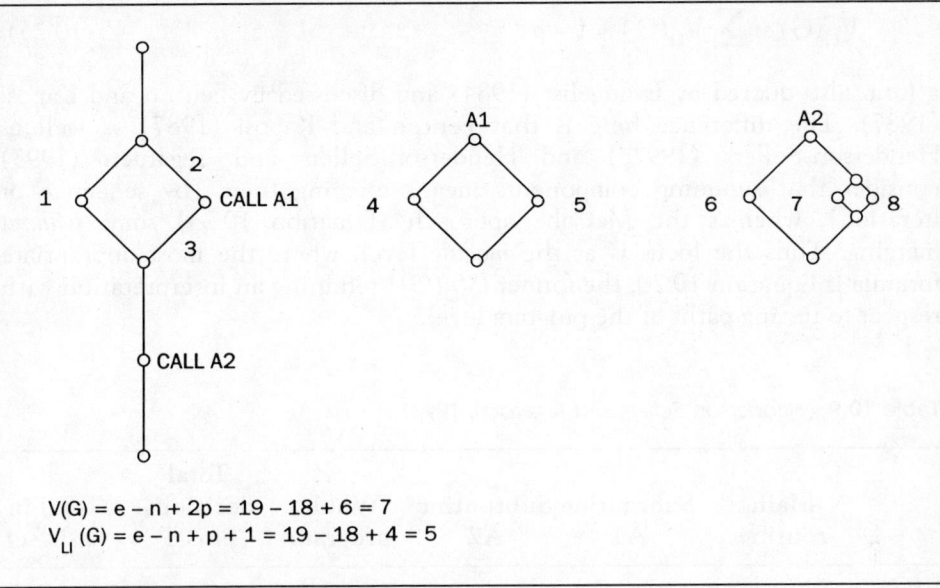

Figure 10.10 *Main routine and two subroutines (A1 and A2), depicted as three disconnected components*

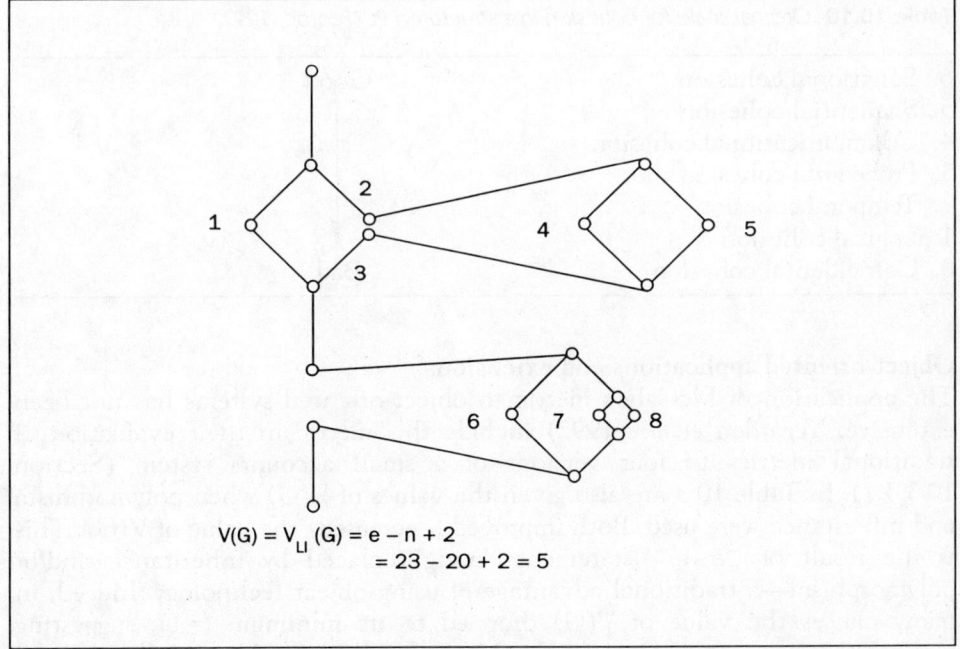

Figure 10.11 *Example of Figure 10.10 redrawn in terms of a single connected graph*

$$V_{LI}(G) = \sum V_{LI}(G_i) + 1 - p \qquad (10.25)$$

a form also quoted by Evangelist (1984) and discussed by Fenton and Kaposi (1987). The difference here is that Fenton and Kaposi (1987) as well as Henderson-Sellers (1992c) and Henderson-Sellers and Tegarden (1993) consider that summing components means merging them (by sequence or iteration), whereas the McCabe approach (Equation 10.24) sums *without* merging. Thus the focus is at the *module* level, where the most appropriate formula is Equation 10.20, the former ($V_{LI}(G)$) retaining an interpretation with respect to testing paths at the program level.

Table 10.9 *(Henderson-Sellers and Tegarden, 1993)*

	Main routine	Subroutine A1	Subroutine A2	Whole program	Total decisions plus 1	Total in basis set
$V(G)$	2	2	3	7	5	5
$V_{LI}(G)$	2	2	3	5		

Table 10.10 *Ordinal scale for cohesion in a structured PL (Fenton, 1991)*

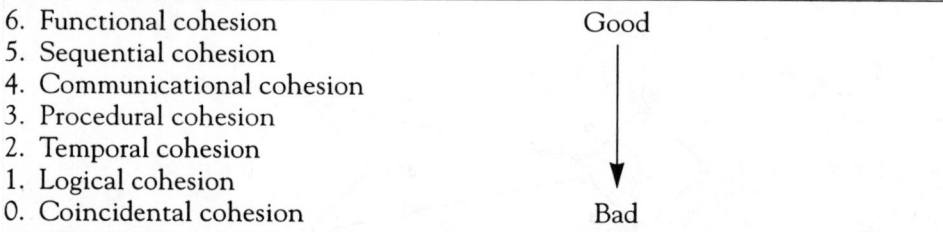

6. Functional cohesion
5. Sequential cohesion
4. Communicational cohesion
3. Procedural cohesion
2. Temporal cohesion
1. Logical cohesion
0. Coincidental cohesion

Object-oriented applications and extensions

The application of McCabe's metric to object-oriented systems has not been extensive. Tegarden *et al.* (1992) include this metric in their evaluation of traditional metrics to four versions of a small accounts system (Section 10.3.3.1). In Table 10.3 are also given the values of $V(G)$ when polymorphism and inheritance were used. Both improved (decreased) the value of $V(G)$. This is the result of Case statements being replaced by inheritance and/or polymorphism—a traditional advantage of using object technology. Indeed, in many classes the value of $V(G)$ dropped to its minimum (=1), suggesting perhaps that in a pure object-oriented system, $V(G)$ would typically be small and perhaps a poor discriminator of complexity at the class level.

Object-oriented "Metrics"

McCabe's metric (Equation 10.22) or the Henderson-Sellers and Tegarden metric (Equation 10.21) can be applied to modularized code in object-oriented systems. This can be evaluated at both module and system level.

A class provides services to the outside world. Each of these services is implemented inside the class as an algorithm, and hence is representable as a DAG, which may be self-contained or may reference other algorithms/code chunks within the class. A small schematic illustration is given in Figure 10.12. Here services S_1 and S_2 are autonomous; services S_3 and S_4 use the same private method, S_5; and service S_6 subcontracts to another class. At this service level (or more usually method level, insofar as service is the external nomenclature, whereas method, feature, or operation is the internal nomenclature), we can say that features 1 and 2 are represented by the DAGs F_1 and F_2 with cyclomatic complexities of 2 and 3 respectively; features 3 and 4 have complexities of 5 and 6 respectively for the value of $V(G)$ and 4 and 5 for $V_{LI}(G)$; and feature 6 has a value of $V(G)$ ($= V_{LI}(G)$ here), which requires knowledge of the complexity of the target object for the message send. However, it could reasonably be argued that changing the complexity of the external class should *not* alter the complexity of class MEASURE (Figure 10.12). Consequently, the value of $V(G)$ and $V_{LI}(G)$ for F_6 should be reported as 1. Across all the features of a class, one could propose an arithmetic average and standard deviation or variance that could then be used to highlight overly complex structures: the class method complexity and class method variance. Thus the average cyclomatic complexity would appear to be:

$$\overline{V_G} = \frac{\sum_{i=1}^{6} V(F_i)}{6} = 3.3 \text{ and } \overline{V_{LI}(G)} = 3.0$$

However, of potentially more interest is the application at the class–class level (a system-design metric—Section 10.3.1). Rather than view each class as a module whose internal complexity we need to incorporate (cf. McCabe and Butler, 1989), we could propose making each class a node and each "service call" an edge. Figure 10.13 illustrates this procedure applied to the simple system of Figure 10.5. There is, however, an obvious disadvantage in the application of cyclomatic complexity at this interclass level; that is, the basic assumptions of $V(G)$ require that graphs be strongly connected. In Figure 10.13, the connections do not represent the flow of control in the same way as nodes and edges in a DAG of a method represent a chronological chain. More realistically, system-level interclass connections should be measured by fan-in/fan-out *except* for the scenario known as use cases, pioneered by Ivar Jacobson in his Objectory methodology (see Section 3.3.6). These really do reflect a control flow across objects and an extension of McCabe's (1976) metric could be developed for them in the future.

Indeed, this interaction and complementarity between the fan-in/fan-out metric and cyclomatic complexity can be exploited further in the context of

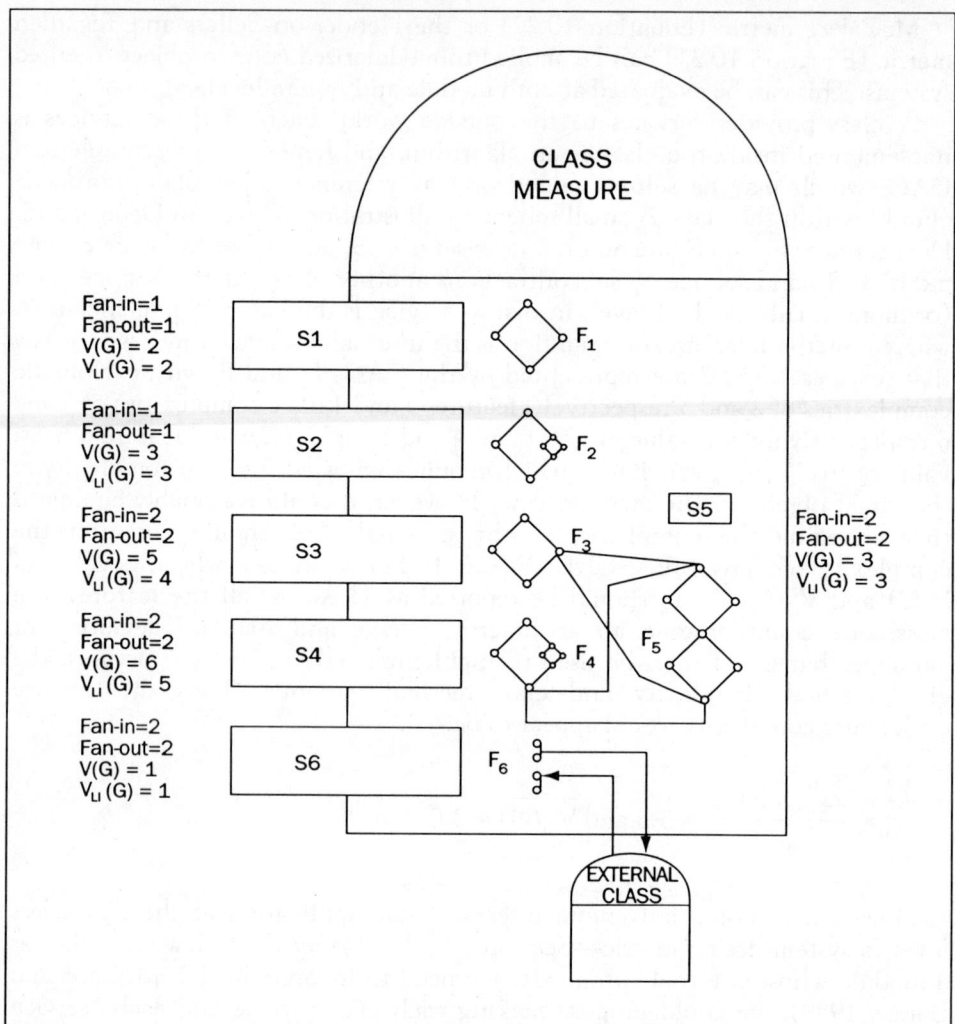

Figure 10.12 *Application of cyclomatic complexity measures to class internals*

object-oriented systems, since they possess more abstraction/modularization levels than a traditional system. If we equate the modularization level of subprogram with class, then at a more detailed level, modularization exists within classes since each feature (operation or attribute) can itself be regarded as a modularized chunk, offering (possibly) an external interface to other classes as well as links to other features in the same class (including private features). Thus we can propose depicting the internal structure of a single class as a set of coupled chunks. At the system level, the related chunks (nodes), as we noted earlier, are classes (Figure 10.5). At the class internal level, the same measures

Object-oriented "Metrics"

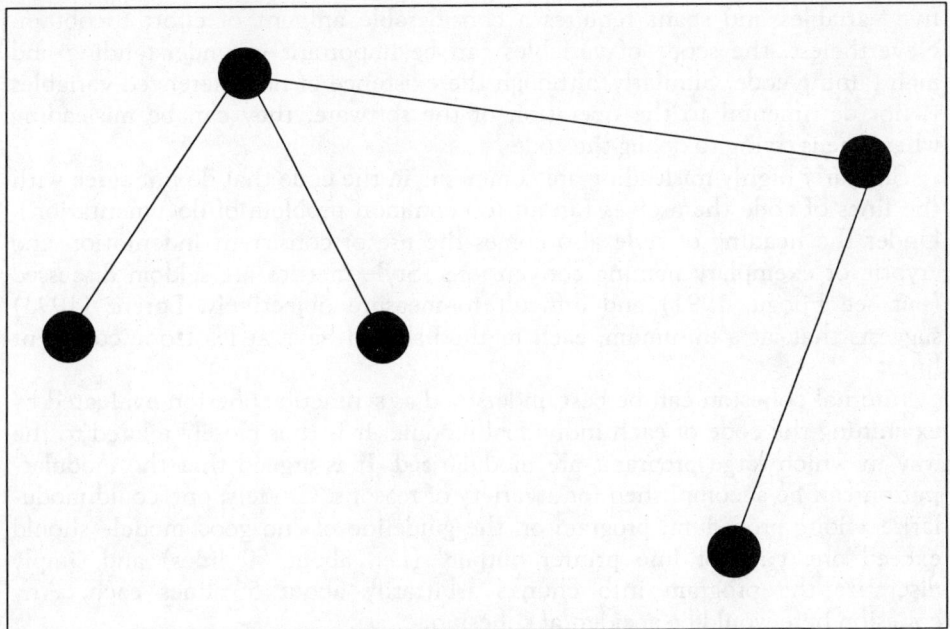

Figure 10.13 *DAG corresponding to Figure 10.5*

apply, but now the nodes are features (see Figure 2.23 in Section 2.4.2). For each feature we can calculate a fan-in and/or a fan-out value and then for the total class, the overall value can be given by Equation 10.11. For the class shown in Figure 10.12 this would give a value of $\overline{S_C}$ from Equation 10.11 as $\overline{S_C} = \frac{18}{5} = 3.6$, which takes into account all the internal features. Such a measure would seem to be appropriate for maintenance. However, in the Specification Phase, private features should be hidden. Thus *all* services offered in the interface have an apparent fan-out of unity. Thus, in these early phases, the value of $\overline{S_C}$ must always be 1 $(= (\Sigma_{i=1}^{n} 1)/n)$. At the system level, then, the fan-out values shown in Figure 10.5 would be useful (calculated earlier). From Equation 10.9, the system complexity for this small, five-class system would be $2 = (\frac{10}{5})$. These calculations highlight the need for further evaluation of the applicability of fan-in/fan-out and cyclomatic complexity measures to object systems, as well as emphasizing the urgent need for different metrics at different lifecycle stages—an area still awaiting detailed exploration.

10.3.3.3 Other procedural complexity measures

Data structure metrics are discussed by Conte *et al.* (1986, Section 2.3). These include the number of variables, which of these are locally live, what the span of each variable is, and whether the variable is ever referenced. While the number of variables is easily extracted from compiler diagnostics, the notion of live variables and spans requires a considerable amount of effort to obtain. Nevertheless, the scope of variables can be important in understanding and maintaining code. Similarly, although the existence of nonreferenced variables is not detrimental to the operation of the software, they can be misleading when one is trying to debug the code.

Similarly highly misleading are comments in the code that do not agree with the lines of code themselves (an all too common problem of documentation). Under the heading of style also comes the use of consistent indentation and cryptic or exemplary naming conventions. Style metrics are seldom discussed (but see Ejiogu, 1991) and difficult to measure objectively. Lorenz (1993) suggests that, at a minimum, each method should have at least one comment line.

Internal cohesion can be best understood as syntactic cohesion evaluated by examining the code of each individual module. It is thus closely related to the way in which large programs are modularized. It is argued that the modularization can be accomplished for a variety of reasons. Crudely, one could modularize a long procedural program on the guideline of "no good module should exceed one page of line printer output" (i.e., about 50 lines) and simply discretize the program into chunks arbitrarily about 50 lines each. Any cohesion here would be accidental cohesion.

More reasonably, the contents of a module should bear some relationship to each other. In a procedural language such as FORTRAN, COBOL, or C, it is most natural to arrange for the contents of each module to bear a functional cohesion to each other. In other words, decomposition into modules is undertaken on the basis of the code in a single module describing a single piece of functionality. Inevitably in such programs the data needed on which the functions operate will be stored elsewhere, i.e., *outside* that module. Other types of cohesion exist; the one with which we will be most concerned here in object-oriented systems can perhaps be called data cohesion.

Chidamber and Kemerer (1991) suggest a metric to evaluate the internal cohesion by considering the number of disjoint sets formed by the intersection of the n sets created by taking all the instance variables used by each of n methods. A high value for this metric suggests that the methods in the class are not really related to each other nor, therefore, to a single overall abstraction. In this case, it suggests that the class be split into two or more classes.

It should be noted that even here, in our subcategory of objective document measures, the success of any module in attaining a high-quality cohesion (based on whatever cohesion rules are being used—data, ADT, function) relies on human assessment. This demonstrates that the ideological description in Figure 10.4 is unlikely to be attained in practice. Cohesion is measured in a structured program by an ordinal scale as shown in Table 10.10, although the number of fan-ins can also be used (Conte *et al.*, 1986, p109; Card and Glass, 1990, p41) where a higher number of fan-ins indicates a lower cohesion.

An alternative measure of cohesion is proposed by Emerson (1984), who gives (after correcting typographical errors in the source)

$$r_C = \frac{|M_i| \dim M_i}{|VF - \{T\}| \dim VF} \tag{10.26}$$

where the set of nodes, VF, in a directed graph, F, contains a subset $\{M_i\}$, and T is the terminal vertex. The dimension of A is equal to $1 + V_G(A)$. The metric r_C then gives the cohesion of this module to the average cohesion of the reference sets.

Finally, a system measure of cohesion can be given (e.g., Fenton, 1991, p200) as

$$\text{cohesion ratio} = \frac{\text{number of modules having (functional) cohesion}}{\text{total number of modules}} \tag{10.27}$$

(where we might replace "functional" by "abstract" for object-oriented systems). This, however, remains to be quantified for object-oriented systems in terms of how the success of achieving "abstract cohesion" is best measured.

Object-oriented applications and extensions
In object-oriented systems, module decomposition is no longer focused on functionality. Consequently, the cohesion scale of Table 10.10 has been extended by Macro and Buxton (1987) by adding a level 7 of "abstract cohesion." In contrast, Fenton (1991) proposes, not a separate level, but a separate scale for *data cohesion*.

10.3.4 Composite metrics

There is a general requirement to compound these various module and intermodule metrics into the structural or document complexity. Typically, the disparate types of measures used require the development of a composite metric. Some authors try to create a single composite metric by arithmetic combination (often without regard for dimensional analysis considerations); others reason that no single number can encapsulate all the facets of full system complexity and propose the use of vector notation (e.g. Conte et al., 1986, p78) (again frequently without due regard for orthogonality of the components). Conte et al. (1986) note that with a pair of metrics (a,b), there is the problem of establishing a partial ordering such that for two programs, P_i with complexity pair (a_i, b_i) ($i = 1,2$), we can say that P_1 is more complex than P_2 if $a_1 \geq a_2$ and $b_1 \geq b_2$ so long as one of the pairs has a nonequality. The problem arises when $a_1 > a_2$ yet $b_2 > b_1$. This would be less of a problem if a and b were dimensionally consistent such that a scalar could be derived as the vector magnitude.

Pairs of metrics used in this way include two versions of cyclomatic complexity (Myers, 1977), cyclomatic number and operation count (Hansen, 1978), Software Science E and $V(G)$ (Baker and Zweben, 1980), and control flow complexity and data flow complexity (Oviedo, 1980).

10.4 Cognitive complexity model

Cant *et al.* (1992) have proposed a theoretically based approach to complexity metrics by analyzing cognitive models for programmer comprehension of code and the coding process (including debugging and maintenance). This cognitive complexity model (CCM) can be described qualitatively in terms of a "landscape" model (described below) and is encapsulated quantitatively by a set of equations. The underlying rationale for the CCM is the recognition that programmers, in problem solving, use the two techniques of chunking and tracing concurrently and synergistically (e.g., Miller, 1956). In chunking, the software engineer divides up the code mentally into logically related chunks, e.g., an iterative loop or decision block; in tracing, other related chunks are located. Having found that code, programmers will once again chunk in order to comprehend it. Conversely, when programmers are primarily tracing, they will need to chunk in order to understand the effect of the identified code fragments. For example, they may need to analyze an assignment statement in order to determine its effect, or they may need to analyze a control structure in order to understand how it interacts with the assignment statements contained in it, so as to create certain effects.

The effects of chunking and tracing difficulty on complexity can be graphically demonstrated by modeling the various programmer tasks as "landscapes" (Figure 10.14). In this visualization of the chunking and tracing cognitive processes, each chunk is delineated by a pair of markers at a single level. For example, in Figure 10.14, at the top level there is a single chunk visible, delineated by the two markers (A and B); at the second level there are two chunks delineated by the two pairs of markers (C, D and D, E); and at the lowest level there is a single chunk—F, G. Note that although the chunk CD is interrupted by a lower-level chunk, its integrity remains as a result of its semantic integrity. The complexity of the top-level chunk is thus represented by the sum of the two line segments Ax_1 and x_2B, the overall system complexity being visualized by the total distance between the end points of the chunk—A and B.

While reading an upper-level chunk, a dependency requires that the programmer suspend reading of the original code segment because of the need to undertake tracing in order to understand fully the chunk currently being analyzed. The "vertical drop" (e.g., x_1C) represents visually the work required in *tracing* the relevant code section. The length of time and amount of work required to resolve the dependency are a function of the aggregate depth of the dependency "valley" and the aggregate breadth of the dependency "valley." The total *depth* of the "nested valleys" depends on the length of the chain of dependencies that must be traced in order to satisfy the programmer's inquiry and on the difficulty of performing the tracing involved in each link of the chain. In addition, the number of "steps" involved indicates the number of chunks that need to be considered. The total *breadth* of the "nested valleys" is determined by the effort required to understand each chunk in the dependency chain.

Object-oriented "Metrics"

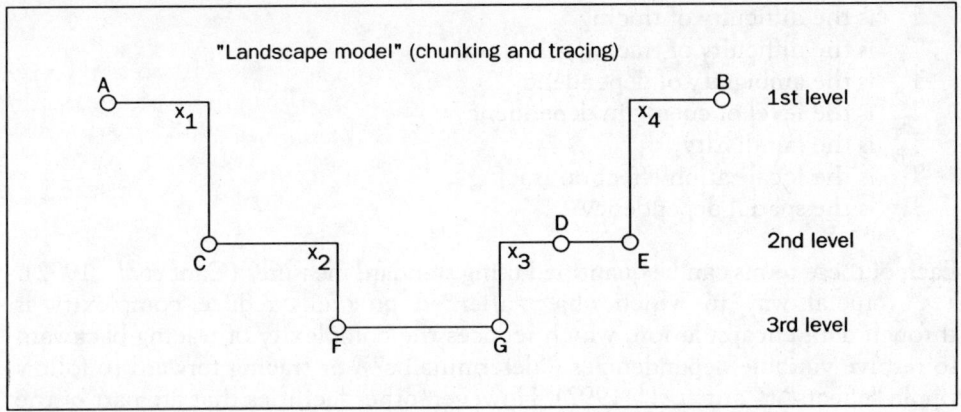

Figure 10.14 *Landscape model of program comprehension (Cant, 1990)*

In mathematical terms, the difficulty of solving a programming inquiry focused on the i-th chunk is described by the complexity, C_i, given by

$$C_i = R_i + \sum_{j \in N} C_j + \sum_{j \in N} T_j \tag{10.28}$$

in which R_i is the difficulty of understanding the immediate (i-th) chunk, N is the set of chunks on which the i-th chunk is directly dependent for a given task, and T_j is the difficulty of tracing a particular dependency.

The functional dependencies of R and T are given by

$$R = R(R_S, R_C, R_E, R_R, R_V, R_D, R_F) \tag{10.29}$$

and

$$T = T(T_L, T_A, T_S, T_C, T_F) \tag{10.30}$$

where

- C_i is the complexity of i-th chunk
- N is the set of chunks on which i-th chunk is dependent
- R_i is the difficulty of understanding i-th chunk
- R_C is the difficulty of comprehending control structure
- R_D is the disruption effect from other dependencies
- R_E is the difficulty of comprehending Boolean expressions
- R_F is the difficulty contributed by familiarity
- R_R is the difficulty contributed by recognizability
- R_S is the difficulty contributed by size
- R_V is the difficulty contributed by visual layout

T is the difficulty of tracing
T_j is the difficulty of tracing j-th chunk
T_A is the ambiguity of dependency
T_C is the level of cueing in dependency
T_F is the familiarity
T_L is the localization effect on tracing
T_S is the spatial dependency

Each of these terms can be quantified using standard measures (Cant et al., 1992).

A crucial way in which object-oriented programs reduce complexity is through data encapsulation, which reduces the complexity of tracing backward to resolve variable dependencies ("determinants"), or tracing forward to follow ripple "effects" (Cant et al., 1992). However, other facilities that are part of the object-oriented paradigm, in particular inheritance, may have varying effects on complexity for different tasks.

A system developed using object-oriented design is organized entirely differently from one developed using structured design. Whereas in structured design, the system is decomposed according to the functions it will perform, in the object-oriented paradigm, systems are decomposed on the basis of the objects that will be manipulated. This involves characterizing the system as a collection of abstract data types.

In terms of the general model of comprehension (Cant et al., 1992) an object-oriented program should result in a shallower landscape (as illustrated in Figure 10.15) than would result from a program developed using structured design, since significantly less tracing is required in order to acquire "variable plans" (which describe the use of variables in particular roles, e.g., as counter variables or storage variables) as a result of the high degree of localization and encapsulation supported by the object-oriented paradigm.

Acquiring a general variable plan for a class is often not sufficient. Sometimes, particularly in debugging or modifying, a programmer will need to trace the exact determinants of a variable or data structure, referred to in an assignment, or alternatively trace the impact of an assignment on the rest of the program. This involves tracing through the execution flow of a program to discover which modules (classes) in the system influence the values of the relevant data structure.

Parameters

Determining which other modules in the program may pass parameters to the module under consideration is a problem common to both object-oriented and procedural languages. It may be a more difficult task in an object-oriented language because in procedural languages the flow of control is usually explicitly understood in terms of the hierarchical model of execution, which matches the model of decomposition. In object-oriented languages, however, the system is decomposed as a set of interacting objects and the exact flow of control is not explicitly modeled as it is in structured design (Meyer, 1988a, p71).

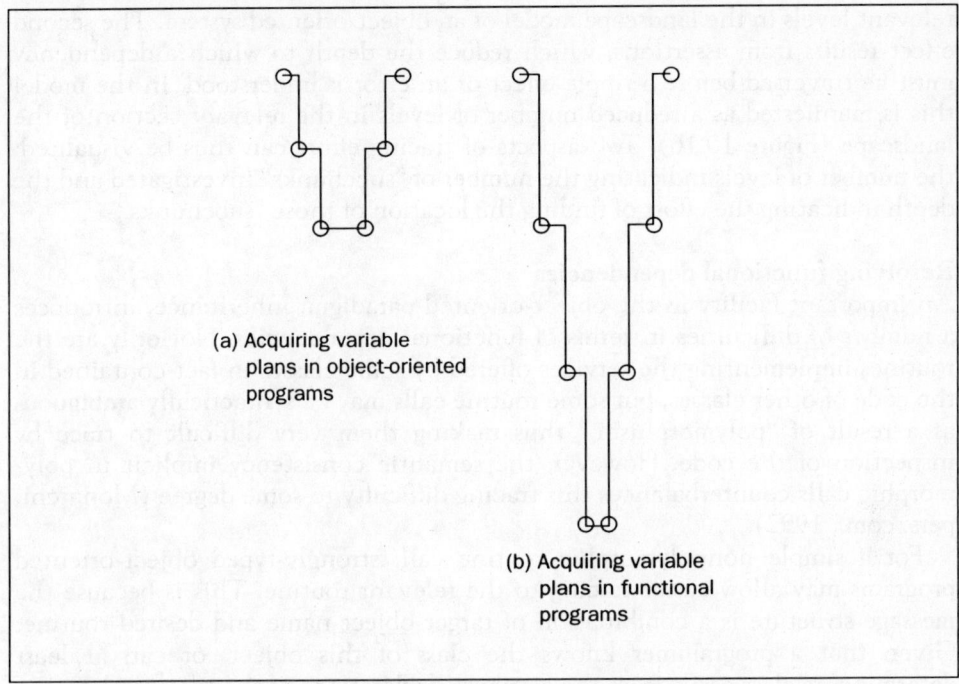

Figure 10.15 *Landscapes for acquiring variable plans in object-oriented programs as compared with programs developed using structured design (Cant, 1990)*

In many object-oriented languages, this problem is attacked by reducing the need to identify the passers of parameters, for example, by use of assertions (Meyer, 1988a, pp111-163; Masotti, 1991). The strict adherence to these "contractual obligations" means that errors are manifested in the routines that cause them and good exception handling mechanisms thus significantly reduce the need to trace calls between classes in order to trace errors. The theory of programming with contractual obligations also reduces the need to trace forward, following modifications. When postconditions are specified correctly, one can ensure that a class will have few, and possibly no, ripple effects because it must meet those conditions. Similarly, one can be sure that if the routine still meets all the preconditions of the classes that it calls, then no ripple effects should be propagated through such called routines. Therefore, correct and strict specification of all post- and preconditions ensures that errors can be isolated in the routine in which they are caused.

In terms of the general model of comprehension (Cant *et al.*, 1992), there are two opposing effects. Firstly, parameters are more difficult to trace in an object-oriented system than in a traditional, structured system, since there is usually no explicit model of the flow of execution, and routines are often called by several different client classes. This is manifested as deeper drops to the relevant levels in the landscape model of an object-oriented system. The second effect results from assertions, which reduce the depth to which a dependency must be traversed before a ripple effect or an error is understood. In the model this is manifested as a reduced number of levels in the relevant section of the landscape (Figure 10.16). Two aspects of tracing effort can thus be visualized: the number of levels indicating the number of "subchunks" investigated and the depth indicating the effort of finding the location of those "subchunks."

Resolving functional dependencies
An important facility in the object-oriented paradigm, inheritance, introduces a number of difficulties in terms of functional dependencies. Not only are the routines implementing the services offered by some classes in fact contained in the code of other classes, but some routine calls may be syntactically ambiguous as a result of "polymorphism," thus making them very difficult to trace by inspection of the code. However, the semantic consistency implicit in polymorphic calls counterbalances this tracing difficulty to some degree (Monarchi, pers. com., 1992).

For a simple nonpolymorphic routine call, strongly-typed object-oriented programs may allow easier tracing to the relevant routine. This is because the message structure is a combination of target object name and desired routine. Given that a programmer knows the class of this object, or can at least determine its class easily from the attribute declarations of the current class, the tracing process is more effectively directed. In a similar way to that in which houses are identified by a number, a street name, and a suburb, a routine is identified by its name and its class. Therefore, resolving basic routine calls may be a simpler process in an object-oriented system than in a traditional system, reflected in the general model of comprehension as a shorter drop between levels of the relevant chunks.

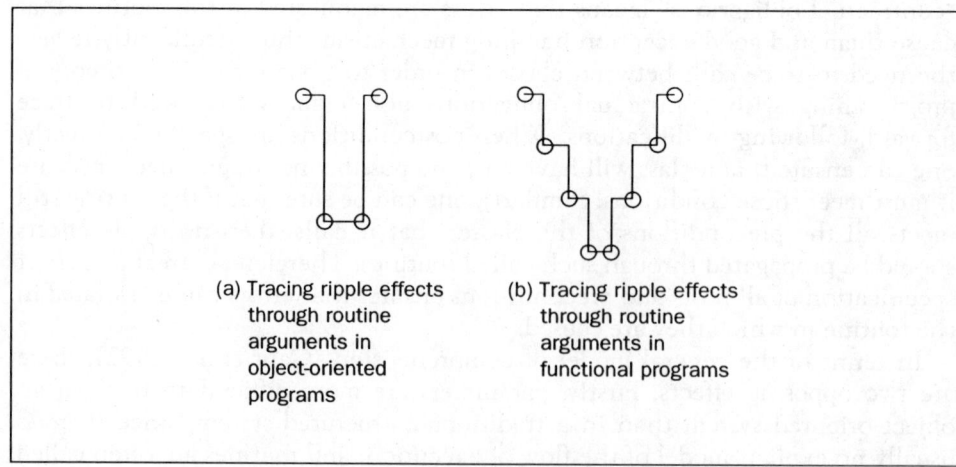

Figure 10.16 *Tracing variable values through routine arguments (Cant, 1990)*

Routines for services located in other classes

The facility of inheritance can cause new difficulties in two respects. Firstly, in simply trying to understand a class, many of the routines available within the class are in fact located in the parent class; in other hierarchies, routines declared in a deferred parent class may not be implemented until a descendant class. In order to understand the entire class, a programmer must therefore consider all the classes from which a class inherits routines or methods. Furthermore, in some object-oriented languages (notably C++) routines may include a reference to the equivalent routine in a superclass, possibly redefining this routine. This means that a routine cannot be fully understood unless the equivalent routine in the "parent class" is understood. In the general model of comprehension, this would mean that a chunk that might have been contained on a single level may be split on to different levels (Figure 10.17). However, at least one tool is available to collapse inheritance hierarchies and thus obviate the need to trace up and down the inheritance tree. In the Eiffel environment, the use of the FLAT tool permits *analysis* of code to be undertaken more simply, thus reducing the inherent complexity during the maintenance phase.

Ambiguity arising out of polymorphism

The second aspect of inheritance that can cause problems is polymorphism. When a polymorphic request for service is issued, one can determine which routine provides the service only if one knows the type of the object referred to

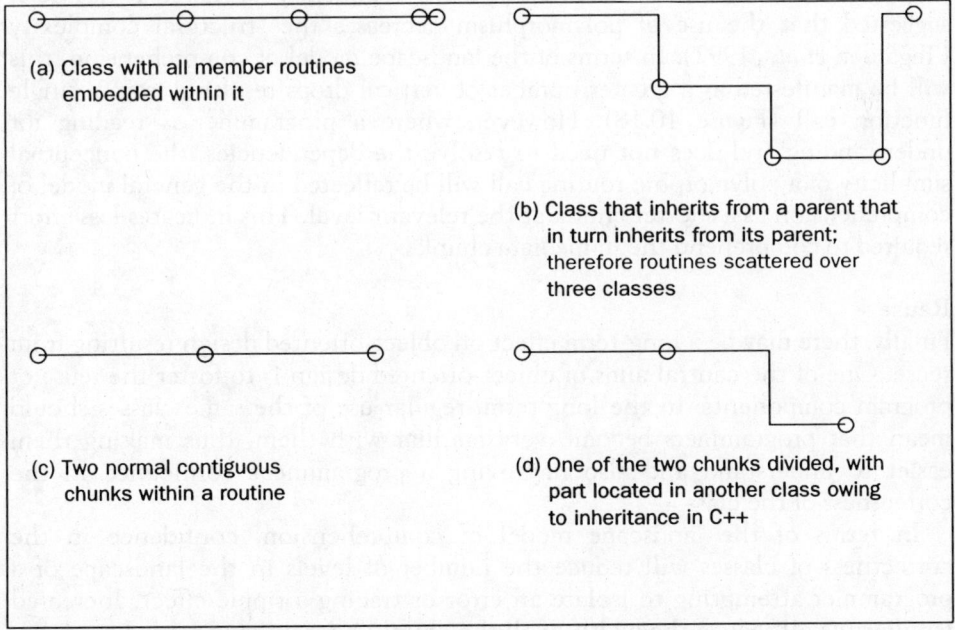

Figure 10.17 *Splitting of classes and chunks caused by inheritance (Cant, 1990)*

by the entity (pointer in C++) specified in the request. Often the type of that object can be known only at run-time. In this case the call is (syntactically) ambiguous when the static code is read. In order for a programmer to understand the possible outcomes of such a call, all the possible routines must be read and understood. Although this would seem to add a large degree of complexity, it could be argued that in order to achieve the same level of flexibility in a normal functional program, a programmer would need to continually embed decision statements to determine which routine should be called.

Clearly, both these methods have advantages and disadvantages. Where a programmer needs to read a called routine in order to understand it, the complexity is reduced by having a decision structure in which the identifiers of all candidate routines are specified. However, where the identifier provides a sufficient indication of the function it performs, it is preferable to have a single call. Since in polymorphic requests for service the nature of the service is usually semantically the same, a single call is conceptually neater. Furthermore, all the candidate routines that might be called would probably be best recognized under the same name. Polymorphism allows this (as also does "operator overloading;" see Stroustrup, 1986, Chapter 6), while the procedural programming alternative does not. The exact effect of polymorphic requests on complexity is contingent upon the programmer's familiarity with the program, and with the called routines in particular, upon the degree of meaning incorporated within the labeling, and also upon the nature of the task being performed by the programmer. If the task requires tracing of the exact flow of control, polymorphism is likely to increase cognitive complexity, although it has been suggested that the use of polymorphism decreases the structural complexity (Tegarden *et al.*, 1992). In terms of the landscape model of comprehension, this will be manifested as a greater number of vertical drops resulting from a single function call (Figure 10.18). However, where a programmer is reading for understanding and does not need to resolve the dependencies, the conceptual simplicity of a polymorphic routine call will be reflected in the general model of comprehension as a shorter chunk at the relevant level. This indicates less effort required to comprehend the immediate chunk.

Reuse
Finally, there may be a long-term effect on object-oriented design resulting from reuse. One of the central aims of object-oriented design is to foster the reuse of program components. In the long term, regular use of the same classes should mean that programmers become very familiar with them, thus making them easier to understand and also improving a programmer's confidence in the correctness of the class.

In terms of the landscape model of comprehension, confidence in the correctness of classes will reduce the number of levels in the landscape of a programmer attempting to isolate an error or tracing a ripple effect. Increased familiarity will reduce the width of all the chunks contained in reused modules, indicating a reduction in the effort required to comprehend them.

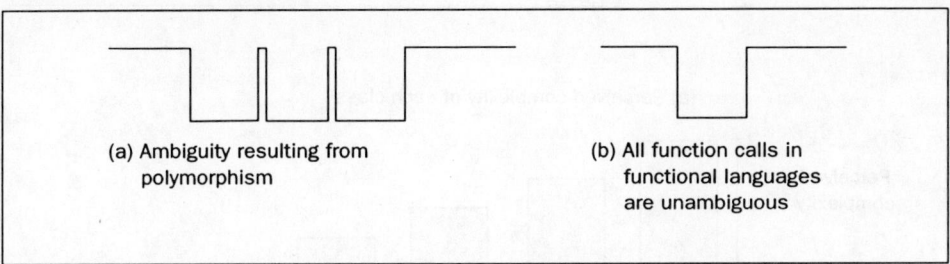

Figure 10.18 *Landscapes illustrating the ambiguity resulting from polymorphism (Cant, 1990)*

Case study

A case study was performed (Cant *et al.*, 1994) to test some of the proposals of Cant *et al.* (1992) as applied here to object-oriented systems. It also serves as an illustration of the nature of the analysis required to fully validate their complexity model and explores the problems that may be encountered.

The study focused on remote dependencies because it was believed that these usually have the greatest impact on complexity out of all the factors considered in the CCM (Cant *et al.*, 1992). This is supported by the empirical research carried out on the metrics of Henry and Kafura (1981) and Shepperd (1990).

The study, carried out within the Australian research arm of a large multinational computer firm, analyzed a C++ project undertaken by a team of 12 (7 of whom were active at any one time). Five classes were examined in this case study. They were chosen from a selection provided by the project manager as representative of different levels of complexity. The classes chosen all contained a similar number of routines and a similar number of lines. The only exception was one class (referred to later as class D) that contained approximately 60% more routines than the others. However, since it was substantially larger, any finding of low complexity would verify that the complexity measure was measuring something other than length and any bias will be against positive findings.

A comparison of the perceived complexity of *understanding* against the predicted complexity value based on comprehension is shown in Figure 10.19. Figure 10.19(a) illustrates the relative ratings of the five classes by two programmers who had substantial experience with them. Figure 10.19(b) illustrates the average number of dependencies in a routine for each class. Figure 10.19(c) illustrates the maximum number of dependencies of any routine in a class. Overall, the figures demonstrate a high correspondence between perceived and predicted complexities. The only striking exception is class D, which, although being the median in terms of its perceived complexity rating, had a very low predicted complexity. This may be due to a distortion in perceived complexity resulting from the fact that D had a much larger number of routines than any of the other classes. This might have made it appear more complex

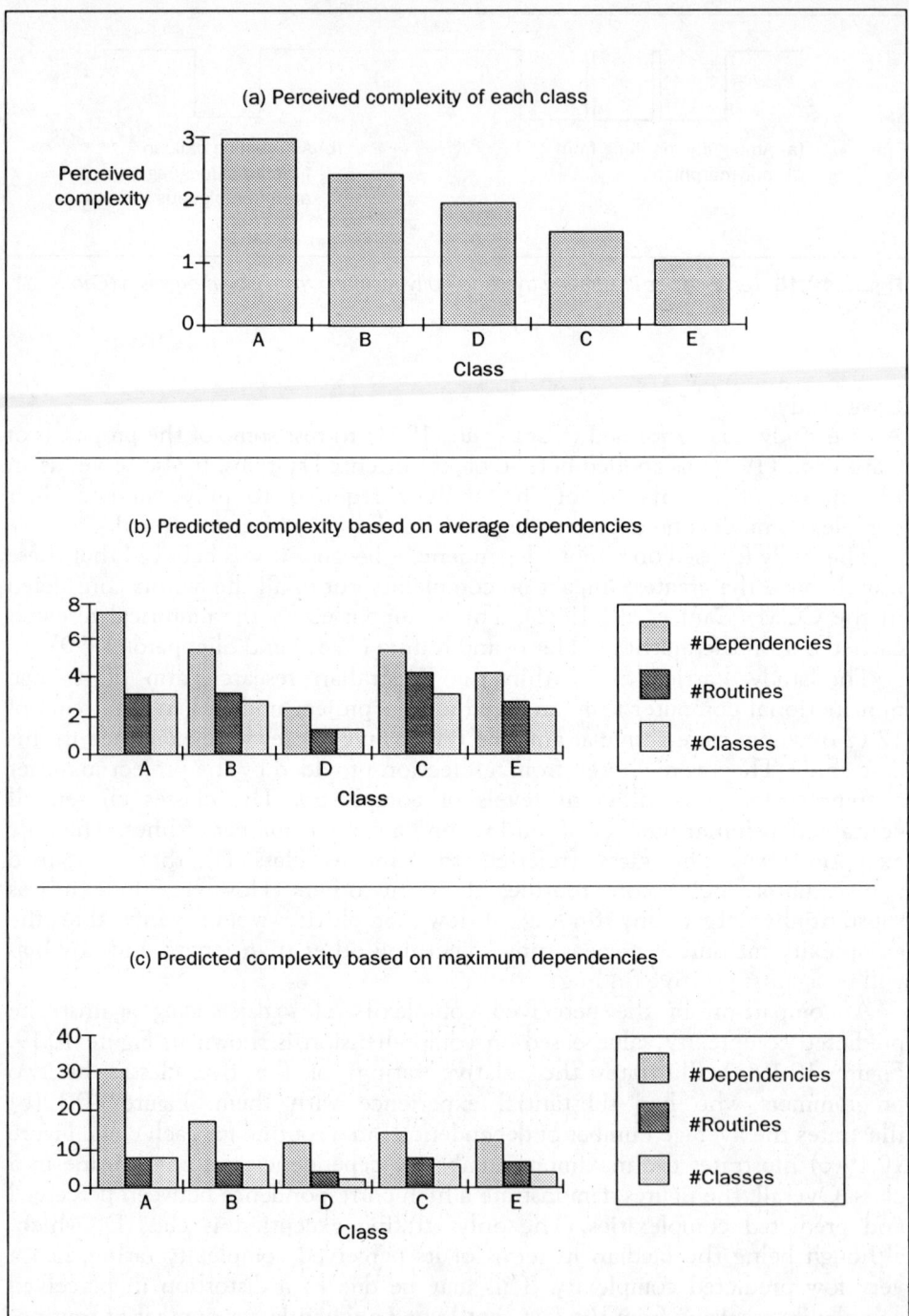

Figure 10.19 *Perceived vs predicted understanding (Cant, 1990)*

than the other classes even though each routine was simpler. An alternative explanation for the high perceived complexity was suggested by one of the team members, who noted that "the maintenance of internal pointers in some of the methods" and the intricacy of some of the algorithms were the main sources of complexity. These would not be exposed by counts of remote dependencies.

A comparison of the perceived complexity of *tracing modifications* with the complexity predicted using remote dependencies appears in Figure 10.20. Once again, the overall trend of predicted complexity is consistent with perceived complexity. The main discrepancy is once again class D. Predicted complexity is substantially lower than perceived complexity for this class. As discussed in the previous section, it is likely that this is due either to the large number of routines or to the internal complexity of the routines, neither of which is measured by a metric based on the number of forward connections.

A comparison of the predicted complexity of *isolating errors* manifested in the classes against the perceived complexity appears in Figure 10.21. Overall, the trends are consistent across all the figures. One exception is the greater average number of dependencies in class A relative to class B. However, Figure 10.21(c) reveals that this is largely due to a single routine in class A that contains a large number of determinants.

A second exception is the greater number of dependencies in E relative to D. However, distortion created by D has already been highlighted. This is probably again a manifestation of the high perceived complexity resulting from internal features of the class.

The applicability of the cognitive complexity model to object systems still awaits final empirical validation. It potentially offers a new type of tool for project management, including as it does cognitive behavioral characteristics.

10.5 Process metrics

A good estimate of schedule and cost of developing software can be of prime importance in getting a software contract, controlling the software development and maintenance process, and allocating optimal resources to different activities. An accurate estimation (and measurement) of software size is important for analyzing and improving the productivity of the software development process.

The cost estimation process is generally regarded (Card and Glass, 1990, p71) as having four stages:

- size estimation
- cost calculation
- schedule development
- performance monitoring leading to periodic adjustments to estimates

The weak link here, according to Verner and Tate (1987) is the first—software sizing (see Section 10.3.3.1).

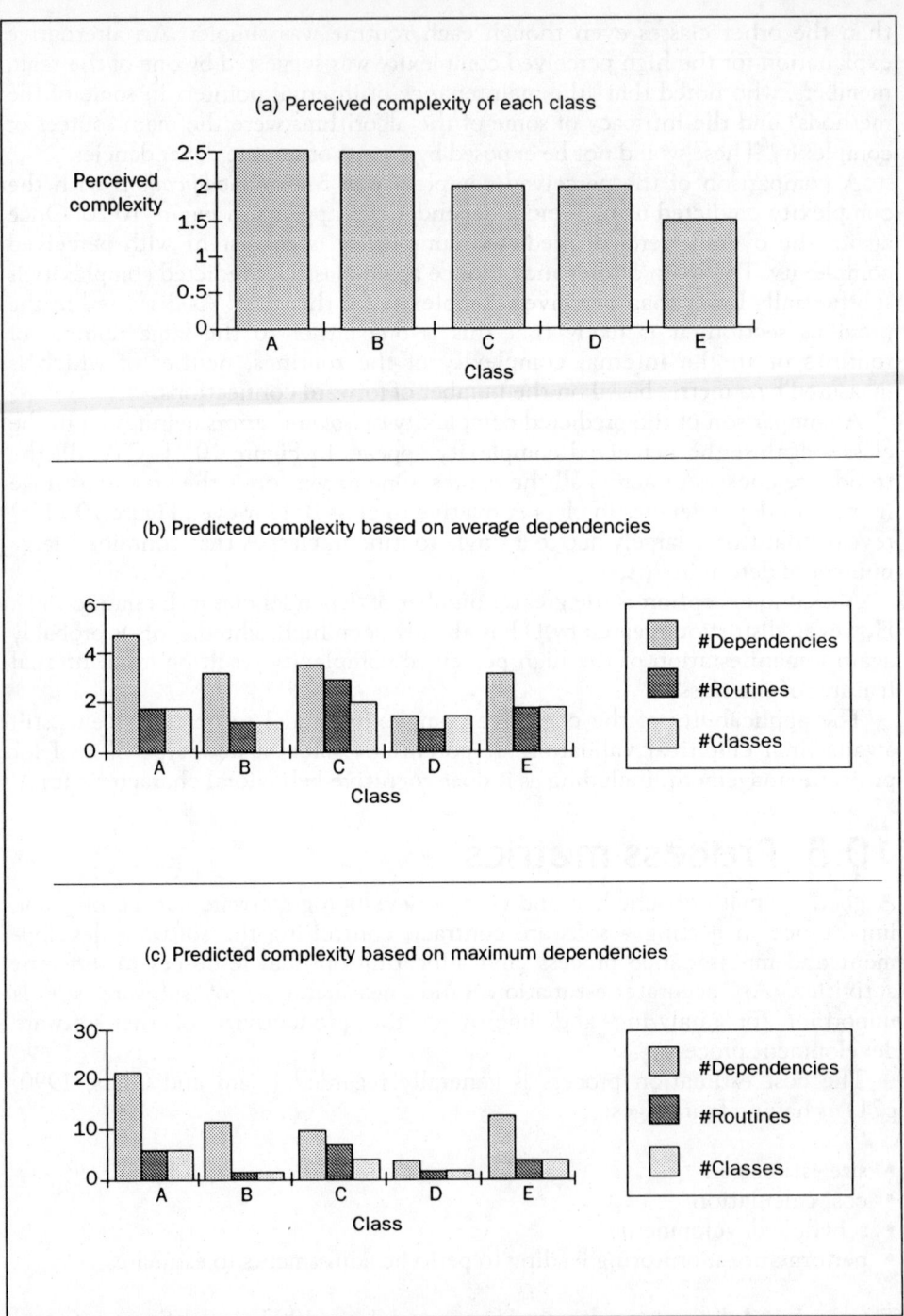

Figure 10.20 *Perceived vs predicted effort for tracing modifications (Cant, 1990)*

Object-oriented "Metrics"

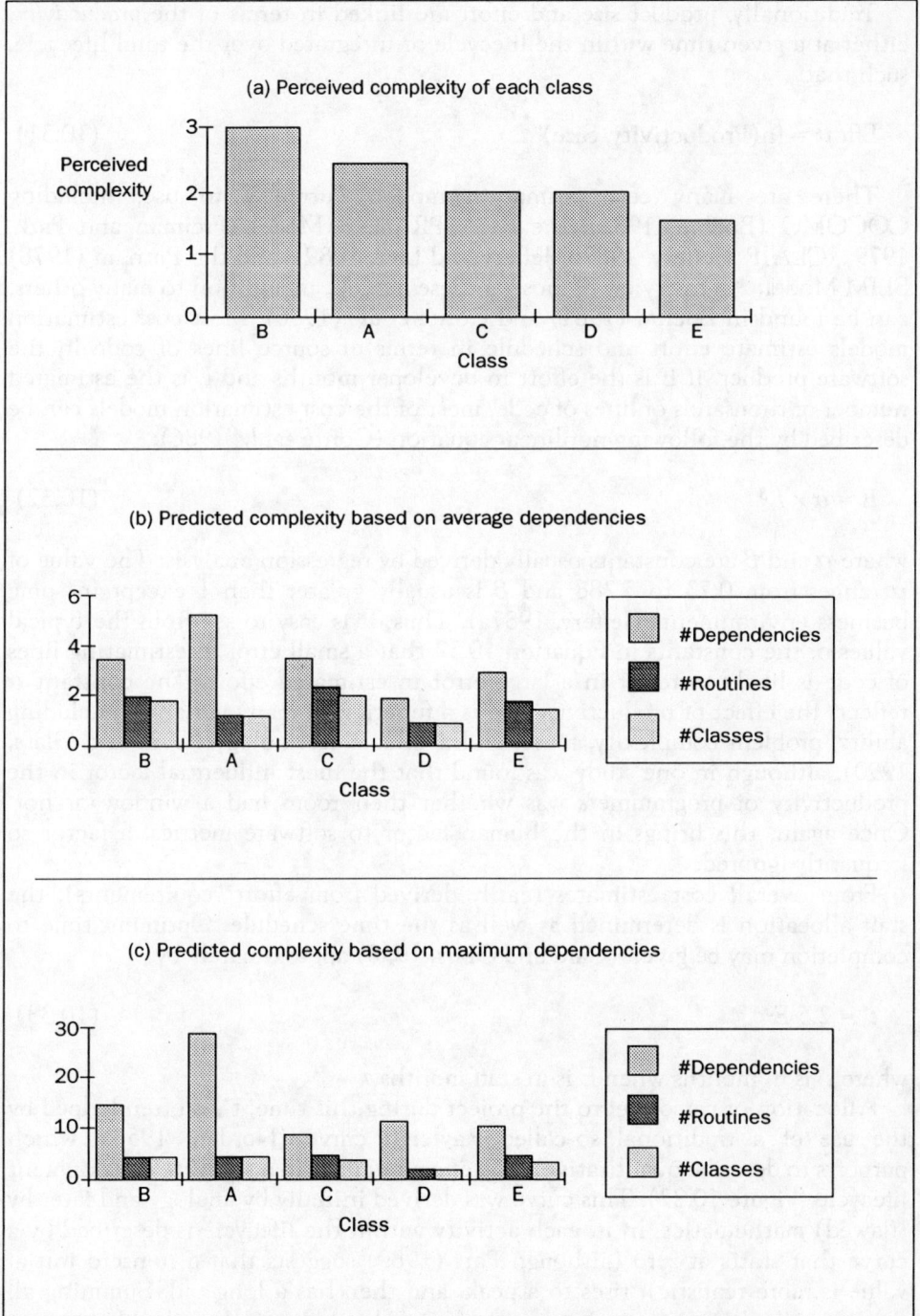

Figure 10.21 Perceived vs predicted effort to isolate errors (Cant, 1990)

Traditionally, product size and effort are linked in terms of the *productivity*, either at a given time within the lifecycle or integrated over the total lifecycle, such that:

Effort = fn(Productivity, Size) (10.31)

There are many cost estimation models currently in use, including COCOMO (Boehm, 1981), the RCA PRICE S Model (Freiman and Park, 1979), CLAIR (Jeffery, 1987b; Jeffery and Low, 1989), and the Putnam (1978) SLIM Model. An overview of most of these models, in addition to many others, can be found in Boehm (1981) and Conte *et al.* (1986). Most cost estimation models estimate effort and schedule in terms of source lines of code in the software product. If E is the effort in developer months and L is the estimated number of thousands of lines of code, most of the cost estimation models can be described by the following nonlinear equation (Conte *et al.*, 1986):

$$E = \alpha \times L^\beta \qquad (10.32)$$

where α and β are constants usually derived by regression analysis. The value of α ranges from 0.73 to 5.288 and β is usually greater than 1 except in some business environments (Jeffery, 1987a). Thus, it is easy to see from the typical values of the constants in Equation 10.32 that a small error in estimating lines of code is likely to result in a large error in estimated effort. The constant α reflects the effect of productivity and is a function of many variables, including ability, problem complexity, reuse, and available technology (Card and Glass, 1990), although in one study was found that the most influential factor in the productivity of programmers was whether their room had a window or not. Once again, this brings in the human factor to software metrics, a factor so frequently ignored.

From overall cost estimates (easily derived from effort requirements), the staff allocation is determined as well as the time schedule. Optimum time to completion may be given (Card and Glass, 1990) approximately by

$$t^* = 2.5 \, E^{0.4} \qquad (10.33)$$

where t^* is in months when E is in staff months.

Allocation of personnel to the project during this time, t^*, is often helped by the use of a traditional so-called Rayleigh curve (Norden, 1958), which purports to describe quantitatively the effort required in a software development lifecycle (Figure 10.22). This curve was derived initially by analogy and later by (flawed) mathematics. In it, each activity within the lifecycle is described by a curve that starts at zero (although Parr (1980) suggests that a nonzero initial value is more realistic), rises to a peak, and then has a long tail. Summing all the lifecycle phases gives a curve of a similar shape that is described by a curve (Putnam, 1978):

Object-oriented "Metrics"

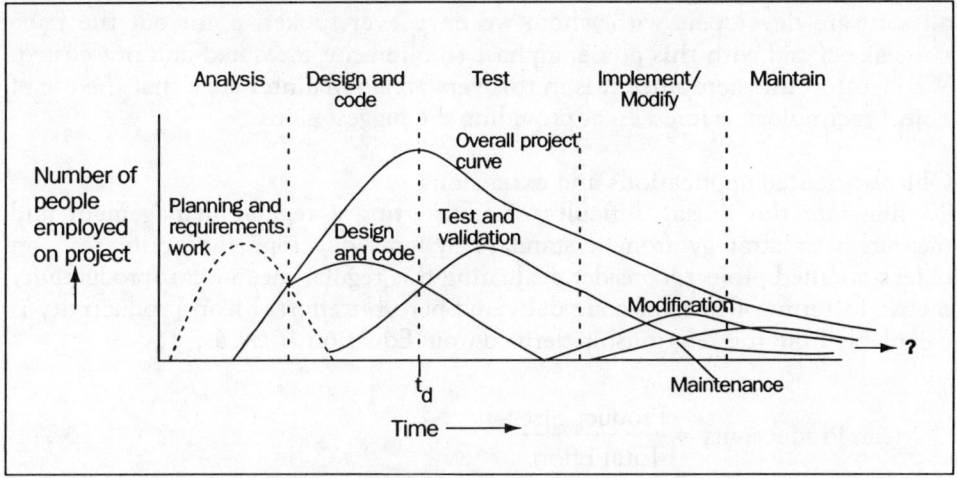

Figure 10.22 *The traditional software development curve of effort as a function of time, often referred to as the Rayleigh curve. As well as the envelope curve, the components are illustrated for the individual lifecycle stages. In general, planning and requirements work are not included in this model (indicated by dotted line). (Norden, © 1958, IBM Corporation— reprinted with permission)*

$$\dot{y} = \frac{K}{t_d^2} t\, e^{-\frac{t^2}{2t_d^2}} \tag{10.34}$$

where $\dot{y}$ is the manpower expressed as a function of time t, the total effort is K (the area under the curve), and t_d is the time to peak manpower (also known as the development time or the elapsed time (Jeffery, 1987c)).

Despite criticism (Parr, 1980; Warburton, 1983; Kitchenham and Taylor, 1985), this description has been found to be useful in some environments (Putnam and Fitzsimmons, 1979; Basili, 1980; Navlakhar, 1990), although in an MIS environment Jeffery (1987c) found the indexes of Putnam's associated equation for productivity, PR, as a function of total effort, K, and elapsed time t_d

$$PR = \text{constant } K^{-0.66} t_d^{1.33} \tag{10.35}$$

to be invalid. He deduced, alternatively, a descriptive equation of

$$PR = \text{constant } K^{-0.47} t_d^{-0.5} \tag{10.36}$$

However, Jeffery (1987c) notes that this regression line is a poor fit to the data, adding caution to the reality of *any* relationship between PR, K, and t_d.

Another anomaly apparent in this curve is that there is an inference that the curve asymptotes to zero at long time, viz., in the maintenance phase, whereas all software developers with whom we have ever spoken point out the large costs associated with this phase, a phase so often not measured and not costed. We mention this here since it is in this very area of maintenance that the use of object technology is foreseen as providing the biggest gains.

Object-oriented applications and extensions
To illustrate the initial difficulty of transferring a regular management and measurement strategy from a standard systems development context to an object-oriented project, consider evaluating this regular mean effort/productivity metric in terms of lines of code delivered per unit effort. Mean productivity is calculable from the relationship derived from Equation 10.31 as:

$$\text{Mean Productivity} = \frac{\text{Product Size}}{\text{Total Effort}} \tag{10.37}$$

This calculation can be undertaken at the "normal" end of the project, defined as when the product is ready to be delivered according to specification. However, in an object-oriented environment it is likely that the developer would then go further and expend additional effort in generalizing the component classes, a process that often reduces the number of lines of code. Thus in the ratio of lines of code (used here as an approximate measure of size) to total effort, the numerator has decreased and the denominator increased—suggesting from Equation 10.37 a significant decrease in mean productivity (Meyer, 1989c). This is counter to our general intuition that object-orientation enhances productivity, thus suggesting that (i) a short-term calculation using this traditional approach does not provide a useful metric for object-oriented development; and (ii) traditional metrics need to be replaced by newly formulated metrics for object-oriented software projects. Generalization costs and a reuse strategy need to be factored into such productivity calculations.

Mutation of this curve to be applicable to object technology requires a visualization of the higher "up-front" effort in the Specification Phase and the lower test and maintenance costs discussed above and in Chapter 9. A schematization was given initially by Thomsett (1990), which is reproduced in Figure 10.23. Now it is possible to fit an equation to this curve of analogous form to Equation 10.34:

$$\dot{y} = K_1 t e^{-\frac{t^2}{2t_1^2}} + K_2(t - t_0) e^{-\frac{(t-t_0)^2}{2(t_2-t_0)^2}} \tag{10.38}$$

(where the time parameters are defined in the figure and the coefficients K_1 and K_2 are related to the area under the graph and represent components of total effort). However, this is merely juggling with equations. There is *absolutely no* causal, quantifiable relationship underlying this curve as presented in Figure

Object-oriented "Metrics"

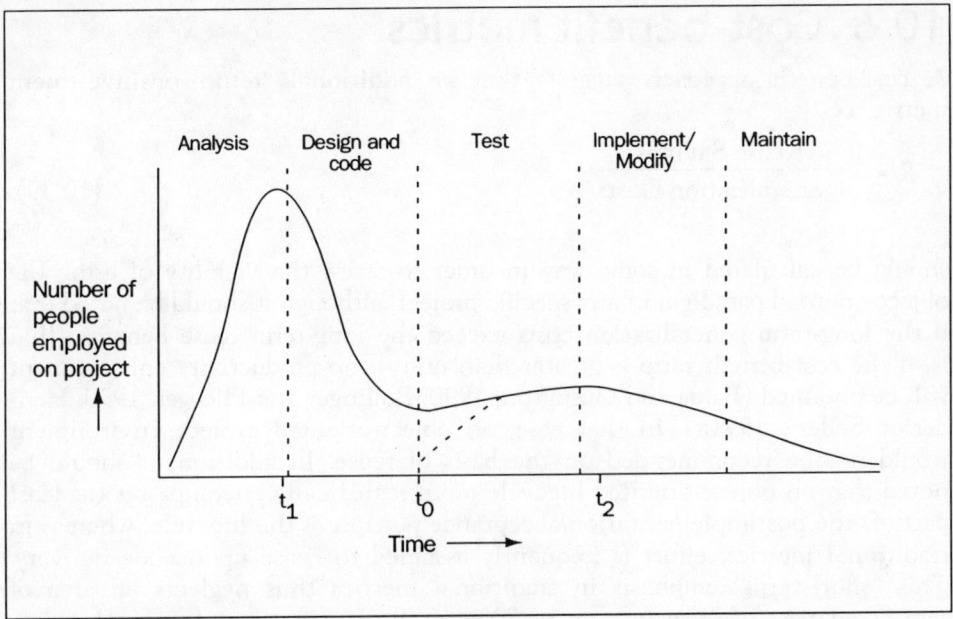

Figure 10.23 *Schematic object-oriented software development curve illustrating the additional effort required in design (Thomsett, 1990)*

10.23. Instead, what is required is the development of an appropriate model rather than intuitive curve sketching. In other words, this curve is qualitatively descriptive and *not* quantitatively predictive. We *do not* recommend that you use the numbers from it for cost estimation.

When working with OOSE/Objectory, Jacobson *et al.* (1992) propose to collect the following process metrics for object-oriented systems:

- total development time;
- development time in each process and each subprocess;
- time spent in modification of reused components;
- fault counts;
- quality assurance costs.

as well as other costs of introducing the new technology that are harder to quantify.

Lorenz (1993) supports the collection of data on time per application class, fault counts, and extent and difficulty of reuse (Table 10.4) and advocates counting the number of classes and methods thrown away during the process. This is seen to be a good indicator of increasing quality of object-oriented code as sizes shrink when the power of OT is being increasingly utilized.

10.6 Cost-benefit metrics

A cost-benefit approach suggests that an additional "return-on-investment metric" of

$$R = \frac{\text{Reuse Savings}}{\text{Generalization Costs}} \quad (10.39)$$

should be calculated in some way in order to assess the viability of using the object-oriented paradigm in any specific project, although it should be noted that if the long-term generalization costs exceed the long-term reuse benefits (that is, if the cost-benefit ratio is greater than unity), no productivity enhancement will be obtained (Balda and Gustafson, 1990; Bollinger and Pfleeger, 1990; Henderson-Sellers, 1991a). In that case, an object-oriented project environment would not be recommended on the basis of reuse. In addition, it should be noted that an object-oriented lifecycle more realistically encompasses (at least part of) the postimplementation/acceptance portion of the lifecycle, whereas in traditional metrics, effort is frequently assumed to cease upon code delivery. This "short-term" emphasis in traditional metrics thus neglects an area of significant cost of software—up to 70% of all software costs being related to postacceptance phases (e.g., Meyer, 1988a, p7). Indeed, it is likely that the class design and implementation could take considerably longer, since generalization and code reuse are one of the aims of the object-oriented lifecycle in order that maintenance costs (often, unwisely, excluded from project development costs) can be dramatically reduced. In addition, it is likely that system testing time will be considerably reduced (e.g., Booch and Vilot, 1990a). Consequently, the traditional software metrics, either in terms of source lines of code or function points, will inevitably indicate a further decrease of productivity (in addition to that mentioned above), since they do not address the subsequent phase of program maintenance.

The general conclusion, as outlined above, is that the very different structural approach adopted in an object-oriented design and implementation suggests that traditional metrics cannot be applied unreservedly in this new environment of object-oriented software development (Moreau and Dominick, 1989, 1990; Jeffery, 1990; Constantine, 1990). New concerns need to be considered. These include allowing for code reuse, for effort spent in creating generalized classes for future use (to be stored in class libraries) as well as for the cost of locating and managing stored library modules. As in traditional metrics, the new metrics needed for object-oriented software development should be aimed at (i) size and productivity—for overall project estimates; and (ii) dynamic allocation of personnel at various stages in the lifecycle. The major differences lie in the *reuse of code* to achieve the same functionality and the additional effort required on project number i (on generalization) in order to reap the benefit of code reuse in projects $i + 1$ et seq.

So far, there is a direct comparison with procedural implementation and the

Object-oriented "Metrics"

size metrics should be of similar magnitude (Moreau and Dominick, 1990). Hence productivity gains will be measured by allowing for generalization and reuse, and by comparing the result with Equation 10.37 (interpreted as a representation of effort or cost rather than size by assuming a linear relationship as a first-order approximation between cost and size in order merely to simplify the algebra. This maintains a focus on *concepts* rather than on mathematical manipulation and developing an underpinning model of the process).

10.6.1 Generalization and reuse

An object-oriented development environment supports design and code reuse, the most straightforward type of reuse being the use of a library class (of code) that perfectly suits the requirements. Perhaps more commonly, a new class will be constructed by using inheritance. In this case a fraction, I, of the old code is effectively reused and a fraction $(1 - I)$ written anew (assuming there are l of these in our system of N classes). If the cost of finding and understanding any class in a library is F, then the cost of reusing k classes without modification is simply

$$C_R = \sum_{i=1}^{k} F = kF \tag{10.40}$$

and the cost of reusing l classes with modification is

$$C_M = \sum_{i=k+1}^{k+l} [s_i(1 - I)_i + F] \tag{10.41}$$

since there is a fixed cost, F, for finding a class irrespective of whether it will be used "as is" or modified. Since the cost of designing and implementing *new* classes, C_D, is essentially given by Equation 10.13 (for the final m classes), then the total cost, C, is given by:

$$C = C_R + C_M + C_D \tag{10.42}$$

Since the cost of the project without reuse would be S, then the reuse savings, for a project in which generalization costs are zero, are $S - C$.

In order to complete the calculation of net savings and to calculate a return-on-investment (ROI) from Equation 10.39, the generalization costs need to be evaluated. In general, if a project of size N produces P reusable classes ($P \leq N$), which need an extra effort (cost) of generalization of g_i, then Equation 10.42 must have an additional term (cf. also Bollinger and Pfleeger, 1990) of

$$C_G = \sum_{i=1}^{P} g_i \tag{10.43}$$

where g_i will, in general, depend upon the class size, s_i, since it is reasonable to assume that in many cases a class with more features will be more expensive to generalize, although this will depend on the semantic "richness" of the class and its features. Thus Equation 10.39 (ROI) can be written as:

$$R = \frac{S-(C+C_G)}{C_G} = \frac{S-C}{C_G} - 1 \tag{10.44}$$

In other words, reuse is beneficial if the reuse savings $(S - C)$ are greater than the generalization costs.

Generalization costs are, at present, very difficult to assess empirically. Nevertheless, conceptually we can consider costing the development of reused classes *either* against the projects in which they are used *or* against the project in which they first arose. Although the former is more appealing, it is more difficult since (i) cost accounting could be difficult if the model remained unused for some time; and (ii) the cost should presumably be amortized over the number of projects that use this class, a number that in general is unknown. To carry out amortization then, some fixed and agreed depreciation rate and amortization period would need to be introduced. In the second case (cost to the originating project), the current project would bear the cost of refining (generalizing) object classes for acceptance into the corporate library. In an organization where the software is to be developed for internal use, this presents little problem; but for third-party software developers and vendors, such overheads are unlikely to find favor with the current clients. Indeed, the different aspects of reuse as viewed by developers of reusable products and consumers of the latter introduce additional issues of investment and economic feasibility (Bollinger and Pfleeger, 1990)— issues beyond the scope of their investigation.

Another component of the cost-benefit equation is how an organization views its software. Many companies treat software as a capital cost, which depreciates over time (Adams and Burbeck, 1992). Consequently, the role of maintenance (ongoing short-term investments) only delays the obsolescence of the asset value of the software. It does *not* increase the value of the asset. If reusable software is viewed in such terms, it will be extremely difficult to argue a case for reuse from an economic standpoint. Rather, Adams and Burbeck (1992) argue, reusable business software components should be viewed as personnel assets that accrue over time. In personnel terms, an inexperienced employee matures within the organization so that his or her worth to the company grows over time. Software assets, too, can appreciate in value over time as they are honed to higher quality, are increasingly reused, and play a more significant role in the day-to-day business of the company. Consequently, a long-term investment strategy is called for in order to achieve maximum return on investment (Adams and Burbeck, 1992).

So far, the analysis has focused on *project* costs and savings, essentially assuming that the company is employing a reuse strategy. However, it should be noted that on an individual project basis, Equation 10.44 implies that the maximum benefit is to be gained by minimizing generalization costs, in other words, by using classes from the library but not contributing classes to the library. It is therefore vital that the application of the ROI calculation either include amortized generalization costs (as discussed above) and/or be applied to long-term evaluations for assessing the viability of reuse within the organization. Hence we could average the values of R over several projects, say over Q projects. Thus the mean ROI ratio $\bar{R}$ is given by:

$$\bar{R} = \frac{1}{Q} \sum_{q=1}^{Q} R_q = \frac{1}{Q} \sum_{q=1}^{Q} (\frac{S-C}{C_G} - 1)_q$$

$$= \frac{1}{Q} \sum_{q=1}^{Q} (\frac{S-C}{C_G})_q - 1 \qquad (10.45)$$

An alternative measure of long-term ROI could be:

$$R_Q = \frac{\sum_{q=1}^{Q} (S - C - C_G)_q}{\sum_{q=1}^{Q} C_{G_q}} \qquad (10.46)$$

This states that the ROI index, R_Q, is the ratio of the cumulative benefits (reuse savings) over Q projects to the cumulative generalization costs. Both R_Q and $\bar{R}$ provide potentially useful, if slightly different, metrics for assessing the efficacy of reuse, positive values of the metrics indicating that an advantage can be gained from a reuse strategy.

The validity of these two equations, as compared with the project-specific ROI given by Equation 10.44, is illustrated here using a simple simulation model. Simulations were undertaken for various values for:

- generalization unit cost;
- reuse unit cost;
- percentages of new classes useful for library;
- number of classes reusable from library per project.

10.6.2 Simulation of ROI over a number of projects

As a simple illustration of the efficacy of Equations 10.45 and 10.46, a simulation model has been constructed. In this model, it is necessary to assume appropriate values for k, l, m, and P as well as an initial value for the size of the library. To simplify (without loss of general applicability), we here consider a set of Q projects, each of which contains 100 classes. For each project, a fraction of these, say 50%, are available as library classes. (We assume for simplicity here that $l = 0$.) Furthermore, we assume that in each project a fraction, say 10%, of the *new* classes can be generalized and added to the library. Assuming no disparity between classes (viz., independence of i), the total cost function is:

$$C = kF + (100 - k)s + gP \qquad (10.47)$$

Reuse savings are then given by

$$100s - (kF + (100 - k)s + gP) \qquad (10.48)$$

and the project ROI (Equation 10.44) is

$$\frac{100s - (kF + (100 - k)s + gP)}{gP} \qquad (10.49)$$

Balda and Gustafson (1990) note that on the basis of evaluations in a non-object-oriented environment, reasonable on-costs for developing a reusable component take about 25% more effort (equivalent here to $g = 0.25 \times s$). They also balance the costs of developing a reusable component and then reusing it $n - 1$ times against the cost of developing it from scratch n times. Here we incorporate such ideas in a more extensive calculation.

Figure 10.24(a) plots the variation in total cost of each of the first 20 projects (Expression 10.47), reuse savings (Expression 10.48) and generalization costs (Equation 10.43) over the 20 projects; and Figure 10.24(b) plots the individual project ROI and the two organizational ROI measures (R and R_Q) over the same 20 projects. Values for the parameters are, here, $F = 2$, $g = 2.5$, and $s = 10$ with an initial library size of 10. It can be seen that projects costs fall monotonically as savings increase. The rate of return on successive projects is positive for all projects (as illustrated here in Figure 10.24(b))—if there are *no* library classes available initially, then the ROI becomes greater than zero for the *third* project, thus stressing the advantage of working in a language environment where library classes already exist. Such an environment gives a "headstart" to an object-oriented environment, compared with a traditional, non-object-oriented reuse environment. Thus the savings from reuse become self-evident and these figures suggest savings on the third or later projects, confirming earlier speculations that, in general, reuse benefits may not start until the second or third project. Although not shown here, the size of the library increases monotonically from the initial 10 to a final value of 126 at the end of the twentieth project.

A second simulation is shown in Figure 10.25 for different parameter values. This represents a significantly more pessimistic calculation in that the costs of reuse are substantially greater: $F = 5$, $s = 10$, $g = 10$ (viz., generalization *doubles* the cost per class). Nevertheless, the graphs still support an ROI > 0 after the completion of the sixth project (Figure 10.25(b)).

Finally (Figure 10.26), we investigated a different scenario in which only 10%[31] of required classes were available in the library, such that more investment

---

31. Generally, we observe that in practice values around 50% (or greater) are not uncommon.

Object-oriented "Metrics"

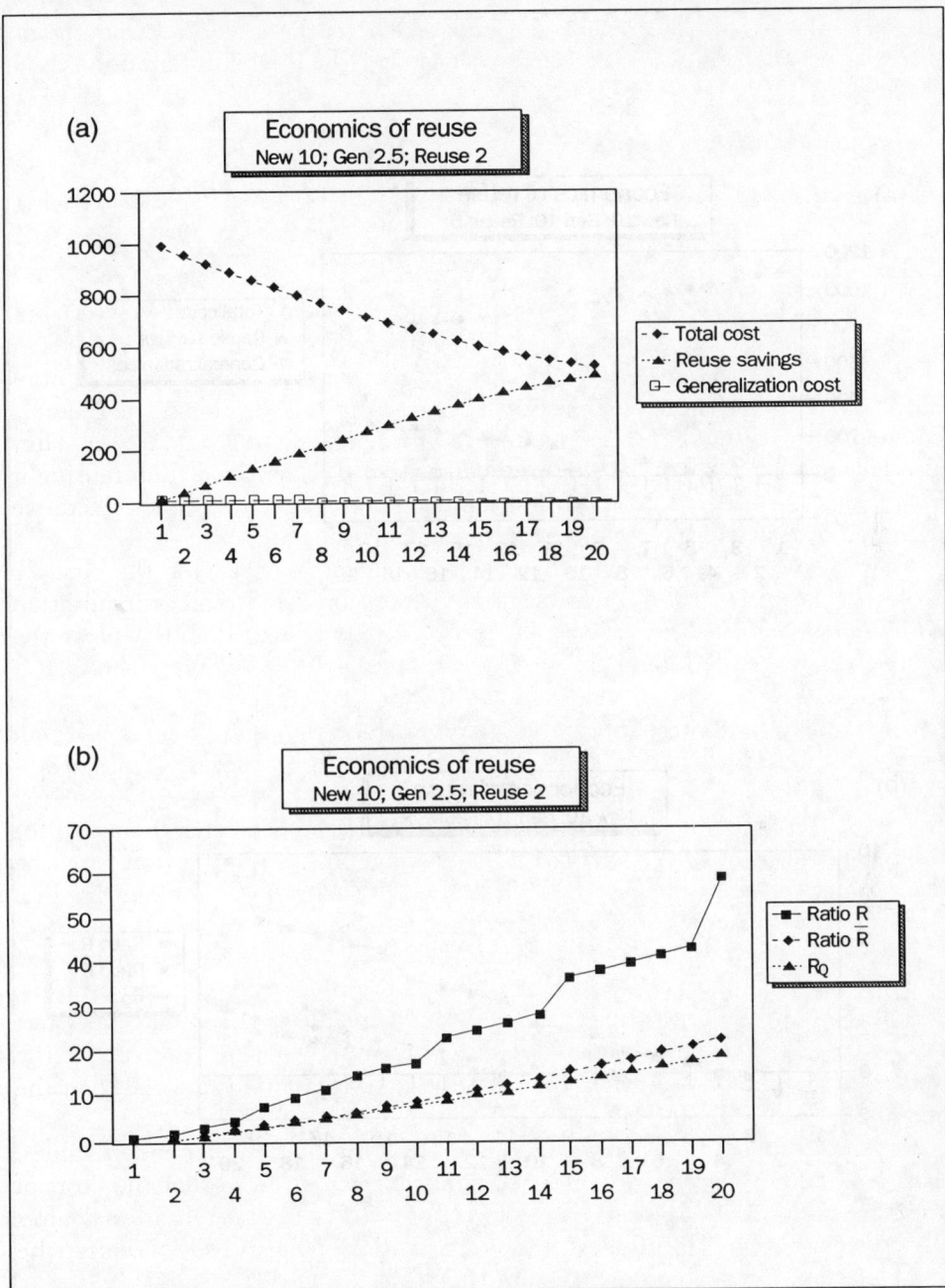

Figure 10.24 *Economics of reuse simulation model results for new costs = 10; generalization costs = 2.5; and reuse locational costs = 2: (a) plots of total cost, reuse savings, and generalization costs; (b) plots of ROI ratios—individual project ratio, R, and the two proposed cumulative ratios, $\overline{R}$ and R_Q (Henderson-Sellers, 1993)*

524 — Chapter 10

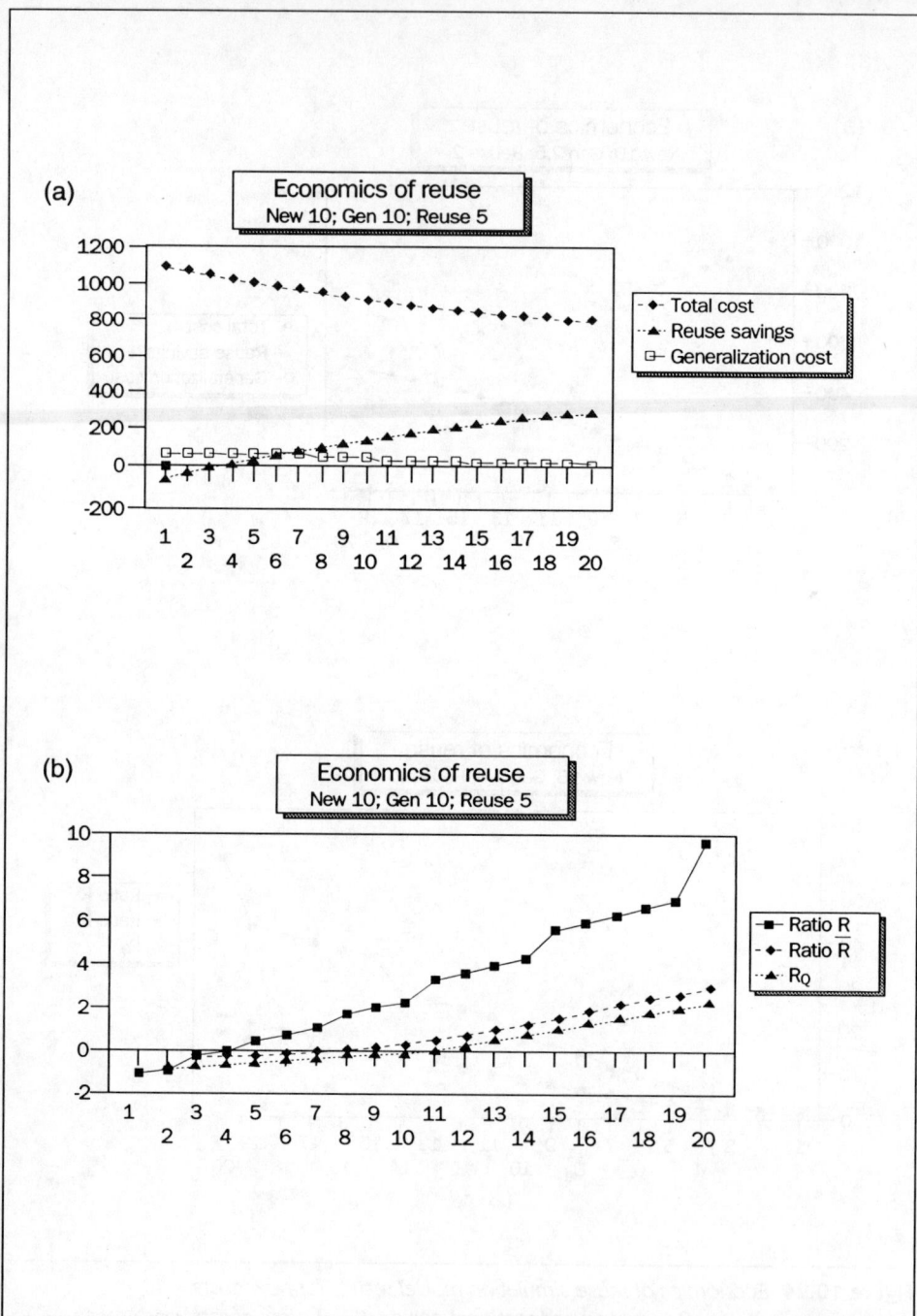

Figure 10.25 *As for Figure 10.24 but with generalization costs = 10 and reuse locational costs = 5 (Henderson-Sellers, 1993)*

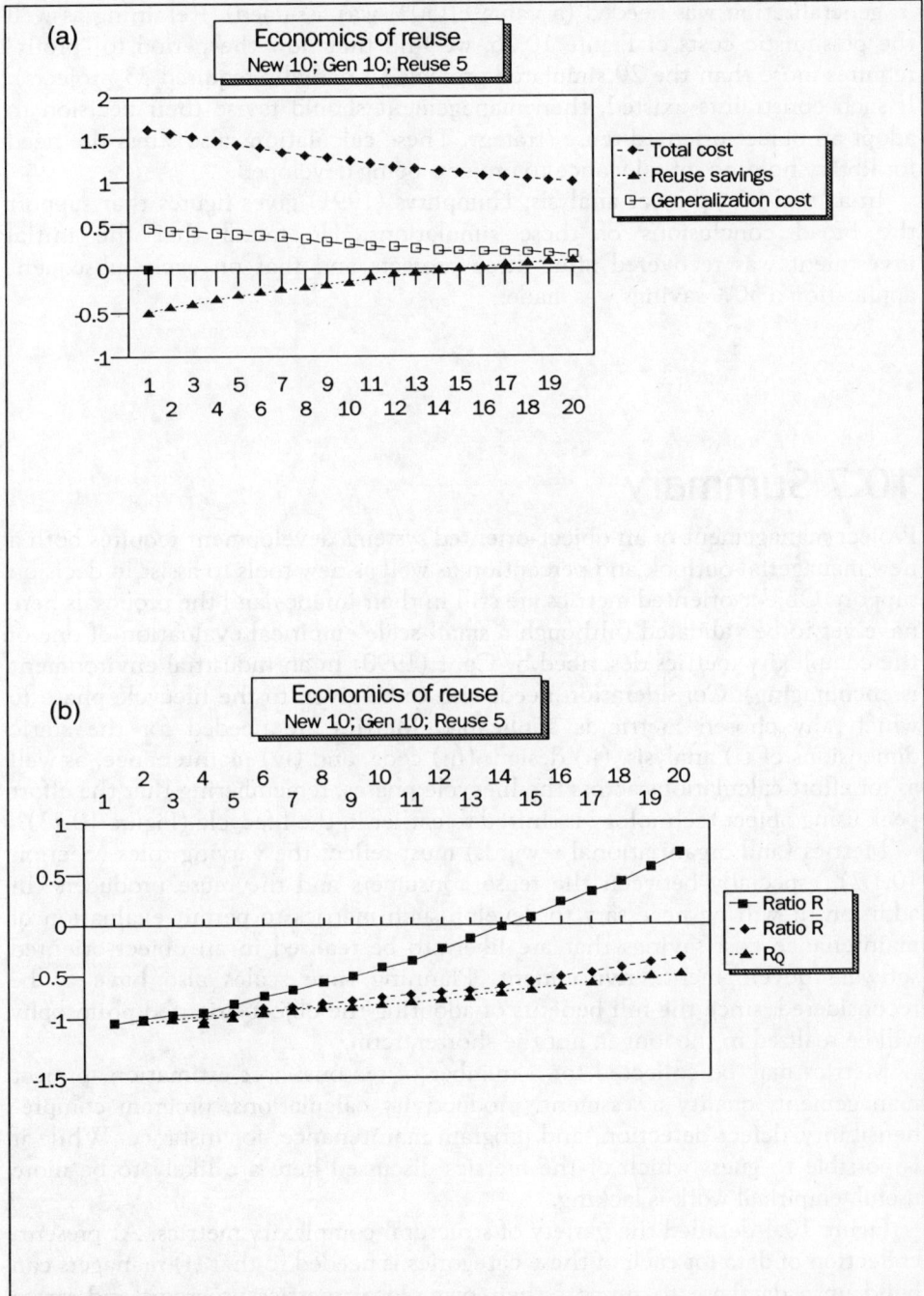

Figure 10.26 As for Figure 10.25 but with only 10% of classes available in library and with half the classes developed being candidates for generalization (Henderson-Sellers, 1993)

in generalization was needed (a value of 50% was assumed). Retaining as well the pessimistic costs of Figure 10.26, we find that now the period to "profit" requires more than the 20 simulated projects (it actually required 33 projects). If such constraints existed, then management should revise their decision to adopt an object-oriented reuse strategy. These calculations also stress the need for library holdings of relevance to projects being developed.

In a "real-life" project analysis, Humphrys (1991) gives figures that support the broad conclusions of these simulations. He found that the initial investment was recovered after three projects and that on each subsequent application a 50% savings was made.

10.7 Summary

Project management of an object-oriented systems development requires both a new managerial outlook and perception as well as new tools to assist in decision support. Object-oriented metrics are still in their infancy and the proposals here have yet to be validated (although a small-scale empirical evaluation of one of the complexity metrics described by Cant (1990) in an industrial environment is encouraging). Consideration needs also to be given to the lifecycle phase to which any chosen metric is applicable. Metrics are needed for the static dimensions of (i) analysis, (ii) design, (iii) code, and (iv) maintenance, as well as for effort calculations across the lifecycle phases, remembering that the effort peak using object technology is shifted to earlier in the lifecycle (Figure 10.23).

Metrics (and organizational rewards) must reflect the varying roles (Section 10.1.2), especially between the reuse consumers and the reuse producers. In addition, it will be necessary to develop such metrics to permit evaluation of maintenance cost savings that are likely to be realized in an object-oriented software development environment. Planning time scales also have to be reconsidered, since the full benefits of adopting the object-oriented philosophy will be realized in the longer, not the shorter, term.

Metrics may be collected for a number of reasons: cost estimation, project management, quality assessment, productivity calculations, program comprehensibility, defect detection, and program maintenance, for instance. While it is possible to guess which of the metrics discussed here are likely to be more useful, empirical work is lacking.

Figure 10.4 detailed the variety of structural complexity metrics. At present, collection of data for each of these categories is needed so that (i) managers can build up a database to support their own, local metrics programs and (ii) a database can be built up to assist researchers in developing a theoretically sound and more widely applicable metrics set.

Currently, a metrics program should probably include in its data collection at least the following:

- fan-out (coupling)
- average (and standard deviation) of number of methods per class
- average (and standard deviation) of method size
- average (and standard deviation) of complexity of methods (e.g., using cyclomatic complexity)
- mean and maximum depth of inheritance hierarchies
- reuse ratio, U
- specialization ratio, S
- time spent in development (effort)
- time spent on generalization; as well as
- a qualitative evaluation of the semantic cohesion of each class.

All these metrics will need to be evaluated empirically using case studies before final recommendations can be made. In the interim, however, we trust that the reflection of the state of the art in this chapter provides information useful for project managers until well-validated metrics and their supporting tools become commercially available.

POSTSCRIPT

The Future of Object Technology

Although many tout OO as "the computing of the 1990s and the next century," many will ask, "Why should we succumb to this new technology and adopt the object-oriented philosophy with all its investment in learning a new mindset?" "We only adopted a relational database two years ago; why should we now switch to an object-oriented database? Perhaps there'll be something even better in another couple of years." And how can we really tell? We don't know for sure, but it's the perception of many of us that the object-oriented approach to software engineering has a reasonably lengthy lifetime ahead of it. The recent emergence of the Object Management Group (Barber, 1991) within the computer industry, as well as a high degree of interest and involvement from all major hardware and software vendors, substantiate that forecast.

In the United Kingdom, May 1990 saw the formation of the Object Interest Group (OIG)(Plant, 1992b). Fourteen large UK companies, two government departments, and one university were the founder members. Their initial goal was to understand and assess the potential for OT and to get hard evidence to support any conclusions. This evidence then provides encouragement to the large-scale suppliers of methods, tools, and software support. The OIG consulted 35 practitioners and companies worldwide, and their report concluded that "Object orientation is potentially one of the most powerful technologies ever to become available to the IT industry and its users. As such it demands high calibre management. It is not a panacea but a high power tool—dangerous if misused but capable of great things" (Plant, 1992b, p4).

As commercial organizations adopt technology, what are the components of object-orientation that they will perceive as maturing fastest? We would suggest that there are four major areas: project management, metrics (both discussed in this book), objectbase management systems (see, e.g., Ahmed et al., 1992), and distributed object systems (see, e.g., Nascimento and Dollimore, 1992). In addition, the next few years are likely to see a consolidation of SDLC methodologies and notations and the emergence and establishment of new (or newer versions of existing) OOPLs. Some of these will include OO COBOL, OOSQL, and FORTRAN90 in the scientific and engineering areas (although the latter is not a true OOPL). Other OOPLs "waiting in the wings" (actually in the research labs) include Emerald, Beta, and Self. Visual programming will become more common, using tools such as ObjectVision, Visual BASIC (not truly OO but strongly influenced by the paradigm), and Visual C++ as well as new programming environments such as those based on Smalltalk and Eiffel Version 3.

Perhaps even further in the future from a commercial viewpoint are (i) formal methods for object-oriented information systems and (ii) metamodeling. Both of these are discussed briefly below.

Formal methods
Formal methods are often not considered to be within the scope of the information systems manager, possibly because of their perceived difficulty, being based on pure mathematical and logic notation. In fact, this difficulty can be illusory. Studies by Swatman (1992) on introducing these ideas into commercial IS departments in Western Australia show that once the mental barrier of "mathematics" had been broken down, the IS practitioners found the hardest ideas to come to grips with were those of abstraction (Section 2.2) rather than the formal methods themselves.

Within the OO world, significant advances have been made in the development of formal methods, usable within industry, in the form of Object-Z (Duke et al., 1991), a formal notation designed specifically for object-oriented systems. An example template for a class SUBSCRIBER (which is part of an EDI system), written in Object-Z (Swatman and Swatman, 1992), is on the opposite page.

Jones (1991) exhorts all IS managers to move toward adopting a formal methodology as part of their move toward quality products. This has been echoed by Meyer (1992d). It is likely that, in the future, formal methods will be seen less as a niche interest and more as mainstream software engineering, especially when the use of OT, with its emphasis on quality, is advocated.

Metamodels
There are a number of levels of abstraction in any modeling process—a concept stressed in Chapters 2 and 3 especially. Each of the methodologies described in

```
┌─ Subscriber ─────────────────────────────────────────────
│   ┌─ sid : SubscriberId ──────────────────────────────────
│   │  mbox : ℙ Document
│   │  ∀ d : mbox • d.sub = sid
│
│   ┌─ INIT ────────────────────────────────────────────────
│   │  mbox = ∅
│
│   ┌─ ReceiveMail ─────────────────────────────────────────
│   │  Δ(mbox)
│   │  d? : Document
│   │  d?.sub = sid
│   │  mbox' = mbox ∪ {d?}
│
│   ┌─ SendMail ────────────────────────────────────────────
│   │  d! : Document
│   │  d!.sub = sid
│   │  d!.ref = NULL
│
│   ┌─ ReadMail ────────────────────────────────────────────
│   │  Δ(mbox)
│   │  ∃ d : mbox • d.code ∉ dom reply
│   │         mbox' = mbox \ {d}
│
│   ┌─ ReplyToMail ─────────────────────────────────────────
│   │  Δ(mbox)
│   │  d! : Document
│   │  ∃ d : mbox • d.code ∉ dom reply
│   │         d!.code = reply(d.code) ∧ d!.ref = d.ref
│   │         d!.subs = sid ∧ dom d!.info = form(d!.code)
│   │         mbox' = mbox \ {d}
└──────────────────────────────────────────────────────────
```

Chapter 3 can be both (i) instantiated (i.e., at a lower level of abstraction), where an individual project utilizes the guidelines of the methodology, and (ii) generalized to a higher level of abstraction. At this higher level, we have a model that attempts to represent knowledge about the overall OO SDLC. Examples of these models are the waterfall, fountain, and spiral models. Thus each of the methodologies (e.g., OMT, MOSES, RDD) are themselves instantiations of the metamethodological model. In principle, this process is infinitely recursive (Hofstadter, 1979, p110 *et seq.*), such that a metameta-methodological model would represent SDLCs independent of paradigm such as function-oriented or object-oriented.

In the realm of research, the commercial developer will see the fruits of this labor in new methodologies that are less *ad hoc* than at present, thus providing a sounder and more reliable framework for software development. Indeed, with the newer methodologies we are beginning already to see these research ideas emerge into mainstream software engineering. For example, on the basis of metamodeling ideas, it can be shown that any OO methodology should have strong guidelines on how and when and to what degree to use iterative and recursive techniques; how to assess when the iteration and recursion are completed; and also how to assess during mid-cycle what percentage has already been completed and what work still remains.

The future

The question remains as to when/if object technology will become the *dominant* paradigm for software development. The dominant technology is the one that can be recommended without justification. For example, in most current commercial organizations, suggesting that a system be coded in COBOL would raise no eyebrows. At present, however, suggesting a Smalltalk implementation would lead to significant documentation having to be produced to justify the suggestion. It is clear that object-orientation is not, with a few small exceptions, the dominant development paradigm in commercial organizations, although firms are increasingly committing themselves to OO as the dominant paradigm for them. Perhaps such use should be regarded as a niche—dominance occurs when these views are accepted industry-wide, not just in a few "far-seeing" organizations (Fichman and Kemerer, 1993). It should be remembered (Gabriel, 1992) that high-quality products are not necessarily those that become dominant or the industry *de facto* standard. If quality is the goal of our profession, then object technology offers us the most efficacious route we have yet developed. Can we seize the opportunity?

APPENDIX

Suggested Answers to Study Examples

The first six study examples follow a single example. This is in the musical domain and is built up recursively and iteratively.

Exercise 1—set in Section 2.6

Question restated
In this first exercise, we offer the following short requirements specification:

> A piece of music consists of several movements, each movement consisting of many notes. Each composition may be assumed to be either a solo piece or an orchestral piece and is therefore performed by a soloist or by a full orchestra.

What are the O/Cs and their relationships here?

Some suggestions for consideration in answering Exercise 1
Figure A1.1 identifies the composition as being made up of (i.e., is an aggregate of) one or more movements. Each movement is itself an aggregate of notes.

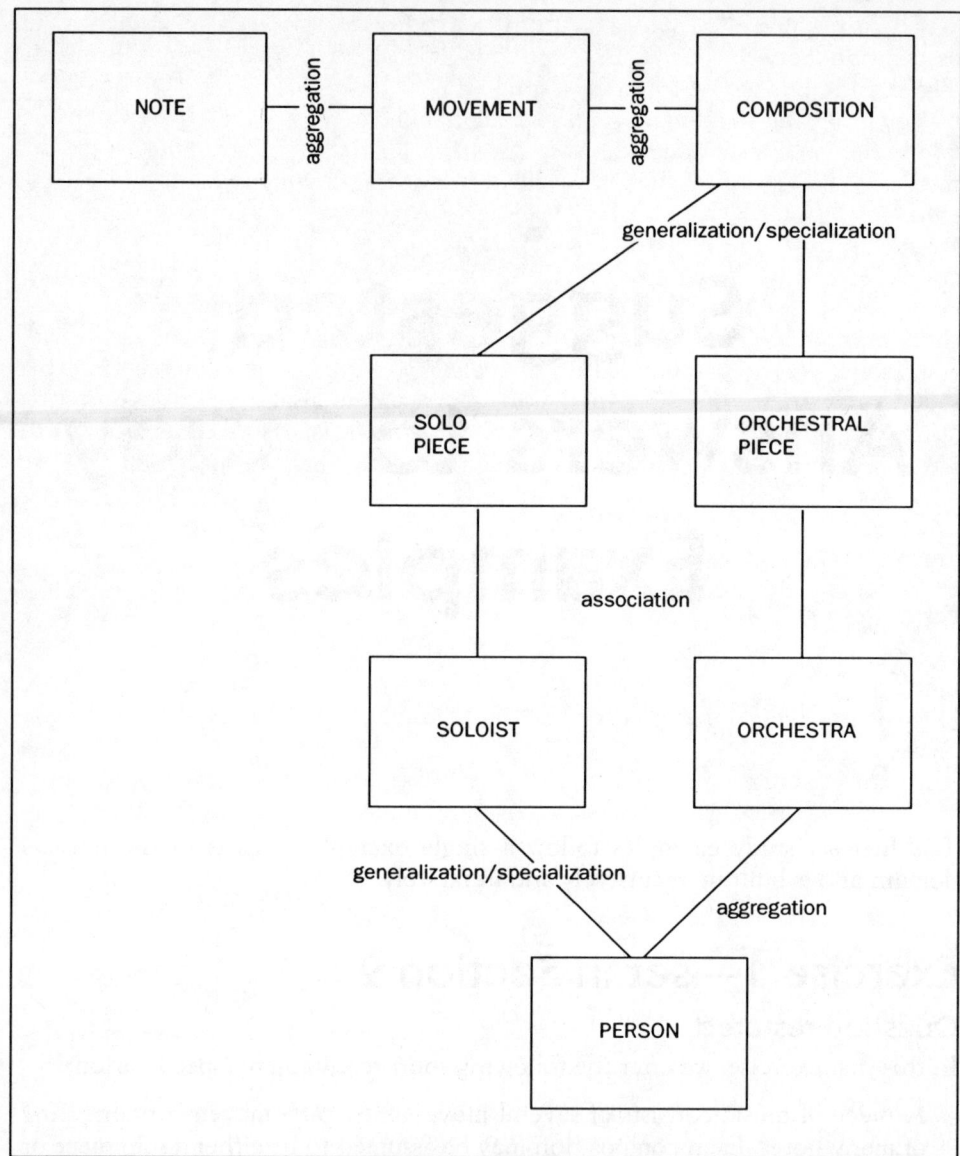

Figure A1.1

Compositions are intended for performance. One type of composition is that for performance by a solo player. Thus a solo composition or solo piece is a special sort of composition, special in that it is intended for performance by a single player. Thus SOLO PIECE is a specialization of COMPOSITION. Similarly, ORCHESTRAL PIECE is a specialization of COMPOSITION.

Suggested Answers to Study Examples — 535

The solo piece is played by a solo performer. *Is-played-by* indicates an association between SOLOIST and SOLO PIECE. Similarly, an ORCHESTRAL PIECE *Is-played-by* an ORCHESTRA.

So far, on the right-hand side of the diagram, there is symmetry between the two branches. Further consideration, perhaps a little beyond the initial requirements, would identify that SOLOIST is a type of PERSON (specialization). However, an ORCHESTRA is *not* a type of PERSON; rather, an ORCHESTRA is an aggregation of PERSONs. (The cynics might say that an ORCHESTRA was composed of a whole bunch of SOLOISTs!)

It should be noted that there is some ambiguity in the requirements in that the noun phrases "composition" and "piece of music" are used. These are essentially synonymous and only one class is required to model both. This redundancy in information in requirements documentation is also noted by Wirfs-Brock *et al.* (1990). They note that the initial list of candidate classes will likely be thinned down on a more detailed inspection.

Exercise 2—set in Section 5.12

Question restated

In classical and popular music, a musical composition consists of several movements, each of which is built up of chords or individual notes, grouped in bars with a given time signature and key signature. The music is scored on one or more staves.

In the specific context of building software designed to produce a printed score, identify the relationships and depict them using the MOSES notation.

Some suggestions for consideration in answering Exercise 2

The context is that of classical music able to be displayed on conventional manuscript paper, premarked with staves. The particular concerns are to do with lining up notes and chords on their respective beats within the bar or measure.

Our initial attempt (Figure A2.1) showed that, using MOSES "tablets," a COMPOSITION was an aggregation of MOVEMENTs. Each MOVEMENT could be regarded as an aggregate of BARs. But is a BAR an aggregate of NOTEs or CHORDs, or of both? The first attempt might argue that a BAR contains both NOTEs and CHORDs (as shown in Figure A2.1). Furthermore, a CHORD is made up of several notes. A cardinality of 1 chord consisting of between 2 to n notes seems reasonable. While this is reasonable in the stated domain, for the musicians, perhaps wanting to write software for musical analysis or composition, the more strict definition of a chord as being at least a triad (of three notes) might be important. (Here two notes would form an interval.)

This solution seems to work ... except that there is no sign of STAVEs. Figure A2.2 redresses this balance. Staves are potentially tricky since they are sort of orthogonal to bars. Nevertheless, for a second iteration the analysis diagram of Figure A2.2 seems to be potentially useful. Here also another modification is

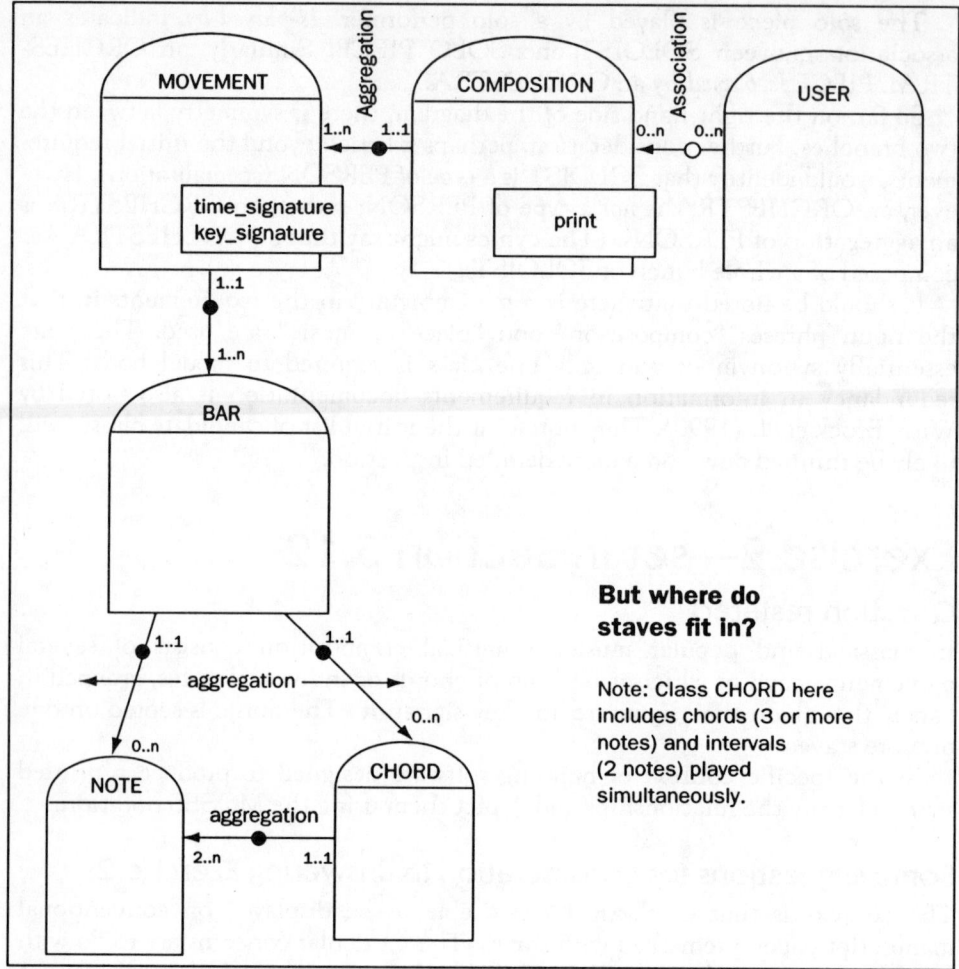

Figure A2.1

made. For the score-printing domain, it might be argued that in aligning notes on beats in the bar on one or more staves we simply need to know about combinations of one or more notes, and that the distinction between chords and intervals discussed above is entirely irrelevant. Consequently, we propose that the CHORD is an aggregate of one or more NOTEs.

Exercise 3—set in Section 6.5

Question restated
Consider again the example you undertook in Exercise 2. In this exercise, we suggest that you translate that example into a simple initial O/C Model, using

Suggested Answers to Study Examples

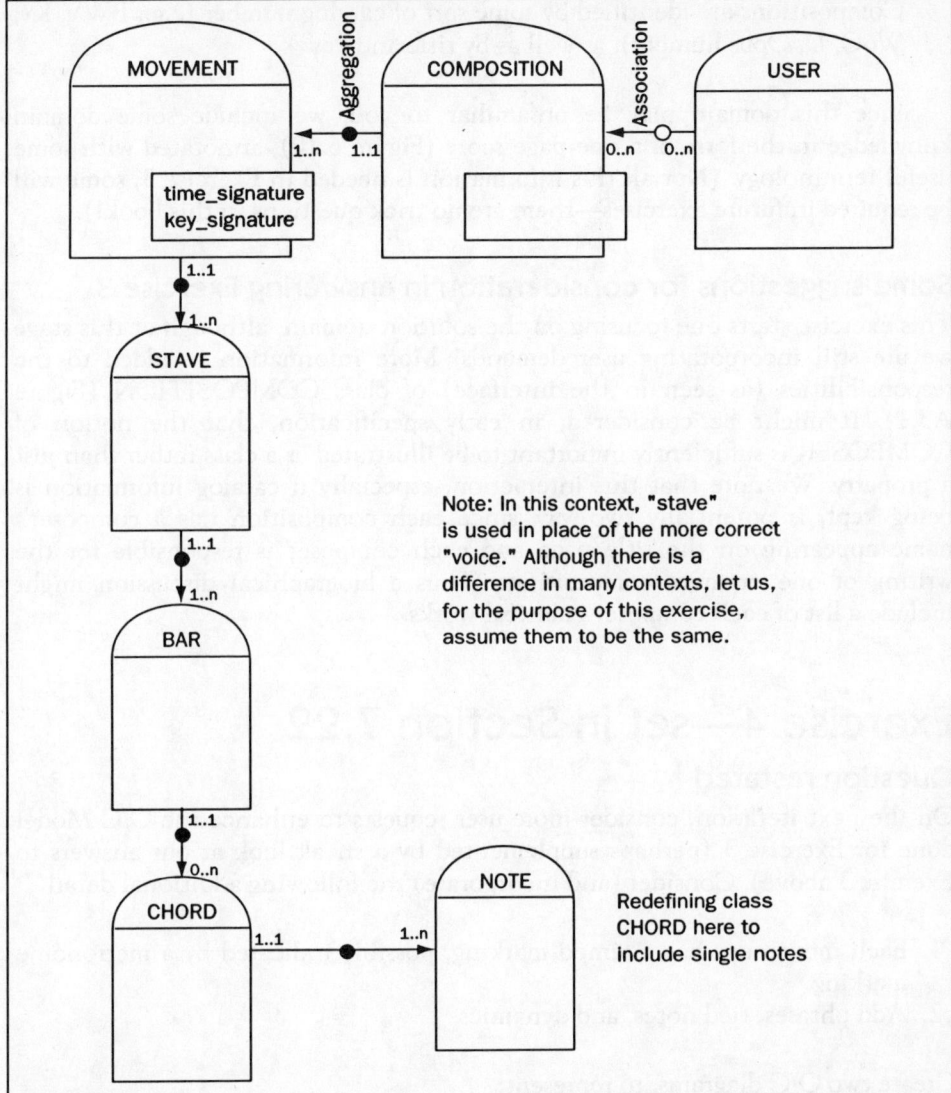

Figure A2.2

the MOSES notation given in Chapter 5. As you do this, begin to add more detail (iteratively added by the user!). As well as information on compositions and movements, please consider the following:

1. A note has a pitch and duration.
2. Compositions are written by a composer.
3. A composer has a year of birth and (sometimes/often) a year of death and a nationality.

4. Compositions are identified by some sort of catalog number (e.g., BWV, Kv, WoO, D, Opus number), as well as by title and key.

Since this domain may be unfamiliar to you, we include some domain knowledge in the form of a one-page score (Figure 6.10), annotated with some useful terminology. (Not all this information is needed in Exercise 3; some will be required in future exercises—there are no trick questions in this book!).

Some suggestions for consideration in answering Exercise 3

This exercise starts one focusing on the solution domain, although at this stage we are still incorporating user demands! More information is added to the responsibilities (as seen in the interface) of class COMPOSITION (Figure A3.1). It might be considered, in early specification, that the notion of COMPOSER is sufficiently important to be illustrated as a class rather than just a property. We note that this interaction, especially if catalog information is being kept, is potentially two-way, since each composition has a composer's name appearing on the title page and each composer is responsible for the writing of one or more compositions. Thus a biographical discussion might include a list of each composer's musical works.

Exercise 4—set in Section 7.22

Question restated

On the next iteration, consider more user requests to enhance the O/C Model done for Exercise 3 (perhaps supplemented by a sneak look at our answers to Exercise 3 above). Consider (and incorporate) the following additional detail:

1. Each movement has a tempo marking, possibly indicated by a metronome marking.
2. Add phrases, tied notes, and dynamics.

Create two O/C diagrams, to represent:

(a) associations
(b) aggregations

Some suggestions for consideration in answering Exercise 4

First, we need to consider the technical details of the extra user requirements, which may throw us back to the Investigation Phase, consideration of domain knowledge and another iteration through the Specification Phase. We note (from Figure 6.10) that a tempo marking is usually written as a note value

Suggested Answers to Study Examples 539

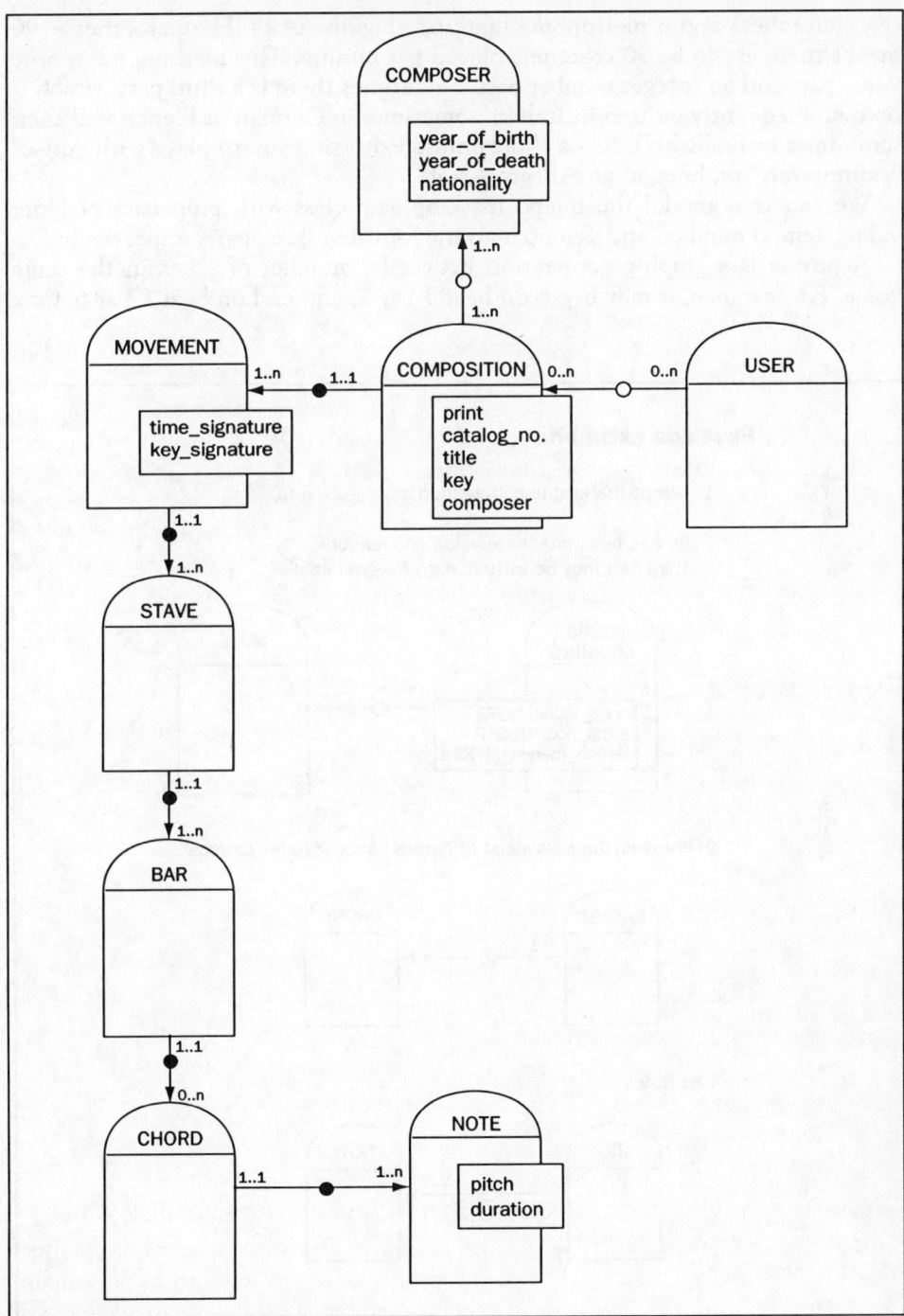

Figure A3.1

(e.g., crotchet) and a metronome marking (Figure A4.1). Here crotchet = 90 means there are to be 90 crotchets played per minute. This marking has a note value part and an integer number part. Sometimes there is a third part, which is textual. Frequently written in Italian, sometimes in German or French and even sometimes in English(!), it is a short phrase exhorting you to play "with gusto," "expressively" or, here, as an Allegro Assai.

We can thus model the tempo marking as a class with properties of Note value, Tempo number, and Tempo marking for these three parts respectively.

A phrase is a graphic connection between a number of notes in the same voice. For instance, it may begin on beat 3 bar 2, and end on beat 1 bar 6. One

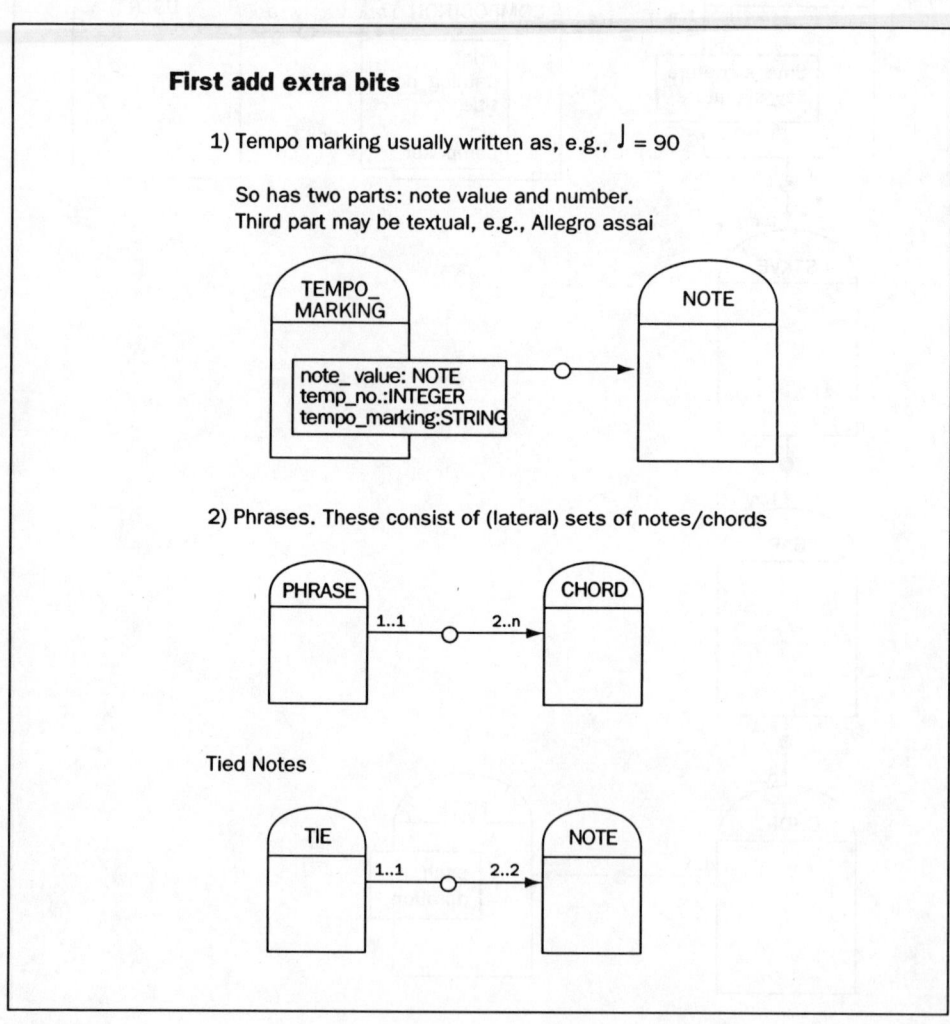

Figure A4.1

Suggested Answers to Study Examples — 541

phrase therefore consists of many notes/chords (strictly more than one) (Figure A4.1). On the other hand, tied notes can be thought of in pairs (although these pairs sometimes overlap). Thus one TIE connects two NOTEs.

Dynamics are potentially complicated. The main emphasis here (for printing a score) is that the dynamic markings, such as loudness, softness, and crescendo (Figure A4.2), need to be attached to specific notes or phrases. Thus when we move towards a detailed specification, we need to worry about placing these accurately, as specified by a particular beat number in the bar, e.g., third beat or even the third quarter beat after the second beat (Figure A4.3). To identify spatial locations as a percentage of the linear distance between bar lines, we will need to identify (i) the smallest subdivision of the bar and (ii) the distance for a particular dynamic marking in terms of a number of these subdivisions. This discussion suggests that now we should consider identifying

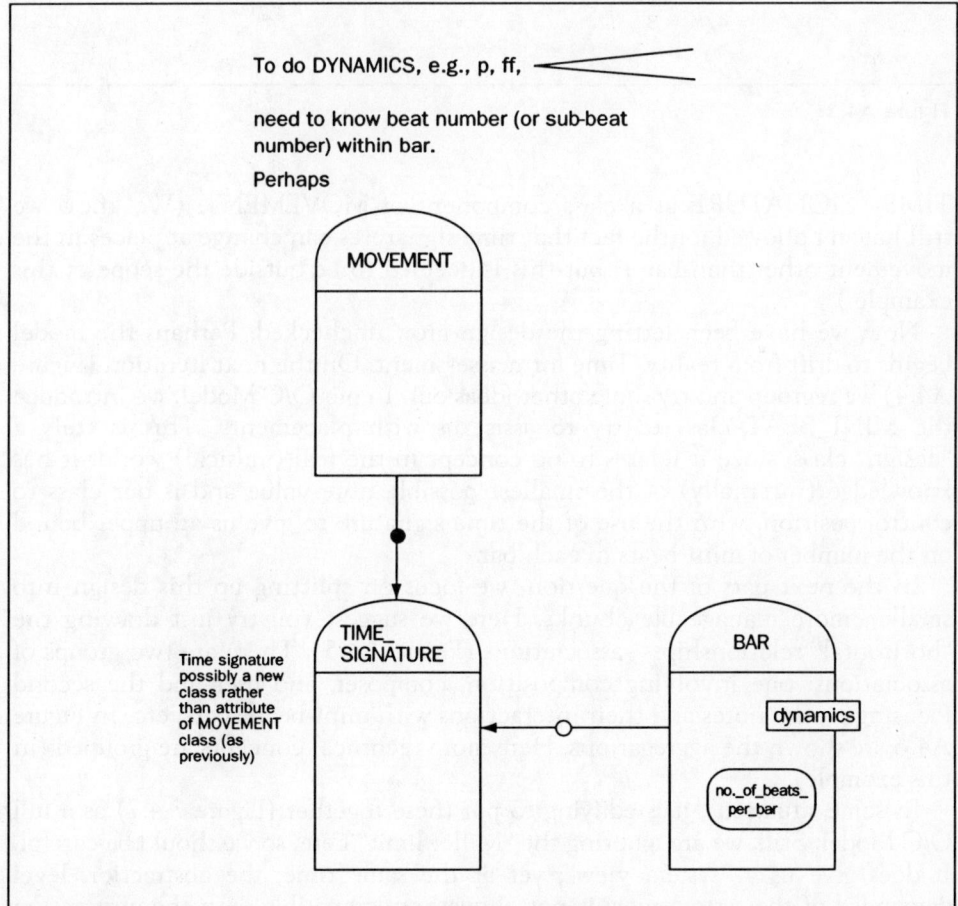

Figure A4.2

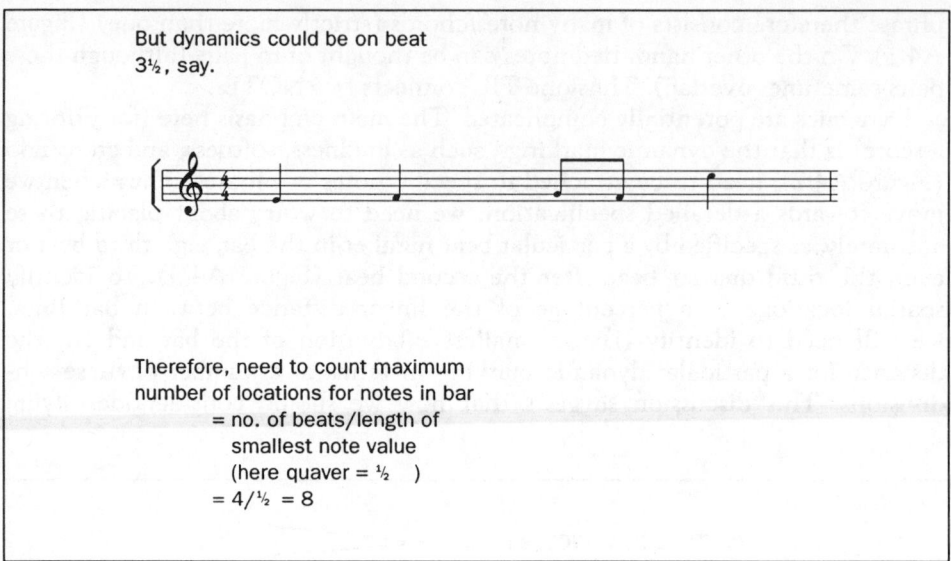

Figure A4.3

TIME_ SIGNATURE as a class component of MOVEMENT. (We know we still haven't allowed for the fact that time signatures can change at places in the movement other than bar 1; but this is deemed to be outside the scope of this example.)

Now, we have been letting the design grow unchecked. Perhaps the model begins to drift from reality. Time for reassessment. On the next iteration (Figure A4.4) we regroup and try some other ideas out. In our O/C Model, we introduce the MINI_BEAT class to try to assist us with placements. This is truly a "design" class, since it relates to no concept in the real (musical) world. It has knowledge (internally) of the smallest possible note value and is our class to control position, with the use of the time signature to give us an upper bound on the number of mini-beats in each bar.

In the next part of the question, we focus on splitting up this design into smaller, more manageable chunks. Here we suggest you try just drawing the "horizontal" relationships—associations (Figure A4.5). There are two groups of associations: one involving composition, composer, and user and the second focusing on the notes and their interactions with mini-beats, bars, etc. In Figure A4.6 are shown the aggregations. Here more technical concepts are grouped (in this example).

In some situations, it is edifying to put these together (Figure A4.7) as a full O/C Model. Still, we are ignoring the "Miller limit" here, so we should be careful. It does give us a "system view"; yet at the same time, the abstraction level demanded of the system view is not altogether compatible with the abstraction details in some of the classes (especially those at the bottom of this figure).

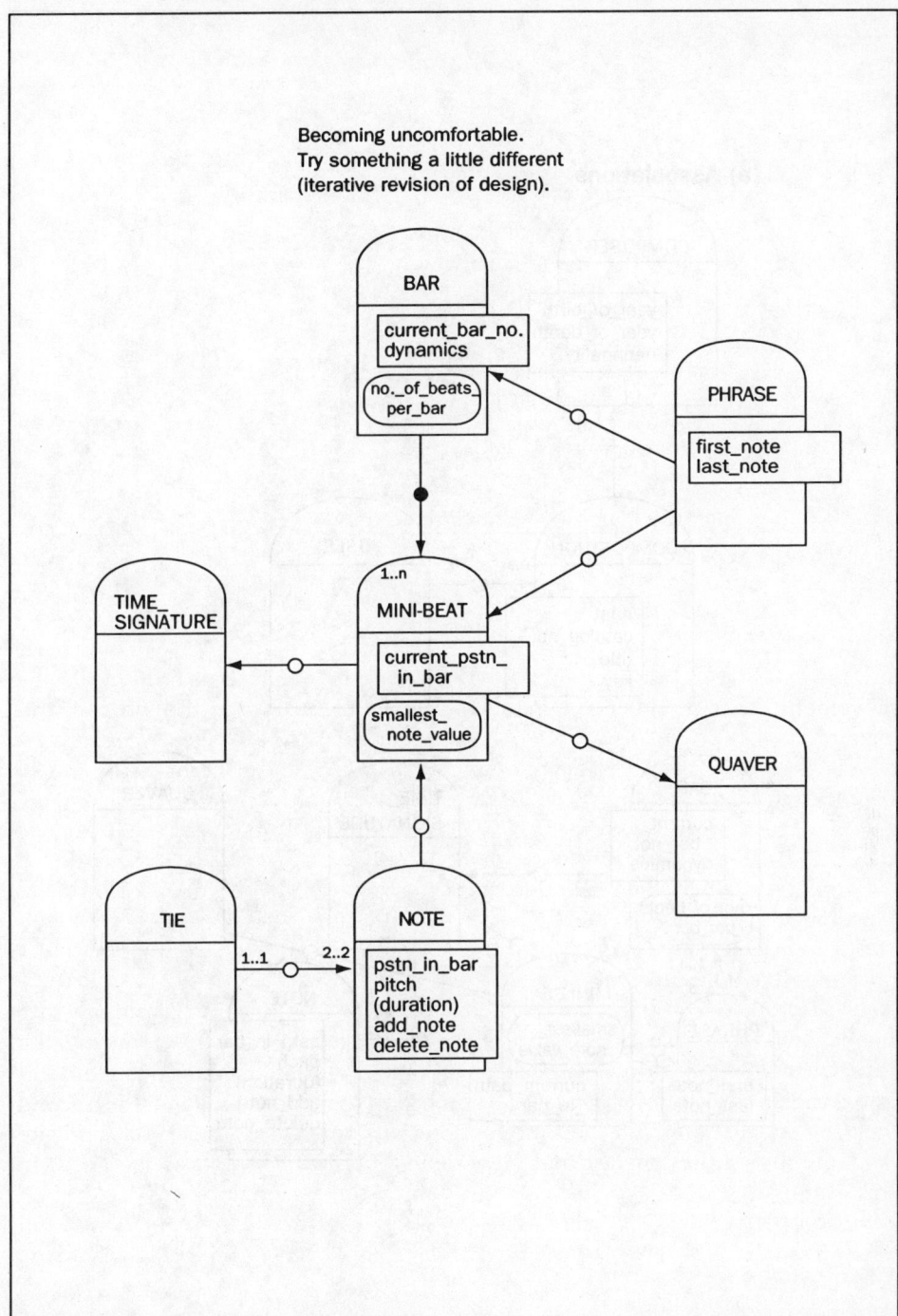

Figure A4.4

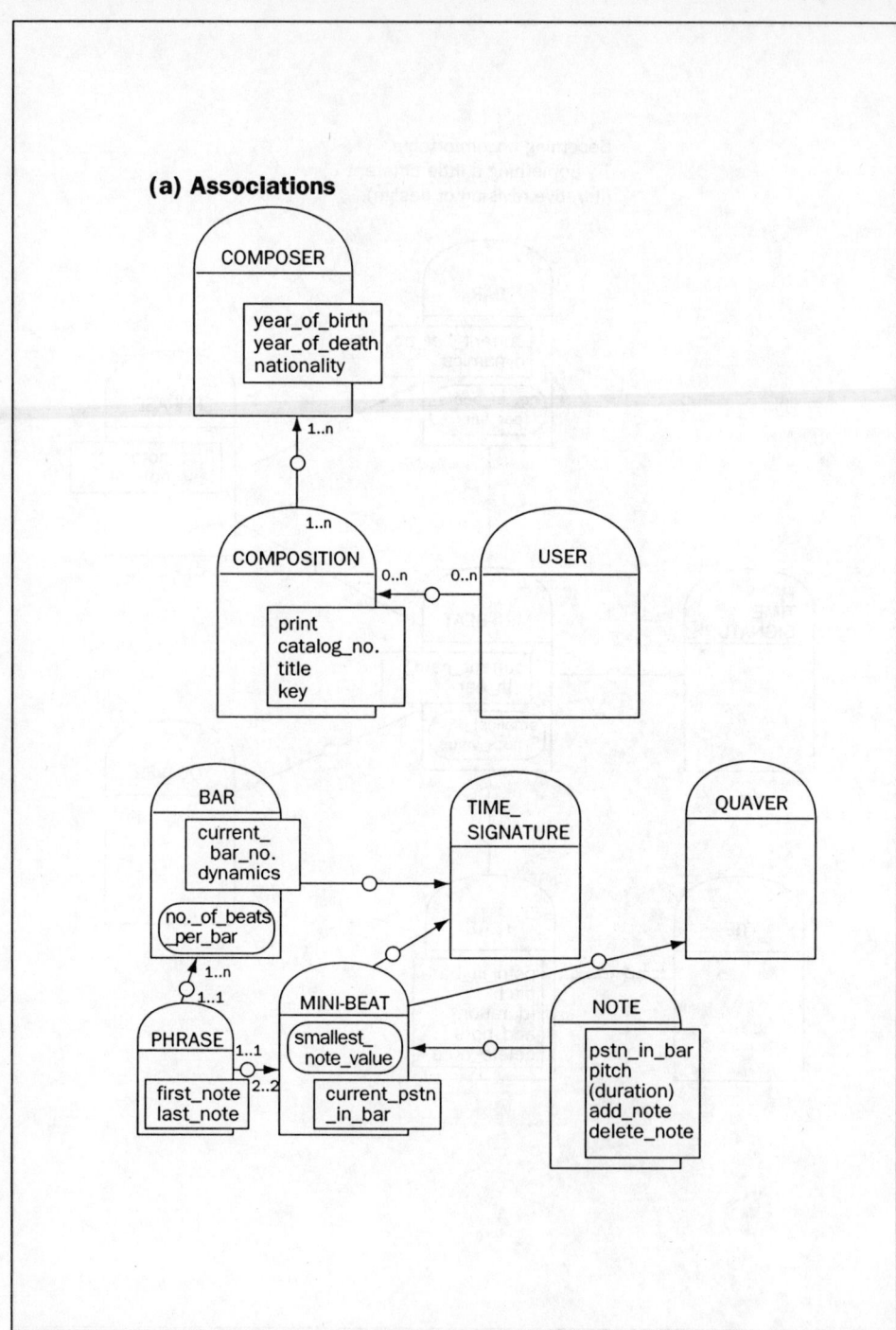

Figure A4.5

Suggested Answers to Study Examples

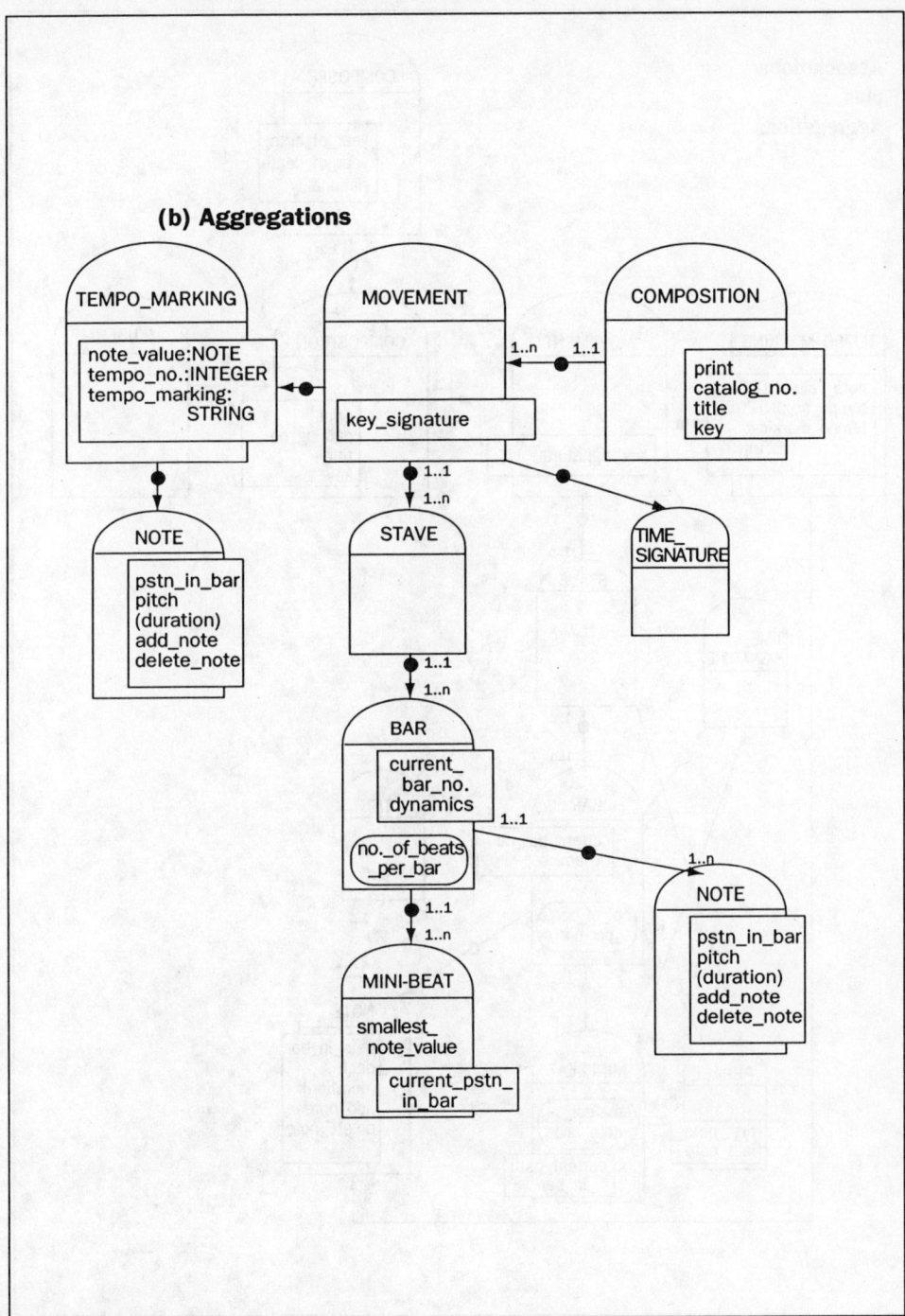

Figure A4.6

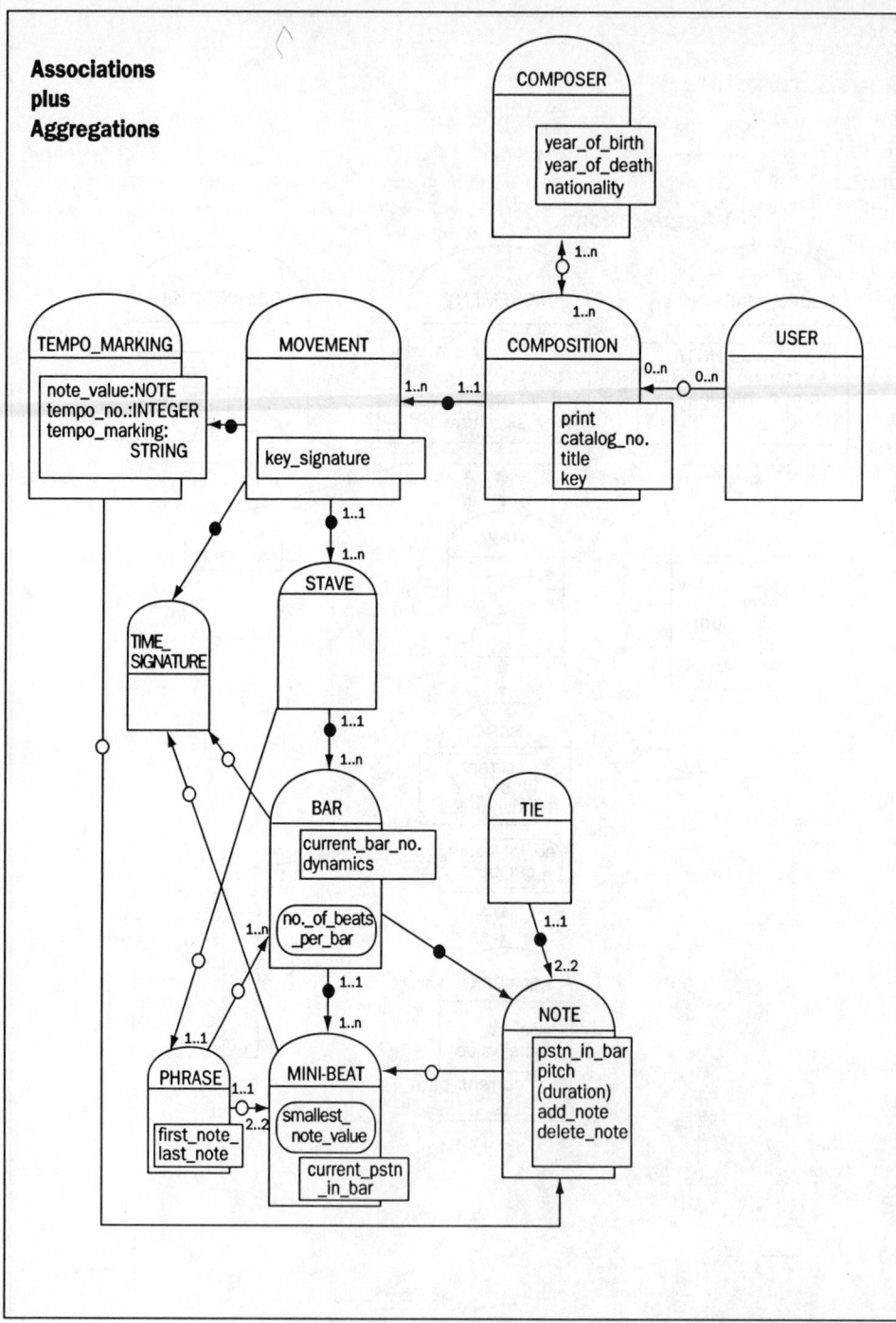

Figure A4.7

Suggested Answers to Study Examples — 547

Exercise 5—set in Section 7.22

Question restated

We can now use layering concepts and subsystems to revise our music printing system in Exercise 4. For this system, start by drawing a layer-1 O/C Model. Identify which classes need expanding to layer-2 and draw these more detailed diagrams. Continue to "zoom in" on these classes until you get to the "bottom layer" where library classes become evident.

Complement these stacked O/C diagrams by inheritance hierarchy diagrams and, if possible, by class specifications (CSs) and/or contracts.

Some suggestions for consideration in answering Exercise 5

We do not expect you necessarily to undertake a full design and we will not fill this Appendix with all the details. Here is a flavor only.

In the O/C Model, the top layer (Layer 1) shows three classes/subsystems (Figure A5.1): COMPOSER, COMPOSITION, and USER. We might indicate

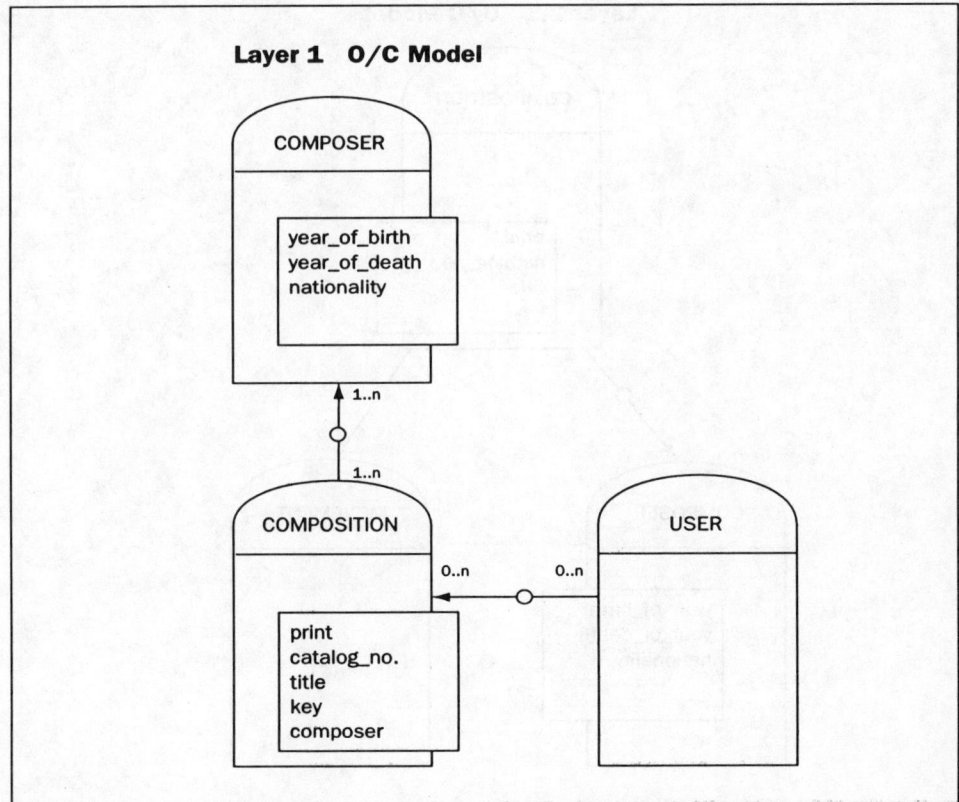

Figure A5.1

some cardinalities and some of the key services. In this level-1 O/C Model, each of these classes needs further elucidation: COMPOSER is shown in more detail in the layer-2 diagram (2.2), COMPOSITION in 2.1, and USER in 2.3.

At the second layer, Figure A5.2 shows the more detailed O/C Model for COMPOSITION (2.1). Here we see connections both to COMPOSER and MOVEMENT. The class MOVEMENT is a high-abstraction-level type of class and needs to be explained—in layer 3.1 (Figure A5.3). Here a MOVEMENT is seen to use the services of four classes: TEMPO_MARKING, STAVE, TIME SIGNATURE, and KEY_SIGNATURE. Of these, only TEMPO_MARKING and STAVE have any more interesting details. These details are shown in layer 4 (4.1 and 4.2) (Figures A5.4 and A5.5). At this bottom level (Figure A5.5) (and moving on through the lifecycle) we have a *very* detailed O/C Model. We will probably want to use "pin-out" diagrams; we will almost certainly be at the level of showing library classes. In level 4, however, we have not yet reached the library class level and can further expand the BAR class into other classes (Figure A5.6).

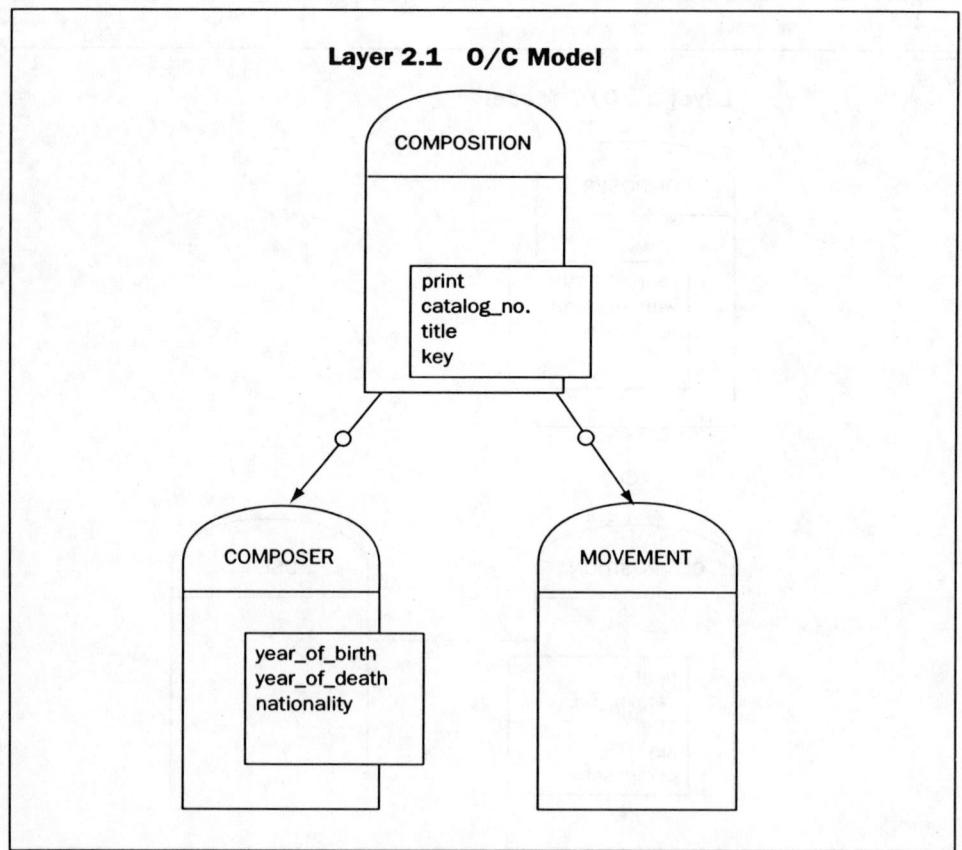

Figure A5.2

Suggested Answers to Study Examples 549

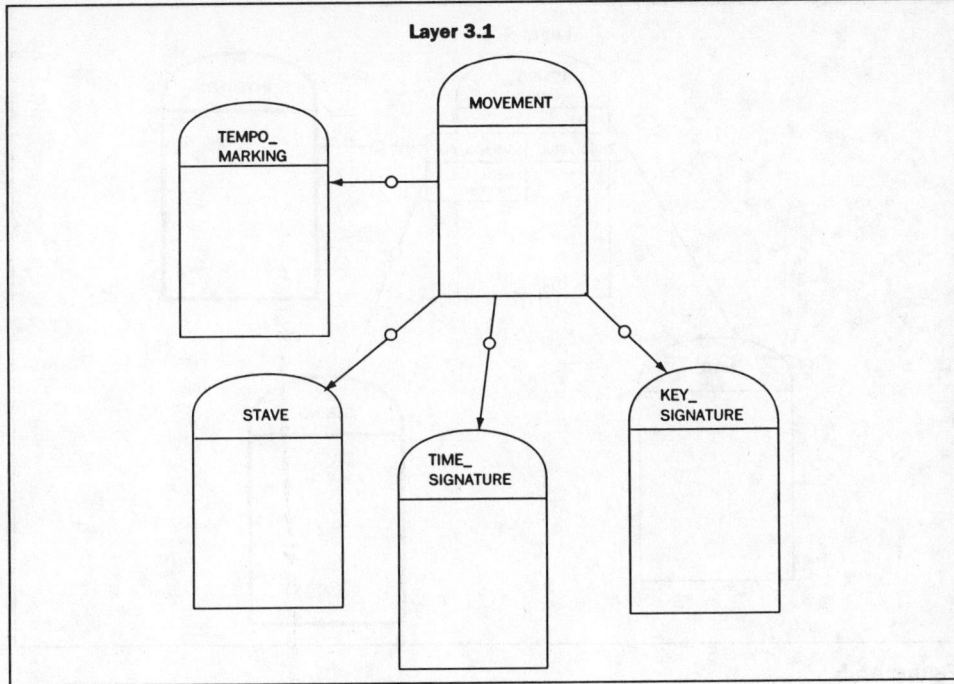

Figure A5.3

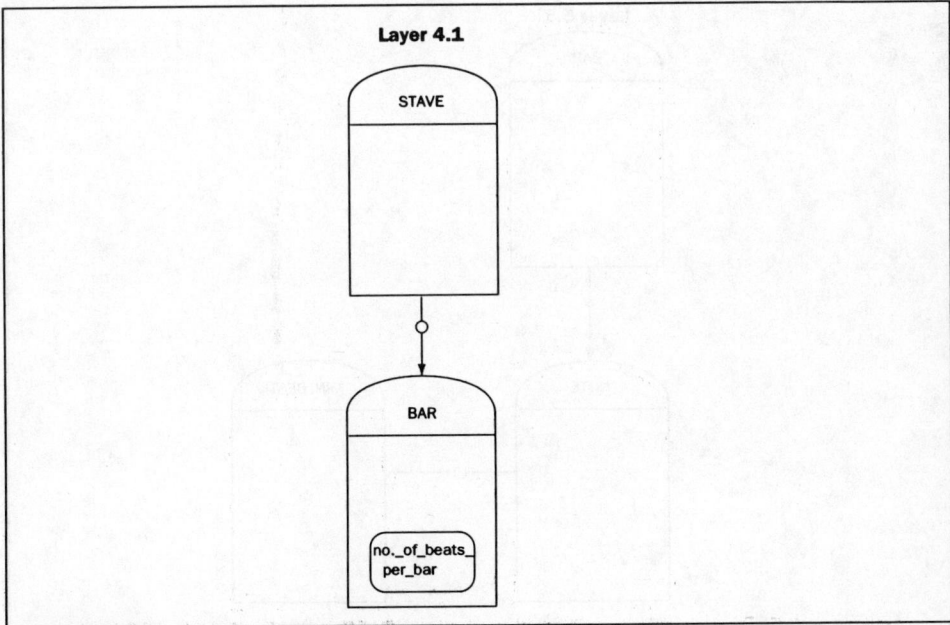

Figure A5.4

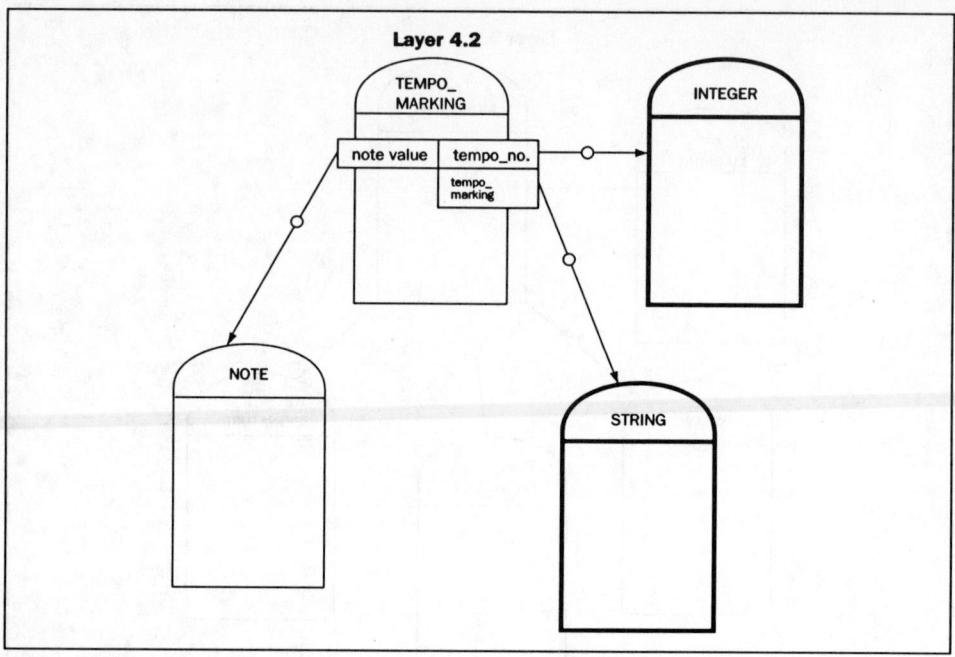

Figure A5.5

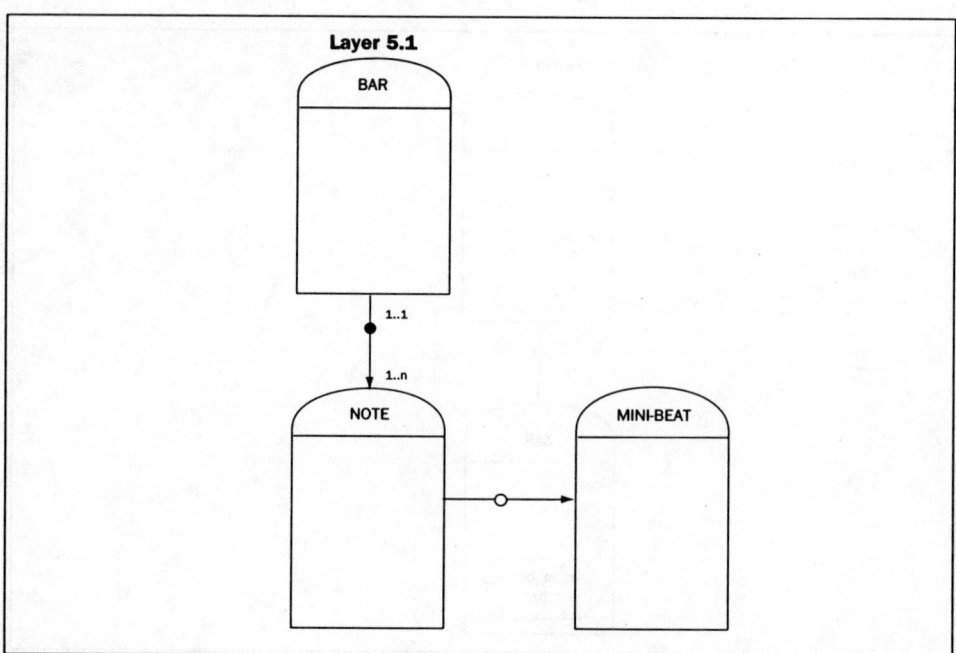

Figure A5.6

Suggested Answers to Study Examples — 551

These diagrams complete the interface, which is described fully in a Class Specification (CS), although neither this nor the associated Contract Tables (CT) are shown here. However, the internal detail/implementation detail still needs elucidating. Figure A5.7 depicts the Services Structure Model (SSM) for the BAR class, written using structured techniques; here pseudocode seems adequate.

Exercise 6—set in Section 7.22

Question restated

Consider the problem statement of Exercise 3 (at the end of Chapter 6) and its solution as an O/C Model derived in that exercise. Construct an appropriate *Implementation Phase diagram* that will also include the following information:

(a) A note may be a semibreve, a minim, a crotchet, or a quaver.
(b) A piece may be played by a soloist or by an orchestra.

Also consider separate inheritance diagram(s) that would complement the client–server diagrams corresponding to the O/C Model derived in Exercise 3. Are the identified inheritance relationships for specification or for implementation?

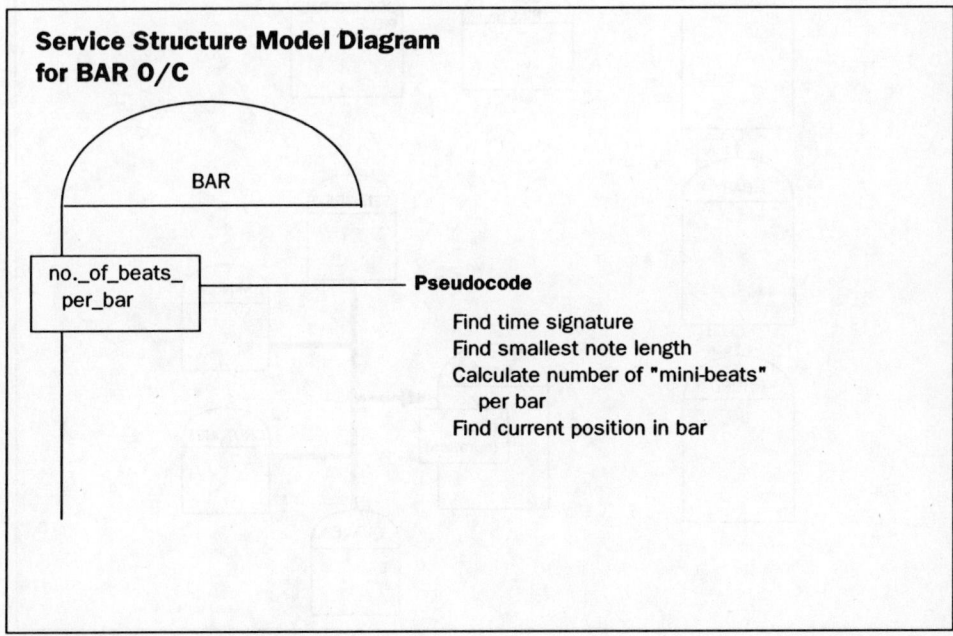

Figure A5.7

Some suggestions for consideration in answering Exercise 6

This should by now be relatively straightforward. This new information is taken through its Specification Phase and finally we derive the Implementation Phase diagram of Figure A6.1. The only additions are two inheritance hierarchies. SOLO_PIECE is a piece of music (a composition) that is played by a soloist. So a SOLO_PIECE is a type of COMPOSITION, as is ORCHESTRAL_PIECE. The second hierarchy relates different valued notes as subtypes of class NOTE.

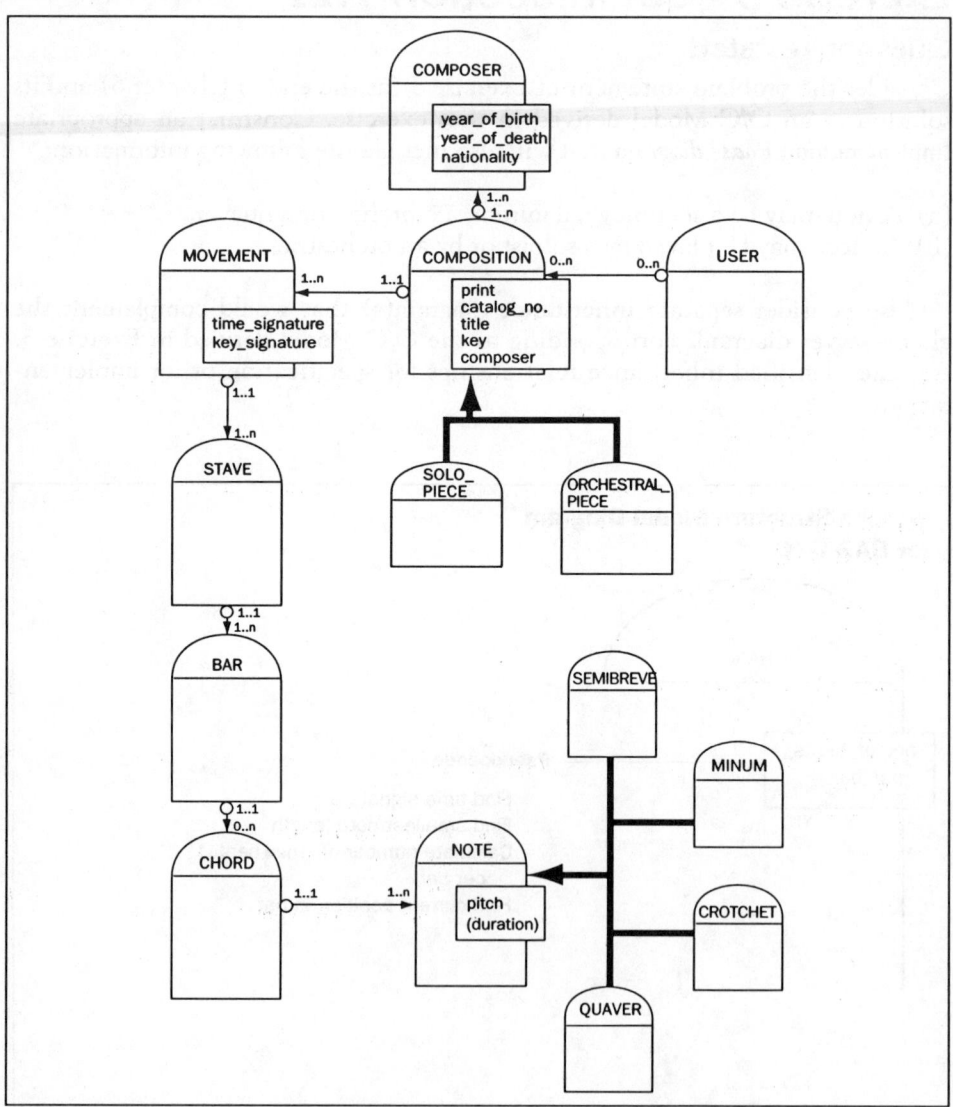

Figure A6.1

Here there are two possibilities: (i) to retain *duration* as a service that is given a numeric value for its length and (ii) to pull out (as here) the individual notes, e.g., SEMIBREVE as separate classes. Since NOTEs are a major feature of our typesetting package, it is reasonable to expect that this second option might be more beneficial. We will have to see in later iterations!

Figure A6.2 shows the more normal method of presentation of inheritance structures as separate diagrams. In this case they all depict inheritance for specification.

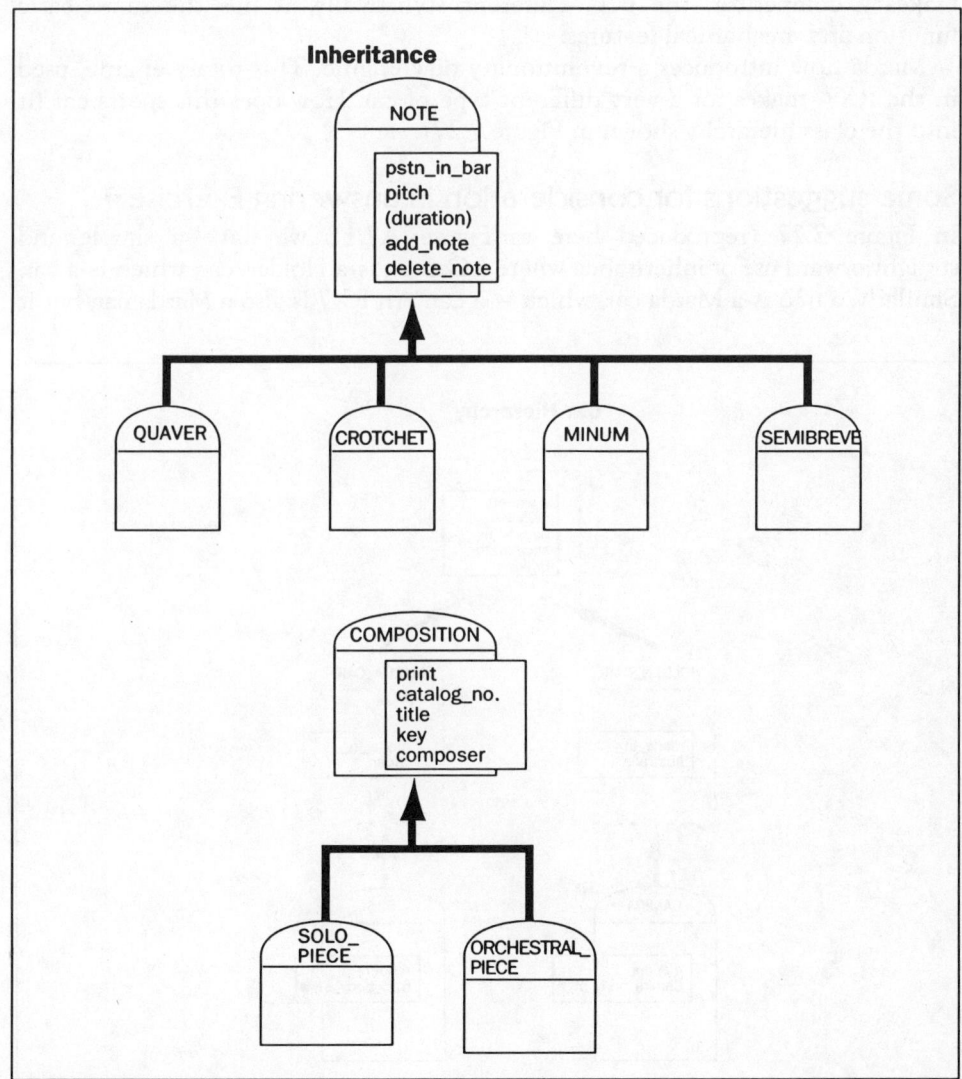

Figure A6.2

Exercise 7—set in Section 7.22

Question restated

As a little digression from music, this exercise considers buying a new car—well, not actually buying, more modeling a small number of makes and models to illustrate some object-oriented concepts discussed in Chapter 7.

In our simplified global market for cars there are but two manufacturers: in Australia there is Holden and in Japan there is Mazda. Holden's first model is a sedan/wagon known as the Camira—very standard in all its features. Mazda makes a competitor, the 626. Different stylistically, it has the same basic function and mechanical features.

Mazda now introduces a revolutionary new engine. This rotary engine, used in the RX7, makes for a very different type of car. How does this sports car fit into the class hierarchy shown in Figure 7.27?

Some suggestions for consideration in answering Exercise 7

In Figure 7.27 (reproduced here as Figure A7.1), we have a simple and straightforward use of inheritance where a Camira **is-a** Holden car, which **is-a** car. Similarly, a 626 **is-a** Mazda car, which **is-a** car. An RX7 is also a Mazda car, but it

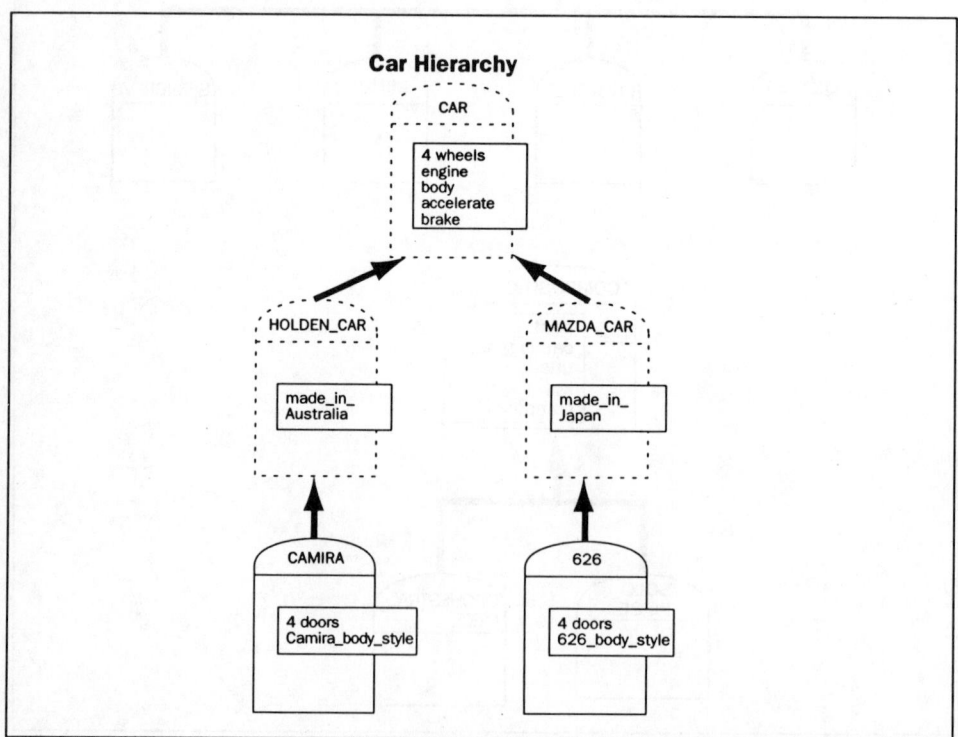

Figure A7.1

Suggested Answers to Study Examples

has a different style of engine. Here all the supertypes are abstract classes—hence a dotted icon is used. Figure A7.2 gives a straightforward answer: that the RX7 is a type of Mazda car. Here the class RX7 inherits features of Mazda car (e.g., made in Japan) and from its parent, CAR, the attributes of four wheels, engine, body, etc. However, now we must rethink, because "engine" as an attribute of CAR in Figure A7.1 implicitly meant "piston-engine." In Figure A7.2, RX7 thus inherits "piston-engine" and must overwrite this feature with its own "rotary engine," as well as its own specific "RX7-ish" attributes.

Overwriting like this is not very satisfactory and doesn't lead to reusability. Also, if "engine" of CAR (not "piston-engine") only applies to a subset of the "leaves" of the inheritance tree, perhaps it shouldn't be placed so high in the hierarchy. Figure A7.3 suggests moving piston-engine down to the HOLDEN_CAR class and through the MAZDA_CAR class into a special subset of Mazdas

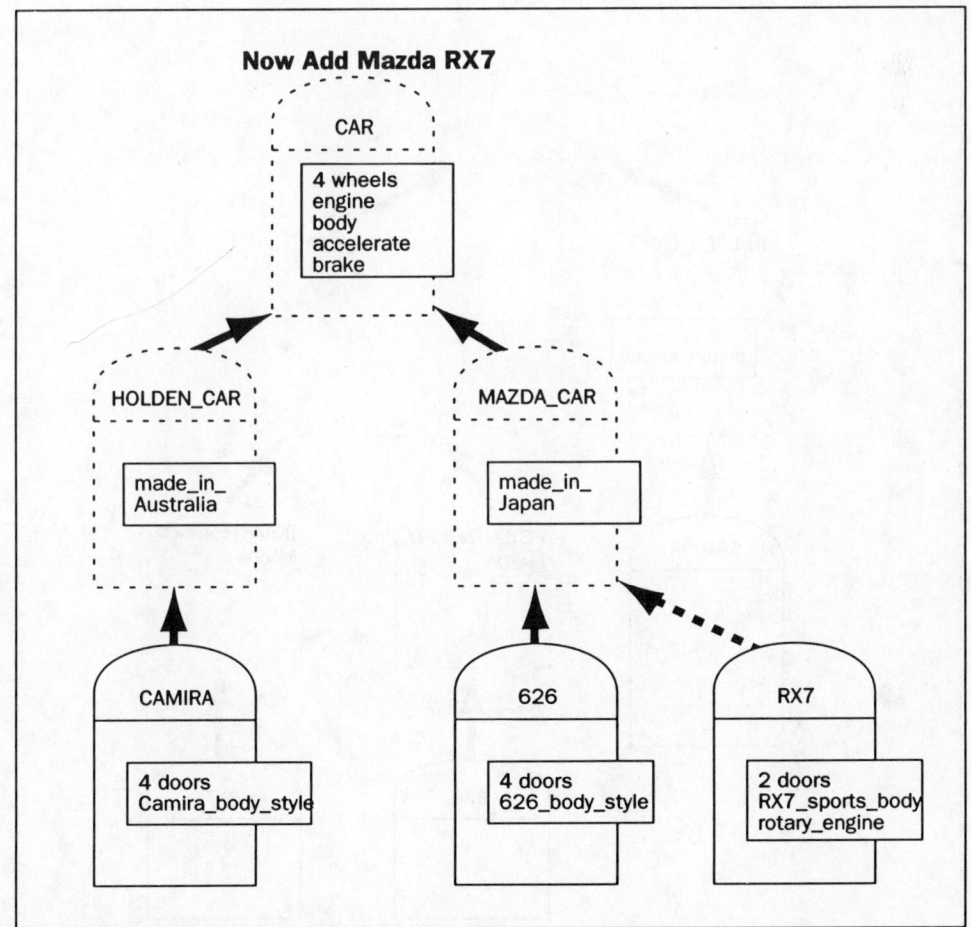

Figure A7.2

represented by the class PISTON-ENGINED_MAZDA. Thus piston-engined Mazdas and rotary-engined Mazdas both inherit from a common parent of Mazda car and support their own particular form of engine.

Maybe. But perhaps we should elevate the difference in engines higher, since at present we define piston-engined cars twice: in the HOLDEN_CAR class and in the PISTON-ENGINED_MAZDA class, which incidentally represents an unhelpful asymmetry in the modeling. Figure A7.4 represents more symmetry with four subclasses of CAR. Then all specific models inherit from two classes: one for the engine and one for the manufacturer. The problem here

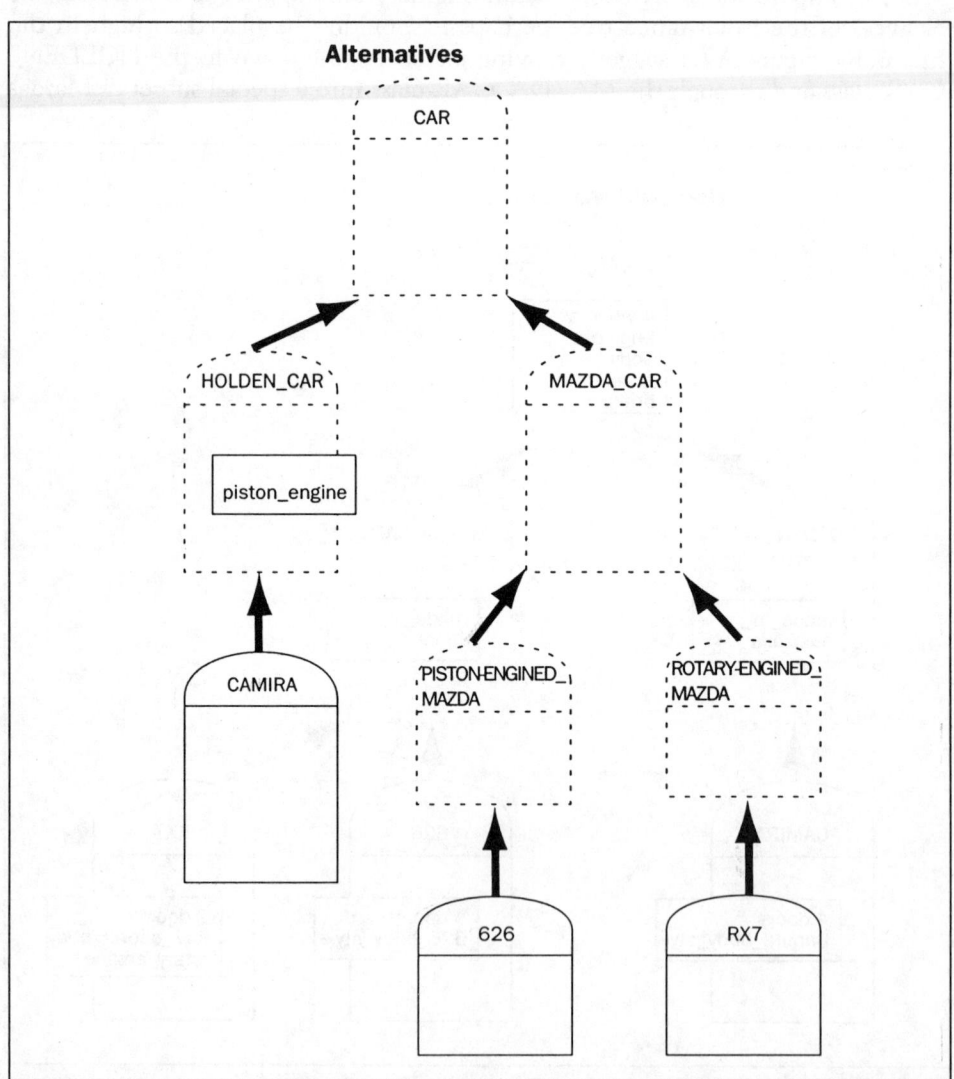

Figure A7.3

(as discussed by McGregor and Korson, 1993) is that of overlapping subtypes. In other words, our four basic subclasses are overlapping. *All* cars *must* inherit from *two* of these four. There are no examples inheriting from only one. Thus the four subclasses of class CAR don't so much as subset CAR but subset it *twice*—using two different characteristics with which to do the subsetting (here manufacturer and engine type).

The problem here is the implicit assumption that we should solve the problem using *only* inheritance. Inheritance is very seductive. Probably a better answer (and an approach that probably should be taken further, beyond the initial answer proposed here) is to represent the engine as a client–server relationship rather than trying to force it into the inheritance hierarchy. Thus a CAR **has-a** ENGINE (Figure A7.5), which can then be subsetted (subtyped) into classes PISTON-ENGINE and ROTARY-ENGINE. Now there are no overlapping subtypes.

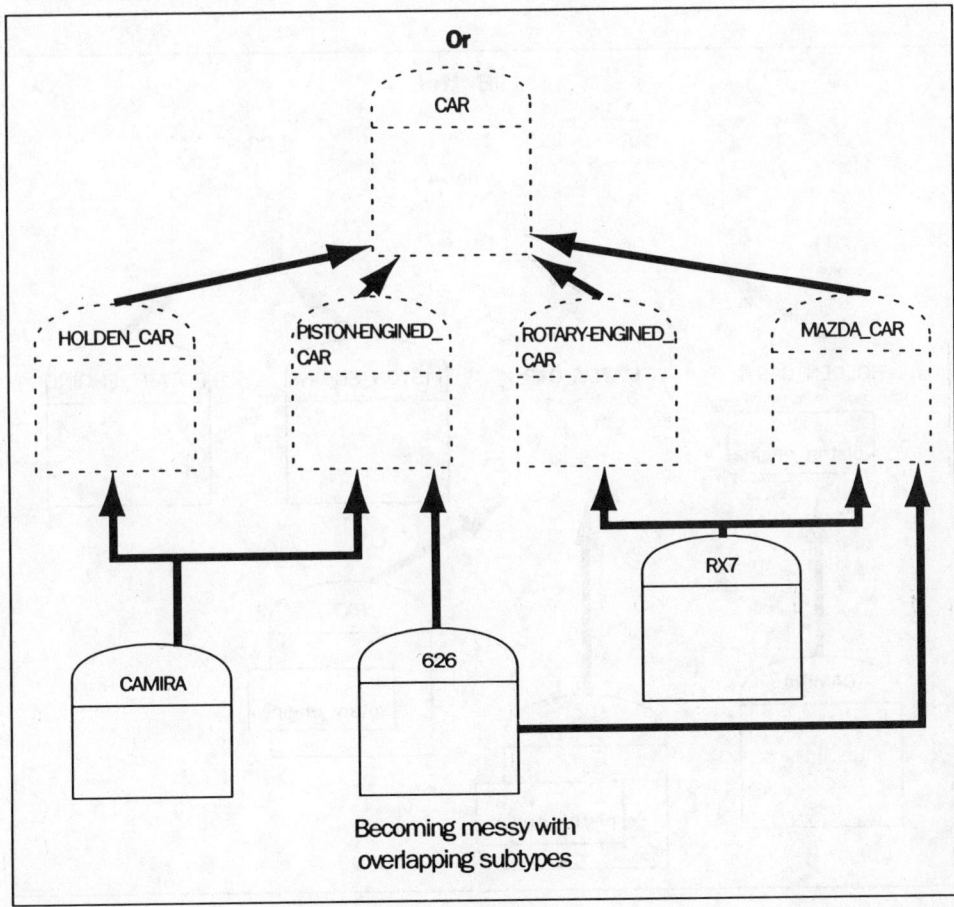

Figure A7.4

Exercise 8—set in Section 8.4

Question restated

The car market (Exercise 7 in Chapter 7) is widening. Customers can make a free choice between the Holden Camira, the Ford Falcon, the Mazda 626, and the Mazda RX7. Mechanics are needed to service the vehicles, but they need special training for the RX7. Further, there is rumored to be a new three-wheeler about to enter the market, but no one seems sure which manufacturer is producing it.

Develop an Implementation Phase O/C Model that will maintain sufficient flexibility and reusability to encompass these possible market directions.

Some suggestions for consideration in answering Exercise 8

One solution (probably a first iteration) is shown in Figure A8.1. As a first attempt, we keep the structure of Figure A7.5 but add the ability for cars to have varying numbers of wheels. This can be done by adding an abstract service

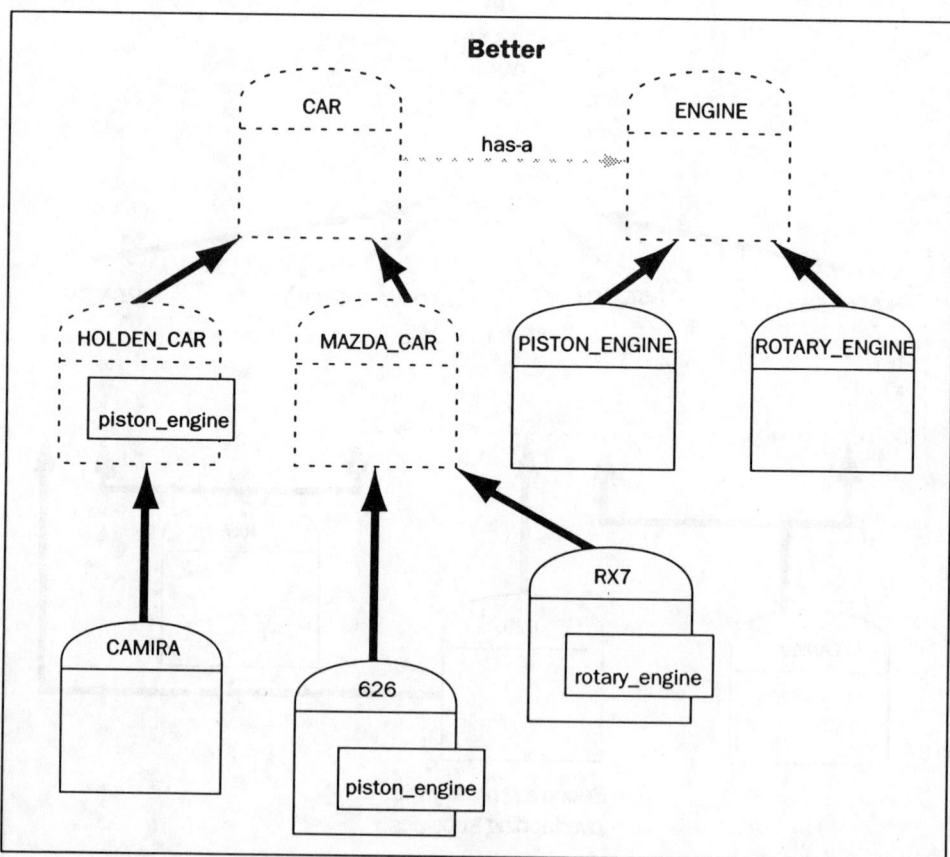

Figure A7.5

Suggested Answers to Study Examples 559

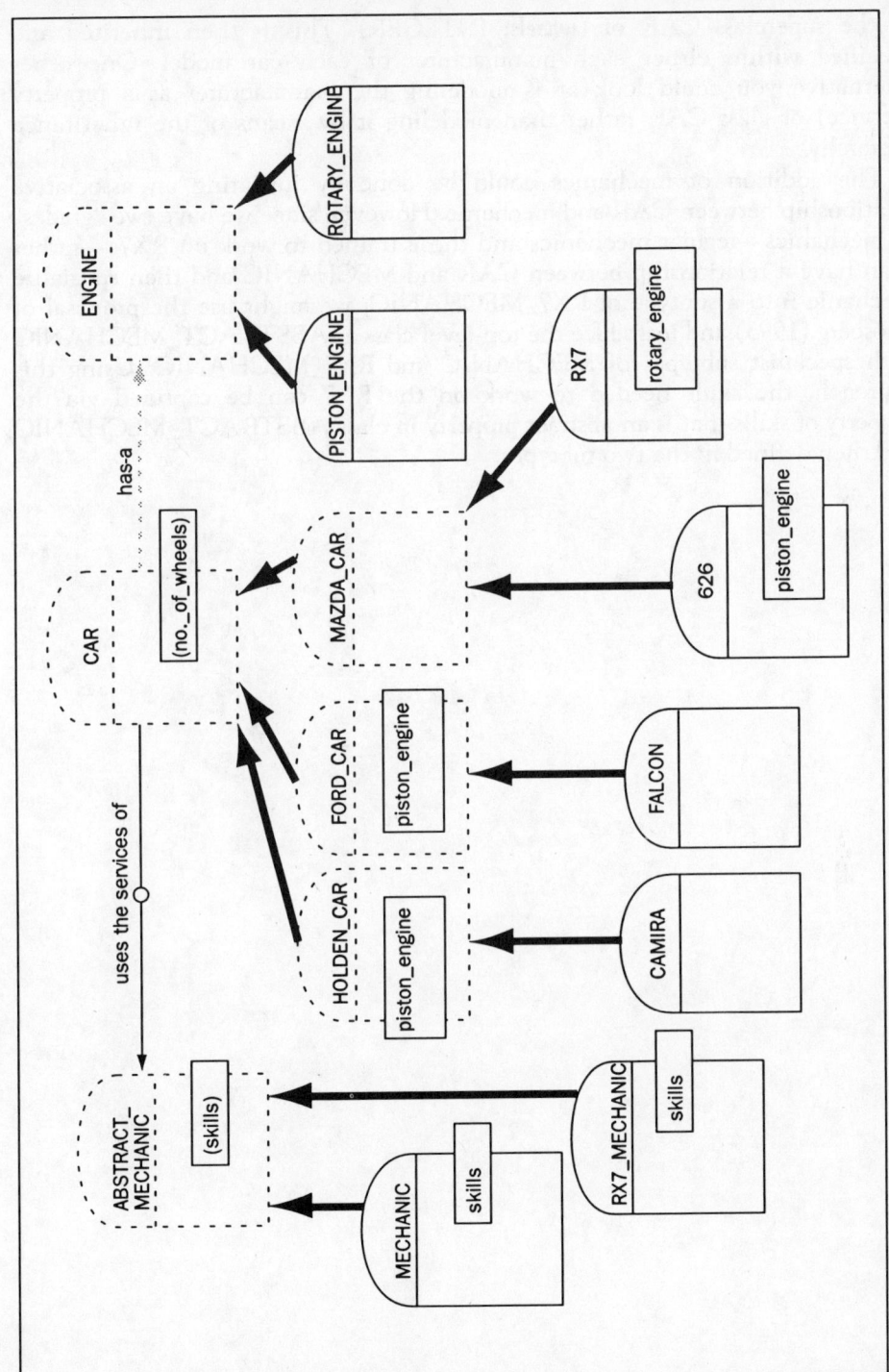

Figure A8.1

to the superclass CAR of (*wheels*: INTEGER). This is then inherited and specified within either each manufacturer or each car model. One other alternative you could look at is modeling the manufacturer as a property (service) of class CAR rather than modeling it by means of the inheritance hierarchy.

The addition of mechanics could be done by initiating an associative relationship between CAR and mechanic. However, since we have two "grades" of mechanics—regular mechanics and those trained to work on RX7s—rather than have a relationship between CAR and MECHANIC and then specialize mechanic into a subtype of RX7_MECHANIC, we might use the proposal of Grosberg (1993) and introduce the top-level class as ABSTRACT_MECHANIC with specialist subtypes of MECHANIC and RX7_MECHANIC. Using this approach, the skills needed to work on the RX7 can be captured via the property of skills that is an abstract property in class ABSTRACT_MECHANIC and then defined in the two subtypes.

Further Reading

There are a number of journals devoted to object technology:

Journal of Object-Oriented Programming
OOPS Messenger
Object Magazine
Hotline on Object-Oriented Technology (ceased publication early 1993)
Object-Oriented Systems (commenced publication 1994)

In addition, there are broadsheets on object technology such as *Object-Oriented Strategies*, and language-specific journals such as *The C++ Report*, *Smalltalk Report*, and *Eiffel Outlook*.

References

Abbott, R. J., 1983, Program design by informal English descriptions, *Comms. ACM*, 26(11), 882–894

Adams, M., and Lenkov, D., 1990, Object-oriented COBOL: the next generation, *Hotline on Obj.-Oriented Technology*, 2(2), 12–15

Adams, M., and Lenkov, D., 1992, Object-oriented COBOL: powerful new capabilities in a compatible form, *Object Magazine*, 1(6), 63–68

Adams, S., 1992a, Return on investment: development environments for the lifecycle (part 3 of a series), *Hotline on Obj.-Oriented Technology*, 3(12), 1, 7–8

Adams, S., 1992b, Constant quality management (part 4 of a series), *Hotline on Obj.-Oriented Technology*, 4(1), 5–8

Adams, S., and Burbeck, S., 1992, Software assets by design, *Object Magazine*, 2(4), A–C

Adelson, B., and Soloway, E., 1985, The role of domain experience in software design, *IEEE Trans. Software Eng.*, 11(11), 1351–1360

Ahmed, S., Wong, A., Sriram, D., and Logcher, R., 1992, Object-oriented database management systems for engineering: a comparison, *J. Obj.-Oriented Programming*, 5(3), 27–44

Alabiso, B., 1988, Transformation of data flow analysis models to object oriented design, *OOPSLA '88 Proceedings*, ACM, 335–353

Albrecht, A. J., 1979, Measuring application development productivity, *Proc. Joint SHARE/GUIDE/IBM Application Development Symposium*, October, 34–43

Albrecht, A. J., and Gaffney, J. E., Jr., 1983, Software function, source lines of code, and development effort prediction: a software science validation, *IEEE Trans. Software Eng.*, SE–9(6), 639–648

Anders, M., 1992, How frameworks enable application portability, *Hotline on Obj.-Oriented Technology*, 3(8), 13–15, 19

Antebi, M., 1990, Issues in teaching C++, *J. Obj.-Oriented Programming*, 3(4), 11–21

Arnold, J., and Early, M., 1988, Object-oriented design environments in process control, *Proceedings of the ISA/89, International Conference and Exhibition on Advances in Instrumentation and Control*, 44 (part 3), 1237–1245

Arnold, P., Bodoff, S., Coleman, D., Gilchrist, H., and Hayes, F., 1991, An evaluation of five object-oriented development methods, *JOOP Focus on Analysis and Design*, 107–121

Arnold, P., Bodoff, S., Coleman, D., Gilchrist, H., and Hayes, F., 1992, Criteria for comparing object-oriented development methods, paper prepared for Workshop on Object-Oriented Software Engineering Practice, Denver, February 1992

Arthur, L. J., 1985, *Measuring Programmer Productivity and Software Quality*, John Wiley and Sons, New York, 292pp

Atkinson, M., Bancilhon, F., DeWitt, D., Dittrich, K., Maier, D., and Zdonik, S., 1989, The Object-Oriented Database System Manifesto, Proceedings of the First International Conference on Deductive and Object-Oriented Databases, Kyoto, Japan

Atwood, T., 1990, Conversation with Tom Atwood, Chairman of Object Design, Inc., *J. Object-Oriented Programming*, 2(6), 78–80

Auer, K., 1989, Which object-oriented language should we choose?, *Hotline on Obj.-Oriented Technology*, 1(1), 1, 3–6

Bachman, B., and Marasco, J., 1992, Project results: benefits of OOD on large systems, Rational, Santa Clara, CA, 9pp

Baetjer, H., and Tulloh, W., 1992, Evolving markets for software components, *Hotline on Obj.-Oriented Technology*, 4(1), 9–11

Bailin, S. C., 1989, An object-oriented requirements specification method, *Comms. ACM*, 32(5), 608–623

Baker, A. L., and Zweben, S. H., 1980, A comparison of measures of control flow complexity, *IEEE Trans. Software Eng.*, SE–6(6), 506–512

Balda, D. M., and Gustafson, D. A., 1990, Cost estimation models for the reuse and prototype software development life-cycles, *ACM SIGSOFT Software Engineering Notes*, 15(3), 42–50

Baldwin, J. M. (ed.), 1940, *Dictionary of Philosophy and Psychology*, Peter Smith, New York

Balzer, R., 1981, Transformational implementation: an example, *IEEE Trans. Software Eng.*, SE–7(1), 3–14

Balzer, R., Cheatham, T. E., and Green, C., 1983, Software technology in the 1990s: using a new paradigm, *IEEE Computer*, 16(11), 39–45

Bancilhon, F., and Delobel, C., 1991, Recent advances in O-O DBMS, TOOLS '91 Tutorial Notes, 4th International Conference and Exhibition, March 4–8, Paris

Barber, G. R., 1991, The Object Management Group, *Hotline on Obj.-Oriented Technology*, 2(5), 17–19

Barnes, D., Bliss, P., Gould, B., and Vallentine, H., 1991, *Water and Wastewater Engineering Systems*, Pitman, Bath, UK, 573pp

Barrett, M. L., and Simsion, G. C., 1992, A review of diagramming notations for object oriented development, in TOOLS9 (ed. J. Potter and B. Meyer), Prentice Hall, UK

Barry, D., 1993, ODBMS feature listing, *Object Magazine*, 2(5), 48–53

Basili, V. R., 1980, Resource models, in *Tutorial on Models and Metrics for Software Management and Engineering*, (ed. V. Basili), IEEE, 4–9

Basili, V. R., and Turner, A. J., 1975, Iterative enhancement: a practical technique for software development, *IEEE Trans. Software Eng.*, SE–1(4), 390–396

Beck, K., and Cunningham, W., 1989, A laboratory for teaching object-oriented thinking, *OOPSLA '89, SIGPLAN Notices*, 24(10), 1–6

Beeri, C., 1990, A formal approach to object-oriented databases, *Data and Knowledge Engineering*, 5, 353–382

Belcher, K., 1991, Object-orientation—the COBOL approach, *Object Magazine*, 1(1), 74–83

Bellin, D., 1992, Object training: harder than it looks, *Hotline on Obj.-Oriented Technology*, 3(11), 4–5

Bennett, L., 1991, Accepting object technology, *Hotline on Obj.-Oriented Technology*, 3(2), 1–4

Berard, E. V., 1990a, Life-cycle approaches, *Hotline on Obj.-Oriented Technology*, 1(6), 1, 3–4

Berard, E. V., 1990b, Understanding the recursive/parallel life-cycle, *Hotline on Obj.-Oriented Technology*, 1(7), 10–13

Berard, E. V., 1990c, Object-oriented requirements analysis, *Hotline on Obj.-Oriented Technology*, 1(8), 9–11

Berard, E. V., 1991, Abstraction, encapsulation, and information hiding, unpublished manuscript (made available on usenet comp.object bulletin board)

Berard, E. V., 1992a, *A Comparison of OO Development Methodologies*, Berard Software Engineering, Maryland, USA

Berard, E. V., 1992b, *Essays on Object-Oriented Software Engineering*, Prentice Hall, Englewood Cliffs, New Jersey, 392pp

Berge, C., 1973, *Graphs and Hypergraphs*, North-Holland Publishing Co., London

Berman, C., and Gur, R., 1988, NAPS—a C++ project case study, *1988 USENIX C++ Conference*, 137–149

Beynon-Davies, P., 1992, Entity models to object models; object-oriented analysis and database design, *Inf. Software Technol.*, 34(4), 255–262

Bielak, R., 1992, Eiffel and object oriented database management systems (part 1), *Eiffel Outlook*, 2(4), 6–9

Birtwistle, G., Dahl, O. J., Myrhaug, B., and Nygaard, K., 1973, *Simula Begin*, Studentliteratur (Lund) and Auerbach Pub., New York

Blair, G. S., Gallagher, J. J., and Malik, J., 1989, Genericity vs inheritance vs delegation vs conformance vs ..., *J. Obj.-Oriented Programming*, 2(3), 11–17

Blair, G. S., Malik, J., Nicol, J. R., and Walpole, J., 1990, A synthesis of object-oriented and functional ideas in the design of a distributed software engineering environment, *Software Engineering Journal*, 5(3), 194–204

Blair, G., Gallagher, J., Hutchinson, D., and Sheperd, D., 1991, *Object-Oriented Languages, Systems and Applications*, Halstead Press, New York

Bliss, H. E., 1940–1953, Bibliographic classification/extended by systematic auxiliary schedule for composite specification and notation, Wilson, New York

Bobrow, D. G., 1989, The object of desire, *Datamation*, 35(9), 37–41

Boehm, B. W., 1975, The high cost of software, in *Practical Strategies for Developing Large Software Systems* (ed. E. Horowitz), Addison-Wesley, Reading, MA

Boehm, B. W., 1981, *Software Engineering Economics*, Prentice Hall, Englewood Cliffs, NJ

Boehm, B. W., 1986, A spiral model of software development and enhancement, ACM *Software Engineering Notes*, 11(4), 14–24

Boehm, B. W., 1988, A spiral model of software development and enhancement, *IEEE Computer*, 21(5), 61–72

Bollinger, T. B., and Pfleeger, S. L., 1990, Economics of reuse: issues and alternatives, *Inf. Software Technol.*, 32, 643–652

Bollobás, B., 1979, *Graph Theory: An Introductory Course*, Springer-Verlag, New York, 180pp

Booch, G., 1983, *Software Engineering with Ada*, 1st ed., Benjamin/Cummings, Menlo Park, CA, 580pp

Booch, G., 1986, Object-oriented development, *IEEE Trans. Software Eng.*, 12(2), 211–221

Booch, G., 1987, *Software Engineering with Ada*, 2nd ed., Benjamin/Cummings, Menlo Park, CA, 580pp

Booch, G., 1991, *Object Oriented Design with Applications*, Benjamin/Cummings, Menlo Park, CA, 580pp

Booch, G., 1992, The Booch method: notation, *Computer Language*, Part 1, September, 47–70; Part 2, October, 37–55

Booch, G., and Vilot, M., 1990a, Object-oriented design. Evolving an object-oriented design, *C++ Report*, 2(8), 11–13

Booch, G., and Vilot, M., 1990b, Object-oriented design. Inheritance relationships, *C++ Report*, 2(9), 8–11

Booch, G., and Vilot, M., 1990c, The design of the C++ Booch components, *SIGPLAN Notices*, 25(10), 1–11

Borland, 1990, World Tour, Sydney, Australia, October 4, 1990

Bourque, P., and Côté, V., An experiment in software sizing with structured analysis metrics, *J. Syst. Software*, 15(2), 159–172

Bracha, G., and Cook, W., 1990, Mixin-based inheritance, *ECOOP/OOPSLA '91 Procs.*, ACM, 303–311

Brachman, R. J., 1985, "I lied about the trees" or, defaults and definitions in knowledge representation, *AI Magazine*, 6(3), 80–93

Brooks, F. P., Jr., 1975, *The Mythical Man-Month*, Addison-Wesley, Reading, MA

Brown, R. G., 1992, From data modeling to object modeling, *Hotline on Obj.-Oriented Technology*, 3(8), 7–12

Byrne, S., 1992, GNU Smalltalk, *Smalltalk Report*, 1(8), 1–4

Caldiera, G., and Basili, V., 1991, Identifying and qualifying reusable software components, *IEEE Computing*, 24(2), 61–70

Cant, S. N., 1990, The cognitive complexity of programs developed using the object-oriented paradigm, unpubl. Honours Thesis, School of Information Systems, University of New South Wales, Australia, 173pp

Cant, S. N., Jeffery, D. R., and Henderson-Sellers, B., 1992, A conceptual model of cognitive complexity of elements of the programming process, CITR Report No. 57, University of New South Wales, Australia

Cant, S. N., Henderson-Sellers, B., and Jeffery, D. R., 1994, Application of cognitive complexity metrics to object-oriented programs, *J. Obj.-Oriented Programming*

Card, D. N., and Agresti, W. W., 1987, Resolving the Software Science anomaly, *J. Syst. Software*, 7(1), 29–35

Card, D. N., and Glass, R. L., 1990, *Measuring Software Design Quality*, Prentice Hall, Englewood Cliffs, NJ

Carrington, D., Duke, D., Duke, R., King, D., Rose, G., and Smith, G., 1990, Object Z: An object-oriented extension to Z, in *Formal Description Techniques II (FORTE 89)*, (ed. S. Vuong), North Holland Publishing Co., Amsterdam

Cattell, R. G. G., 1992, *Object Data Management: Object-Oriented and Extended Relational Database Systems*, Addison-Wesley, Sydney, 318pp

Chan, M. L., and Henderson-Sellers, B., 1990, Corporate object-oriented development environment (CODE), *ACM SIGSOFT, Software Engineering Notes*, 15(1), 42–43

Chen, P., 1976, The entity-relationship model: towards a unified view of data, *ACM Trans. on Database Systems*, 1(1), 9–36

Chidamber, S., and Kemerer, C., 1991, Towards a metric suite for object-oriented design, in *Proc. OOPSLA '91, Sigplan Notices*, 26(11), 197–211

Coad, P., 1991, OOA & OOD: a continuum of representation, *J. Obj.-Oriented Programming*, 3(6), 55–56

Coad, P., and Yourdon, E., 1990, *Object-Oriented Analysis*, 1st ed., Prentice Hall, Englewood Cliffs, NJ, 232pp

Coad, P., and Yourdon, E., 1991a, *Object-Oriented Analysis*, 2nd ed., Prentice Hall, Englewood Cliffs, NJ, 233pp

Coad, P., and Yourdon, E., 1991b, *Object-Oriented Design*, Prentice Hall, Englewood Cliffs, NJ, 197pp

Colbert, E., 1989, The object-oriented software development method: a practical approach to object-oriented development, *TRI–Ada 89 Proceedings*, 16pp

Coleman, D., and Hayes, F., 1991a, Lessons from Hewlett-Packard's experience of using object-oriented technology, *Technology of Object-oriented Languages and Systems, TOOLS 4* (ed. J Bézivin & B. Meyer), Prentice Hall, Hemel Hempstead, 327–333

Coleman, D., and Hayes, F., 1991b, Getting the best from objects: the experiences of Hewlett-Packard, *Hotline on Obj.-Oriented Technology*, 2(10), 6–12

Coleman, D., Hayes, F., and Bear, S., 1992, Introducing objectcharts or how to use statecharts in object-oriented design, *IEEE Trans. Software Engineering*, 18(1), 9–18

Coleman, D., Arnold, P., Bodoff, S., Dollin, C., Gilchrist, H., Hayes, F., and Jeremaes, P., 1993, *Object-Oriented Development: The Fusion Method*, Prentice Hall Inc.

Connell, J. M., 1991, Adopting objects—a path, *Hotline on Obj.-Oriented Technology*, 3(2), 5–8

Constantine, L. L., 1990a, public communication at The Object-Oriented Systems Symposium, Digital Consulting Pacific, Sydney, June

Constantine, L. L., 1990b, Objects by teamwork, *Hotline on Obj.-Oriented Technology*, 2(1), 1, 3–6

Constantine, L. L., 1992, CASE and cognition, *Computer Language*, 9(1), 110–112

Conte, S. D., Dunsmore, H. E., and Shen, V. Y., 1986, *Software Engineering Metrics and Models*, Benjamin/Cummings, Menlo Park, CA

Côté, V., and St-Denis, R., 1992, Bridging the gap between CASE tools and project management through a decision support system based on metrics, *IEEE Compsac*, 300–309

Côté, V., Bourque, P., Oligny, S., and Rivard, N., 1988, Software metrics: an overview of recent results, *J. Syst. Software*, 8(2), 121–131

Coulter, N. S., 1983, Software Science and cognitive psychology, *IEEE Trans. Software Eng.*, SE-9(2), 166–171

Cox, B. J., 1986, *Object Oriented Programming: An Evolutionary Approach*, Addison-Wesley, Reading, MA, 274pp

Cox, B. J., 1988, *Objective-C Interpreter Version 4.0 User's Reference Manual*, Stepstone Inc., Sandy Hook, CT

Cox, B. J., 1990a, There is a silver bullet, *Byte*, 15(10), 209–218

Cox, B. J., 1990b, Planning the software industrial revolution, *IEEE Software*, 7(11), 25–33

Cox, B. J., 1992, What if there is a silver bullet?, *J. Obj.-Oriented Programming*, 5(3), 8–9, 76

Curtis, B., 1979, In search of software complexity, in *Workshop on Quantitative Software Models*, IEEE, New York, 95–106

Davis, A. M., 1988, A taxonomy for the early stages of the software development life cycle, *J. Systems and Software*, 8, 297–311

Davis, A., Bersoff, E., and Comer, E., 1988, A strategy for comparing alternative software development life cycle models, *IEEE Trans. Software Eng.*, 14(10), 1453–1460

Davis, J. S., 1984, Chunks: a basis for complexity measurement, *Information Processing and Management*, 20(1), 119–127

de Champeaux, D., 1991, Object-oriented analysis and top-down software development, *European Conference on Object-oriented Programming 1991, Lecture Notes in Computer Science*, No. 512, Springer-Verlag, Berlin, 360–376 de Champeaux, D., Burnham, J., and Wirfs-Brock, R., 1991, Object-oriented Domain Analysis Workshop, report on the Domain Analysis Workshop, OOPSLA'91

de Champeaux, D., and Faure, P., 1992, A comparative study of object-oriented analysis methods, *J. Object-Oriented Programming*, 5(1), 21–33

Dellinger, R. L., 1992, Achieving zero-cost portability today, *Hotline on Obj.-Oriented Technology*, 4(2), 1, 8–9

DeMarco, T., 1978, *Structured Analysis and System Specification*, Yourdon Press, New York

Deming, W. E., 1981, Improvement of quality and productivity through action by management, *National Productivity Review*, Winter 1981/82, 12–22

Dennis, S., 1992, Implementing objects in a real-time multi-processor system, 1992 Object-Oriented Conference, Sydney, May 4–5, Technology Training Corporation

de Paula, E. G., and Nelson, M. L., 1991, Designing a class hierarchy, *Technology of Object-Oriented Languages and Systems: TOOLS5* (ed. T. Korson, V. Vaishnavi, and B. Meyer), Prentice Hall, New York, 203–218

Dewey, M., 1876, Classification and subject index: for cataloguing and arranging the books and pamphlets of a library, Amherst, MA

Dewhurst, S. C., and Stark, K. T., 1987, Out of the C world comes C++, *Computer Language*, 4(2), 29–36

Dictionary of Computing, (2nd ed.), 1986, Oxford University Press, Oxford, 416pp

Dittrich, K. R. (ed.), 1988, *Advances in Object-Oriented Database Systems*, Lecture Notes in Computer Science, 334, Springer-Verlag, Berlin, 373pp

Dobbie, G., 1991, Object oriented database systems: a survey, Procs. 14th Aust. Comp. Sci. Conf., University of New South Wales, Feb. 6–8, 1991, *Australian Computer Science Communications*, 13(1), 10.1–10.11

Dock, P., 1992a, OOD: research or ready?, *Hotline on Obj.-Oriented Technology*, 3(9), 7–9

Dock, P., 1992b, Object methods, *Hotline on Obj.-Oriented Technology*, 3(12), 4–6

Drake, J. M., Xie, W., and Tsai, W. T., 1992a, Document-Driven Analysis: description and formalism, *J. Obj.-Oriented Programming*, 5(7), 33–50

Drake, J., Tsai, W. T., Lee, H. J., and Zualkernan, I., 1992b, A case study to evaluate three object-oriented analysis techniques, paper presented at *Workshop on Object-Oriented Software Engineering Practice*, Denver, February

Dreger, J. B., 1989, *Function Point Analysis*, Prentice Hall, Englewood Cliffs, NJ

D'Souza, D., 1992, Teacher! Teacher!, *J. Obj.-Oriented Programming*, 5(2), 12–17

Dué, R. T., 1993, In pursuit of object engineering, *Hotline on Object-Oriented Technology* 4(4), 7–9

Duff, C., and Howard, B., 1990, Migration patterns, *Byte*, 15(10), 223–232

Duke, R., King, P., Rose, G., and Smith, G., 1991, The Object-Z Specification Language Version 1, Software Verification Research Centre, University of Queensland, Technical Report No. 91-1

Dunsmore, H. E., 1984, Software metrics: an overview of an evolving methodology, *Information Processing and Management*, 20(1–2), 183–192

Eckel, B., 1989, *Using C++*, McGraw-Hill, Berkeley, CA, 617pp

Edwards, J., 1989, Lessons learned in more than ten years of practical application of the object-oriented paradigm, in *Procs. CASExpo–Europe*, London

Edwards, J., 1990, Ptech: object-oriented methods and tools, Associative Design Technology Seminar, Sydney

Edwards, J. M., 1992, Development of an object-oriented modelling methodology and its application to a water resources problem, University of New South Wales PhD thesis (unpubl.), Sydney, Australia

Edwards, J., Gallagher, D., and Henderson-Sellers, B., 1991, A seamless integration of engineering and economic models for the water industry, *International Symposium on Hydrology and Water Resources (IAHS)*, Perth, October, vol. 2, 359–364

Edwards, J. M., and Henderson-Sellers, B., 1991, A coherent notation for object-oriented software engineering, *Technology of Object-Oriented Languages and Systems: TOOLS5* (ed. T. Korson, V. Vaishnavi, and B. Meyer), Prentice Hall, New York, 405–426

Edwards, J. M., and Henderson-Sellers, B., 1993a, A graphical notation for object-oriented analysis and design, *J. Object-Oriented Programming*, 5(9), 53–74

Edwards, J. M., and Henderson-Sellers, B., 1993b, Application of an object-oriented analysis and design methodology to engineering cost management, *J. Systems Software*, 23(2), 123–138

Ejiogu, L. O., 1991, *Software Engineering with Formal Metrics*, QED Technical Publishing Group, Boston, 334pp

Elshoff, J. L., 1978, An investigation into the effects of the counting method used on Software Science Measurement, *ACM SIGPLAN Notices*, 13(2), 30–45

Emerson, T. J., 1984, A discriminant metric for module cohesion, *Int. Conf. SE*, 1984, 294–303

Evangelist, W. M., 1983, Software complexity metric sensitivity to program structuring rules, *J. Systems Software*, 3(3), 231–243

Evangelist, W., 1984, An analysis of control flow complexity, COMPSAC 84, IEEE, 388–396

Fedra, K., and Loucks, D., 1985, Interactive computer technology for planning and policy modelling, *Water Res. Res.*, 21(2), 114–122

Feghali, I., and Watson, A. H., 1994, Clarification concerning modularization and McCabe's cyclomatic complexity, *Comm. ACM*, 37(4), 91–92

Feldman, P., and Miller, D., 1986, Entity model clustering: structuring a data model by abstraction, *Computer Journal*, 29, 348–360

Fenton, N. E., 1991, *Software Metrics: A Rigorous Approach*, Chapman and Hall, London, 337pp

Fenton, N. E., and Kaposi, A. A., 1987, Metrics and software structure, *Inf. Software Technol.*, 29(6), 301–320

References

Fichman, R. G., and Kemerer, C. F., 1993, Adoption of software engineering process innovations: the case of object-orientation, *Sloan Management Review*

Fiedler, S. P., 1989, Object-oriented unit testing, *Hewlett-Packard Journal*, April, 69–74

Firesmith, D. G., 1991, ObjectMaker 2.0: The power of choice, customization and extensibility, *Object Magazine*, 1(4), 70–72

Firesmith, D. G., 1992a, ADM3: a language-independent, object-oriented method for large, real-time systems development, presented at Methodologies and Tools for Real-Time and Object-Oriented Systems Conference 1992, 26pp

Firesmith, D. G., 1992b, ADM–3—a third generation, object-oriented software development method, 1992 Object-Oriented Conference, Sydney, May 4–5, Technology Training Corporation

Firesmith, D. G., 1993, *Object-Oriented Requirements Analysis and Logical Design: A Software Engineering Approach*, John Wiley & Sons Inc., New York, 575pp

Firesmith, D. G., 1994, *Object-Oriented Methods, Standards, and Procedures*, Prentice Hall, US

Foote, B., 1991, A fractal model of the lifecycle of reusable objects, unpublished manuscript

Fortran Forum, 1989, Fortran 8X Draft, May 1989, *SIGPLAN Special Interest Publication on Fortran*, 8(4) (whole issue)

Foskett, D. J., and Bury, S., 1982, Concept organisation and Universal Classifications Systems

Fowler, M., 1991, The use of object-oriented analysis in medical informatics for large integrated systems, *Technology of Object-oriented Languages and Systems 4*, Prentice Hall, UK, 203–214

Frakes, W. B., and Gandel, P. B., 1990, Representing reusable software, *Inf. Software Technol.*, 32, 653–664

Frank, M., 1991, *Object Oriented Design*, book review, *Object Magazine*, 1(4), 68–69

Freeman, C., and Henderson-Sellers, B., 1991, OLMS: the Object Library Management System, *Technology of Object-Oriented Languages and Systems: TOOLS6* (ed. B. Meyer, J. Potter, and M. Tokoro), Prentice Hall, Sydney

Freiman, F. R., and Park, R. E., 1979, Price Software model version 3: an overview, in *Proc. IEEE-PINY Workshop Quantitative Software Models*, October, 32–41

Friedman, R., Ansell, C., and Diamond, S., 1984, The use of models for water resources management, planning and policy, *Water Res. Res.*, 21(7), 793–802

Gabriel, R. P., 1992, Is worse really better?, *J. Obj.-Oriented Programming*, 5(6), 6

Ghezzi, C., Jazayeri, M., and Mandrioli, D., 1991, *Fundamentals of Software Engineering*, Prentice Hall, Englewood Cliffs, NJ

Gibbs, S., Tsichritzis, D., Casais, E., Nierstrasz, O., and Pintado, X., 1990, Class management for software communities, *Comms. ACM*, 33(9), 90–103

Gibson, E., 1990, Objects—born and bred, *Byte*, 15(10), 245–254

Gibson, E., 1991, Flattening the learning curve: educating object-oriented developers, *J. Obj.-Oriented Programming*, 3(6), 24–29

Goldberg, A., 1985, *Smalltalk-80: The Interactive Programming Environment*, Addison-Wesley, Reading, MA

Goldberg, A., 1991a, Object-oriented project management, TOOLS '91 Tutorial Notes, Paris, March

Goldberg, A., 1991b, The cost of reuse, presentation at TOOLS Pacific 91, December 3, Sydney, Australia

Goldberg, A., 1993, Wishful thinking, *Object Magazine*, 3(1), 88, 87

Goldberg, A., and Robson, D., 1983, *Smalltalk-80: The Language and Its Implementation*, Addison-Wesley, Reading, MA

Goldberg, A., and Rubin, K., 1990, Talking to project managers: organizing for reuse, *Hotline on Obj.-Oriented Technology*, 1(10), 7–11

Gole, A., 1991, Moving from Pascal to C++ (Part 3), *Hotline on Obj.-Oriented Technology*, 2(6), 12–14

Gomaa, H., 1990, Criteria for structuring a system into objects, *Workshop on Finding the Object, ECOOP/OOPLSA 1990* (ed. M. Whiting and D. DeVaney), Ottawa, Canada

Gomaa, H., 1992, An object-oriented domain analysis and modeling method for software reuse, *Procs. HICSS 1992 Conference*, vol. II, Decision Support and Knowledge-Based Systems, IEEE, 46–56

Gorlen, K. E., Orlow, S. M., and Plexico, P. S., 1990, *Data Abstraction and Object-Oriented Programming in C++*, John Wiley and Sons, Chichester, UK, 403pp.

Graham, I., 1991, *Object-Oriented Methods*, Addison-Wesley, Wokingham, UK, 410pp

Graham, I., 1992, Interoperation: combining object-oriented applications with conventional IT, *Object Magazine*, 2(4), 36–37

Graham, I. M., 1994, *Migrating to Object Technology*, Addison–Wesley, Wokingham, UK

Griss, M. L., 1991, Software reuse at Hewlett-Packard, HPL-91-38, 8pp

Griss, M. L., 1992, Software reuse at Hewlett-Packard, presented at Procs Workshop on Object-Oriented Software Engineering Practice, Denver, February

Griss, M. L., Adam, S. S., Baetjer, H. Jr., Cox, B. J., and Goldberg, A., 1991, The economics of software reuse, *Procs. OOPSLA '91*, ACM, 264–270

Grochow, J. M., 1992, Developing strategic business systems using object technology, *Hotline on Obj.-Oriented Technology*, 3(11), 1, 10–12

Grosberg, J. A., 1993, Comments on considering "class" harmful, *Comms. ACM.*, 36(1), 113–114

Guariso, G., and Werthner, H., 1989, *Environmental Decision Support Systems*, Ellis Horwood Ltd., Chichester, England, 240pp

Guttman, M. K., and Matthews, J. R., 1992, Managing a large project: case study of a long-term project at NCR, *Object Magazine*, 2(4), 75–78, 81

Haber, R. N., and Wilkinson, L., 1982, Perceptual components of computer displays, IEEE *Computer Graphics and Applications*, 2(3), 23–35

Halstead, M. H., 1977, *Elements of Software Science*, Elsevier Scientific Publishing Company, Amsterdam

Hamer, P. G., and Frewin, G. D., 1982, M. H. Halstead's Software Science—a critical examination, *Procs. IEEE Sixth Int. Conf. on Software Engineering*, 197–206

Hansen, W. J., 1978, Measurement of program complexity by the pair (cyclomatic number, operator count), *ACM SIGPLAN Notices*, April, 29–33

Harary, F., 1969, *Graph Theory*, Addison-Wesley, Reading, MA, 274pp

Harel, D., 1987, Statecharts: a visual formalism for complex systems, *Sci. Computer Program.*, 8, 231–274

Harmon, P., 1990, Object-oriented systems, *Intelligent Software Strategies*, 6(9), 1–16

Harmon, P., and Sawyer, B., 1991, *Object Craft: A Graphical Programming Tool for Object-Oriented Applications*, Addison-Wesley, Reading, MA, 289pp

Harris, W., 1991, Contravariance for the rest of us, *J. Obj.-Oriented Programming*, 4(7), 10–18

Harrold, M. J., and McGregor, J. D., 1992, Toward a testing methodology for object-oriented software systems, paper presented at *Workshop on Object-Oriented Software Engineering Practice*, Denver, February

Hawryszkiewycz, I. T., 1988, *Information Systems Analysis and Design*, Prentice Hall, Sydney, 373pp

Hayes, F., and Coleman, D., 1991, Coherent models for object-oriented analysis, *Procs. OOPSLA '91*, ACM, 171–183

Heintz, T. J., 1991, Object-oriented databases and their impact on future business database applications, *Inf. Management*, 20, 95–103

Henderson-Sellers, B., 1990, Three methodological frameworks for object-oriented systems development, *Procs. 3rd Intl. Conf., TOOLS3*, (ed. J. Bézivin, B. Meyer, J. Potter, and M. Tokoro), Sydney, 118–131

Henderson-Sellers, B., 1991a, Some metrics for object-oriented software engineering, *Technology of Object-Oriented Languages and Systems: TOOLS6* (ed. B. Meyer, J. Potter, and M. Tokoro), Prentice Hall, Sydney, 131–139

Henderson-Sellers, B., 1991b, Hybrid object-oriented/functional decomposition methodologies for the software engineering lifecycle, *Hotline on Obj.-Oriented Technology*, 2(7), 1–8

Henderson-Sellers, B., 1991c, Parallels between object-oriented software development and total quality management, *Journal of Information Technology*, 6(3), 63–67

Henderson-Sellers, B., 1992a, *A Book of Object-Oriented Knowledge*, Prentice Hall, 297pp

Henderson-Sellers, B., 1992b, Object-oriented information systems: an introductory tutorial, *Australian Computer Journal*, 24(1), 12–24

Henderson-Sellers, B., 1992c, Modularization and McCabe's cyclomatic complexity, *Comms. ACM: Technical Correspondence*, 35(12), 17–19

Henderson-Sellers, B., 1993, The economics of reusing library classes, *J. Obj.-Oriented Programming*, 6(4), 43–50

Henderson-Sellers, B., and Constantine, L. L., 1991, Object-oriented development and functional decomposition, *J. of Obj.-Oriented Programming*, 3(5), 11–17

Henderson-Sellers, B., and Edwards, J. M., 1990, The object-oriented systems life cycle, *Comms. ACM*, 33(9), 142–159

Henderson-Sellers, B., and Edwards, J. M., 1993a, The fountain model for object-oriented system development, *Object Mag.*, 3(2), 71–79

Henderson-Sellers, B., and Edwards, J. M., 1993b, The O-O-O methodology for the object-oriented life cycle, *SIGSOFT Software Engineering Notes*, 18(4), 54–60

Henderson-Sellers, B., and Freeman, B., 1992, Cataloguing and Classification for Object Libraries, *ACM SIGSOFT Software Engineering Notes*, 17(1), 62–64

Henderson-Sellers, B., and Pant, Y. R., 1993, When should we generalize classes to make them reusable?, *Object Magazine*, 3(4), 73–75

Henderson-Sellers, B., and Tegarden, D., 1994, Clarification concerning modularization and McCabe's cyclomatic complexity. Response, *Comms. ACM*, 37(4), 92–94

Henderson-Sellers, B., and Tegarden, D., 1993, The application of cyclomatic complexity to multiple entry/exit modules, Centre for Information Technology Research Report No. 93/2, University of New South Wales, Sydney, Australia, 28pp

Henderson-Sellers, B., Edwards, J. M., and Constantine, L. L., 1992, *The O-O-O/EUON Handbook*, Centre for Information Technology Research Report No. 58, University of New South Wales, Sydney, Australia, 80pp

Henry, S., and Kafura, D., 1981, Software structure metrics based on information flow, *IEEE Trans. Software Eng.*, 7(5), 510–518

Hoare, C. A. R., 1974, Monitors: an operating system structuring concept, *Comms. ACM.*, 17(10), 549–557

Hofstadter, D. R., 1979, *Gödel, Escher, Bach: An Eternal Golden Braid*, Viking Penguin Books, New York, 777pp

Hong, S., van den Goor, G., and Brinkkemper, S., 1992, A comparison of object-oriented analysis and design methodologies, in *Procs. CSN'92—Computing Science in the Netherlands* (ed. J. Dietz), Utrecht

HOOD Working Group, 1989, *HOOD Reference Manual 3.0*, Report WME/89-173/JB, Noordwijk, Netherlands

Hopkins, D., 1990a, An Eiffel experience, *ACS Bulletin* (Victoria Branch), June, 5–8

Hopkins, J. W., 1990b, Object-oriented programming: the next step up, *J. Obj.-Oriented Programming*, 3(1), 66–68

Hopkins, T., and Warboys, B., 1990, Asset management and object-oriented technology, *Hotline on Obj.-Oriented Technology*, 1(11), 12–13

Howard, G. S., 1988, Object oriented programming explained, *J. Systems Management*, 39(7), 13–19

Howard, R., 1992a, What TQM means for OT, *Hotline on Obj.-Oriented Technology*, 3(11), 13–15

Howard, R., 1992b, Eiffel key "product of the year" from Bytex (interview with Roger Osmond of Bytex), *Eiffel Outlook*, 2(4), 20–22

Hughes, J. G., 1991, *Object-Oriented Databases*, Prentice Hall, New York, 280pp

Humphrey, W., 1989, *Managing the Software Process*, Addison-Wesley, Reading, MA

Humphrys, M., 1991, The objective evidence. A real-life comparison of procedural and object-oriented programming, IISL Innovative Solutions Project, IBM Ireland Information Services Ltd (IISL), internal report

Huneke, I., 1991, A review of "Object Oriented Modelling and Design", *OOPS Newsletter*, BCS SIG, Autumn

Hunt, B., 1992, Choosing an object-oriented language, *Hotline on Obj.-Oriented Technology*, 3(12), 9–12

Hurson, A. R., Pakzad, S. H., and Cheng, J-B., 1993, Object-oriented database management systems: evolution and performance issues, *IEEE Computer*, 26(2), 48–60

Iivari, J., 1990, Hierarchical spiral model for information systems and software development. Part 2: design process, *Inf. Software Technol.*, 32(7), 450–458

Iivari, J., 1991, Object-oriented information systems analysis: a framework for object identification, *Procs. HICSS-92*, IEEE, San Diego, 205–218

Ince, D., 1990, Software metrics: an introduction, *Inf. Soft. Technol.*, 32, 297–303

International Federation for Documentation, 1943 to date (irregular), Brussels Universal Decimal Classification. Complete English ed., 4th International ed., British Standards Institute, London

Iscoe, N., 1988, Domain-specific reuse: an object-oriented and knowledge-based approach, 299–308, in *IEEE Tutorial: Software Reuse: Emerging Technology* (ed. W. Tracz), IEEE Computer Society Press, Washington DC

ISE, 1988, *Eiffel: An Introduction*, Interactive Software Engineering, Technical Report, TR–EI–3/GI

Jacobson, I., Christerson, M., Jonsson, P., and Övergaard, G., 1992, *Object-Oriented Software Engineering: A Use Case Driven Approach*, Addison Wesley, Reading, MA, 524pp

Jeffery, D. R., 1987a, A software development productivity model for MIS environments, *J. Syst. Software*, 7(2), 115–125

Jeffery, D. R., 1987b, Time relationship between team size, experience, and attitudes and software development productivity, *IEEE COMPSAC 1987*, 2–8

Jeffery, D. R., 1987c, Time-sensitive cost models in the commercial MIS environment, *IEEE Trans. Software Eng.*, SE13(7), 852–859

Jeffery, D. R., 1990, Software metrics, Half-day seminar presented before the 5th Australian Software Engineering Conference (ASWEC '90), IREE, Sydney, May 22

Jeffery, D. R., and Low, G., 1989, Generic estimation tools in the management of software development, *Procs 1989 Annual Meeting of the Decision Sciences Institute*, November 20–22, 1989, New Orleans, 596–598

Johnson, R. E., and Foote, B., 1988, Designing reusable classes, *J. Obj.-Oriented Programming*, 1(2), 22–35

Joiner, B. L., and Scholtes, P. R., 1986, The quality manager's new job, *Quality Progress*, October, 52–56

Jones, C., 1986, *Programming Productivity*, McGraw-Hill

Jones, C. B, 1991, Does the O-O community need formal methods, *Technology of Object-oriented Languages and Systems 4*, Prentice Hall, 15–18

Jones, R., 1992, Moving up to Eiffel 3, *J. Obj.-Oriented Programming*, 5(5), 69–76

Jones, T. C., 1988, A short history of function points and feature points, ACI Computer Services, 45pp

Joyner, I., 1992, C++??, in *TOOLS9* (ed. J. Potter and B. Meyer), Prentice Hall, UK

Kandibur, M., 1992, Victory is the main object in war, *Object Magazine*, 2(4), 28–30

Kearney, J. K., Sedlmeyer, R. L., Thompson, W. B., Gray, M. A., and Adler, M. A., 1986, Software complexity measurement, *Comms. ACM*, 29(11), 1044–1050

Keller, S., 1991, Moving from Pascal to C++: Part 2, *Hotline on Obj.-Oriented Technology*, 2(5), 14–16

Khoshafian, S., 1990, Insight into object-oriented databases, *Inf. Software Technol.*, 32(4), 274–289

Khoshafian, S., 1993, *Object-Oriented Database*, John Wiley & Sons, New York, 362pp

Kilian, M., 1991, A note on type composition and reusability, *OOPS Messenger*, 2(3), 24–32

Kilov, H., 1990, Generic information modeling concepts: a reusable component library, *Technology of Object-oriented Languages and Systems 4*, Prentice Hall, 187–201

Kilov, H., 1992, From OSI systems management to an interoperable object model: behavioral specification of (generic) relationships, in *Procs. Third Telecommunications Information Networking Architecture Workshop*, January 21–23, Narita, Japan, 23-3-1–23-3-8

Kim, W., and Lochovsky, F. H. (eds.), 1989, *Object-Oriented Concepts, Databases, and Applications*, ACM Press, New York/Addison-Wesley, Reading, MA, 602pp

Kirslis, P., undated, A style for writing C++ classes

Kitchenham, B. A., and Linkman, S. J., 1990, Design metrics in practice, *Inf. Soft. Technol.*, 32, 304–310

Kitchenham, B. A., and Taylor, N. R., 1985, Software project development cost estimation, *J. Systems and Software*, 5, 267–278

Kitchenham, B. A., and Walker, J. G., 1986, The meaning of quality, in *Proc. Conf. Software Engineering 86*, 393–406

Knudsen, J. L., 1988, Name collisions in multiple classification hierarchies, European Conference on Object-Oriented Programming (ECOOP'88), Oslo, Norway, 93–109

Koenig, A., and Stroustrup, B., 1990, Exception handling for C++, *J. Obj.-Oriented Programming*, 3(2), 16–33

Korson, T., and McGregor, J. D., 1990, Object-oriented software design: a tutorial, *Comms. ACM*, 33(9), 40–60

Korson, T., and McGregor, J. D., 1992, Technical criteria for the specification and evaluation of object-oriented libraries, *Software Eng. J.*, 7(2), 85–94

Lahire, P., and Brissi, P., 1991, An integrated query language for handling persistent objects in Eiffel, in *Technology of Object-Oriented Languages and Systems: TOOLS4* (ed. J. Bézivin and B. Meyer), Prentice Hall, New York, 101–114

LaLonde, W., and Pugh, J., 1990, Smalltalk as the first programming language: the Carleton experience, *J. Obj.-Oriented Programming*, 3(4), 60–65

LaLonde, W., and Pugh, J., 1991, Subclassing ≠ subtyping ≠ **is-a**, *J. Obj.-Oriented Programming*, 3(5), 57–62

Laranjeira, L. A., 1990, Software size estimation of object-oriented systems, *IEEE Trans. Software Eng.*, 16(5), 510–522

Leathers, B., 1990a, Cognos and Eiffel: a cautionary tale, *Hotline on Obj.-Oriented Technology*, 1(9), 1, 3, 6–8

Leathers, B., 1990b, OOPSLA panel: OOP in the real world, *ECOOP/OOPSLA '90 Proceedings*, ACM Press, New York, 299–302

Leathers, B., 1992, Thinking the unthinkable: reducing the risk of failure, *Hotline on Obj.-Oriented Technology*, 3(6), 1, 4–6

Leavens, G. T., 1991, Modular specification and verification of object-oriented programs, *IEEE Software*, 8(7), July, 72–80

Lehman, M. M., Stenning, V., and Turski, W. M., 1984, Another look at software design methodology, ACM *Software Engineering Notes*, 9(2), 38–53

Letovsky, S., and Soloway, E., 1986, Delocalized plans and program comprehension, *IEEE Software*, 3(3), 41–49

Levitin, A. V., 1986, How to measure size, and how not to, in *Proc. Tenth COMPSAC 1986*, 314–318.

Lewis, J. A., Henry, S. M., Kafura, D. G., and Schulman, R. S., 1992, On the relationship between the object-oriented paradigm and software reuse: an empirical investigation, *J. Obj.-Oriented Programming*, 5(4), 35–41

Lieberherr, K. J., and Holland, I. M., 1989, Assuring good style for object-oriented programs, *IEEE Software*, 6(9), September, 38–48

Lieberherr, K. J., Holland, I., and Riel, A., 1988, Object-oriented programming: an objective sense of style, *Procs. OOPSLA '88*, ACM Press, 323–334

Lippman, S. B., 1989, *C++ Primer*, Addison-Wesley, Reading, MA, 464pp

Lister, A. M., 1982, Software Science—the emperor's new clothes?, *Aust. Computer J.*, 14(2), 66–70

Loomis, M. E. S., 1990a, OODBMS: The basics, *J. Obj.-Oriented Programming*, 3(1), 77, 79–81

Loomis, M. E. S., 1990b, OODBMS vs. relational, *J. Obj.-Oriented Programming*, 3(2), 79–82

Loomis, M. E. S., 1991, Integrating objects with relational technology, *Object Magazine*, 1(2), 46–60

Loomis, M. E. S., 1993, Object and relational co-operation, *Object Magazine*, 2(5), 35–40

Loomis, M. E. S., Shah, A. V., and Rumbaugh, J. E., 1987, An object modeling technique for conceptual design, *Procs. ECOOP '87*, Springer, New York, 192–202

Lorenz, M., 1991, Real-world reuse, *J. Obj.-Oriented Programming*, 4(7), 35–39

Lorenz, M., 1993, *Object-Oriented Software Development: A Practical Guide*, Prentice Hall, Englewood Cliffs, NJ, 227pp

Love, T., 1993, *Object Lessons*, SIGS Books, New York, 266pp

Loy, P. H., 1990, A comparison of object-oriented and structured development methods, *ACM SIGSOFT, Software Engineering Notes*, 15(1), 44–48

Ma, J., and Edwards, J. M., 1991, Using a ROBM for object library management, *Technology of Object-Oriented Languages and Systems: TOOLS6* (ed. B. Meyer, J. Potter, and M. Tokoro), Prentice Hall, Sydney

McCabe, T. J., 1976, A complexity measure, *IEEE Trans. Soft. Eng.*, 2(4), 308–320

McCabe, T. J., and Butler, C. W., 1989, Design complexity measurement and testing, *Comms. ACM*, 32(12), 1415–1425

McCullough, P., and Deshler, N., 1990, WyCASH+: an application built within an OOP environment, *Hotline on Obj.-Oriented Technology*, 1(10), 1, 3–4

McCullough, P., Atkinson, B., Goldberg, A., Griss, M., and Morrison, J., 1992, Reuse: truth or fiction (panel), *SIGPLAN Notices (Procs. OOPSLA '92)*, 27(10), 41–44

McDowell, B., 1992, Object-Oriented Design in C++, course presented by Object-Oriented Pty Ltd., Sydney, January

McGregor, J. D., and Korson, T., 1993, Supporting dimensions of classification in object-oriented design, *J. Obj.-Oriented Programming*, 5(9), 25–30

McGregor, J. D., and Sykes, D. A., 1992, *Object-Oriented Software Development: Engineering Software for Reuse*, Van Nostrand Reinhold, New York, 352pp

Macro, A., and Buxton, J., 1987, *The Craft of Software Engineering*, Addison-Wesley

Madhavji, N. H., 1991, The process cycle, *Software Eng. J.*, 6(5), 234–242

Maiden, N., 1991, Analogy as a paradigm for specification reuse, *Software Eng. J.*, 6(1), 3–15

Malone, C., 1991, Object oriented design and programming: a case study, in *TOOLS6* (ed. J. Potter, M. Tokor, and B. Meyer), Prentice Hall, Sydney, 119–130

Manola, F., 1993, Object-oriented databases, Tutorial and TOOLS USA '93, Santa Barbara, 3 August

Marsden, J., Pingry, D., and Whinston, A., 1972, Production function theory and the optimal design of wastewater treatment facilities, *Applied Economics*, 4, 279–290

Marsden, J., Pingry, D., and Whinston, A., 1974, Engineering foundations of production functions, *Journal of Economic Theory*, 9, 124–140

Martin, J., and Odell, J. J., 1992, *Object-Oriented Analysis and Design*, Prentice Hall, Englewood cliffs, NJ, 513pp

Masotti, G., 1991, EC++: extended C++, *J. Object-Oriented Programming*, 4(5), 10–20

Mellor, S. J., Shlaer, S., Booch, G., Rumbaugh, J., Salmons, J., Babitsky, T., Adams, S., and Wirfs-Brock, R. J., 1993, Premature methods standardization considered harmful, *J. Obj.-Oriented Programming*, 6(4), 8, 85

Menzies, T., Edwards, J. M., and Ng, K., 1992, The case of the mysterious missing reusable libraries, *Technology of Object-Oriented Languages and Systems: TOOLS9* (ed. B. Meyer and J. Potter), Prentice Hall, Sydney, 421–427

Meyer, B., 1988a, *Object-oriented Software Construction*, Prentice Hall, Hemel Hempstead, 534pp

Meyer, B., 1988b, Harnessing multiple inheritance, *J. Obj.-Oriented Programming*, 1(4), 48–51

Meyer, B., 1989a, From structured programming to object-oriented design: the road to Eiffel, *Structured Programming*, 1, 19–39

Meyer, B., 1989b, Writing correct software, *Dr Dobb's Journal*, 14(12), 48–63

Meyer, B., 1989c, The new culture of software development: reflections on the practice of object-oriented design, *Procs. TOOLS '89*, Paris, November 13–15, 13–23

Meyer, B., 1989d, Course notes for two day seminar, Object-oriented design and programming: a software engineering perspective, Sydney, November, Interactive Software Engineering, Inc., 235pp

Meyer, B., 1990a, Tools for the new culture: lessons from the design of the Eiffel libraries, *Comms. ACM*, 33(9), 68–88

Meyer, B., 1990b, Eiffel and C++: a comparison, unpublished technical note, Interactive Software Engineering, Inc., March, 12pp

Meyer, B., 1992a, *Eiffel: The Language*, Prentice Hall, New York, 594pp

Meyer, B., 1992b, Design by contract, pp1–50, in *Advances in Object-Oriented Software Engineering* (ed. D. Mandrioli and B. Meyer), Prentice Hall, New York, 214pp

Meyer, B., 1992c, Public communication, presentation at the Object-Oriented Special Interest Group of the Australian Computer Society (New South Wales Branch), Sydney, October 14

Meyer, B., 1992d, Software engineering: reflections on a scientific discipline and its educational requirements, seminar presented at University of Technology, Sydney, October 21

Meyer, B., 1992e, Object-oriented technology: a management perspective, Tutorial Notes, TOOLS9, Sydney, December 2

Meyer, B., 1992f, Applying "design by contract", *IEEE Computer*, 25(10), 40–51

Meyer, B., 1992g, The new culture of software development: reflections on the practice of object-oriented design, pp 51–64, in *Advances in Object-Oriented Software Engineering* (ed. D. Mandrioli and B. Meyer) Prentice Hall, New York, 214pp

Meyer, B., 1993, What is an object-oriented environment? Five principles and their application, *J. Obj.-Oriented Programming*, 6(4), 75–81

Miller, G., 1956, The magical number seven, plus or minus two: some limits on our capacity for processing information, *Psychological Review*, 63(2), 81–97

Miller, G., 1975, The magic number seven after fifteen years, *Studies in Long-Term Memory* (ed. A. Kennedy), John Wiley & Sons, Chichester, 358pp

Millikin, M., 1989, Object-orientation: what it can do for you, *Computerworld*, March 13

Monarchi, D. E., and Puhr, G. I., 1992, A research typology for object-oriented analysis and design, *Comms. ACM*, 35(9), 35–47

Moodie, D., 1990, A practical methodology for representation of enterprise data models, Seminar presentation, University of New South Wales, June 13

Moreau, D. R., and Dominick, W. D., 1989, Object-oriented graphical information systems: research plan and evaluation metrics, *J. Systems and Software*, 10, 23–28

Moreau, D. R., and Dominick, W. D., 1990, A programming environment evaluation methodology for object-oriented systems: Part I—The Methodology, *J. Object-Oriented Programming*, 3(1), 38–52

Mori, R., 1989, What lies ahead, *Byte*, 14(1), 346–348

Mori, R., and Kawahara, M., 1990, Superdistribution: the concept and the architecture, *Trans IEICE*, E–73(7)

Mullin, M., 1989, *Object Oriented Program Design With Examples in C++*, Addison-Wesley, Reading, MA, 303pp

Murphy, G., 1991, Experiences applying object-oriented analysis, in *Procs. TOOLS5* (ed. T. Korson, V. Vaitinari, and B. Meyer), Prentice Hall, New York, 249–264

Myers, G. J., 1977, An extension to the cyclomatic measure of program-complexity, *SIGPLAN Notices*, October, 61–64

Myers, G. J., 1978, *Composite Structured Design*, Van Nostrand Reinhold, Wokingham, UK

Nance, R., 1981, The time and state relationships in simulation modelling, *Comms. ACM*, 24(4), 173–179

Nascimento, C., and Dollimore, J., 1992, Behavior maintenance of migrating objects in a distributed object-oriented environment, *J. Obj.-Oriented Programming*, 5(5), 25–33

Navlakhar, J. K., 1990, Choosing a software cost estimation model for your organization: a case study, *Inf. Manage.*, 18, 255–261

Needham, C. D., 1971, *Organising Knowledge in Libraries: An Introduction to Information Retrieval*, 2nd ed. rev., André Deutsch, London

Neighbors, J. M., 1984, The Draco approach to constructing software from reusable components, *IEEE Trans. Software Eng.*, 10(5), 564–574

Nejmeh, B. A., 1988, NPATH: a measure of execution path complexity and its applications, *Comms. ACM*, 31(2), 188–200

Nerson, J.-M., 1990, Case studies in object-oriented analysis, Tutorial Notes, Tools Pacific, Sydney

Nerson, J.-M., 1991, Extending Eiffel toward O-O analysis and design, *Technology of Object-Oriented Languages and Systems: TOOLS5* (ed. T. Korson, V. Vaishnavi, and B. Meyer), Prentice Hall, New York, 377–392

Nerson, J.-M., 1992a, Applying object-oriented analysis and design, *Comms. ACM*, 35(9), 63–74

Nerson, J.-M., 1992b, O-O development of a date and time management cluster, *J. Obj.-Oriented Programming*, 5(1), 39–46

Nerson, J.-M., 1993, Object-Oriented Project Management, Tutorial at TOOLS II, Santa Barbara, August 2

Nolan, R. L., 1979, Managing the crises in data processing, *Harvard Business Review*, 57(2), 115–126

Norden, P. V., 1958, Curve fitting for a model of applied research and development scheduling, *IBM Journal*, July, 232–248

Object Interest Group, 1991, A large scale user's assessment of object-orientation, Dept. Trade and Industry, UK Govt

Odell, J. J., 1991, Object-oriented analysis and design, *JOOP Focus on Analysis and Design*, 74–84

Odell, J. J., 1992a, Dynamic and multiple classification, *J. Obj.-Oriented Programming*, 4(8), 45–48

Odell, J. J., 1992b, More than a programming language, *Object Magazine*, 2(4), 47–49

Olle, T., Sol, H., and Verrijn-Stuart, A., 1982, *Information Systems Design Methodologies: A Comparative Review*, North Holland Publishing Co., Amsterdam, 648pp

Omohundro, J., 1991, The difference between Sather and Eiffel, *Eiffel Outlook*, 1(1), 12–14

Object-Oriented Strategies, 1992 (ed. P. Harmon), The market for OO-software products, 11(3), 1–4

O'Shea, D., 1992, The big prize: acceptance of O-O by the MIS community, *Hotline on Obj.-Oriented Technology*, 3(4), 1, 4–6

Oviedo, E. I., 1980, Control flow, data flow and program complexity, *Proc. COMPSAC 80*, 146–152

Page-Jones, M., 1991a, Object-orientation: stop, look, and listen! *Hotline on Object-Oriented Technology*, 2(3), 1, 3–7

Page-Jones, M., 1991b, TOOLS '91 Tutorial Notes, 4th International Conference and Exhibition, Paris, March 4–8

Page-Jones, M., 1992a, Object orientation: the importance of being earnest, *Object Magazine*, 2(2), 11–14

Page-Jones, M., 1992b, Comparing techniques by means of encapsulation and connascence, *Comms. ACM*, 35(9), 147–151

Page-Jones, M., Constantine, L. L., and Weiss, S., 1990, Modeling object-oriented systems: the Uniform Object Notation, *Computer Language*, 7(10), 69–87

Pant, Y. R., Verner, J. M., and Henderson-Sellers, B., 1994, S/C: a software size/complexity metric (submitted for publication)

Papazoglou, M. P., Georgiadis, P. I., and Maritsas, D. G., 1984, An outline of the programming language Simula, *Computer Languages*, 9, 107–131

Parkhill, D., 1992, Object-oriented technology transfer: techniques and guidelines for a smooth transition, *Object Magazine*, 2(1), 57–59

Parr, F. N., 1980, An alternative to the Rayleigh curve model for software development, *IEEE Trans. Soft. Eng.*, SE-6, 291–296

Pascoe, G. A., 1986, Elements of object-oriented programming, *Byte*, 11(8), 139–144

Perry, D. E., and Kaiser, G. E., 1990, Adequate testing and object-oriented programming, *J. Obj.-Oriented Programming*, 2(5), 13–19

Pfleeger, S. L., 1993, Lessons learned in building a corporate metrics program, *IEEE Software*, 10(3), 67–74

Pinson, L. J., and Wiener, R. S., 1988, *An Introduction to Object-Oriented Programming and Smalltalk*, Addison-Wesley, Reading, MA, 502pp

Plant, N., 1992a, A large-scale users' assessment of object orientation, *Hotline on Obj.-Oriented Technology*, 3(5), 1, 4–6, 9

Plant, N., 1992b, What large-scale IT users want from O-O suppliers, *Hotline on Obj.-Oriented Technology*, 3(7), 6–13

Plews, M., 1993, Programming language study. Evaluating the claims made for object orientation, *Object Magazine*, 3(1), 54–55

Potter, J., 1990, Eiffel 2. 2, *J. Obj.-Oriented Programming*, 3(3), 84–88

Pratap, S., 1992, Objects and reuse, *Hotline on Obj.-Oriented Technology*, 3(12), 16–18

Premerlani, W. J., Blaha, M. R., Rumbaugh, J. E., and Varwig, T. A., 1990, An object-oriented relational database, *Comms. ACM*, 33(11), 99–109

Price, R. T., and Girardi, R., 1990, A class retrieval tool for an object-oriented environment, *Procs. 3rd Intl. Conf., TOOLS3* (ed. J. Bézivin, B. Meyer, J. Potter, and M. Tokoro), Sydney, 26–36

Prieto-Diaz, R., and Freeman, P., 1987, Classifying software for reusability, *IEEE Software*, 4(1), 6–16

Pun, W., and Winder, R., 1990, A design method for object-oriented programming, Department of Computer Science, University College London, Research Note RN/90/51, 17pp

Purchase, J. A., and Winder, R. L., 1991, Debugging tools for object-oriented programming, *J. Obj.-Oriented Programming*, 4(3), 10–27

Putnam, L. H., 1978, A general empirical solution to the macro software sizing and estimation problem, *IEEE Trans. Software Eng.*, SE-4(4), 345–361

Putnam, L. H., and Fitzsimmons, A., 1979, Estimating software costs (Part 3), *Datamation*, 25(12), 137–140

Ramakrishnan, N., 1992, The personalized paradigm, *Object Magazine*, 2(4), 56–57

Ranganathan, S. R., 1958, Classified Catalogue Code: with additional rules for dictionary catalogue, 4th ed., Madras Library Association, Madras, India

Ratjens, M., 1991, Discovering classes and their properties in large-scale management information systems, *Technology of Object-Oriented Languages and Systems*, TOOLS6 (ed. J. Potter, M. Tokoro, and B. Meyer), Prentice Hall, Englewood Cliffs, NJ, 53–65

Ratjens, M., 1994, *The Seminar*, Prentice Hall, Sydney

Reed, D. R., 1992, Pragmatic issues with C++ class libraries, part 1, *C++ Report*, September 1992, 22–25

Rombach, H. D., 1990, Design measurement: some lessons learned, *IEEE Software*, 7(3), March, 17–25

Ross, D. T., Goodenough, J. B., and Irvine, C. A., 1975, Software engineering: process, principles, and goals, *IEEE Computer*, 8(5), 17–27

Rossiter, P. M., 1992, Commercial adoption of object-oriented methods, paper presented at the 1992 Object-Oriented Conference, Sydney, May 4–5, Technology Training Corporation

Rothe, O., and Meyer, W., 1990, ObjectWorks for C++: Product Review, *C++ Report*, 2(8), 22–25

Royce, W. W., 1970, Managing the development of large software systems, *Procs IEEE Wescon*, August, 1–9

Rubin, K. S., and Goldberg, A., 1992, Object behavior analysis, *Comms. ACM*, 35(9), 48–62

Rumbaugh, J., 1987, Relations as semantic constructs in an object-oriented language, *OOPSLA '87 Proceedings*, ACM, 466–481

Rumbaugh, J., 1992a, Horsing around with associations, *J. of Obj.-Oriented Programming*, 4(9), 49–53

Rumbaugh, J., 1992b, An object or not an object?, *J. Obj.-Oriented Programming*, 5(3), 20–25

Rumbaugh, J., and Blaha, M., 1991, Object-oriented modeling, OOPSLA '91 Tutorial, Arizona

Rumbaugh, J., Blaha, M., Premerlani, W., Eddy, F., and Lorensen, W., 1991, *Object-oriented Modeling and Design*, Prentice Hall, Englewood Cliffs, NJ, 500pp

Sakkinen, M., 1988, Comments on 'The Law of Demeter' and C++, *SIGPLAN Notices*, 23(12), 38

Saunders, J. H., 1989, A survey of object-oriented programming languages, *J. Obj.-Oriented Programming*, 1(6), 5–11

Schmucker, K. J., 1986a, MacApp: an application framework, *Byte*, 11(8), 189–193

Schmucker, K. J., 1986b, *Object-Oriented Programming for the Macintosh*, Hayden Book Company, Hasbrouk Heights, New Jersey

Seidewitz, E., and Stark, M., 1987, Towards a general object-oriented software development methodology, *Ada Letters*, 7 (July–August), 54–67

Shah, A., Rumbaugh, J., Hamel, J., and Borsari, R., 1989, DSM: an object-relation modeling language, *Procs. OOPSLA '89*, ACM Press, New Orleans

Sharble, R. C., and Cohen, S. S., 1993, The object-oriented brewery: a comparison of two object-oriented development methods, *ACM SIGSOFT Software Engineering Notes*, 18(2), 60–73

Shaw, R. H., 1991, C++ without objects, *Borland Language Express*, 1(1), 10–13

Sheetz, S. D., Tegarden, D. P., and Monarchi, D. E., 1991, Measuring object-oriented system complexity, in *Proceedings of the First Workshop on Information Technologies and Systems*, MIT Sloan School of Management, Cambridge, MA, December

Shelton, R., 1991. *Object-Oriented Modelling and Design* book review, *Object Magazine*, 1(4), 66–67

Shen, V. Y., Conte, S. D., and Dunsmore, H. E., 1983, Software science revisited: a critical analysis of the theory and its empirical support, *IEEE Trans. Software Eng.*, SE–9(2), 155–165

Shepperd, M., 1988, A critique of cyclomatic complexity as a software metric, *Software Engineering Journal*, 3, 30–36

Shepperd, M., 1990, Early life-cycle metrics and software quality models, *Inf. Software Technol.*, 32(4), 311–316

Shlaer, S., and Mellor, S. J., 1988, *Object-Oriented Systems Analysis: Modeling the World in Data*, Yourdon Press Computing Series, 144pp

Shlaer, S., and Mellor, S. J., 1991, *Object Lifecycles: Modeling the World in States*, Yourdon Press/Prentice Hall, 251pp

Shlaer, S., Mellor, S. J., and Hywari, W., 1991, OODLE: a language-independent notation for object-oriented design, *JOOP Focus on Analysis and Design*, 98–106

Singh, J., 1990, Object modeling, *Hotline on Obj.-Oriented Technology*, 2(2), 8–10

Smart, P. F., Woodfield, S. N., Embley, D. W., and Scott, D. T., 1988, An empirical investigation of the effect of education and tools on software reusability, in *Procs. Seventh Annual International Phoenix Conf. on Computers and Communications*, IEEE Comp. Soc. Press, Washington DC, 224–228

Smeers, Y., and Tyteca, D., 1984a, Variable operating costs of water-meter treatment plants, *Trans. of the Institute of Manufacturing and Control*, 6(3) 173–179

Smeers, Y., and Tyteca, D., 1984b, A geometric programming model for the optical design of wastewater treatment plants, *Operations Research*, 32(2), 314–342

Smith, D. N., 1991, *Concepts of Object-Oriented Programming*, McGraw-Hill, New York

Smith, M. D., and Robson, D. J., 1992, A framework for testing object-oriented programs, *J. Obj.-Oriented Programming*, 5(3), 45–53

Smolander, K., Tahvanainen, V-P., and Lyytinen, K., 1991, How to combine tools and methods in practice—a field study, in *Advanced Information Systems*

Engineering: *Lecture Notes in Computer Science, Procs. of CAiSE91*, Springer-Verlag, Berlin, 195–214

Smolander, K., Lyytinen, K., Tahvanainen, V-P., and Marttiin, P., 1991, MetaEdit—A flexible graphical environment for methodology modelling, in *Procs. Computer-Aided Information Systems Engineering '91 Conference*, Springer-Verlag, Berlin, 168–193

Snyder, A., 1986, Encapsulation and inheritance in object-oriented programming languages, *OOPSLA '86 Proceedings*, ACM Press, 38–45

Snyder, A., 1989, The essence of objects, Hewlett-Packard Laboratories, Technical report STL–89–25

Sollisch, M. J., 1991, Moving from Pascal to C++, *Hotline on Obj.-Oriented Technology*, 2(4), 1–5

Sommerville, I., 1989, *Software Engineering*, 3rd ed., Addison-Wesley, Wokingham, UK, 653pp

Sprague, R., and Carlson, E., 1982, *Building Effective Decision Support Systems*, Prentice Hall, Englewood Cliffs, NJ, 328pp

Stallman, R., 1988, *GDB+ 2.5.0 Manual*, The GNU C++ debugger, MA

Stein, J., 1988, Object-oriented programming and databases, *Dr Dobb's Journal*, March, 18–34

Stepney, S., Barden, R., and Cooper, D., 1992, A survey of object orientation in Z, *Software Eng. J.*, 7(2), 150–160

Stevens, W. P., Myers, G. J., and Constantine, L. L., 1974, Structured design, *IBM Systems Journal*, 13(2), 115–139

Stewart, M. K., 1991, Object projects: what can go wrong, *Hotline on Obj.-Oriented Technology*, 2(6), 15–17

Stone, C., 1992, OMG's 18–24 month view, *Hotline on Obj.-Oriented Technology*, 3(9), 10–13

Stroustrup, B., 1986, *The C++ Programming Language*, 1st ed., Addison-Wesley, Reading, MA, 328pp

Stroustrup, B., 1988, What is object-oriented programming?, *IEEE Software*, 5(3), 1–19

Stroustrup, B., 1991, *The C++ Programming Language*, 2nd ed., Addison-Wesley, Reading, MA, 328pp

Sutcliffe, A. G., 1991, Object-oriented systems development: survey of structured methods, *Inf. Software Technol.*, 33(6), 433–442

Sutton, W. L., 1989, Advanced models of the software process, *ACM SIGSOFT Software Engineering Notes*, 14(4), 156–158

Swatman, P. A., 1992, Increasing formality in the specification of high-quality information systems in a commercial context, unpublished PhD thesis, Curtin University of Technology, Western Australia, 243pp

Swatman, P., and Swatman, P., 1992, Formal specification—an analytic tool for (management) information systems, *J. Inf. Systems*, 2(2), 121–160

Switzer, R., 1993, *Eiffel: An Introduction*, Prentice Hall, Hemel Hempstead, 161pp

Symons, C. R., 1988, Function point analysis: difficulties and improvements, *IEEE Trans. Software Eng.*, SE-14(1), 2–11

Taligent, 1993a, *Lessons Learned from Early Adopters of Object Technology*, Taligent Inc., Cupertino, CA, 16pp

Taligent, 1993b, *Driving Innovation with Technology: The Intelligent Use of Objects*, Taligent Inc., Cupertino, CA, 16pp

Taylor, P., 1992, Experiences with object oriented software development, in *TOOLS9* (ed. J. Potter and B. Meyer), Prentice Hall, UK

Tegarden, D. P., Sheetz, S. D., and Monarchi, D. E., 1992, Effectiveness of traditional software metrics for object-oriented systems, *Procs. HICSS-92*, IEEE, San Diego

Tegarden, D. P., Sheetz, S. D., and Monarchi, D. E., 1993, A software complexity model of object-oriented systems, *Decision Support Systems* (in press)

Tenderich, B., 1992, Business class, *Object Magazine*, 2(2), 43–45

Thomas, D., 1989a, In search of an object-oriented development process, *J. Obj.-Oriented Programming*, 2(1), 60–63

Thomas, D., 1989b, What's in an object?, *Byte*, 14(3), 231–240

Thomas, D., and Jacobson, I., 1989, Managing object-oriented software engineering, Tutorial, *TOOLS '89*, Paris, November 13–15, 52pp

Thomsett, R., 1990, Management implications of object-oriented development, *ACS Newsletter*, October 5–7, 10–12

Thorup, K. K., 1992, Practical experiences with the Sather language, *Eiffel Outlook*, 2(3), 20–22

Thurston, P., 1993, Object oriented databases, *OOPS Newsletter*, 17, Spring, British Computer Society, 8–13

Tsai, W. T., Lopez, M. A., Rodriguez, V., and Volovik, D., 1986, An approach measuring data structure complexity, *COMPSAC 86*, 240–246

Turner, C. D., and Robson, D. J., 1992, The testing of object-oriented programs, Technical Report TR-13/92, Computer Science Division, School of Engineering and Computer Science, University of Durham, England, 64pp

Turner, J. A., 1987, Understanding the elements of system design, in *Critical Issues in Information Systems Research* (ed. R. J. Boland, Jr., and R. A. Hirschheim), John Wiley and Sons, Chichester, UK, 97–111

Uhl, J., and Schmid, H. A., 1990, *A Systematic Catalogue of Reusable Data Types*, Springer–Verlag

Ullman, J. D., 1988, *Principles of Database and Knowledge-base Systems*, vol. I, Computer Science Press

Umphress, D. A., and March, S. G., 1991, Object-oriented requirements determination, *JOOP Focus on Analysis and Design*, 35–40

Urlocker, Z., 1989, Teaching object-oriented programming, *J. Obj.-Oriented Programming*, 2(2), 45–47

Urlocker, Z., 1990, Breaking technical barriers in the 1990s, *J. Obj.-Oriented Programming*, 2(5), 78–80

Van Gigch, J. P., 1991, *System Design Modeling and Metamodeling*, Plenum, New York, 453pp

Vasan, R., 1992, Becoming object-oriented: "build vs buy", *Object Magazine*, 2(1), 61–63

Velho, A., and Carapuca, R., 1992, SOM: a semantic object model, towards an abstract, complete and unifying way to model the real world, *Third Int. Working Conf. on Dynamic Modeling of Information Systems*, June 9–10, The Netherlands

Verner, J. M., 1991, Software size metrics: a review, Technical Report No. 52, University of New South Wales, Kensington, New South Wales, Australia

Verner, J., and Tate, G., 1987, A model for software sizing, *J. Systems Software*, 7, 173–177

Verner, J., and Tate, G., 1988, Estimating size and effort in fourth-generation development, *IEEE Software*, 5, 15–22

Verner, J., and Tate, G., 1992, A software size model, *IEEE Trans. Software Eng.*, 18(4), 265–278

Vickery, B. C., 1975, *Classification and Indexing in Science*, 3rd ed., Butterworths, London

Waldo, J., 1990, O-O benefits of Pascal to C++ conversion, *The C++ Report*, 2(8), 1, 5–7

Walker, I., 1992, Requirements of an OO design method, *Software Eng. J.*, 7(2), 102–113

Wampler, K. D., 1990, The object-oriented programming paradigm (OOPP) and FORTRAN programs, *Computers in Physics*, 4(4), 385–394

Wand, Y., and Weber, R., 1989, An ontological evaluation of systems analysis and design methods, in *Information Systems Concepts: An In-depth Analysis* (ed. E. D. Falkenberg and P. Lindgren), Elsevier Science Publishers (North Holland), Amsterdam, 79–107

Wang, E. L., 1992, The use and abuse of "object-oriented", *Object Magazine*, 2(4), 50–51

Warburton, R. D. H., 1983, Managing and predicting the costs of real-time software, *IEEE Trans. Software Eng.*, SE–9(5), 562–569

Ward, P., 1989, How to integrate object orientation with structured analysis and design, *IEEE Software*, 6(2), 74–82

Ward, P. T., and Mellor, S. J., 1985, *Structured Development for Real-Time Systems*, Yourdon Press, New Jersey

Wasserman, A. I., and Pircher, P. A., 1987, A graphical, extensible integrated environment for software development, *Proc. Second Symp. Practical Software Development Environments*, SIGPLAN Notices, 22(1), 131–142

Wasserman, A. I., Pircher, P. A., and Muller, R. J., 1990, The object-oriented structured design notation for software design representation, *IEEE Computer*, 23(3), 50–63

Wegner, P., 1989, Learning the language, *Byte*, 14(3), 245–253

Wegner, P., 1990, Concepts and paradigms of object-oriented programming, *OOPS Messenger*, 1(1), 7–87

Welke, R. J., 1988, *The CASE Repository: More than another database application*, MetaSystems Ltd., Ann Arbor, MI

Weyuker, E. J., 1988, Evaluating software complexity measures, *IEEE Trans. Software Eng.*, 14(9), 1357–1365

Whitewater Group, 1989, *Actor Language Manual*, Whitewater Group Inc., Evanston, Illinois

Whitten, J., Bentley, L., and Barbur, V., 1989, Systems Analysis and Design Methods, Irwin, Boston, MA, 797pp

Wieringa, R., 1991, Steps towards a method for the formal modelling of dynamic objects, *Data and Knowledge Engineering*, 6(6), 509–540

Wild, F. H., III, 1991, Managing class coupling: apply the principles of structured design to object-oriented programming, *UNIX Review*, 9(10), 44–47

Wilde, N., and Huitt, R., 1992, Issues in the maintenance of object oriented programs, *Procs Workshop on Object-Oriented Software Engineering Practice*, Denver, February

Williams, L. G., 1988, A Behavioral Approach to Software Process Modelling, *ACM SIGSOFT Soft. Eng. Notes*, 14(4), June

Winblad, A. L., Edwards, S. D., and King, D. R., 1990, *Object-Oriented Software*, Addison-Wesley, Reading, MA, 291pp

Winder, R., 1991, *Developing C++ Software*, John Wiley and Sons, Chichester, UK, 400pp

Winkler, J. F. H., 1992, Objectivism: "class" considered harmful, *Comms. ACM*, 35(8), 128–130

Winston, A., 1990, Objective reality, *Unixworld*, 7(4), 72–75

Winston, G., 1982, *The Timing of Economic Activities*, Cambridge University Press, Cambridge, UK, 343pp

Wirfs-Brock, R. J., and Johnson, R. E., 1990, A survey of current research in object-oriented design, *Comms. ACM*, 33(9), 104–124

Wirfs-Brock, A., and Wilkerson, B., 1989a, Variables limit reusability, *J. Obj.-Oriented Programming*, 2(1), 34–40

Wirfs-Brock, R. J., and Wilkerson, B., 1989b, Object-oriented design: a responsibility-driven approach, *OOPSLA '89 Proceedings*, 71–75

Wirfs-Brock, R. J., Wilkerson, B., and Wiener, L., 1990, *Designing Object-Oriented Software*, Prentice Hall, New York, 368pp

Wyatt, B., Kau, K., and Hufnagel, S., 1992, Parallelism in object-oriented languages: a survey, *IEEE Software*, 9(11), November, 56–65

Wybolt, N., 1990, Experiences with C++ and object-oriented software development, *Procs. USENIX C++ Conference*, 1–9

Yap, L.-M., and Henderson-Sellers, B., 1993a, Consistency considerations of object-oriented class libraries, Centre for Information Technology Research Report No. 93/3, University of New South Wales, Sydney, Australia, 110pp

Yap, L.-M., and Henderson-Sellers, B., 1993b, A semantic model for inheritance in object-oriented systems, *Procs. ASWEC93*, IREE, Sydney, Australia, 28–35

Yourdon, E., and Constantine, L. L., 1979, *Structured Design: Fundamentals of a Discipline of Computer Program and Systems Design*, Yourdon Press/Prentice Hall, Englewood Cliffs, NJ, 473pp

Yu, W. D., Smith, D. P., and Huang, S. T., 1991, Software Productivity Measurements, in *Proc. IEEE COMPSAC 1991*, 558–564

Zultner, R., 1988, The Deming approach to software quality engineering, *Quality Progress*, November, 58–64

Zultner, R., 1989, The Deming way to software quality, presented at the Pacific Northwest Software Quality Conference, Zultner & Company, Princeton, NJ

Zuse, H., 1990, *Software Complexity: Measures and Methods*, Walter de Gruyter, Berlin, 605pp

Zweben, S. H., 1990, On the resolution of the Software Science anomaly, *J. Syst. Software*, 12(2), 167–171

Index

Abstract class—see O/C (abstract)
Abstract data type (ADT), 83
Abstraction, 42–46
Actor language, 94
Actors, 344–345
Ada, 91
ADT—see Abstract data type
Aggregation, 56, 57–59, 323
Assertions, 15, 97–98
Association, 56, 57, 324–326
Attributes, 51–52
Automatic garbage collection, 99

Behavior, 51, 281–282
(see also Services)
Bottom-up development, 25
Business planning, 268–270, 419

C++, 84, 86, 88, 91–92, 94–95, 314, 429, 452–457
Candidate O/Cs, 323
Cardinalities, 323–324
CASE technology, 439, 441–444
Class—see O/C
Class Specification (CS), 397–401
Classification, 44, 432–434
Client–server versus inheritance, 26
CLOS, 91–92
Cluster model, 121
COBOL—see OO COBOL
Cognitive Complexity Model (CCM), 343, 502–511

Commands, 54
Commercial adoption, 134
example projects—see Industry case studies
first project—see Migration
Communication, 54–56
Competitive edge, 14, 24–25
Complexity, 14, 468–470, 479, 500–501
McCabe, 492–499
Comp.object FAQ, 38
Concurrency, 136
Connascence, 475
Contracts, 52–54, 295–298
CORBA, 38, 459–460
Correctness, 7
Cost–Benefit Analysis (CBA), 270, 520
Cost estimation, 465–466, 514–517
Costs, 417, 420
Coupling, 342, 472–476
CRC cards, 440–441
Critical Success Factors (CSFs), 269–270
Cyclomatic complexity— see Complexity, McCabe

Database (OO)—see Objectbases
Data dependency, 10, 16–18
Deferred classes—see Abstract class
Design
by contract, 295–298
reuse of—see Frameworks
Domain analysis, 107, 329

Ease of use, 14
ECWAT, 362
Eiffel, 84, 85, 87, 91–92, 93, 299, 314, 458
Encapsulation, 15, 49
Entity-relationship diagrams, 434–435
Event Model (EM), 300–302, 383–386
Exception handling, 99
Extensibility, 8

Fan-out, 342, 473–476
FAQ—see Comp.object (FAQ)
Features, 86
Feasibility study, 270
Finding objects—see O/C identification
Formal methods, 37–38, 530
Fortran, 90, 95
Fountain lifecycle model— see Systems development lifecycle (fountain model)
Fractal lifecycle model—see Systems development lifecycle (fractal model)
Frameworks, 429
Functional decomposition, 110–111
Future (the), 532

Garbage collection—see Automatic garbage collection
Generalization, 46, 282, 394–397, 413–414, 519–521
for reuse, 302–314

Genericity, 97, 314
Geometric shapes example, 307–312
GUI, 402–411

Hierarchy—see Inheritance hierarchy
Historical perspective, 1, 90
Hybrid language—see OOPL (hybrid)
Hybrid methodologies—see Systems development lifecycle methodologies (hybrid)

Identity, 47
Implementation, 286, 355–356
Industry case studies, 452–459
Information hiding, 49
Inheritance hierarchies, 303–304, 315–322, 489–491
 depth of, 313, 490
 generalization hierarchies, 6–62, 316–321
 implementation inheritance hierarchies, 321–322
 refinement of, 306–314
Inheritance
 dimensions of, 66–70
 implementation, 60
 multiple, 26, 62–65, 318–321, 322
 repeated, 64–65
 single, 59–62, 66–70
 specialization, 61–62
 specification, 61–62
 Venn diagram representation, 150
Inheritance Model (IM)—see MOSES notation
Integrity, 9
Interactions—see Relationships
Invariant, 298–299, 334
Iteration, 401
Iteration plan, 326–327
Iterative Development Process (IDP), 151, 275 (see also MOSES (IDP))

Key advantages—see Software engineering (advantages)

Learning curve, 2–3, 26–27
Layering diagrams—see MOSES notation (complexity management techniques: layering)
Libraries, 23, 30, 282–283, 302, 303, 327–330, 429–437, 488–489
Lifecycle—see Systems development lifecycle

Maintenance, 12–14, 37, 293
Management issues—see Project management
McCabe complexity—see Complexity, McCabe
Measurement theory, 462–464
Member functions—see Methods
Memory management—see Automatic garbage collection
Message, 56
Message passing, 82–84
MetaEdit, 443
Metamodelling, 38, 104–105, 136, 530–532
Methods, 84
Methodologies—see Systems development lifecycle methodologies
Metrics, 24, 30, 341–343, 461–527
Migration, 2–3
 caveats, 21
Migration path, 35, 447–452
Milestones—see MOSES (deliverables)
"Miller" limit, 343, 502
Mindset, 2
Mixin, 48
Modeling, 48, 105
Modularity, 15
MOSES (Methodology for Object-oriented Software Engineering of Systems), 193–414
 activities, 206, 295 et seq.

Build Stage, 271
Business Planning Stage, 268 et seq.
 deliverables, 194, 200–201, 208–209, 271, 273, 277, 279, 285, 288, 291, 296, 299, 302, 314, 330, 334, 338, 349, 352, 357
Delivery Stage, 272–273
documentation—see MOSES (deliverables)
Enhancement Period, 268, 273
evaluating for completeness, 361–363
Growth Period, 268
IDP, 205
Implementation Phase, 285 et seq., 321, 412–413
Investigation Phase, 277 et seq.
lifecycle model, 200, 206–207
notation—see MOSES notation
phases, 199, 200–206
Planning Phase, 275 et seq.
process lifecycle, 197–199, 274 et seq.
product lifecycle, 195–197
Review Phase, 288 et seq.
Specification Phase, 279 et seq., 300, 436
MOSES notation, 211–264
 aggregation, 223–225
 association, 221–223
 bibliography example, 254–264
 BNF description, 218
 brainstorming, 254
 cardinality, 225
 CASE tool support, 253–254
 Class Specification, 229–234
 client–server relationships, 226
 complexity management techniques, 212, 243–253
 layering, 249–252

Index

selective visibility, 250, 253
sheets, 244–247
subsystems, 247–248
contracts, 234–236
embedded structures, 225
Event Model, 237–240
exception handling, 227
"friends", 227
genericity, 215
inheritance, 220–221
Inheritance Model, 242–243
library class, 213, 216
objectcharts, 240–242
objects, 219
O/C Model, 212–229
persistence, 213, 216
services, 213–215, 217
Service Structure Model, 236
tablet, 213 et seq
trace, 239, 389–391
whiteboarding, 254–255
Multiple inheritance (MI)—see Inheritance (multiple)
Music
definitions, 292–294
MVC, 92

NICE, 43
Nolan curve, 447
Notation, 29
—see individual methodology entries under Systems development lifecycle methodologies

Object
definition of, 83
Objectbases, 30–35
Objectchart, 240–242, 330–335, 347, 386–391
Object/Class(es) (O/C)
abstract, 48
and subclass or superclass—see Inheritance
definition of, 46–49, 83
embedded, 225
hierarchy—see Inheritance
identification, 27, 335–337
instantiation from—see Instantiation
specification—see MOSES notation (Class Specification)
ObjectCraft, 446
Object Interest Group, 529–530
Object model, 28
refining, 283
Objective-C, 91, 92, 95
Object Management Group, 459–460
Object Modeling Technique—see System development lifecycle methodologies (OMT)
Object-oriented databases—see Objectbases
Object-oriented paradigm, 41 et seq.
current and emerging issues, 27–38
recent issues, 25–27
Object-oriented programming languages (OOPL), 78–99, 287
choice of, 96–97
comparison, 91–92
definition of, 79–81
hybrid, 94
Object-oriented techniques
business advantages, 5
when to use, 5
Object-oriented triangle, 75–78
ObjectMaker, 441–442
Object Pascal, 91–92
Objectworks/VisualWorks, 444–446
Object-Z, 37–38, 297, 530–531
OOSD (Object-Oriented Structured Design)—see Software through Pictures
Open-Closed Principle, 312, 428
Operations, 51–52, 346–347
Optimization, 305, 338

Paradigm Plus, 442–443

Persistence, 90, 337
Polymorphism, 70–71
Postcondition, 297, 298, 334
Precondition, 297, 334
Process metrics, 464–467, 511–514
Productivity, 10, 516
Product culture, 8
Product metrics, 468–501
Programming in the large, 29
Project management, 23, 29, 114–115, 415–427
tools, 275–327
Properties, 51–52, 348–349
Protocols, 82
Prototyping, 4, 118, 122, 123, 148, 278, 338, 352, 418
PTech, 188–192, 444

Quality, 9, 290, 303, 338–341, 424–426
Queries, 54

Relationships, 26, 56–73, 281, 323–326
confusion between, 71–73
Repeated inheritance—see Inheritance (repeated)
Requirements analysis—see User requirements
Responsibilities—see Services
Responsibility-driven, 19, 49, 136
Reusability, 8–9
Reusable libraries—see Libraries; and Reuse
Reuse, 23, 24, 30, 313, 420–422, 427–429, 508, 519–520
metrics, 491
Robustness, 7
ROI, 518–526
Roles, 73–75
organizational, 426–427
Routine—see Methods

Sather, 93–94
Scenarios, 278, 300–302, 343–346, 370–373, 381–382
Seamless transition, 10–12, 13, 19, 20, 118

Selective visibility—see MOSES notation (complexity management techniques: selective visibility)
Semantic cohesion, 479
Services, 49–51, 346–349
Simula, 90, 91
Size
    function points, 483–484
    LOC, 480–481
    object-oriented, 484–486
    Software Science, 482–483
    tokens, 481–483
Smalltalk, 88–89, 91, 92
Software engineering (advantages), 6–14, 38–39
Software through Pictures, 186, 444
Specialization, 44–46
Spiral lifecycle model—see Systems development lifecycle (spiral model)
Standards, 38, 460
State Transition Diagram (STD), 330
Strategic investment and strategic planning, 6, 23, 24, 273, 418, 421, 448, 520
Style, 35–37
Subsystem
    coordination, 349–350
    identification, 350–352
Sydney Harbour Bridge, 188
System Architect, 443
Systems development lifecycle methodologies, 22, 28–29, 133 et seq

ADM3/4, 167–175
Berard, 178–182
BON, 182–184
Booch, 141–146
Coad and Yourdon, 153–159
comparison of, 134–136, 167
DDA, 184–185
De Champeaux, 185–186
Firesmith—see ADM3/4
Fusion, 186
Graham—see SOMA
Henderson-Sellers and Edwards—see O-O-O
hybrid methodologies, 129–133
Jacobson et al.—see Objectory
Lorenz, 149–153
Martin and Odell, 184
Nerson—see BON
OBA, 184
Objectory, 163–166
OMT, 137–141
O-O-O, 159–163
OOSD, 186–188
RDD 146–149
Rubin and Goldberg—see OBA
Rumbaugh et al.—see OMT
Shlaer/Mellor, 175–178
SOMA, 158–159
strengths and weaknesses, 105–106
Wirfs-Brock et al.—see RDD
Systems development lifecycle, 103–129
    fountain model, 111–121, 274

    fountain model for subsystems, 114–121
    fractal model, 123
    iterative nature of—see Iterative Development Process
    McGregor and Sykes 125–126
    spiral model, 121–123
    waterfall model, 103, 107–111

Template—see Genericity
Terminology of objects and classes, 46–78
Testing, 37, 283, 287, 289, 352–355
3GL, 90, 94
Tools, 438–446
Top-down development, 25
Traces—see MOSES notation (traces)
Training in OO, 451
Transitions, 333–334,
Turbo Pascal, 91

Use cases, 153, 166
User-defined type—see Abstract data type
User requirements, 278, 356–357
Uniform Object Notation (UON), 211

Verification and validation—see Testing

Wastewater treatment case study, 361–414
Waterfall lifecycle model—see Systems development lifecycle (waterfall model)